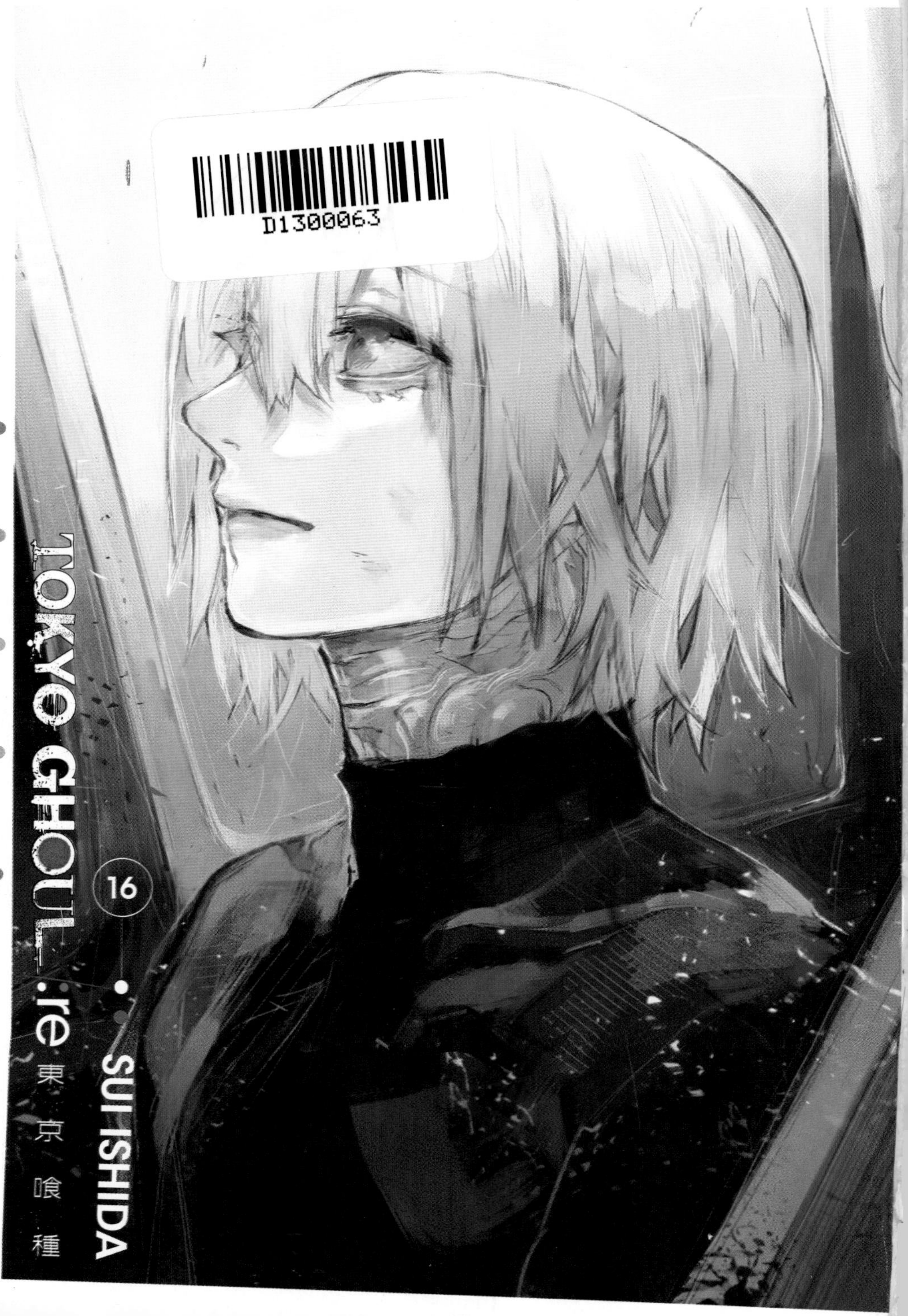
TOKYO GHOUL :re
東京喰種
16
SUI ISHIDA

TOKYO GHOUL:re 16 CONTENTS

東　京　喰　　種

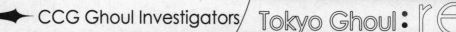

CCG Ghoul Investigators / Tokyo Ghoul:re

The CCG is the only organization in the world that investigates and solves Ghoul-related crimes. Founded by the Washu Family, the CCG developed and evolved Quinques, a type of weapon derived from Ghouls' Kagune. Quinx, an advanced, next-generation technology where humans are implanted with Quinques, is currently under development.

Urie Squad

Qs (Quinx) ● Investigators implanted with Quinques. They all ● live together in a house called the Chateau.

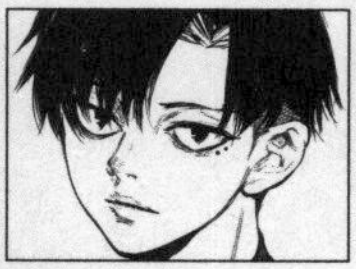

● Kuki Urie

Senior Investigator

New Quinx squad leader and most talented fighter in the squad. Demonstrating leadership after the death of Shirazu. Appointed head of S2 Squad.

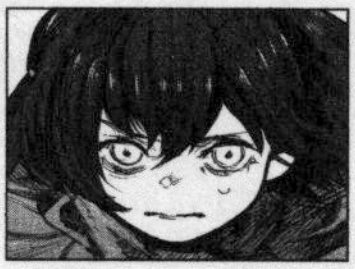

● Saiko Yonebayashi

Rank 2 Investigator

Supporting Urie as deputy squad leader while playing with her subordinates. Very bad at time management and a sucker for games and snacks.

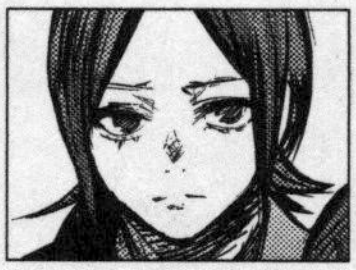

● Toma Higemaru

Rank 3 Investigator

Discovered his Quinx aptitude before enrolling in the academy. Looks up to Urie. Comes from a wealthy family.

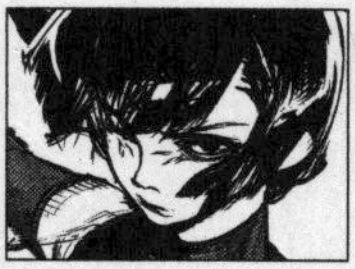

● Ching-li Hsiao

Rank 1 Investigator

From Hakubi Garden like Hairulhei. Skilled in hand-to-hand combat. Came to Japan from Taiwan as a child.

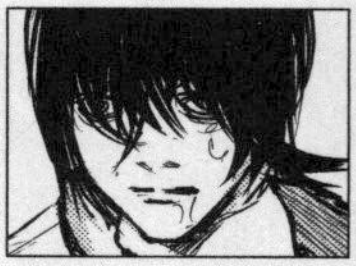

● Shinsanpei Aura

Rank 2 Investigator

Nephew of Special Investigator Kiyoko Aura. Unlike his aunt, who graduated at the top of her class, his grades were not that great.

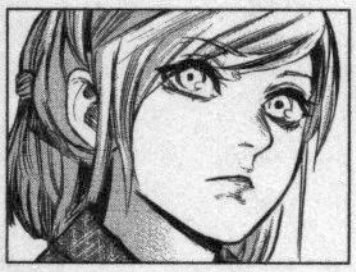

● Akira Mado

Former-Assistant Special Investigator

Mentor to Haise. Takes after her father. Determined to eradicate Ghouls. Discharged from the CCG after aiding a Ghoul during the Rushima operation. Working with Amon.

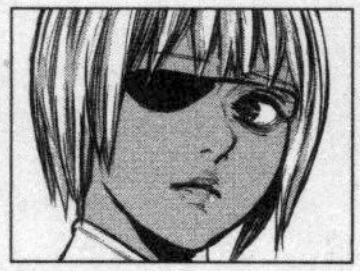

● Toru Mutsuki

Rank 1 Investigator

Assigned female at birth, he transitioned after the Quinx procedure. Struggling with the lie he has been living with...

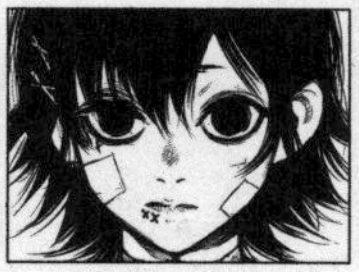

● Juzo Suzuya

Special Investitgator

Promoted to special investigator at 22, a feat previously only accomplished by Kisho Arima. A maverick who fights with knives hidden in his prosthetic leg. Appointed head of S3 Squad.

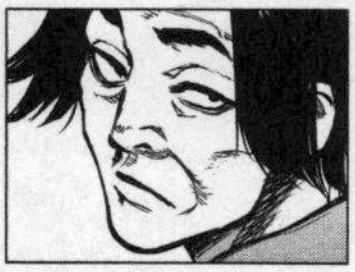

● Itsuki Marude

Special Investitgator

Leads Countermeasure II. Working independently to rebuild the CCG due to his doubts about the Washu.

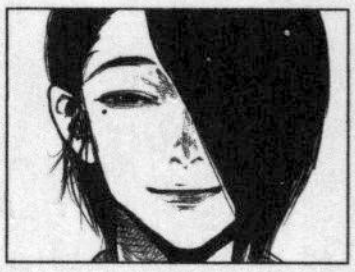

● Kichimura Washu

CCG Bureau Chief

Mysterious investigator related to the Washu family. Developed the Oggai for Tokyo Dissolution, a plan to eradicate all Ghouls.

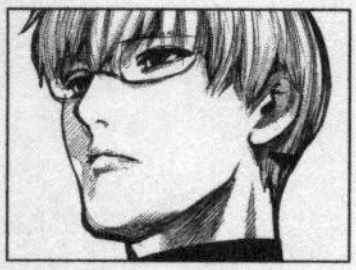

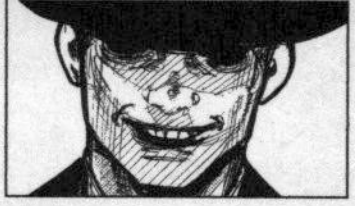

● Kisho Arima

Special Investigator

An undefeated investigator respected by many at the CCG. Killed at Cochlea by the One-Eyed King.

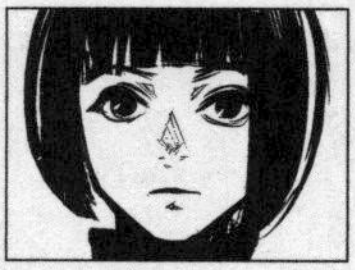

● Kori Ui

Special Investigator

Promising investigator formerly with the Arima Squad. Became a special investigator at a young age, but has a stubborn side. Assistant to the new bureau chief.

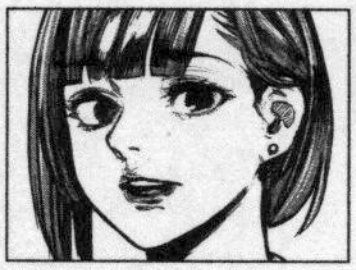

● Kimi Nishino

Medical student who studied under Akihiro Kano. Specializes in Ghoul research. Currently investigating the Dragon.

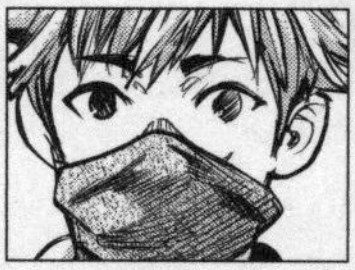

● Hideyoshi Nagachika

Kaneki's best friend. Worked behind the scenes as Scarecrow, suggesting the CCG and Ghouls join forces to save Kaneki.

Special Operations Investigator V

● Kaiko

Armed operatives who appear when the CCG is in crisis. Secret advisers to the Washu family. Currently under Furuta's command.

Tokyo Ghoul :re • Ghouls

They appear human, but have a unique predation organ called Kagune and can only survive by feeding on human flesh. They are the nemesis of humanity. Besides human flesh, the only other thing they can ingest is coffee. Ghouls can only be wounded by a Kagune or a Quinque made from a Kagune.

Clown Masks

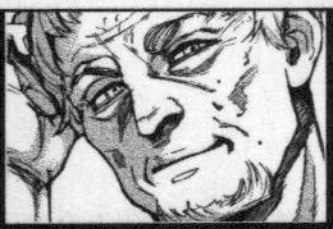

Donato Porpora
A Clown. Used his position as the priest of an orphanage to prey on kids. Kotaro Amon's adoptive father.

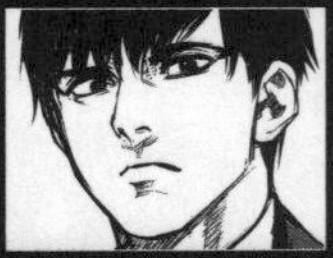

Kotaro Amon
Known as Floppy after getting Kakuho transplant surgery, but makes a miraculous recovery with Rc Suppressants. Reunited with his former-colleague Akira Mado.

The Goat

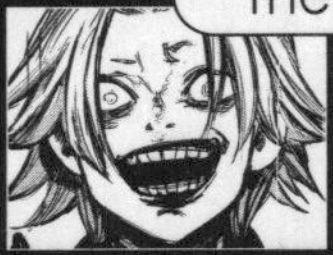

The Owl
The current incarnation of investigator Seido Takizawa after Professor Kano implanted him with a Kakuho.

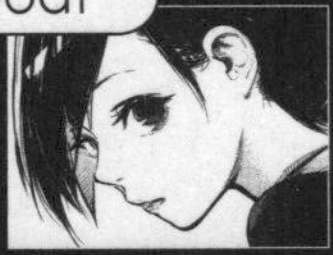

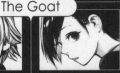

Touka Kirishima
Former manager of Café :re who wanted to carry on the traditions of Anteiku. Pregnant with Kaneki's child.

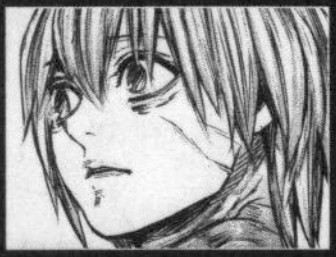

Ken Kaneki
Served as the Qs Squad mentor as Haise Sasaki. A half-Ghoul who has succeeded Kisho Arima as the One-Eyed King. Leader of the Goat, an anti-human organization based in the underground 24th Ward. Working to feed noncombatant Ghouls and stealing Quiques to render the CCG powerless. Recently married Touka Kirishima but then transformed into the Dragon after ingesting Furuta and the Oggai. Rescued by Touka and the Qs.

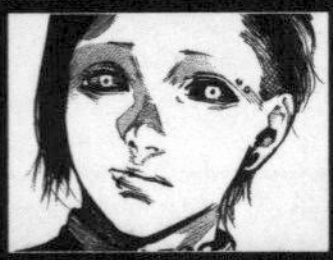

Uta
Owner of HySy Artmask Studio. Made Kaneki and Qs' masks.

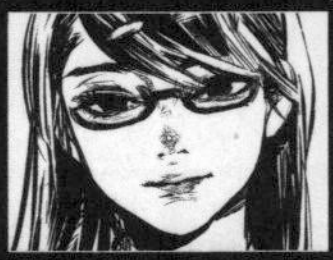

Rize
Ghoul belonging to V. Her kakuho was transplanted into Kaneki, Furuta and the Oggai by Dr. Kano.

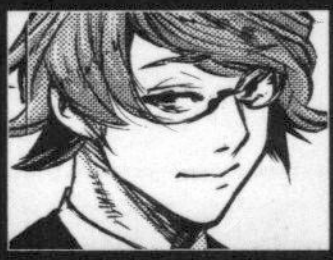

Nishiki Nishio
The Ghoul known as Orochi. Tracking the Aogiri Tree.

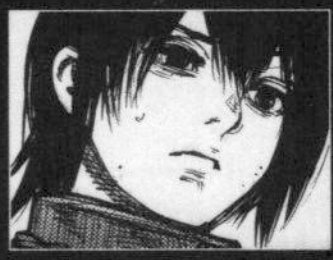

Ayato Kirishima
Touka's younger brother. A Rate SS Ghoul known as the Rabbit. Exploring the lowest level of the 24th Ward.

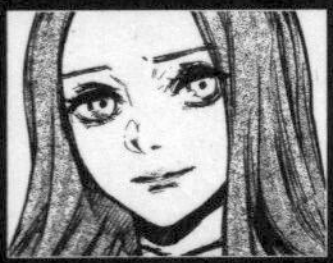

Itori
Owner of bar Helter Skelter. Values information.

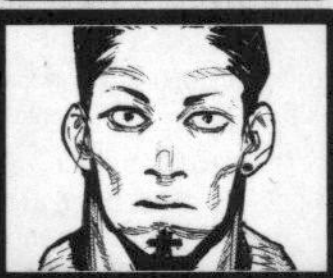

Banjo
Ayato's lieutenant during his Aogiri Tree days.

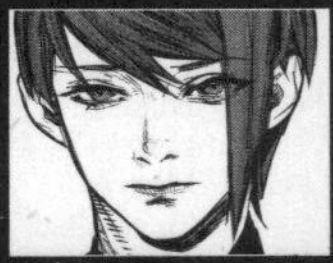

Shu Tsukiyama
A gourmet Ghoul. Continues to follow Ken Kaneki after the dissolution of his family's conglomerate.

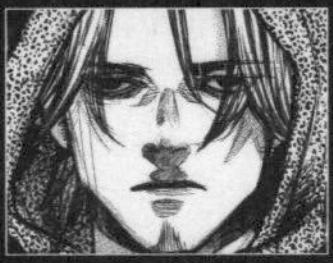

Renji Yomo
Former Café :re barista. Touka and Ayato's uncle.

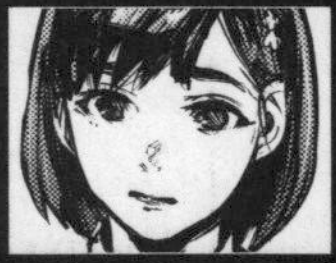

Hinami Fueguchi
Freed from Cochlea by Kaneki.

So far in :re

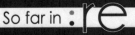

Ken Kaneki succeeded Kisho Arima as the One-Eyed King and formed the anti-human organization Goat after the conflicts at Cochlea and Rushima, hoping to create a world where Ghouls and humans can coexist peacefully. Meanwhile, the Washu Family's dark side has been made public and Nimura Furuta, now known as Kichimura Washu, has been appointed new Bureau Chief of the CCG. He hopes to completely eradicate and displace all Ghouls from Tokyo with the Oggai. Kaneki and Touka finally tie the knot, but under orders from Furuta, the Oggai and Suzuya Squad crash the celebration. Backed into a corner, Kaneki consumes the Oggai and transforms into a dragon-like monstrosity before rising to the surface. The Ghouls decide to join forces with the CCG to save Kaneki and the city, and their alliance leads to recovering Kaneki from inside the monster's massive body. However, Furuta can't contain his excitment as the countdown to total human Ghoulification winds down...

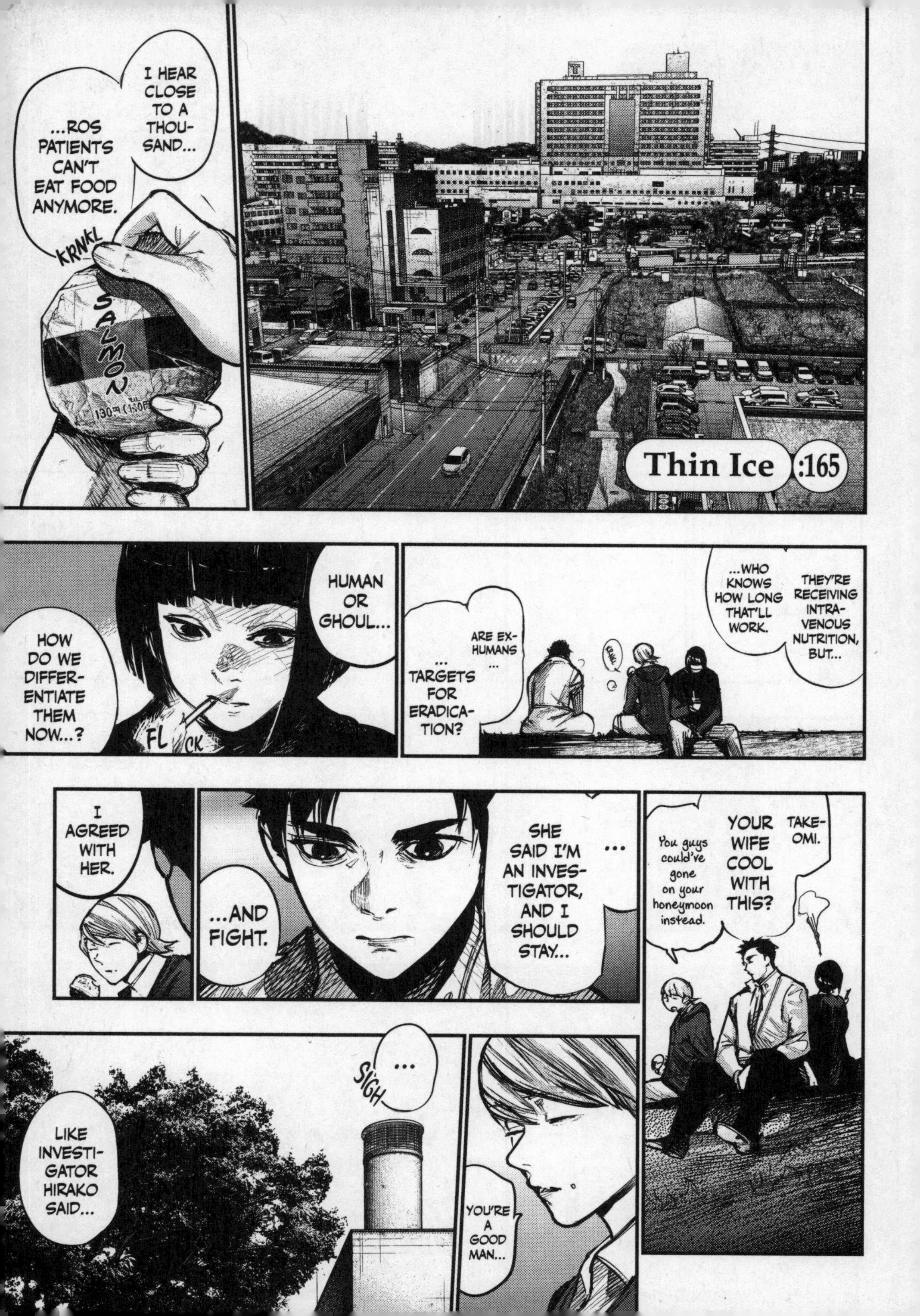
Thin Ice :165
I HEAR CLOSE TO A THOUSAND...
...ROS PATIENTS CAN'T EAT FOOD ANYMORE.
KRNKL
SALMON
130円
THEY'RE RECEIVING INTRAVENOUS NUTRITION, BUT...
...WHO KNOWS HOW LONG THAT'LL WORK.
KRNKL
ARE EX-HUMANS...
...TARGETS FOR ERADICATION?
HUMAN OR GHOUL...
HOW DO WE DIFFERENTIATE THEM NOW...?
FLICK
TAKE-OMI.
YOUR WIFE COOL WITH THIS?
You guys could've gone on your honeymoon instead.
...
SHE SAID I'M AN INVESTIGATOR, AND I SHOULD STAY...
...AND FIGHT.
I AGREED WITH HER.
YOU'RE A GOOD MAN...
...
SIGH
LIKE INVESTIGATOR HIRAKO SAID...

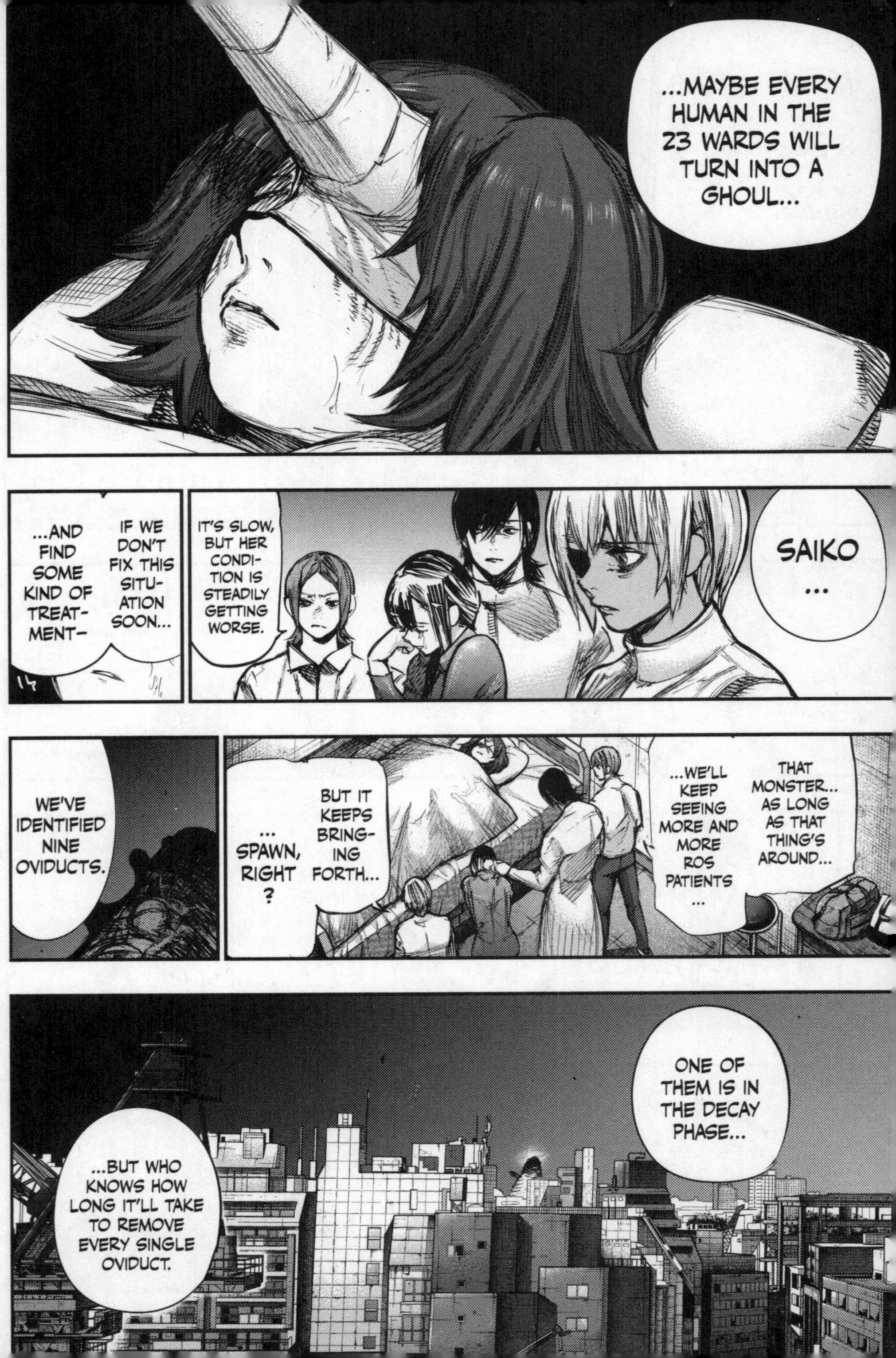
...MAYBE EVERY HUMAN IN THE 23 WARDS WILL TURN INTO A GHOUL...
SAIKO ...
IT'S SLOW, BUT HER CONDITION IS STEADILY GETTING WORSE.
IF WE DON'T FIX THIS SITUATION SOON...
...AND FIND SOME KIND OF TREATMENT–
THAT MONSTER... AS LONG AS THAT THING'S AROUND...
...WE'LL KEEP SEEING MORE AND MORE ROS PATIENTS ...
BUT IT KEEPS BRINGING FORTH...
... SPAWN, RIGHT ?
WE'VE IDENTIFIED NINE OVIDUCTS.
ONE OF THEM IS IN THE DECAY PHASE...
...BUT WHO KNOWS HOW LONG IT'LL TAKE TO REMOVE EVERY SINGLE OVIDUCT.

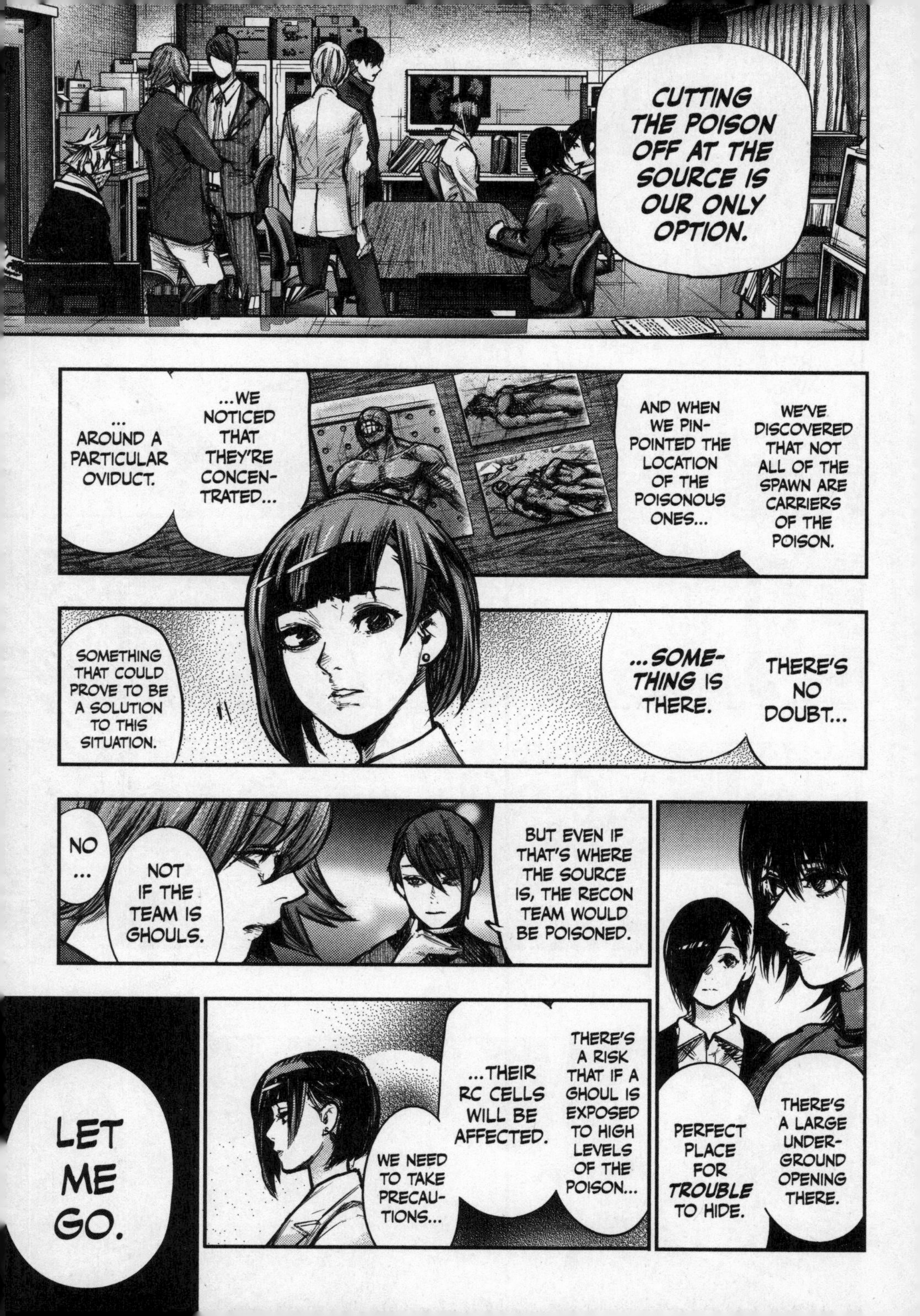
CUTTING THE POISON OFF AT THE SOURCE IS OUR ONLY OPTION.
WE'VE DISCOVERED THAT NOT ALL OF THE SPAWN ARE CARRIERS OF THE POISON.
AND WHEN WE PIN-POINTED THE LOCATION OF THE POISONOUS ONES...
...WE NOTICED THAT THEY'RE CONCEN-TRATED...
...AROUND A PARTICULAR OVIDUCT.
THERE'S NO DOUBT...
...*SOME-THING* IS THERE.
SOMETHING THAT COULD PROVE TO BE A SOLUTION TO THIS SITUATION.
THERE'S A LARGE UNDER-GROUND OPENING THERE.
PERFECT PLACE FOR *TROUBLE* TO HIDE.
BUT EVEN IF THAT'S WHERE THE SOURCE IS, THE RECON TEAM WOULD BE POISONED.
NO...
NOT IF THE TEAM IS GHOULS.
THERE'S A RISK THAT IF A GHOUL IS EXPOSED TO HIGH LEVELS OF THE POISON...
...THEIR RC CELLS WILL BE AFFECTED.
WE NEED TO TAKE PRECAU-TIONS...
LET ME GO.

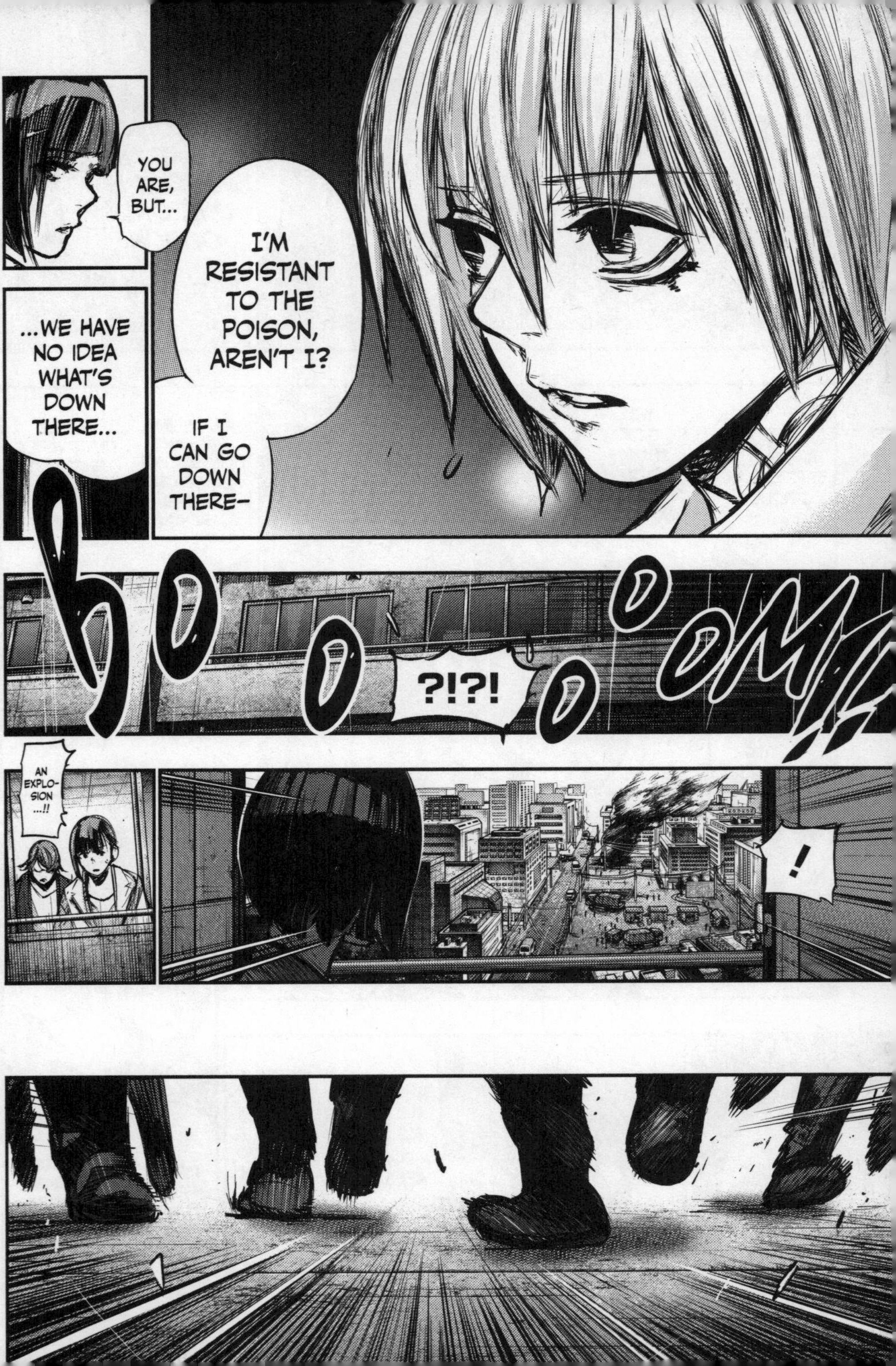
I'M RESISTANT TO THE POISON, AREN'T I?
IF I CAN GO DOWN THERE–
YOU ARE, BUT...
...WE HAVE NO IDEA WHAT'S DOWN THERE...
BOOOOOM!!
?!?!
!
AN EXPLOSION ...!!

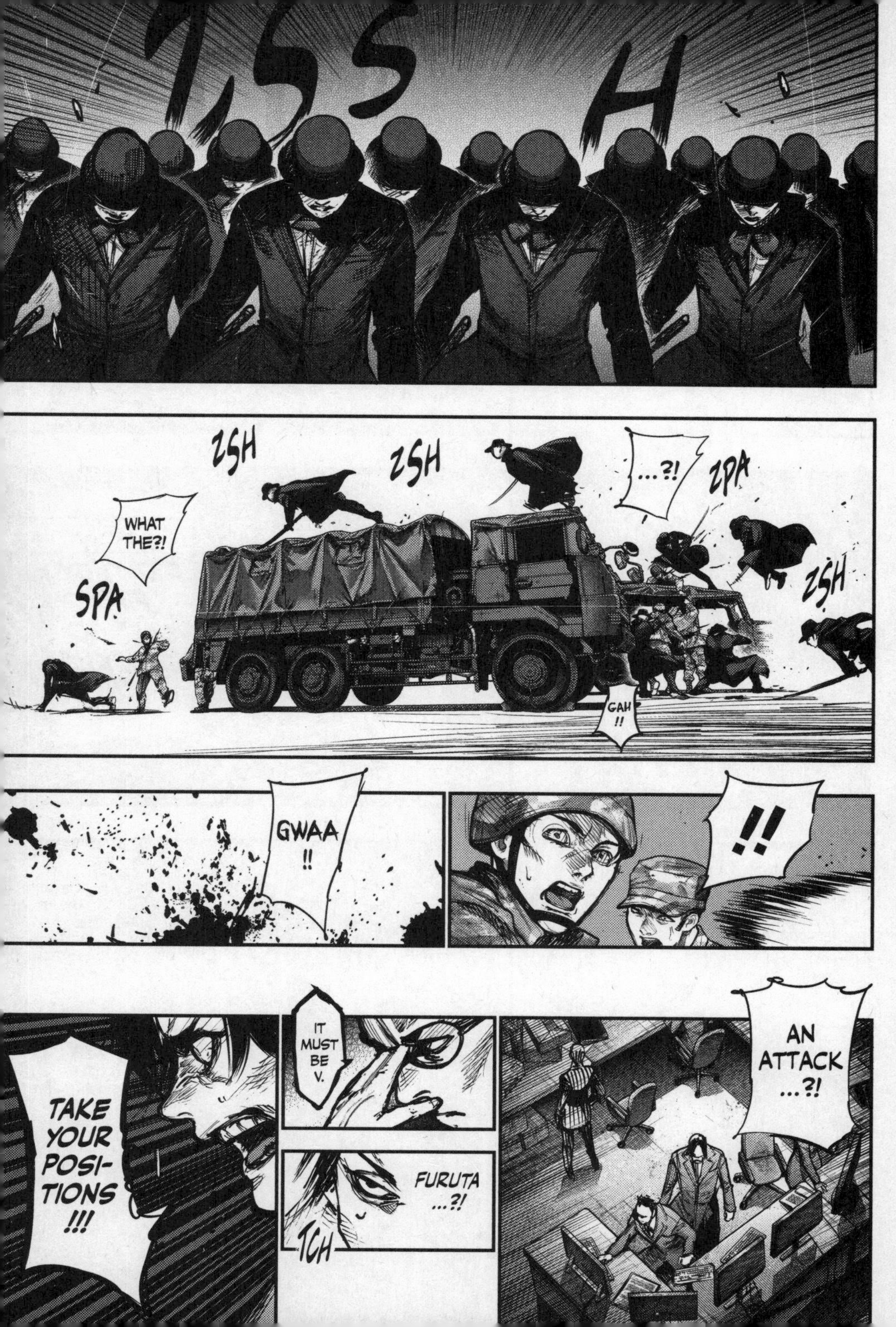
ZSSH
...?!
ZPA
ZSH
ZSH
ZSH
WHAT THE?!
SPA
GAH!!
!!
GWAA!!
AN ATTACK...?!
IT MUST BE V.
FURUTA...?!
TCH
TAKE YOUR POSI-TIONS!!!

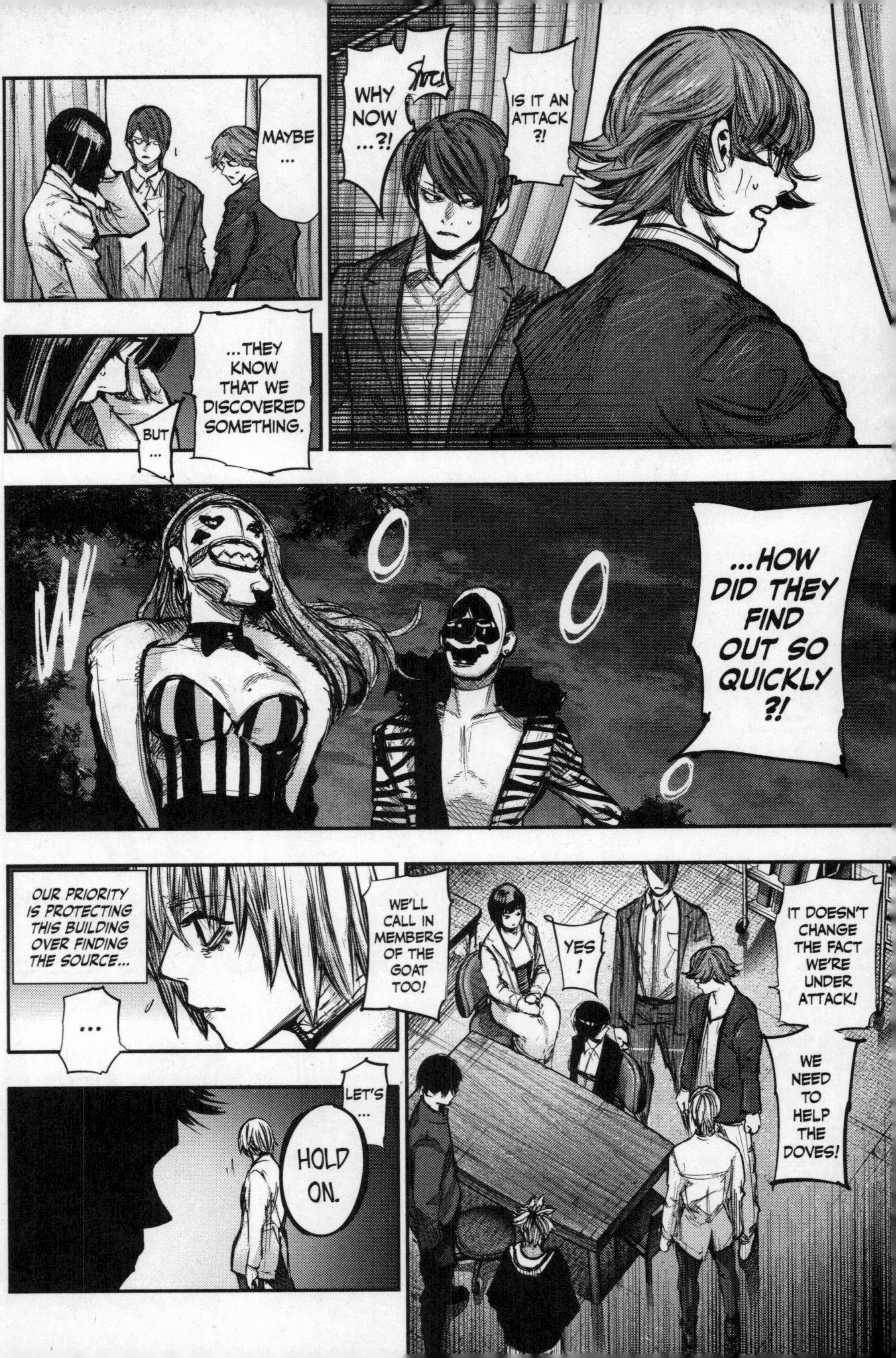
IS IT AN ATTACK ?!
WHY NOW ...?!
MAYBE ...
...THEY KNOW THAT WE DISCOVERED SOMETHING.
BUT ...
...HOW DID THEY FIND OUT SO QUICKLY ?!
IT DOESN'T CHANGE THE FACT WE'RE UNDER ATTACK!
WE NEED TO HELP THE DOVES!
YES !
WE'LL CALL IN MEMBERS OF THE GOAT TOO!
OUR PRIORITY IS PROTECTING THIS BUILDING OVER FINDING THE SOURCE...
...
LET'S ...
HOLD ON.

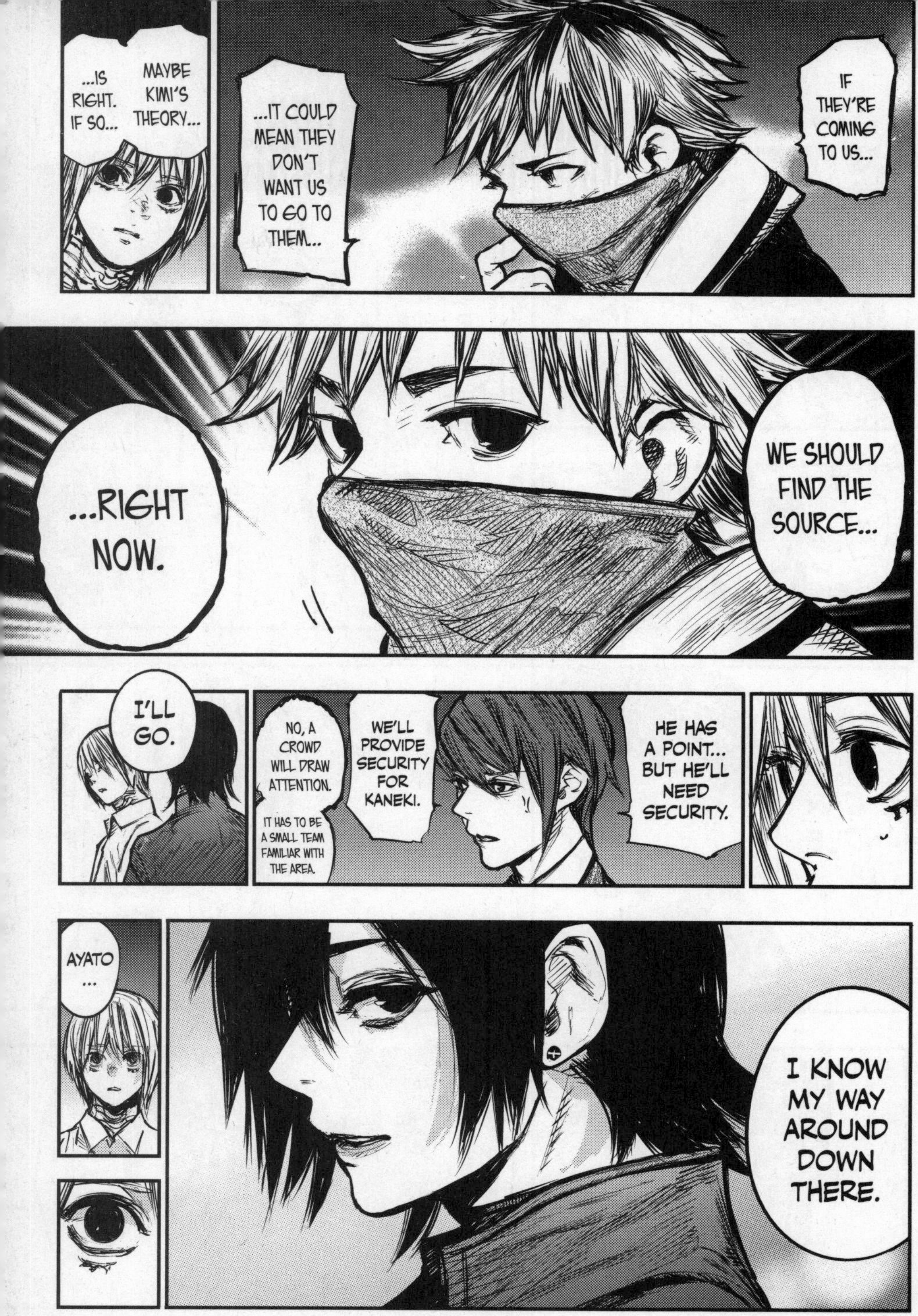
IF THEY'RE COMING TO US...
...IT COULD MEAN THEY DON'T WANT US TO GO TO THEM...
MAYBE KIMI'S THEORY...
...IS RIGHT. IF SO...
WE SHOULD FIND THE SOURCE...
...RIGHT NOW.
HE HAS A POINT... BUT HE'LL NEED SECURITY.
WE'LL PROVIDE SECURITY FOR KANEKI.
NO, A CROWD WILL DRAW ATTENTION.
IT HAS TO BE A SMALL TEAM FAMILIAR WITH THE AREA.
I'LL GO.
I KNOW MY WAY AROUND DOWN THERE.
AYATO ...

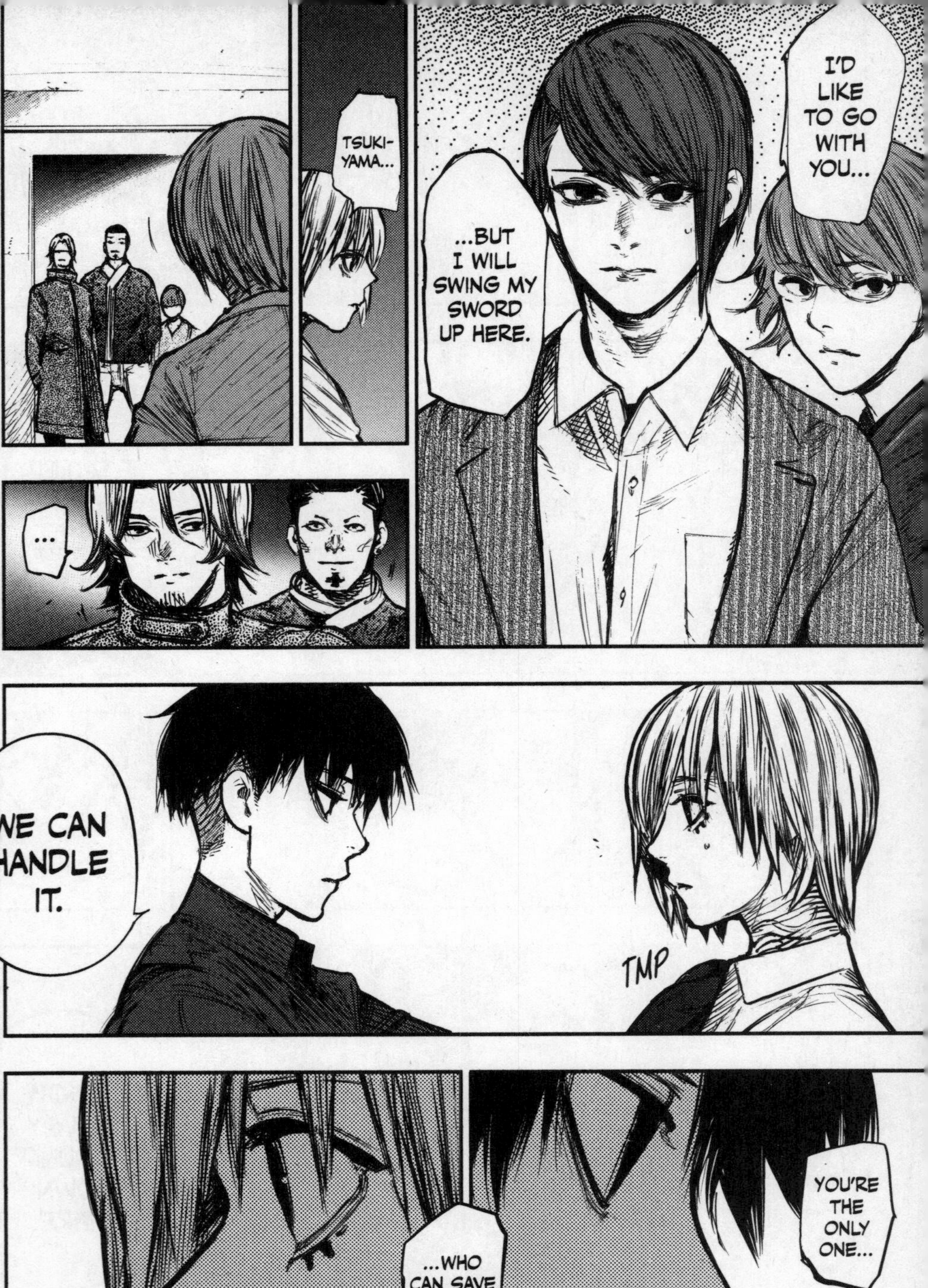
I'D LIKE TO GO WITH YOU...
...BUT I WILL SWING MY SWORD UP HERE.
TSUKI-YAMA...
...
WE CAN HANDLE IT.
TMP
YOU'RE THE ONLY ONE...
...WHO CAN SAVE YONE-BAYASHI.

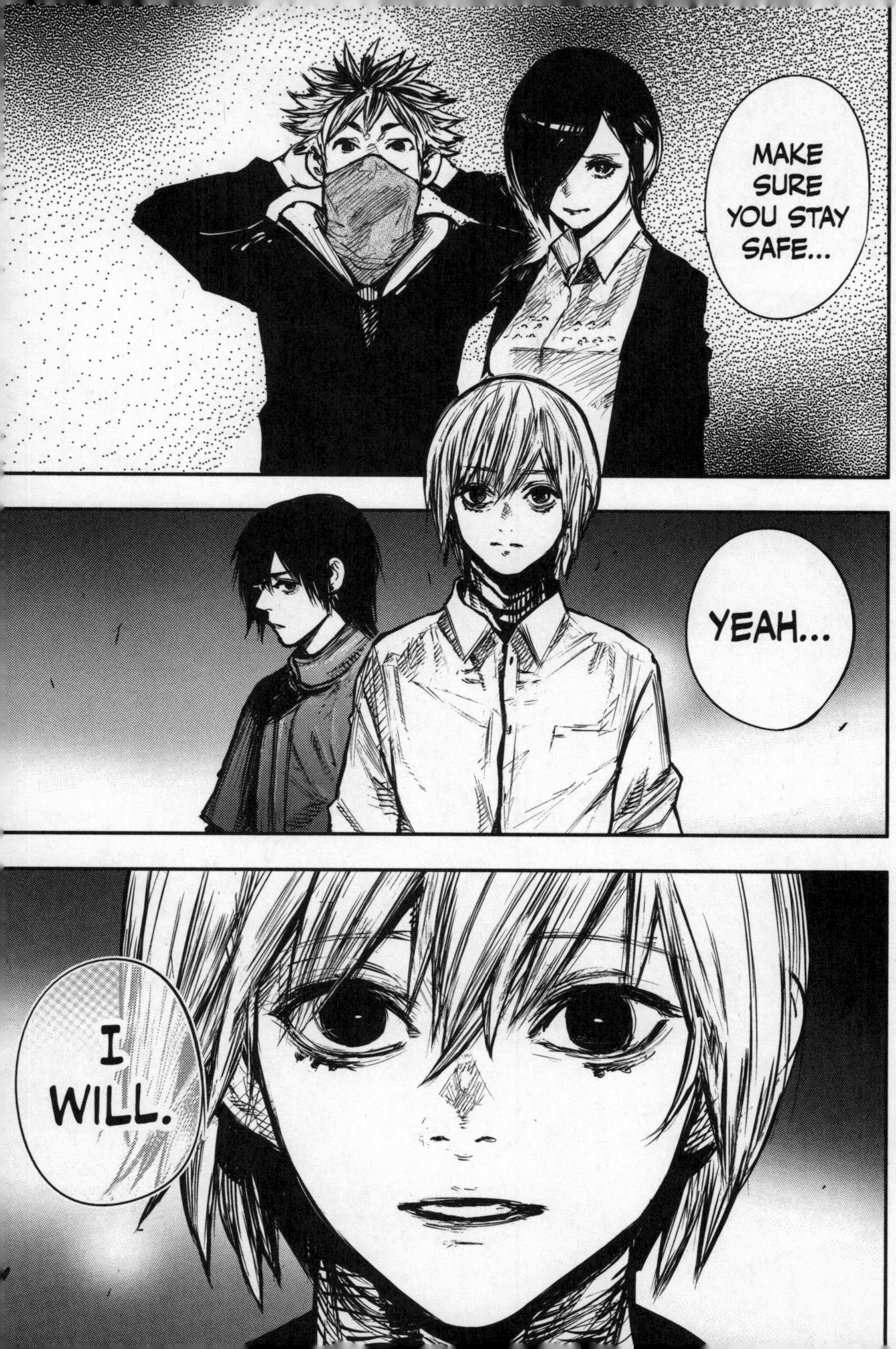
MAKE SURE YOU STAY SAFE...
YEAH...
I WILL.

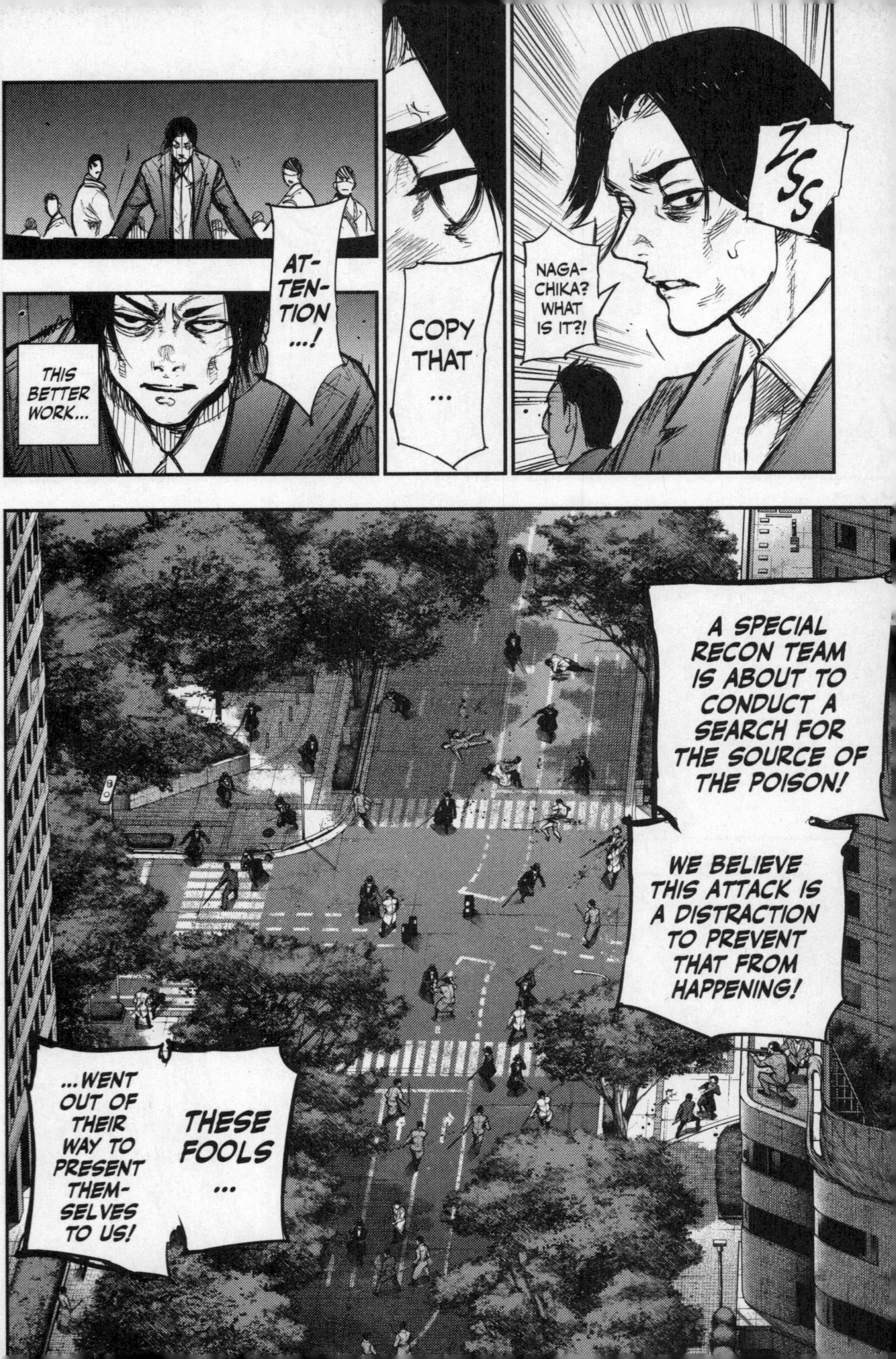
ZSS
NAGA-CHIKA? WHAT IS IT?!
COPY THAT ...
ATTENTION ...!
THIS BETTER WORK...
A SPECIAL RECON TEAM IS ABOUT TO CONDUCT A SEARCH FOR THE SOURCE OF THE POISON!
WE BELIEVE THIS ATTACK IS A DISTRACTION TO PREVENT THAT FROM HAPPENING!
THESE FOOLS ...
...WENT OUT OF THEIR WAY TO PRESENT THEMSELVES TO US!

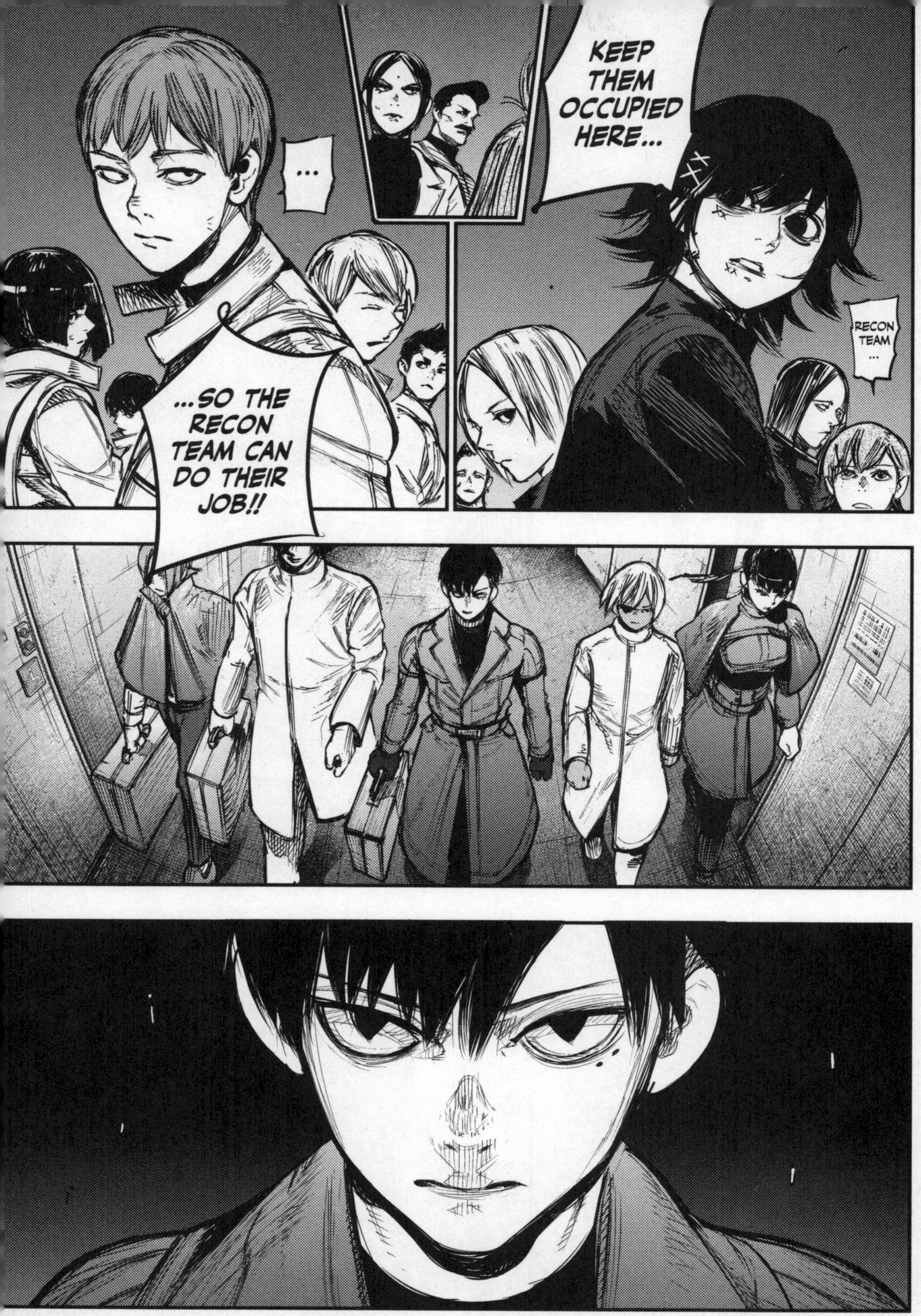
KEEP THEM OCCUPIED HERE...
RECON TEAM ...
...
...SO THE RECON TEAM CAN DO THEIR JOB!!

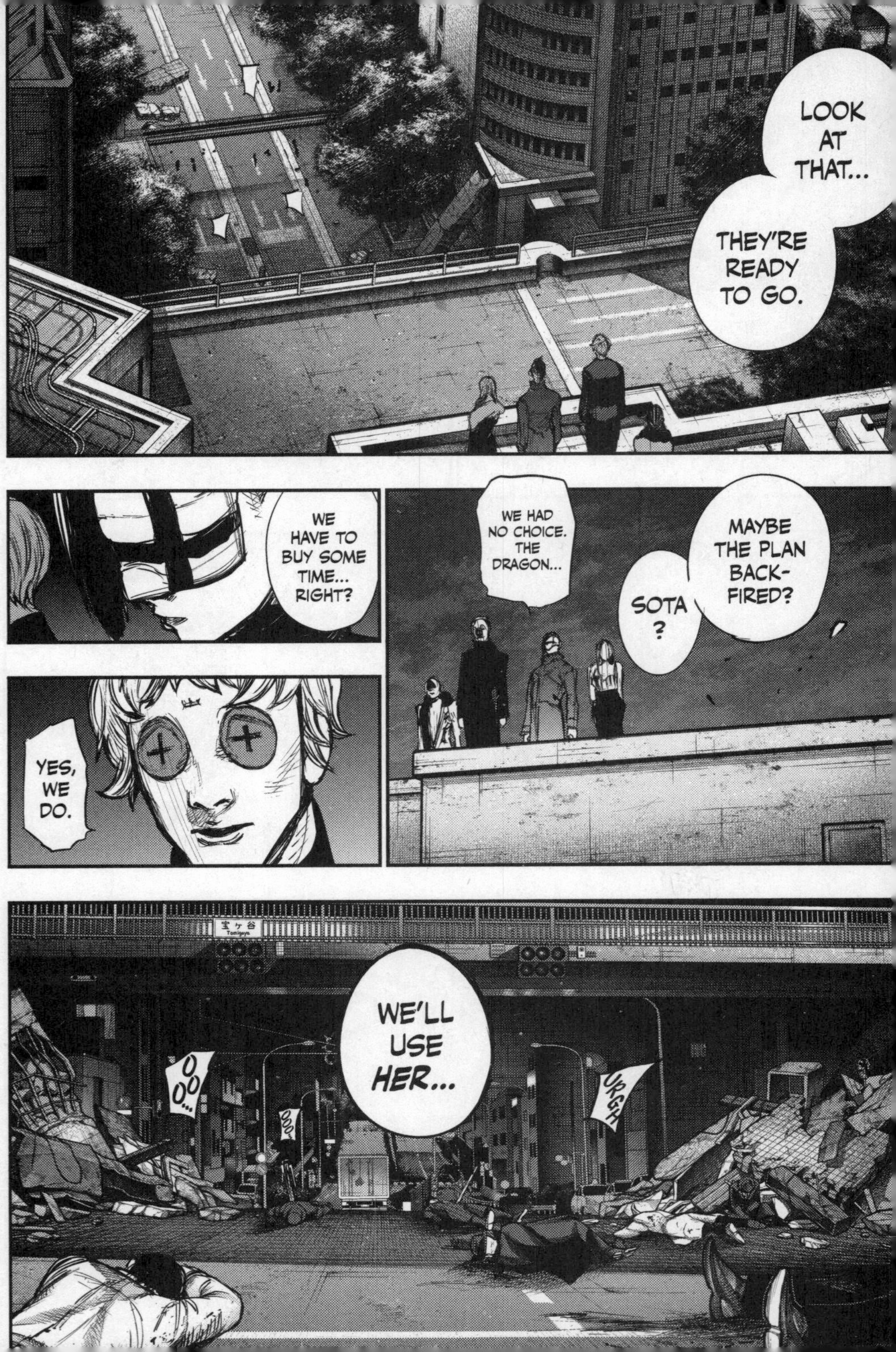
LOOK AT THAT...
THEY'RE READY TO GO.
MAYBE THE PLAN BACK-FIRED?
SOTA?
WE HAD NO CHOICE. THE DRAGON...
WE HAVE TO BUY SOME TIME... RIGHT?
YES, WE DO.
宝ヶ谷 Tomigaya
URGH
WE'LL USE *HER*...
OOO...

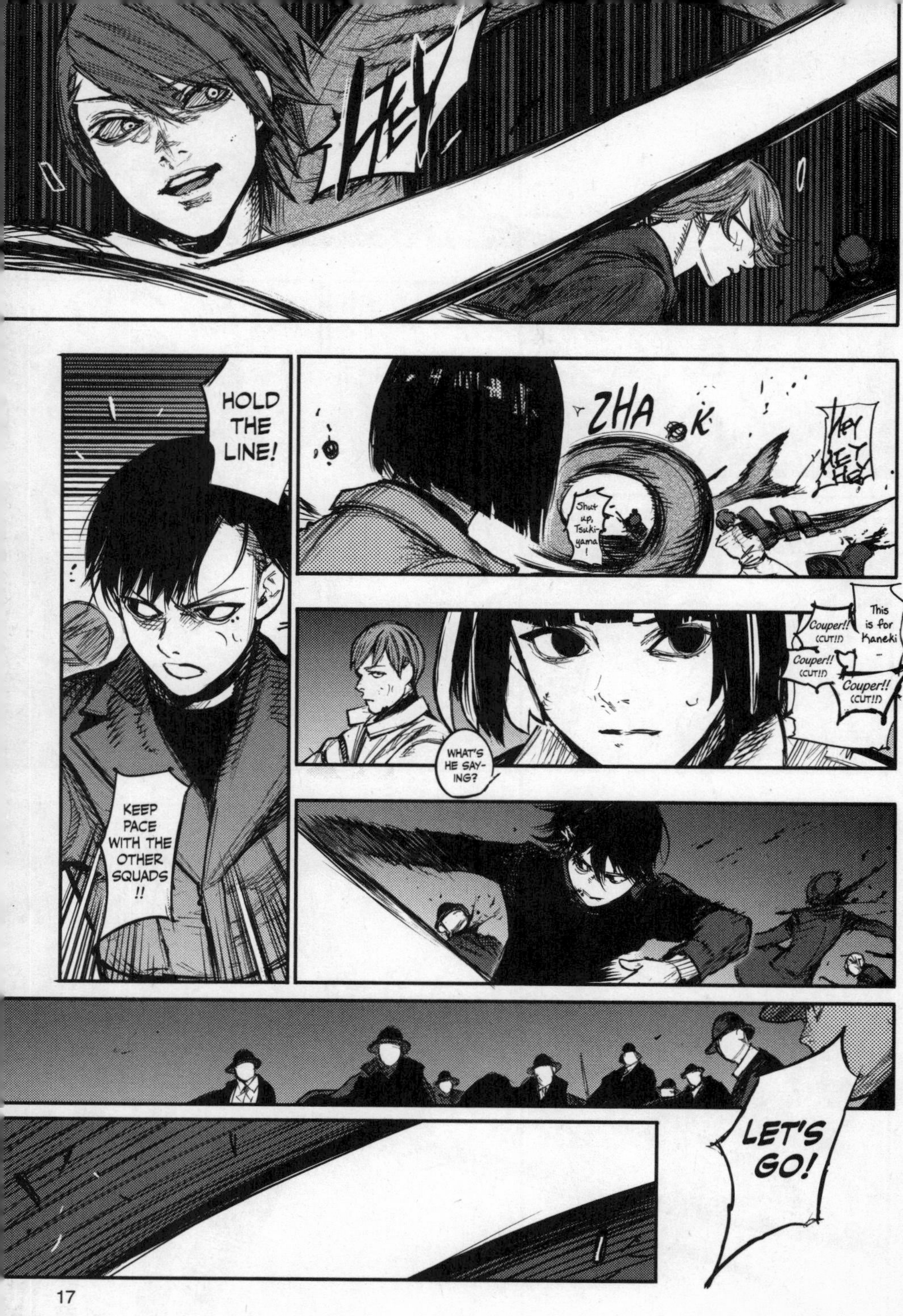
HEY
HEY HEY HEY
ZHAK
Shut up, Tsukiyama!
This is for Kaneki...
Couper!! (CUT!!)
Couper!! (CUT!!)
Couper!! (CUT!!)
WHAT'S HE SAYING?
HOLD THE LINE!
KEEP PACE WITH THE OTHER SQUADS!!
LET'S GO!

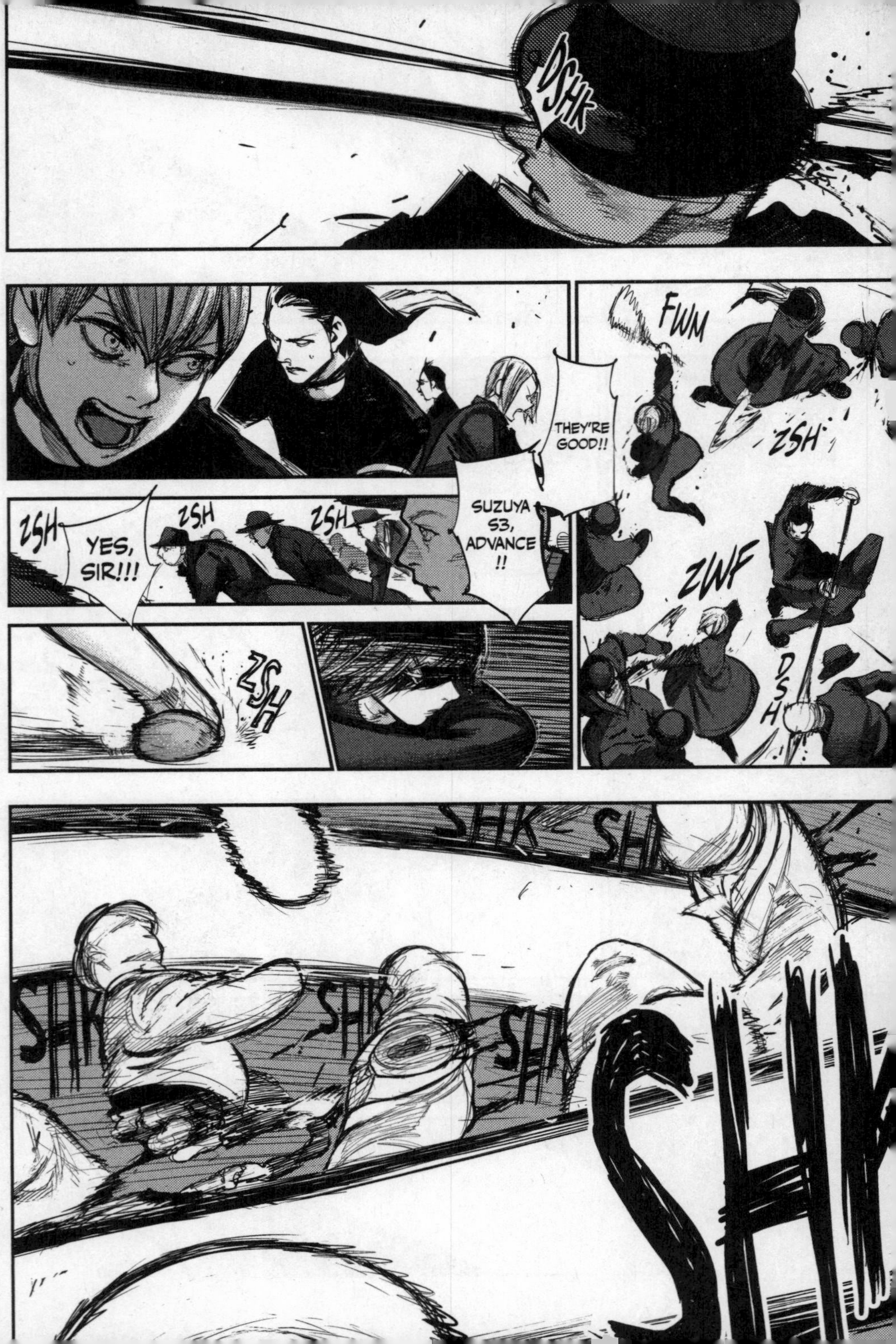
DSHK
FWUM
ZSH
ZWF
DSH
THEY'RE GOOD!!
SUZUYA S3, ADVANCE!!
ZSH
ZSH
ZSH
YES, SIR!!!
ZSH
SHK
SHK
SHK
SHK
SHK
SHK

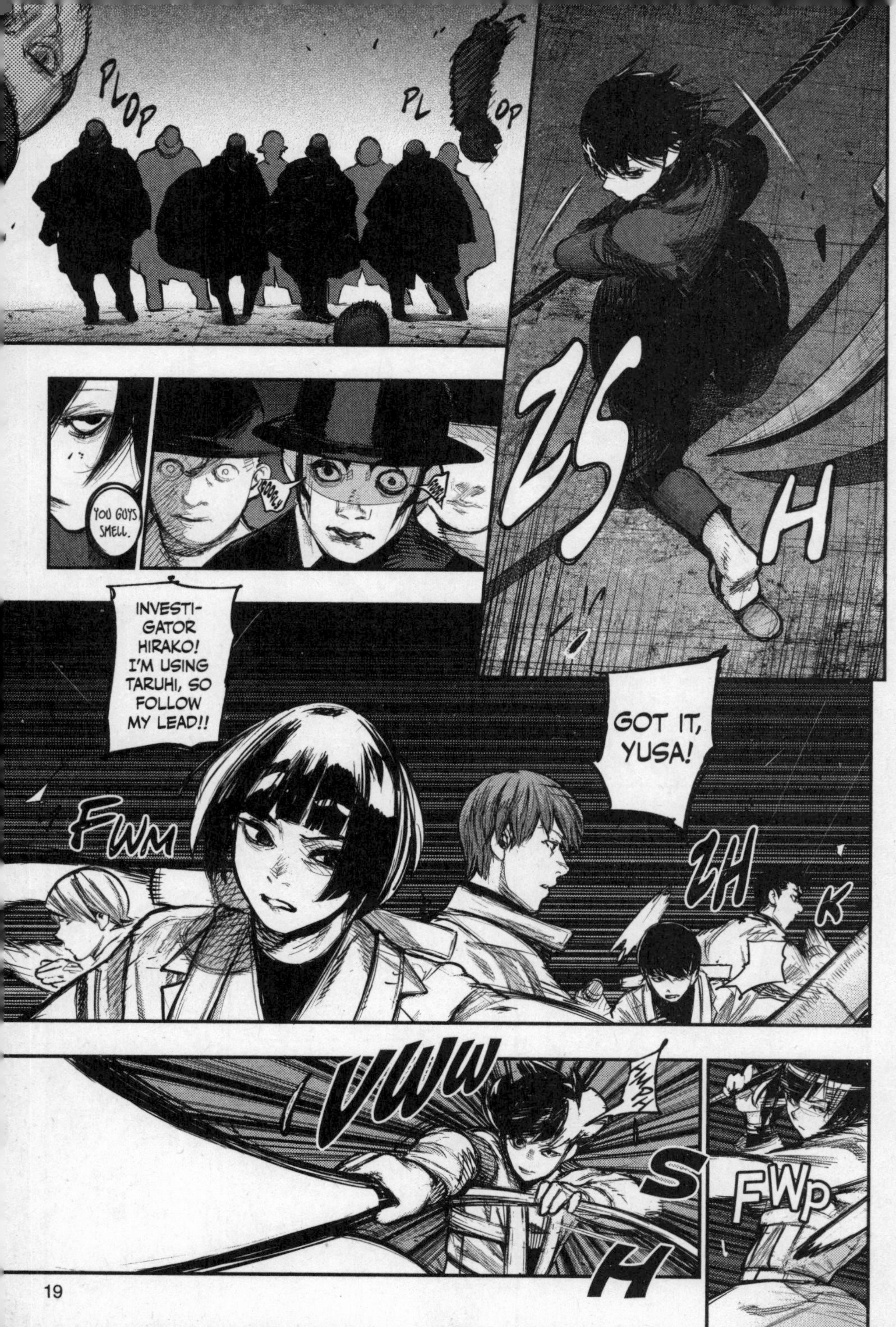
ZS
H
!
PLOP
PL
OP
GOOGLY
YOU GUYS SMELL.
GOT IT, YUSA!
INVESTI-GATOR HIRAKO! I'M USING TARUHI, SO FOLLOW MY LEAD!!
ZH
K
FWM
FWP
VWW
HMPH
S
H

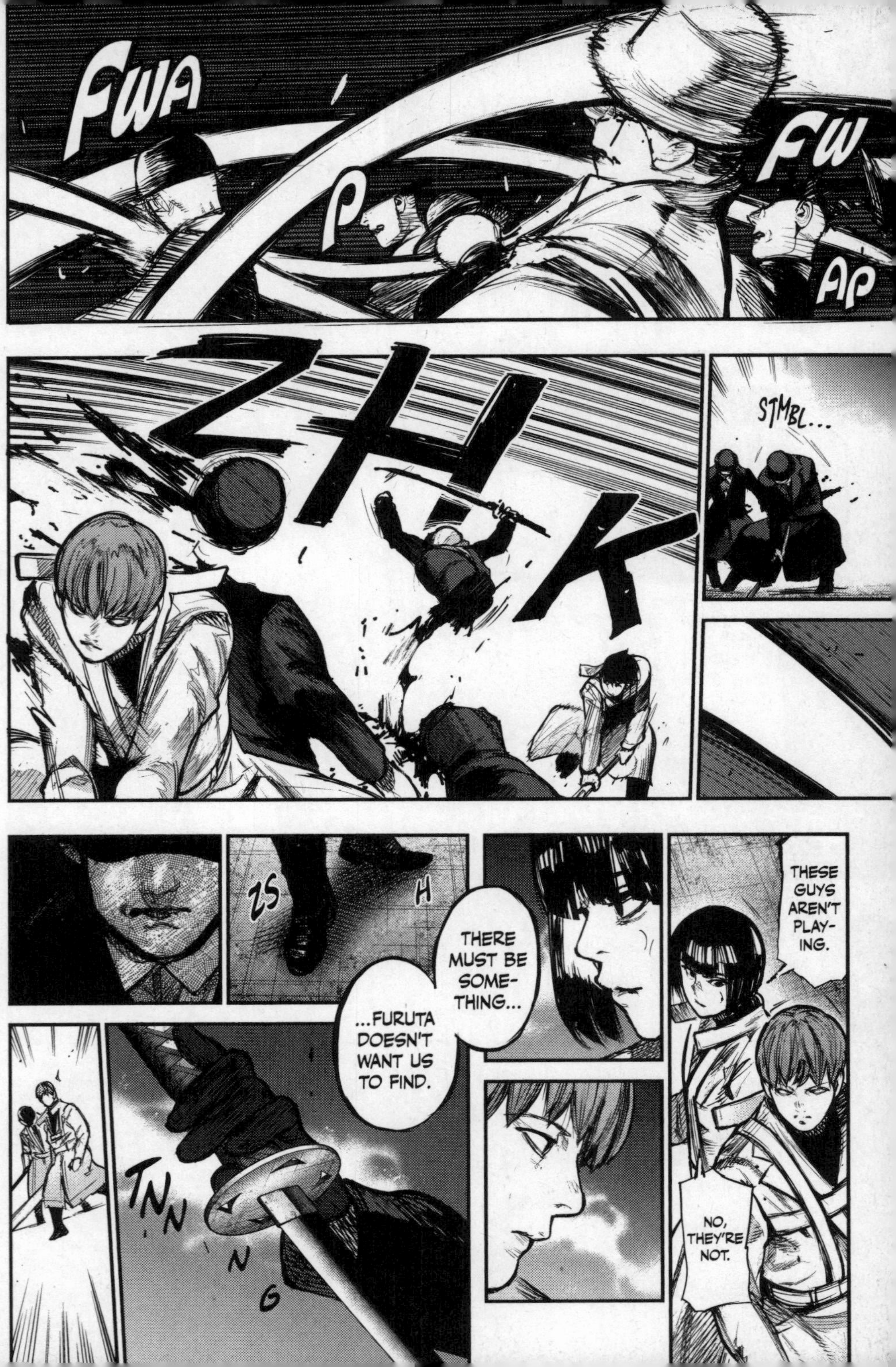
FW
AP
FWA
P
STMBL...
ZHK
THESE GUYS AREN'T PLAY-ING.
THERE MUST BE SOME-THING...
...FURUTA DOESN'T WANT US TO FIND.
ZSH
NO, THEY'RE NOT.
TNNNG

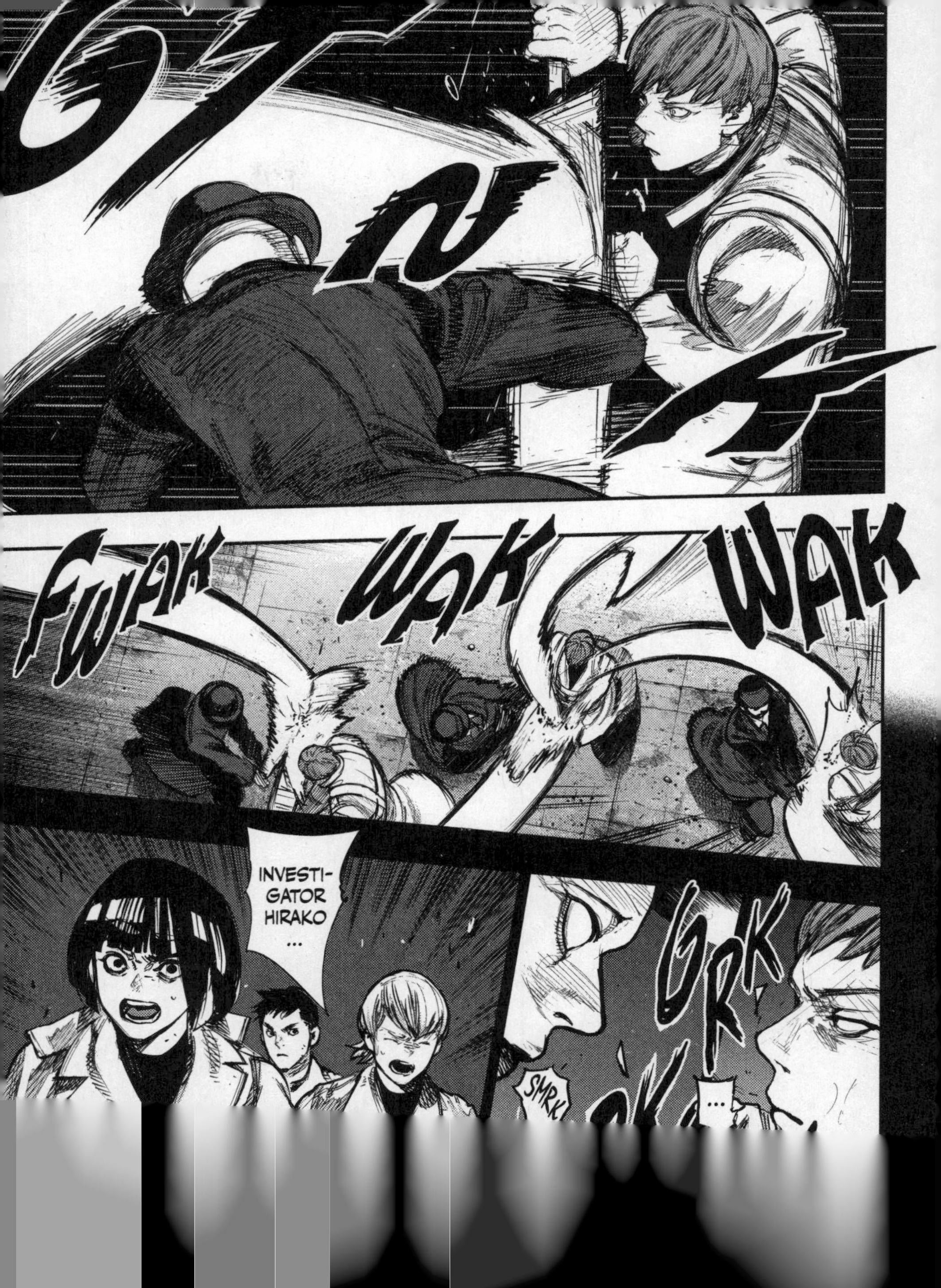
WAK
WAK
FWAK
GRK
SMRK
...
INVESTI-
GATOR
HIRAKO
...

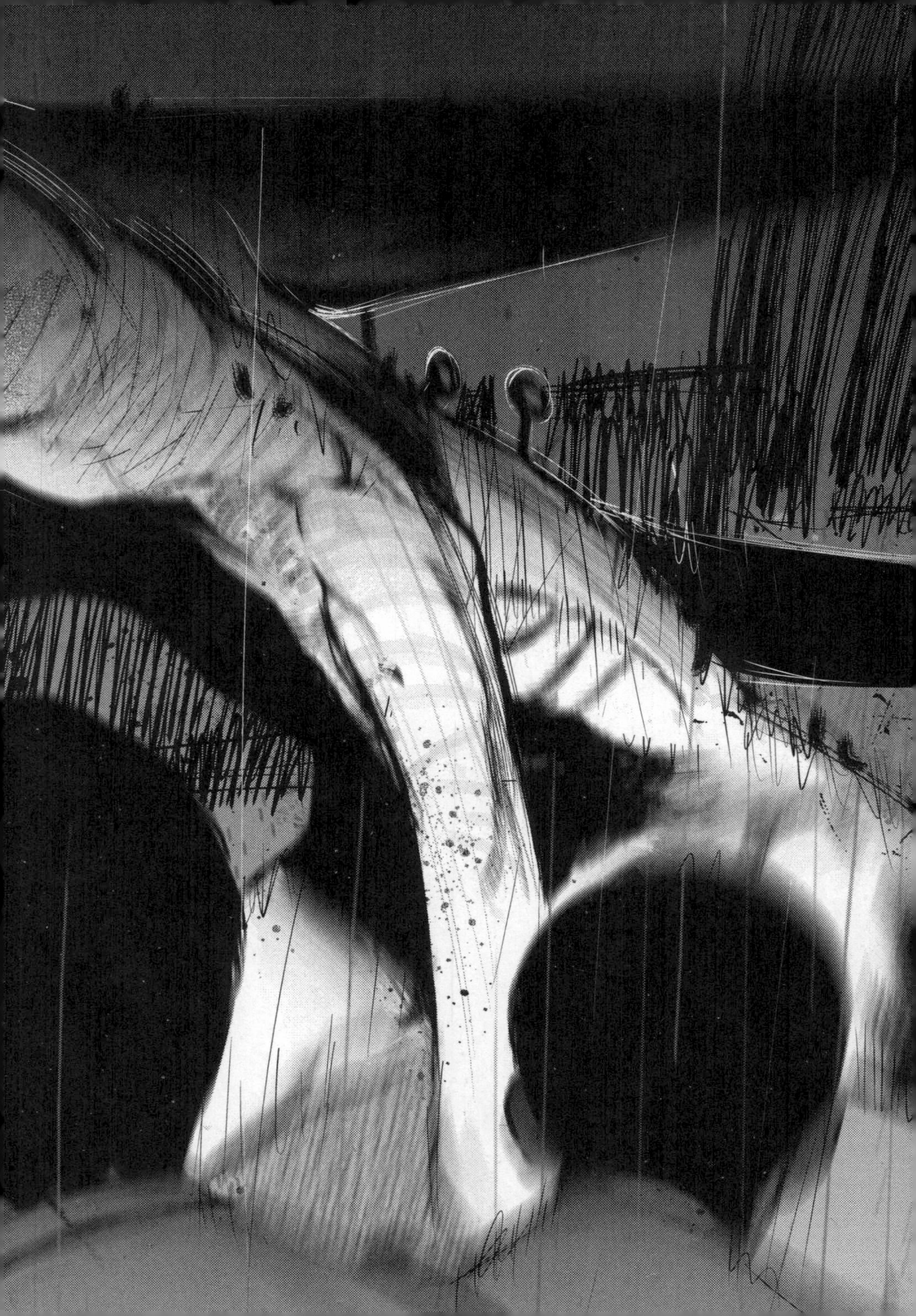

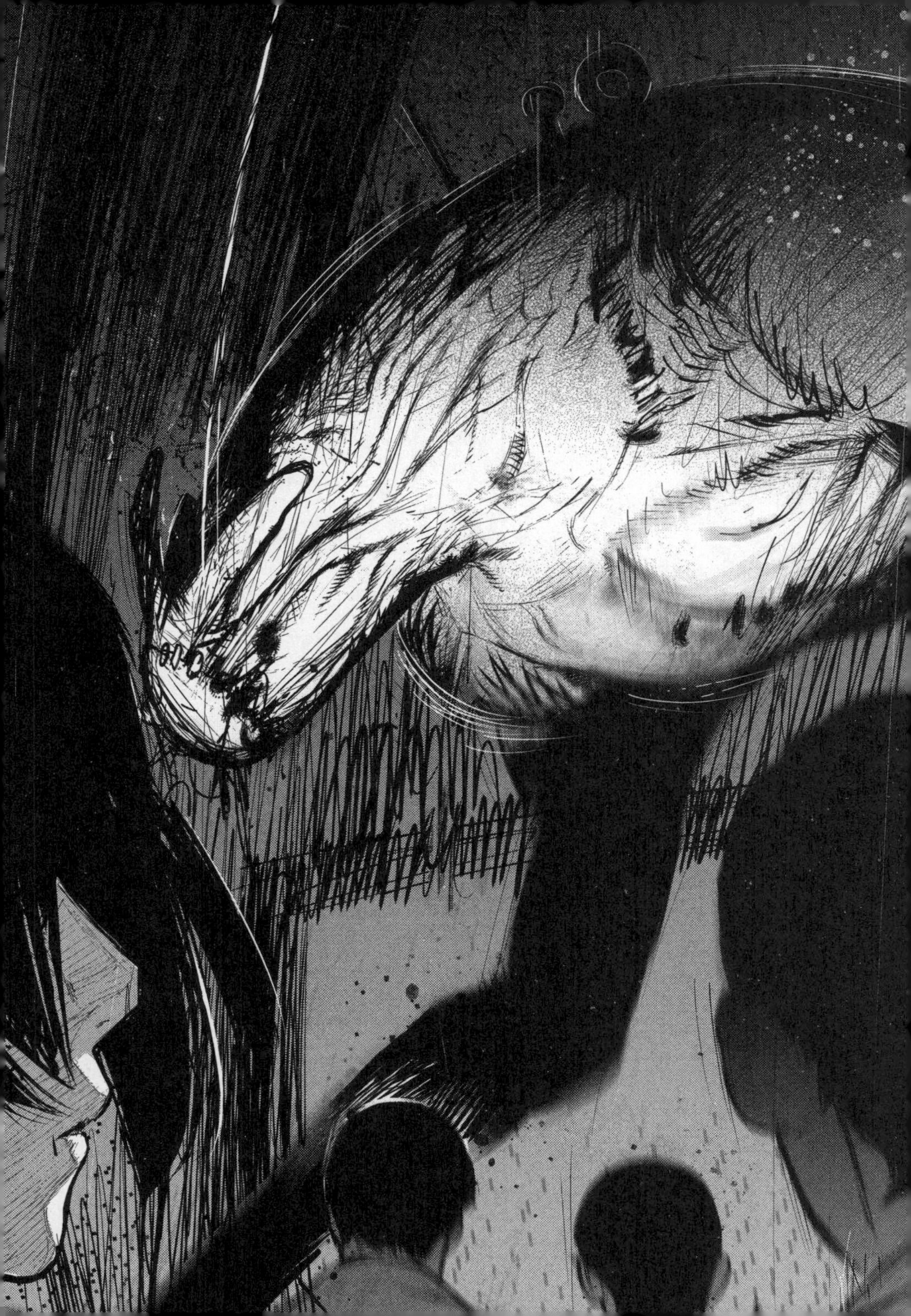

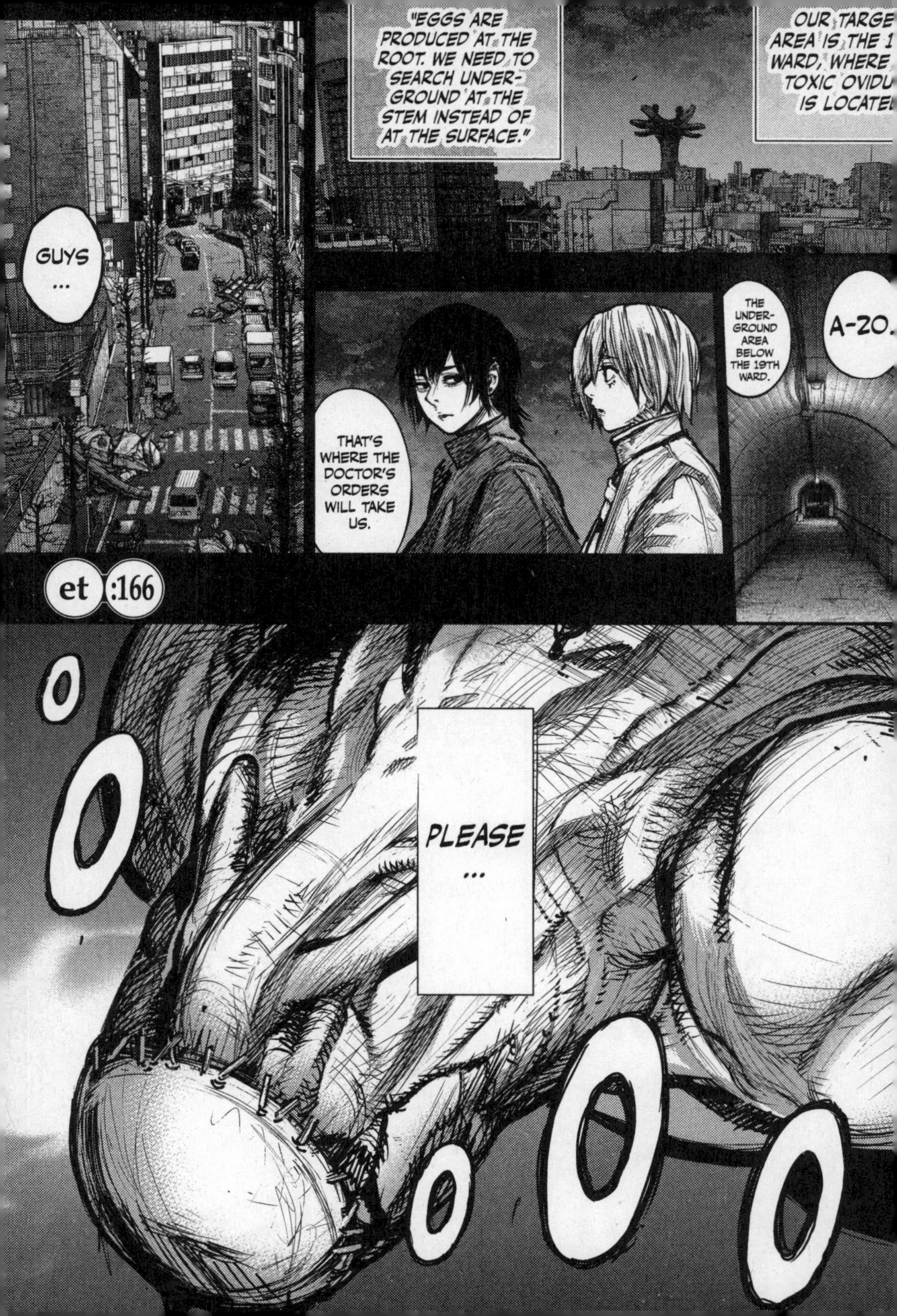
OUR TARGE AREA IS THE 1 WARD, WHERE TOXIC OVIDU IS LOCATE
"EGGS ARE PRODUCED AT THE ROOT. WE NEED TO SEARCH UNDERGROUND AT THE STEM INSTEAD OF AT THE SURFACE."
A-ZO.
THE UNDERGROUND AREA BELOW THE 19TH WARD.
THAT'S WHERE THE DOCTOR'S ORDERS WILL TAKE US.
GUYS ...
et :166
PLEASE ...
O
O
O
O
O
O

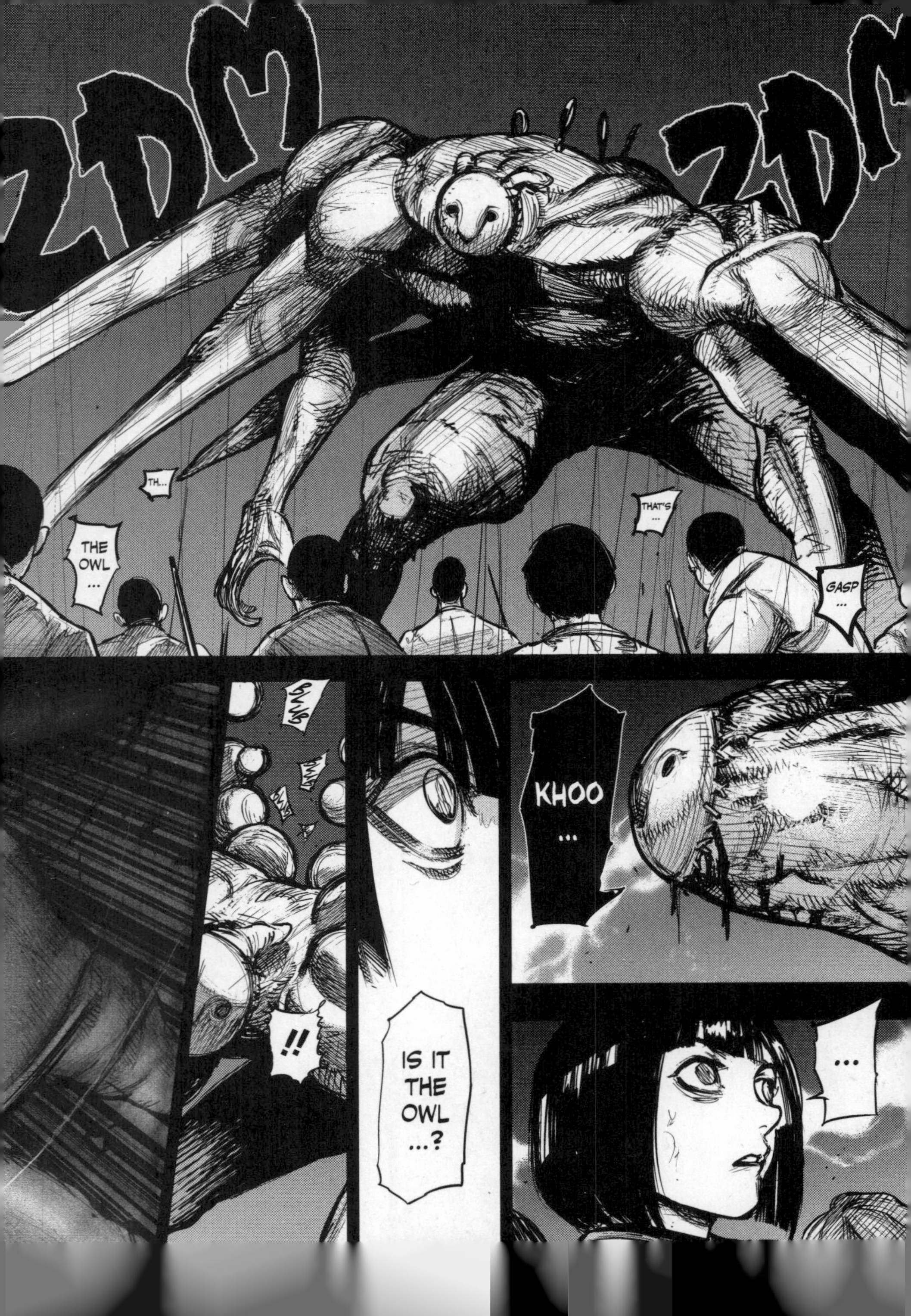
ZDM
ZDM
THAT'S ...
TH...
GASP ...
THE OWL ...
KHOO ...
...
IS IT THE OWL ...?
!!

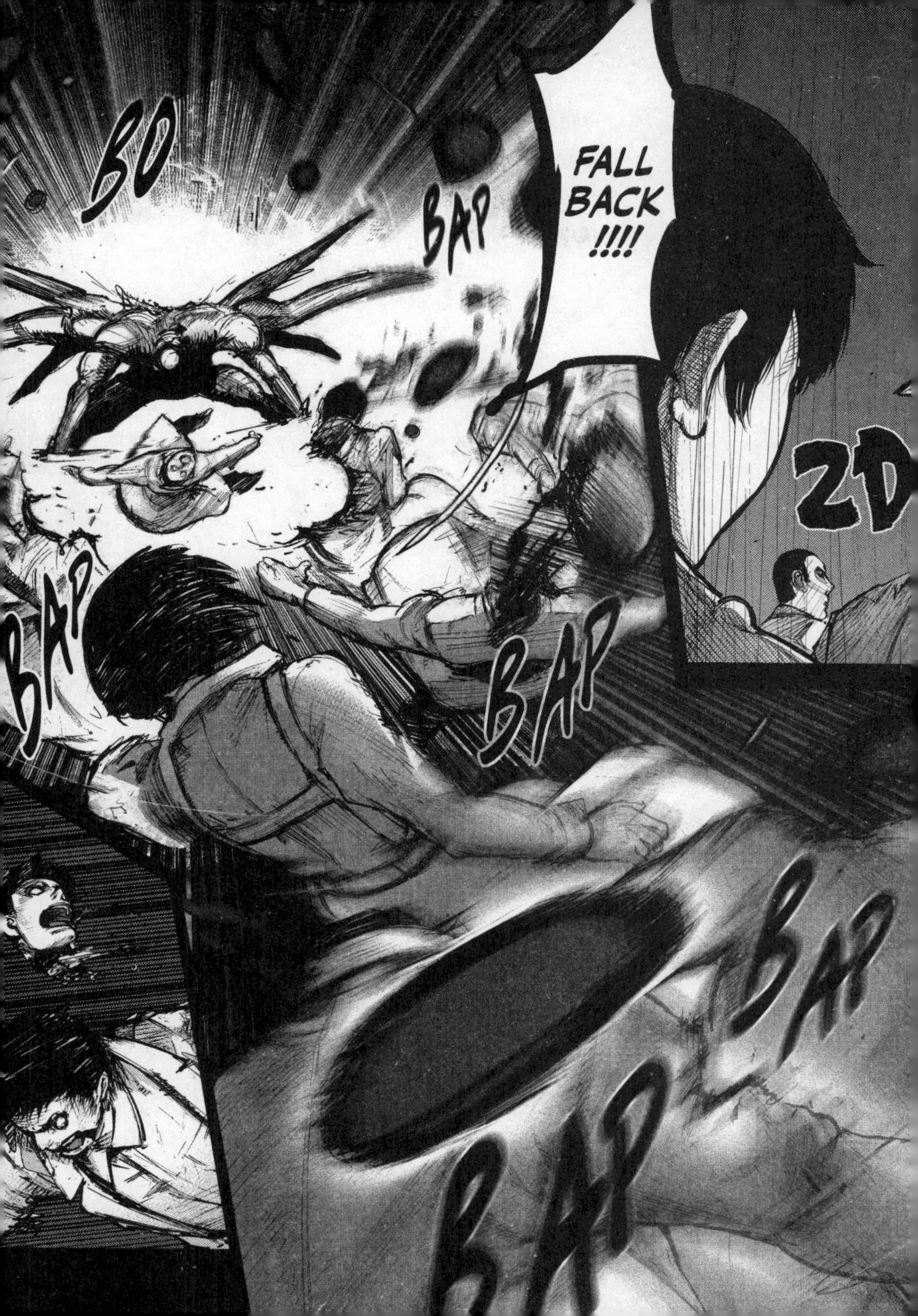
FALL BACK!!!!
ZD
BAP
BO
BAP
BAP
BAP
BAP
BAP

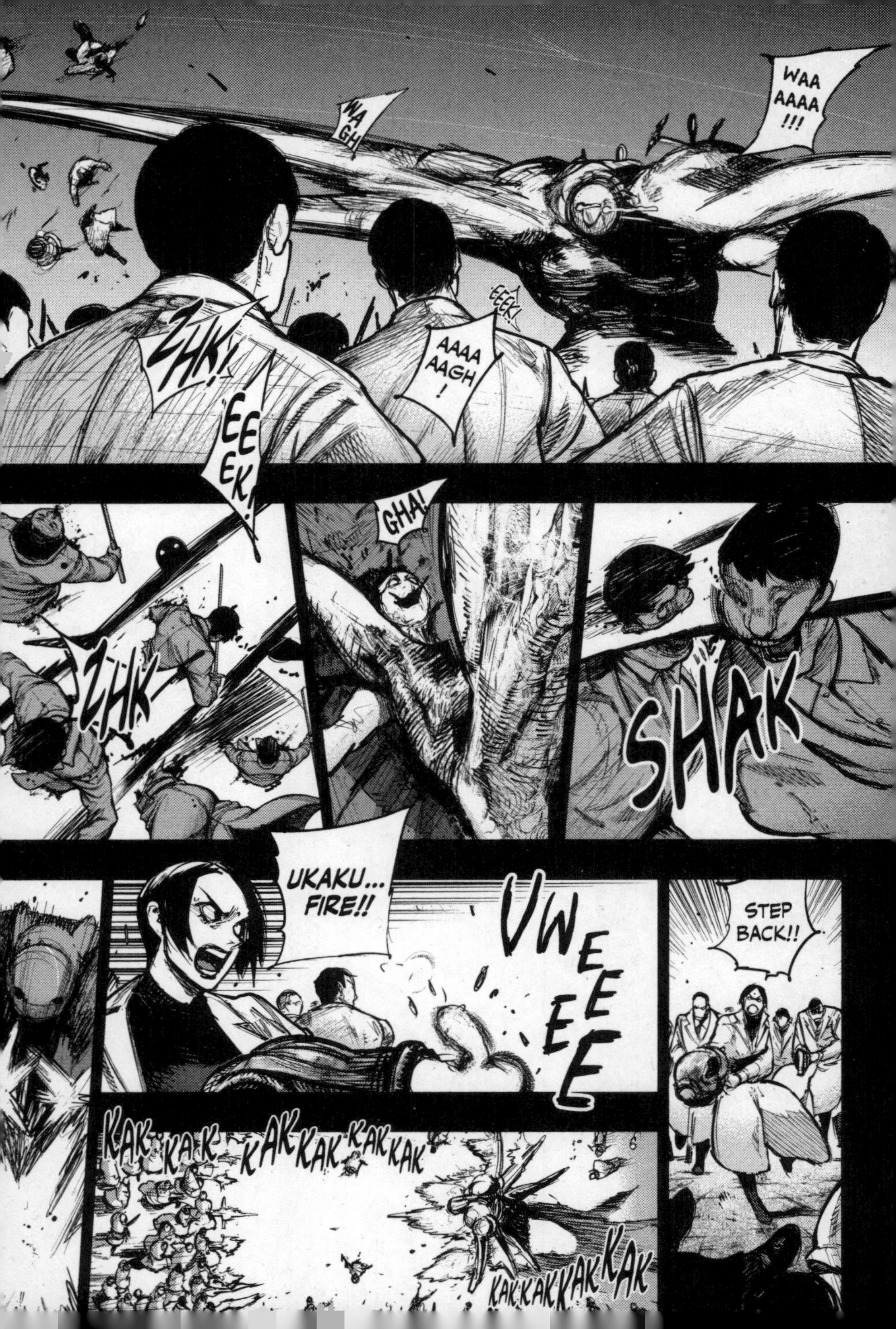
WAA AAAA !!!
WAGH
EEEK!
AAAA AAGH !
ZHK!
EEEK!
SHAK
GHA!
ZHK
STEP BACK!!
UWEEEEE
UKAKU... FIRE!!
KAK KAK KAK KAK
KAK KAK KAK KAK KAK KAK KAK

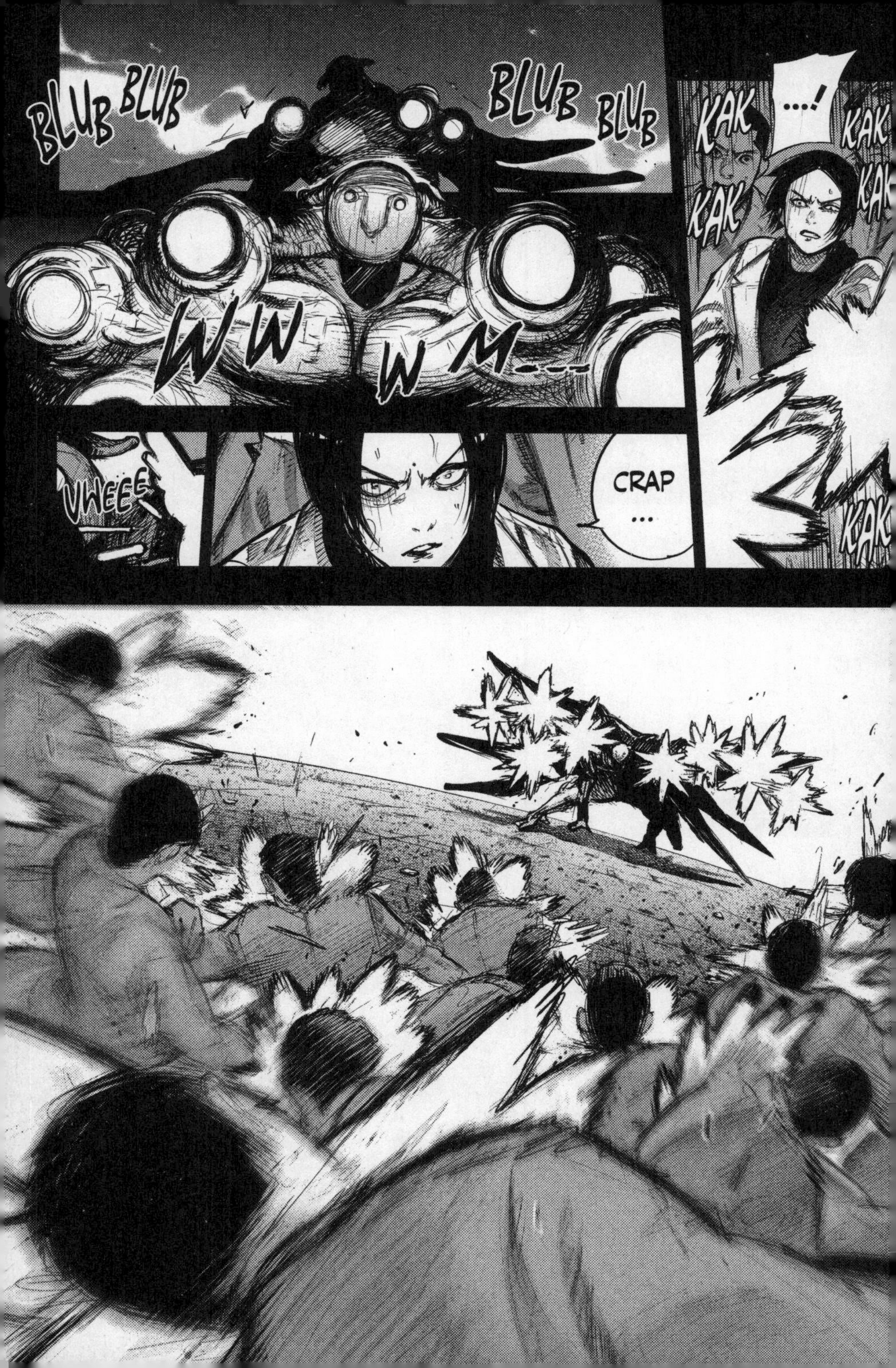
KAK
...!
KAK
KAK
KAK
KAK
BLUB
BLUB
BLUB
BLUB
WWWM...
CRAP ...
UWEEE

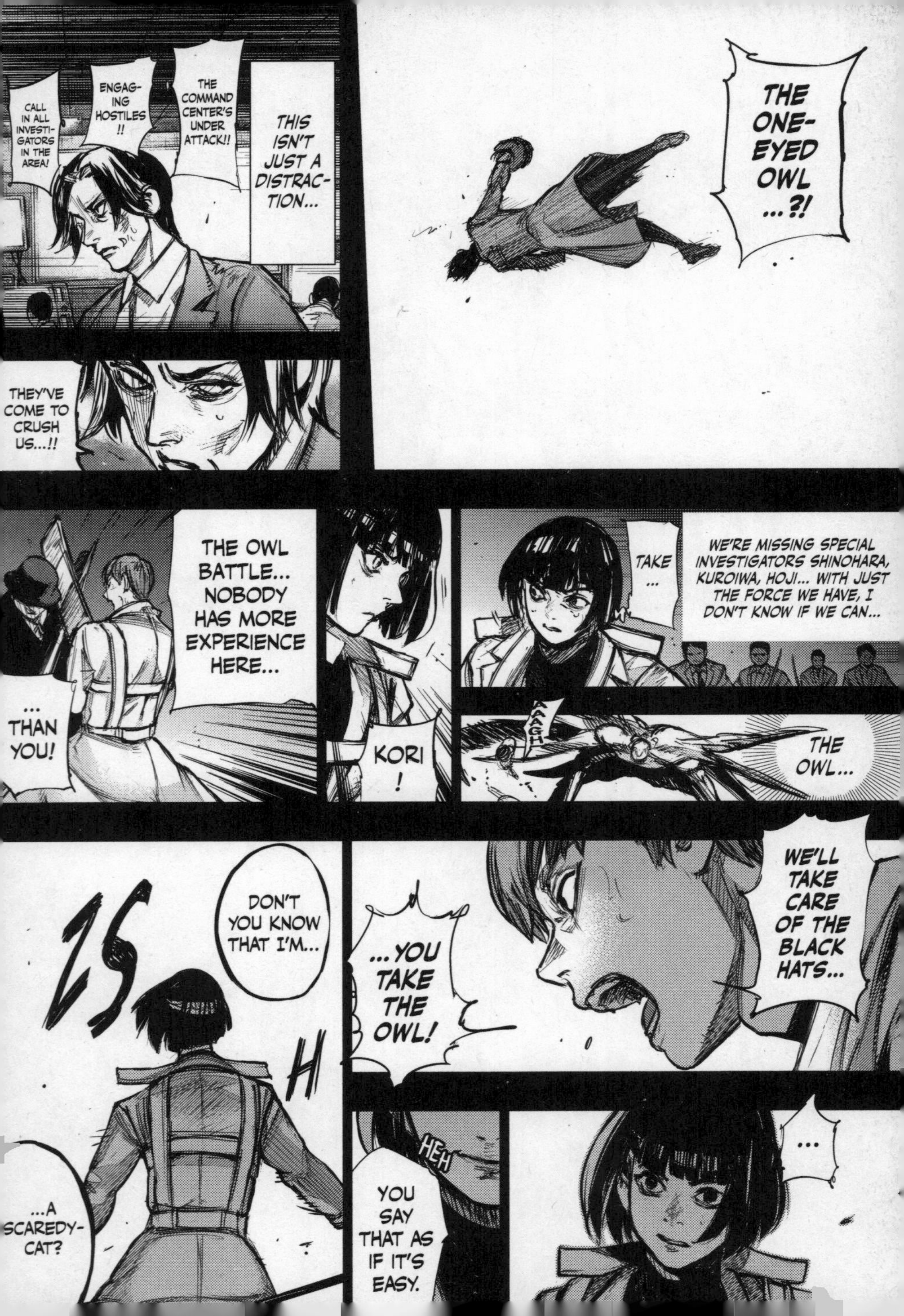
THE ONE-EYED OWL ...?!
THIS ISN'T JUST A DISTRACTION...
THE COMMAND CENTER'S UNDER ATTACK!!
ENGAGING HOSTILES !!
CALL IN ALL INVESTIGATORS IN THE AREA!
THEY'VE COME TO CRUSH US...!!
WE'RE MISSING SPECIAL INVESTIGATORS SHINOHARA, KUROIWA, HOJI... WITH JUST THE FORCE WE HAVE, I DON'T KNOW IF WE CAN...
TAKE ...
THE OWL...
KORI !
THE OWL BATTLE... NOBODY HAS MORE EXPERIENCE HERE...
... THAN YOU!
WE'LL TAKE CARE OF THE BLACK HATS...
...YOU TAKE THE OWL!
...
HEH
YOU SAY THAT AS IF IT'S EASY.
DON'T YOU KNOW THAT I'M...
...A SCAREDY-CAT?

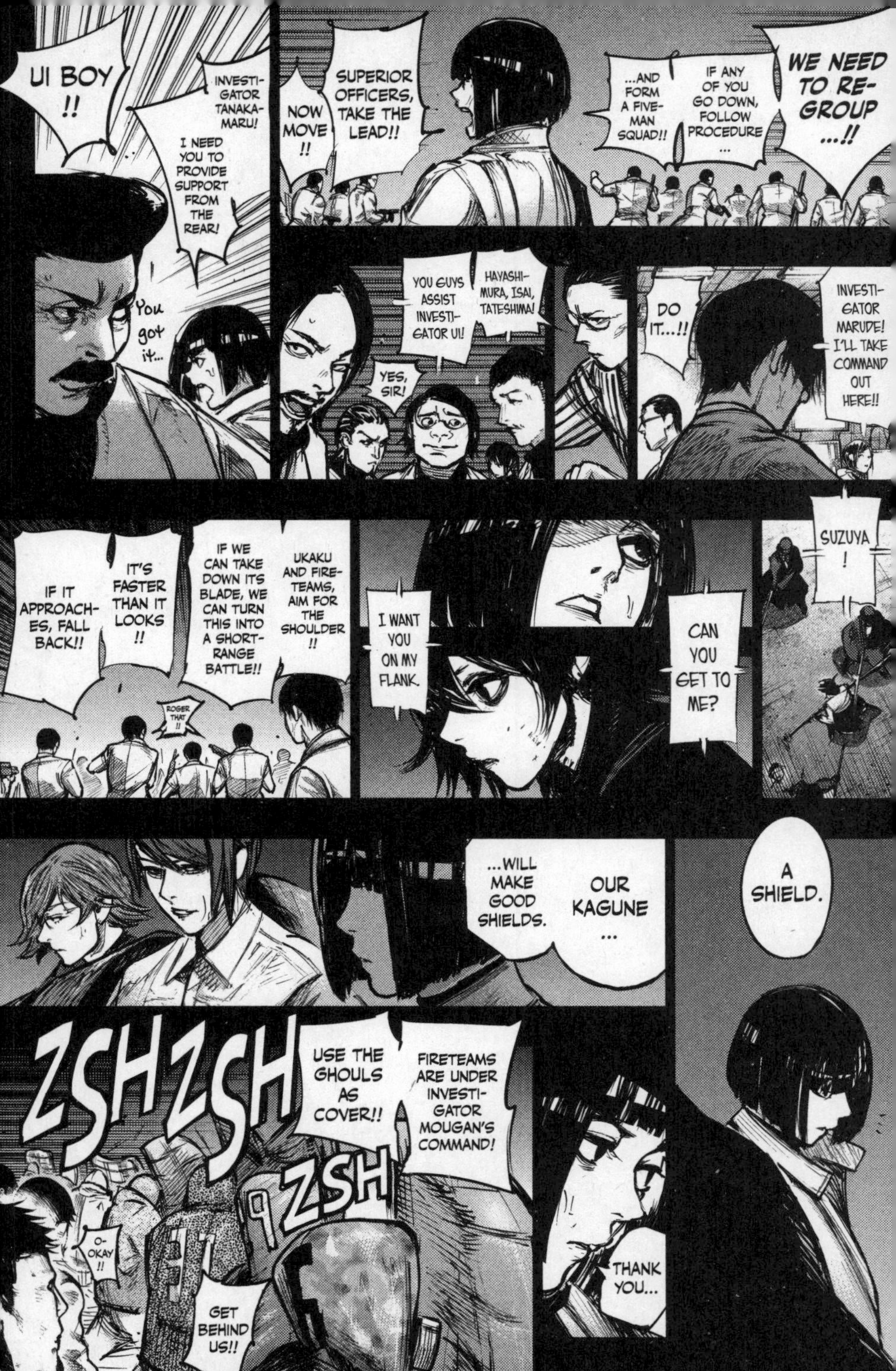

WE NEED TO RE-GROUP ...!!
IF ANY OF YOU GO DOWN, FOLLOW PROCEDURE ...
...AND FORM A FIVE-MAN SQUAD!!
SUPERIOR OFFICERS, TAKE THE LEAD!!
NOW MOVE !!
INVESTIGATOR MARUDE! I'LL TAKE COMMAND OUT HERE!!
DO IT...!!
HAYASHIMURA, ISAI, TATESHIMA!
YOU GUYS ASSIST INVESTIGATOR UI!
YES, SIR!
UI BOY !!
INVESTIGATOR TANAKAMARU!
I NEED YOU TO PROVIDE SUPPORT FROM THE REAR!
You got it...
SUZUYA !
CAN YOU GET TO ME?
I WANT YOU ON MY FLANK.
UKAKU AND FIRETEAMS, AIM FOR THE SHOULDER !!
IF WE CAN TAKE DOWN ITS BLADE, WE CAN TURN THIS INTO A SHORT-RANGE BATTLE!!
IT'S FASTER THAN IT LOOKS !!
IF IT APPROACHES, FALL BACK!!
ROGER THAT !!
A SHIELD.
OUR KAGUNE ...
...WILL MAKE GOOD SHIELDS.
THANK YOU...
FIRETEAMS ARE UNDER INVESTIGATOR MOUGAN'S COMMAND!
USE THE GHOULS AS COVER!!
ZSHZSH
ZSH
O-OKAY !!
GET BEHIND US!!

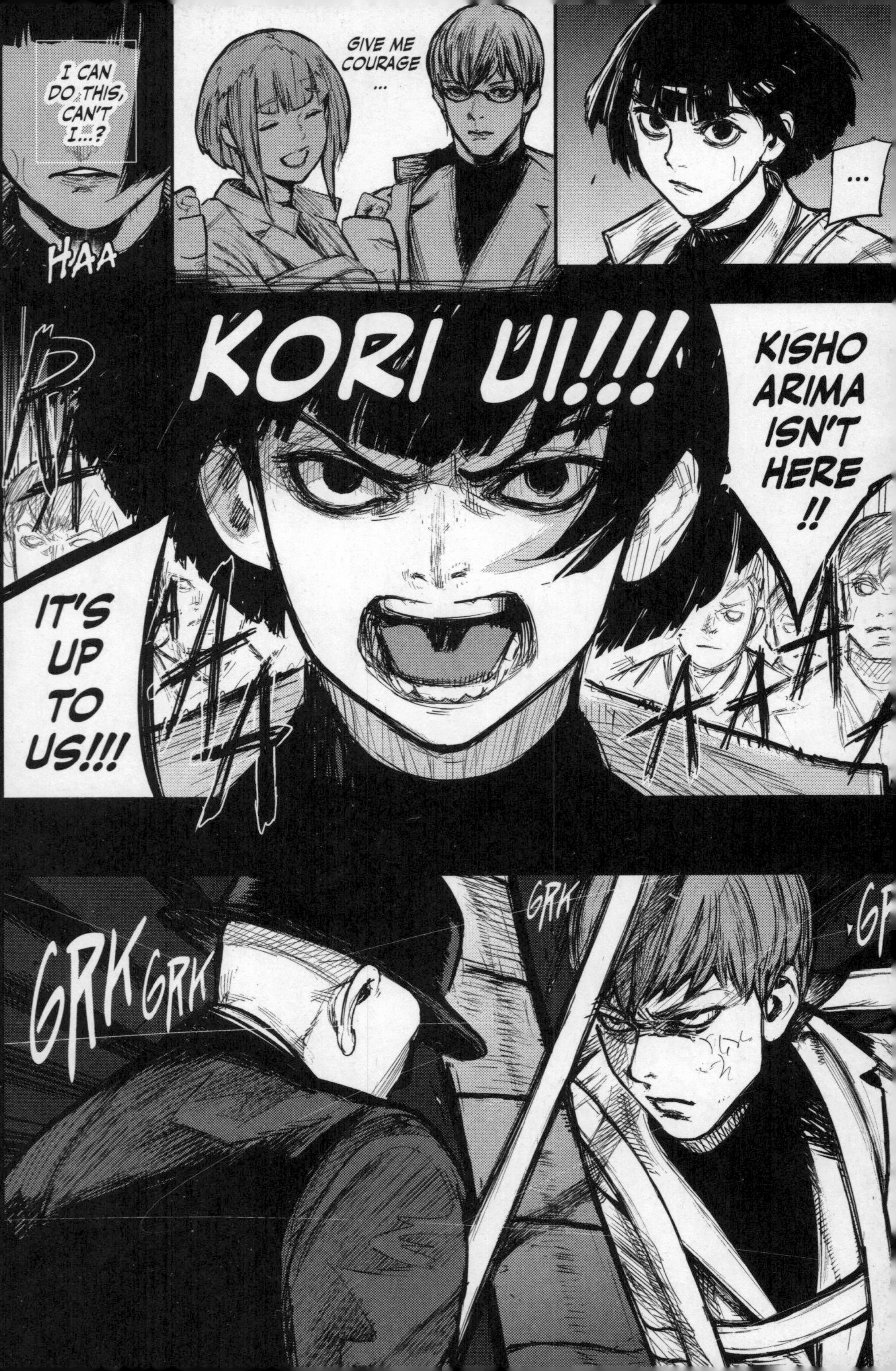
...
GIVE ME COURAGE ...
I CAN DO THIS, CAN'T I...?
HAA
KORI UI!!!!
KISHO ARIMA ISN'T HERE !!
IT'S UP TO US!!!
GRK
GRK GRK

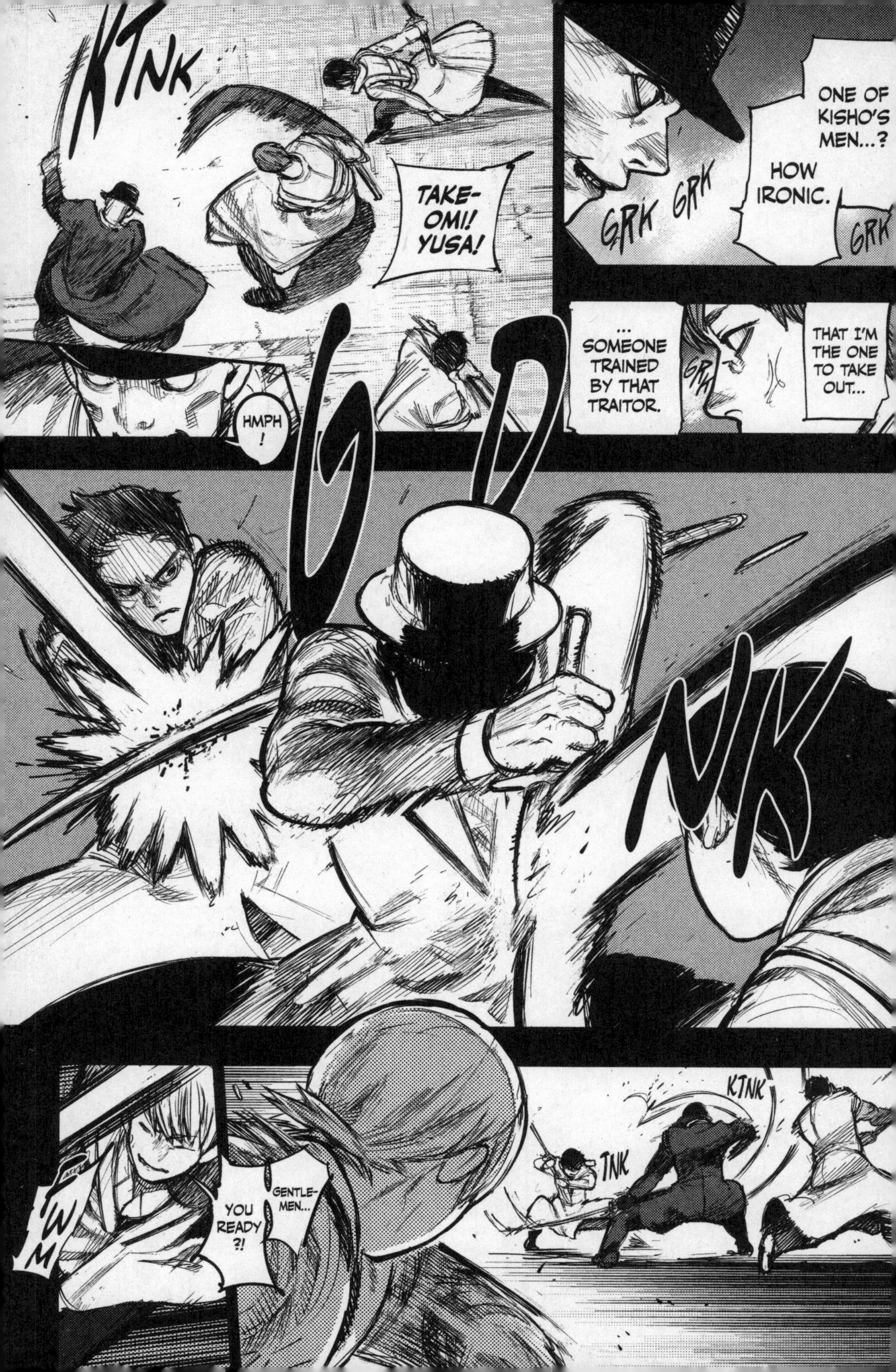
ONE OF KISHO'S MEN...?
HOW IRONIC.
GRK GRK
GRK
THAT I'M THE ONE TO TAKE OUT...
... SOMEONE TRAINED BY THAT TRAITOR.
GRK
KTNK
TAKE-OMI! YUSA!
HMPH!
GONK
KTNK
TNK
GENTLE-MEN...
YOU READY?!
FWM

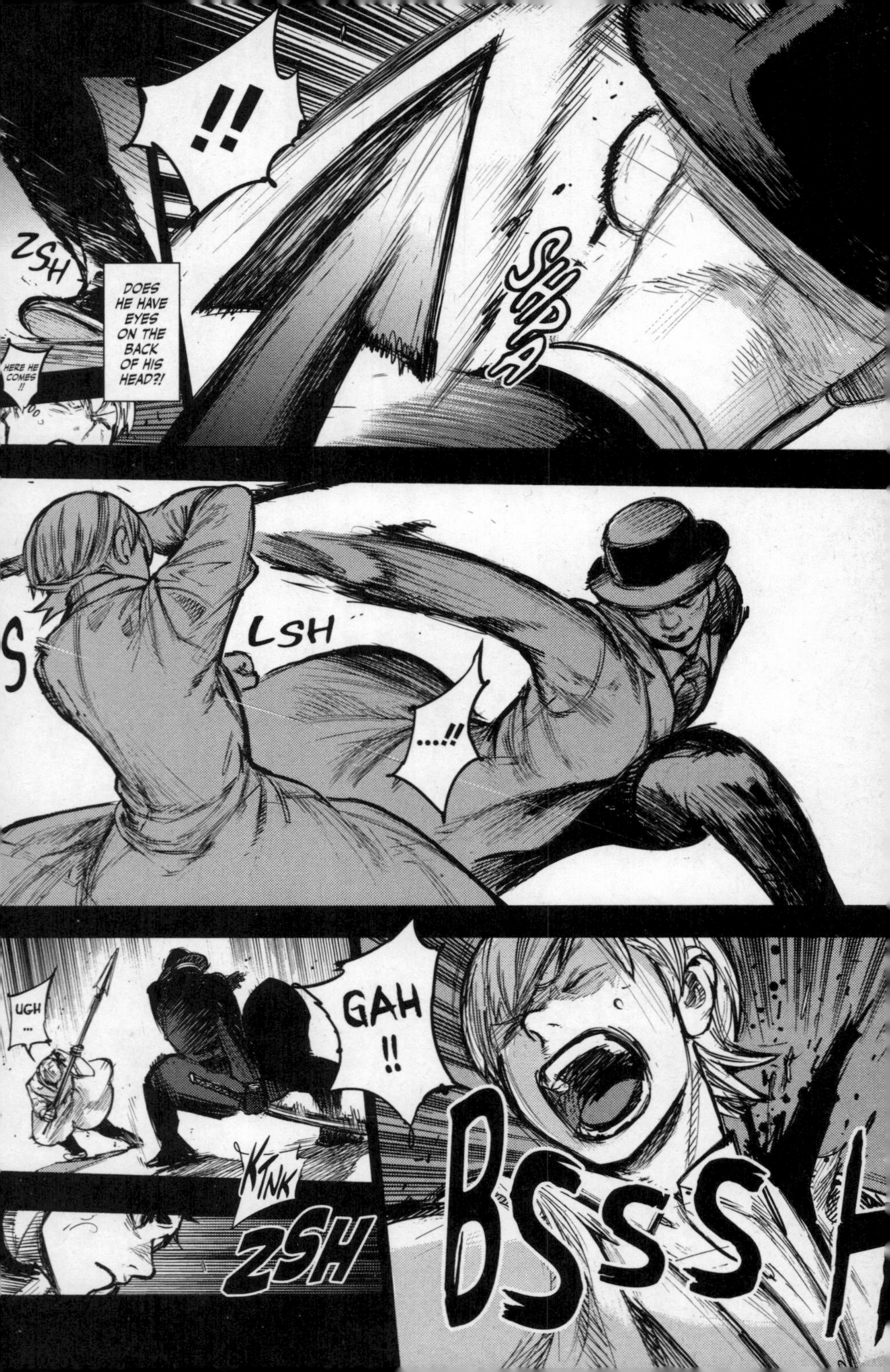
SHPA
!!
ZSH
DOES HE HAVE EYES ON THE BACK OF HIS HEAD?!
HERE HE COMES !!
....!!
LSH
S
BSSSH
GAH !!
KINK
ZSH
UGH ...

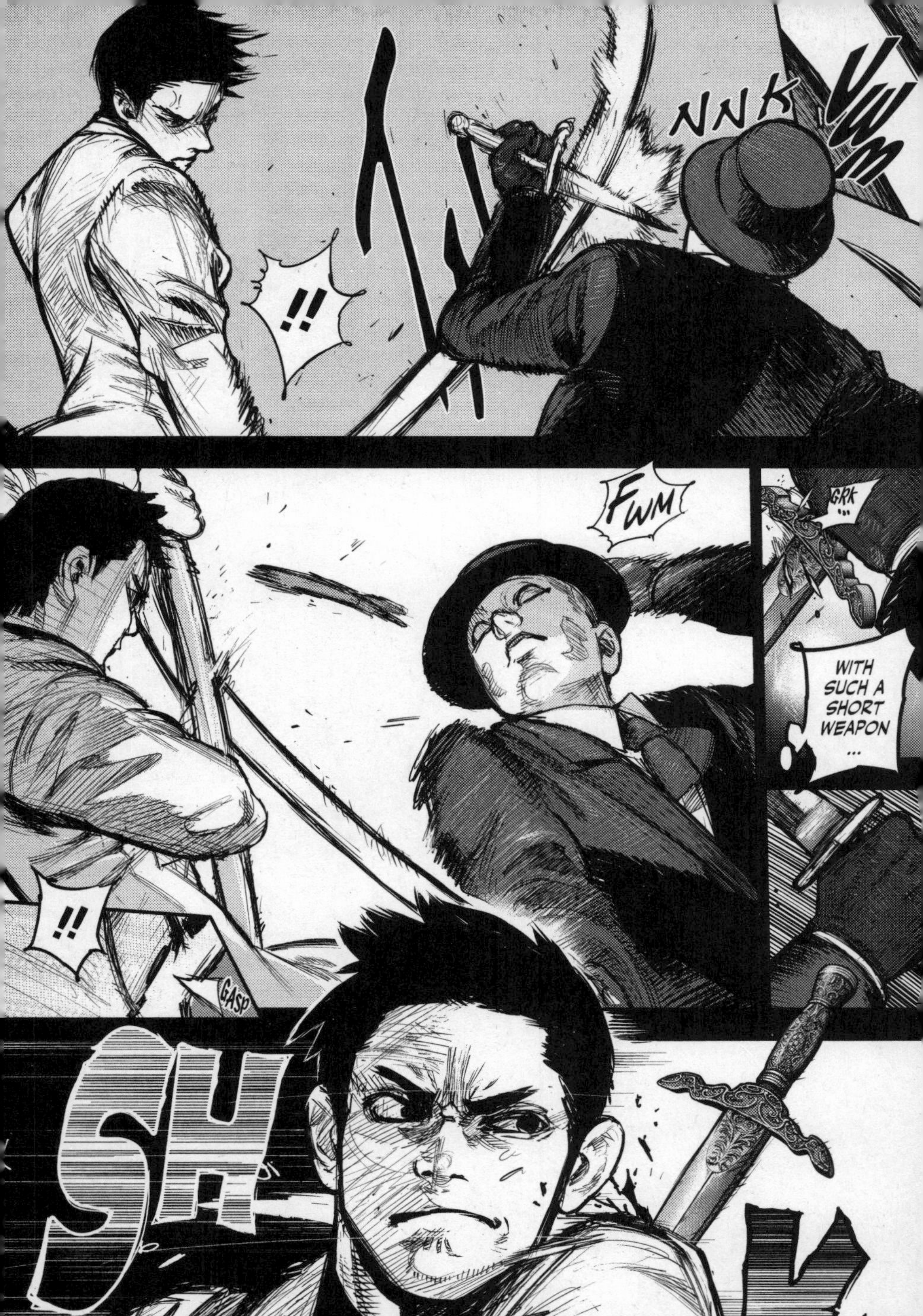
NNK
!!
GRK...
WITH SUCH A SHORT WEAPON...
FWM
!!
GASP
SH

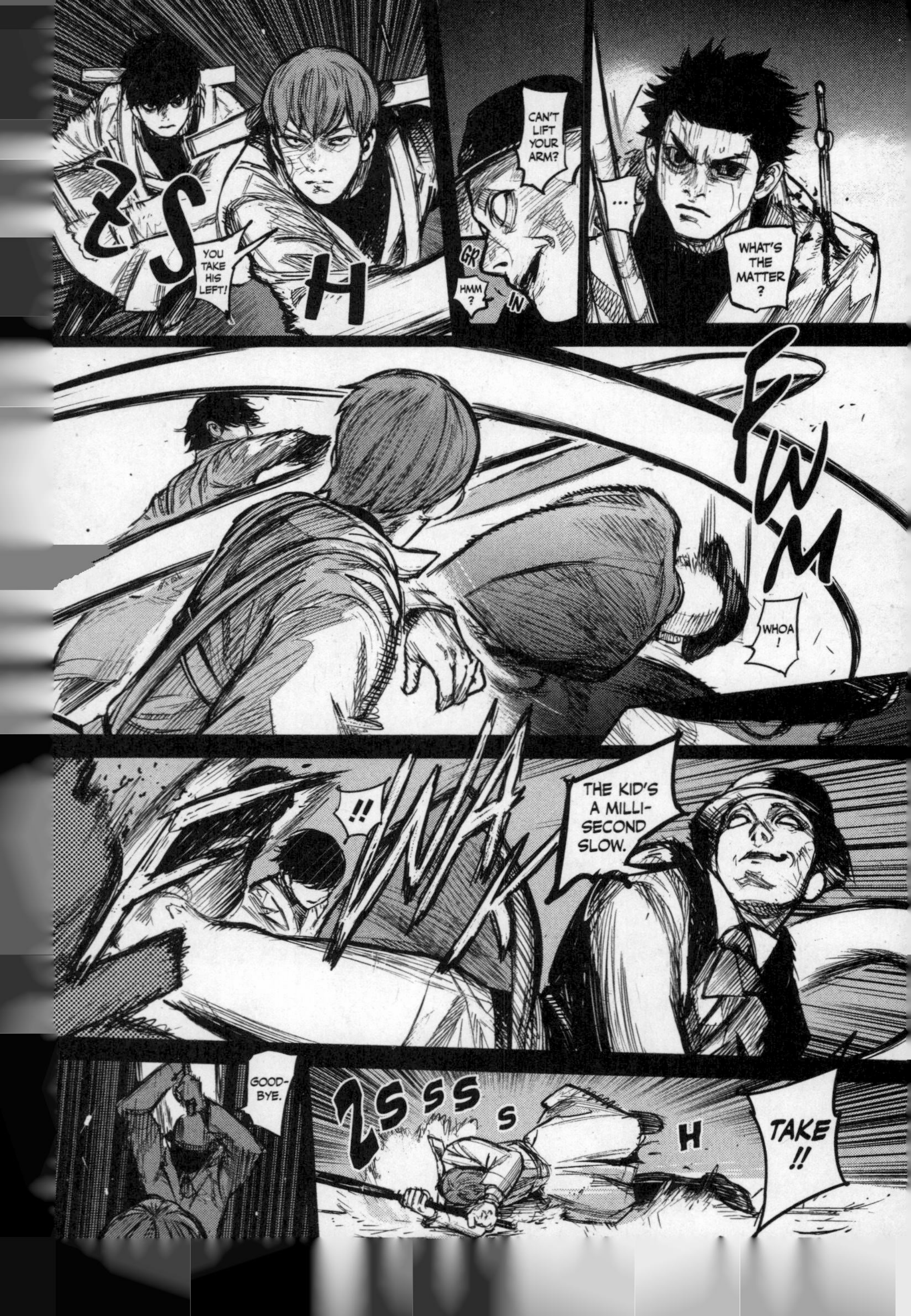
...
WHAT'S THE MATTER?
CAN'T LIFT YOUR ARM?
GRIN
HMM?
YOU TAKE HIS LEFT!
ZSH
WHOA!
THE KID'S A MILLI-SECOND SLOW.
!!
TAKE!!
ZSSSSH
GOOD-BYE.

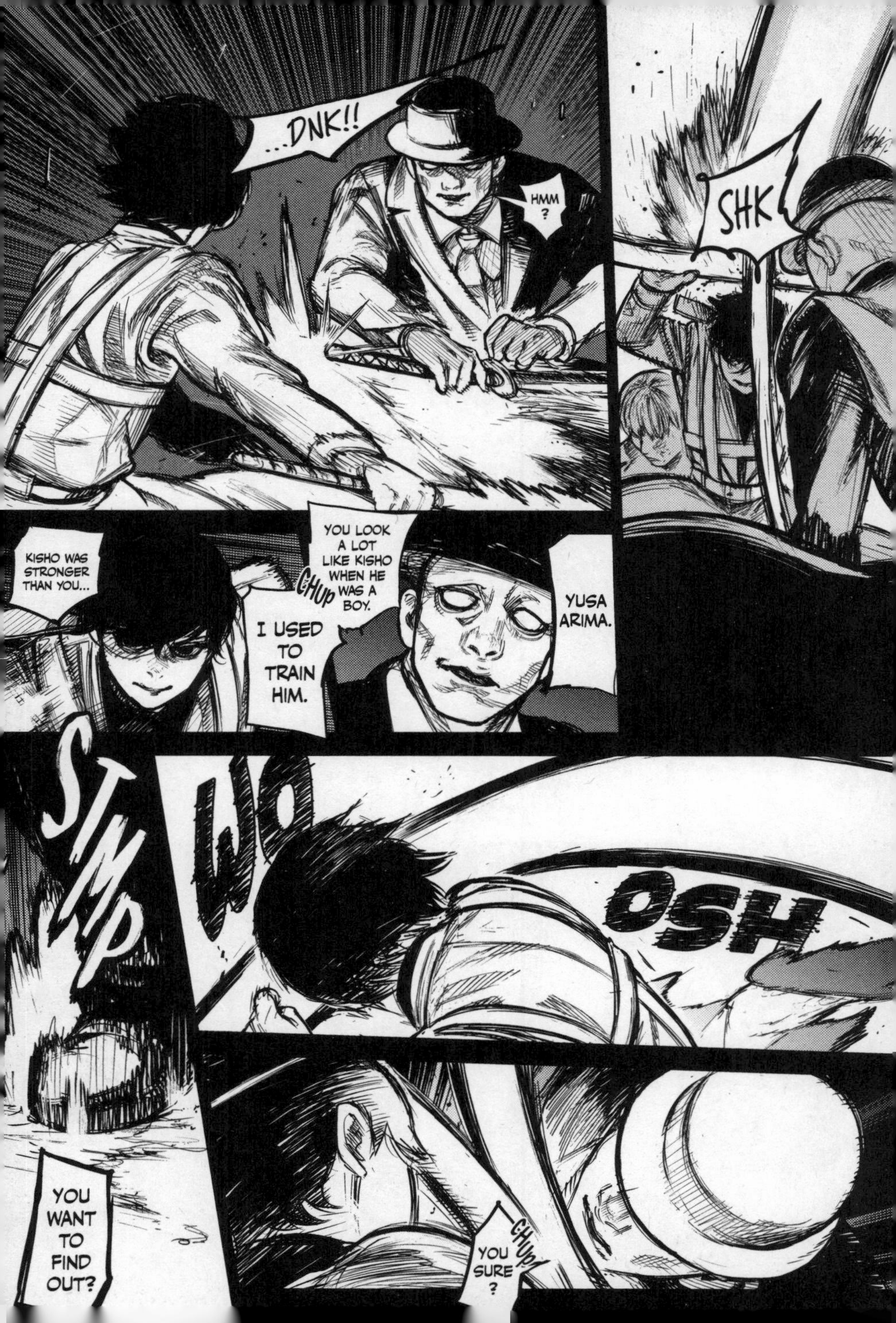

SHK
...DNK!!
HMM?
YUSA ARIMA.
YOU LOOK A LOT LIKE KISHO WHEN HE WAS A BOY.
CHUP
I USED TO TRAIN HIM.
KISHO WAS STRONGER THAN YOU...
WOOSH
CHUP
YOU SURE?
STMP
YOU WANT TO FIND OUT?

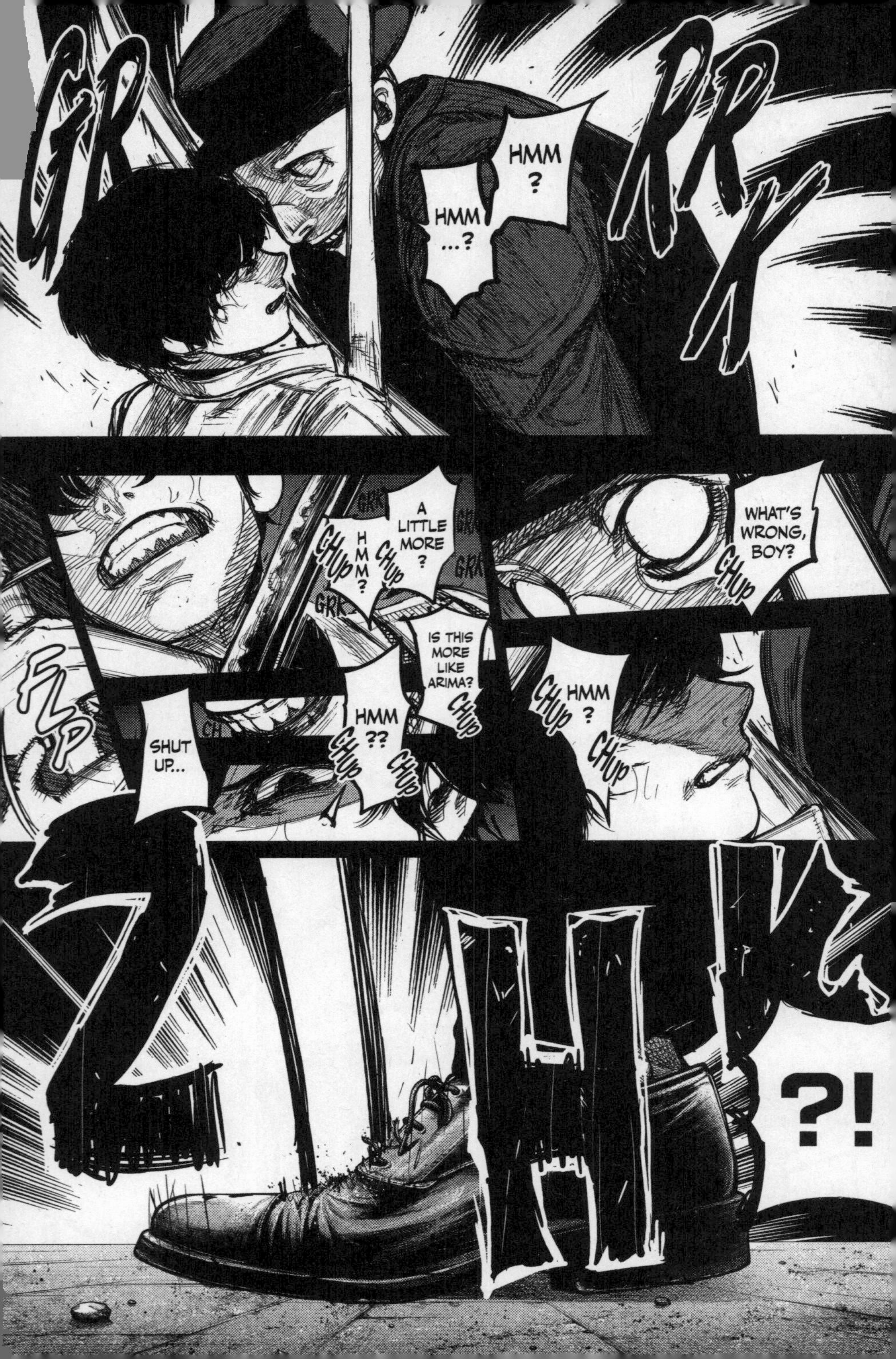
GR
RRX
HMM ?
HMM ...?
WHAT'S WRONG, BOY?
CHUP
GRK
A LITTLE MORE ?
HMM HMM?
CHUP
CHUP
GRK
GRK
GRK
HMM ?
CHUP
CHUP
IS THIS MORE LIKE ARIMA?
CHUP
HMM ??
CHUP
CHUP
SHUT UP...
FLP
CH
?!

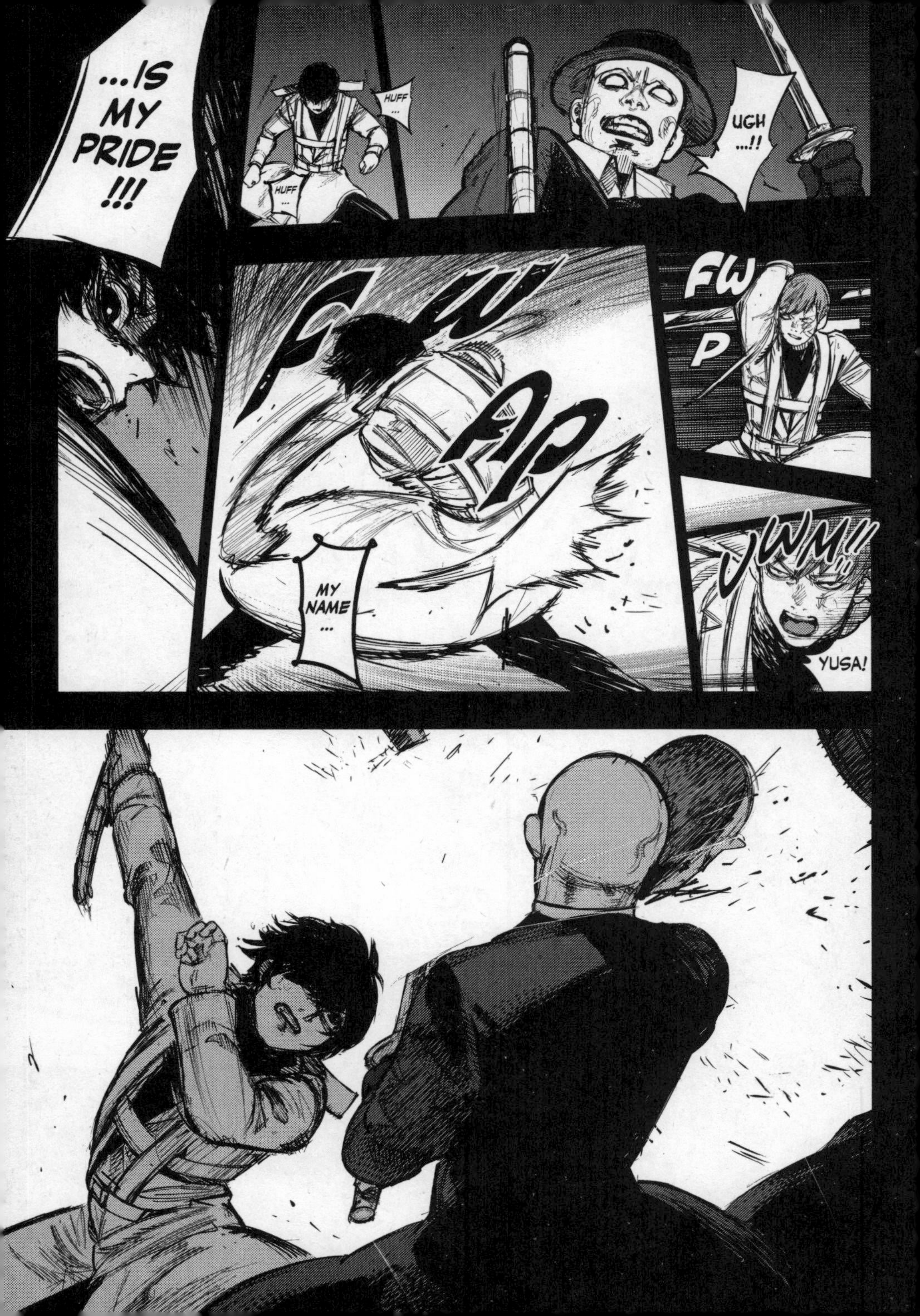
UGH ...!!
HUFF ...
HUFF ...
...IS MY PRIDE !!!
FW P
YUSA!
FWAP
MY NAME ...

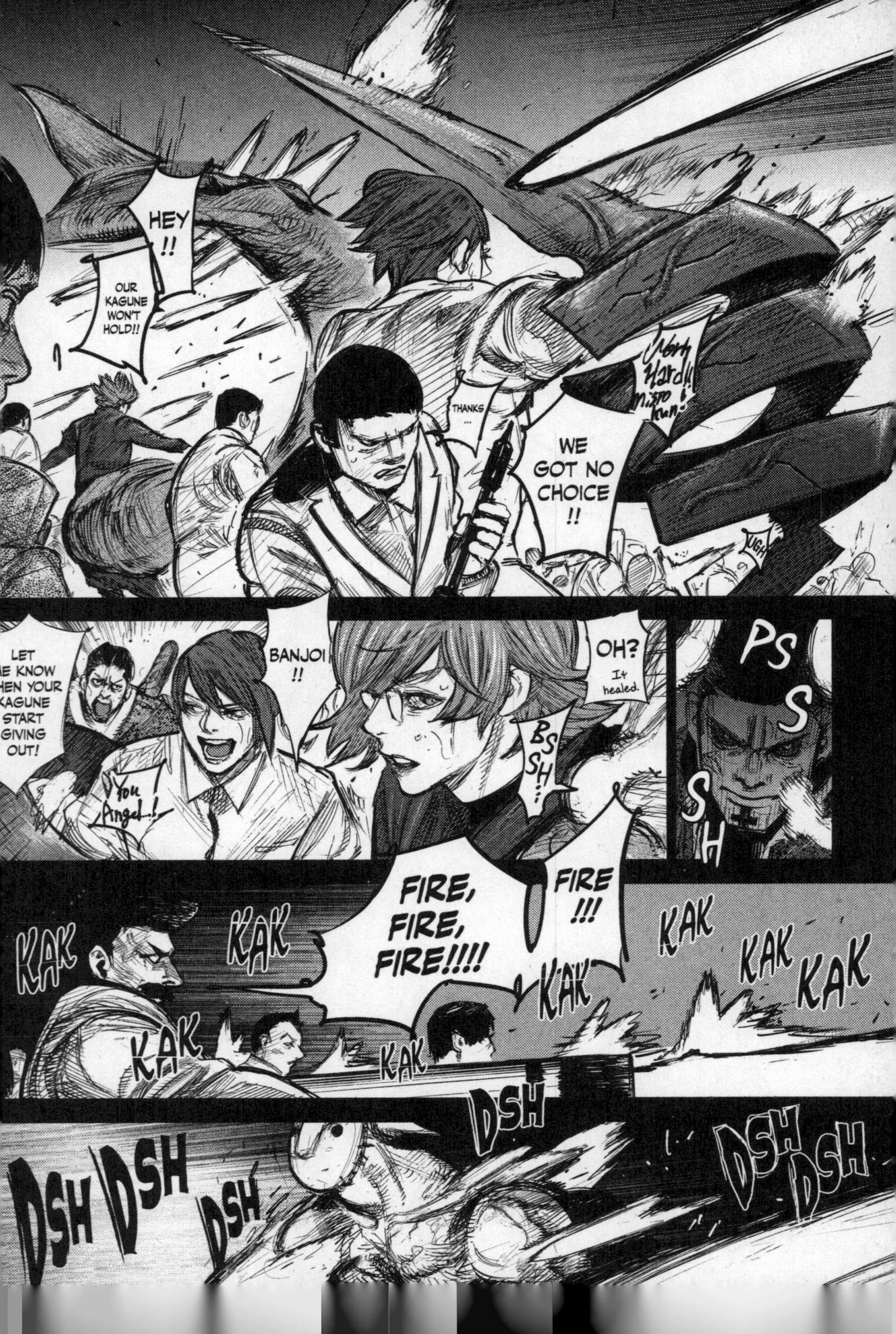
Work Hard!!
WE GOT NO CHOICE !!
THANKS ...
HEY !!
OUR KAGUNE WON'T HOLD!!
UGH
PSSSH
OH? It healed.
BSSH
BANJOI !!
LET ME KNOW WHEN YOUR KAGUNE START GIVING OUT!
You Angel...!
FIRE !!!
FIRE, FIRE, FIRE!!!!
KAK KAK KAK KAK
KAK KAK KAK KAK
DSH DSH DSH
DSH DSH DSH

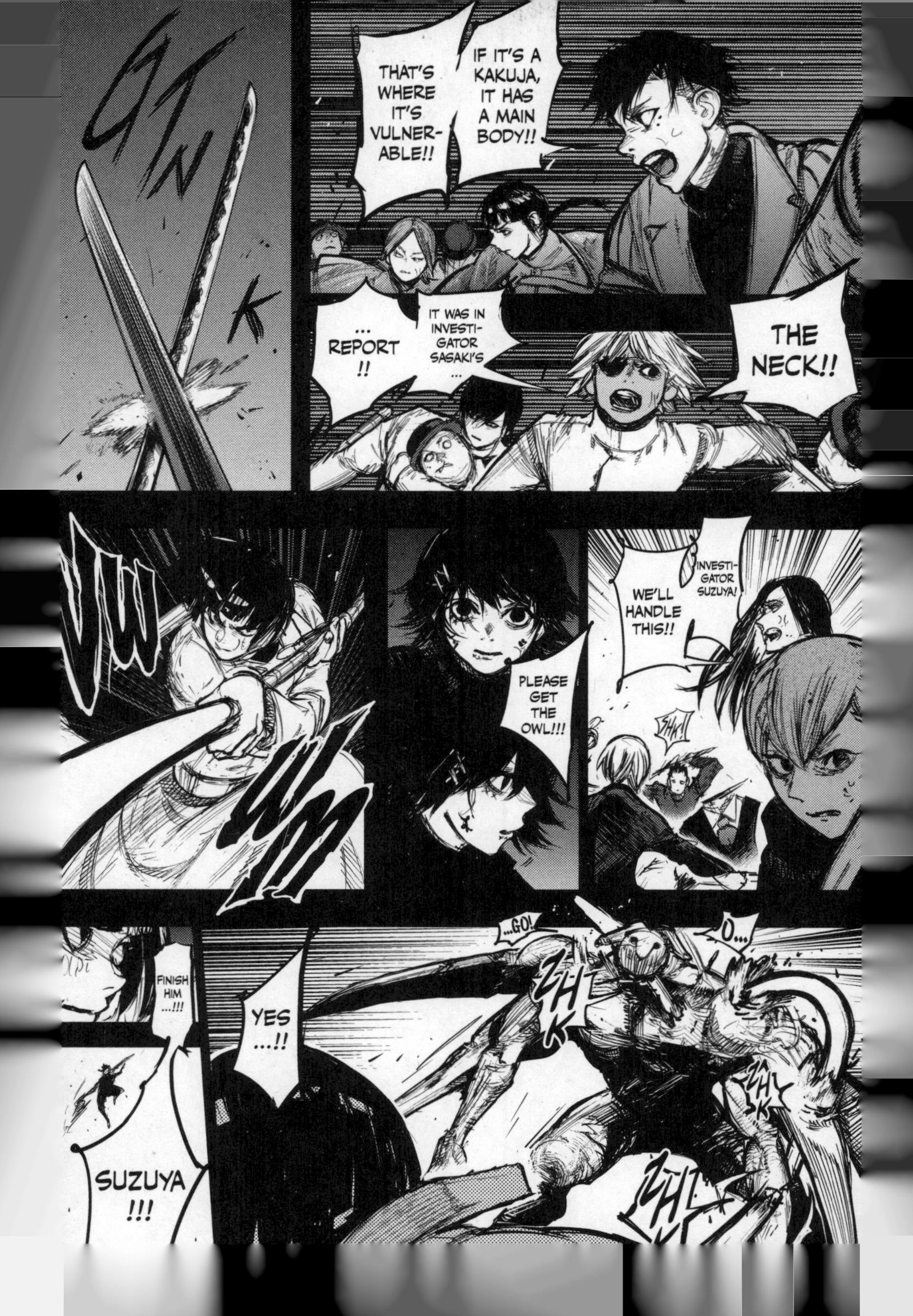
IF IT'S A KAKUJA, IT HAS A MAIN BODY!!
THAT'S WHERE IT'S VULNERABLE!!
THE NECK!!
IT WAS IN INVESTIGATOR SASAKI'S ...
... REPORT !!
INVESTIGATOR SUZUYA!
WE'LL HANDLE THIS!!
SHK!
PLEASE GET THE OWL!!!
O...
...GO!
YES ...!!
FINISH HIM ...!!!
SUZUYA !!!

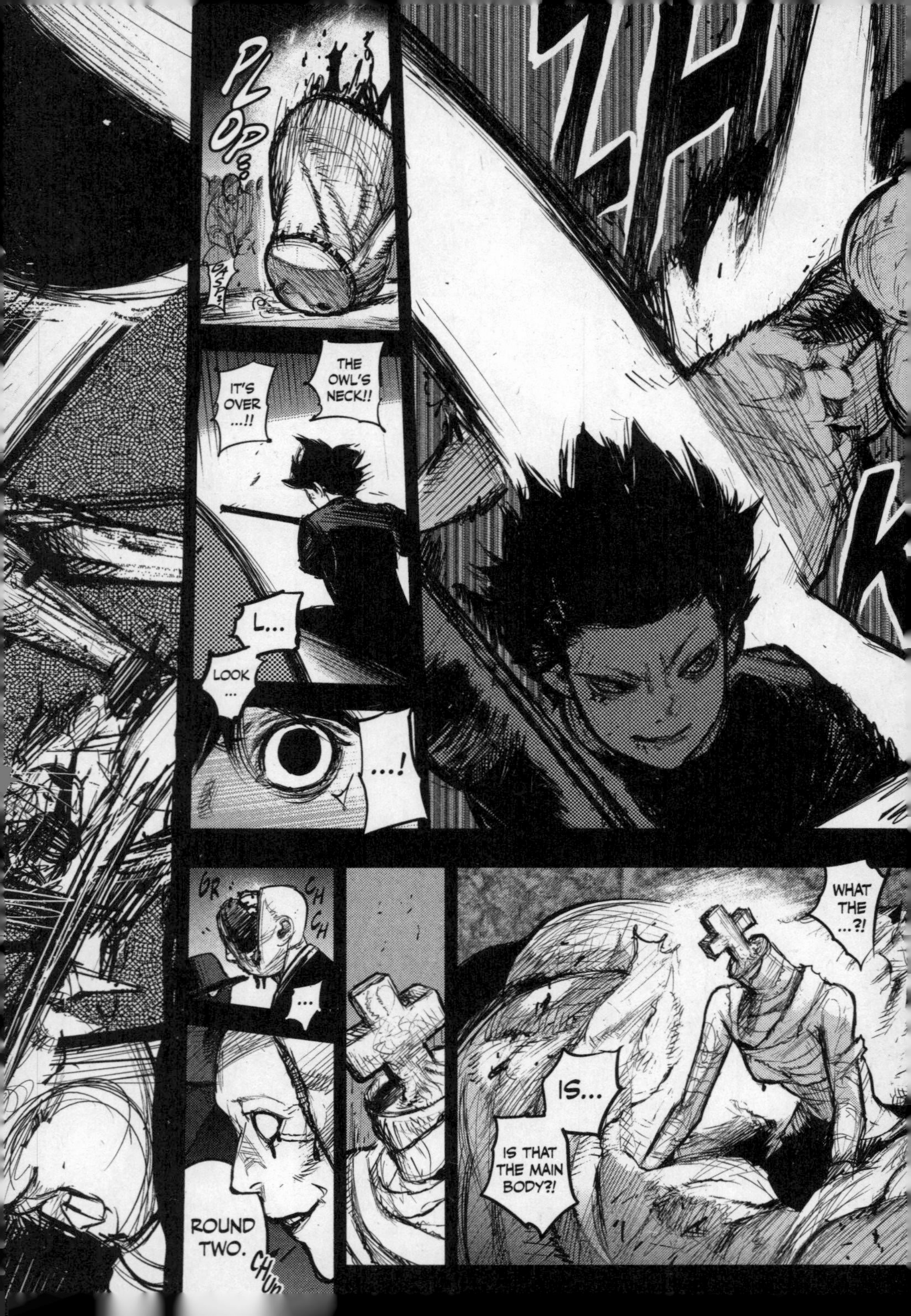
PLOP
GASP
THE OWL'S NECK!!
IT'S OVER ...!!
L...
LOOK ...
...!
WHAT THE ...?!
IS...
IS THAT THE MAIN BODY?!
GR
CH CH
...
ROUND TWO.
CHUN

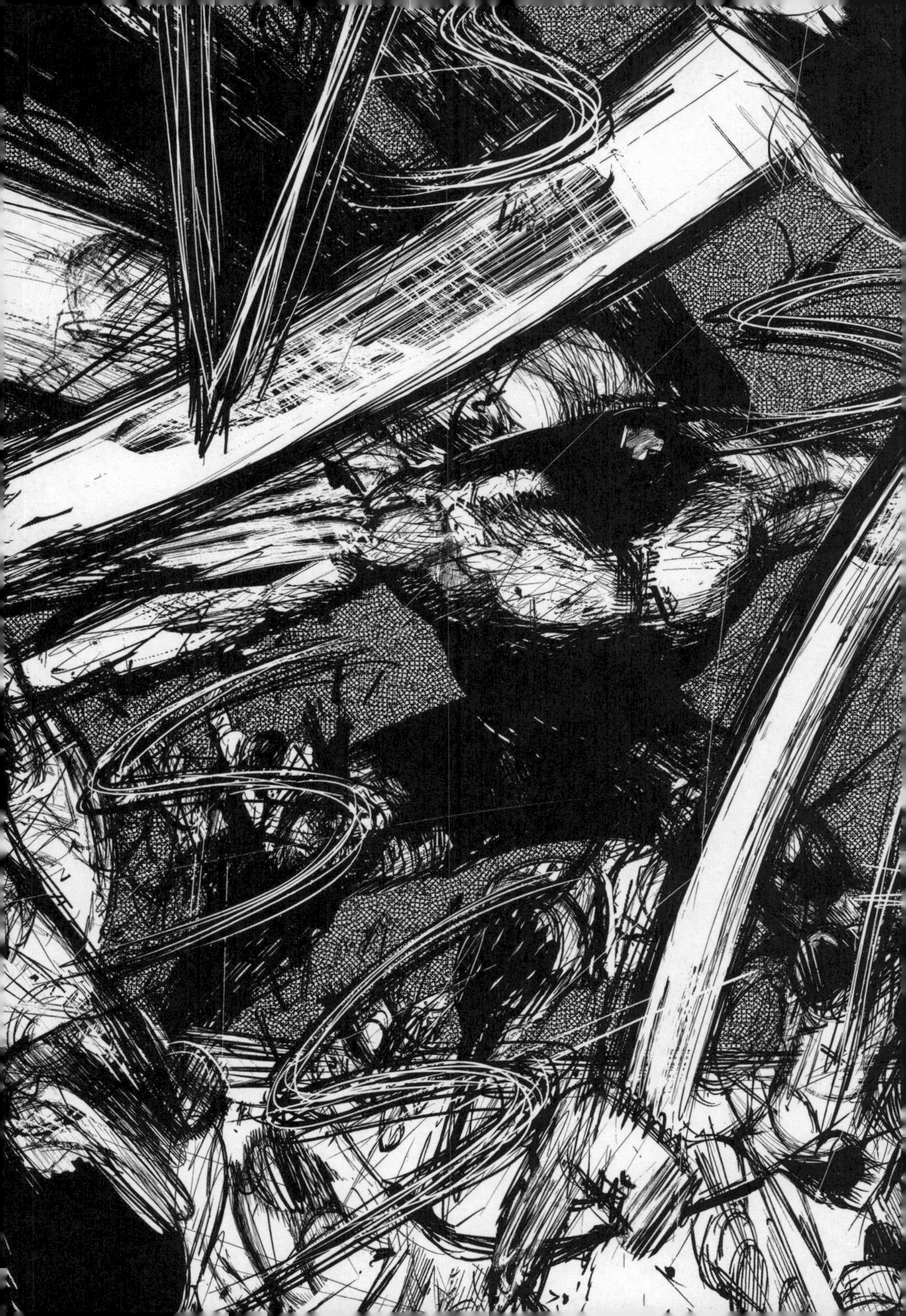

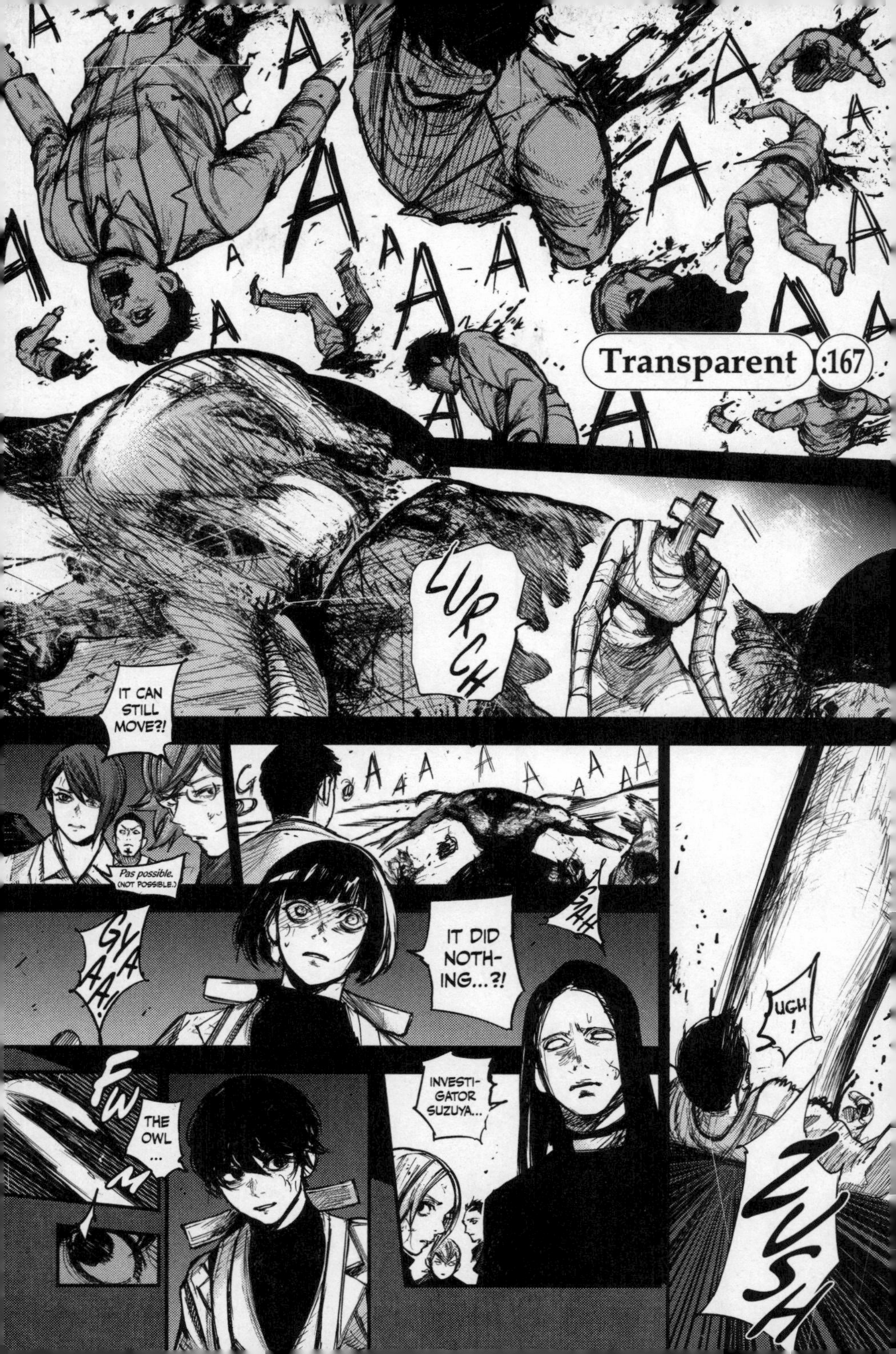
Transparent :167
LURCH
IT CAN STILL MOVE?!
UGH!
ZUSH
GAAAAAAAAA
Pas possible. (NOT POSSIBLE.)
GAH
IT DID NOTHING...?!
GYAAA!!
INVESTIGATOR SUZUYA...
THE OWL...
FWM

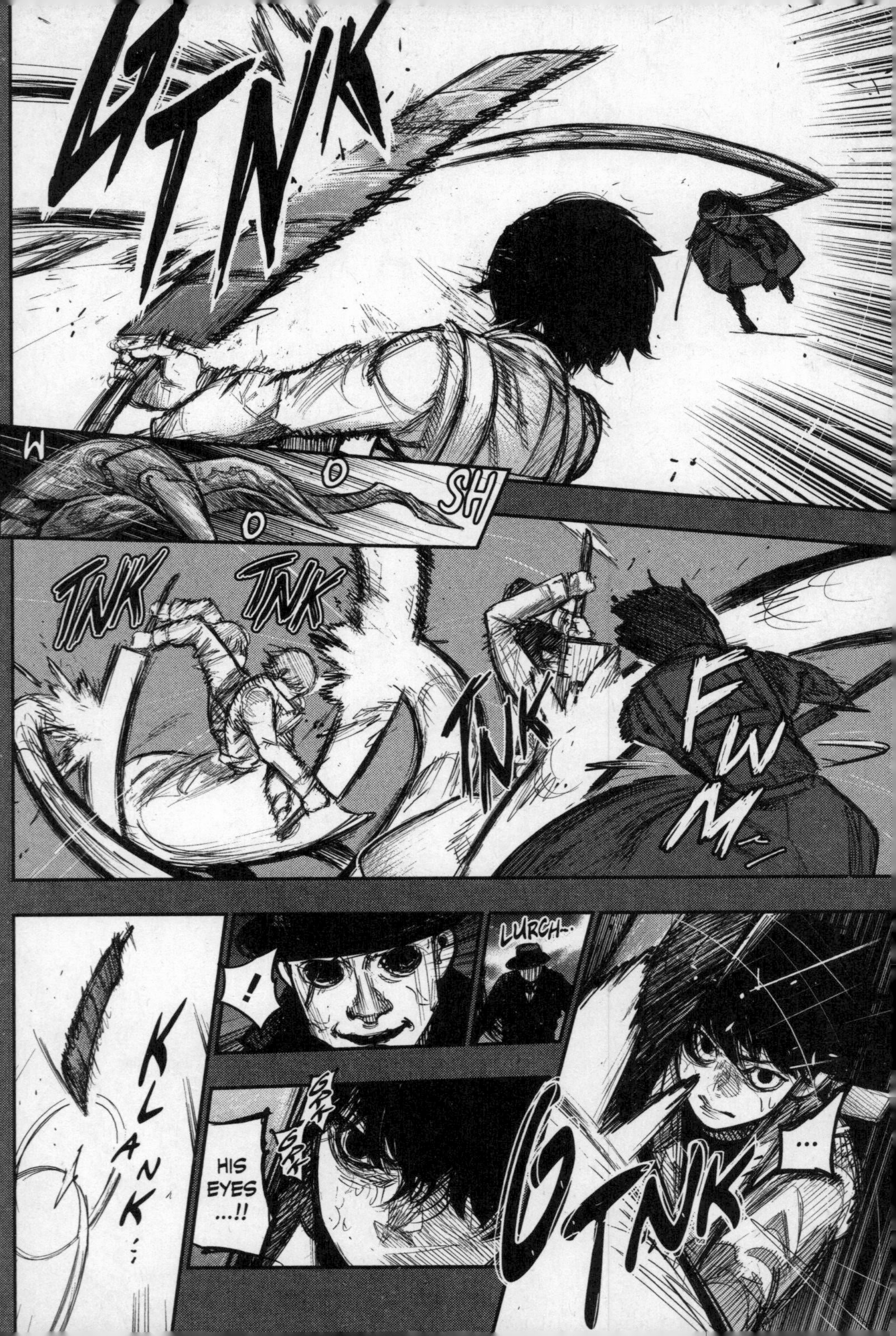
GTNK
WOOSH
FWM
TNK
TNK
TNK
...
GTNK
LURCH..
!
GRK GRK
HIS EYES ...!!
KLANK..

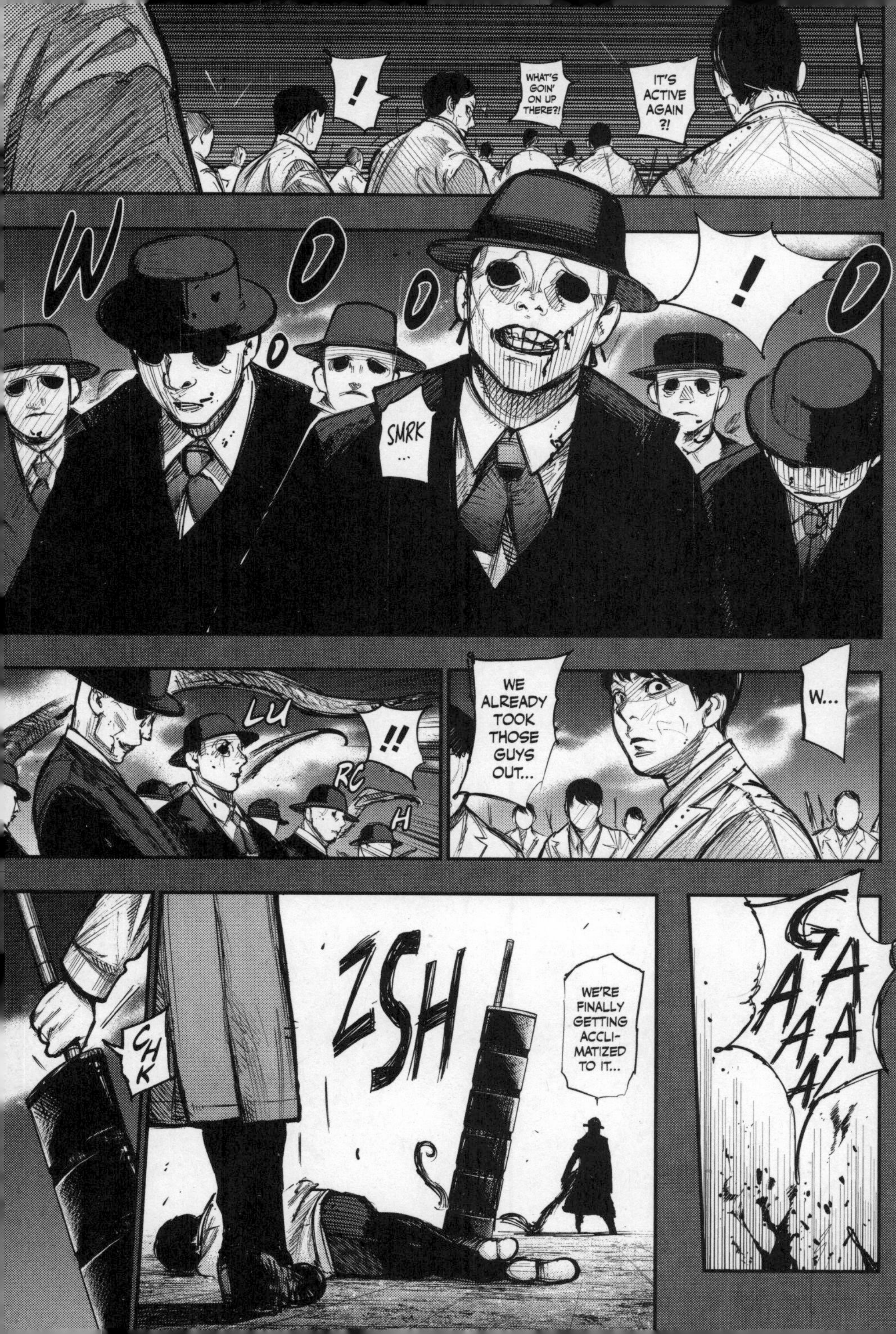
IT'S ACTIVE AGAIN?!
WHAT'S GOIN' ON UP THERE?!
!
!
WOOOOOO
SMRK...
W...
WE ALREADY TOOK THOSE GUYS OUT...
!!
LURCH
GAAAAA
WE'RE FINALLY GETTING ACCLI-MATIZED TO IT...
ZSH
CHK

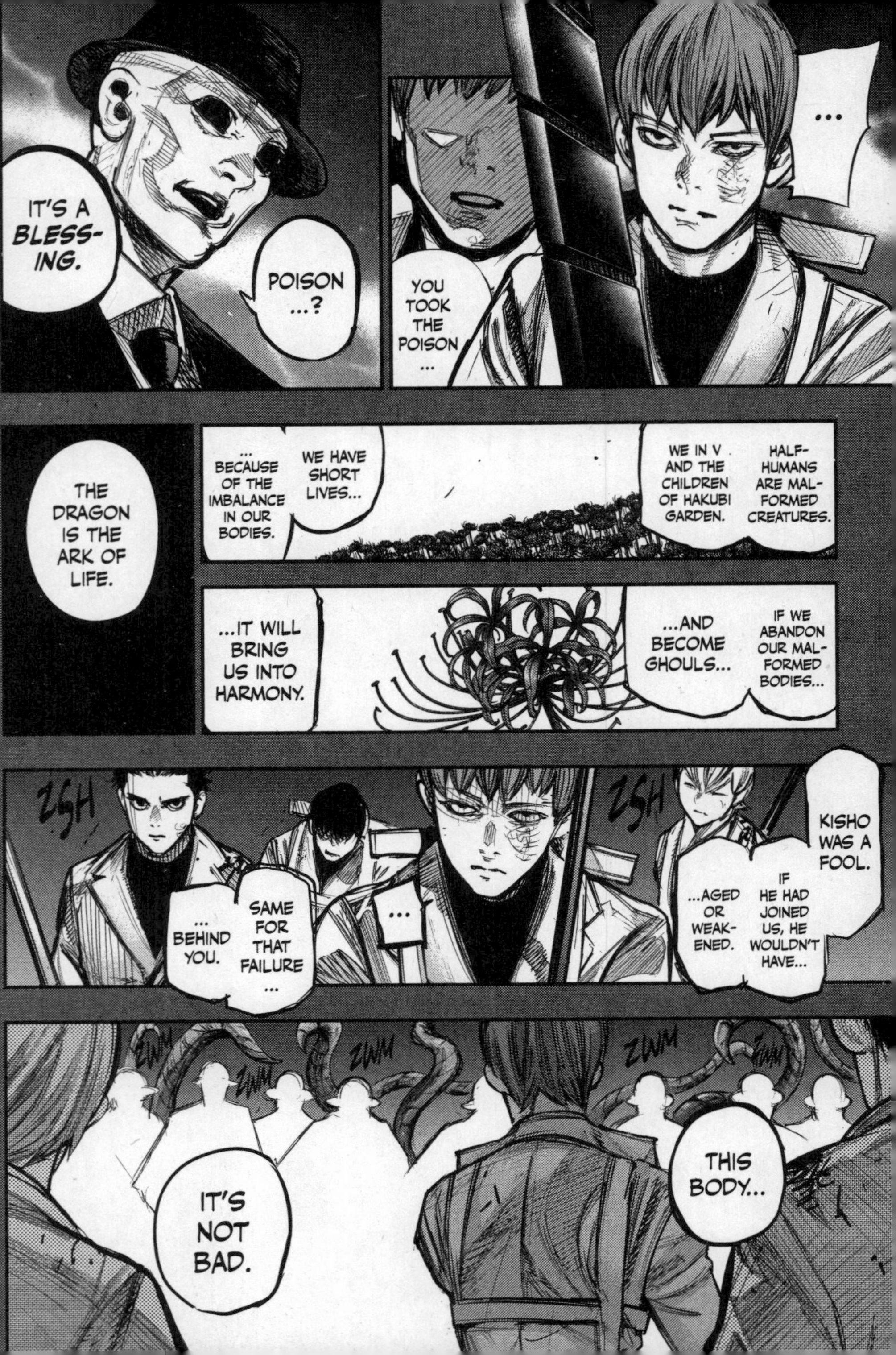
...
YOU TOOK THE POISON ...
POISON ...?
IT'S A BLESSING.
HALF-HUMANS ARE MALFORMED CREATURES.
WE IN V AND THE CHILDREN OF HAKUBI GARDEN.
WE HAVE SHORT LIVES...
... BECAUSE OF THE IMBALANCE IN OUR BODIES.
IF WE ABANDON OUR MALFORMED BODIES...
...AND BECOME GHOULS...
...IT WILL BRING US INTO HARMONY.
THE DRAGON IS THE ARK OF LIFE.
ZSH
KISHO WAS A FOOL.
IF HE HAD JOINED US, HE WOULDN'T HAVE...
...AGED OR WEAKENED.
...
SAME FOR THAT FAILURE ...
... BEHIND YOU.
ZSH
ZWM
ZWM
ZWM
ZWM
ZWM
THIS BODY...
IT'S NOT BAD.

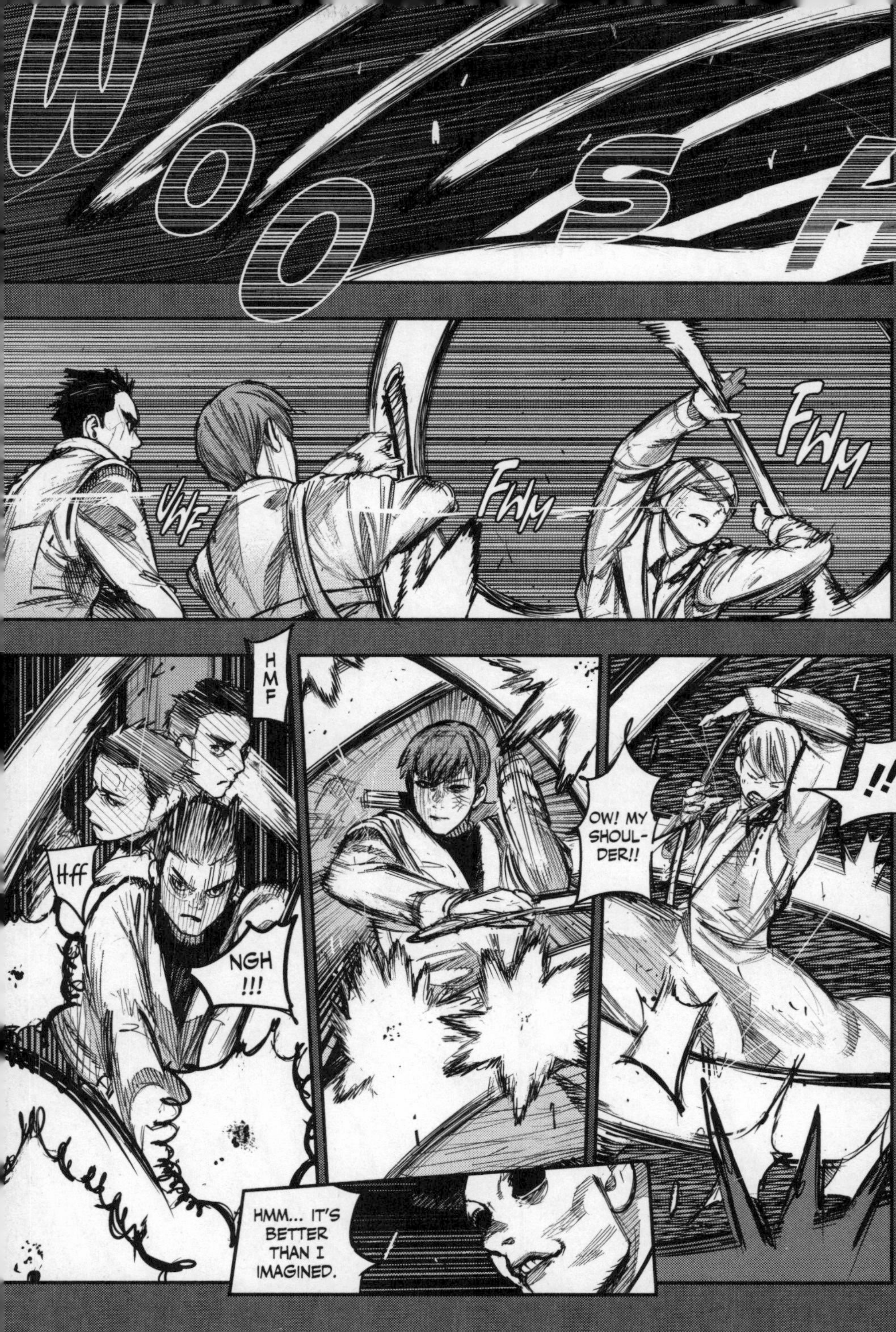
WOOSH
FWM
FWM
UMF
!!
OW! MY SHOUL-DER!!
HMF
Hff
NGH !!!
HMM... IT'S BETTER THAN I IMAGINED.

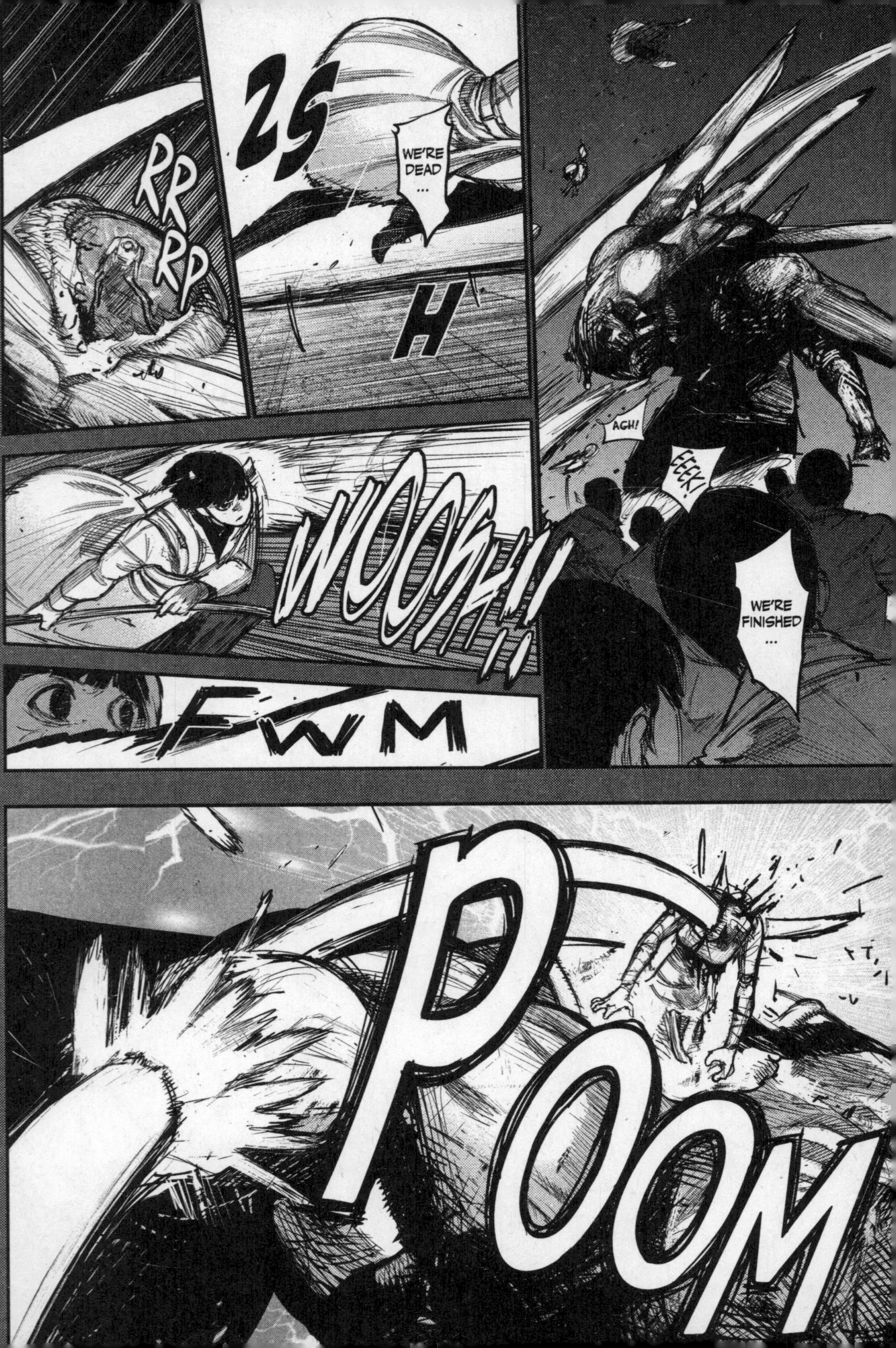
AGH!
EEEK!
WE'RE FINISHED ...
ZS
WE'RE DEAD ...
H
RRRP
WOOSH!!
FWM
POOM

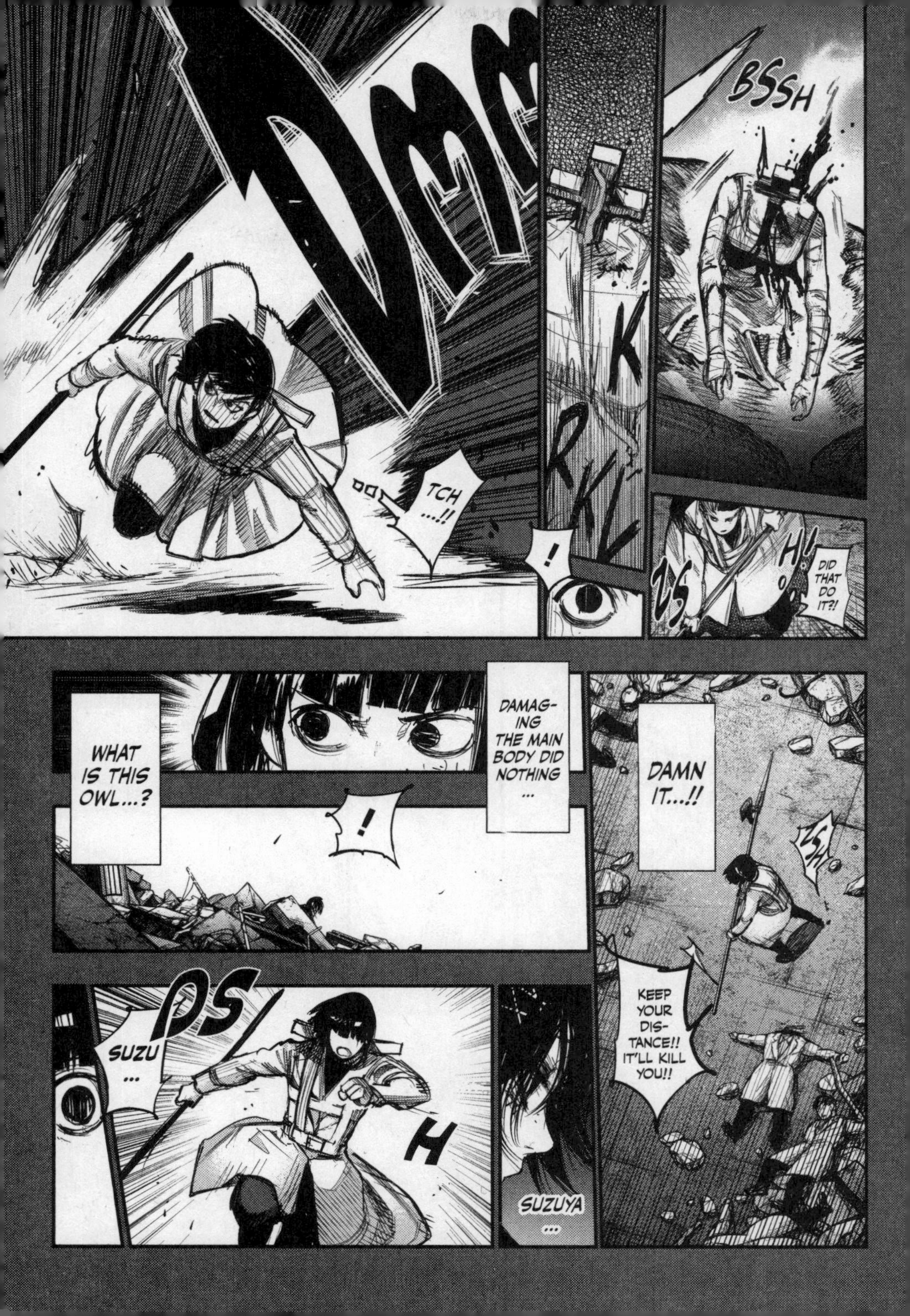
BSSH
DID THAT DO IT?!
K
R
K
!
TCH ...!!
DAMN IT...!!
KEEP YOUR DISTANCE!! IT'LL KILL YOU!!
DAMAGING THE MAIN BODY DID NOTHING ...
WHAT IS THIS OWL...?
!
SUZUYA ...
DS
SUZU ...
H

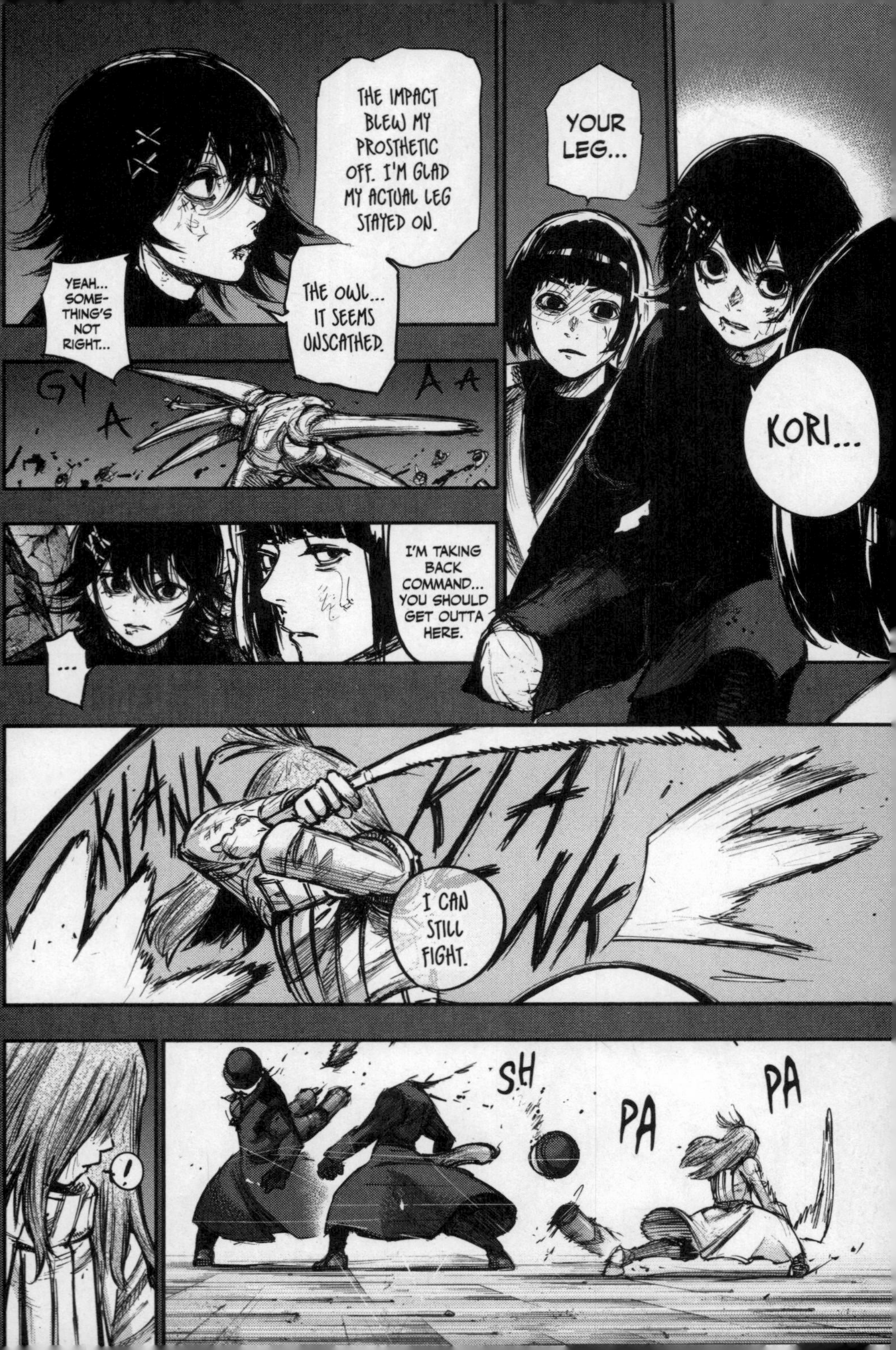
YOUR LEG...
KORI...
THE IMPACT BLEW MY PROSTHETIC OFF. I'M GLAD MY ACTUAL LEG STAYED ON.
THE OWL... IT SEEMS UNSCATHED.
YEAH... SOMETHING'S NOT RIGHT...
GY A A A
I'M TAKING BACK COMMAND... YOU SHOULD GET OUTTA HERE.
...
KLANK
KA
NK
I CAN STILL FIGHT.
SH
PA
PA
!

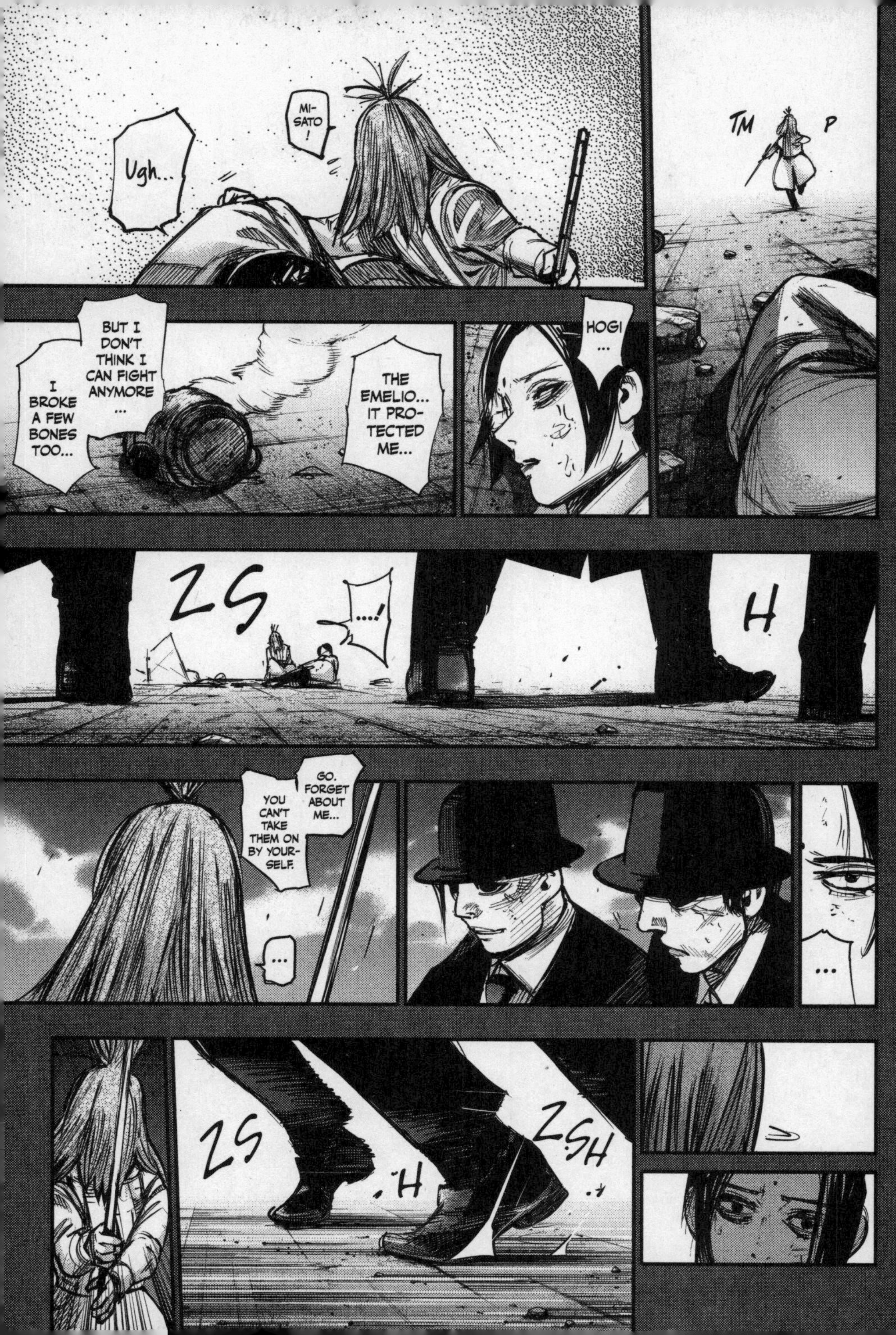
TMP
MI-SATO!
Ugh...
HOGI...
THE EMELIO... IT PROTECTED ME...
BUT I DON'T THINK I CAN FIGHT ANYMORE...
I BROKE A FEW BONES TOO...
H
...!
ZS
...
GO. FORGET ABOUT ME...
YOU CAN'T TAKE THEM ON BY YOURSELF.
...
ZSH
H
ZS

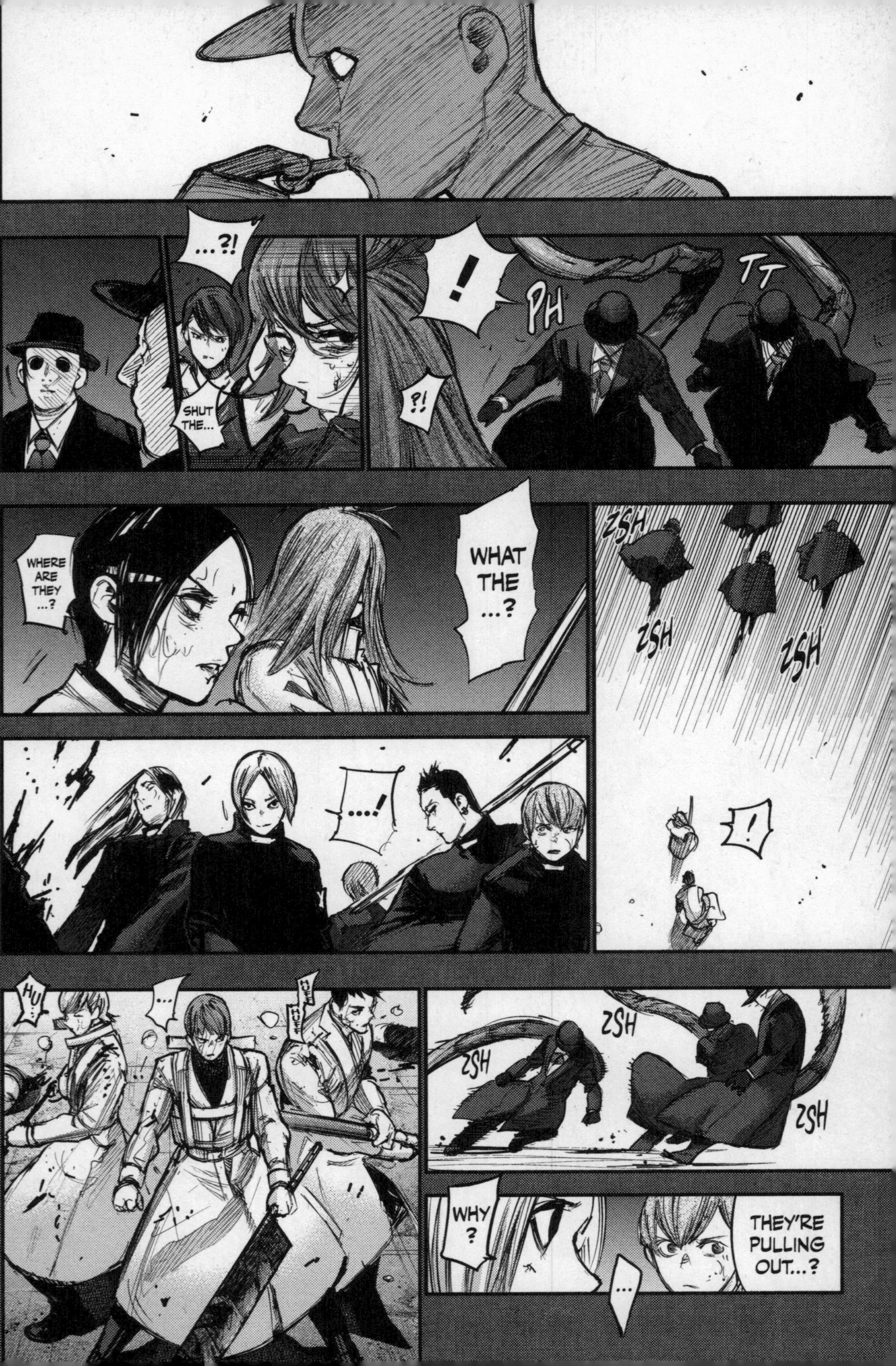
TT
PH
!
...?!
?!
SHUT THE...
ZSH
ZSH
ZSH
!
WHAT THE ...?
WHERE ARE THEY ...?
...!
ZSH
ZSH
ZSH
THEY'RE PULLING OUT...?
WHY ?
...
HUFF HUFF
...
HU...

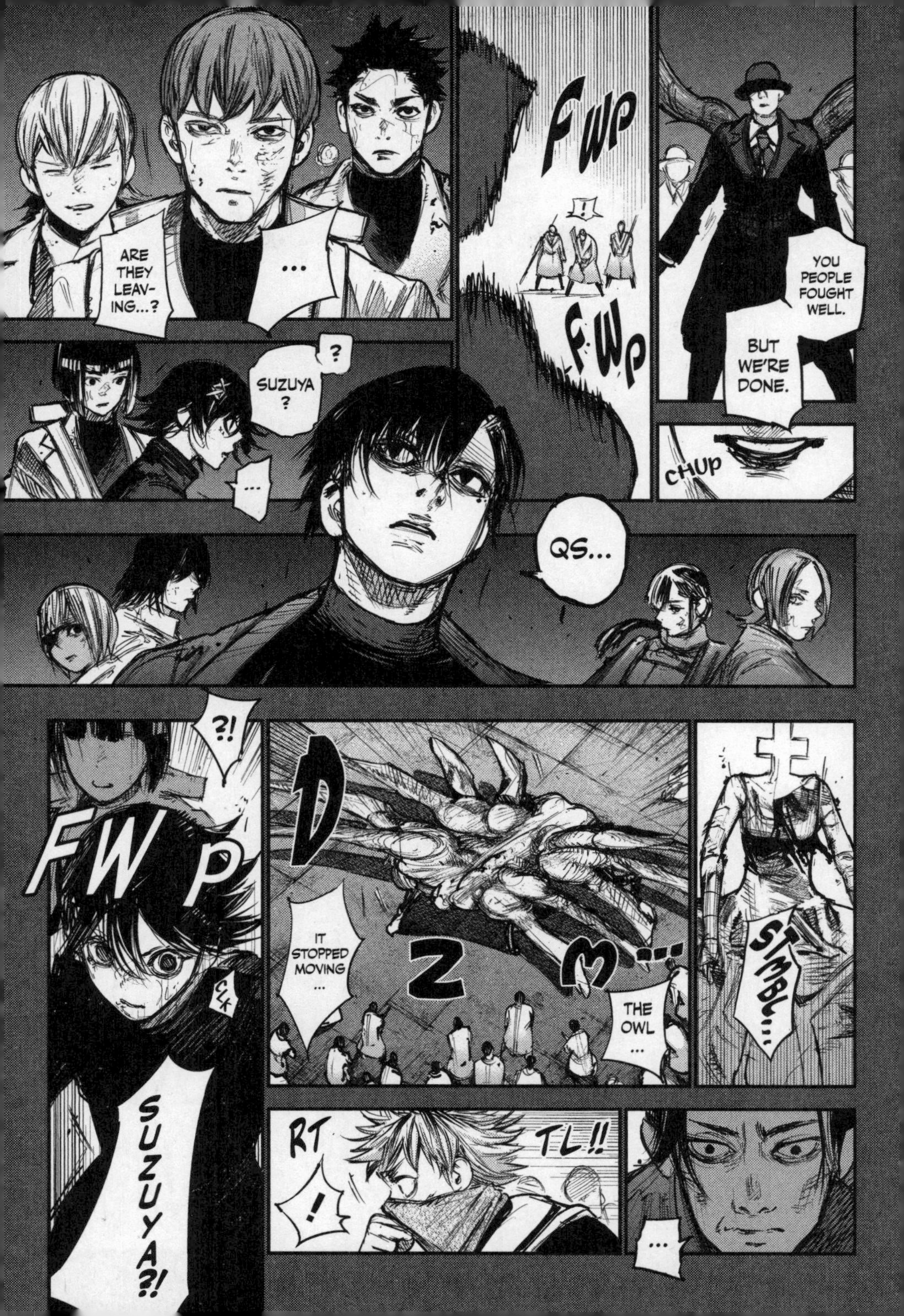
YOU PEOPLE FOUGHT WELL.
BUT WE'RE DONE.
CHUP
FWP
!
FWP
...
ARE THEY LEAV-ING...?
?
SUZUYA?
...
QS...
STMBL...
D
ZM...
THE OWL...
IT STOPPED MOVING...
?!
FWP
CLK
SUZUYA?!
...
TL!!
RT
!

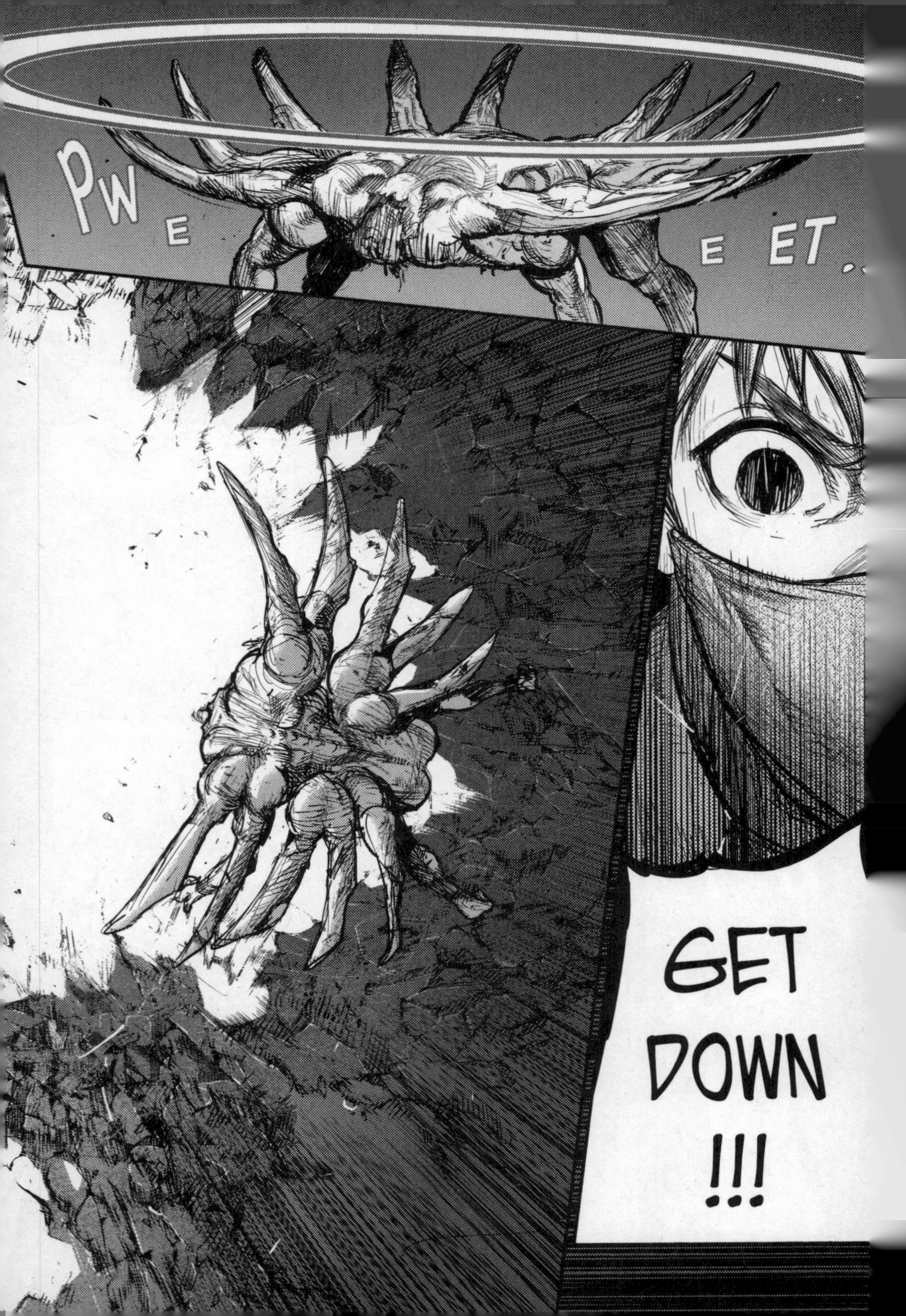
PWEEET...
GET DOWN!!!

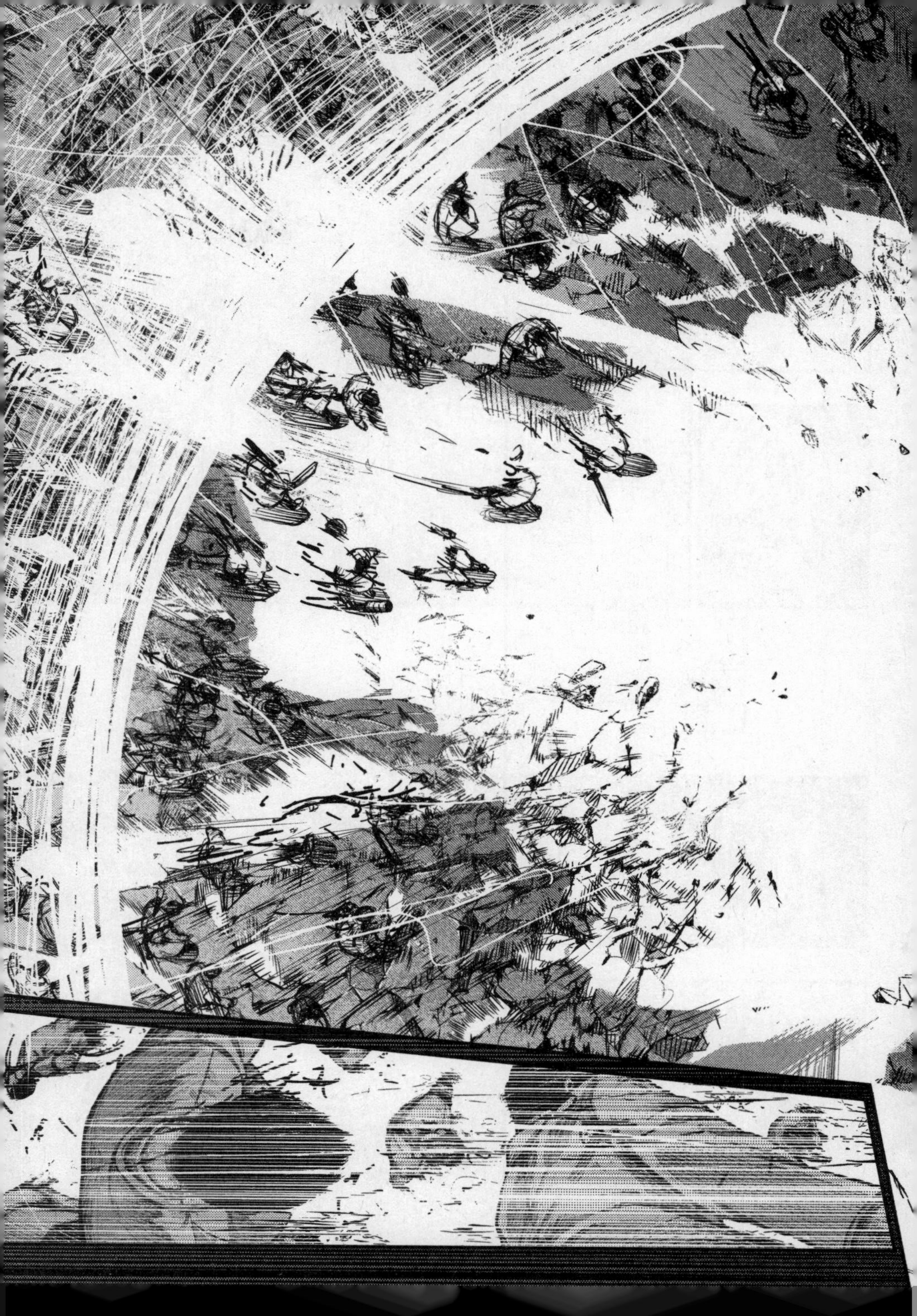

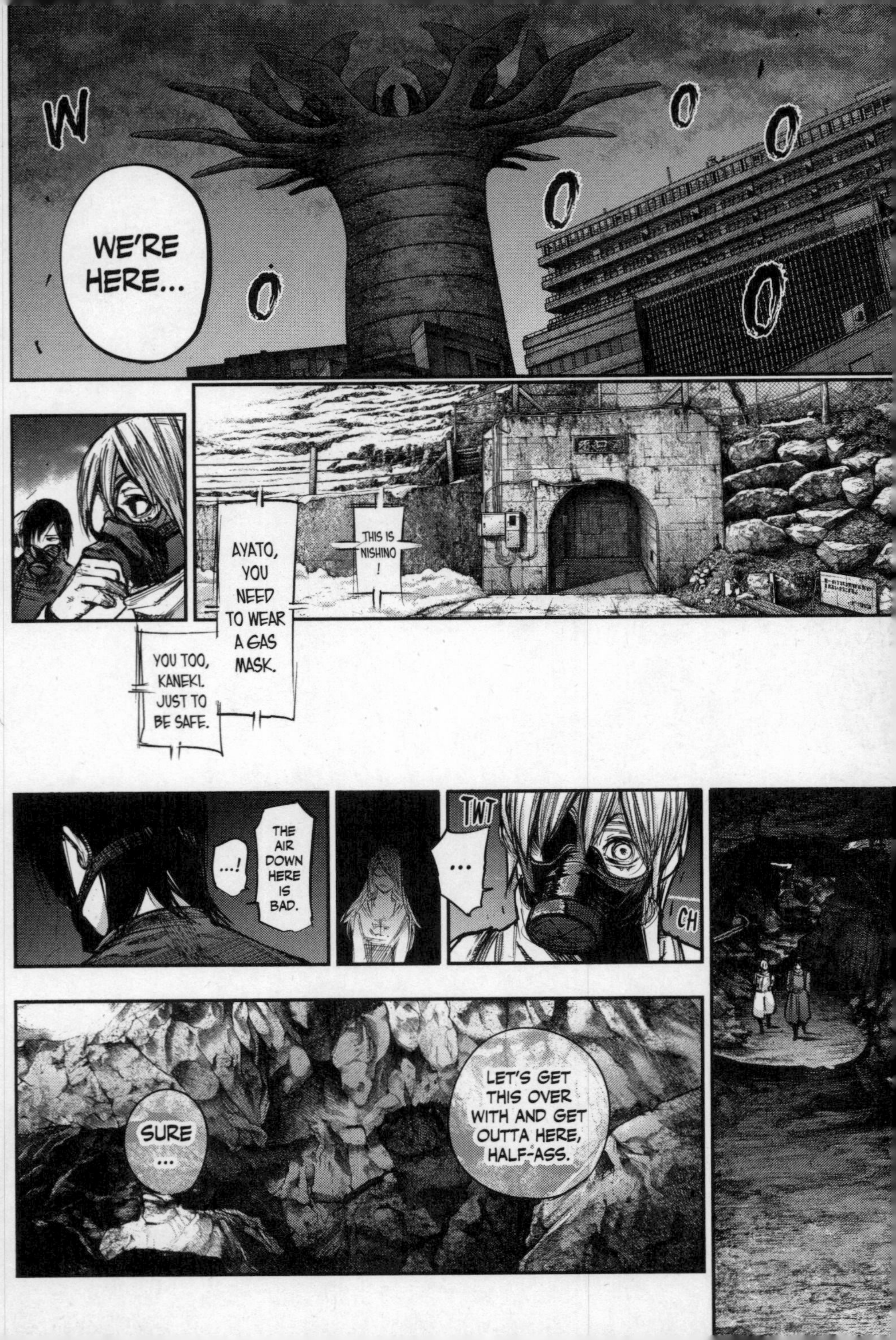
WOOOOO
WE'RE HERE...
THIS IS NISHINO!
AYATO, YOU NEED TO WEAR A GAS MASK.
YOU TOO, KANEKI. JUST TO BE SAFE.
TWT
...
CH
THE AIR DOWN HERE IS BAD.
...!
LET'S GET THIS OVER WITH AND GET OUTTA HERE, HALF-ASS.
SURE...

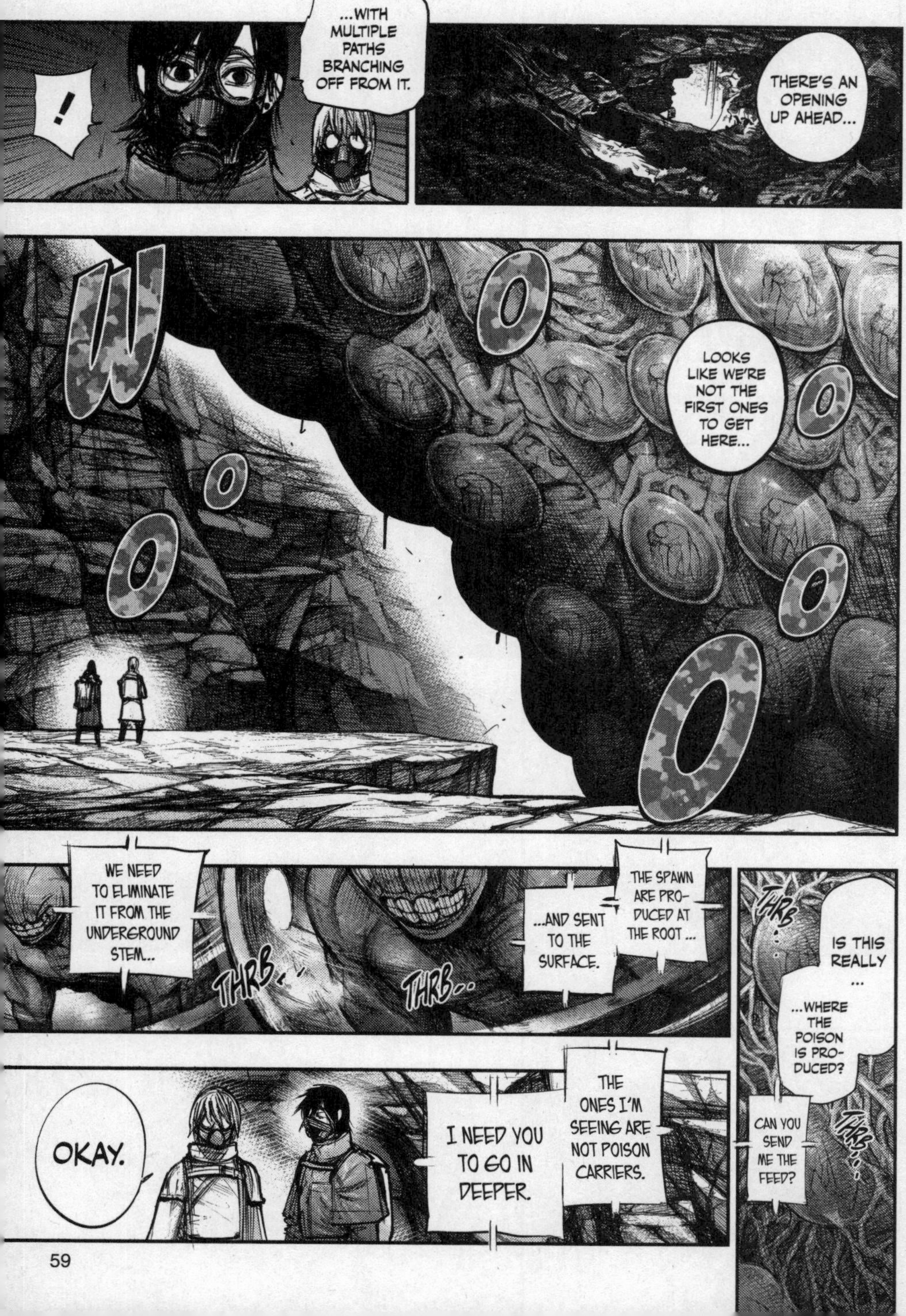
THERE'S AN OPENING UP AHEAD...
...WITH MULTIPLE PATHS BRANCHING OFF FROM IT.
!
WOOOOOO
LOOKS LIKE WE'RE NOT THE FIRST ONES TO GET HERE...
THRB...
IS THIS REALLY ...
...WHERE THE POISON IS PRODUCED?
THRB...
CAN YOU SEND ME THE FEED?
THE SPAWN ARE PRODUCED AT THE ROOT...
...AND SENT TO THE SURFACE.
THRB...
WE NEED TO ELIMINATE IT FROM THE UNDERGROUND STEM...
THRB...
THE ONES I'M SEEING ARE NOT POISON CARRIERS.
I NEED YOU TO GO IN DEEPER.
OKAY.

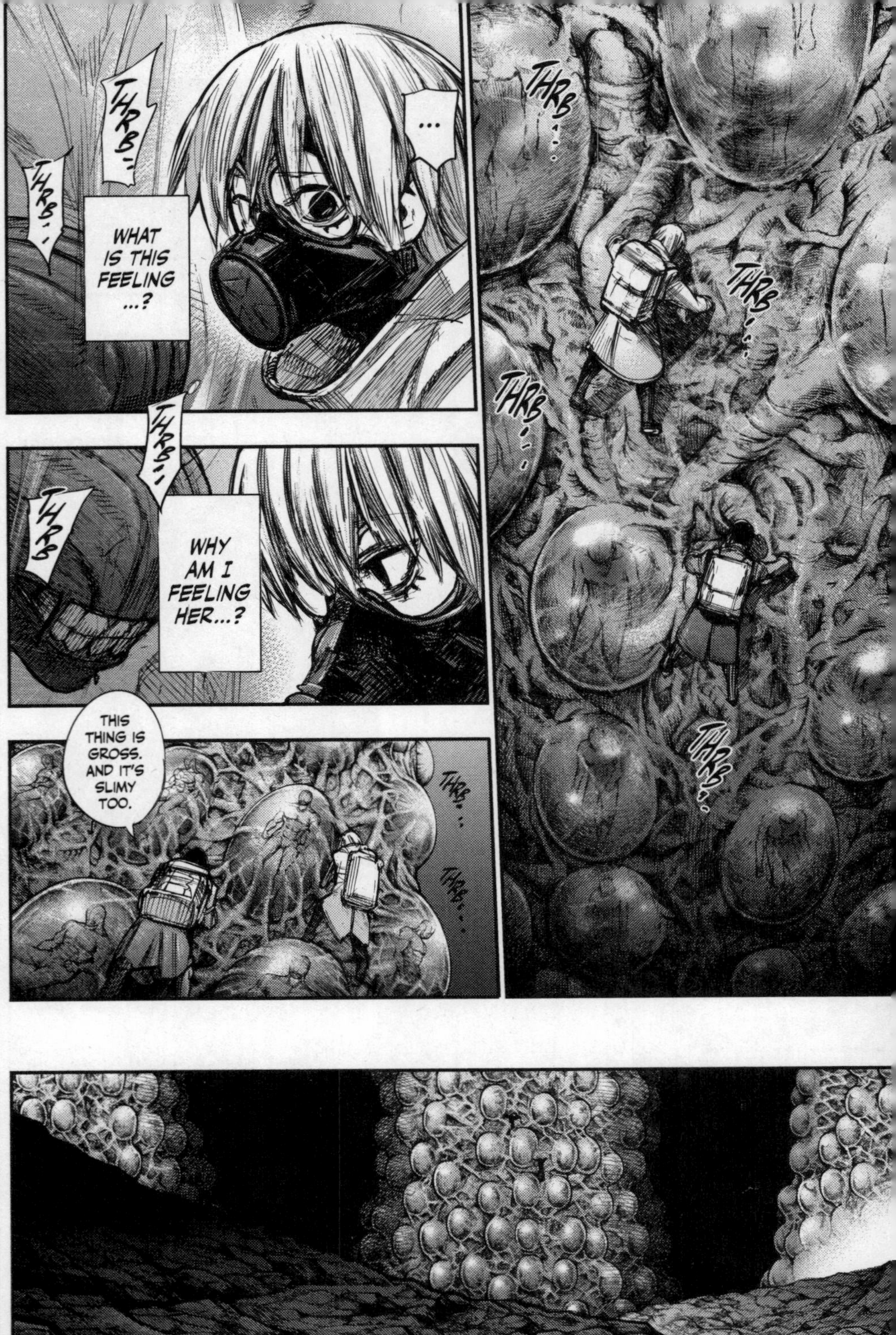
THRB...
THRB...
THRB...
THRB...
...
THRB...
THRB...
WHAT IS THIS FEELING ...?
THRB...
THRB
WHY AM I FEELING HER...?
THIS THING IS GROSS. AND IT'S SLIMY TOO.
THRB...
THRB...

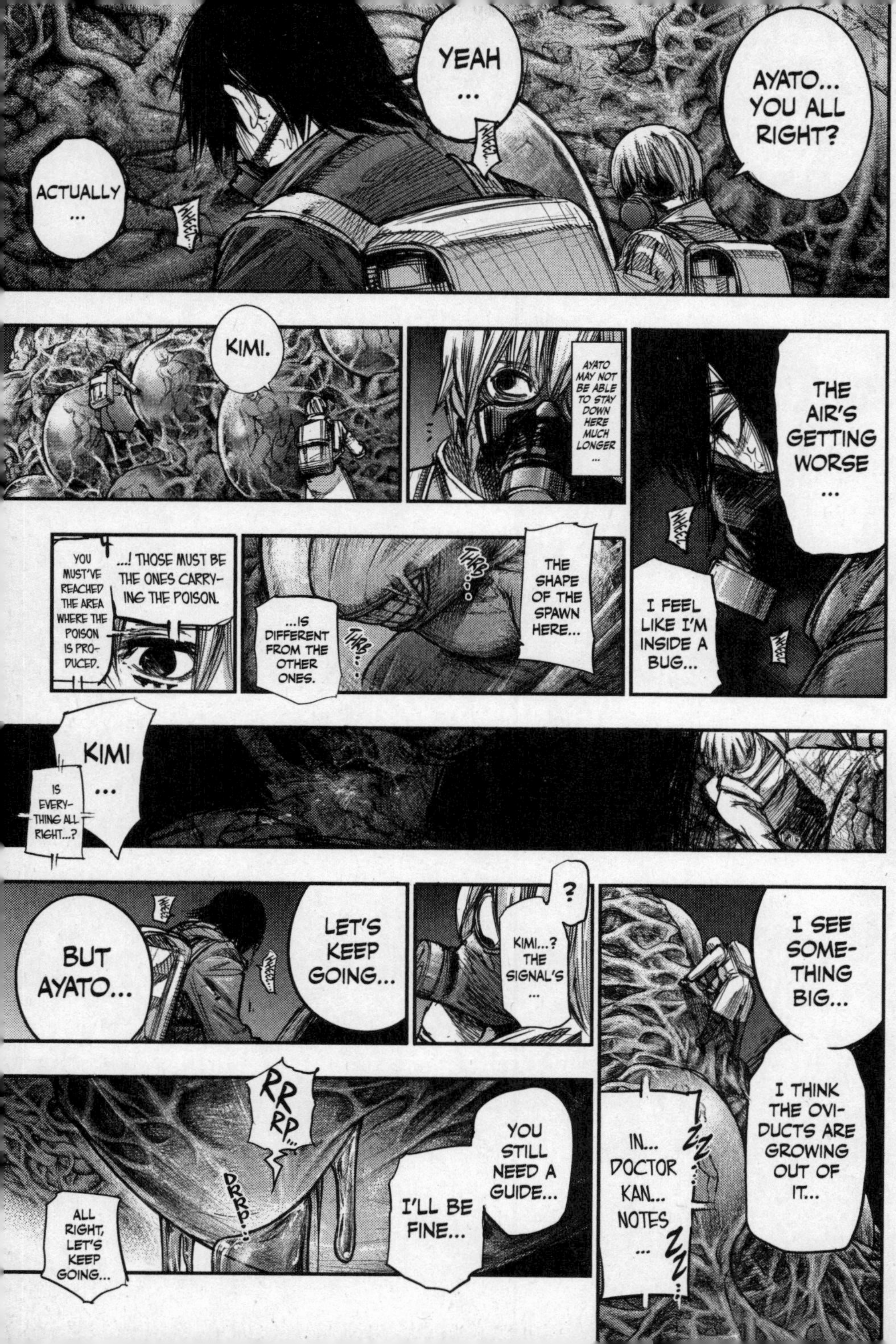
AYATO... YOU ALL RIGHT?
YEAH ...
ACTUALLY ...
THE AIR'S GETTING WORSE ...
I FEEL LIKE I'M INSIDE A BUG...
AYATO MAY NOT BE ABLE TO STAY DOWN HERE MUCH LONGER ...
KIMI.
THE SHAPE OF THE SPAWN HERE...
...IS DIFFERENT FROM THE OTHER ONES.
THRB...
...! THOSE MUST BE THE ONES CARRYING THE POISON.
YOU MUST'VE REACHED THE AREA WHERE THE POISON IS PRODUCED.
KIMI ...
IS EVERYTHING ALL RIGHT...?
I SEE SOMETHING BIG...
I THINK THE OVIDUCTS ARE GROWING OUT OF IT...
IN... DOCTOR KAN... NOTES ...
?
KIMI...? THE SIGNAL'S ...
LET'S KEEP GOING...
BUT AYATO...
RRRP...
YOU STILL NEED A GUIDE...
I'LL BE FINE...
DRRRP...
ALL RIGHT, LET'S KEEP GOING...

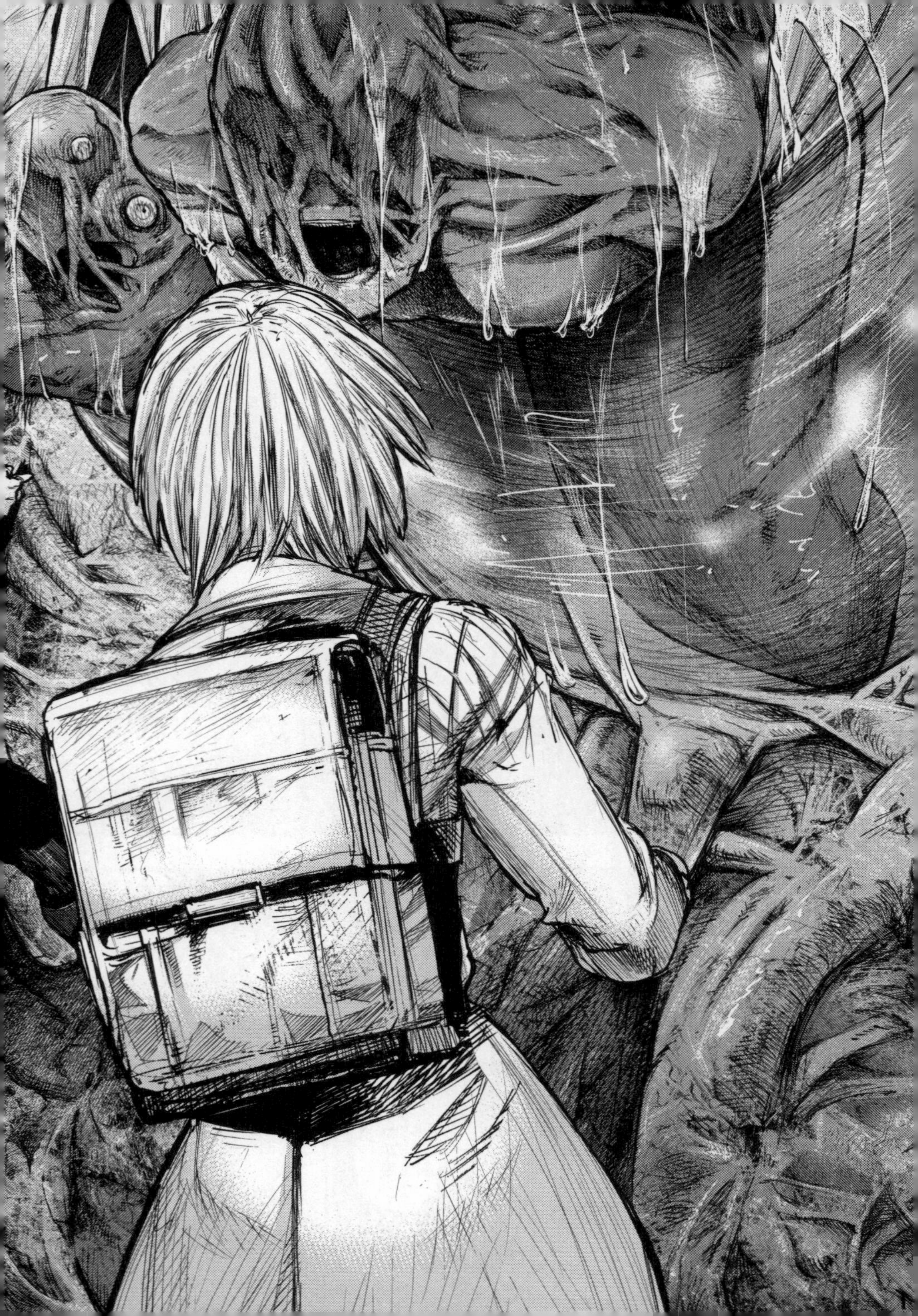

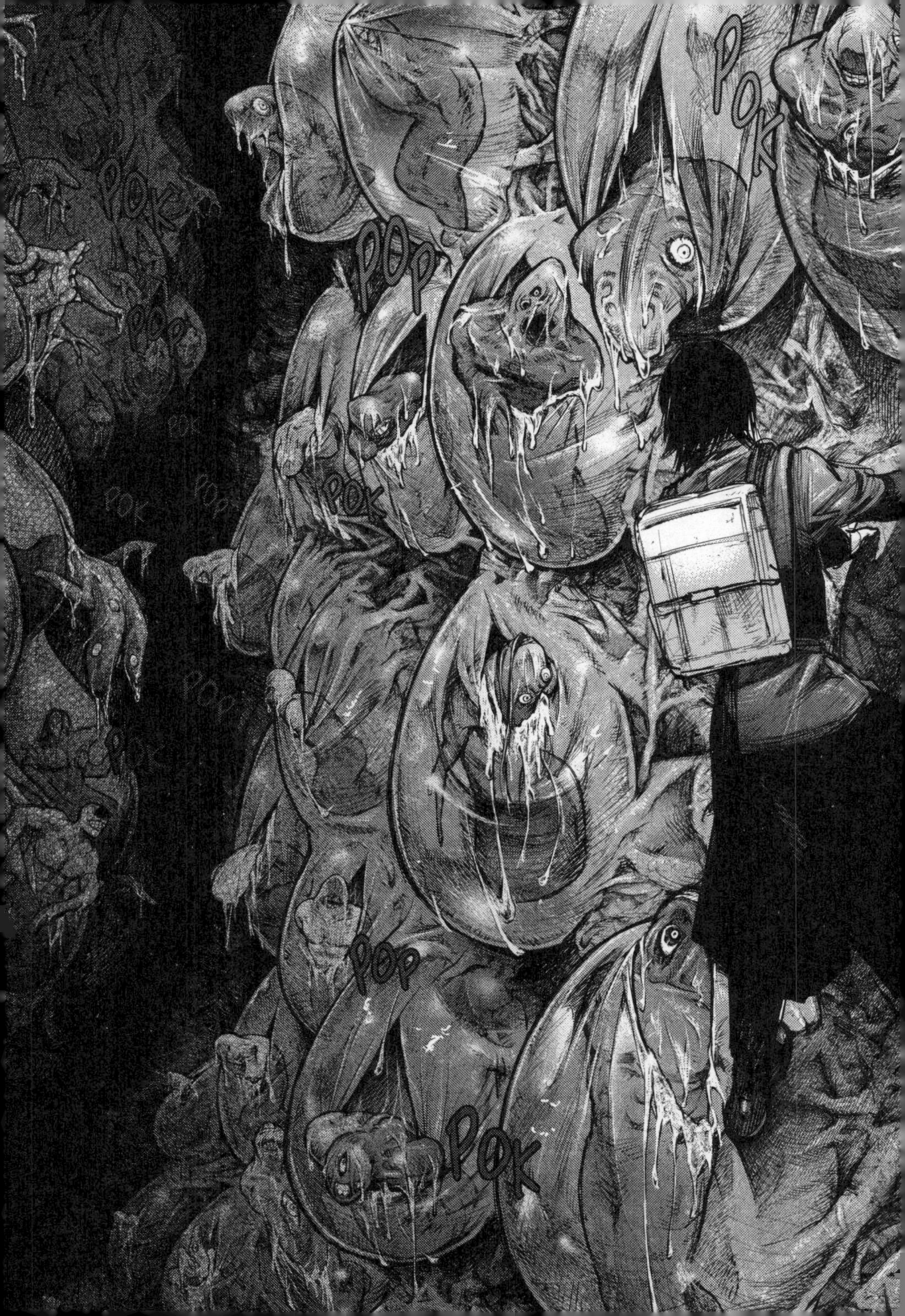
POK
POP
POK
POP
POK

TOKYO GHOUL:re

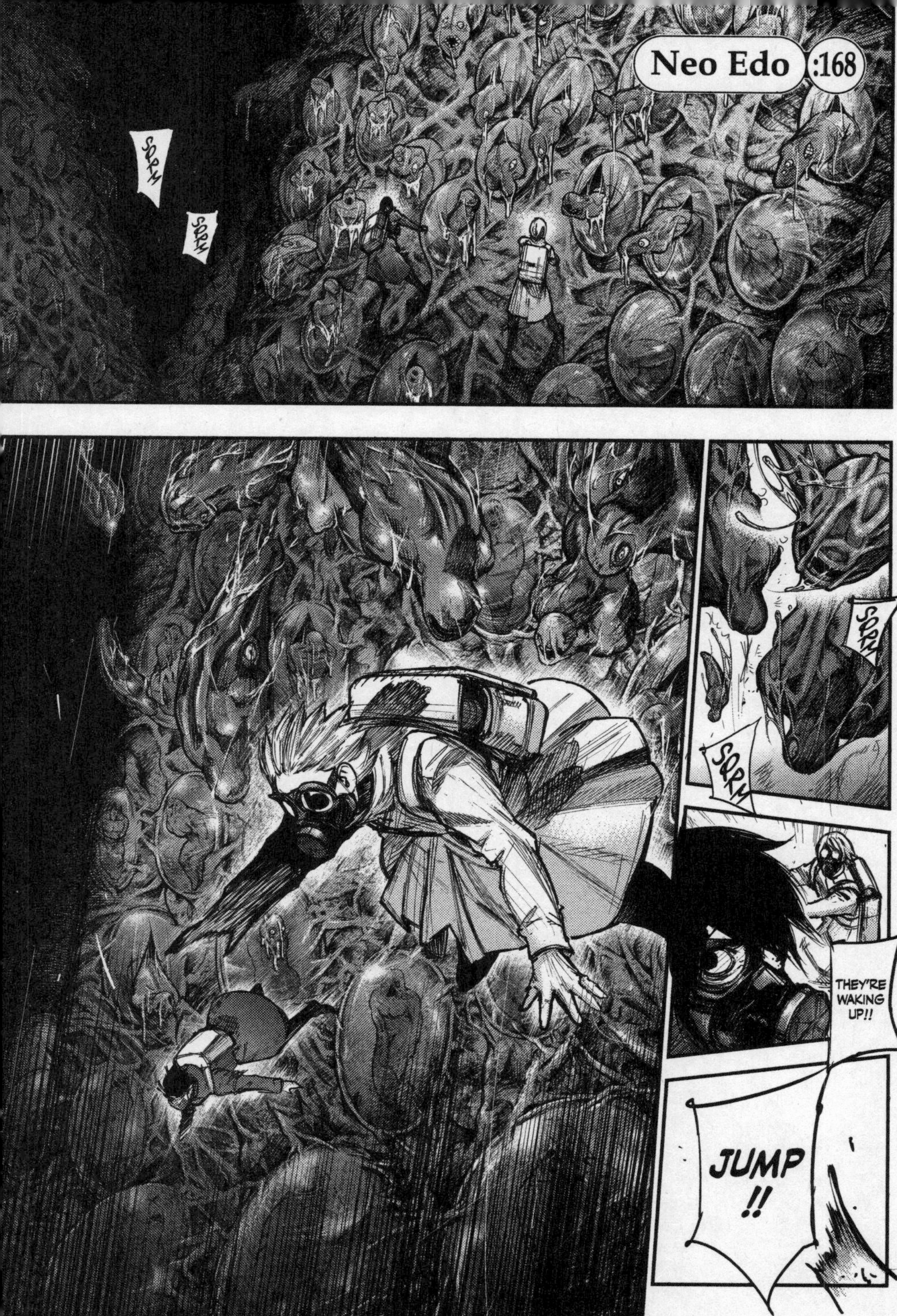
Neo Edo :168
SQRM
SQRM
SQRM
SQRM
THEY'RE WAKING UP!!
JUMP !!

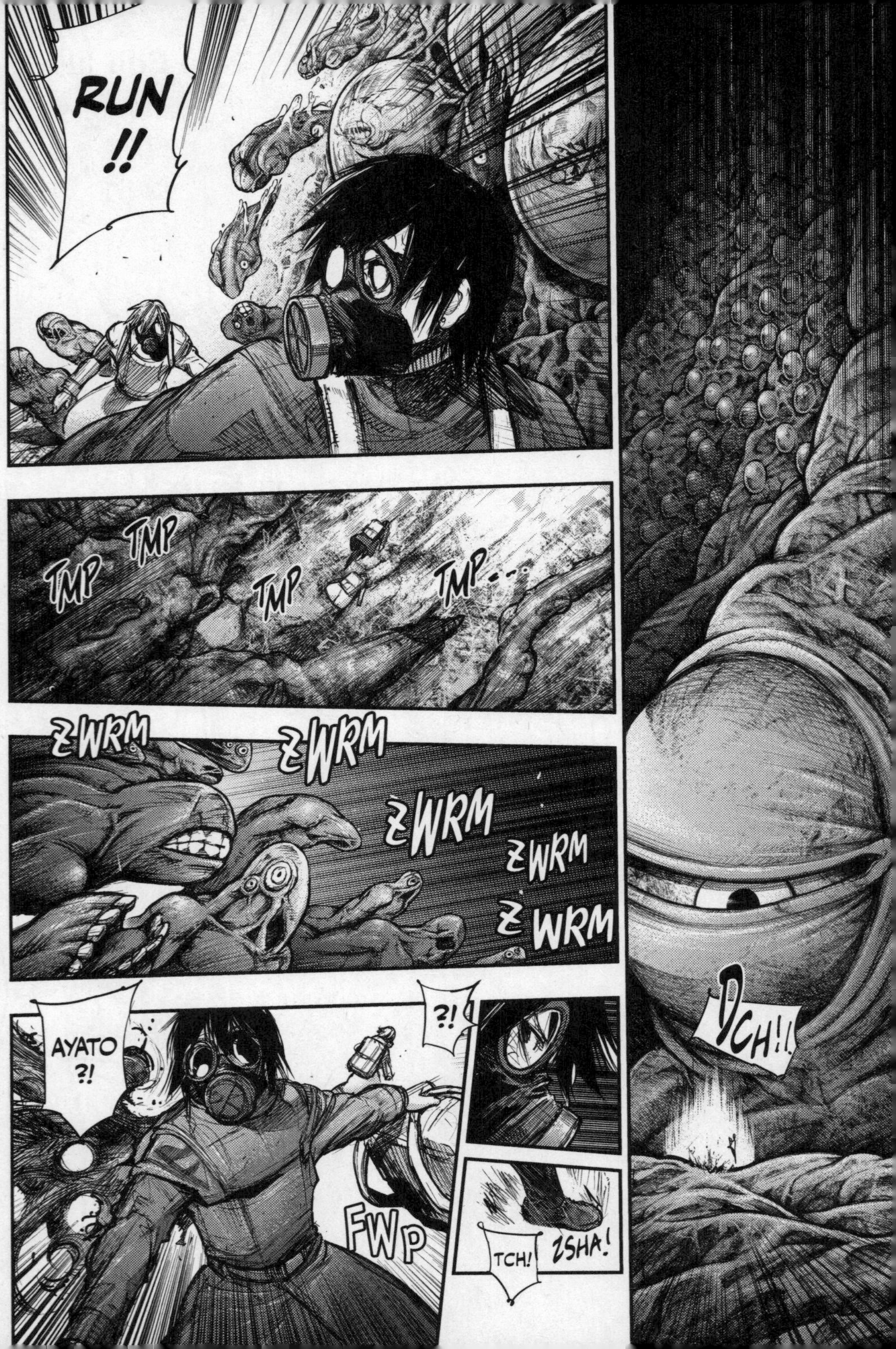

DCH!!
RUN!!
TMP
TMP
TMP
TMP...
ZWRM
ZWRM
ZWRM
ZWRM
ZWRM
?!
TCH!
ZSHA!
AYATO ?!
FWp

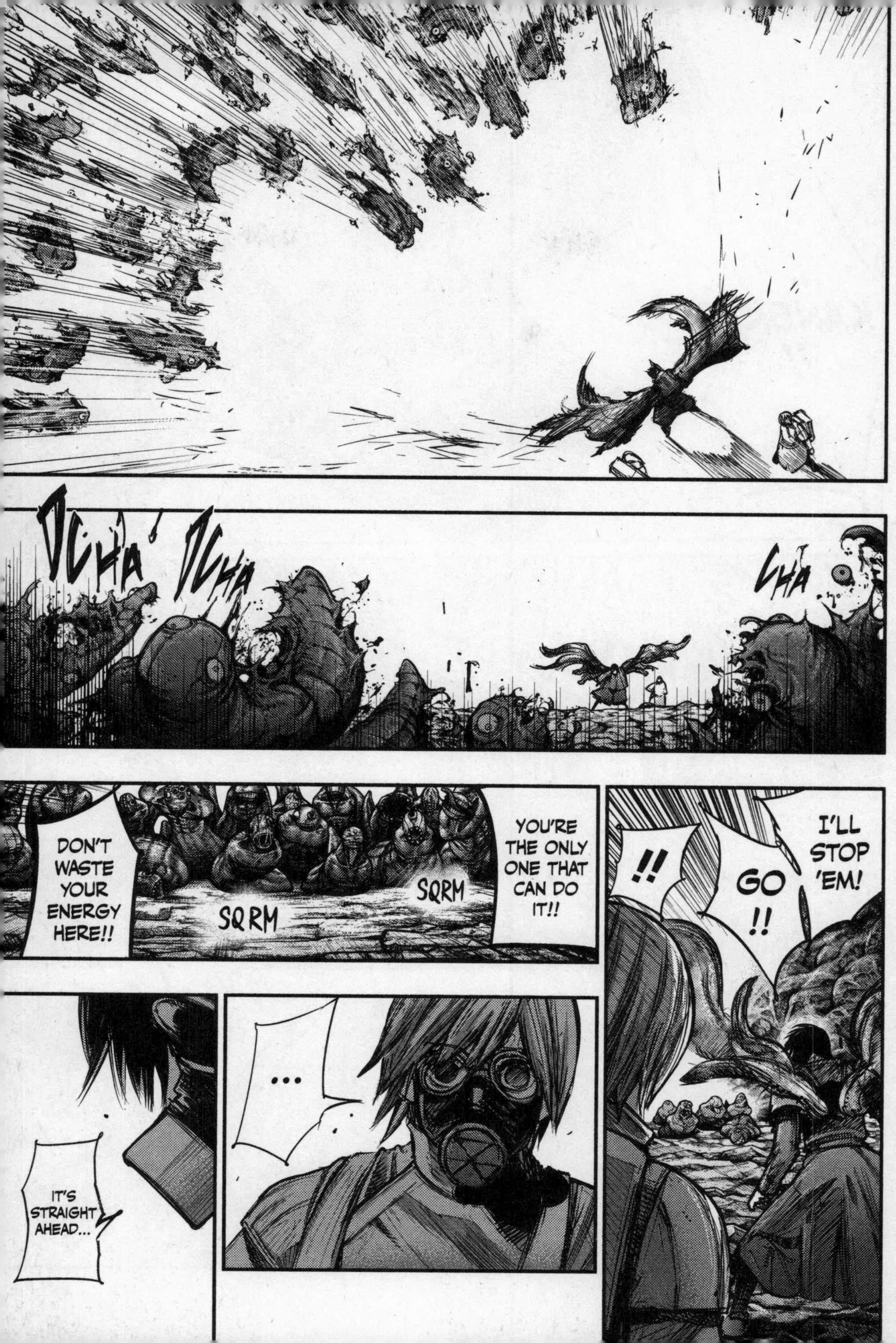
CHA
DCHA
DCHA
I'LL STOP 'EM!
GO!!
!!
YOU'RE THE ONLY ONE THAT CAN DO IT!!
SQRM
SQRM
DON'T WASTE YOUR ENERGY HERE!!
...
IT'S STRAIGHT AHEAD...

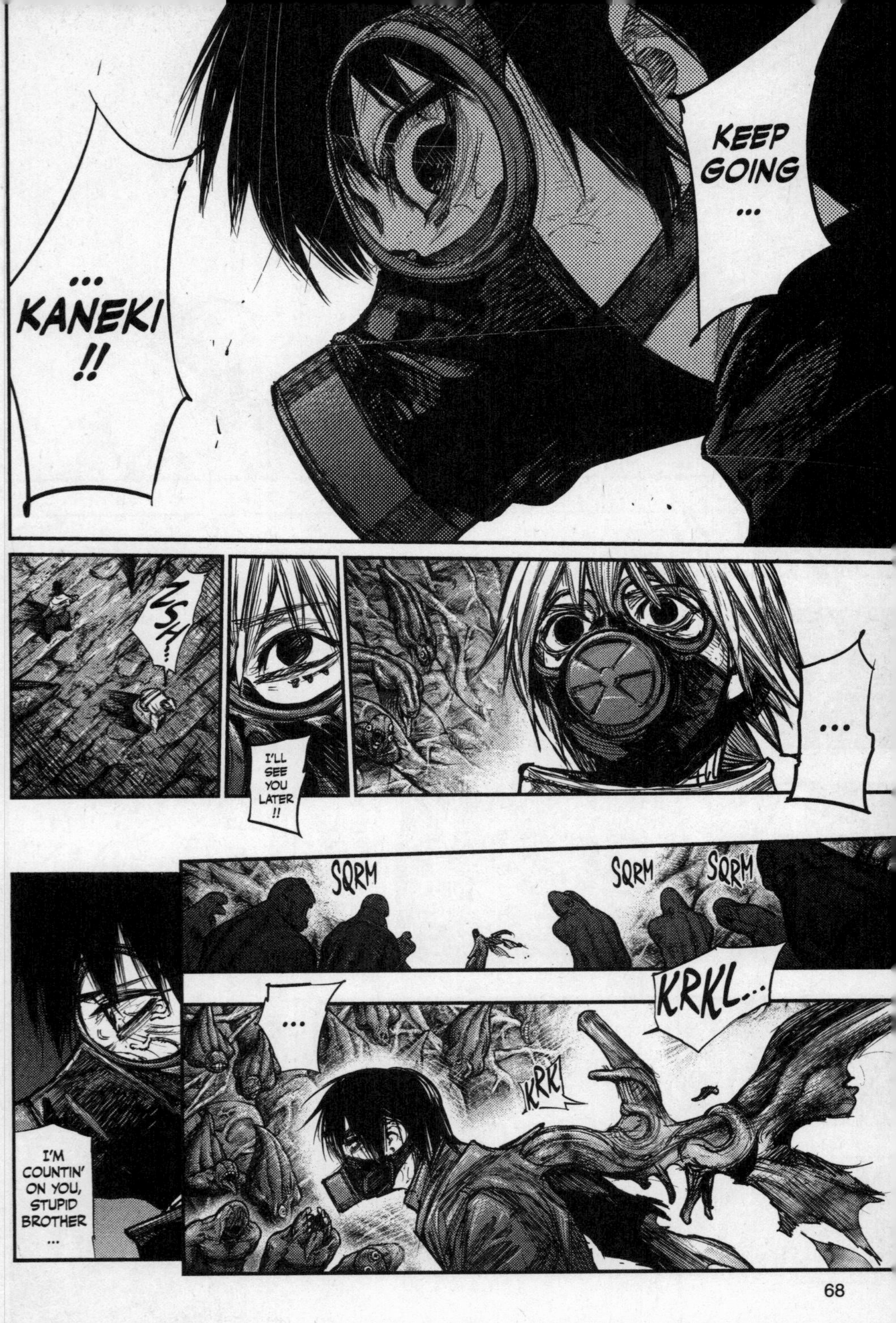
KEEP GOING ...
... KANEKI !!
...
I'LL SEE YOU LATER !!
ZSH...
SQRM
SQRM
SQRM
KRKL...
...
KRK
I'M COUNTIN' ON YOU, STUPID BROTHER ...

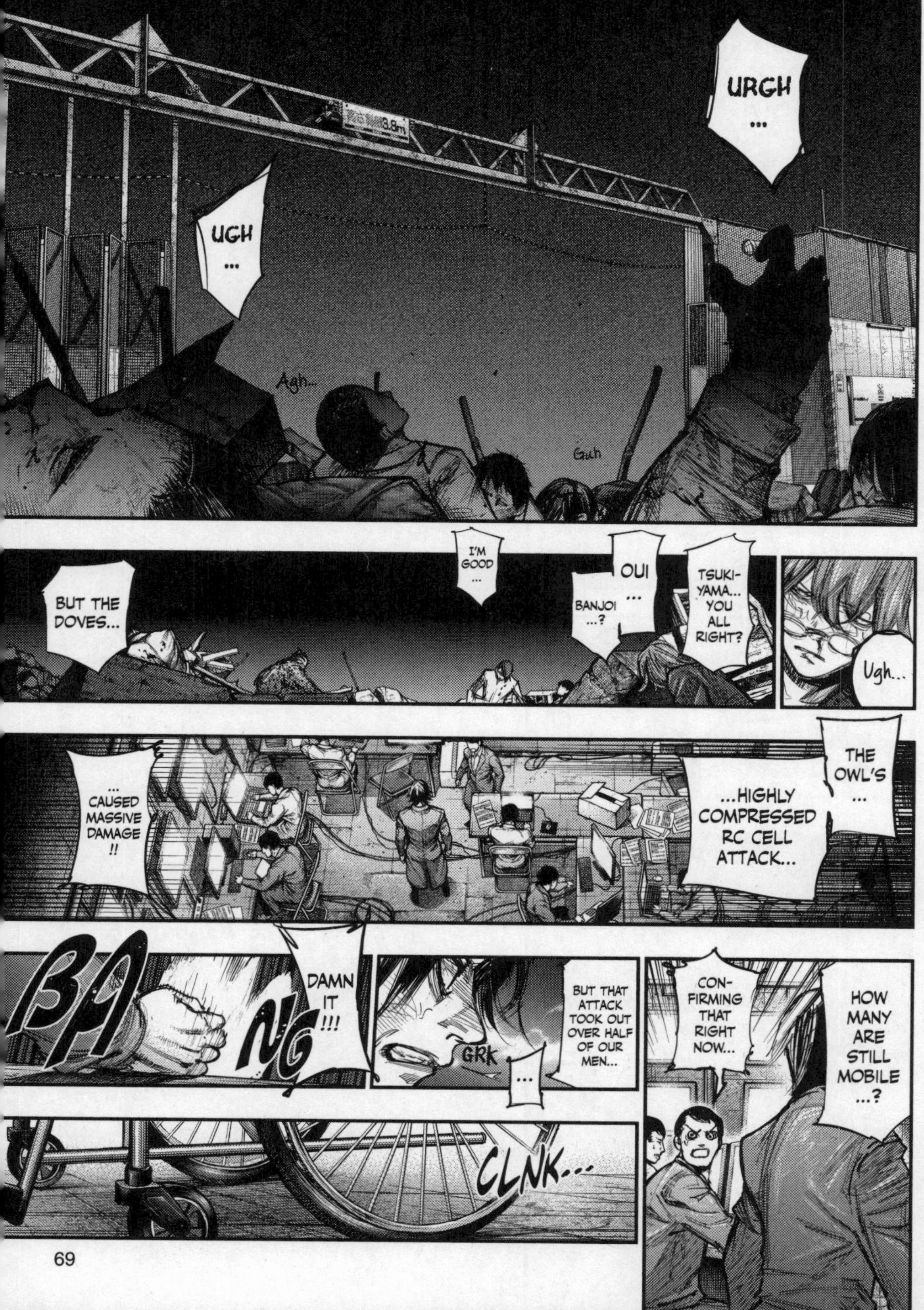
URGH ...
UGH ...
Agh...
Guh
Ugh...
TSUKI-YAMA... YOU ALL RIGHT?
OUI ...
BANJOI ...?
I'M GOOD ...
BUT THE DOVES...
THE OWL'S ...
...HIGHLY COMPRESSED RC CELL ATTACK...
... CAUSED MASSIVE DAMAGE !!
HOW MANY ARE STILL MOBILE ...?
CON-FIRMING THAT RIGHT NOW...
BUT THAT ATTACK TOOK OUT OVER HALF OF OUR MEN...
GRK
...
DAMN IT !!!
BANG
CLNK...

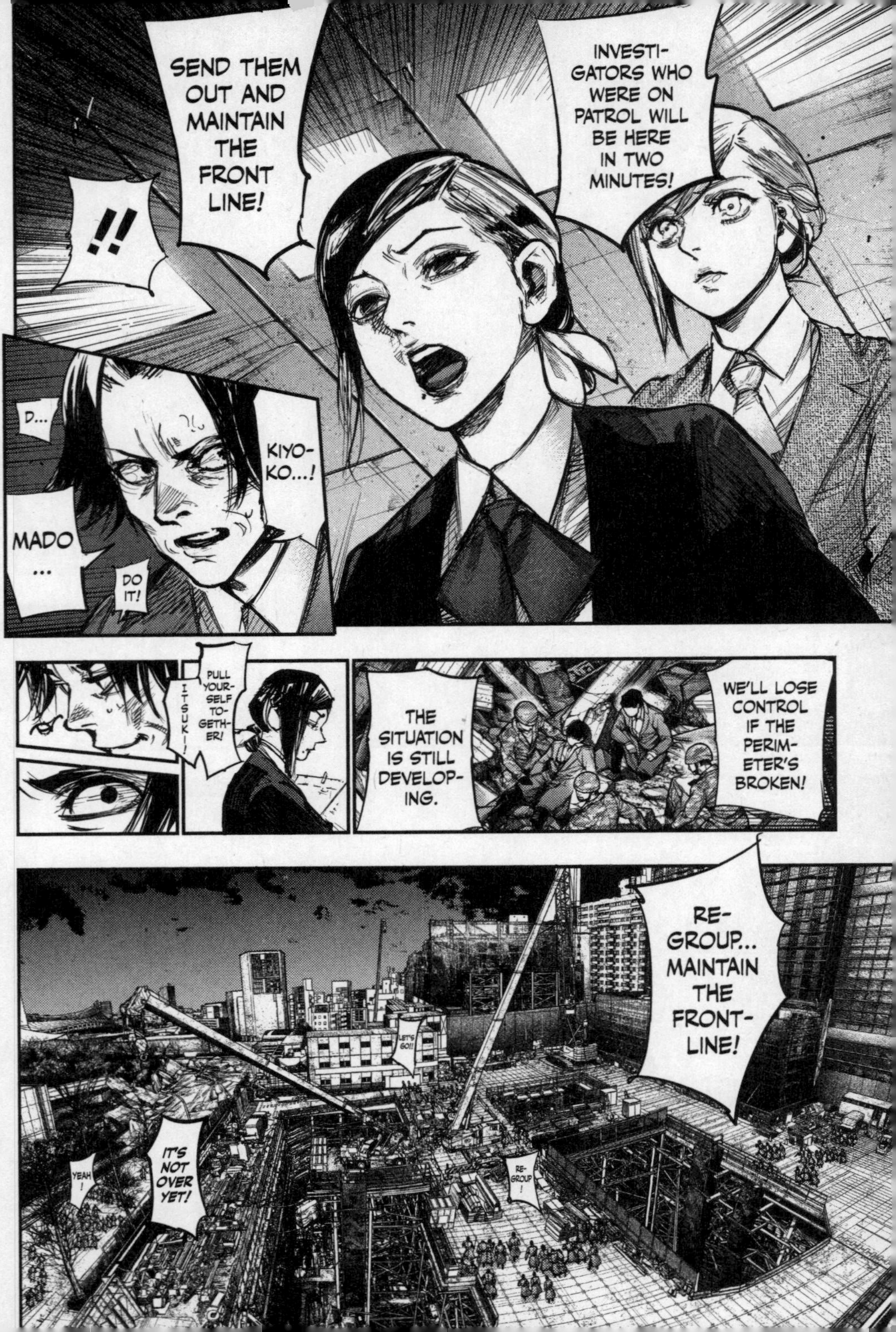
INVESTIGATORS WHO WERE ON PATROL WILL BE HERE IN TWO MINUTES!
SEND THEM OUT AND MAINTAIN THE FRONT LINE!
!!
KIYOKO...!
D...
MADO...
DO IT!
WE'LL LOSE CONTROL IF THE PERIMETER'S BROKEN!
THE SITUATION IS STILL DEVELOPING.
PULL YOURSELF TOGETHER!
ITSUKI...!
REGROUP... MAINTAIN THE FRONT-LINE!
LET'S GO!!
REGROUP!
IT'S NOT OVER YET!
YEAH!

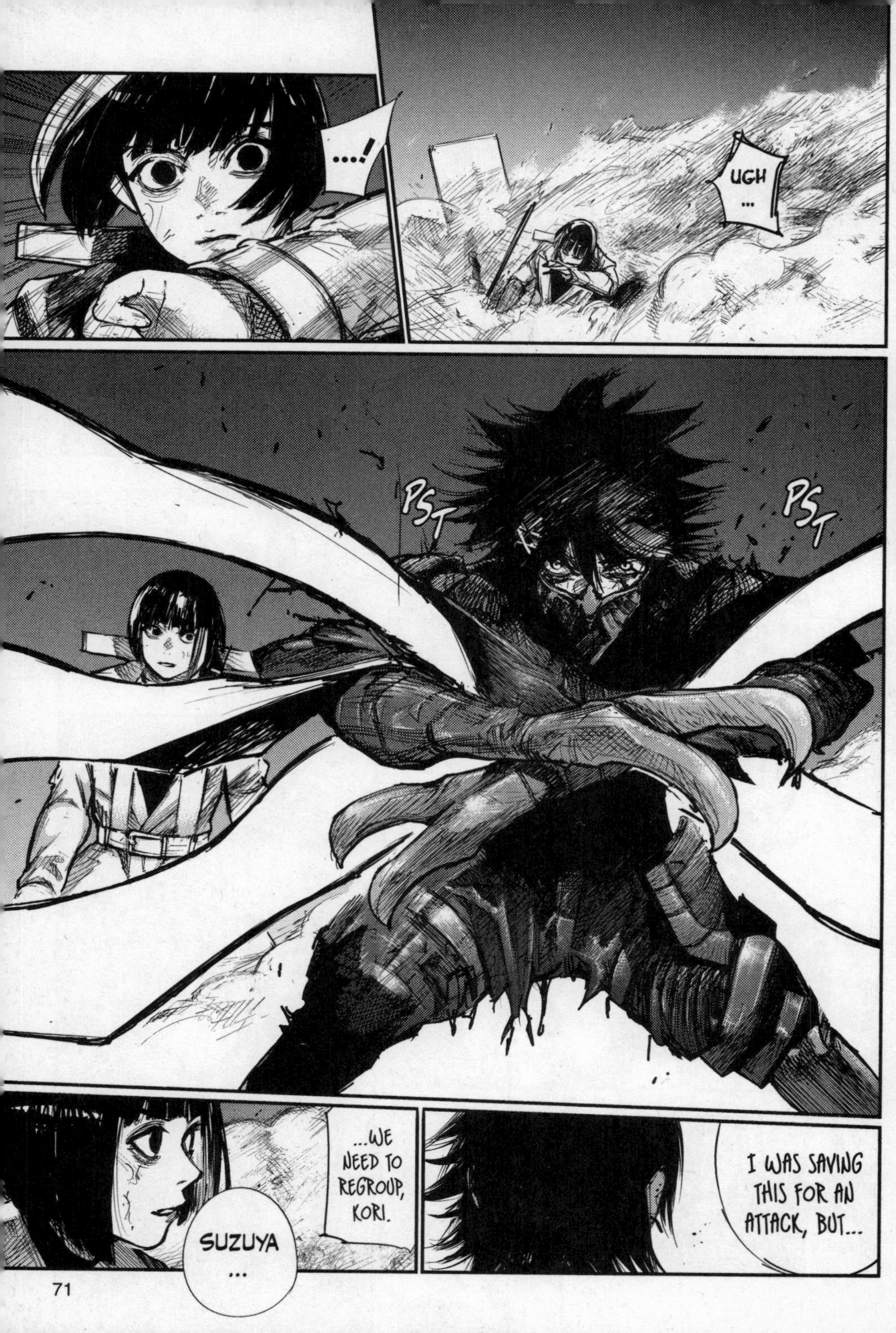
UGH ...
...!
PST
PST
I WAS SAVING THIS FOR AN ATTACK, BUT...
...WE NEED TO REGROUP, KORI.
SUZUYA ...

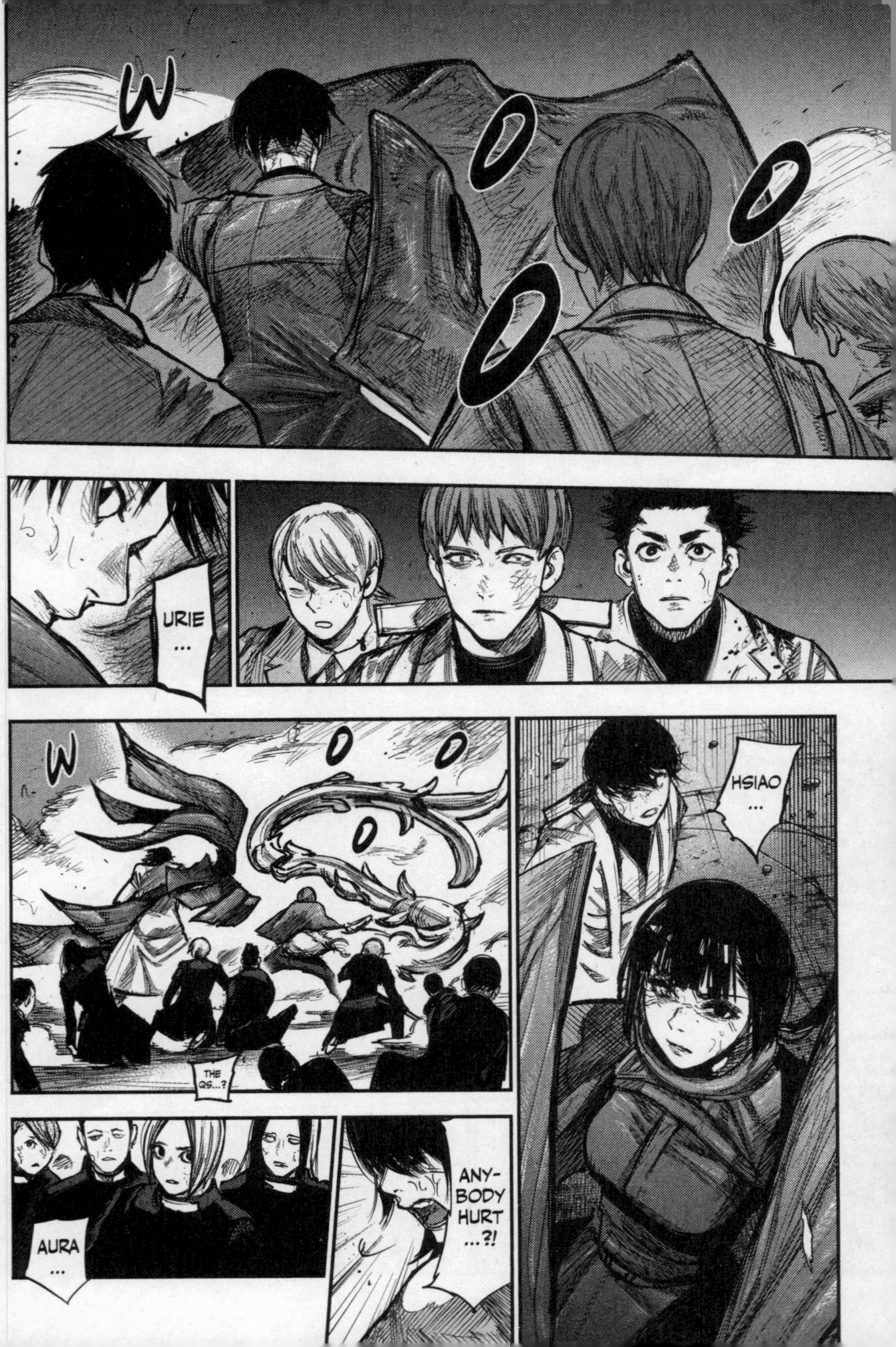
WOOOO
URIE ...
HSIAO ...
WOOO
THE QS...?
ANY-BODY HURT ...?!
AURA ...

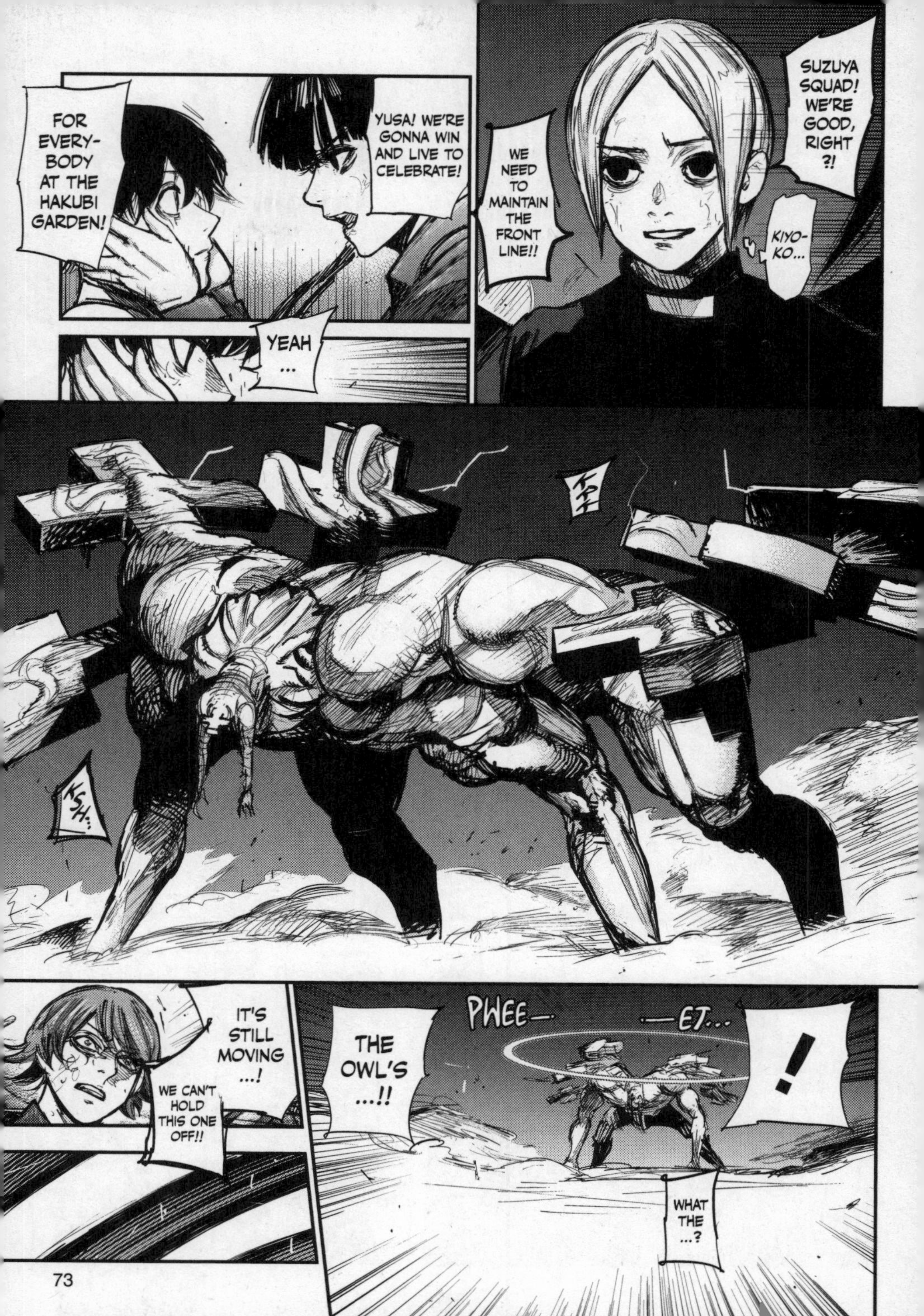
SUZUYA SQUAD! WE'RE GOOD, RIGHT?!
WE NEED TO MAINTAIN THE FRONT LINE!!
KIYO-KO...
YUSA! WE'RE GONNA WIN AND LIVE TO CELEBRATE!
FOR EVERY-BODY AT THE HAKUBI GARDEN!
YEAH ...
KSH...
!
PWEE— —ET...
THE OWL'S ...!!
WHAT THE ...?
IT'S STILL MOVING ...!
WE CAN'T HOLD THIS ONE OFF!!

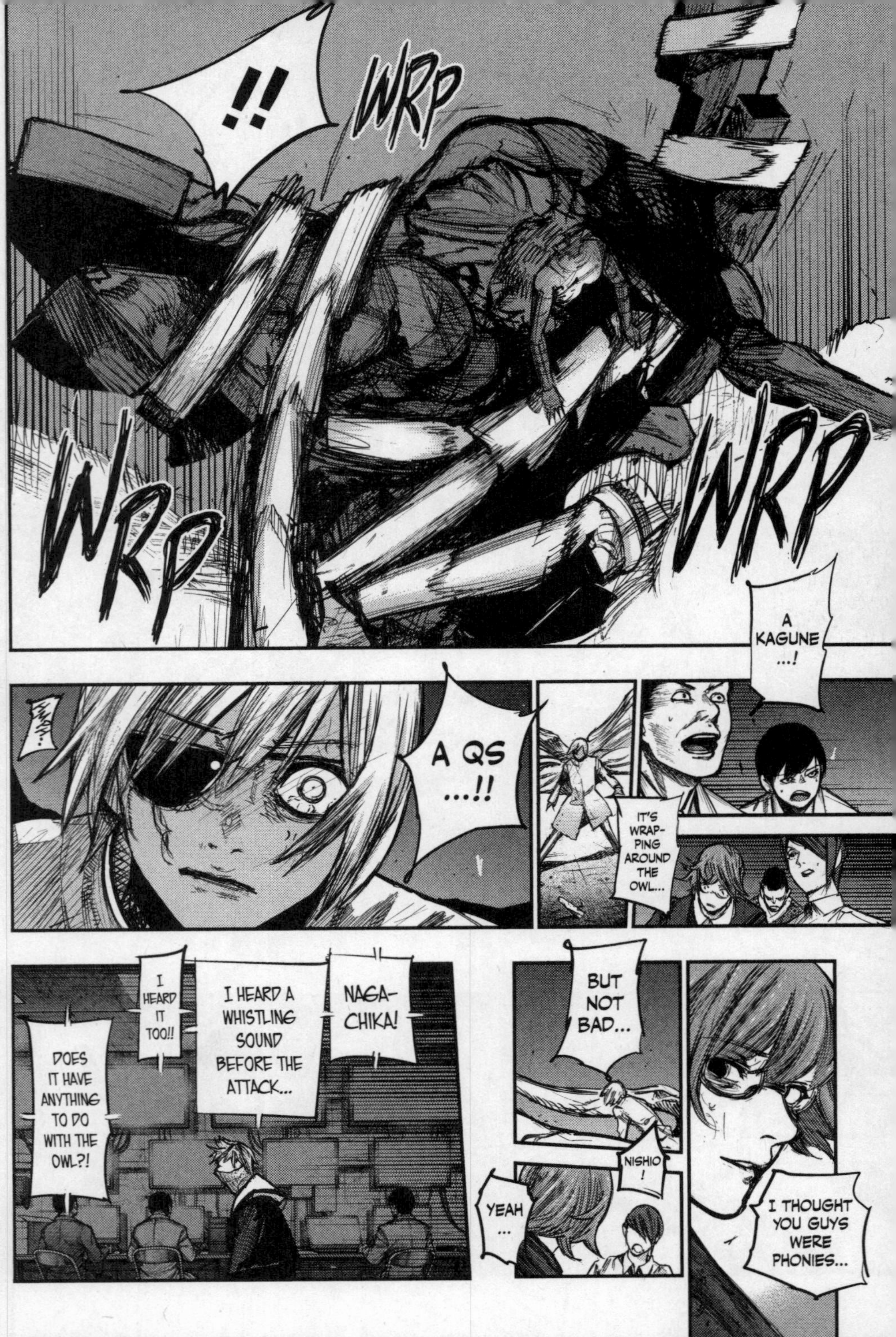
WRP
!!
WRP
WRP
A KAGUNE ...!
IT'S WRAPPING AROUND THE OWL...
A QS ...!!
I THOUGHT YOU GUYS WERE PHONIES...
BUT NOT BAD...
NISHIO!
YEAH ...
NAGA-CHIKA!
I HEARD A WHISTLING SOUND BEFORE THE ATTACK...
I HEARD IT TOO!!
DOES IT HAVE ANYTHING TO DO WITH THE OWL?!

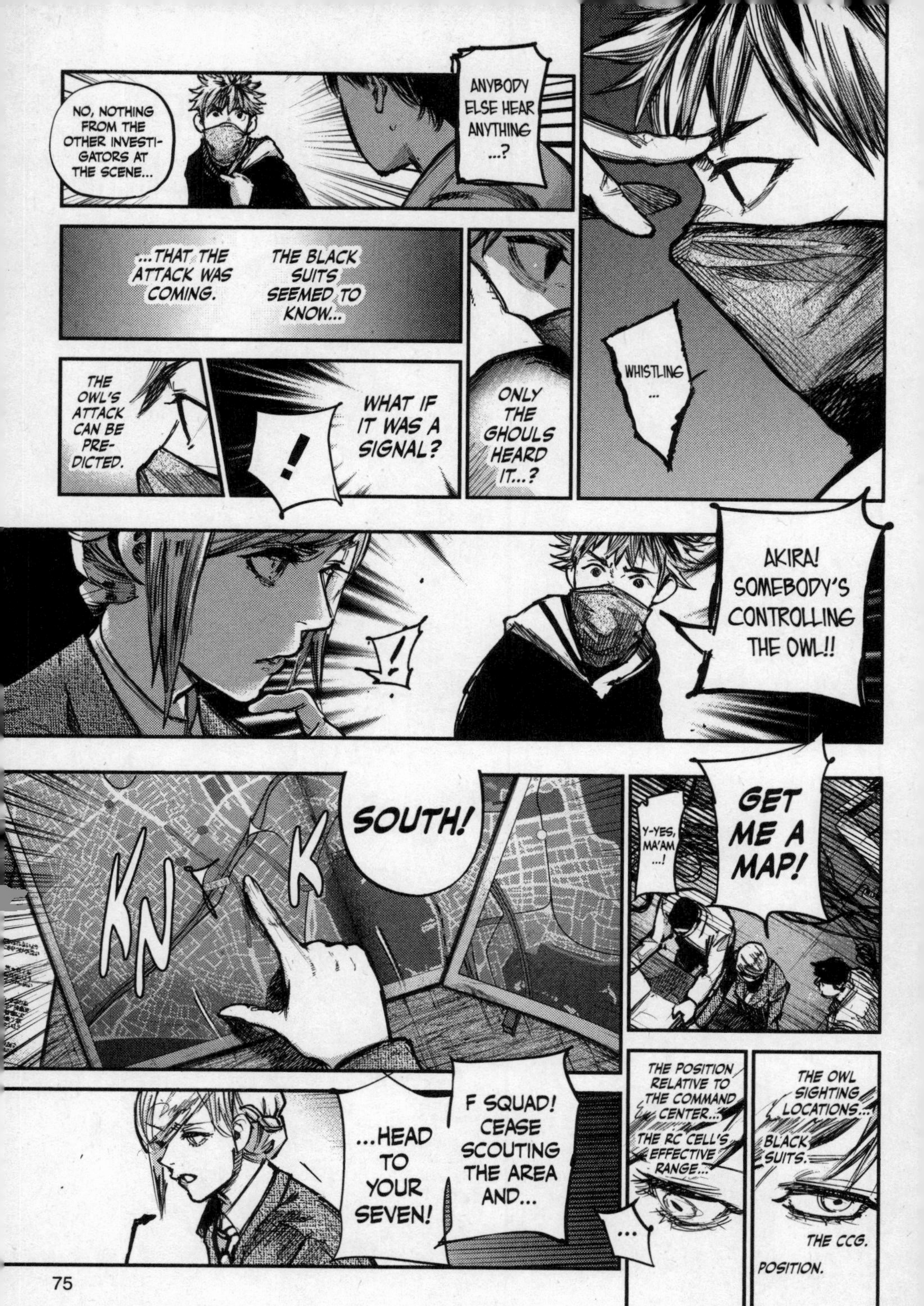
WHISTLING...
ANYBODY ELSE HEAR ANYTHING...?
NO, NOTHING FROM THE OTHER INVESTIGATORS AT THE SCENE...
ONLY THE GHOULS HEARD IT...?
THE BLACK SUITS SEEMED TO KNOW...
...THAT THE ATTACK WAS COMING.
WHAT IF IT WAS A SIGNAL?
!
THE OWL'S ATTACK CAN BE PREDICTED.
AKIRA! SOMEBODY'S CONTROLLING THE OWL!!
!
GET ME A MAP!
Y-YES, MA'AM...!
SOUTH!
KN K
THE OWL SIGHTING LOCATIONS...
BLACK SUITS.
THE CCG.
POSITION.
THE POSITION RELATIVE TO THE COMMAND CENTER...
THE RC CELL'S EFFECTIVE RANGE...
...
F SQUAD! CEASE SCOUTING THE AREA AND...
...HEAD TO YOUR SEVEN!

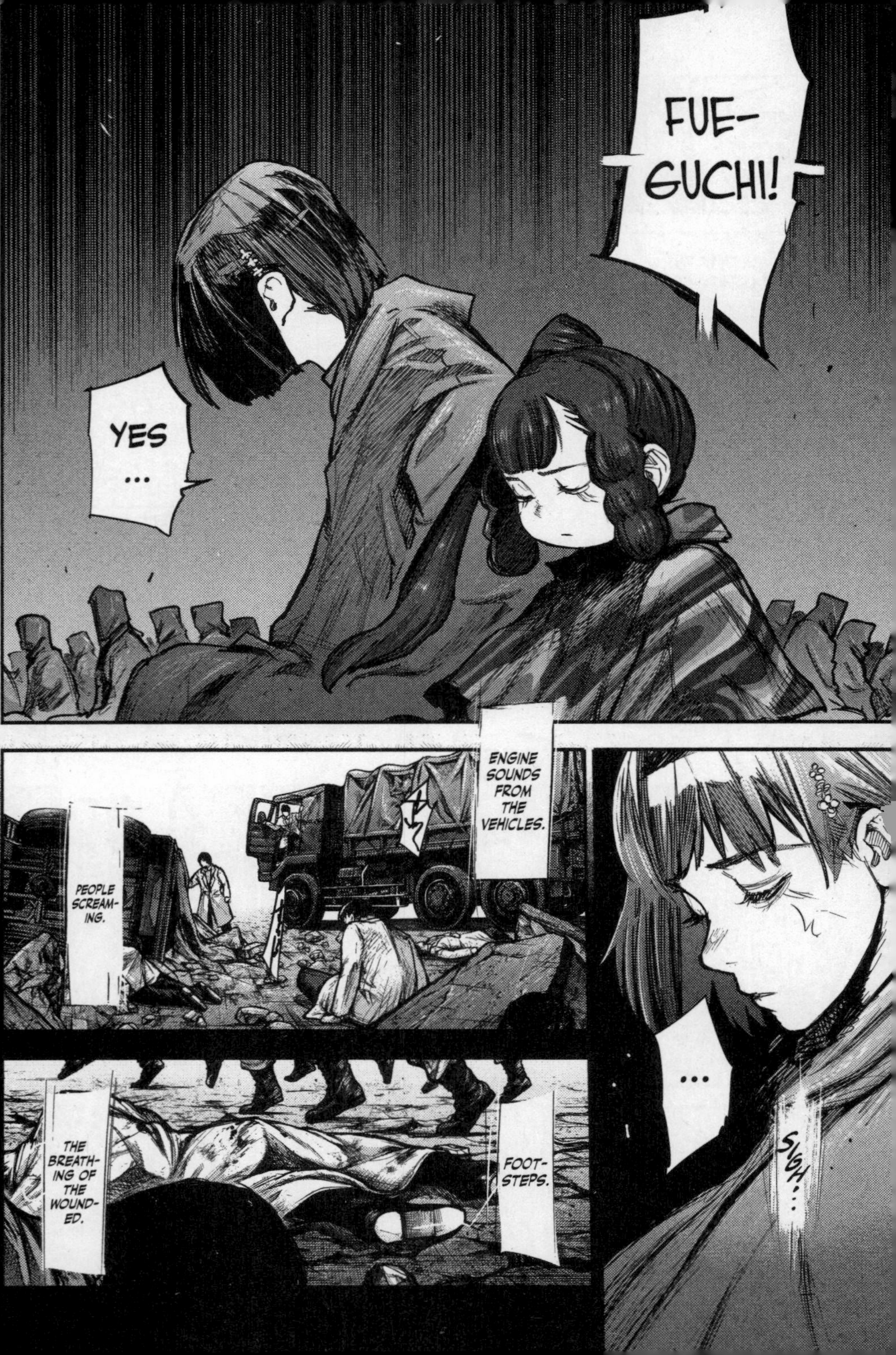
FUE-GUCHI!
YES ...
...
SIGH...
ENGINE SOUNDS FROM THE VEHICLES.
PEOPLE SCREAMING.
FOOTSTEPS.
THE BREATHING OF THE WOUNDED.

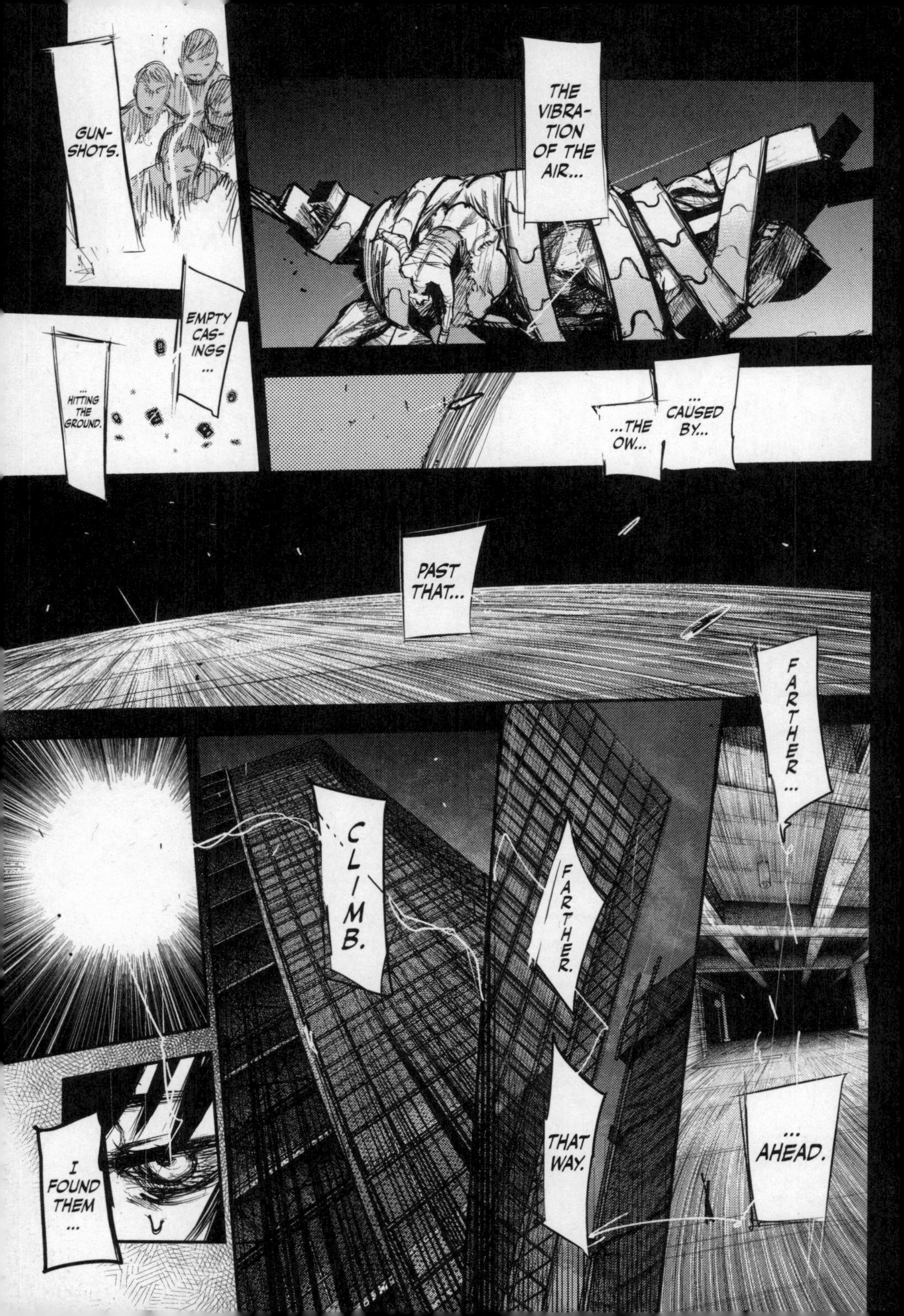
THE VIBRATION OF THE AIR...
GUNSHOTS.
...CAUSED BY...
...THE OW...
EMPTY CASINGS...
...HITTING THE GROUND.
PAST THAT...
FARTHER...
...AHEAD.
FARTHER.
THAT WAY.
CLIMB.
I FOUND THEM...

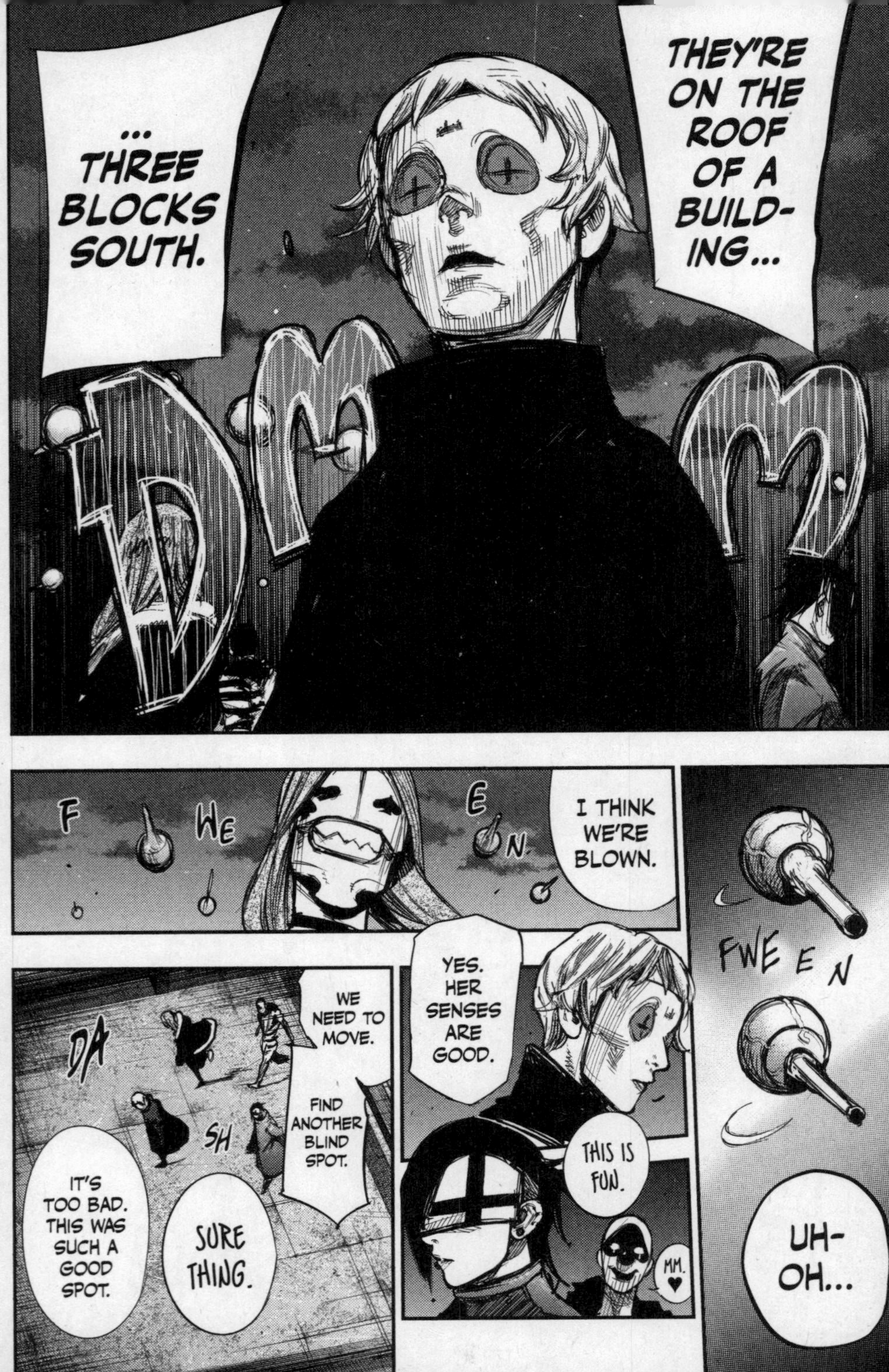
THEY'RE ON THE ROOF OF A BUILD-ING...
... THREE BLOCKS SOUTH.
DMM
FWEEN
UH-OH...
F WE E N.
I THINK WE'RE BLOWN.
YES. HER SENSES ARE GOOD.
THIS IS FUN.
MM. ♥
WE NEED TO MOVE.
FIND ANOTHER BLIND SPOT.
DA
SH
SURE THING.
IT'S TOO BAD. THIS WAS SUCH A GOOD SPOT.

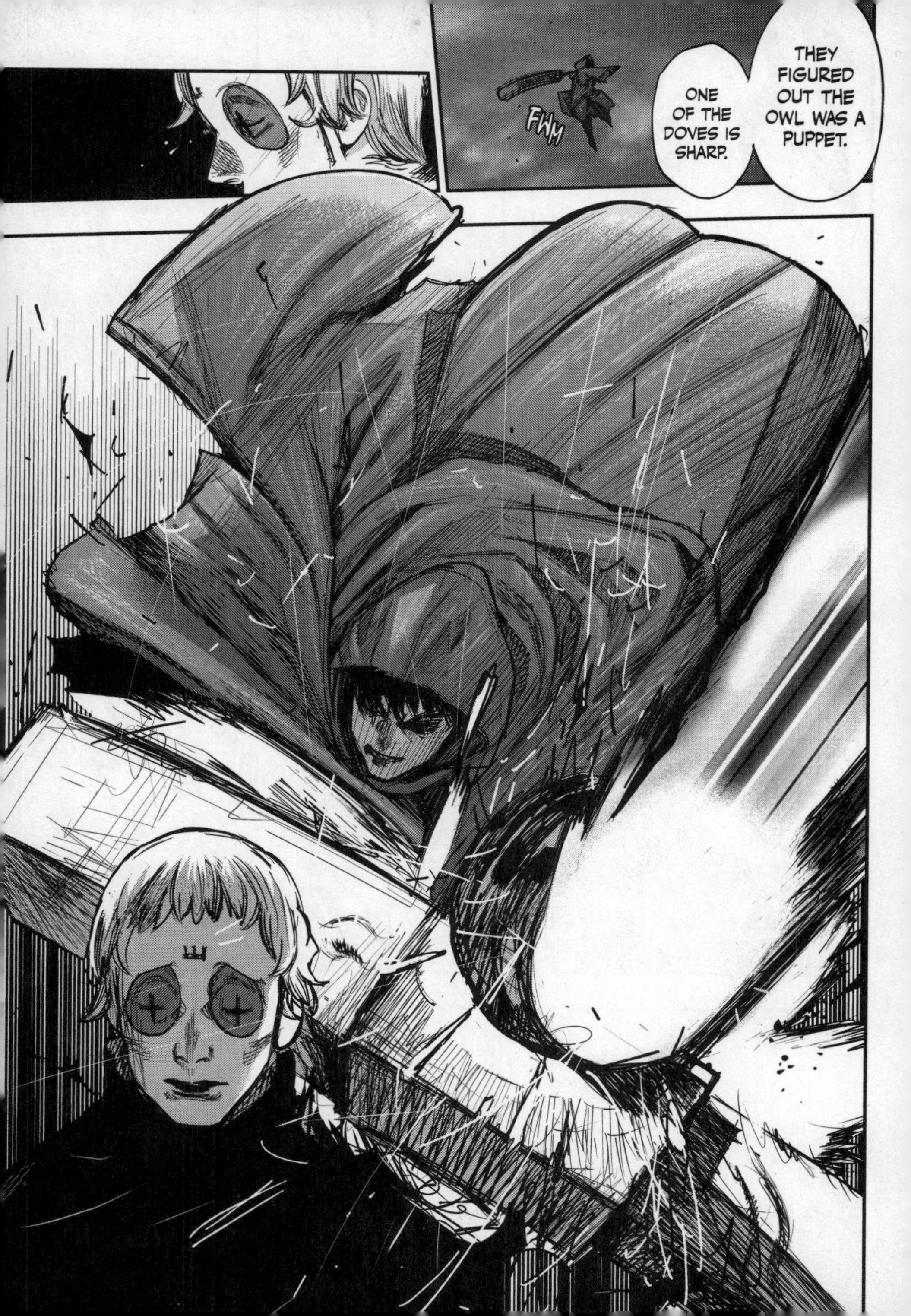
THEY FIGURED OUT THE OWL WAS A PUPPET.
ONE OF THE DOVES IS SHARP.
FWM

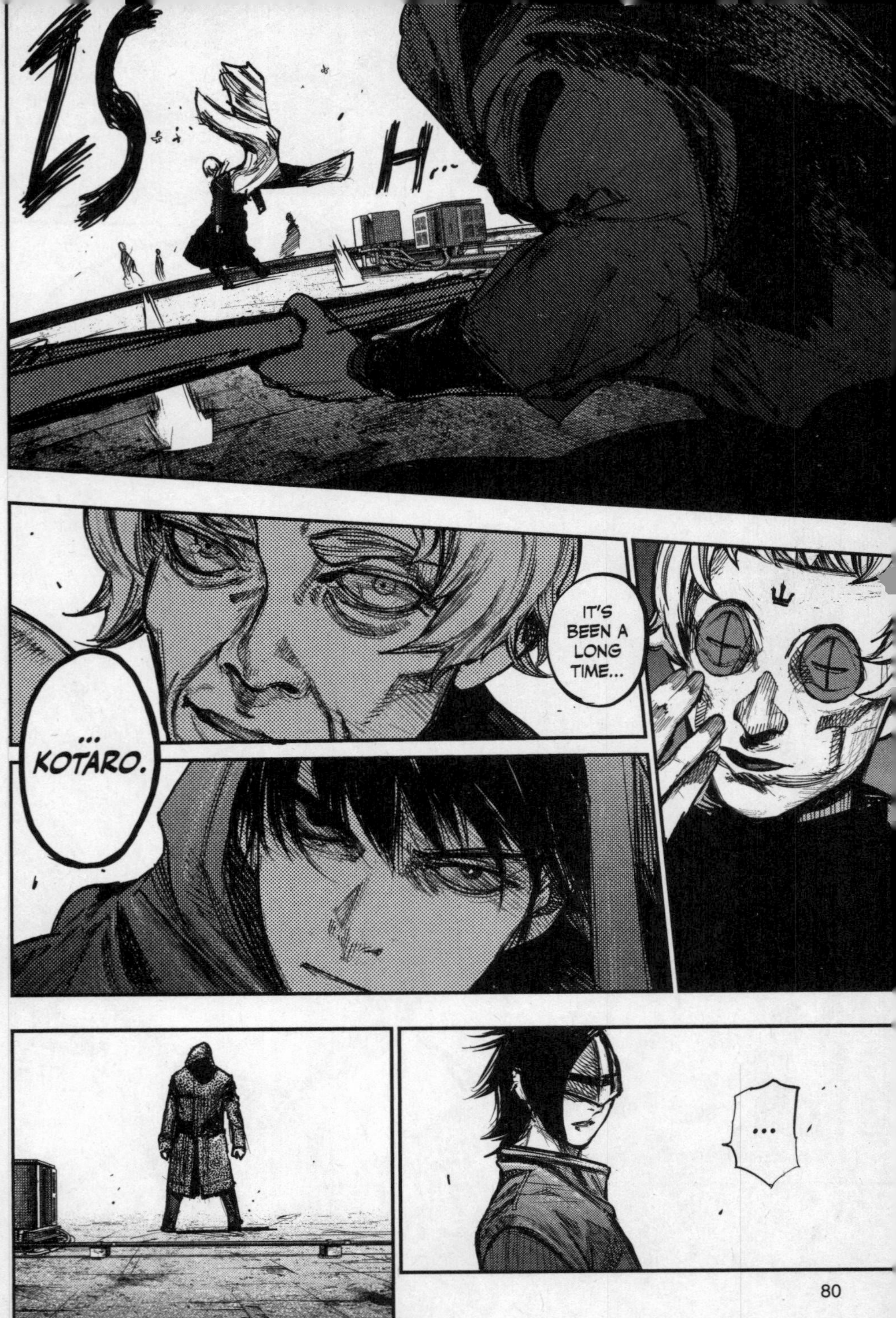

ZSSH...
IT'S BEEN A LONG TIME...
...KOTARO.
...

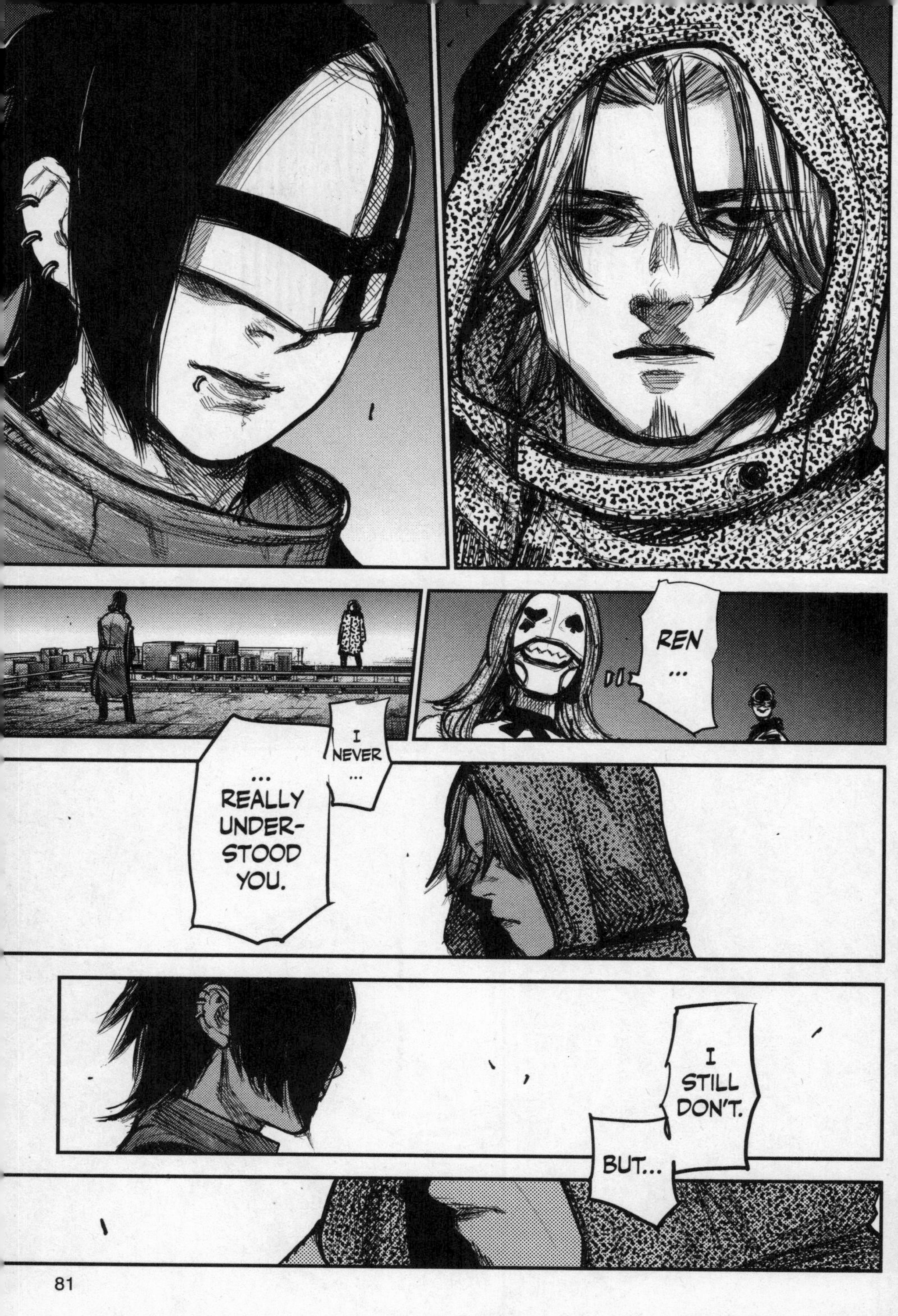
REN ...
I NEVER ...
... REALLY UNDER-STOOD YOU.
I STILL DON'T.
BUT...

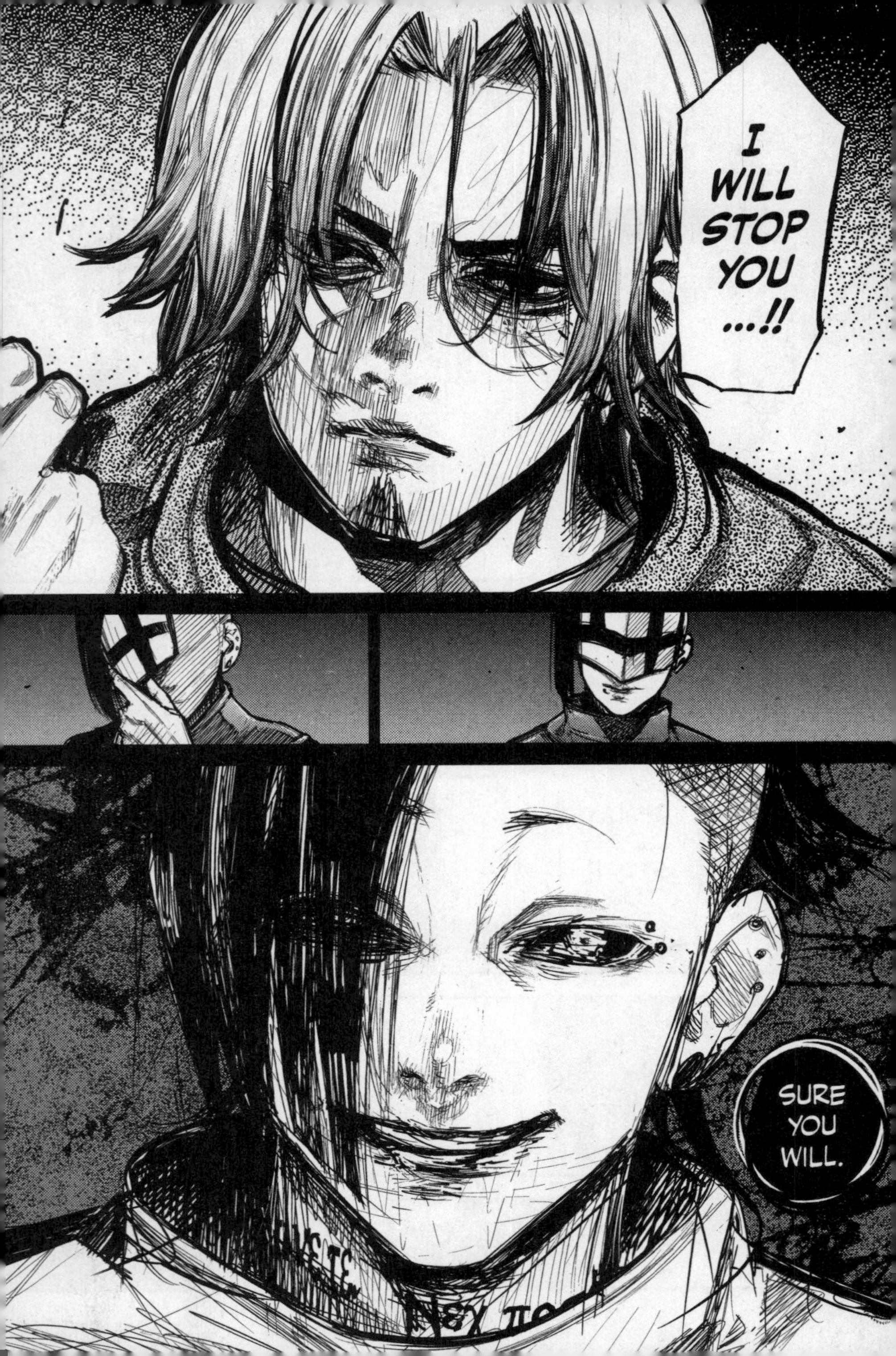
I WILL STOP YOU ...!!
SURE YOU WILL.

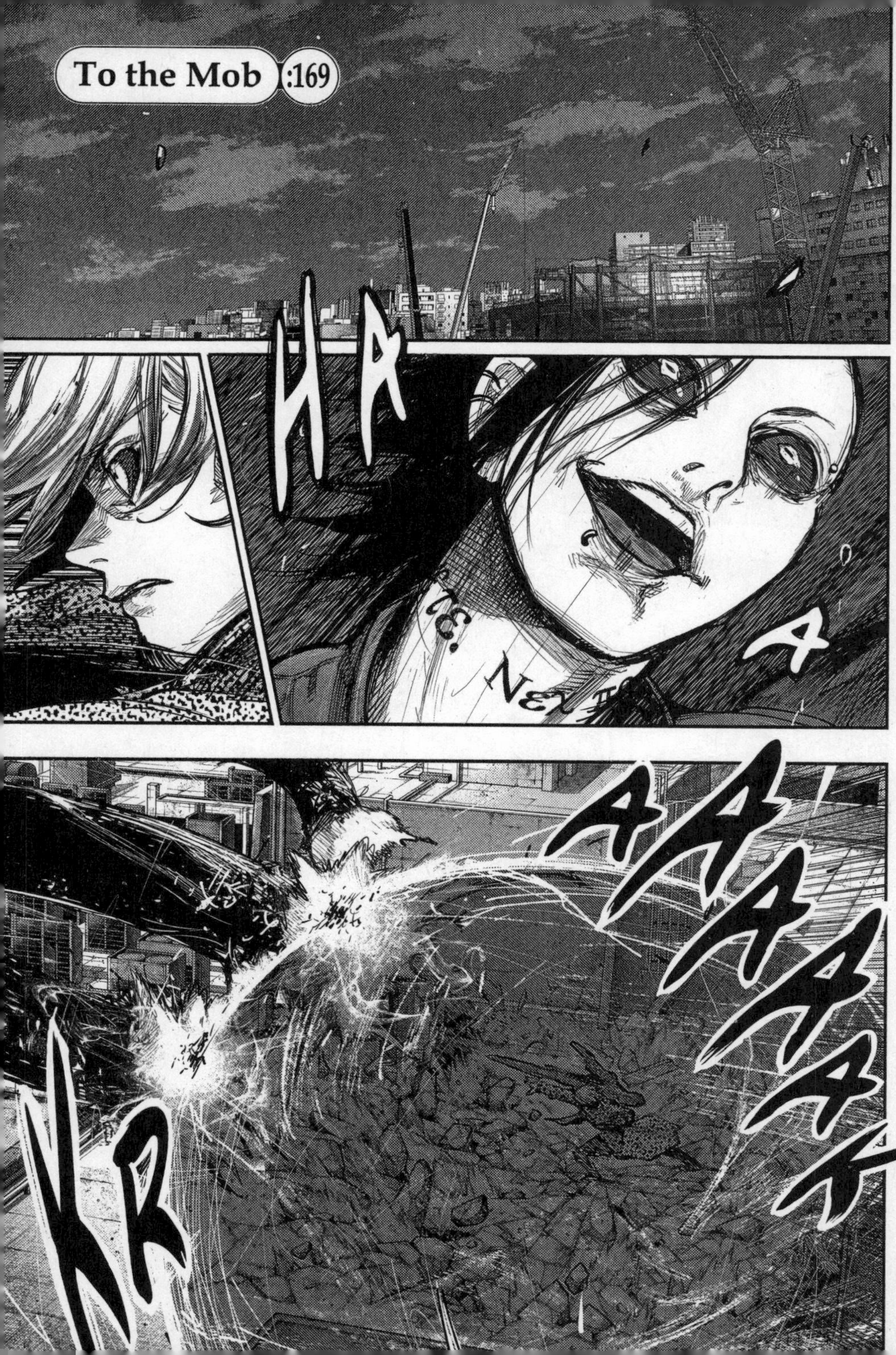
To the Mob :169
HA
A
AAAAAK
KR

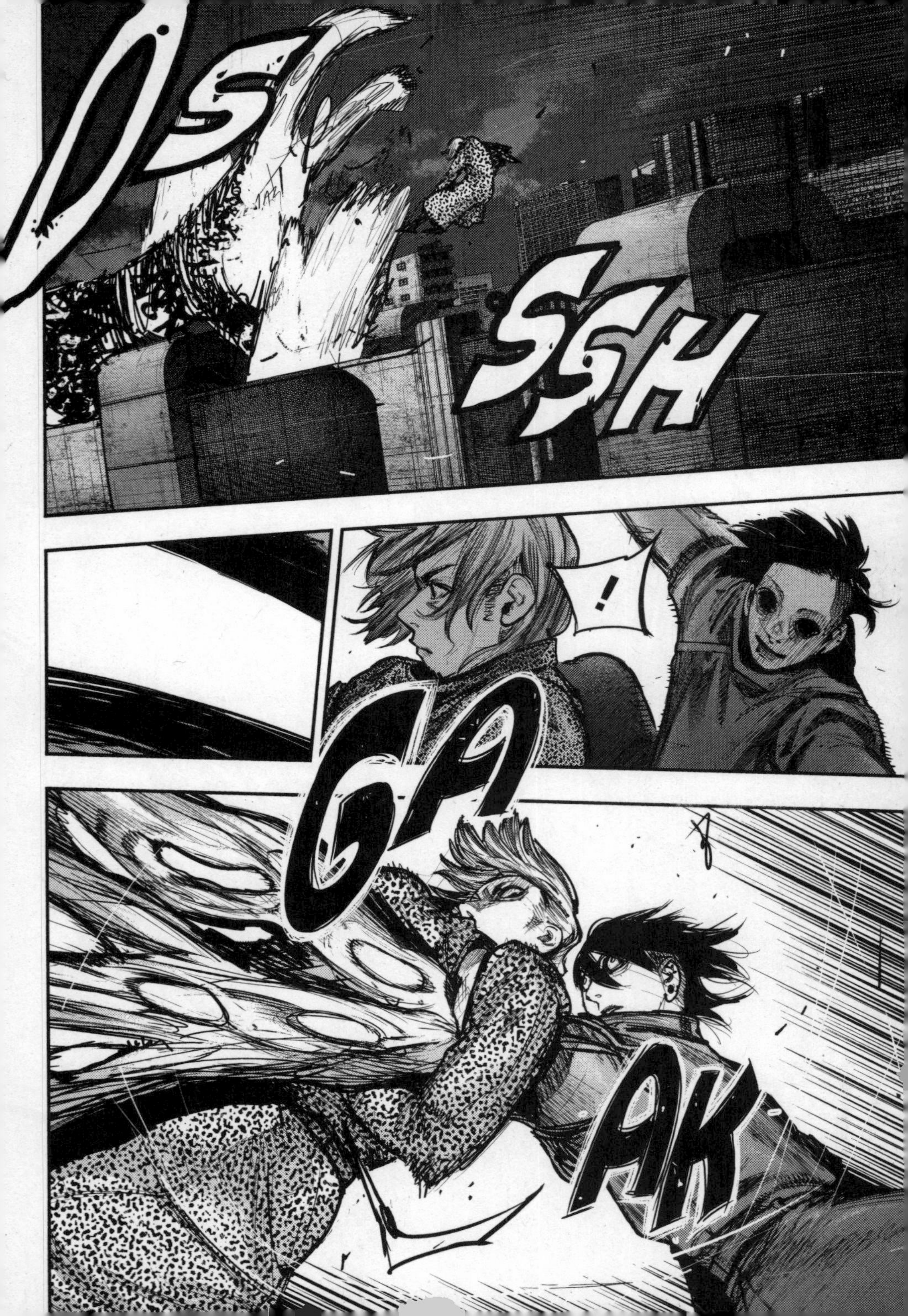
SSH
!
AK

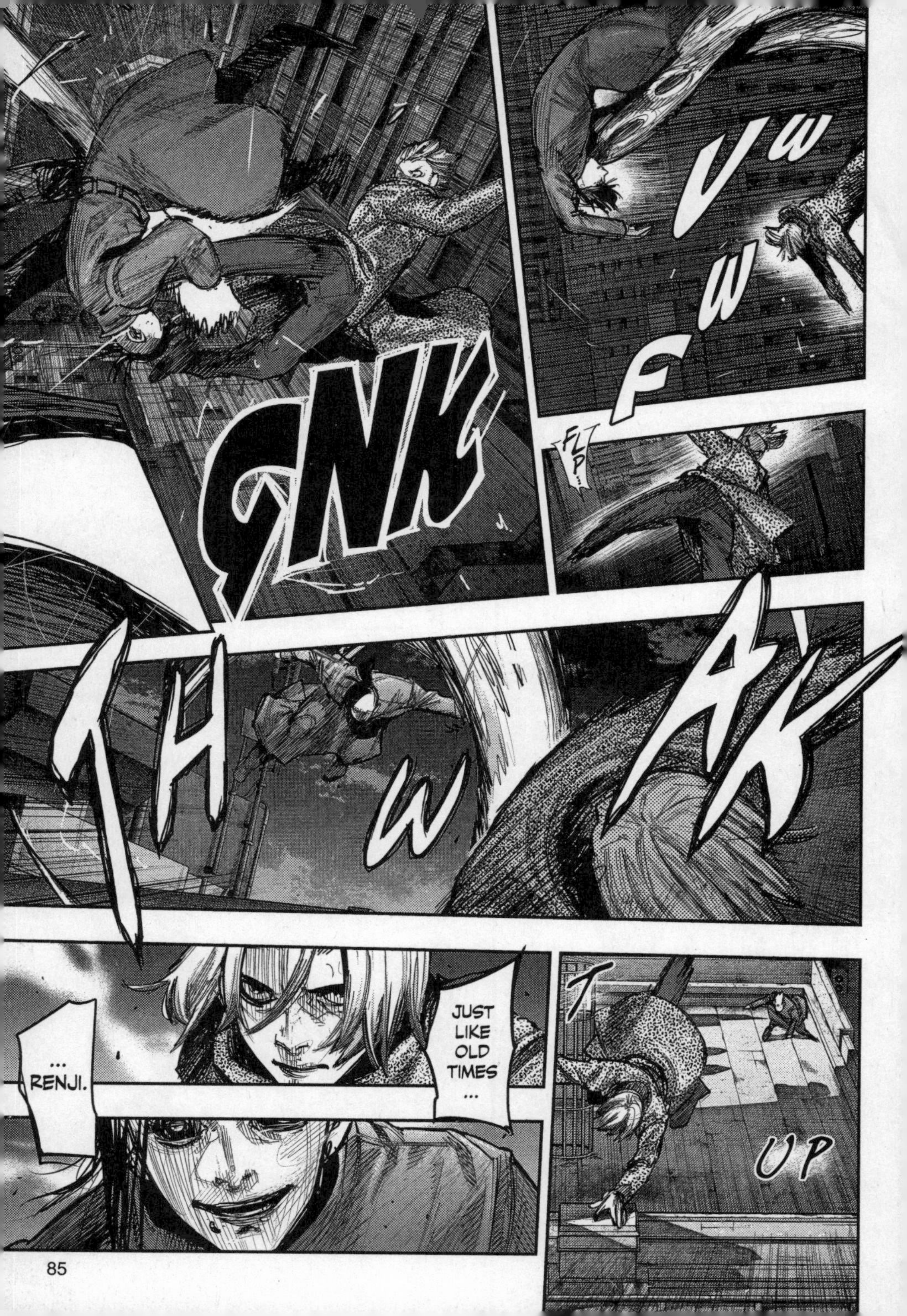
FLP...
GNK
THWAK
TUP
JUST LIKE OLD TIMES...
...RENJI.

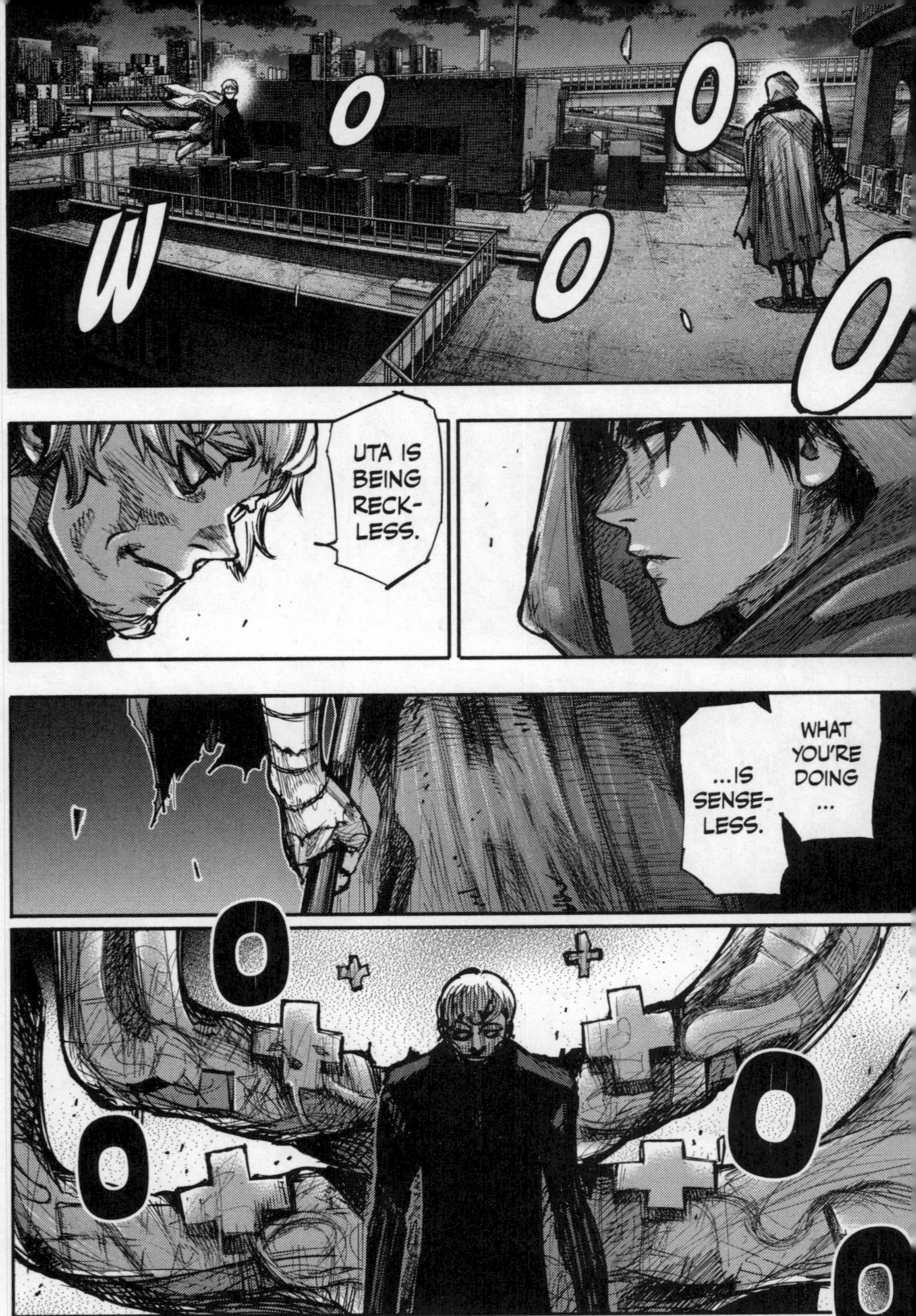
WOOOO
UTA IS BEING RECKLESS.
WHAT YOU'RE DOING...
...IS SENSELESS.
OOOO

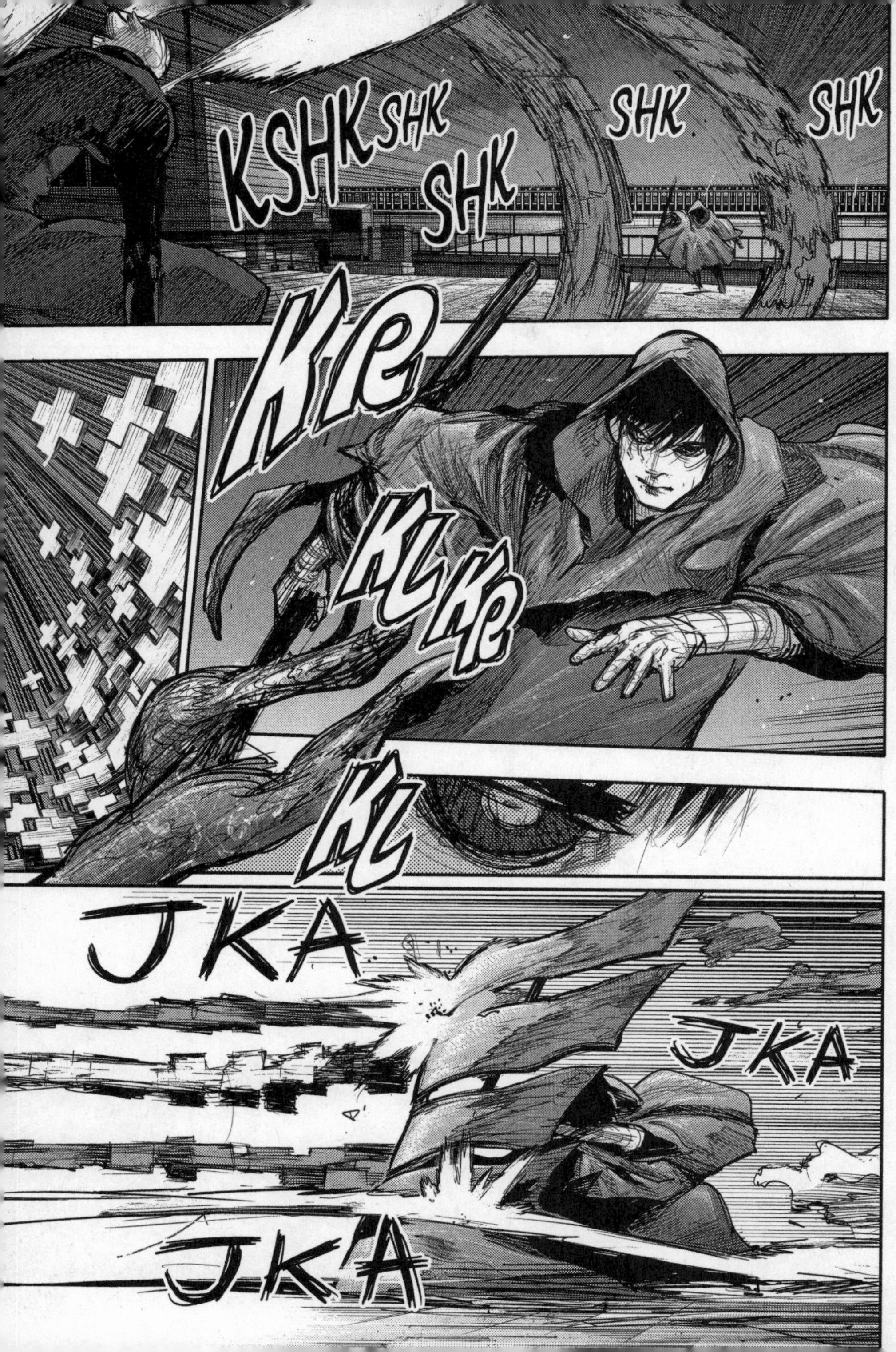
SHK
SHK
SHK
KSHK
SHK
JKA
JKA
JKA

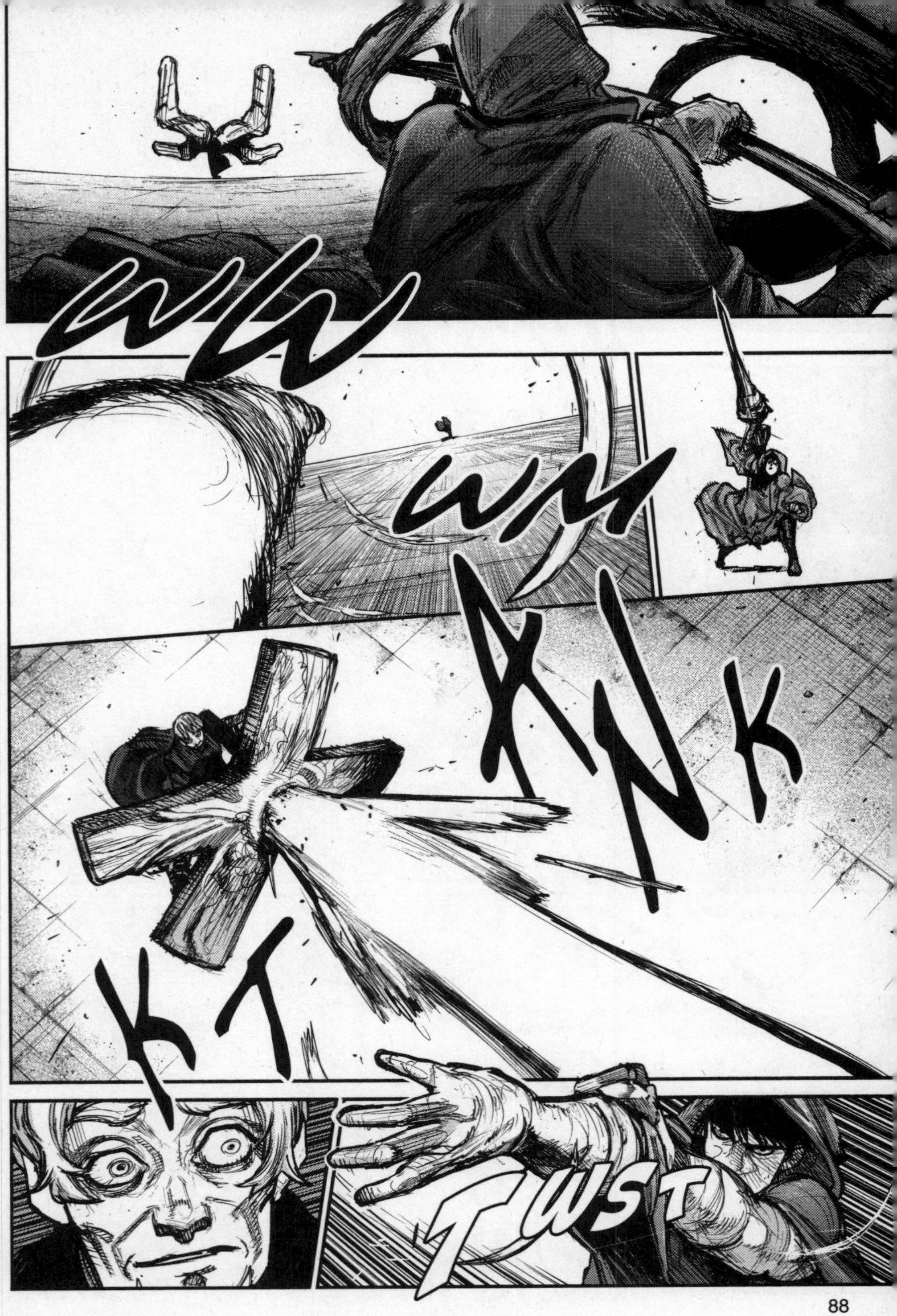

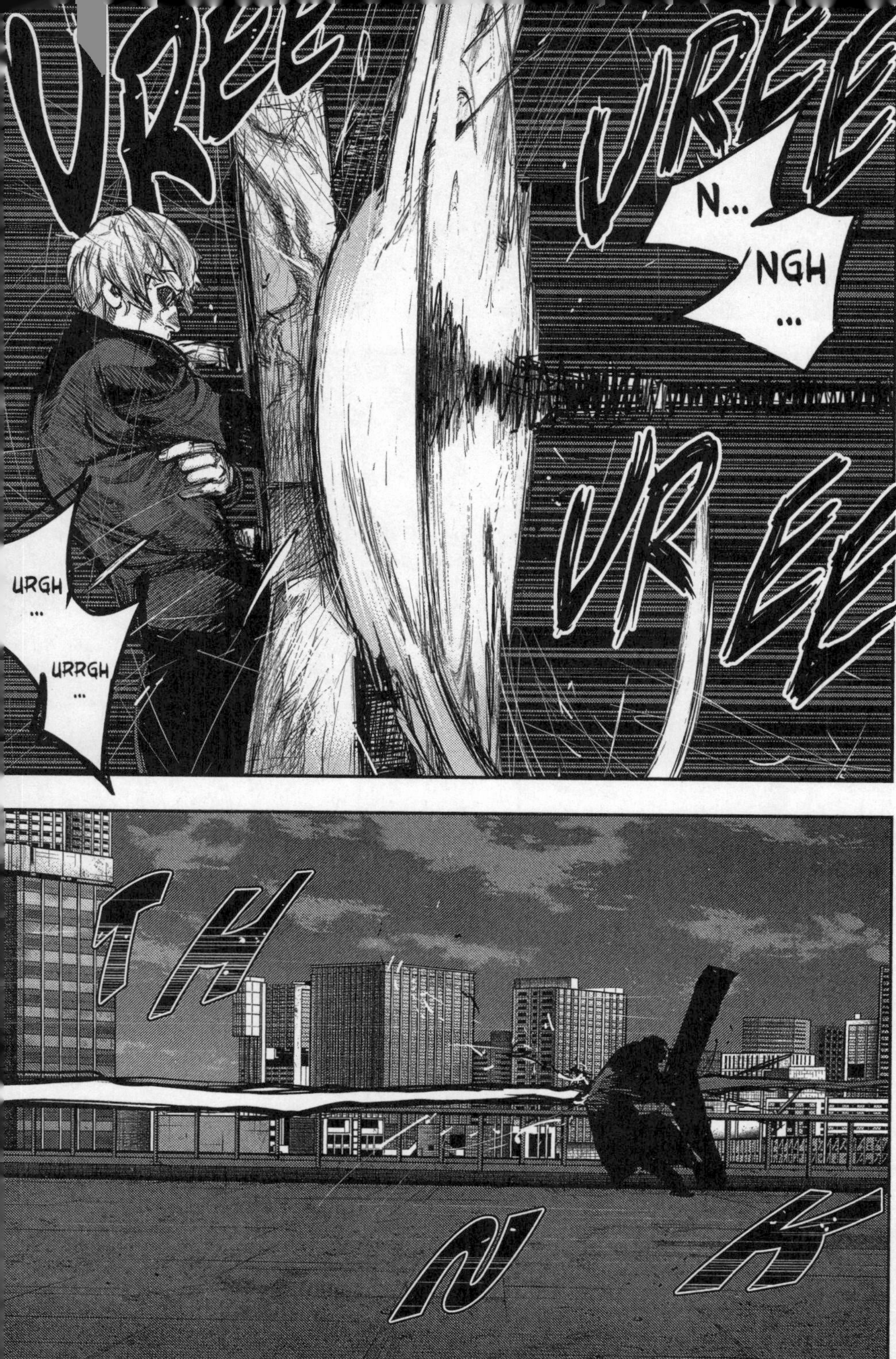
N... NGH ...
URGH ...
URRGH ...

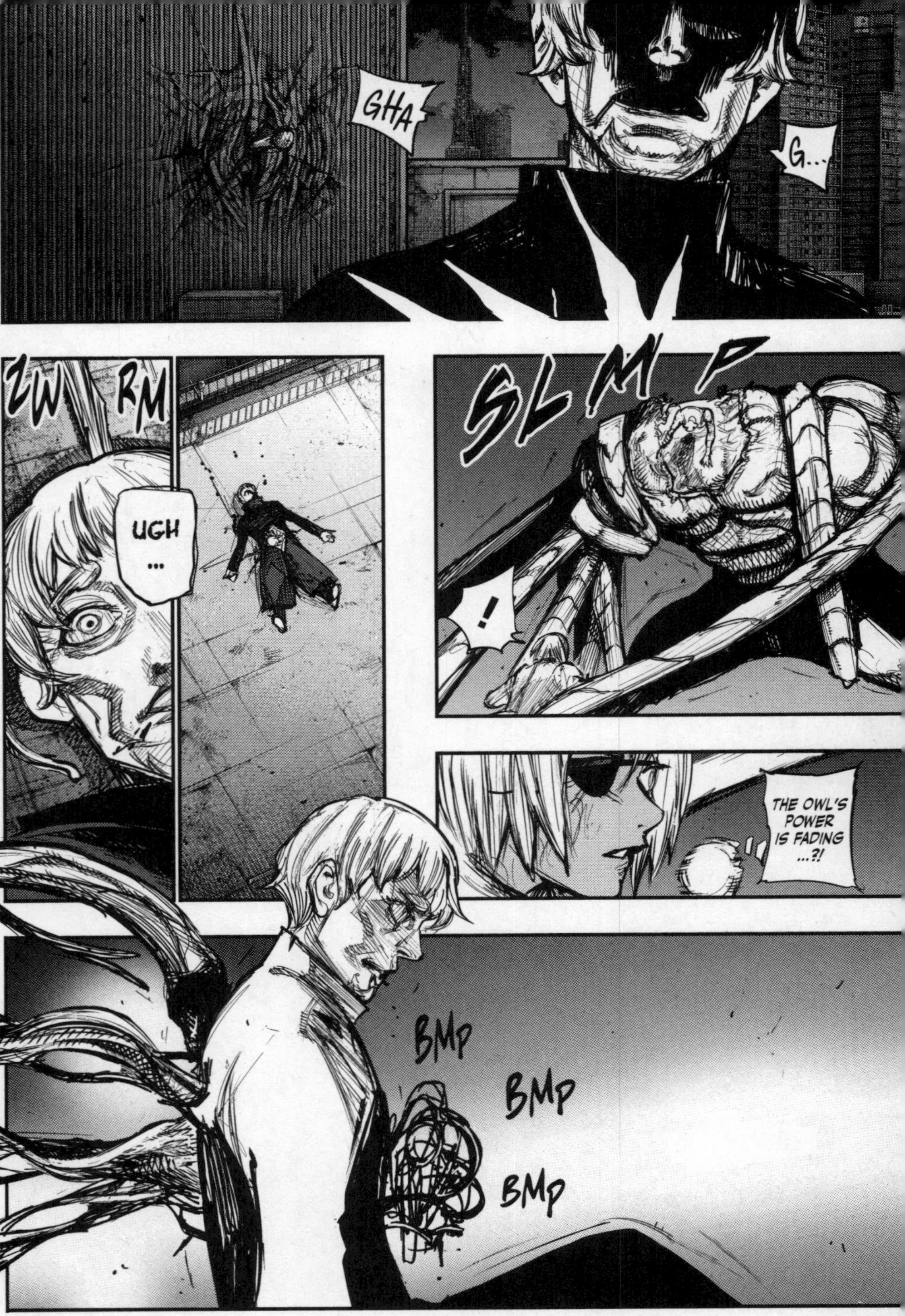
GHA
G...
SLMP
!
THE OWL'S POWER IS FADING ...?!
ZWRM
UGH ...
BMP
BMP
BMP

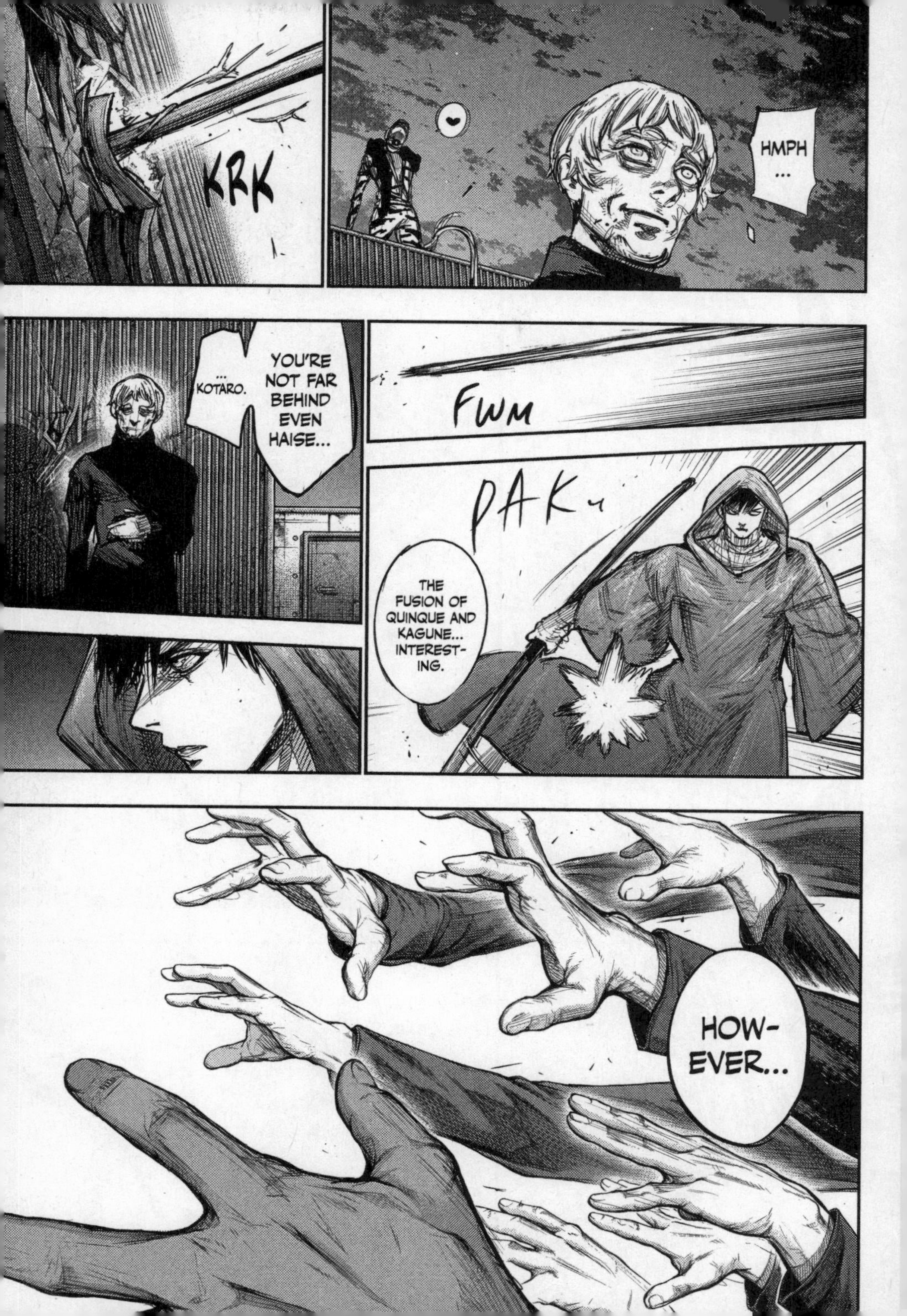
HMPH ...
KRK
FWM
PAK
THE FUSION OF QUINQUE AND KAGUNE... INTEREST-ING.
... KOTARO. YOU'RE NOT FAR BEHIND EVEN HAISE...
HOW-EVER...

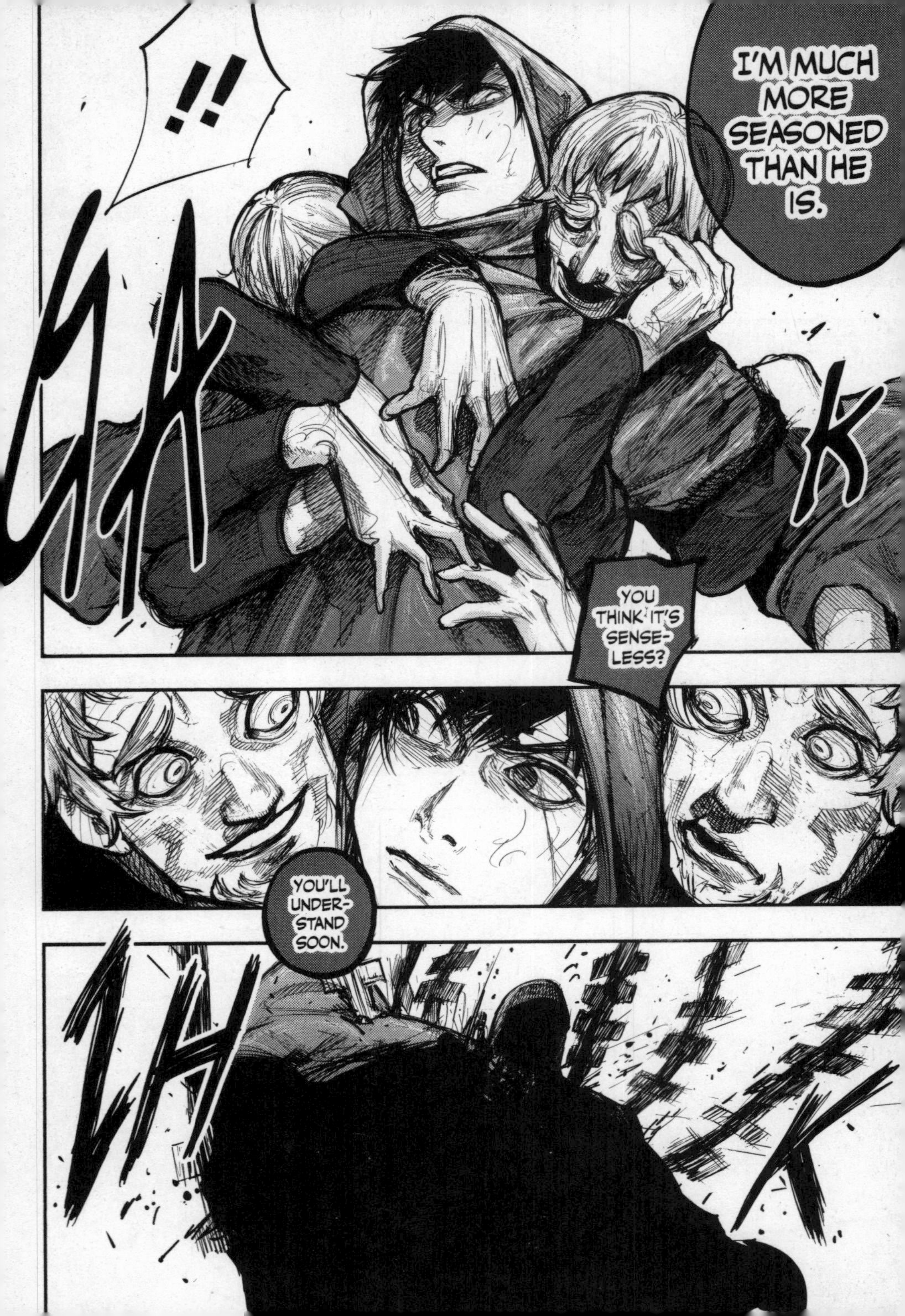
I'M MUCH MORE SEASONED THAN HE IS.
!!
GYAK
YOU THINK IT'S SENSE-LESS?
YOU'LL UNDER-STAND SOON.
ZH

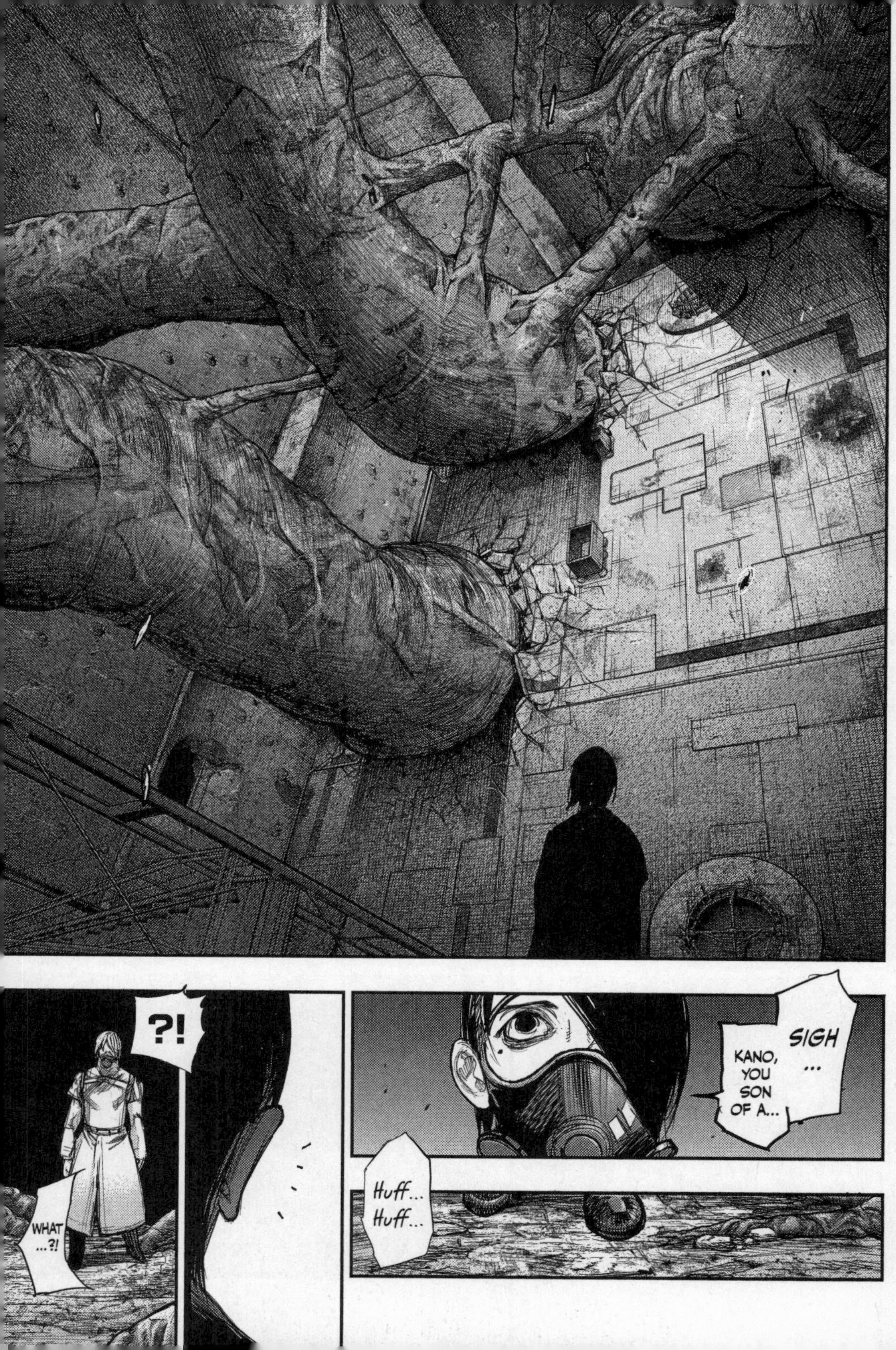
SIGH ...
KANO, YOU SON OF A...
Huff... Huff...
?!
WHAT ...?!

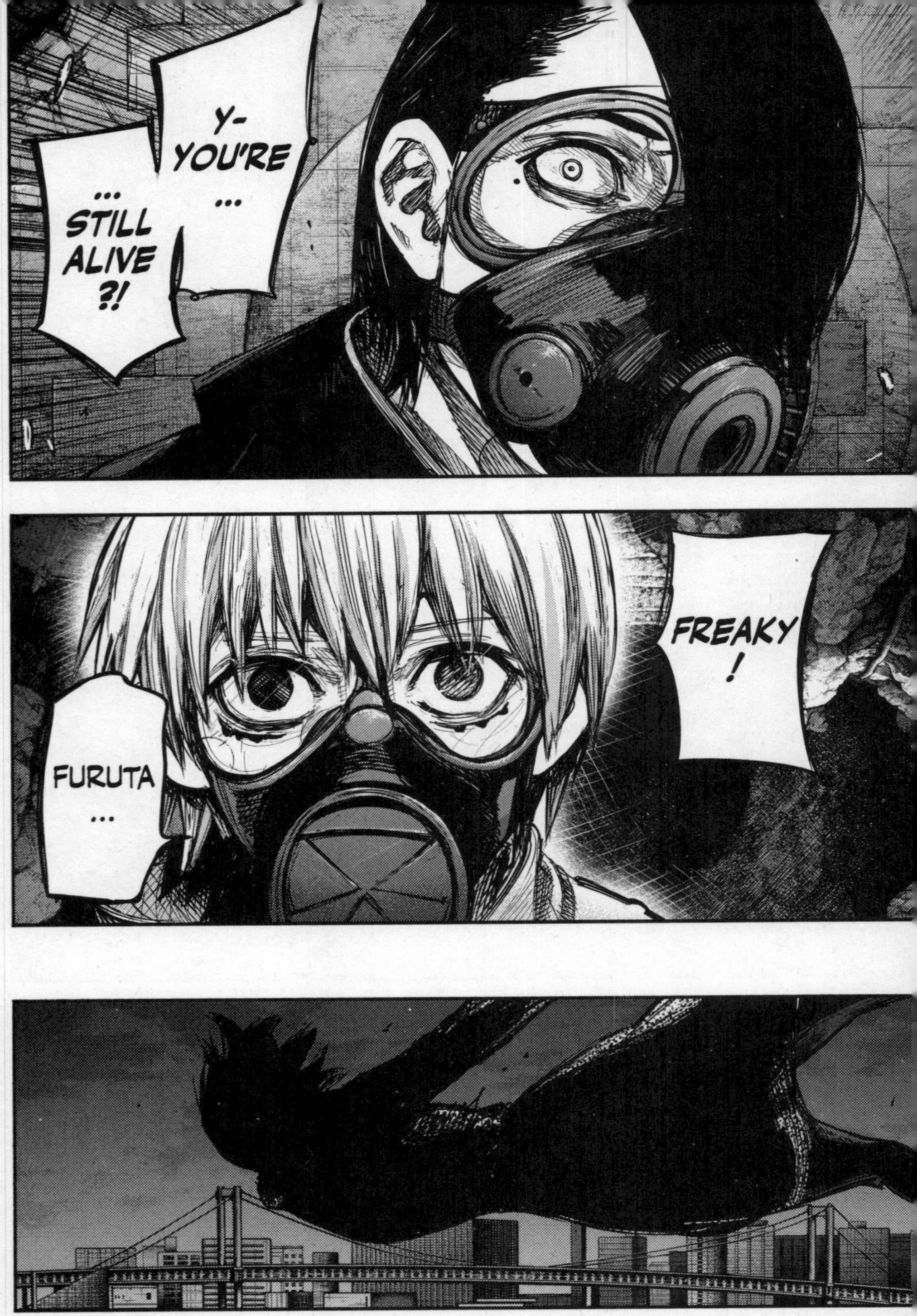
Y-YOU'RE ...
... STILL ALIVE ?!
FREAKY!
FURUTA ...

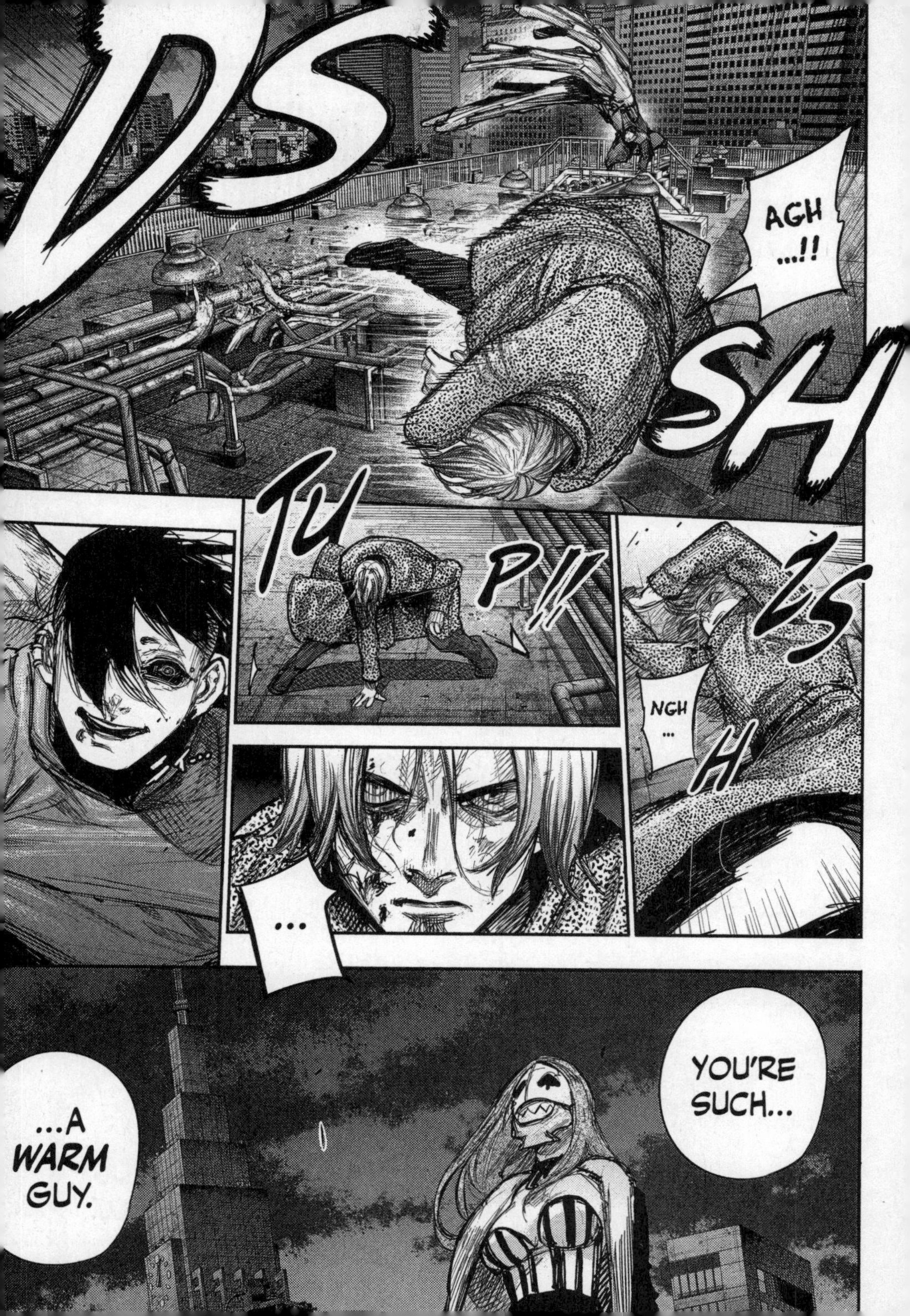
AGH ...!!
DS
SH
ZS
H
NGH ...
TU
P!!
...
YOU'RE SUCH...
...A WARM GUY.

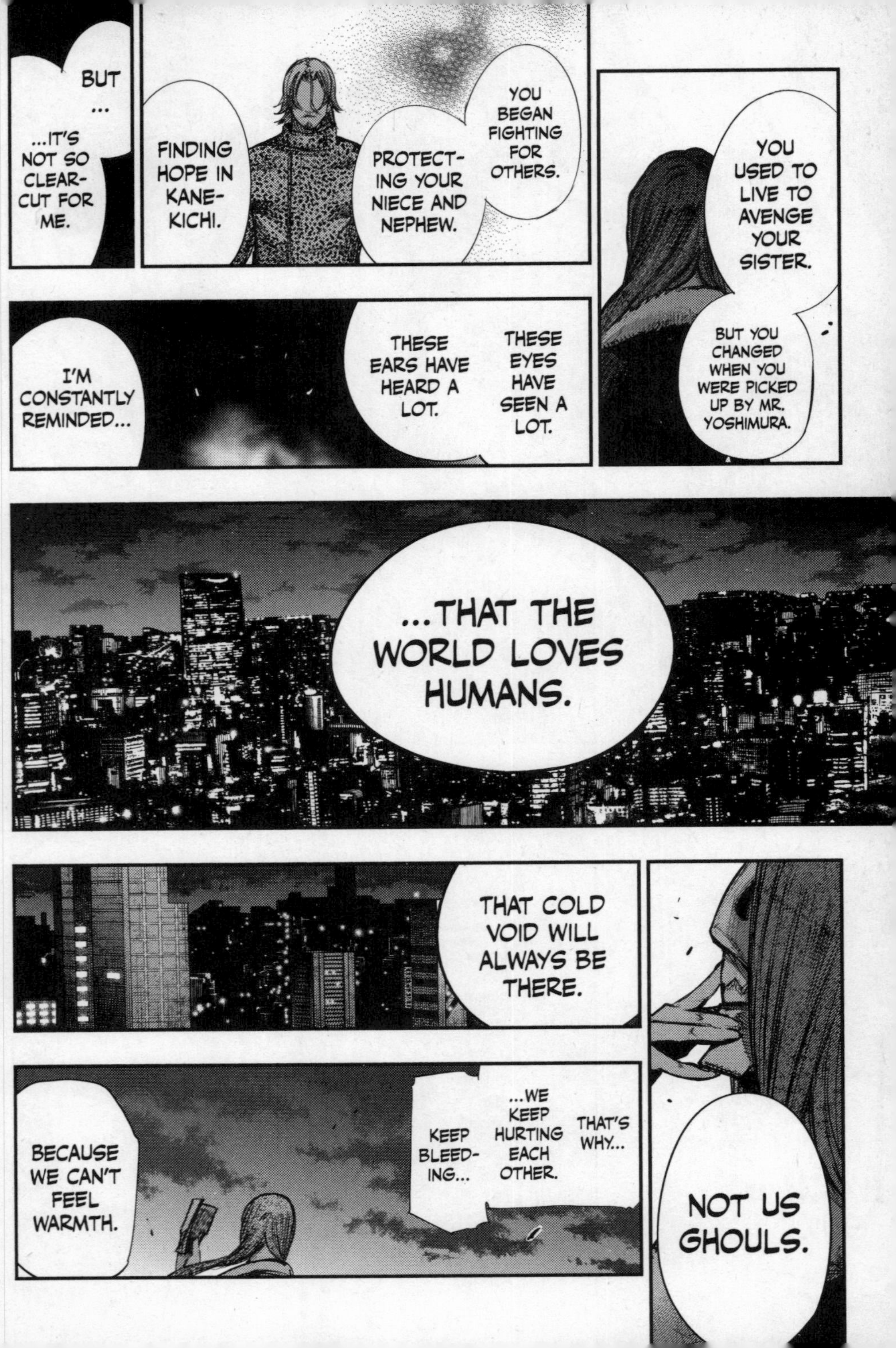
YOU USED TO LIVE TO AVENGE YOUR SISTER.
BUT YOU CHANGED WHEN YOU WERE PICKED UP BY MR. YOSHIMURA.
YOU BEGAN FIGHTING FOR OTHERS.
PROTECTING YOUR NIECE AND NEPHEW.
FINDING HOPE IN KANEKICHI.
BUT ...
...IT'S NOT SO CLEAR-CUT FOR ME.
THESE EYES HAVE SEEN A LOT.
THESE EARS HAVE HEARD A LOT.
I'M CONSTANTLY REMINDED...
...THAT THE WORLD LOVES HUMANS.
NOT US GHOULS.
THAT COLD VOID WILL ALWAYS BE THERE.
THAT'S WHY...
...WE KEEP HURTING EACH OTHER.
KEEP BLEEDING...
BECAUSE WE CAN'T FEEL WARMTH.

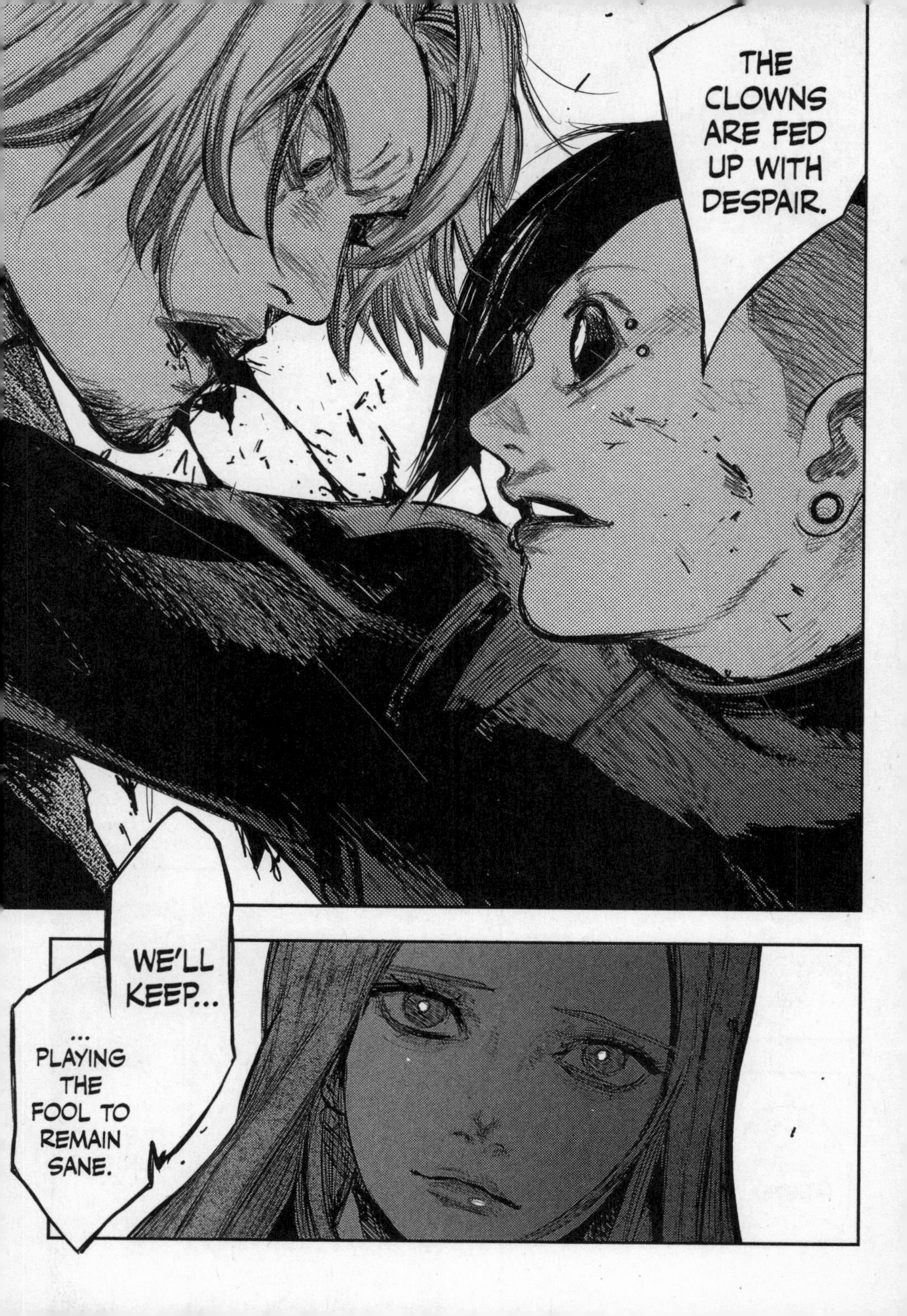
THE CLOWNS ARE FED UP WITH DESPAIR.
WE'LL KEEP...
...PLAYING THE FOOL TO REMAIN SANE.

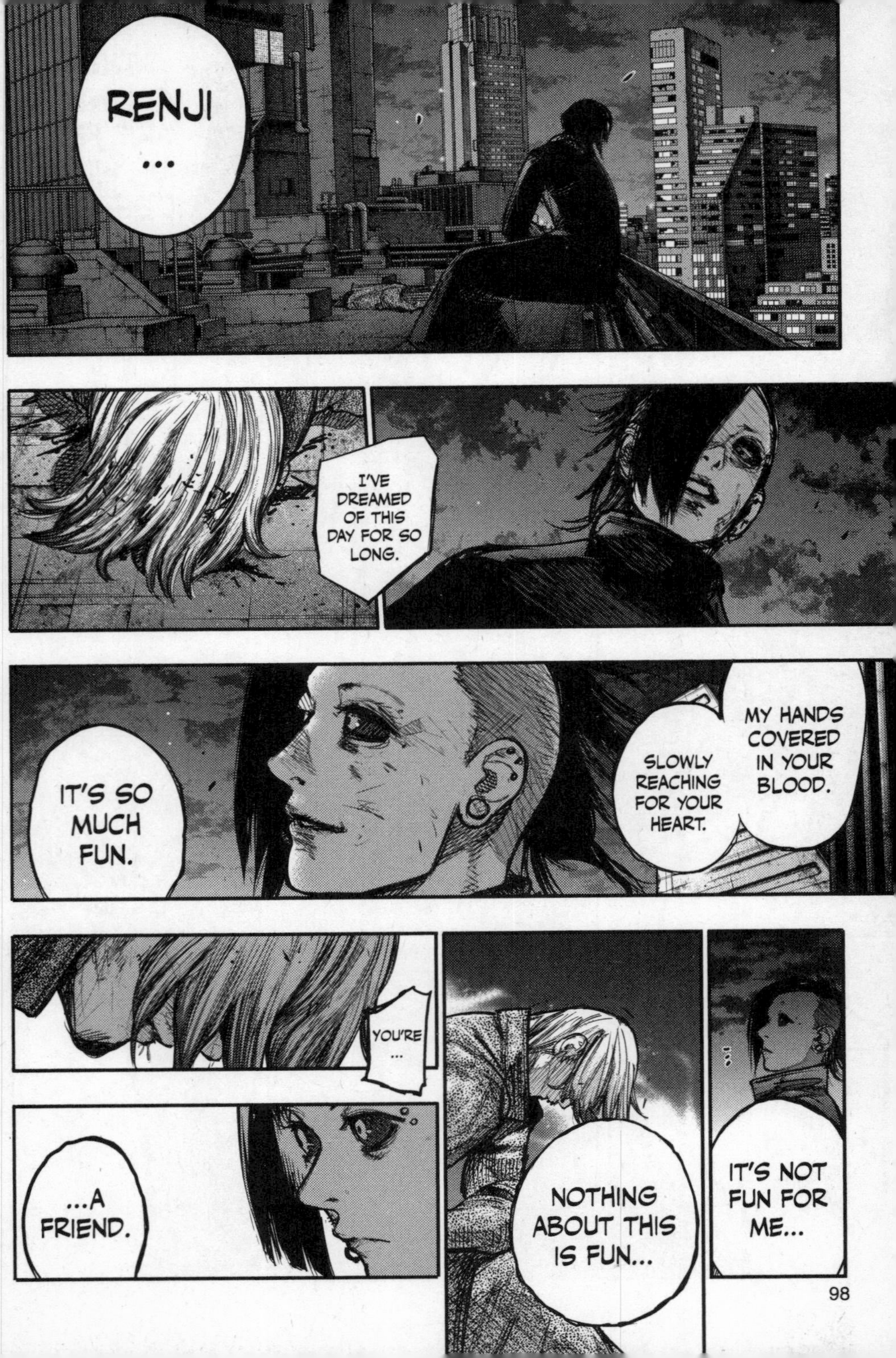
RENJI ...
I'VE DREAMED OF THIS DAY FOR SO LONG.
MY HANDS COVERED IN YOUR BLOOD.
SLOWLY REACHING FOR YOUR HEART.
IT'S SO MUCH FUN.
...
IT'S NOT FUN FOR ME...
NOTHING ABOUT THIS IS FUN...
YOU'RE ...
...A FRIEND.

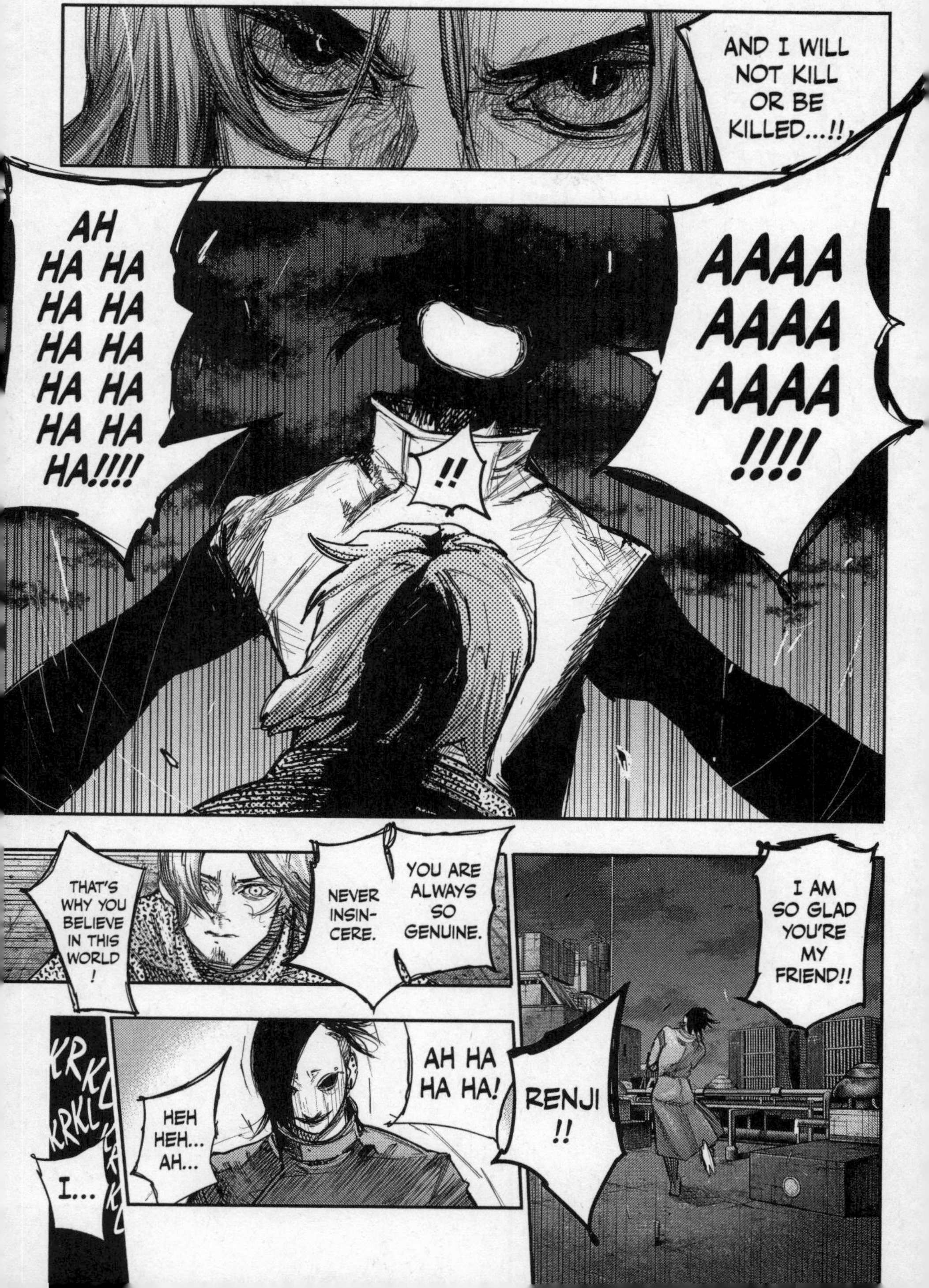
AND I WILL NOT KILL OR BE KILLED...!!
AAAA AAAA AAAA !!!!
AH HA HA HA HA HA HA HA HA HA HA HA HA!!!!
!!
I AM SO GLAD YOU'RE MY FRIEND!!
RENJI !!
YOU ARE ALWAYS SO GENUINE.
NEVER INSIN- CERE.
THAT'S WHY YOU BELIEVE IN THIS WORLD !
AH HA HA HA!
HEH HEH... AH...
KRKL KRKL
I...

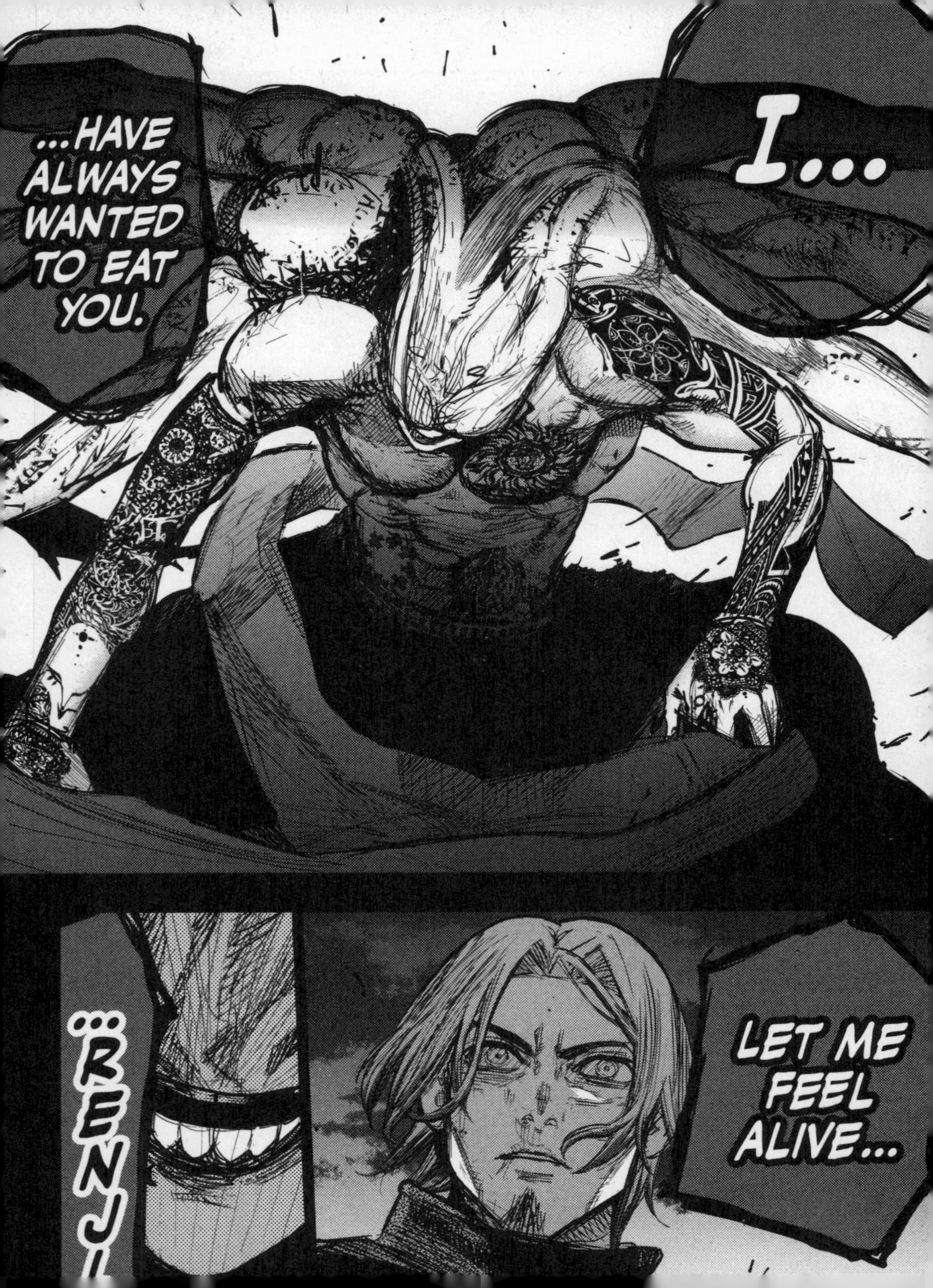
I...
...HAVE ALWAYS WANTED TO EAT YOU.
LET ME FEEL ALIVE...
..RENJ

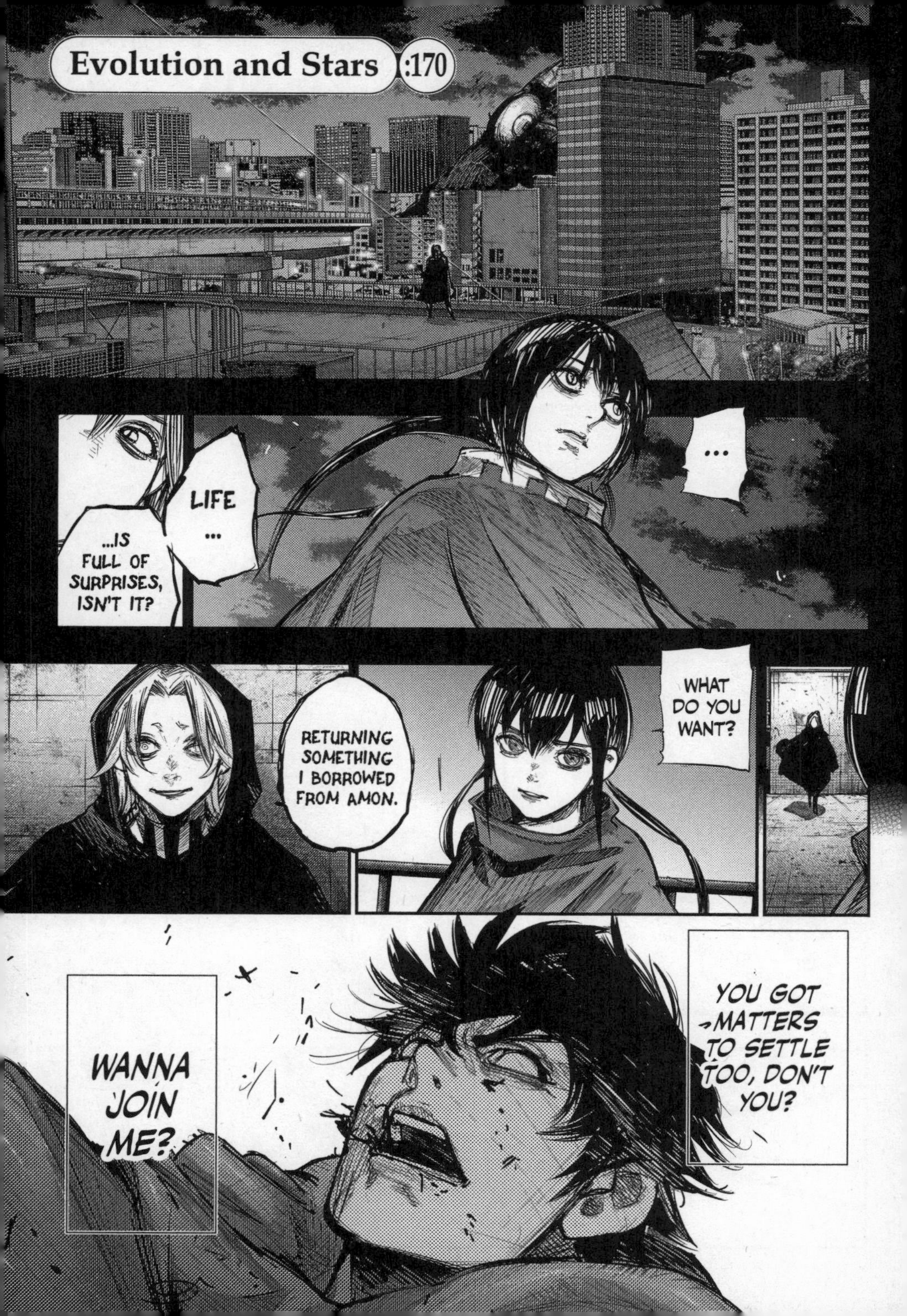
Evolution and Stars :170
...
LIFE ...
...IS FULL OF SURPRISES, ISN'T IT?
WHAT DO YOU WANT?
RETURNING SOMETHING I BORROWED FROM AMON.
YOU GOT MATTERS TO SETTLE TOO, DON'T YOU?
WANNA JOIN ME?

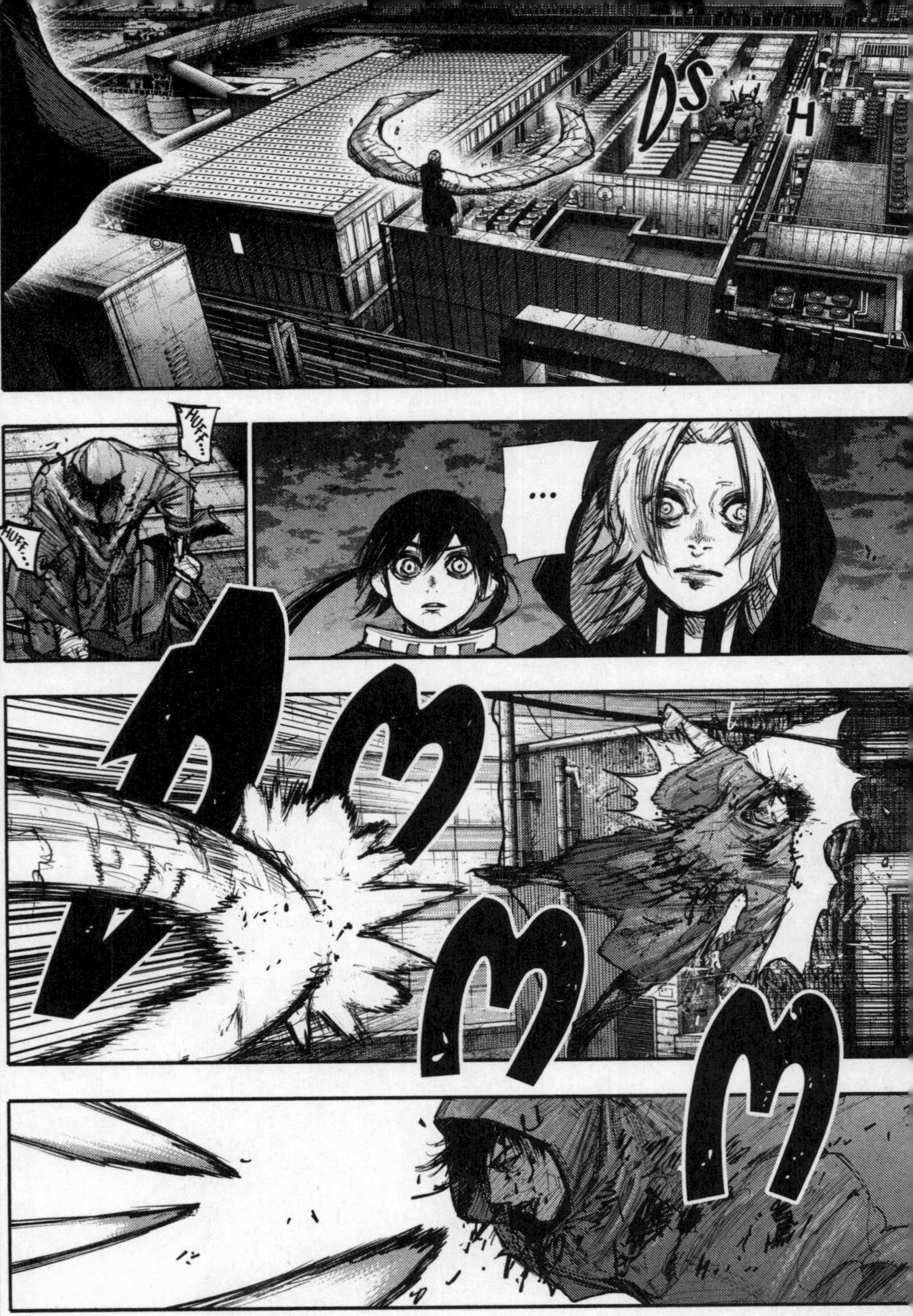
DSH
...
HUFF...
HUFF...

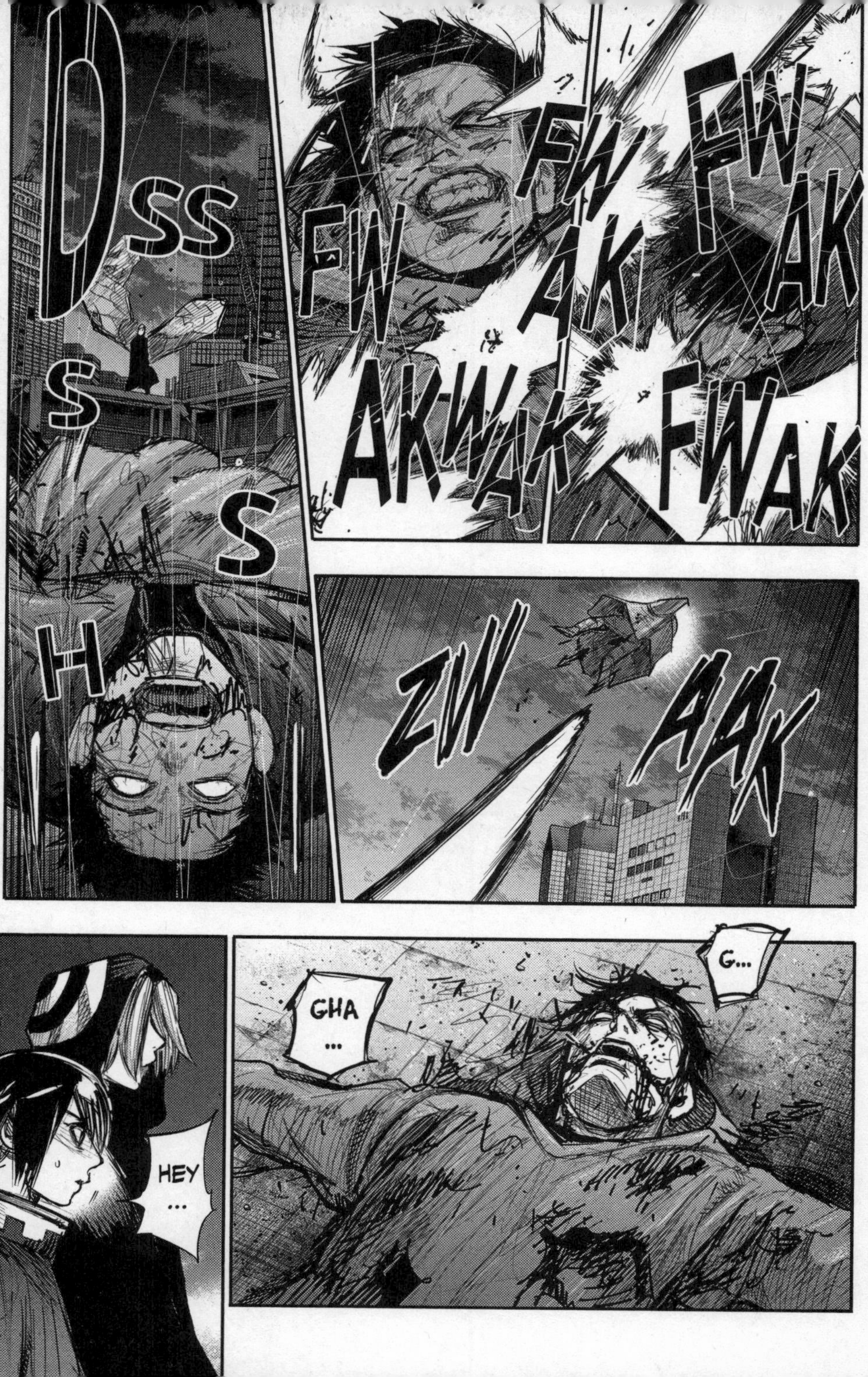
FWAK
FWAK
FW
FW
AK
FW
FW
AK
AKWAK
ZWAAK
DSSSSH
G...
GHA ...
HEY ...

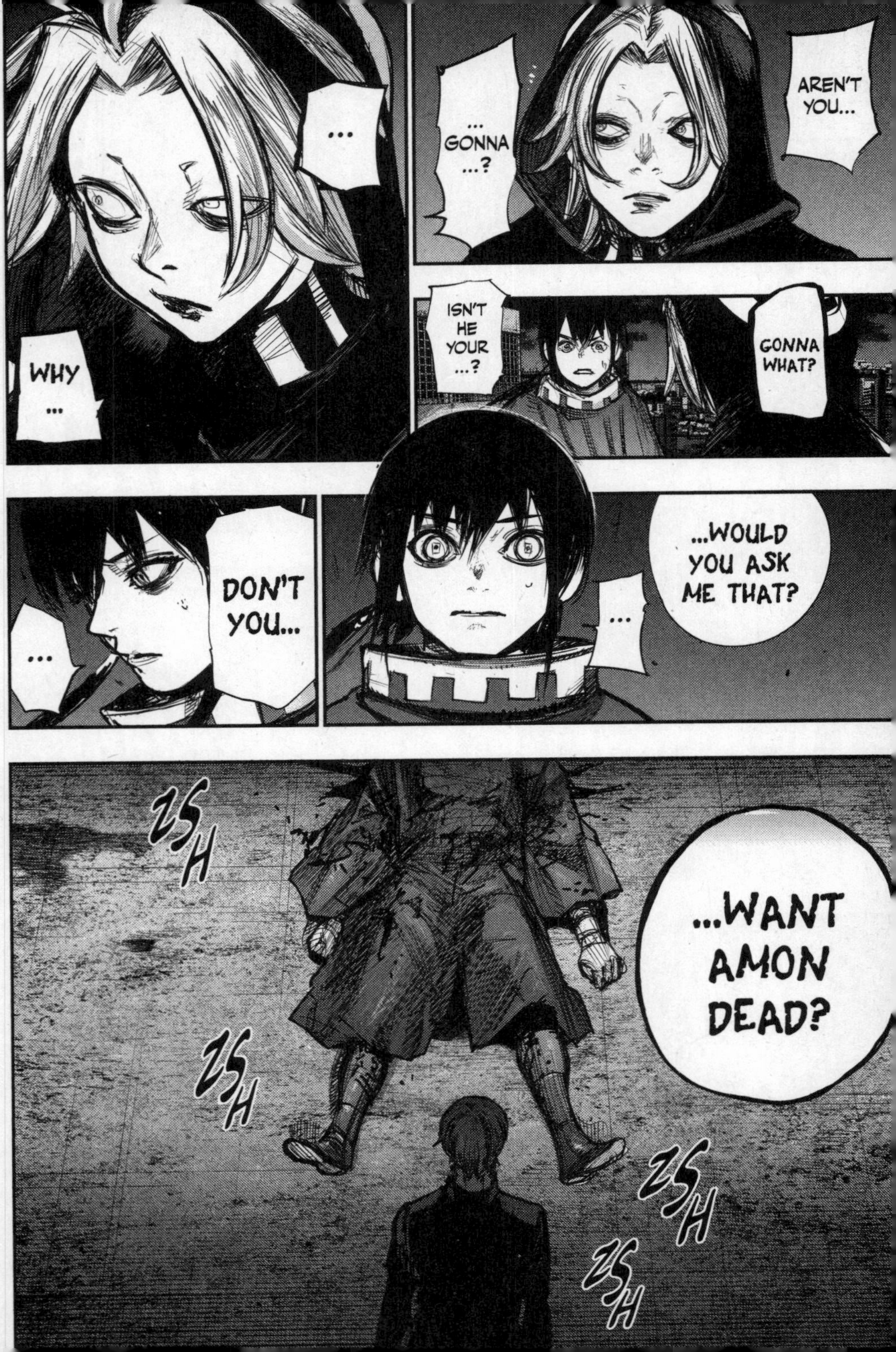
AREN'T YOU...
... GONNA ...?
GONNA WHAT?
ISN'T HE YOUR ...?
...
WHY ...
...WOULD YOU ASK ME THAT?
...
DON'T YOU...
...
ZSH
...WANT AMON DEAD?
ZSH
ZSH
ZSH

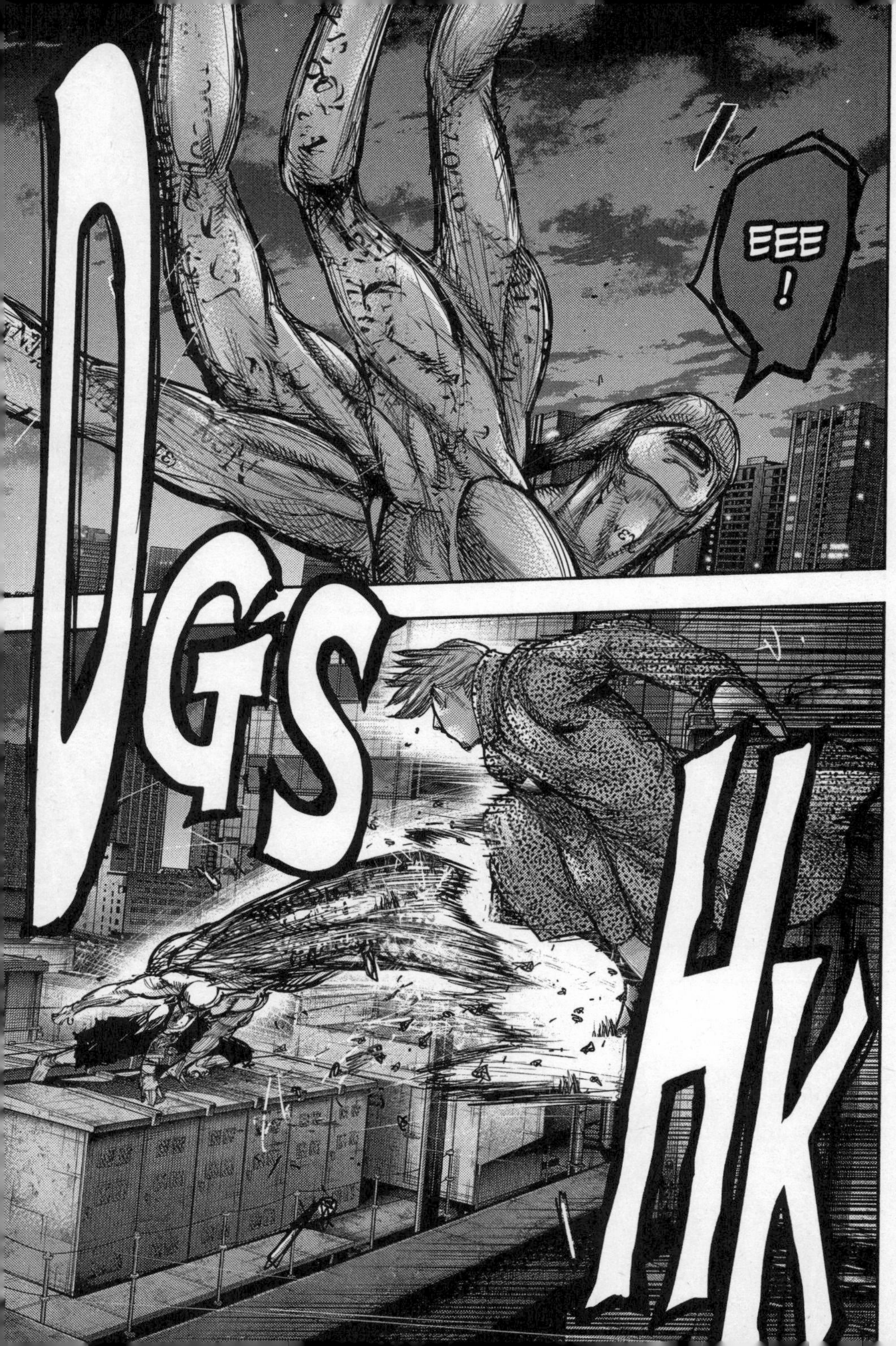
EEE!
DGSHK

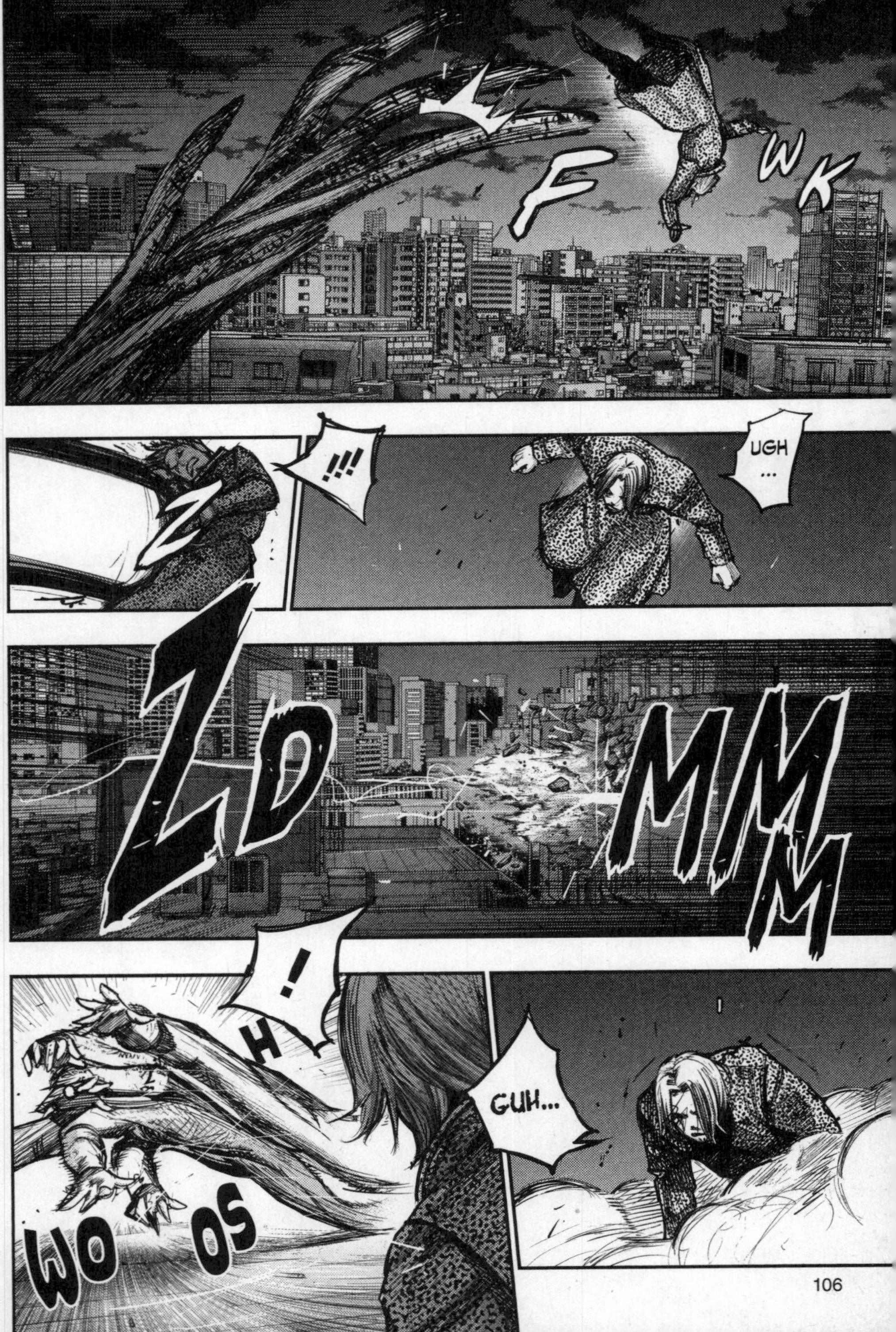
F
W K
UGH ...
!!!
Z D
MM M
GUH...
!
H
WO OS

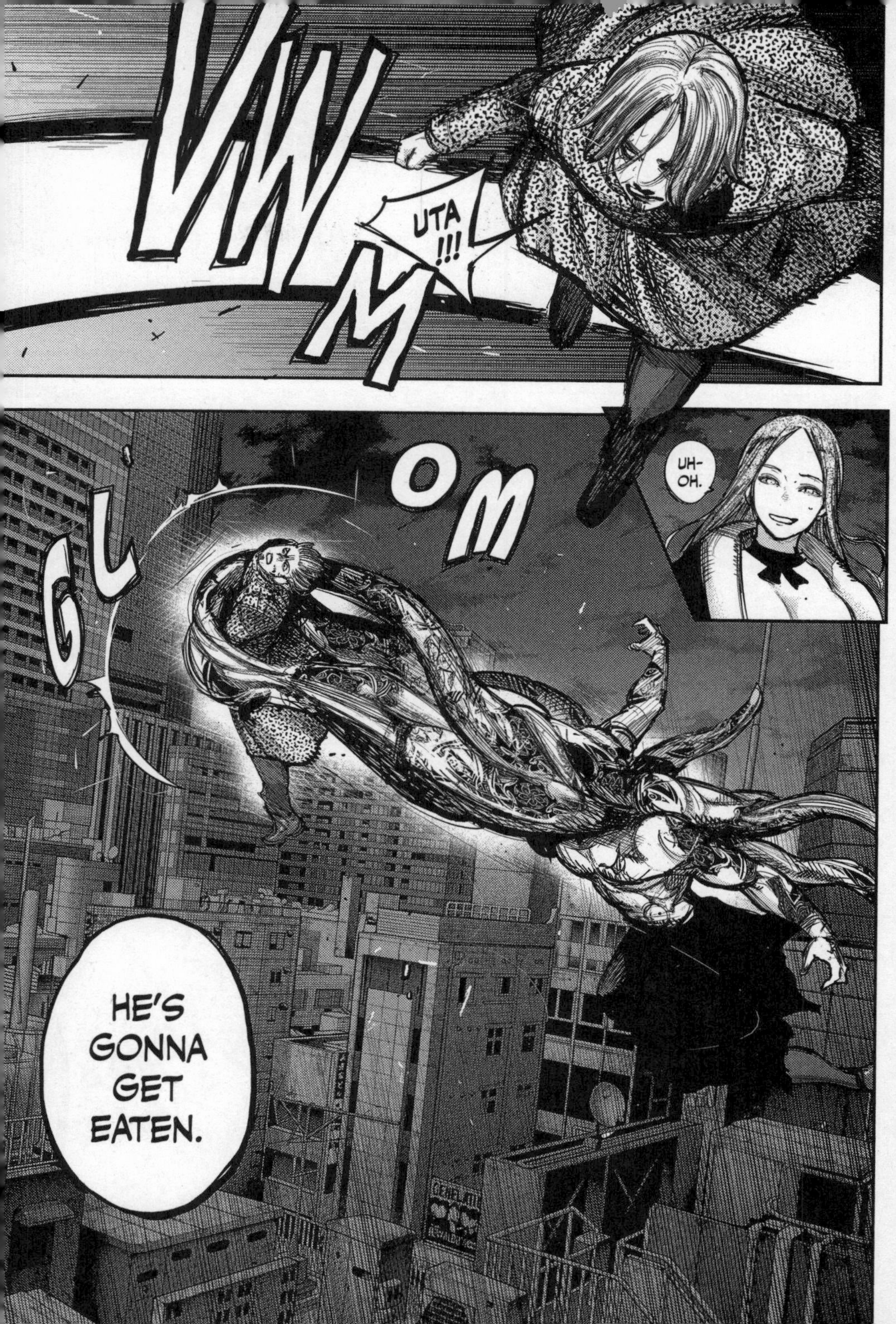
VWM
UTA!!!
UH-OH.
GLOMM
HE'S GONNA GET EATEN.

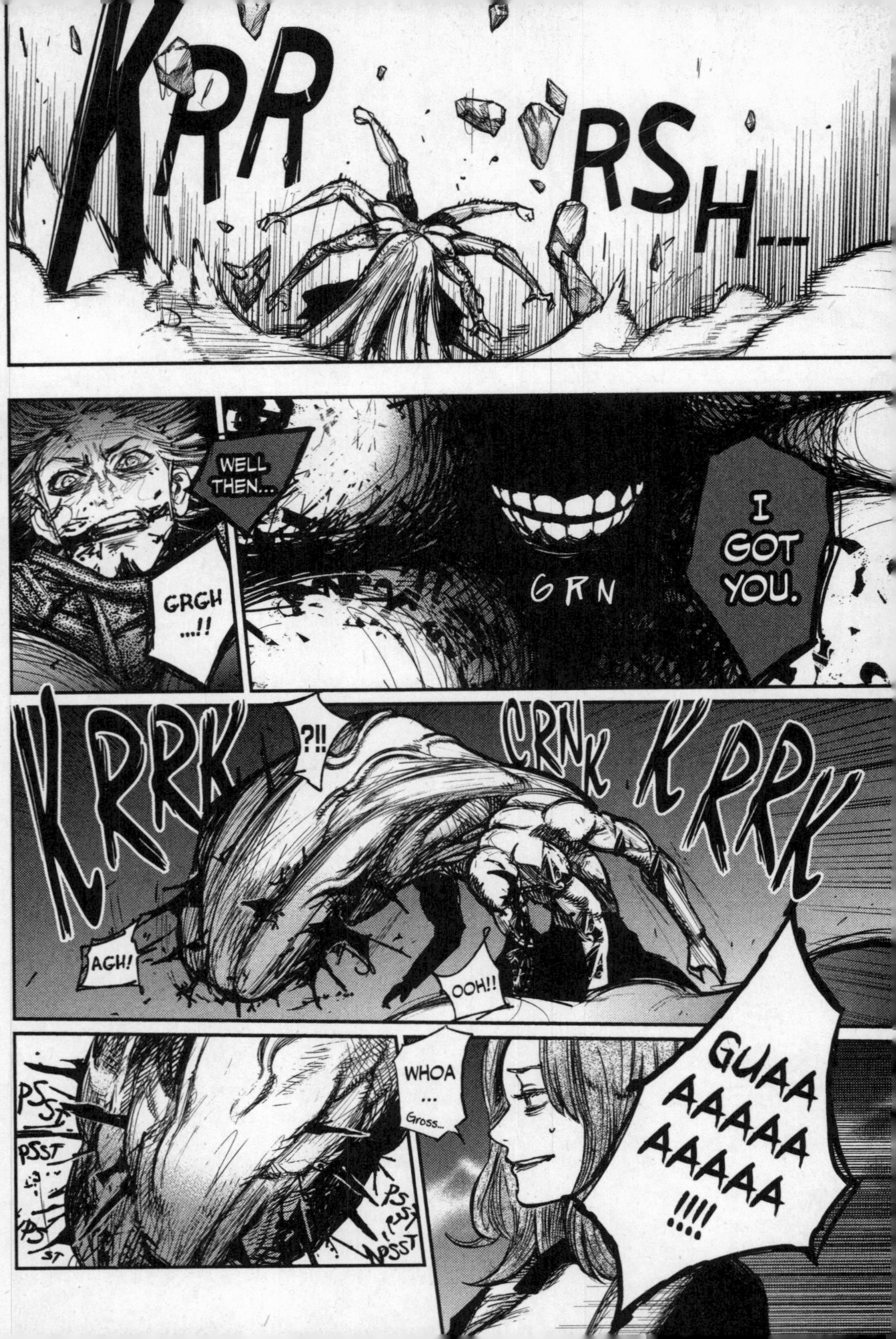
KRRRSH...
I GOT YOU.
GRN
WELL THEN...
GRGH ...!!
CRNK
KRRK
?!!
KRRK
OOH!!
AGH!
GUAAAAAAAAAAAAA!!!!
WHOA...
Gross...
PSST
PSST
PSST
PSST
PSST

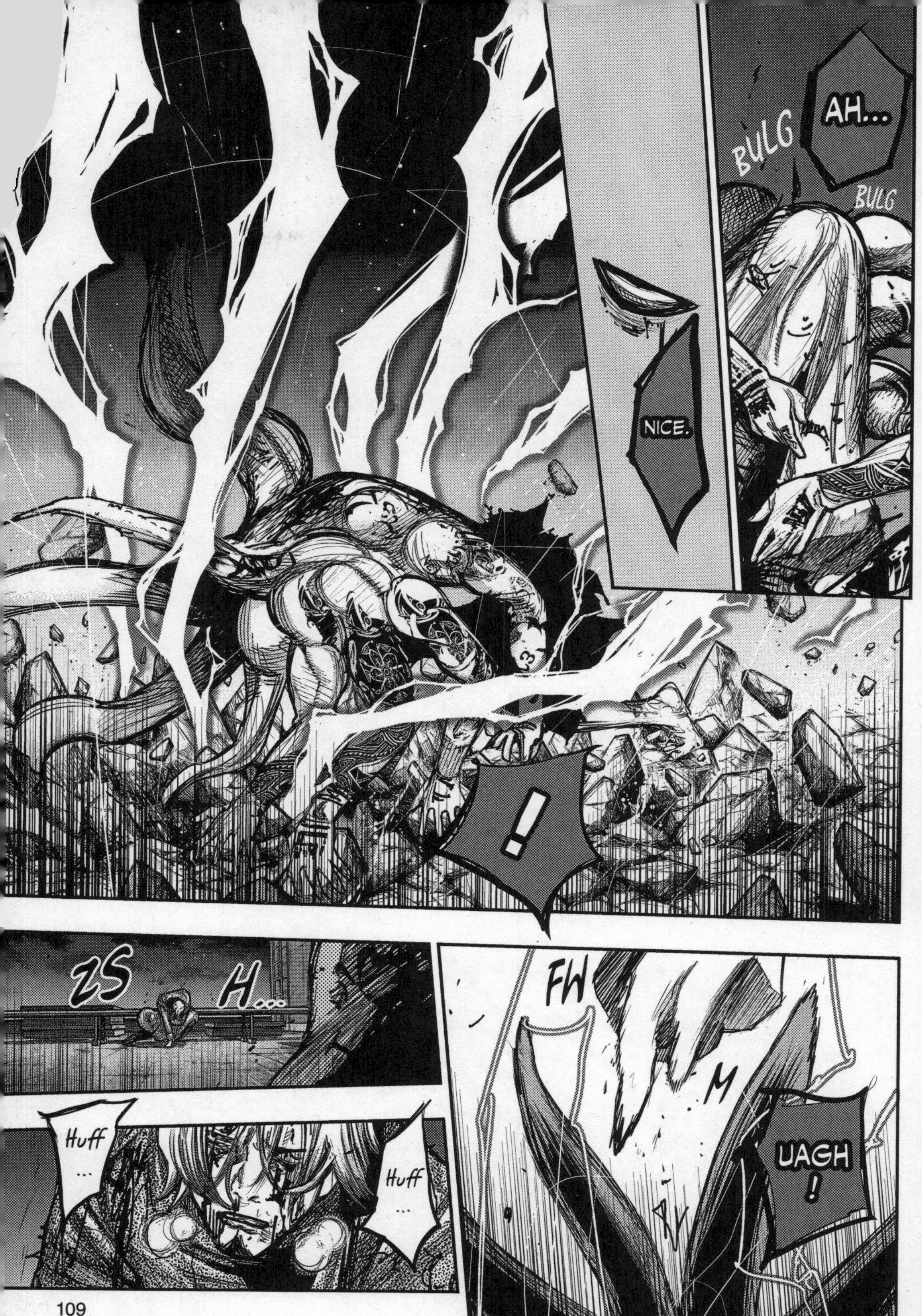
BULG
AH...
BULG
NICE.
!
FW
M
UAGH
!
ZS
H...
Huff
...
Huff
...

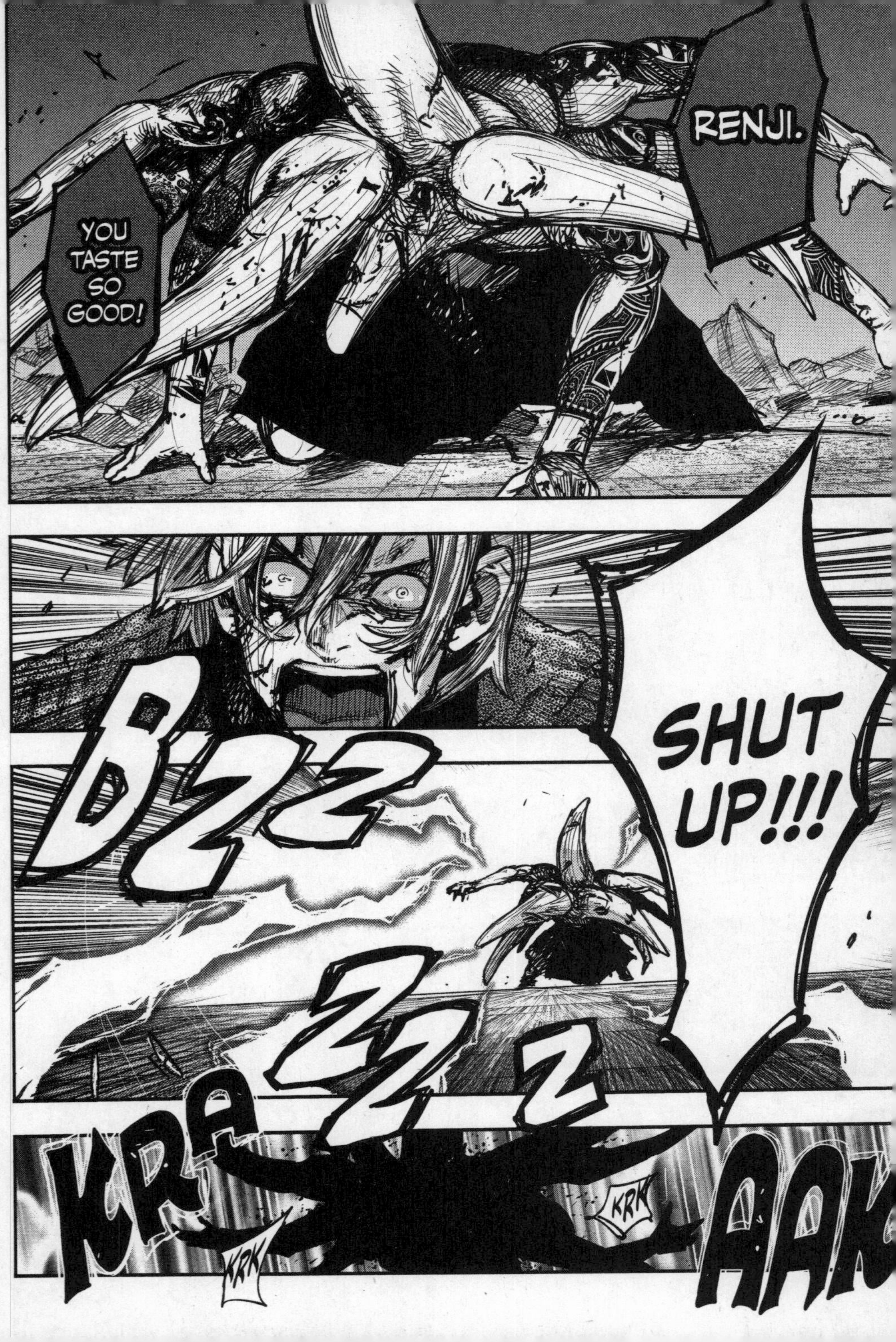
RENJI.
YOU TASTE SO GOOD!
SHUT UP!!!
BZZ
ZZZ
KRA
AAK
KRK
KRK

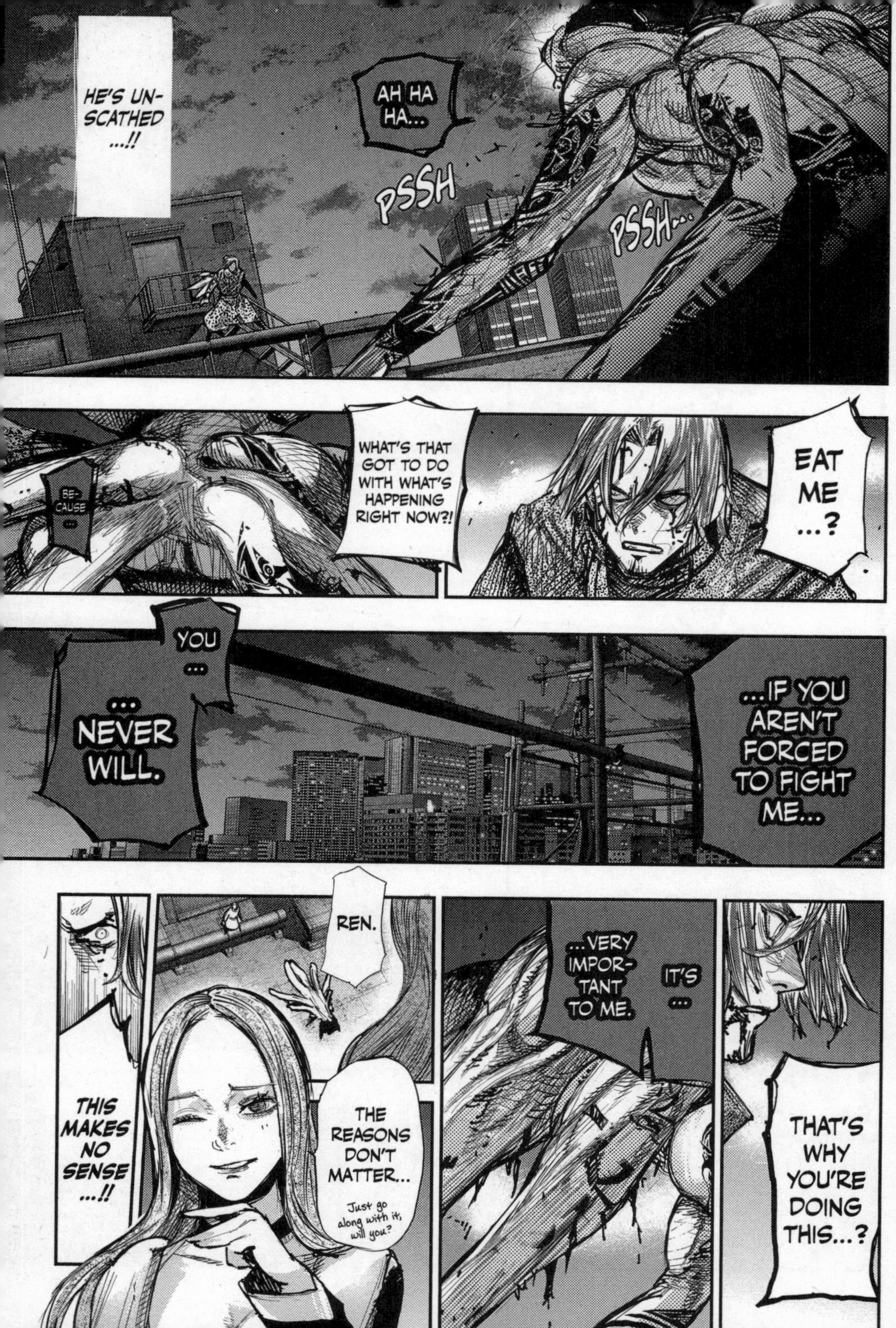
AH HA HA...
HE'S UN-SCATHED ...!!
PSSH...
PSSH
EAT ME ...?
WHAT'S THAT GOT TO DO WITH WHAT'S HAPPENING RIGHT NOW?!
... BE-CAUSE ...
...IF YOU AREN'T FORCED TO FIGHT ME...
YOU ...
... NEVER WILL.
THAT'S WHY YOU'RE DOING THIS...?
IT'S ...
...VERY IMPOR-TANT TO ME.
REN.
THE REASONS DON'T MATTER...
Just go along with it, will you?
THIS MAKES NO SENSE ...!!

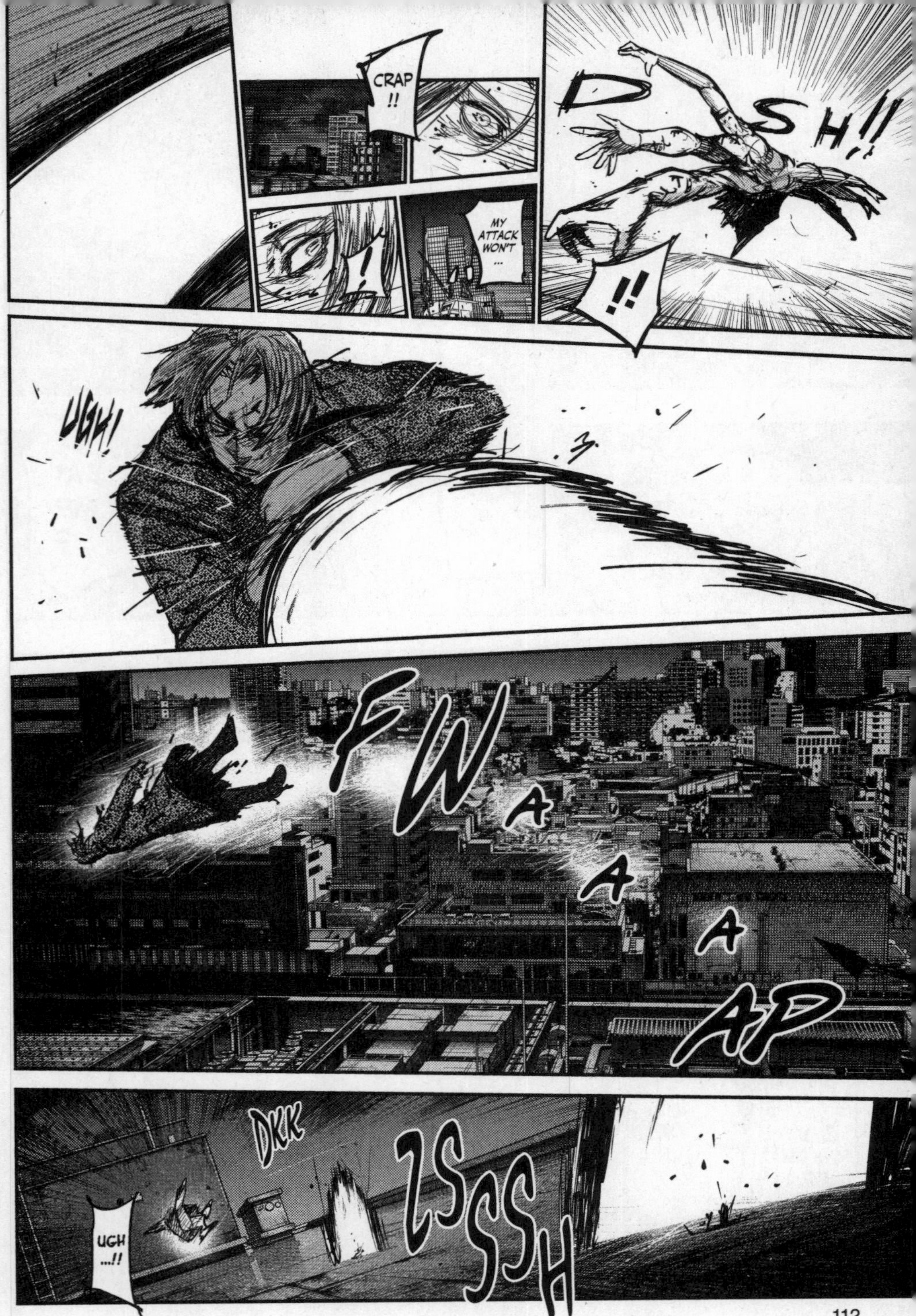
DSH!!
!!
CRAP!!
MY ATTACK WON'T ...
!
UGH!
FWAAAAP
ZSSSH
DKK
UGH...!!

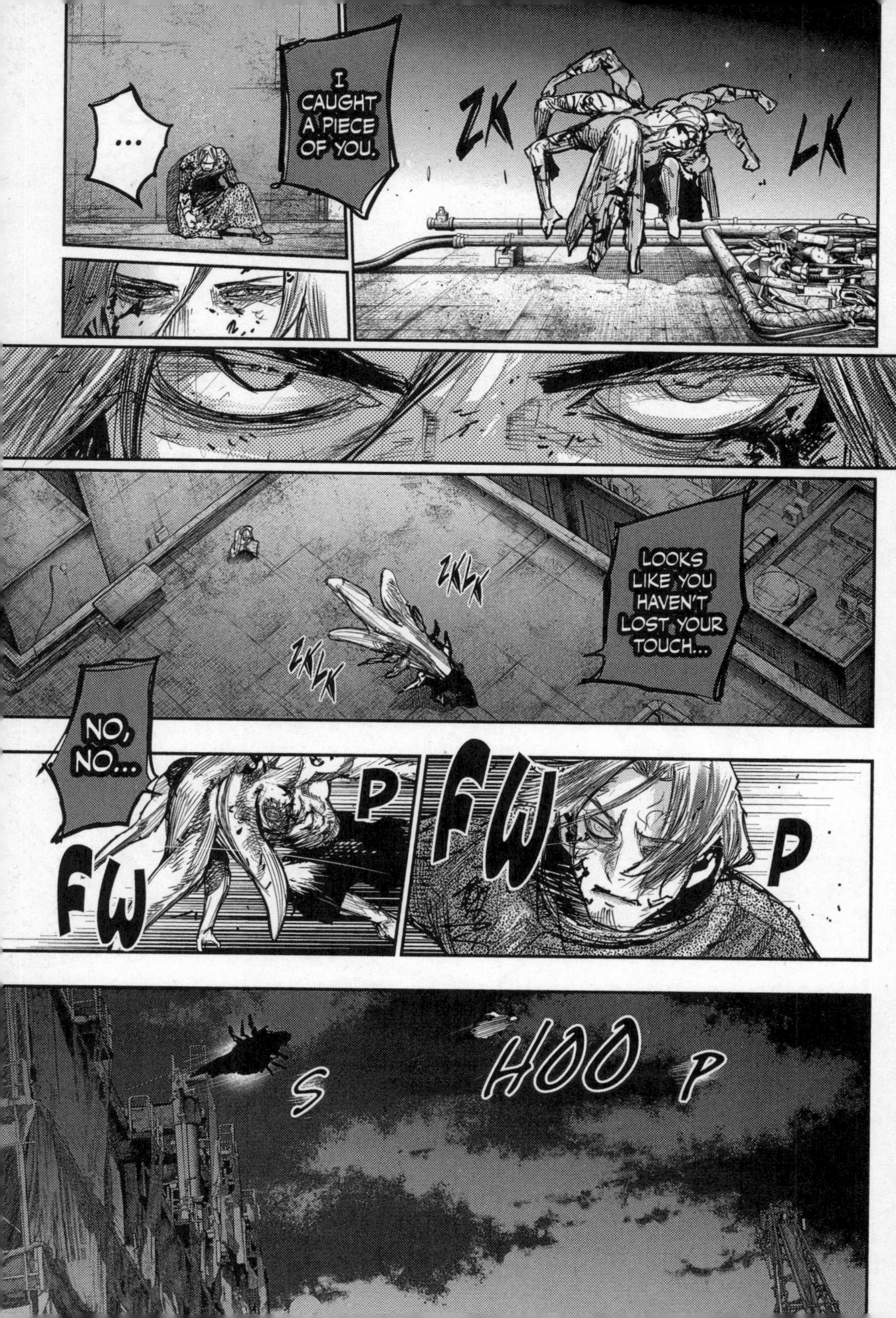
ZK
LK
I CAUGHT A PIECE OF YOU.
...
LOOKS LIKE YOU HAVEN'T LOST YOUR TOUCH...
ZKLK
ZKLK
FW
P
NO, NO...
P
FW
S
HOO
P

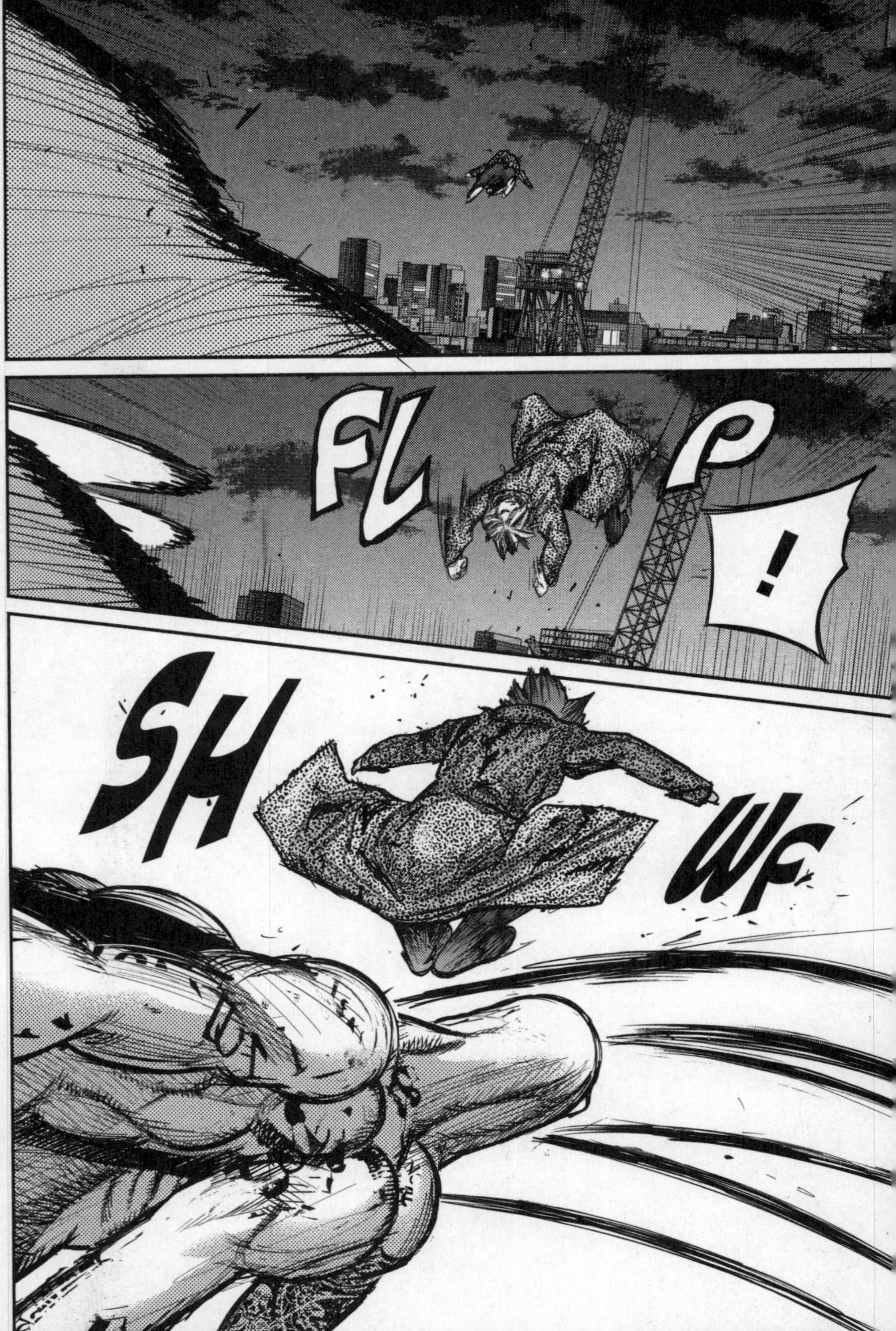

FL P
!
SH WF

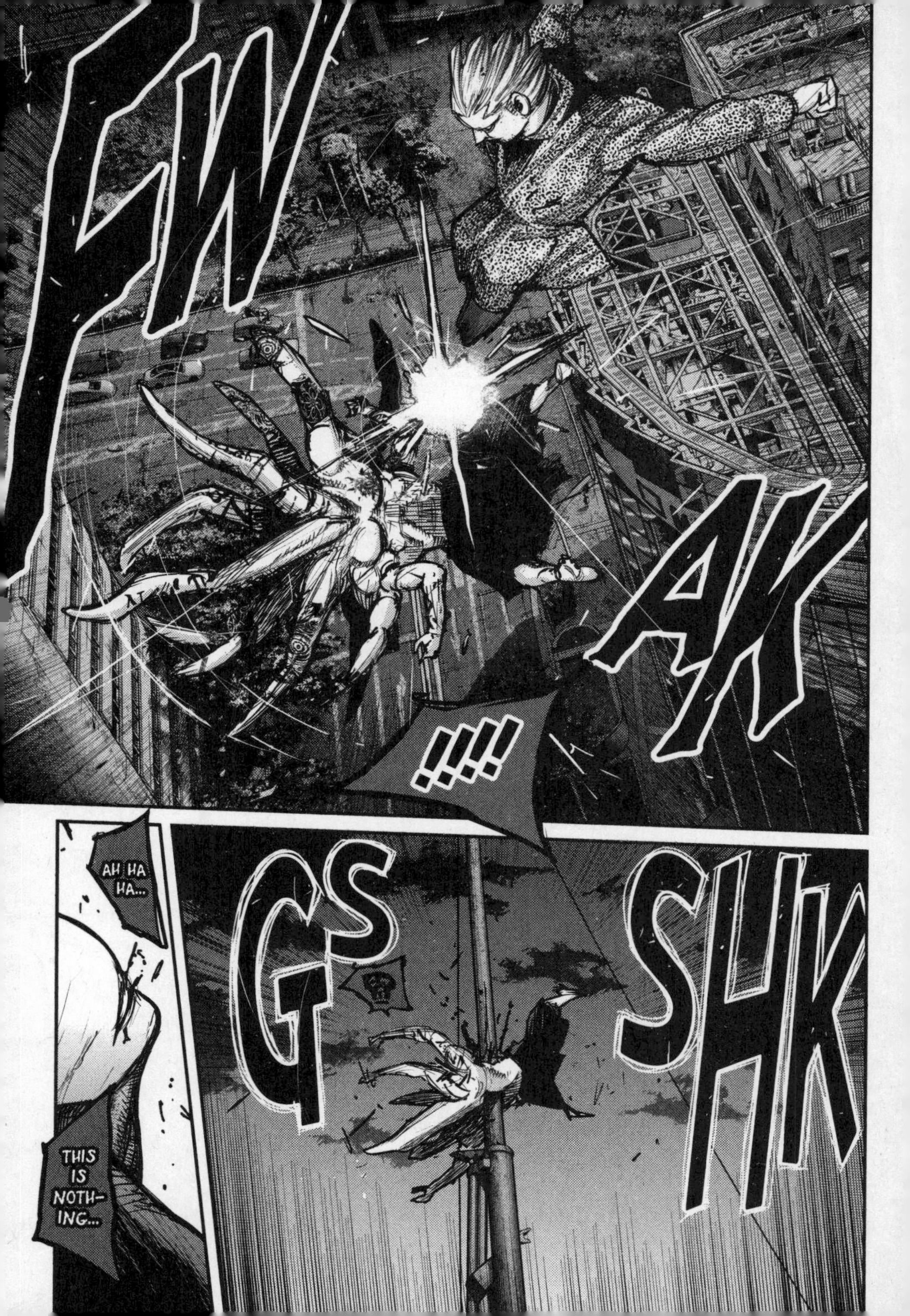
AK
FW
!!!!
SHK
GST
AH HA HA...
THIS IS NOTH-ING...

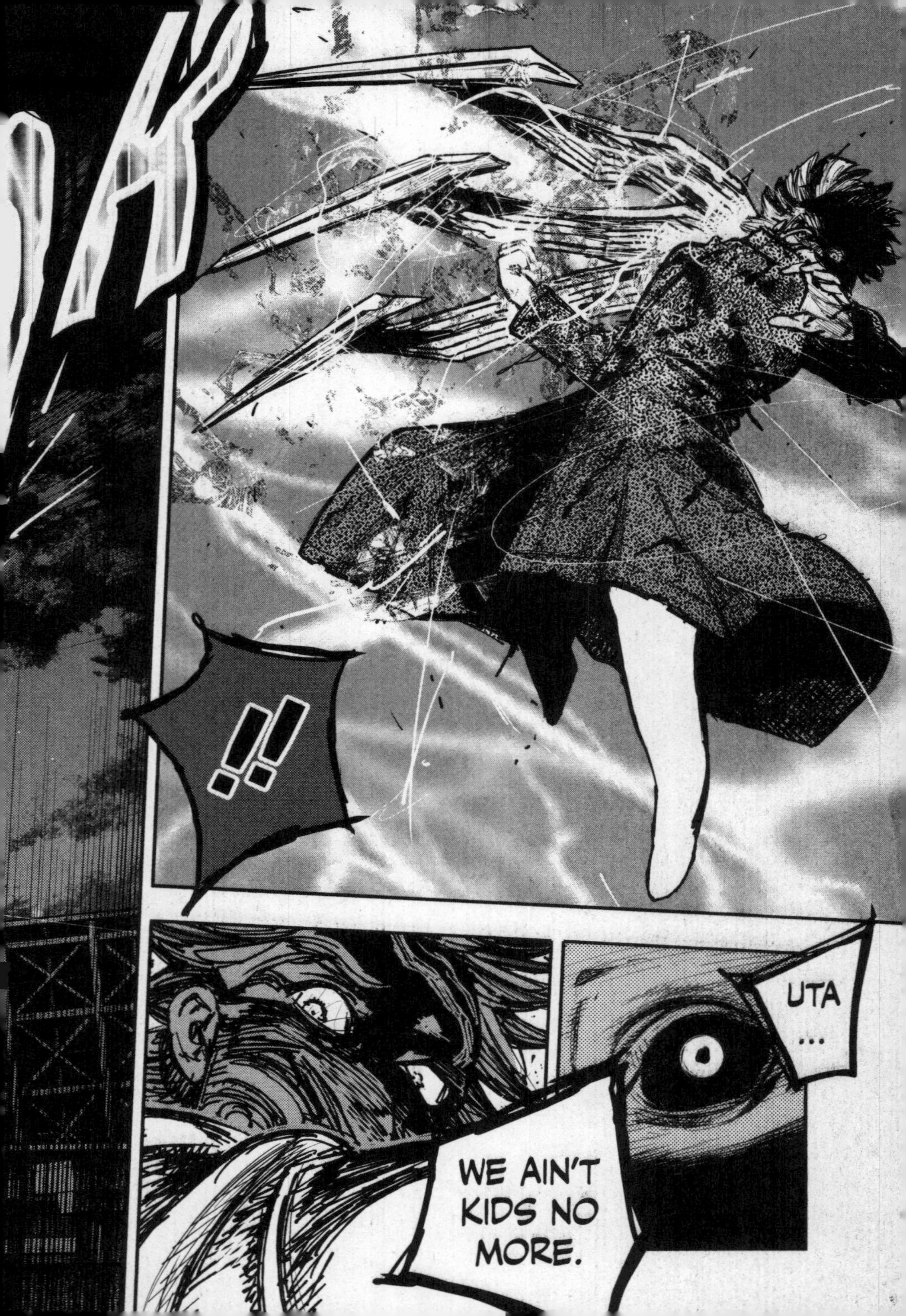
!!
UTA ...
WE AIN'T KIDS NO MORE.

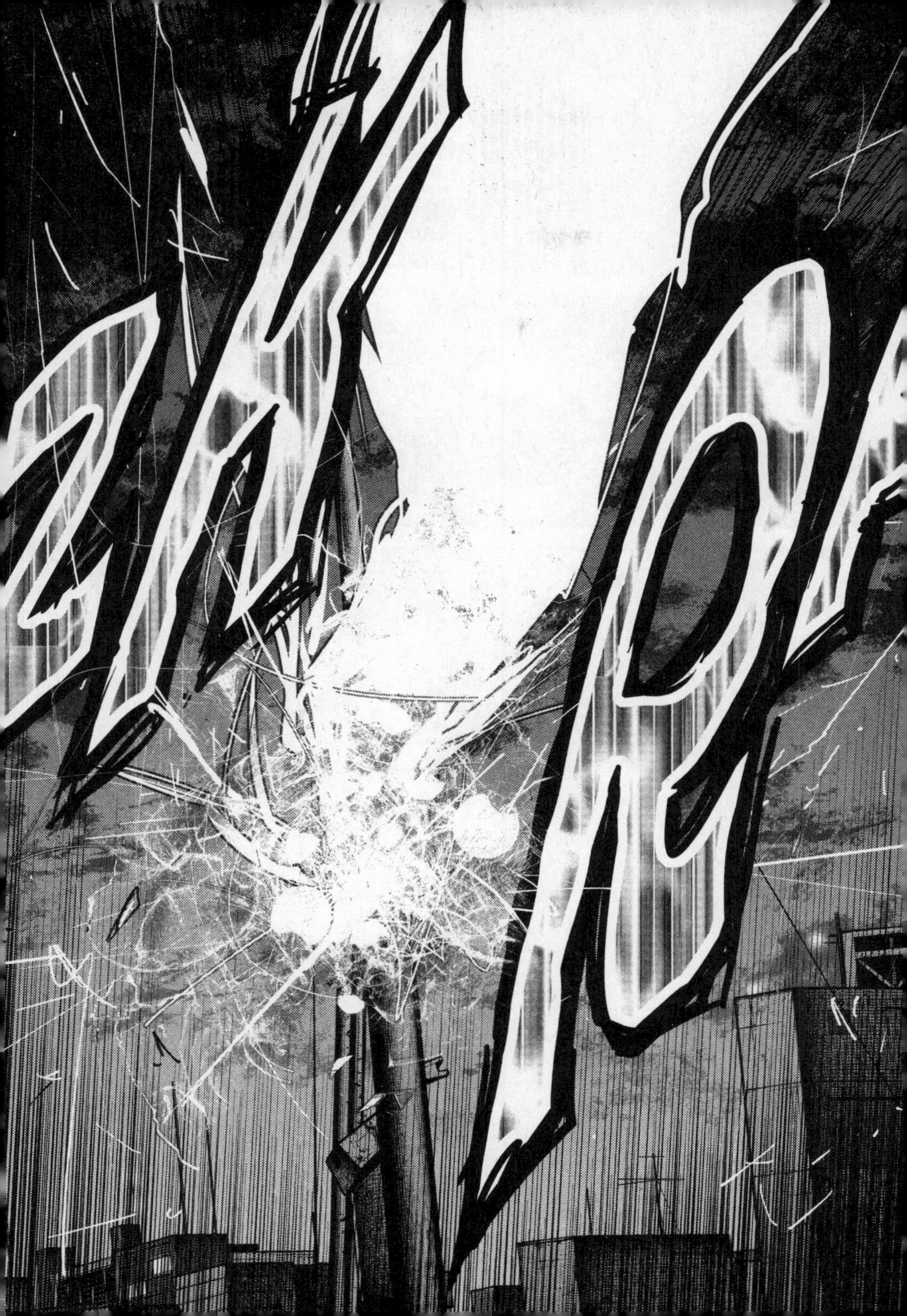

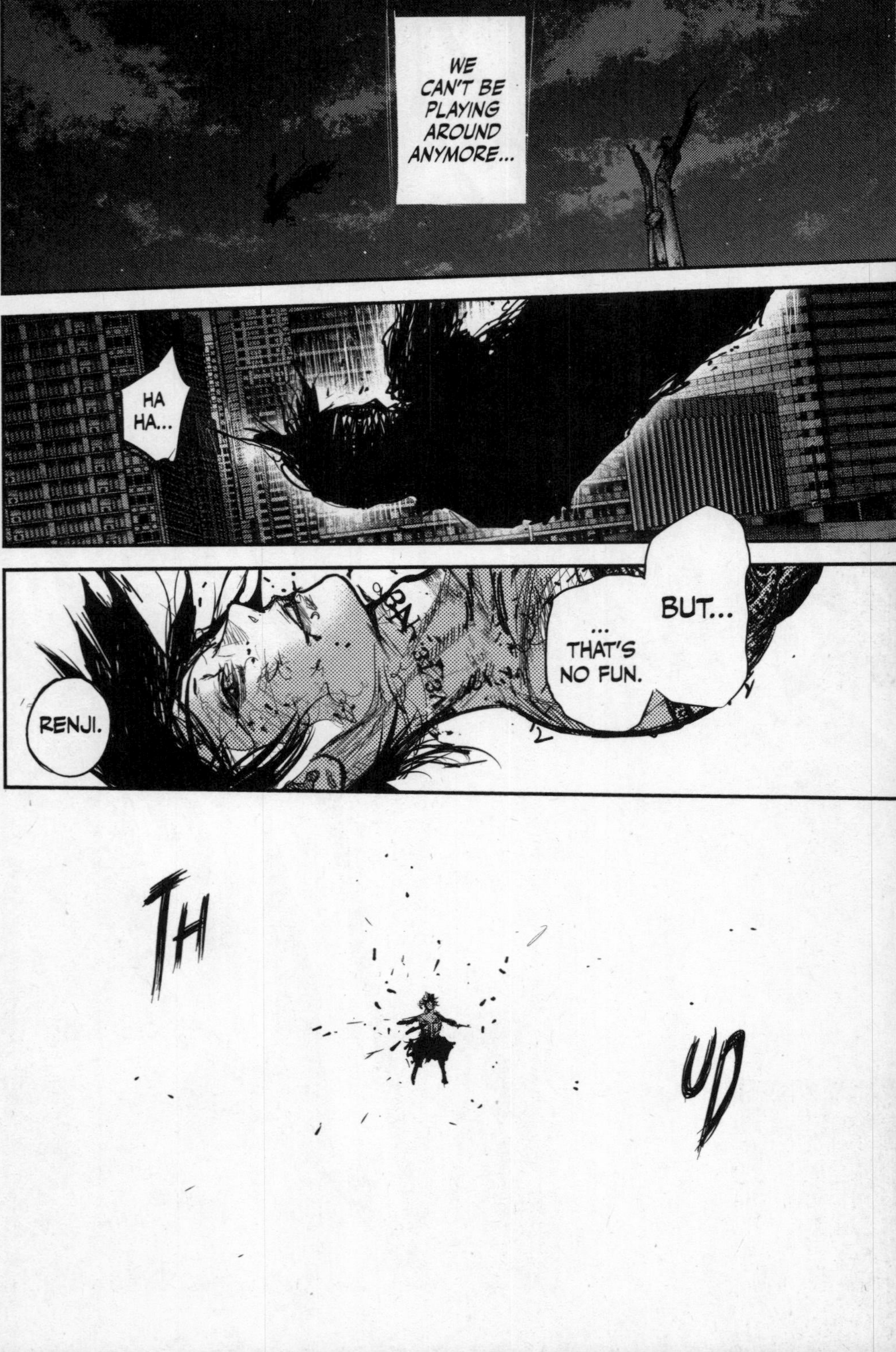
WE CAN'T BE PLAYING AROUND ANYMORE...
HA HA...
BUT...
... THAT'S NO FUN.
RENJI.
THUD

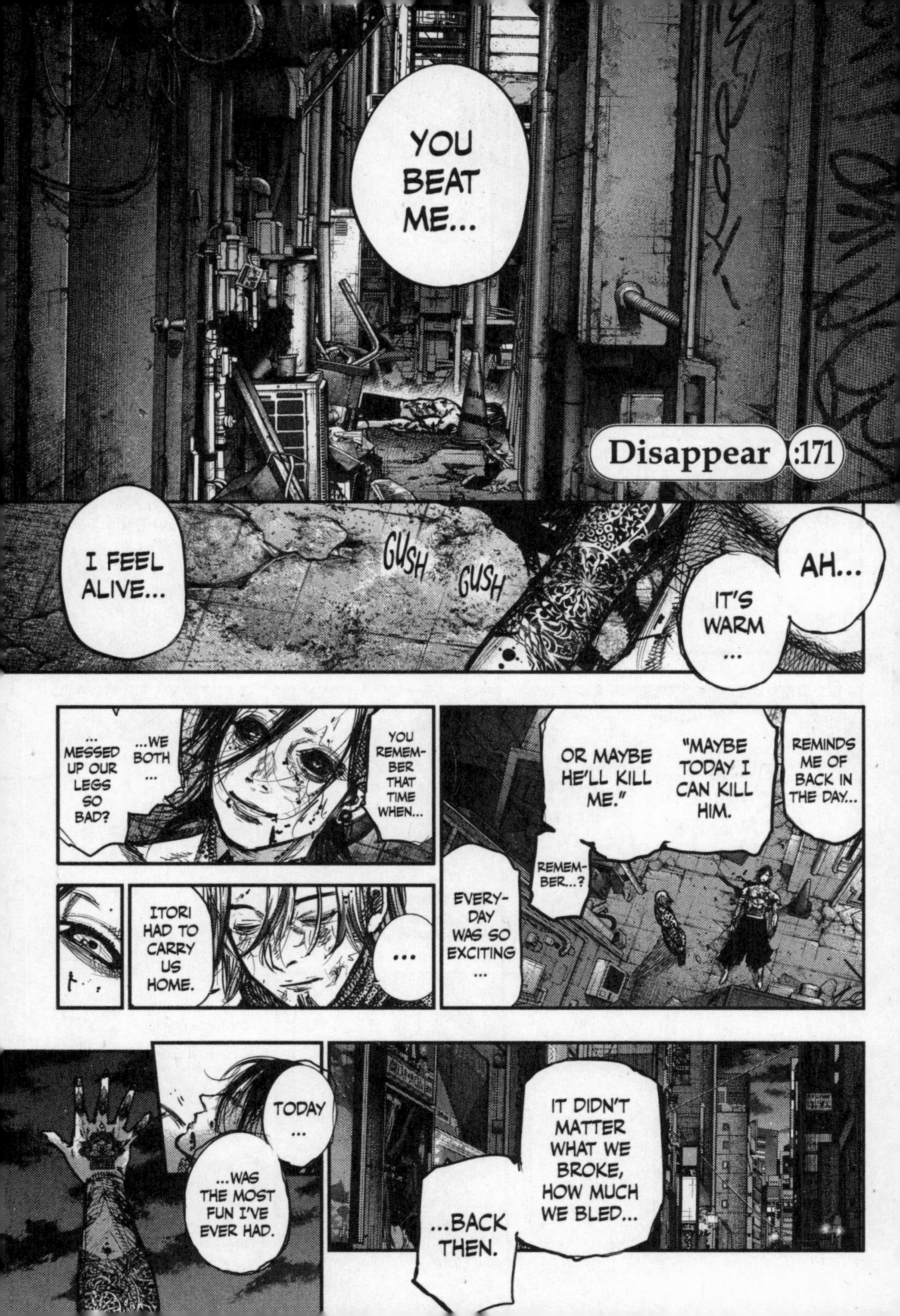
Disappear :171
YOU BEAT ME...
AH...
IT'S WARM ...
GUSH
GUSH
I FEEL ALIVE...
REMINDS ME OF BACK IN THE DAY...
"MAYBE TODAY I CAN KILL HIM.
OR MAYBE HE'LL KILL ME."
REMEMBER...?
EVERYDAY WAS SO EXCITING ...
YOU REMEMBER THAT TIME WHEN...
...WE BOTH ...
... MESSED UP OUR LEGS SO BAD?
...
ITORI HAD TO CARRY US HOME.
IT DIDN'T MATTER WHAT WE BROKE, HOW MUCH WE BLED...
...BACK THEN.
TODAY ...
...WAS THE MOST FUN I'VE EVER HAD.

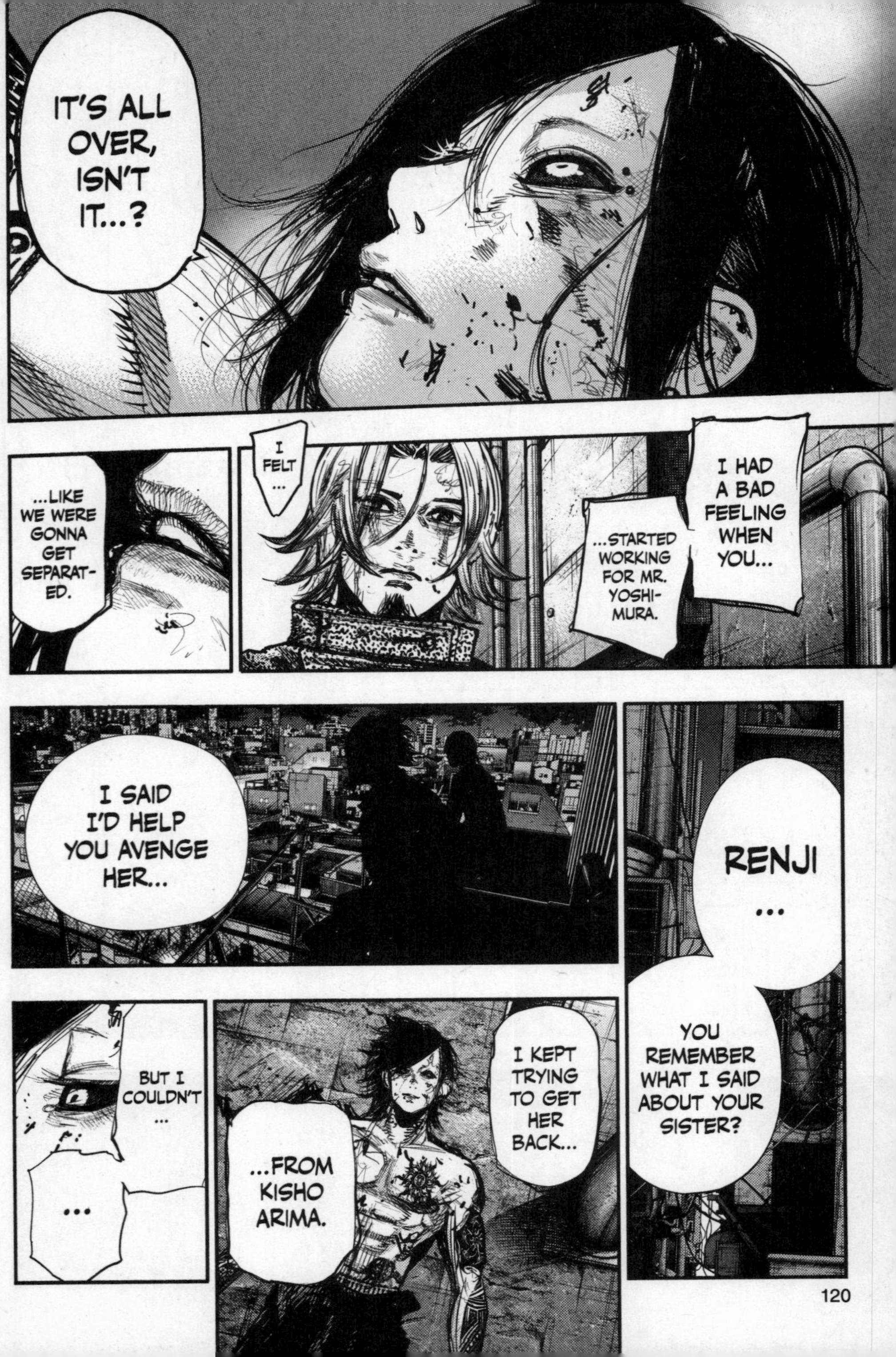
IT'S ALL OVER, ISN'T IT...?
I HAD A BAD FEELING WHEN YOU...
...STARTED WORKING FOR MR. YOSHIMURA.
I FELT ...
...LIKE WE WERE GONNA GET SEPARAT-ED.
RENJI ...
YOU REMEMBER WHAT I SAID ABOUT YOUR SISTER?
I SAID I'D HELP YOU AVENGE HER...
I KEPT TRYING TO GET HER BACK...
...FROM KISHO ARIMA.
BUT I COULDN'T ...
...

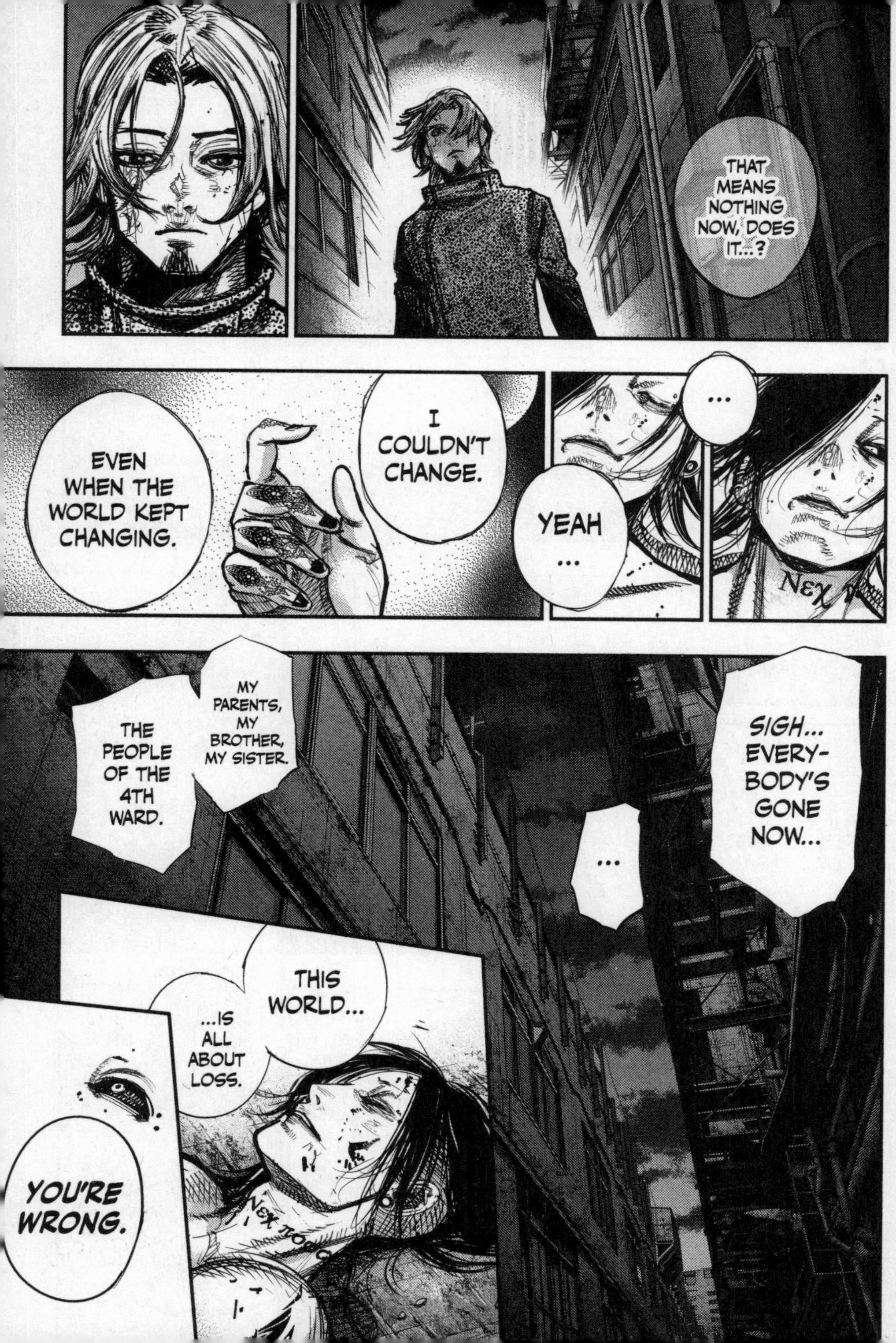
THAT MEANS NOTHING NOW, DOES IT...?
...
YEAH ...
I COULDN'T CHANGE.
EVEN WHEN THE WORLD KEPT CHANGING.
SIGH... EVERY-BODY'S GONE NOW...
...
MY PARENTS, MY BROTHER, MY SISTER.
THE PEOPLE OF THE 4TH WARD.
THIS WORLD...
...IS ALL ABOUT LOSS.
YOU'RE WRONG.

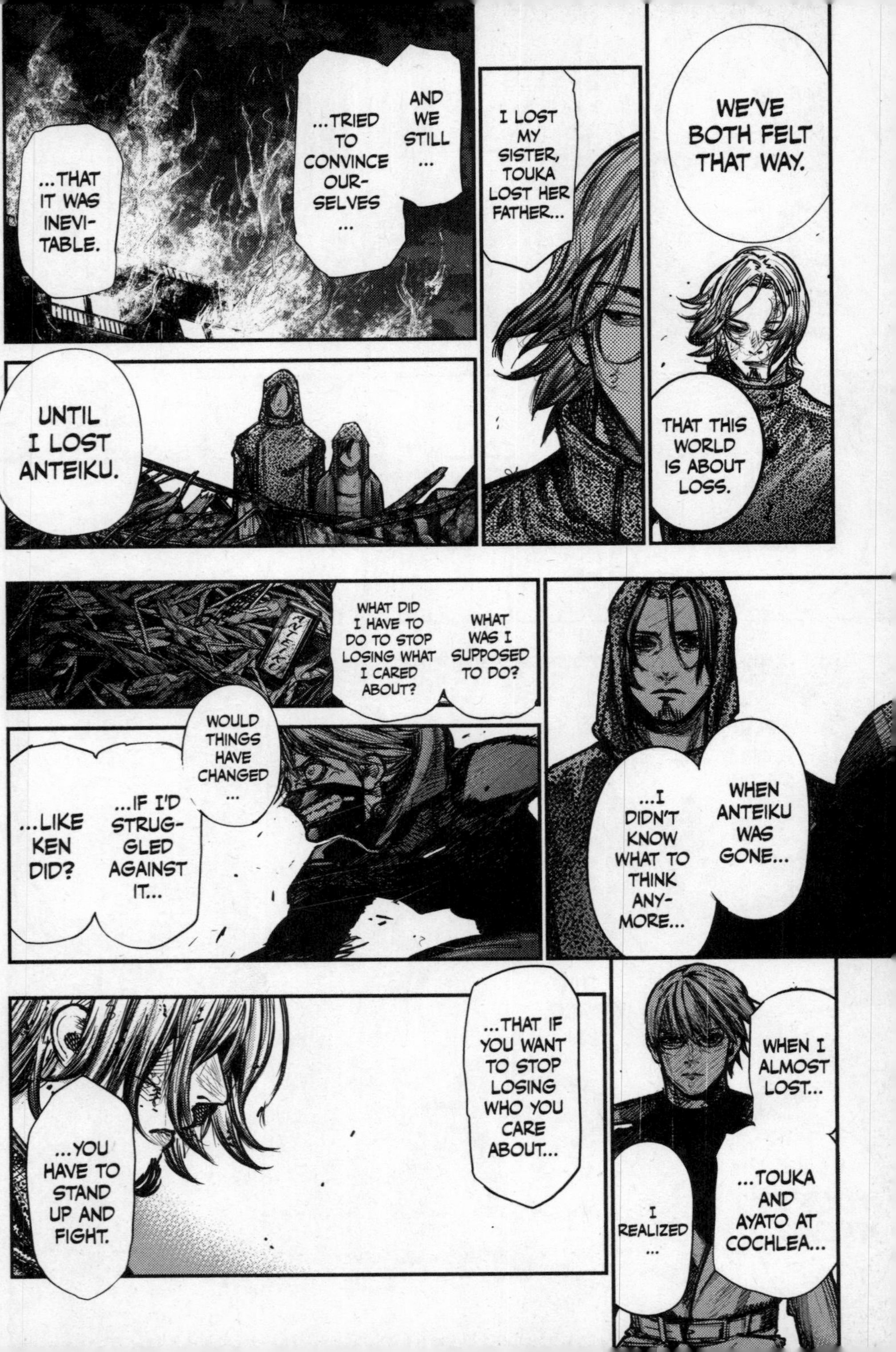
WE'VE BOTH FELT THAT WAY.
THAT THIS WORLD IS ABOUT LOSS.
I LOST MY SISTER, TOUKA LOST HER FATHER...
AND WE STILL...
...TRIED TO CONVINCE OUR-SELVES...
...THAT IT WAS INEVI-TABLE.
UNTIL I LOST ANTEIKU.
WHEN ANTEIKU WAS GONE...
...I DIDN'T KNOW WHAT TO THINK ANY-MORE...
WHAT WAS I SUPPOSED TO DO?
WHAT DID I HAVE TO DO TO STOP LOSING WHAT I CARED ABOUT?
ANTEIKU
WOULD THINGS HAVE CHANGED...
...IF I'D STRUG-GLED AGAINST IT...
...LIKE KEN DID?
WHEN I ALMOST LOST...
...TOUKA AND AYATO AT COCHLEA...
I REALIZED...
...THAT IF YOU WANT TO STOP LOSING WHO YOU CARE ABOUT...
...YOU HAVE TO STAND UP AND FIGHT.

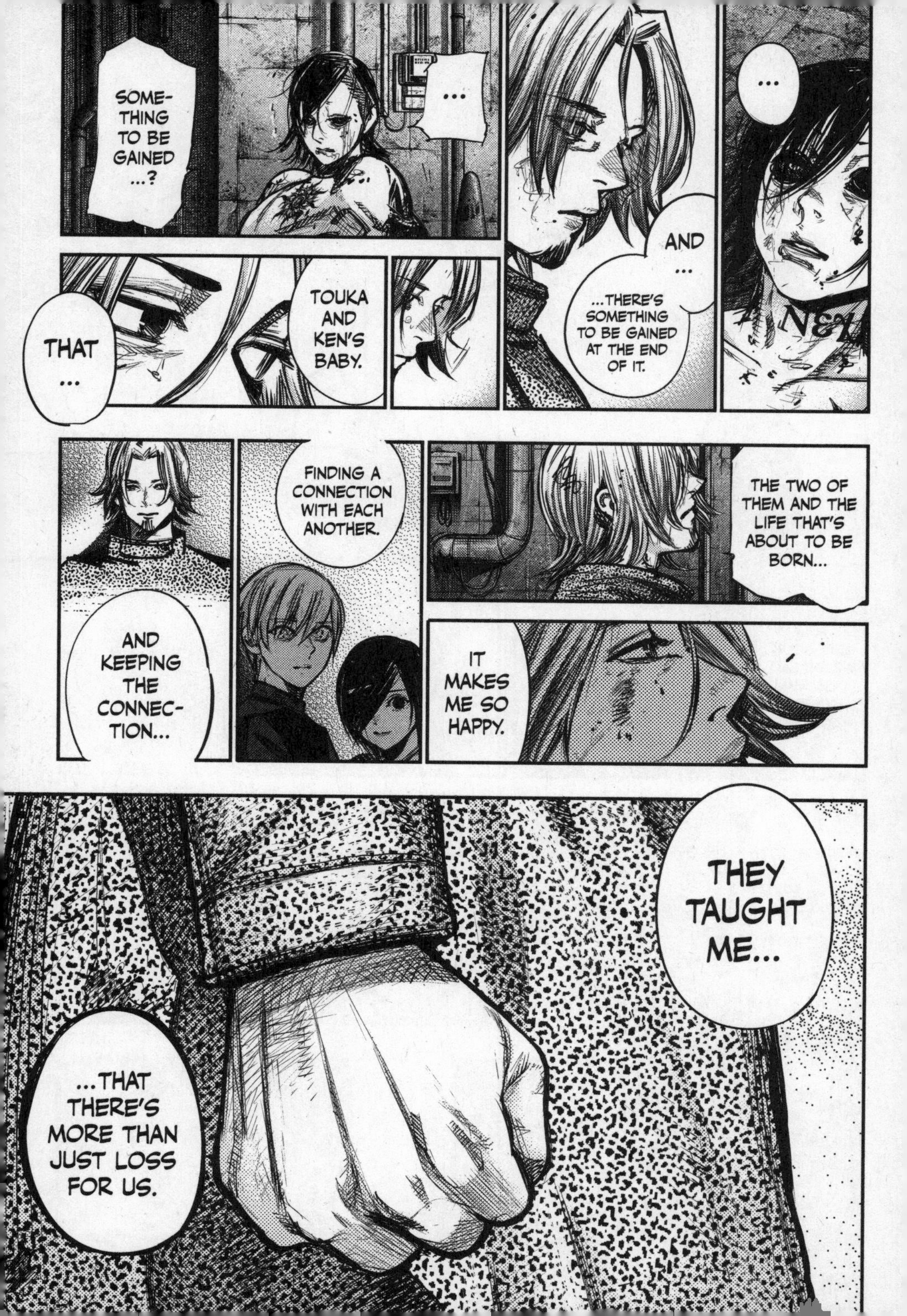
...
AND ...
...THERE'S SOMETHING TO BE GAINED AT THE END OF IT.
...
SOME-THING TO BE GAINED ...?
TOUKA AND KEN'S BABY.
THAT ...
THE TWO OF THEM AND THE LIFE THAT'S ABOUT TO BE BORN...
IT MAKES ME SO HAPPY.
FINDING A CONNECTION WITH EACH ANOTHER.
AND KEEPING THE CONNEC-TION...
THEY TAUGHT ME...
...THAT THERE'S MORE THAN JUST LOSS FOR US.

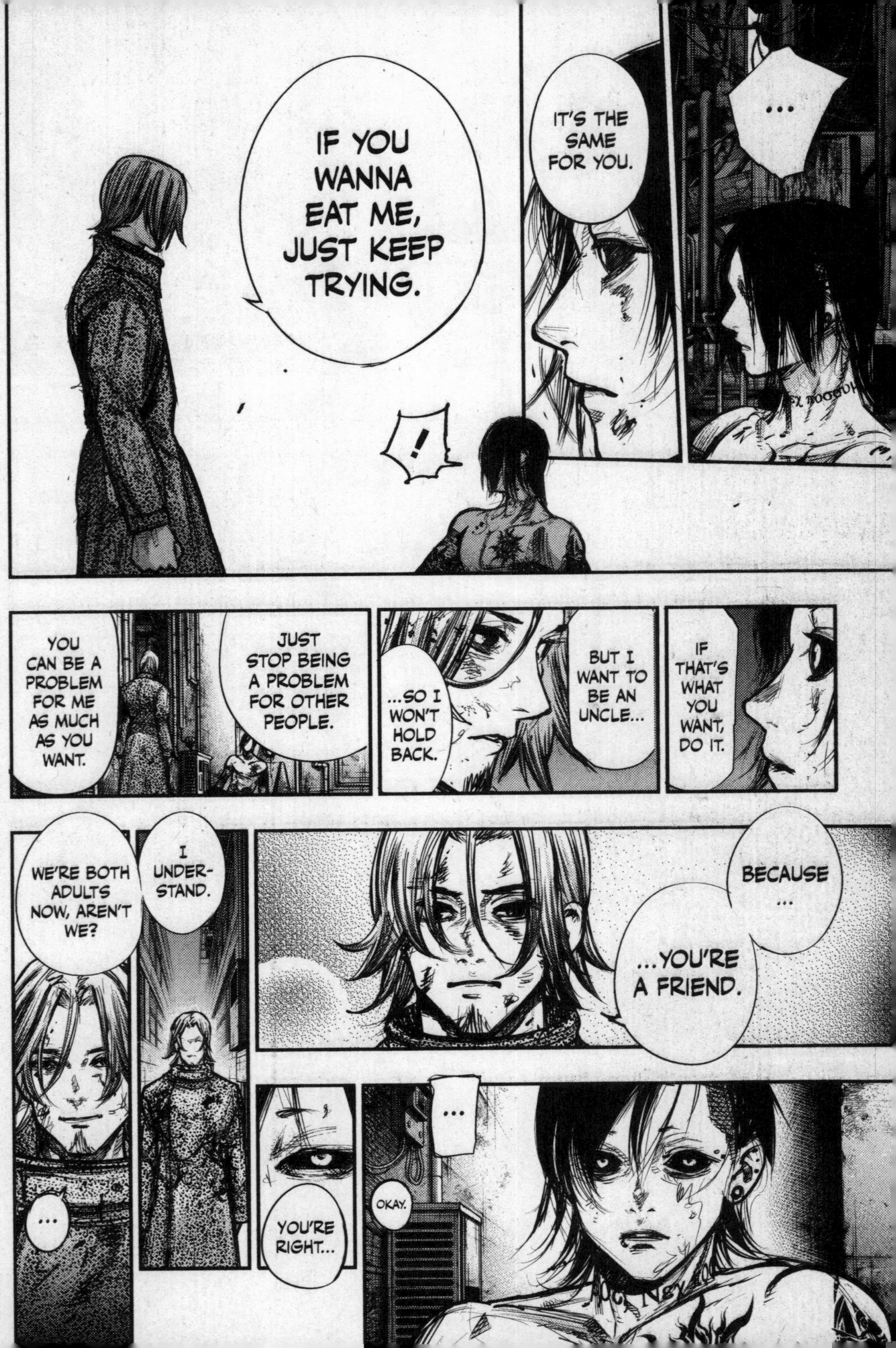
...
IT'S THE SAME FOR YOU.
IF YOU WANNA EAT ME, JUST KEEP TRYING.
!
IF THAT'S WHAT YOU WANT, DO IT.
BUT I WANT TO BE AN UNCLE...
...SO I WON'T HOLD BACK.
JUST STOP BEING A PROBLEM FOR OTHER PEOPLE.
YOU CAN BE A PROBLEM FOR ME AS MUCH AS YOU WANT.
BECAUSE ...
...YOU'RE A FRIEND.
...
OKAY.
YOU'RE RIGHT...
I UNDER-STAND.
WE'RE BOTH ADULTS NOW, AREN'T WE?
...

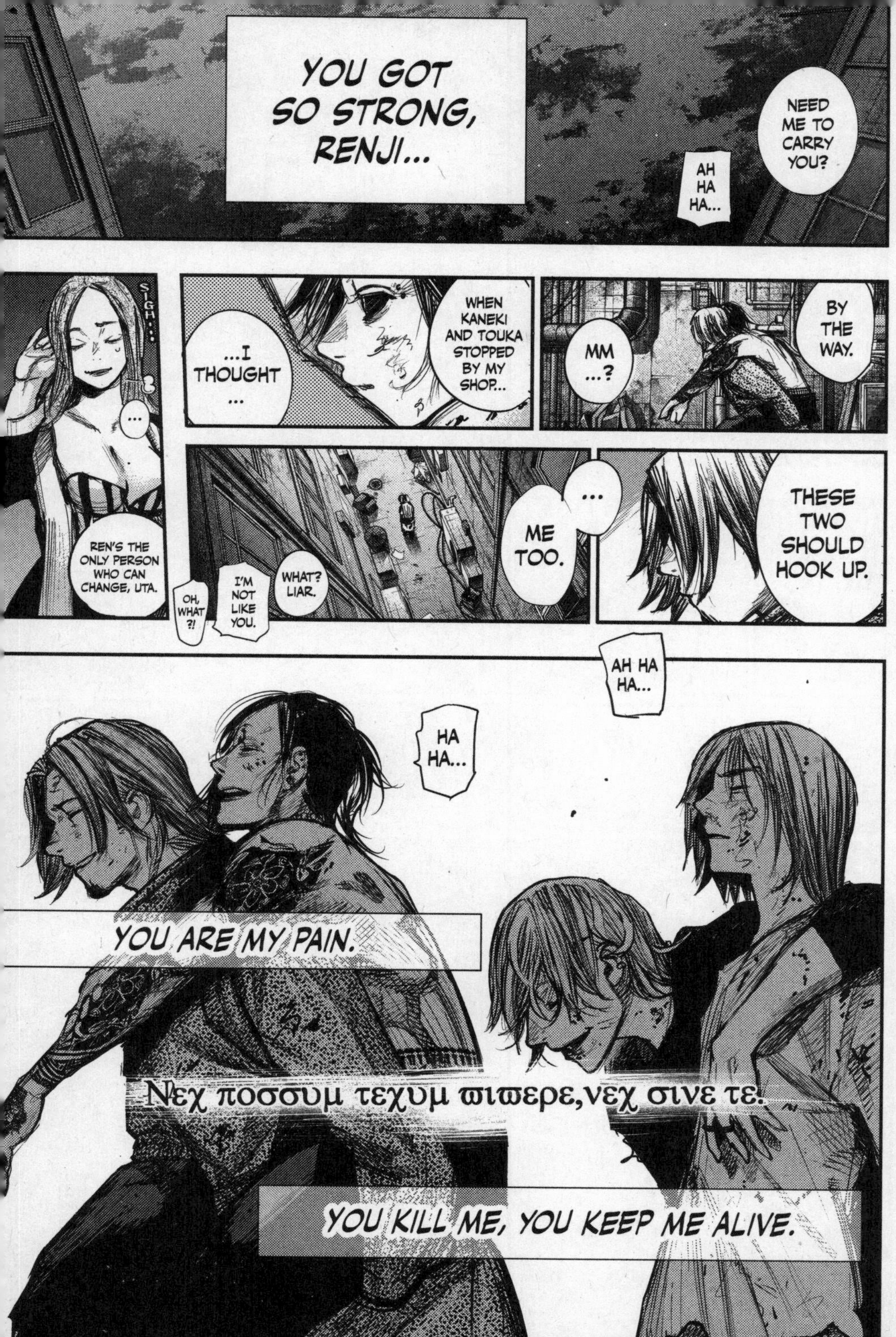
NEED ME TO CARRY YOU?
AH HA HA...
YOU GOT SO STRONG, RENJI...
BY THE WAY.
MM ...?
WHEN KANEKI AND TOUKA STOPPED BY MY SHOP...
...I THOUGHT ...
THESE TWO SHOULD HOOK UP.
...
ME TOO.
WHAT? LIAR.
I'M NOT LIKE YOU.
OH, WHAT ?!
SIGH...
...
REN'S THE ONLY PERSON WHO CAN CHANGE, UTA.
AH HA HA...
HA HA...
YOU ARE MY PAIN.
Νεχ ποσσυμ τεχυμ ϖιϖερε,νεχ σινε τε.
YOU KILL ME, YOU KEEP ME ALIVE.

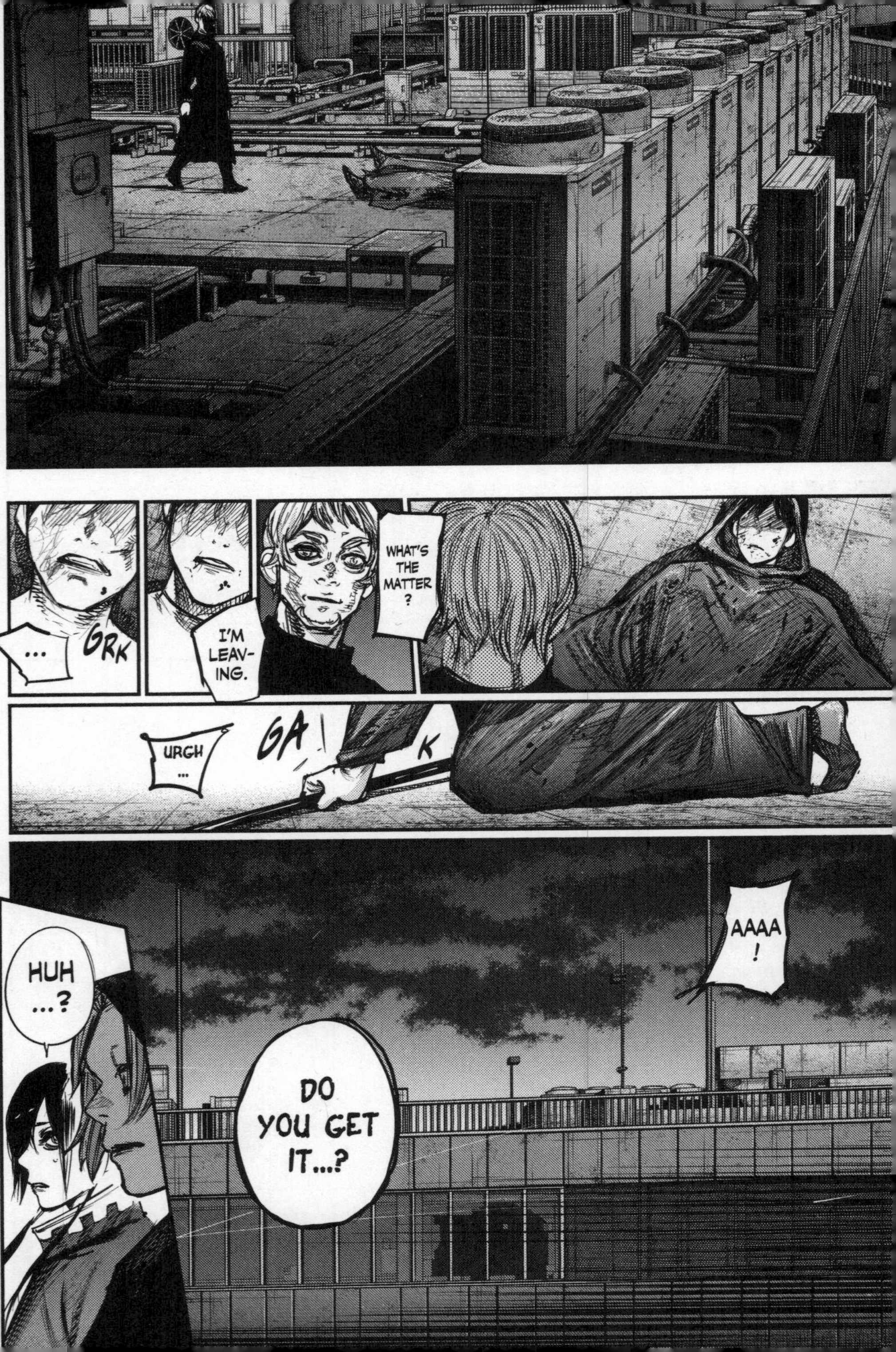
WHAT'S THE MATTER ?
I'M LEAV-ING.
GRK
...
GA K
URGH ...
AAAA !
DO YOU GET IT...?
HUH ...?

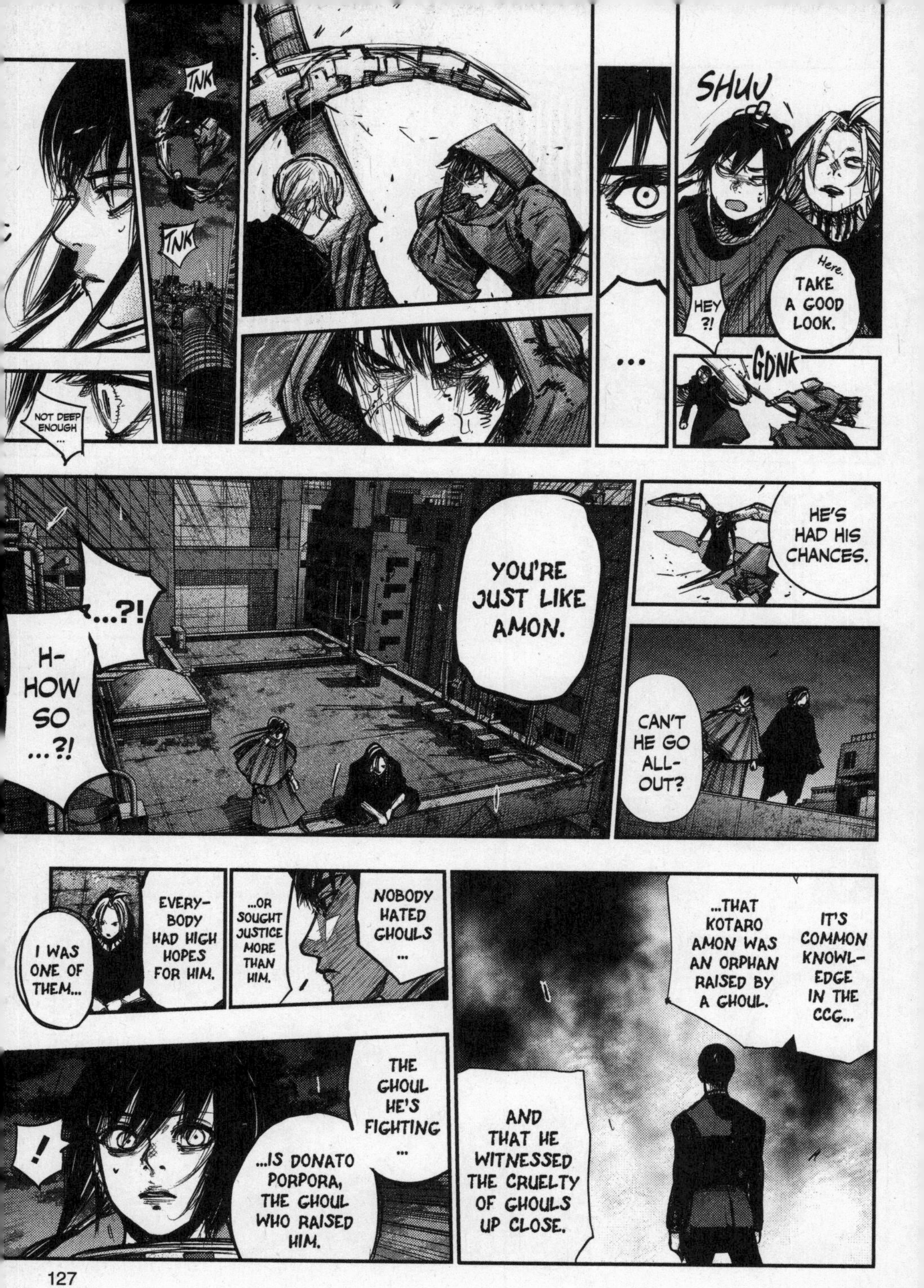

SHUV
Here. TAKE A GOOD LOOK.
HEY?!
GDNK
...
TNK
TNK
NOT DEEP ENOUGH...
HE'S HAD HIS CHANCES.
CAN'T HE GO ALL-OUT?
YOU'RE JUST LIKE AMON.
...?!
H-HOW SO...?!
IT'S COMMON KNOWLEDGE IN THE CCG...
...THAT KOTARO AMON WAS AN ORPHAN RAISED BY A GHOUL.
AND THAT HE WITNESSED THE CRUELTY OF GHOULS UP CLOSE.
NOBODY HATED GHOULS...
...OR SOUGHT JUSTICE MORE THAN HIM.
EVERYBODY HAD HIGH HOPES FOR HIM.
I WAS ONE OF THEM...
THE GHOUL HE'S FIGHTING...
...IS DONATO PORPORA, THE GHOUL WHO RAISED HIM.
!

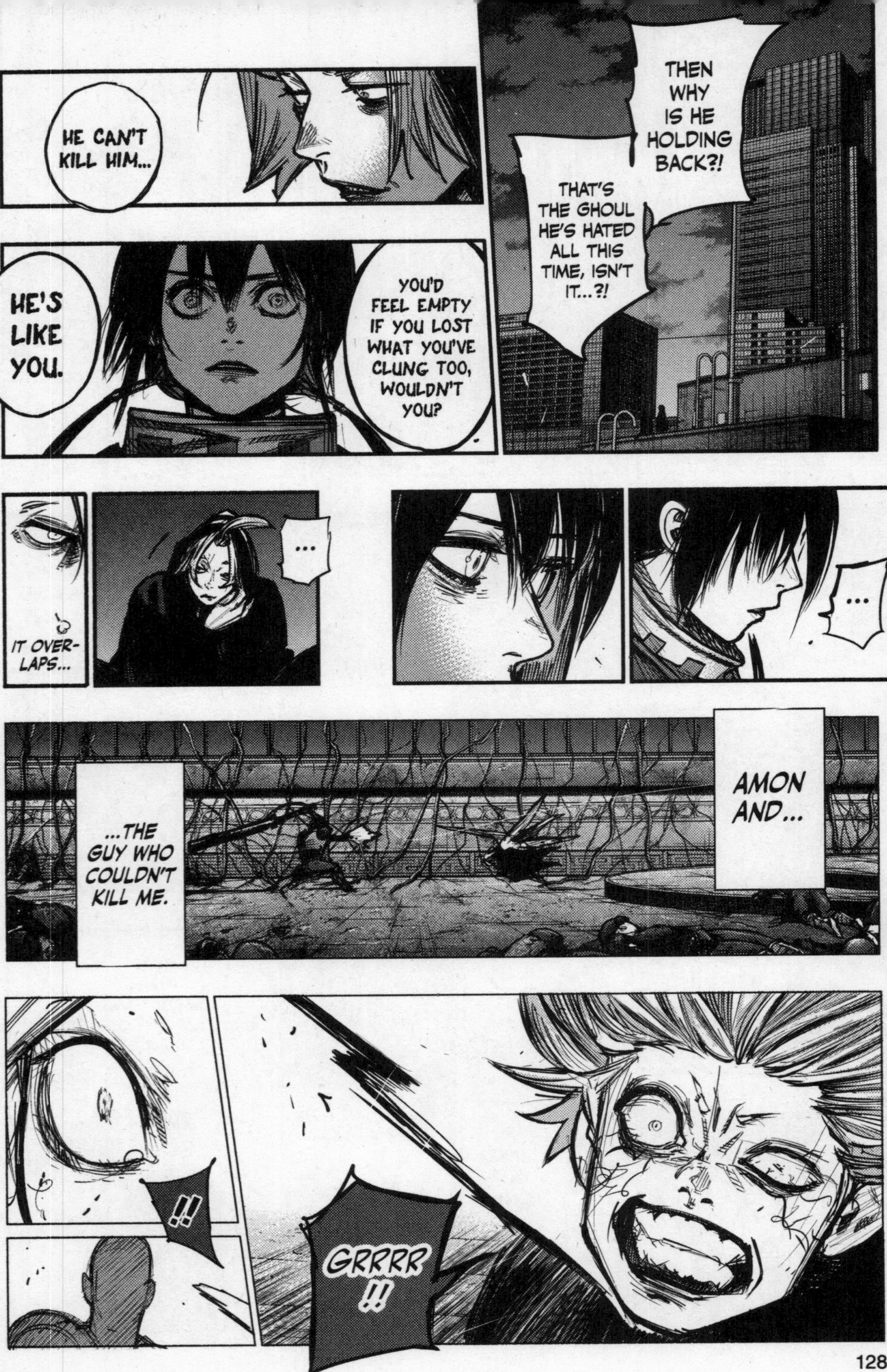
THEN WHY IS HE HOLDING BACK?!
THAT'S THE GHOUL HE'S HATED ALL THIS TIME, ISN'T IT...?!
HE CAN'T KILL HIM...
YOU'D FEEL EMPTY IF YOU LOST WHAT YOU'VE CLUNG TOO, WOULDN'T YOU?
HE'S LIKE YOU.
...
...
IT OVER-LAPS...
AMON AND...
...THE GUY WHO COULDN'T KILL ME.
GRRRR!!
!!

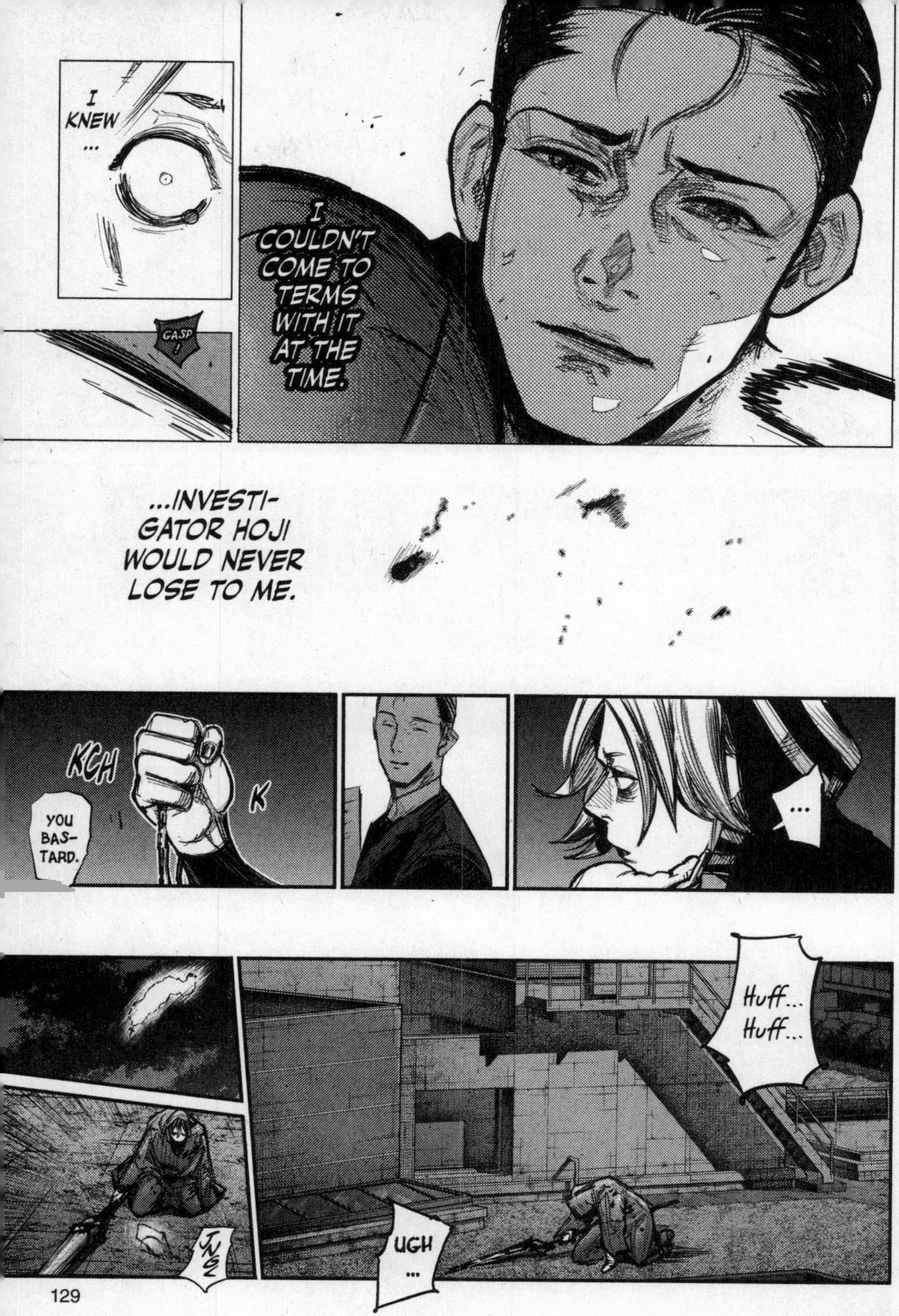
I COULDN'T COME TO TERMS WITH IT AT THE TIME.
I KNEW ...
GASP!
...INVESTIGATOR HOJI WOULD NEVER LOSE TO ME.
...
KCH
K
YOU BASTARD.
Huff... Huff...
UGH ...
JNG

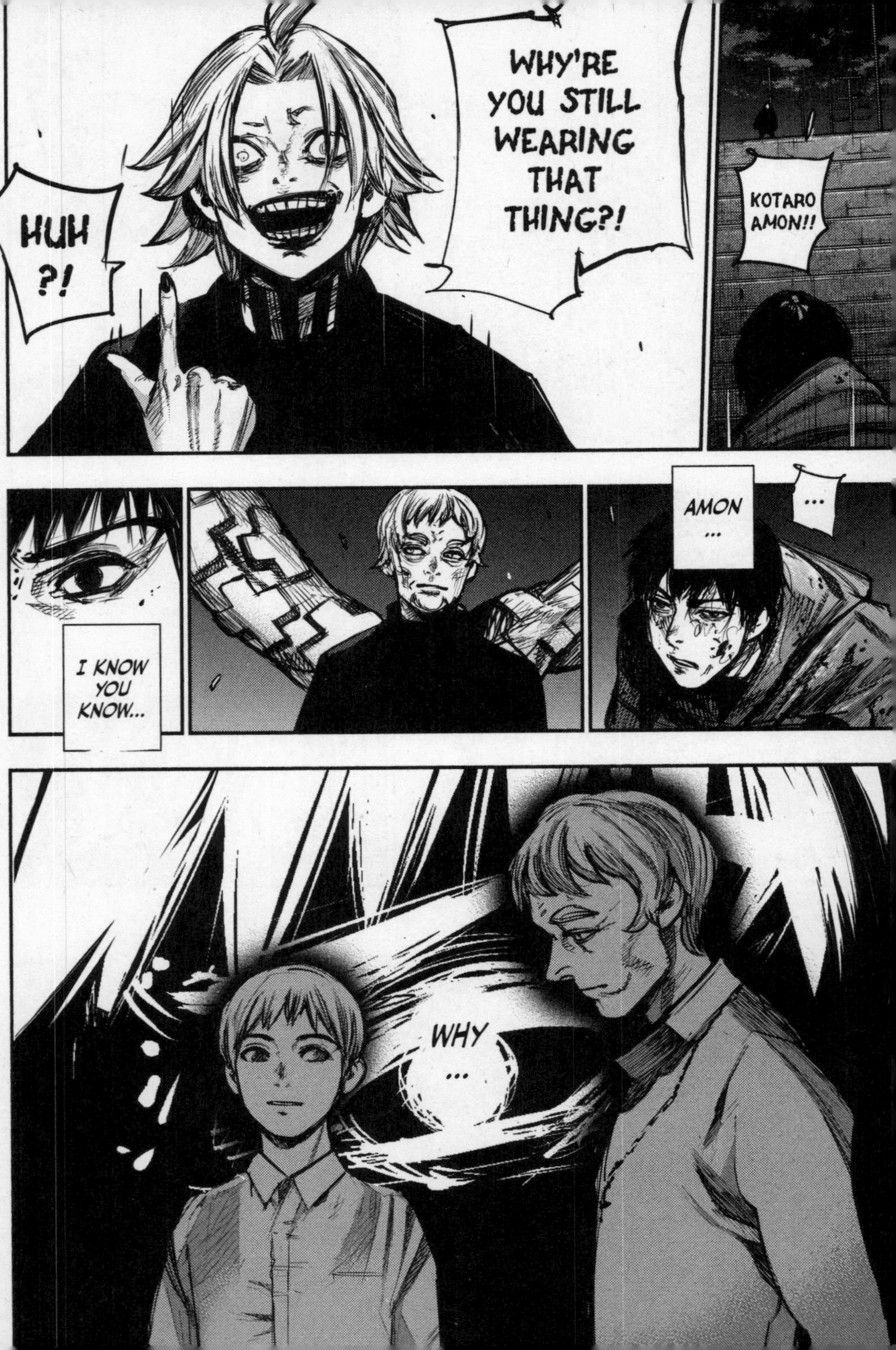
KOTARO AMON!!
WHY'RE YOU STILL WEARING THAT THING?!
HUH ?!
...
AMON ...
I KNOW YOU KNOW...
WHY ...

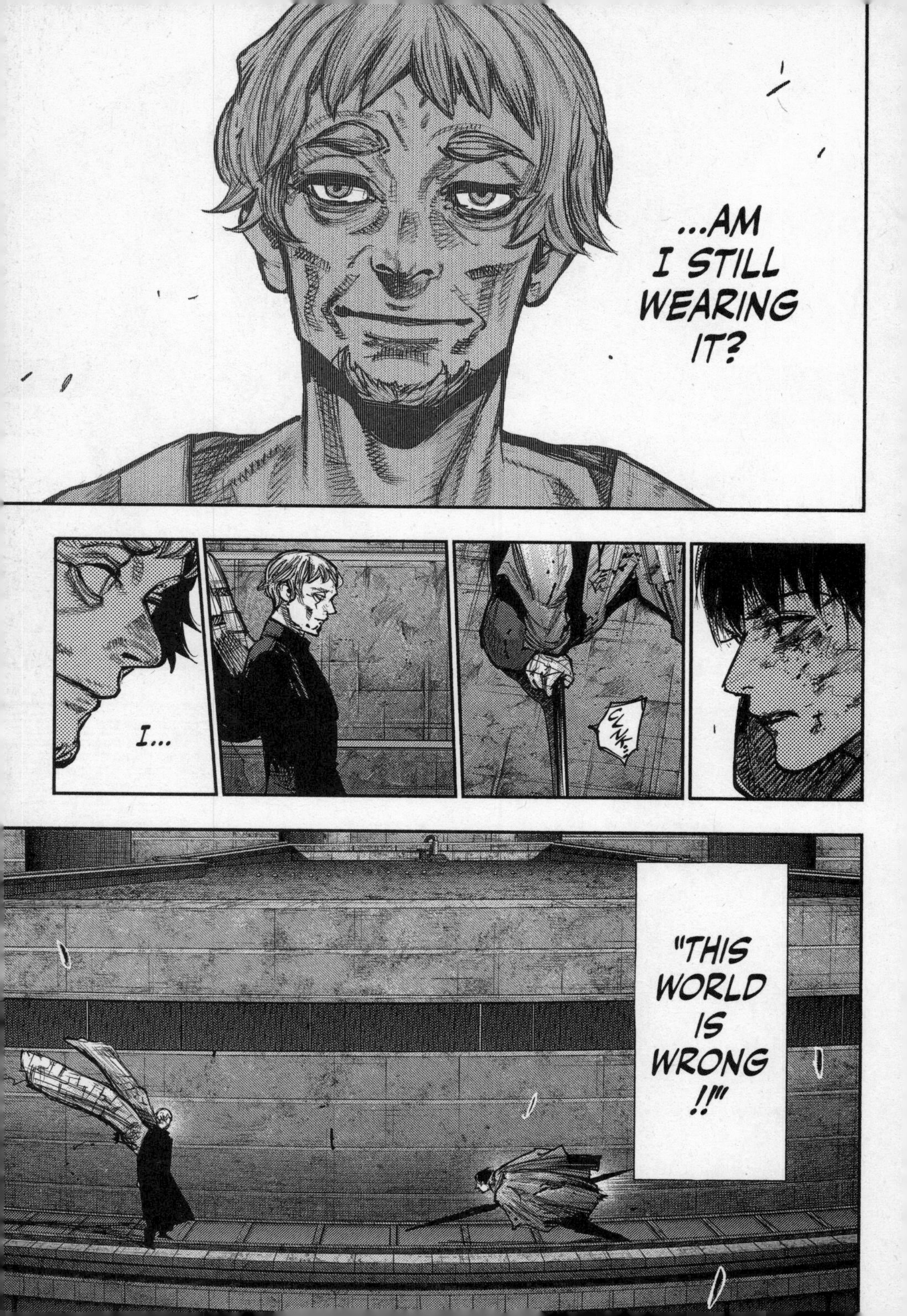
...AM I STILL WEARING IT?
CLINK...
I...
"THIS WORLD IS WRONG!!"

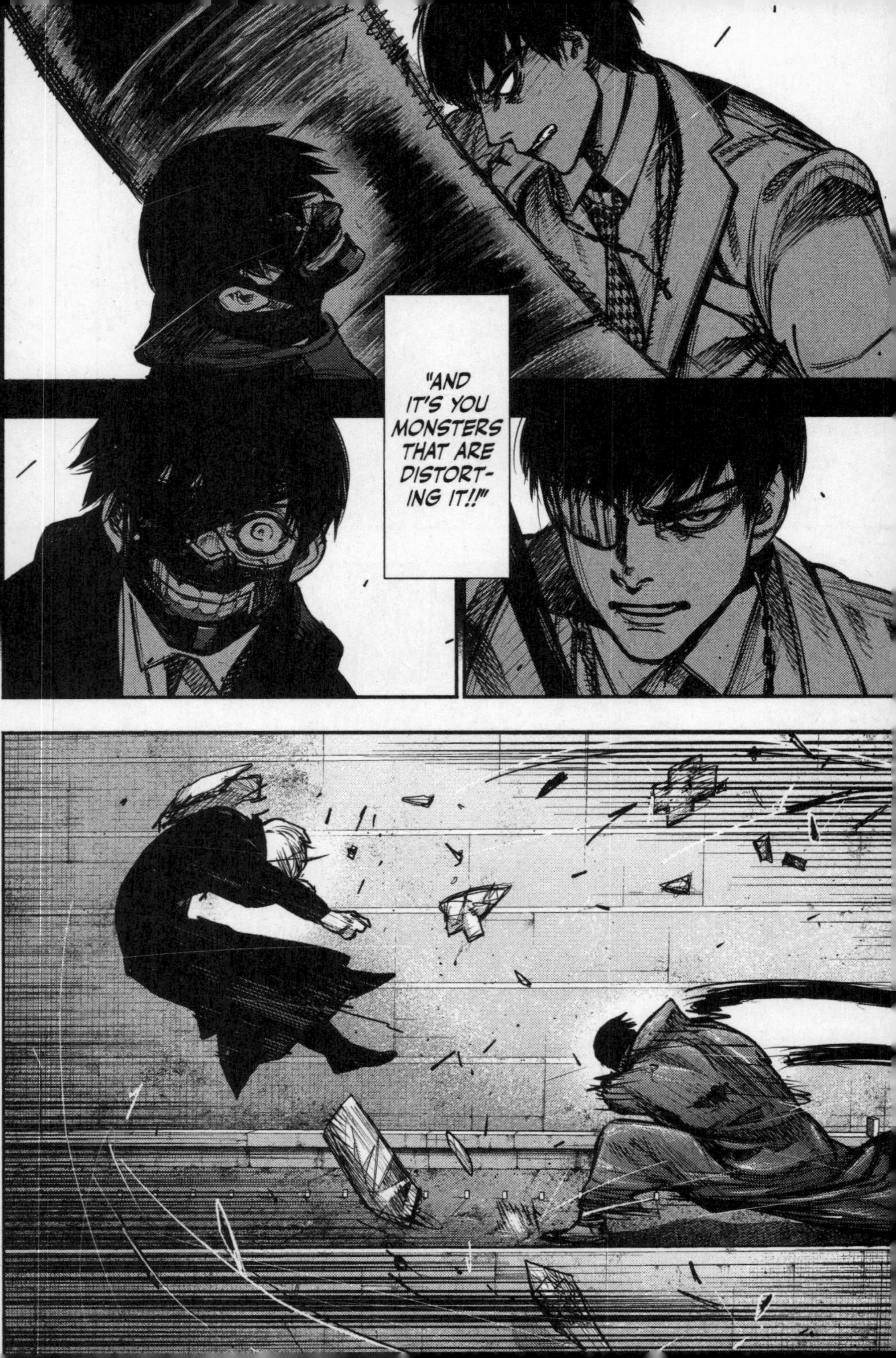
"AND IT'S YOU MONSTERS THAT ARE DISTORT-ING IT!!"

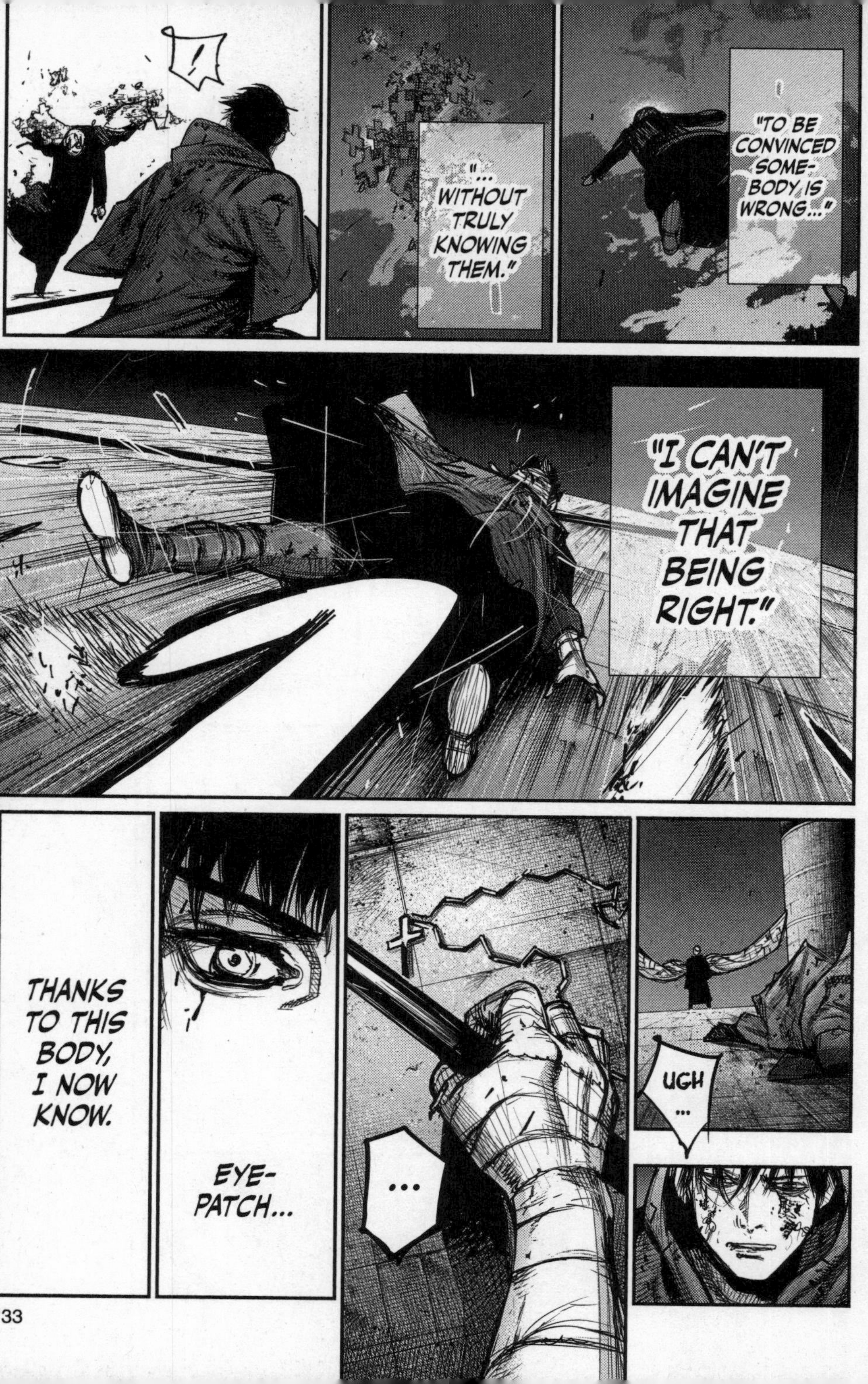

"TO BE CONVINCED SOMEBODY IS WRONG..."
"...WITHOUT TRULY KNOWING THEM."
!
"I CAN'T IMAGINE THAT BEING RIGHT."
UGH...
...
EYE-PATCH...
THANKS TO THIS BODY, I NOW KNOW.

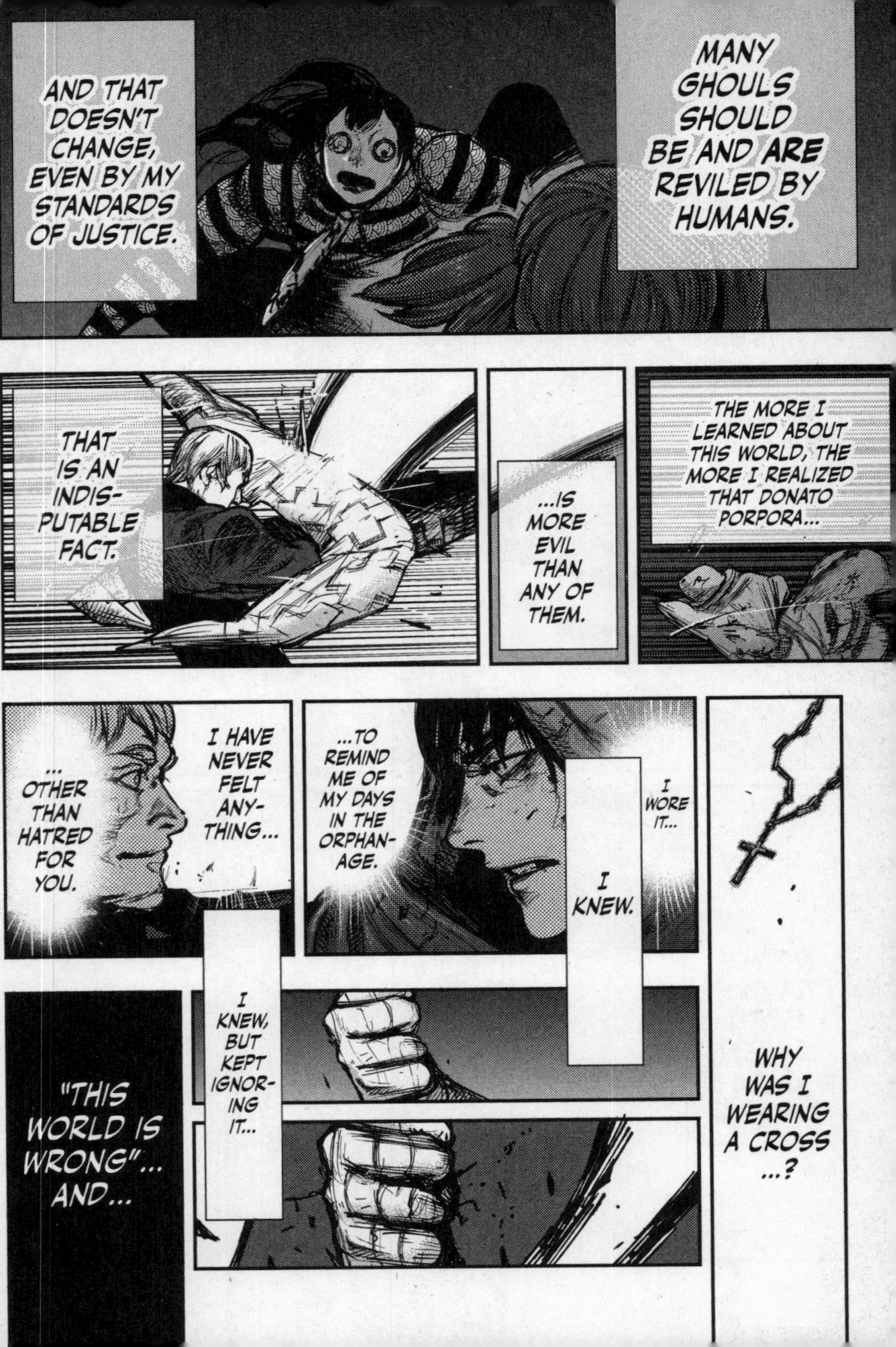
MANY GHOULS SHOULD BE AND ARE REVILED BY HUMANS.
AND THAT DOESN'T CHANGE, EVEN BY MY STANDARDS OF JUSTICE.
THE MORE I LEARNED ABOUT THIS WORLD, THE MORE I REALIZED THAT DONATO PORPORA...
...IS MORE EVIL THAN ANY OF THEM.
THAT IS AN INDIS-PUTABLE FACT.
WHY WAS I WEARING A CROSS ...?
I WORE IT...
...TO REMIND ME OF MY DAYS IN THE ORPHAN-AGE.
I KNEW.
I HAVE NEVER FELT ANY-THING...
...OTHER THAN HATRED FOR YOU.
I KNEW, BUT KEPT IGNOR-ING IT...
"THIS WORLD IS WRONG"... AND...

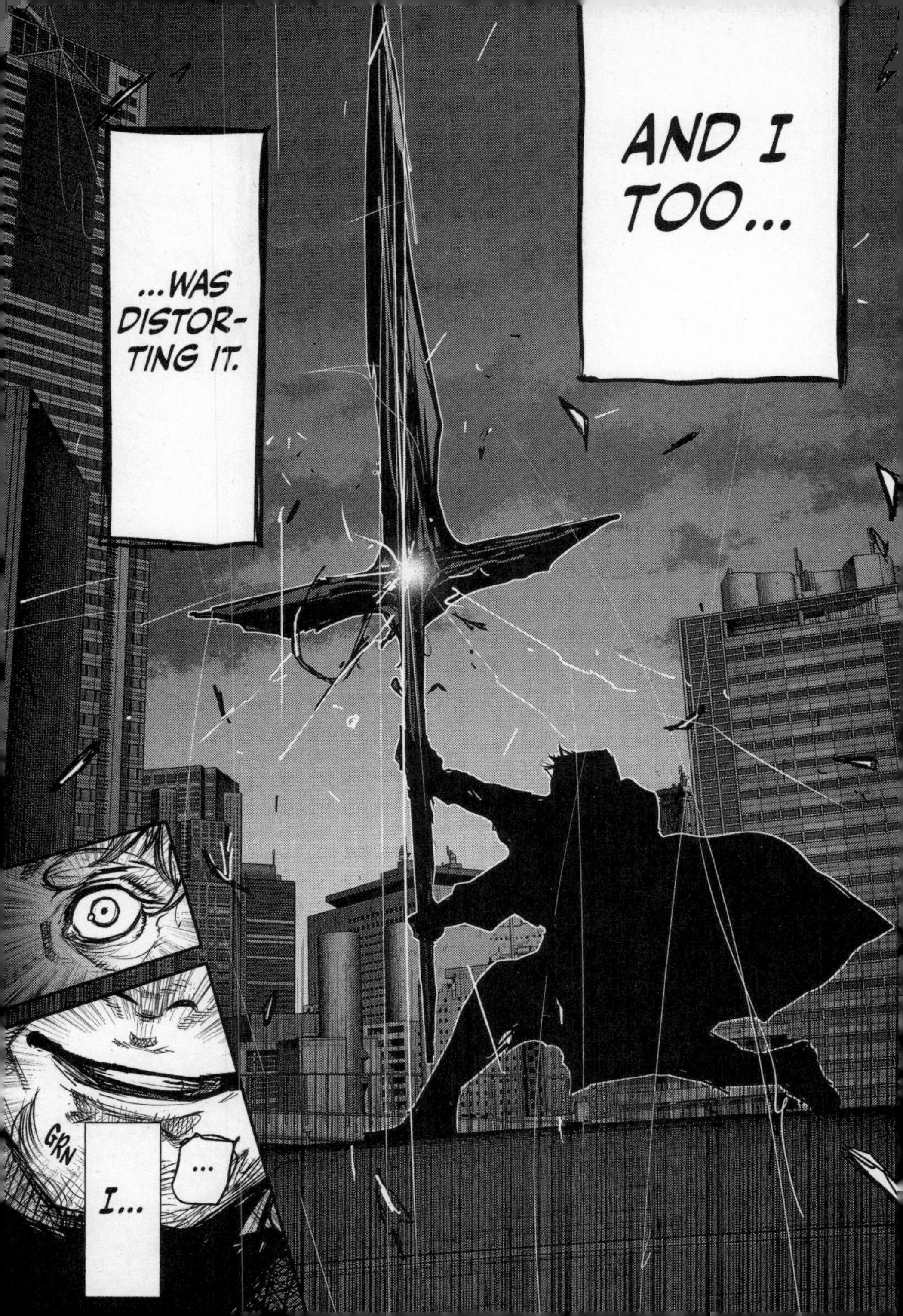
AND I TOO...
...WAS DISTORTING IT.
GRN
...
I...

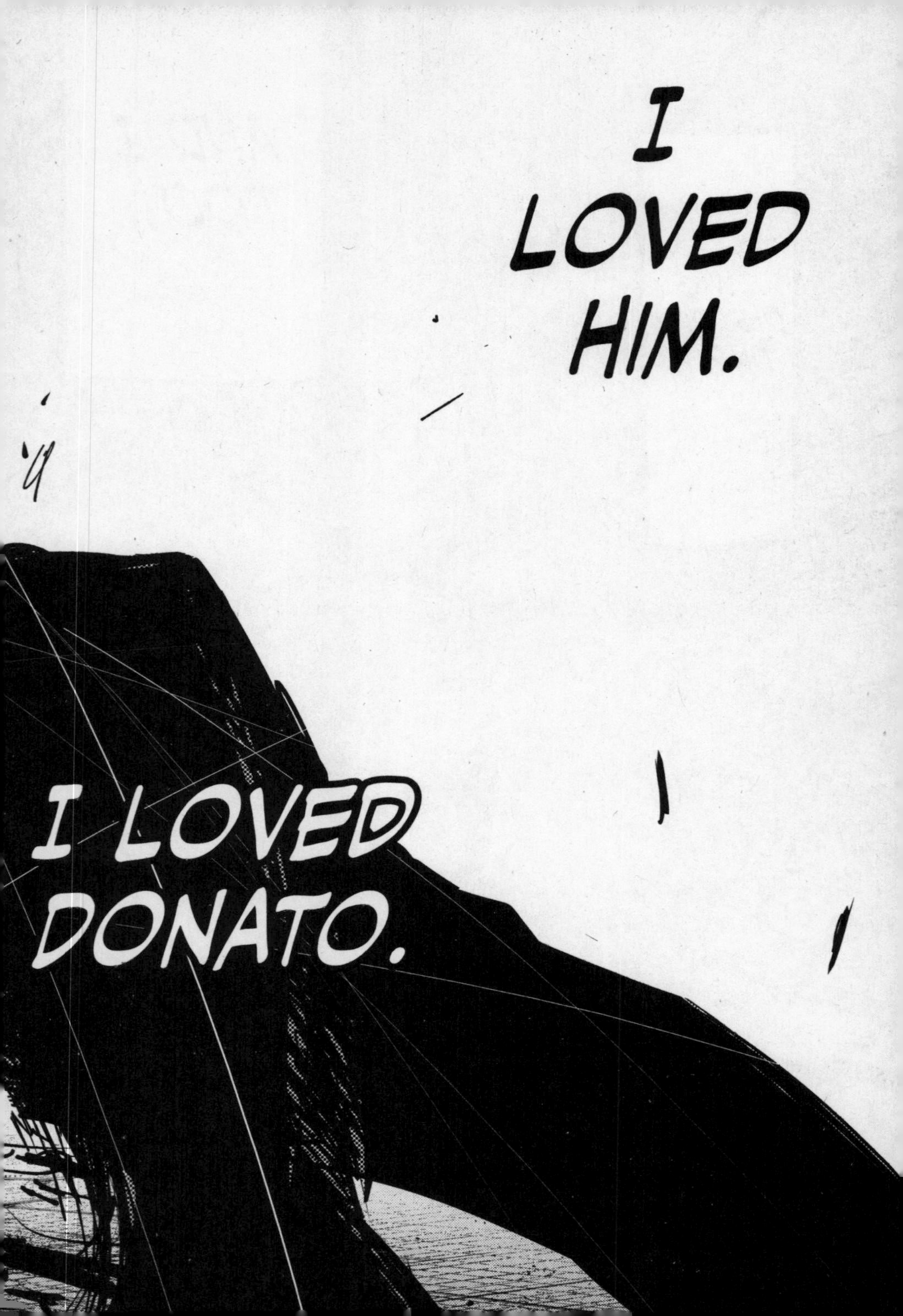
I LOVED HIM.
I LOVED DONATO.

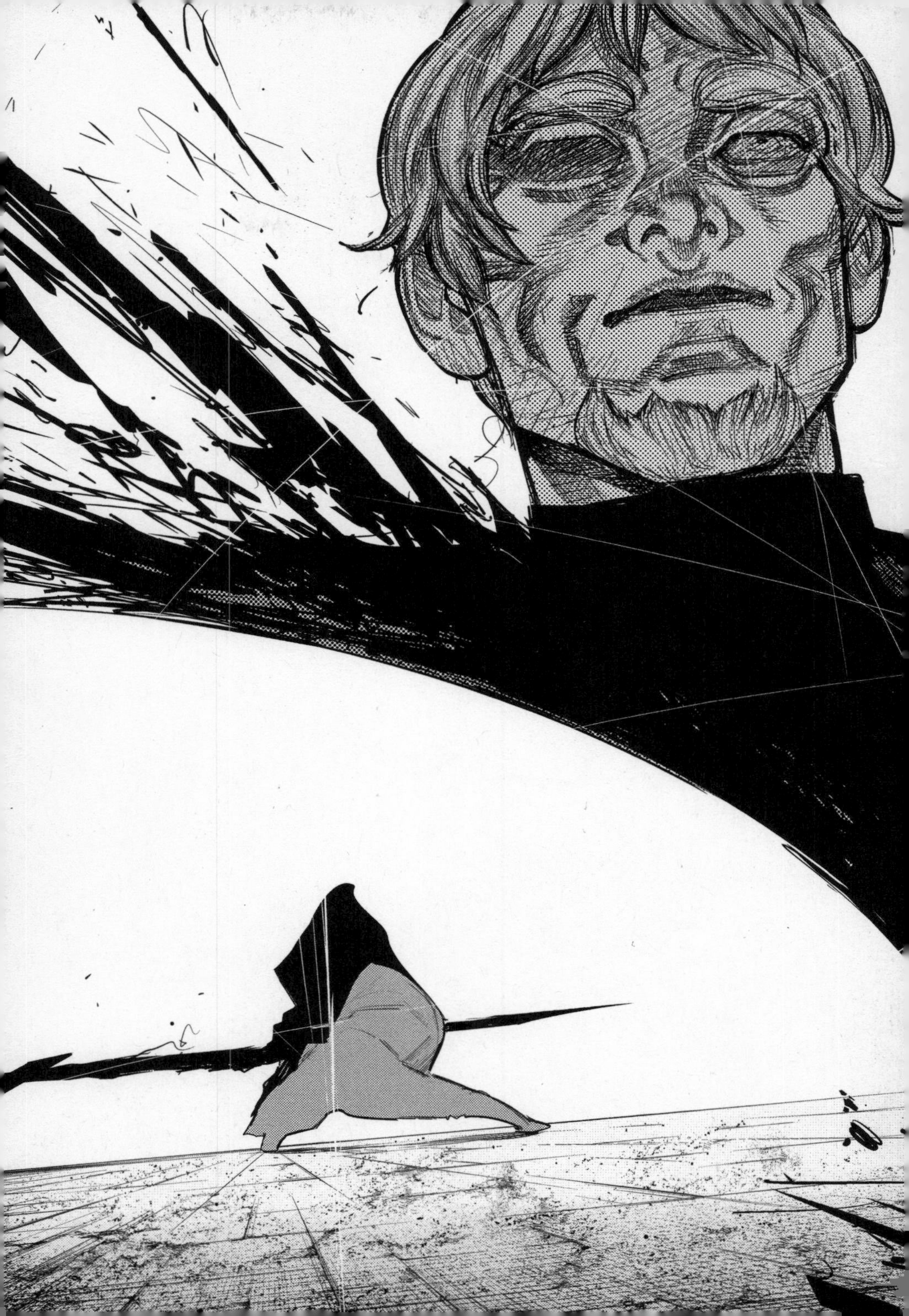

TOKYO GHOUL:re

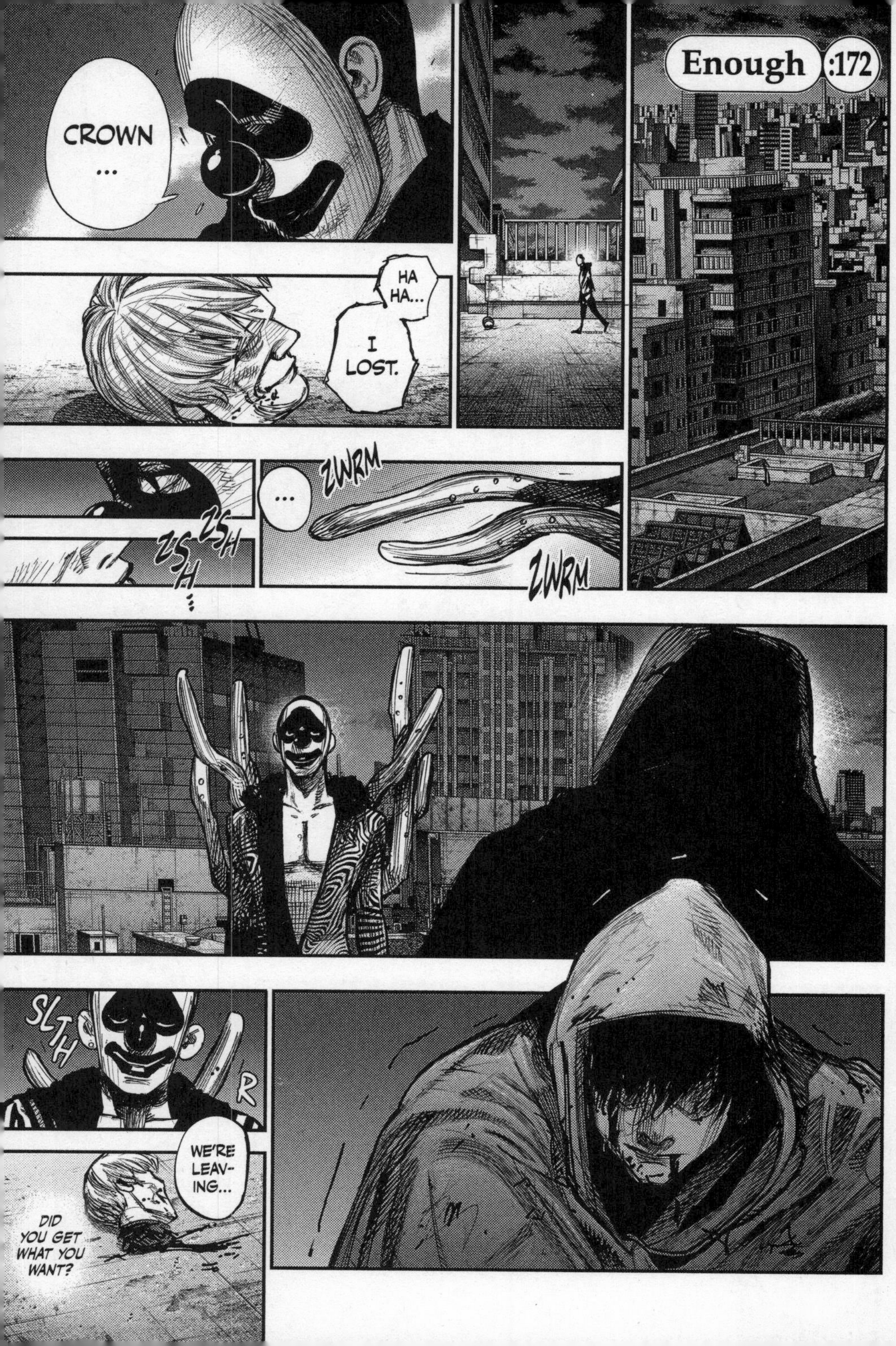

Enough :172
CROWN ...
HA HA...
I LOST.
...
ZWRM
ZWRM
ZSH
ZSH
SLTH
R
WE'RE LEAVING...
DID YOU GET WHAT YOU WANT?

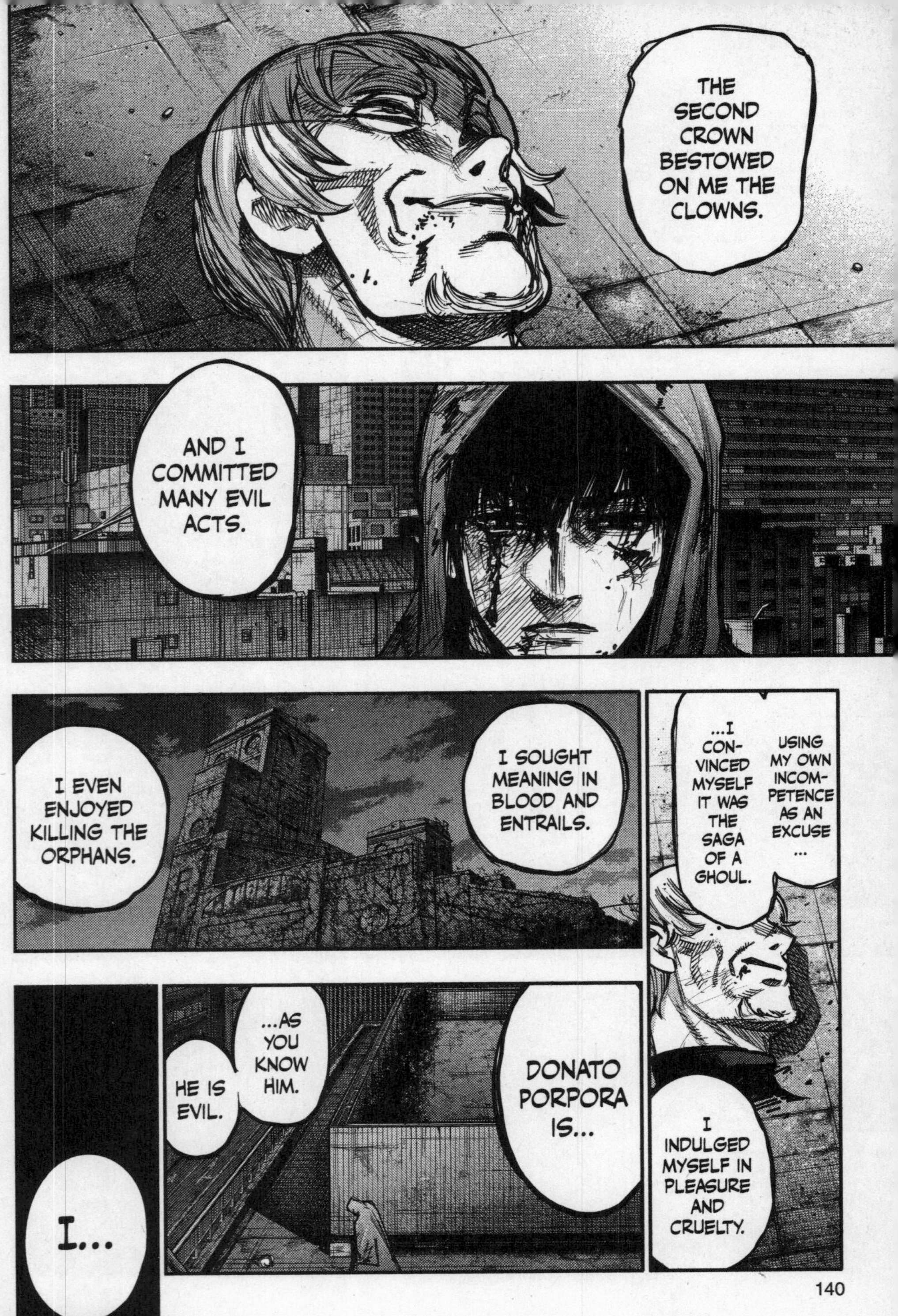
THE SECOND CROWN BESTOWED ON ME THE CLOWNS.
AND I COMMITTED MANY EVIL ACTS.
USING MY OWN INCOMPETENCE AS AN EXCUSE ...
...I CONVINCED MYSELF IT WAS THE SAGA OF A GHOUL.
I INDULGED MYSELF IN PLEASURE AND CRUELTY.
I SOUGHT MEANING IN BLOOD AND ENTRAILS.
I EVEN ENJOYED KILLING THE ORPHANS.
DONATO PORPORA IS...
...AS YOU KNOW HIM.
HE IS EVIL.
I...

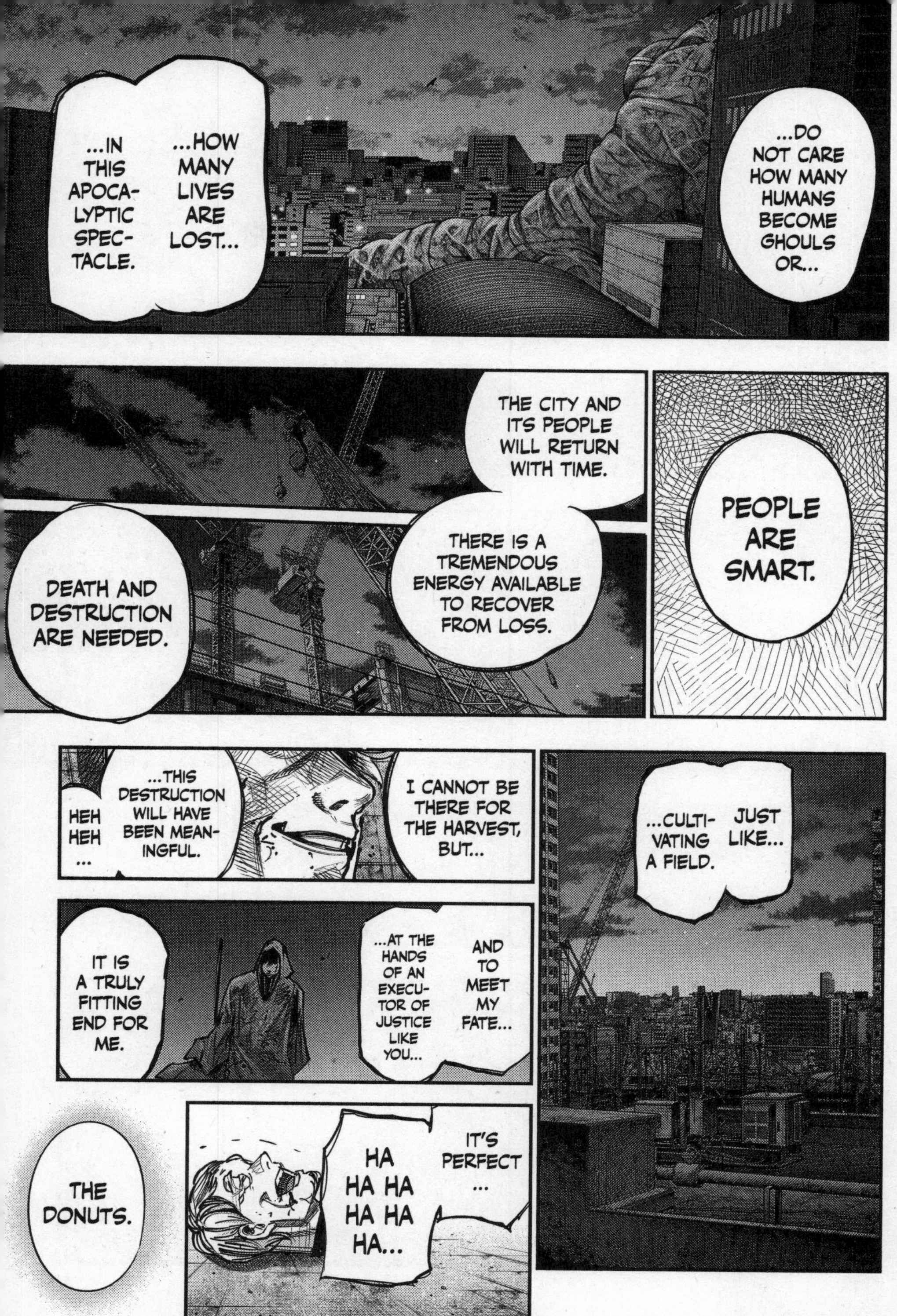
...DO NOT CARE HOW MANY HUMANS BECOME GHOULS OR...
...HOW MANY LIVES ARE LOST...
...IN THIS APOCALYPTIC SPECTACLE.
PEOPLE ARE SMART.
THE CITY AND ITS PEOPLE WILL RETURN WITH TIME.
THERE IS A TREMENDOUS ENERGY AVAILABLE TO RECOVER FROM LOSS.
DEATH AND DESTRUCTION ARE NEEDED.
JUST LIKE...
...CULTIVATING A FIELD.
I CANNOT BE THERE FOR THE HARVEST, BUT...
...THIS DESTRUCTION WILL HAVE BEEN MEANINGFUL.
HEH HEH ...
AND TO MEET MY FATE...
...AT THE HANDS OF AN EXECUTOR OF JUSTICE LIKE YOU...
IT IS A TRULY FITTING END FOR ME.
IT'S PERFECT ...
HA HA HA HA HA HA...
THE DONUTS.

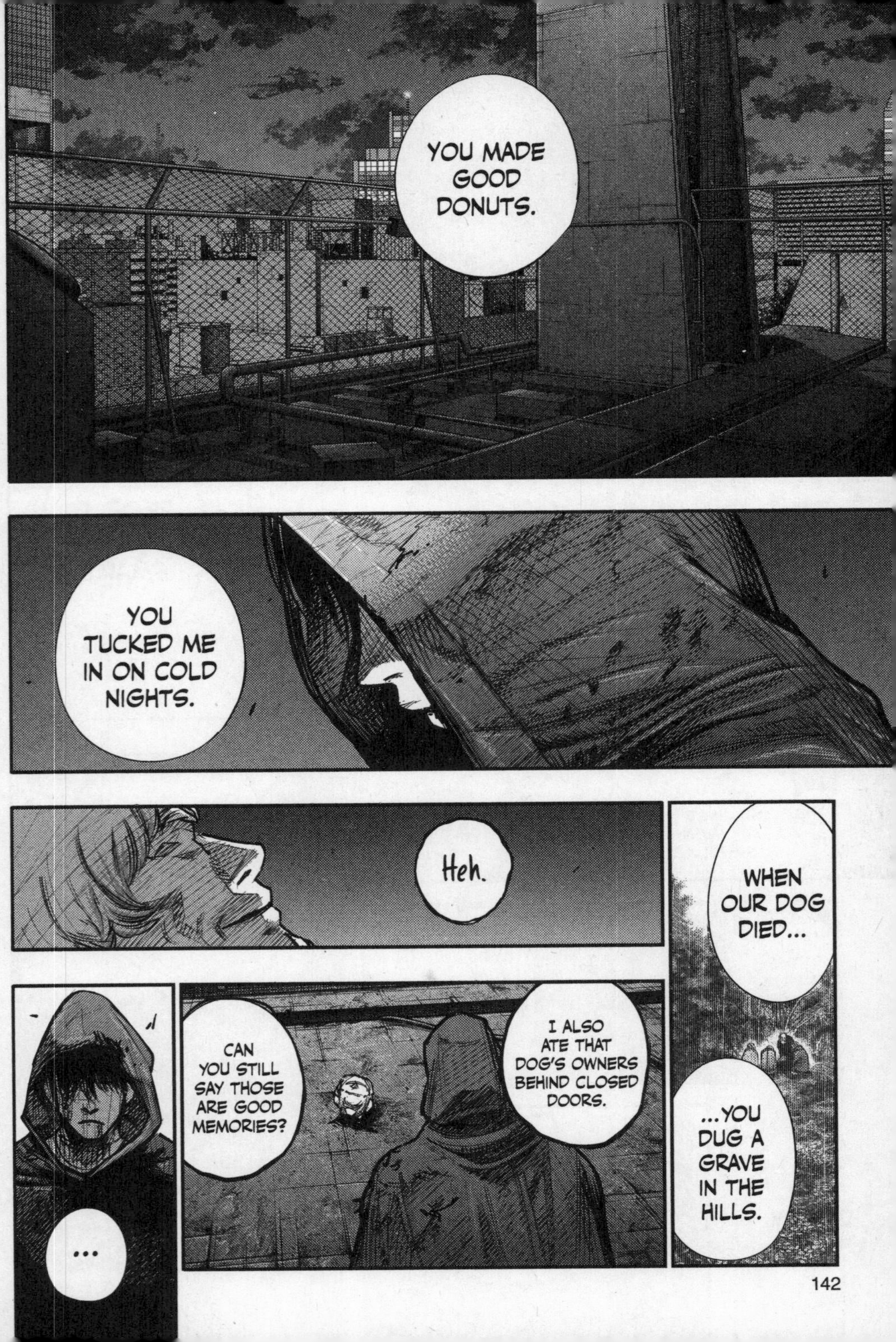
YOU MADE GOOD DONUTS.
YOU TUCKED ME IN ON COLD NIGHTS.
WHEN OUR DOG DIED...
...YOU DUG A GRAVE IN THE HILLS.
Heh.
I ALSO ATE THAT DOG'S OWNERS BEHIND CLOSED DOORS.
CAN YOU STILL SAY THOSE ARE GOOD MEMORIES?
...

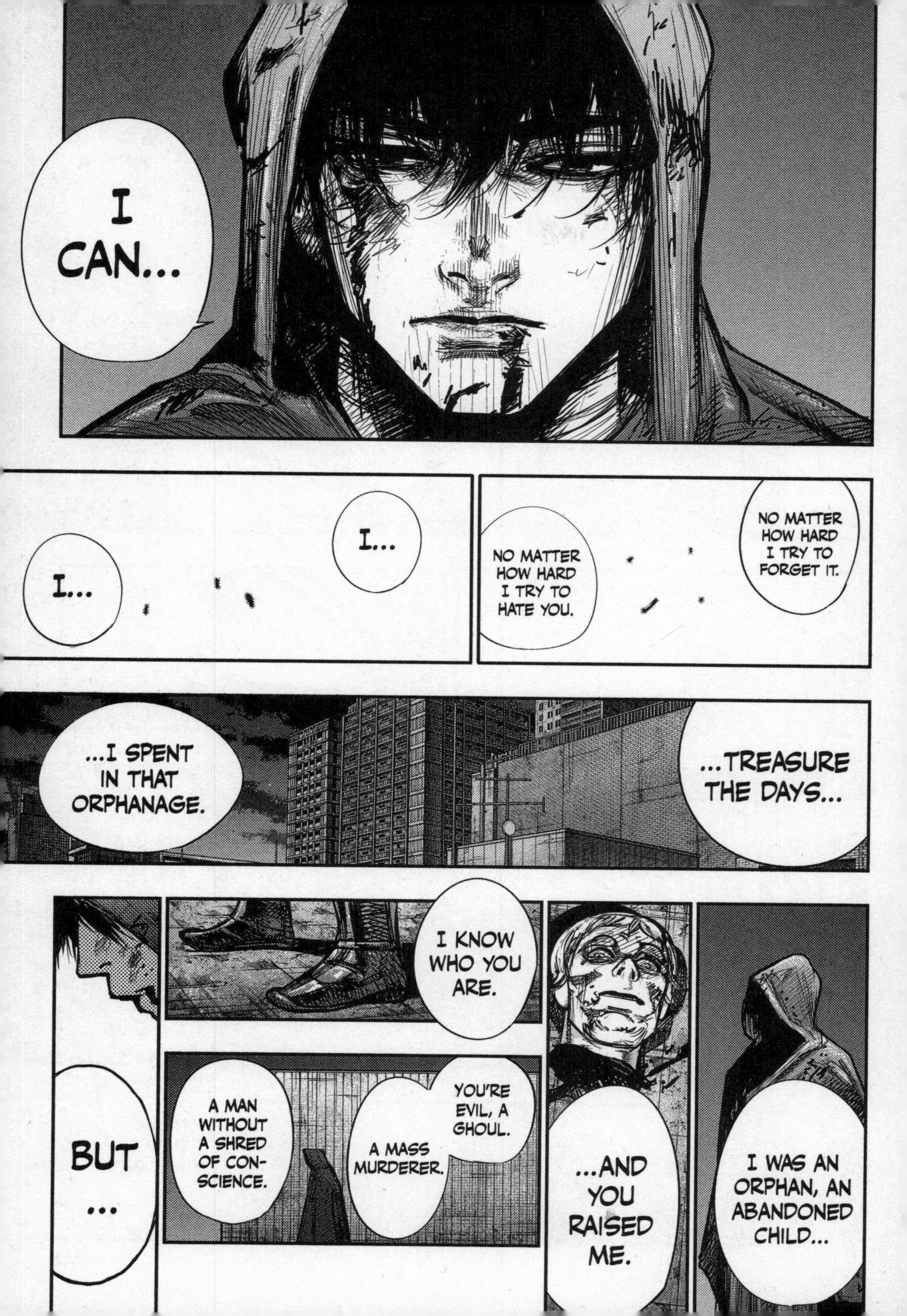
I CAN...
NO MATTER HOW HARD I TRY TO FORGET IT.
NO MATTER HOW HARD I TRY TO HATE YOU.
I...
I...
...TREASURE THE DAYS...
...I SPENT IN THAT ORPHANAGE.
I WAS AN ORPHAN, AN ABANDONED CHILD...
...AND YOU RAISED ME.
I KNOW WHO YOU ARE.
YOU'RE EVIL, A GHOUL.
A MASS MURDERER.
A MAN WITHOUT A SHRED OF CON-SCIENCE.
BUT ...

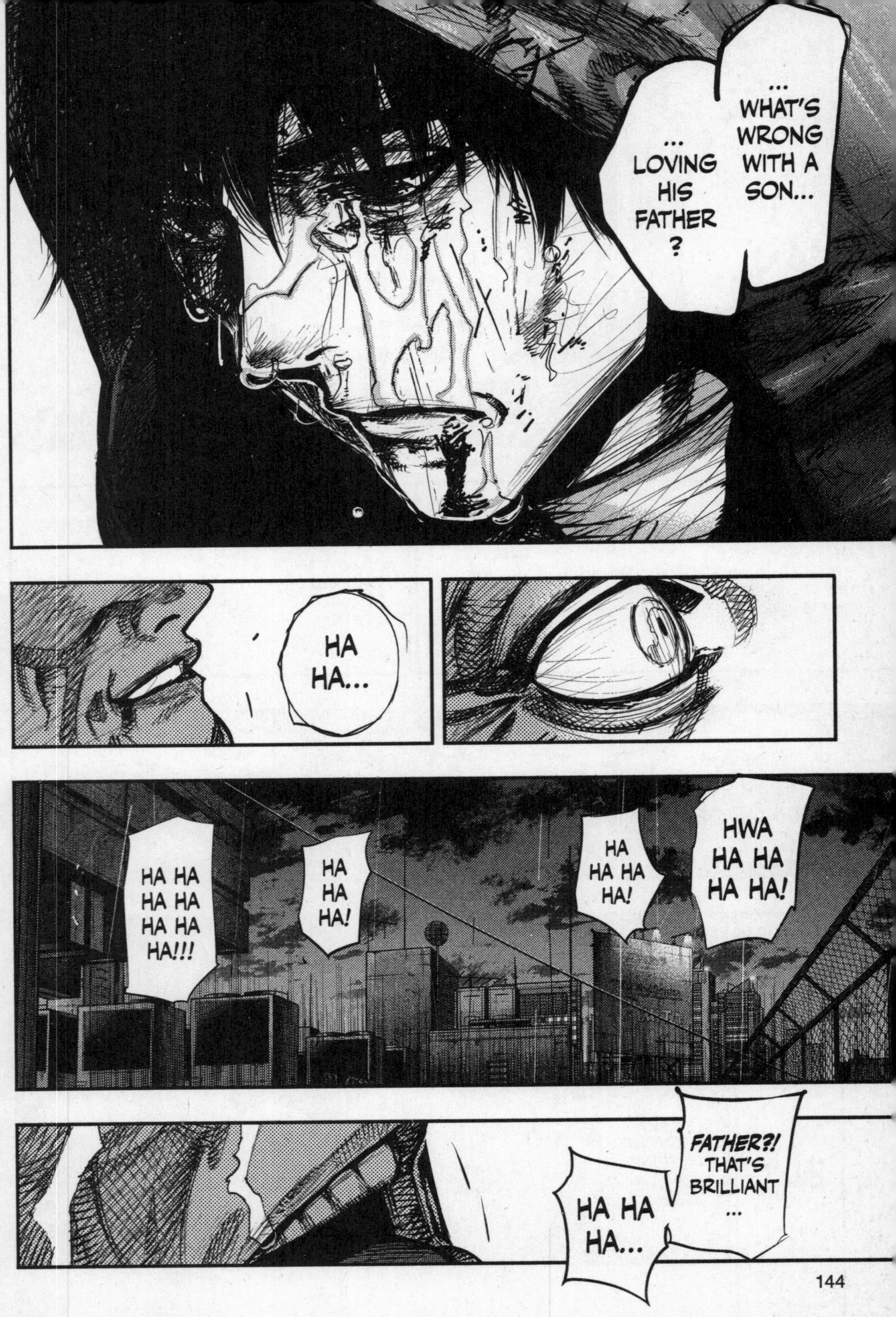
... WHAT'S WRONG WITH A SON...
... LOVING HIS FATHER ?
HA HA...
HWA HA HA HA HA!
HA HA HA HA!
HA HA HA!
HA HA HA HA HA HA HA!!!
FATHER?! THAT'S BRILLIANT ...
HA HA HA...

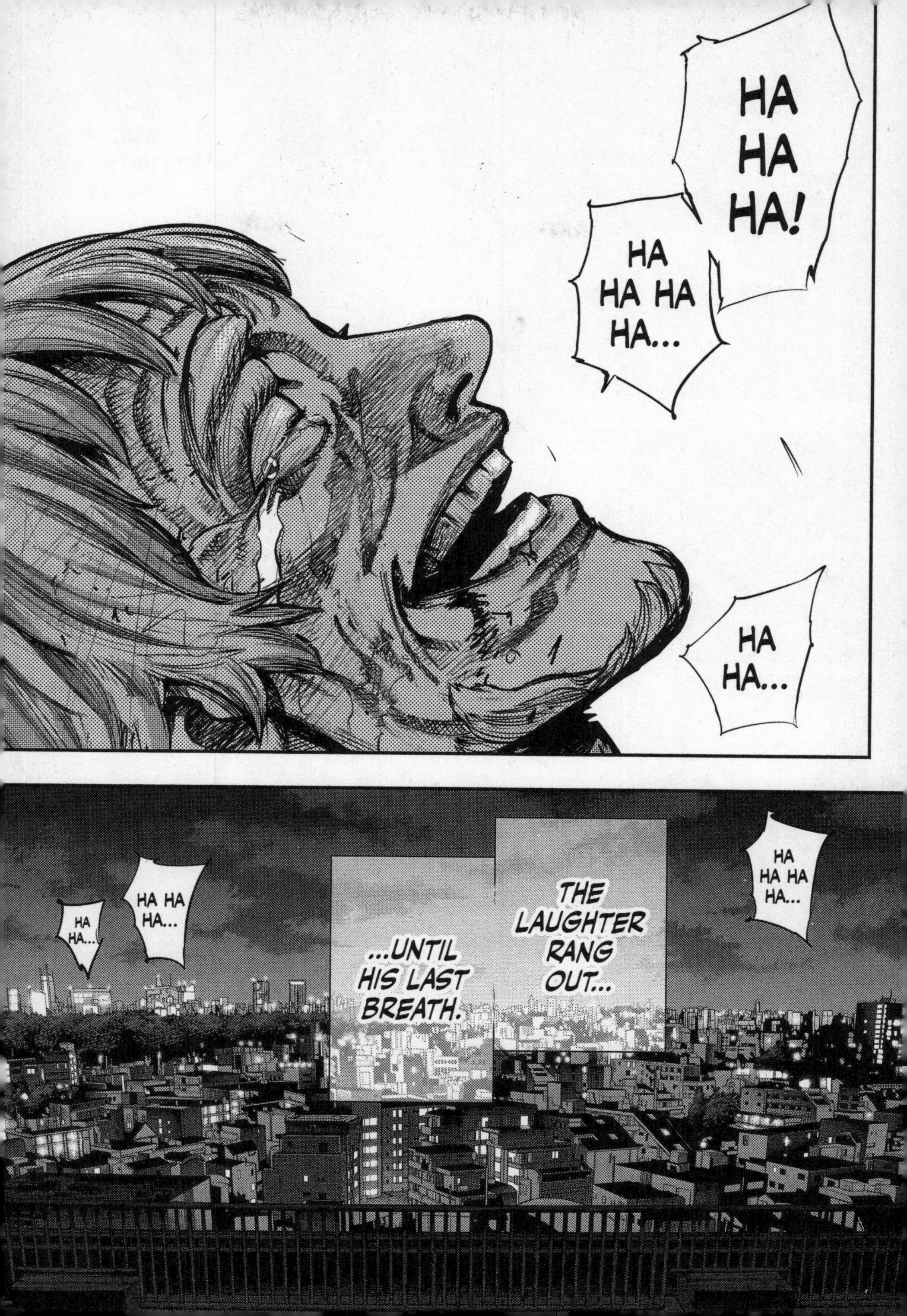
HA HA HA!
HA HA HA HA...
HA HA...
HA HA HA HA...
THE LAUGHTER RANG OUT...
...UNTIL HIS LAST BREATH.
HA HA HA...
HA HA...

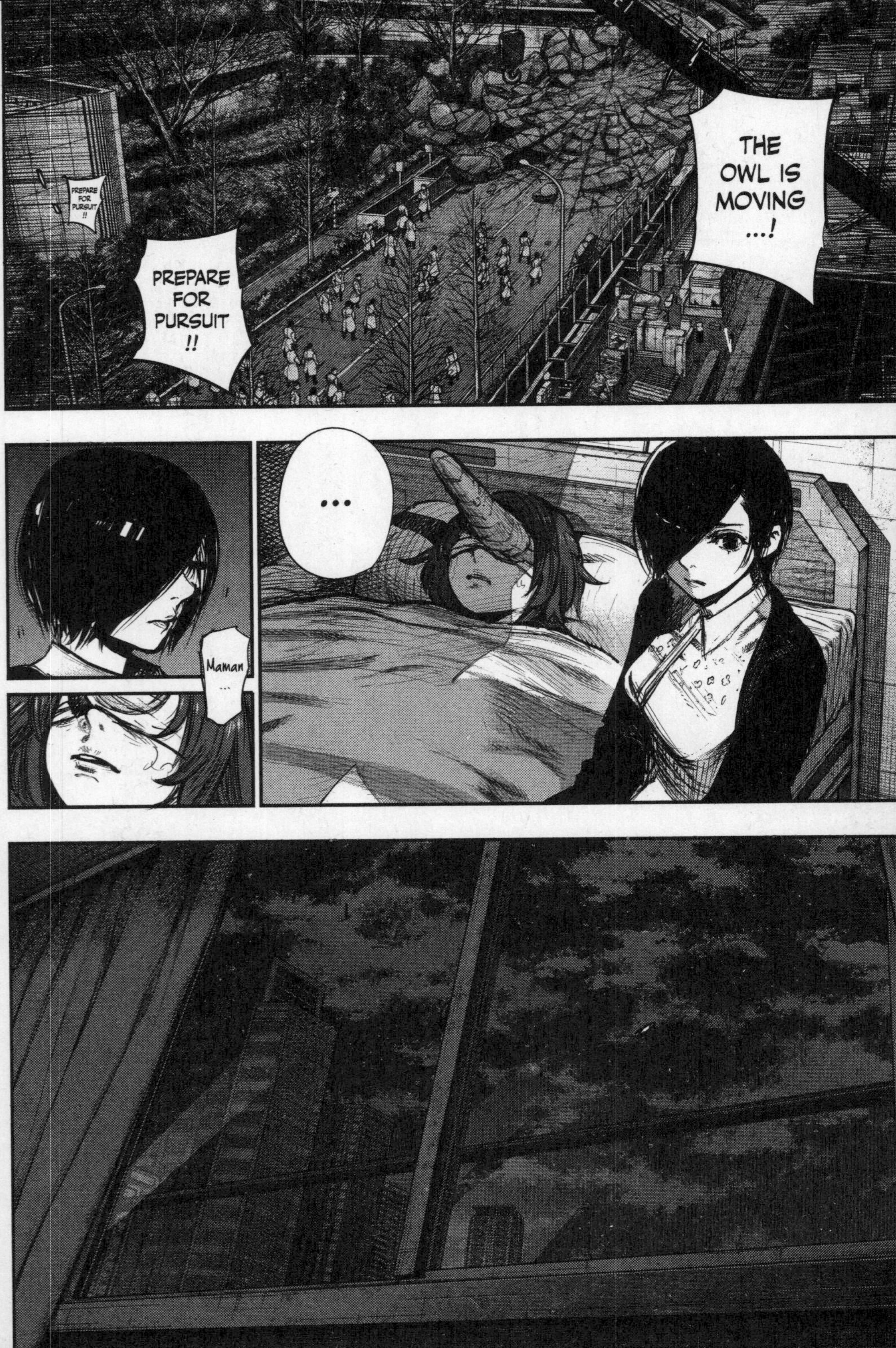
THE OWL IS MOVING ...!
PREPARE FOR PURSUIT !!
PREPARE FOR PURSUIT !!
...
Maman ...

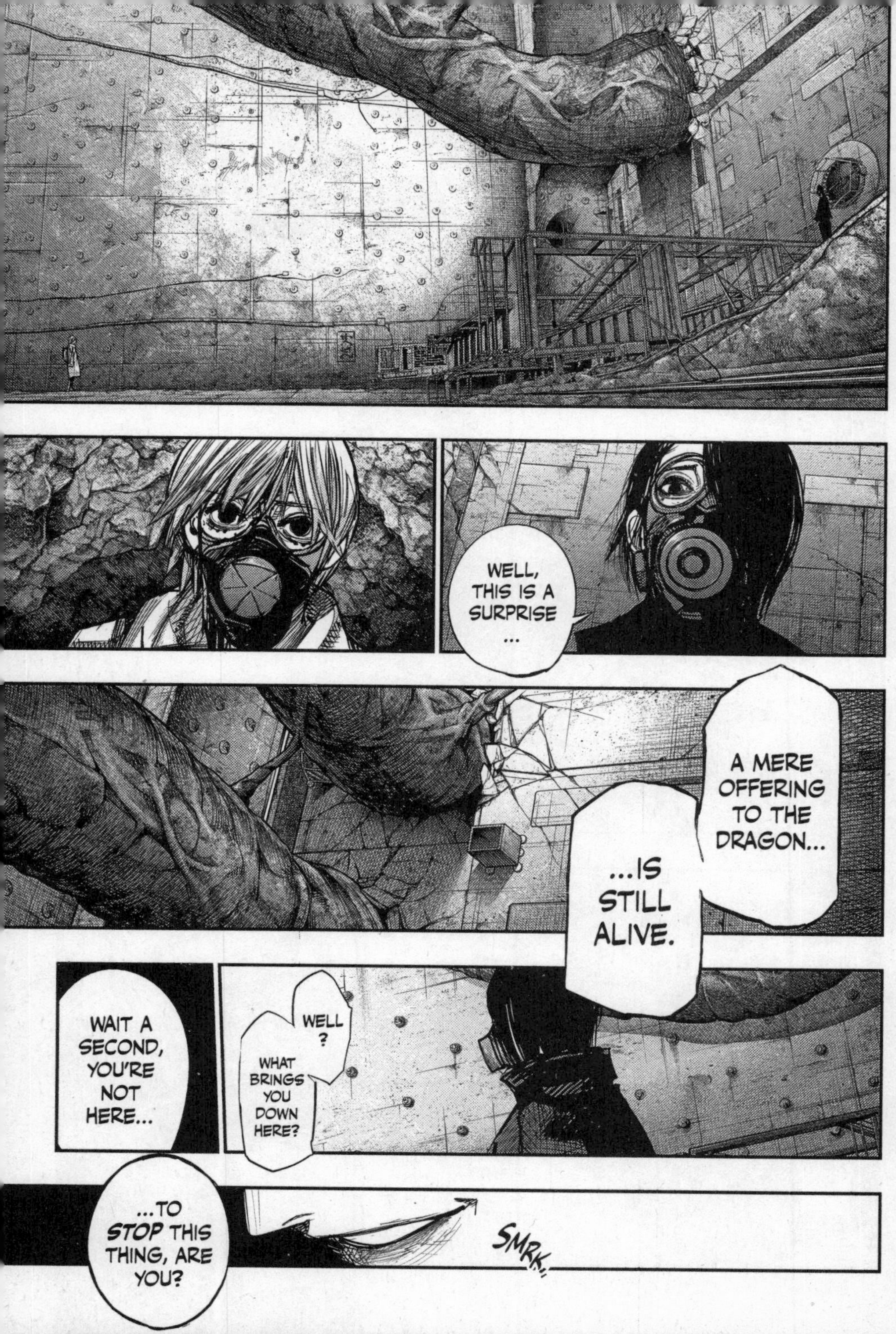

WELL, THIS IS A SURPRISE ...
A MERE OFFERING TO THE DRAGON...
...IS STILL ALIVE.
WELL?
WHAT BRINGS YOU DOWN HERE?
WAIT A SECOND, YOU'RE NOT HERE...
...TO STOP THIS THING, ARE YOU?
SMRK...

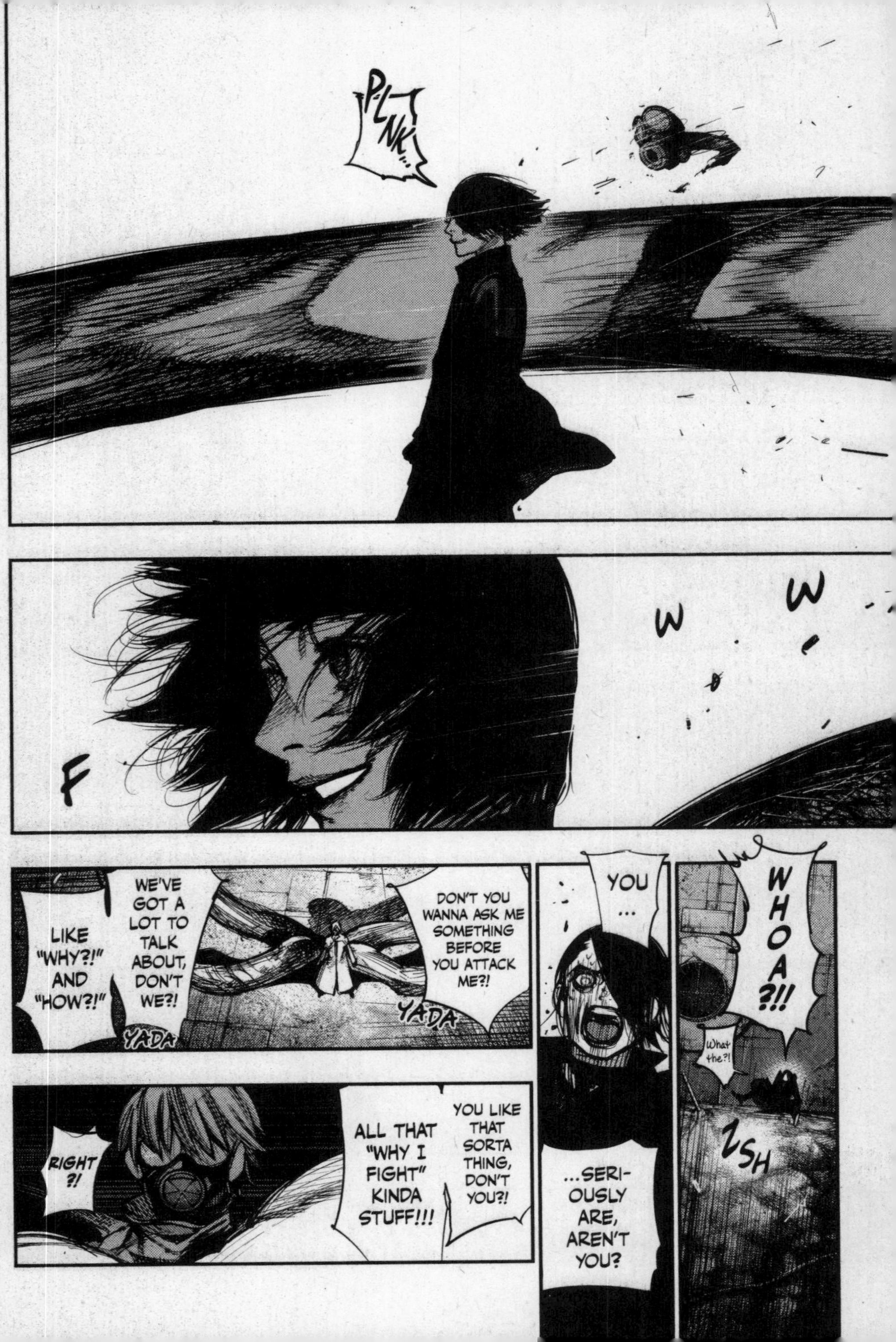
PLINK...
FWW
WHOA?!!
What the?!
ZSH
YOU ...
...SERIOUSLY ARE, AREN'T YOU?
DON'T YOU WANNA ASK ME SOMETHING BEFORE YOU ATTACK ME?!
WE'VE GOT A LOT TO TALK ABOUT, DON'T WE?!
LIKE "WHY?!" AND "HOW?!"
YADA
YADA
YOU LIKE THAT SORTA THING, DON'T YOU?!
ALL THAT "WHY I FIGHT" KINDA STUFF!!!
RIGHT?!

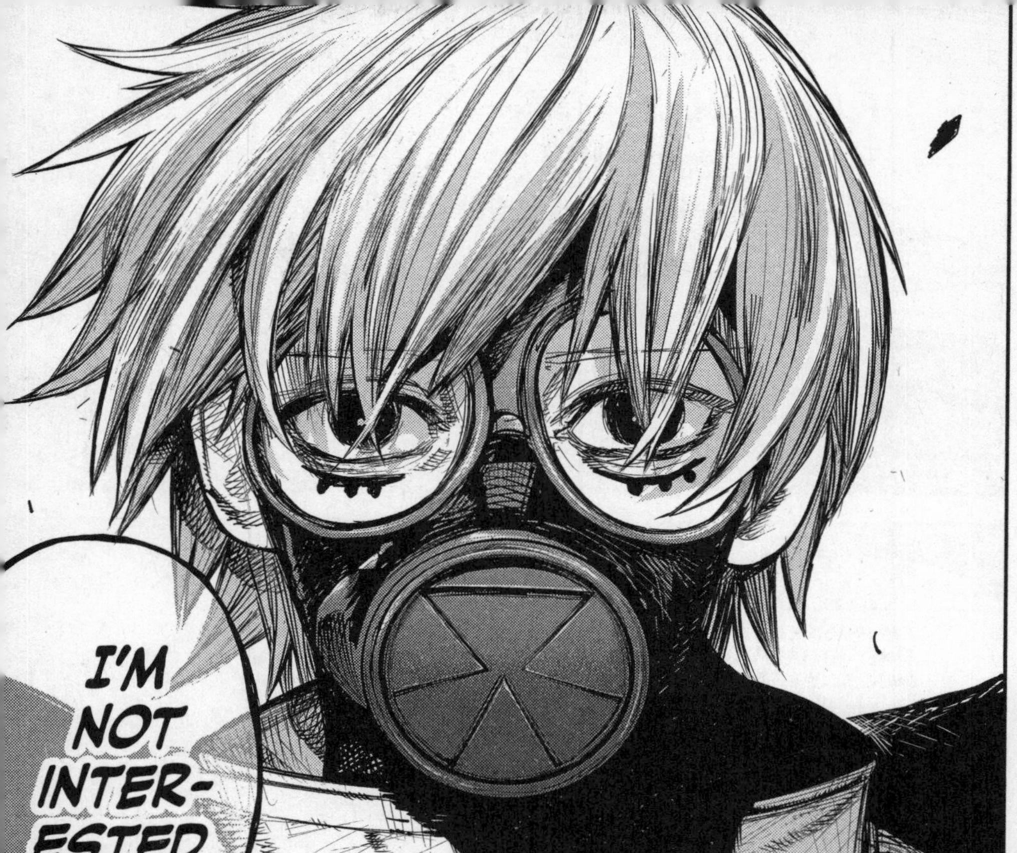
I'M NOT INTER-ESTED.
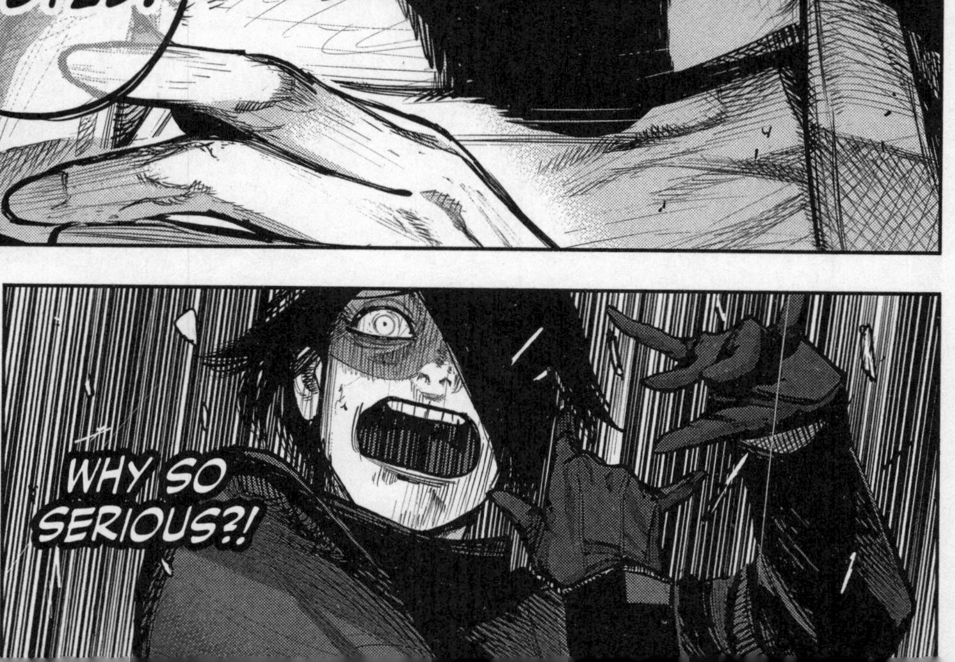
WHY SO SERIOUS?!

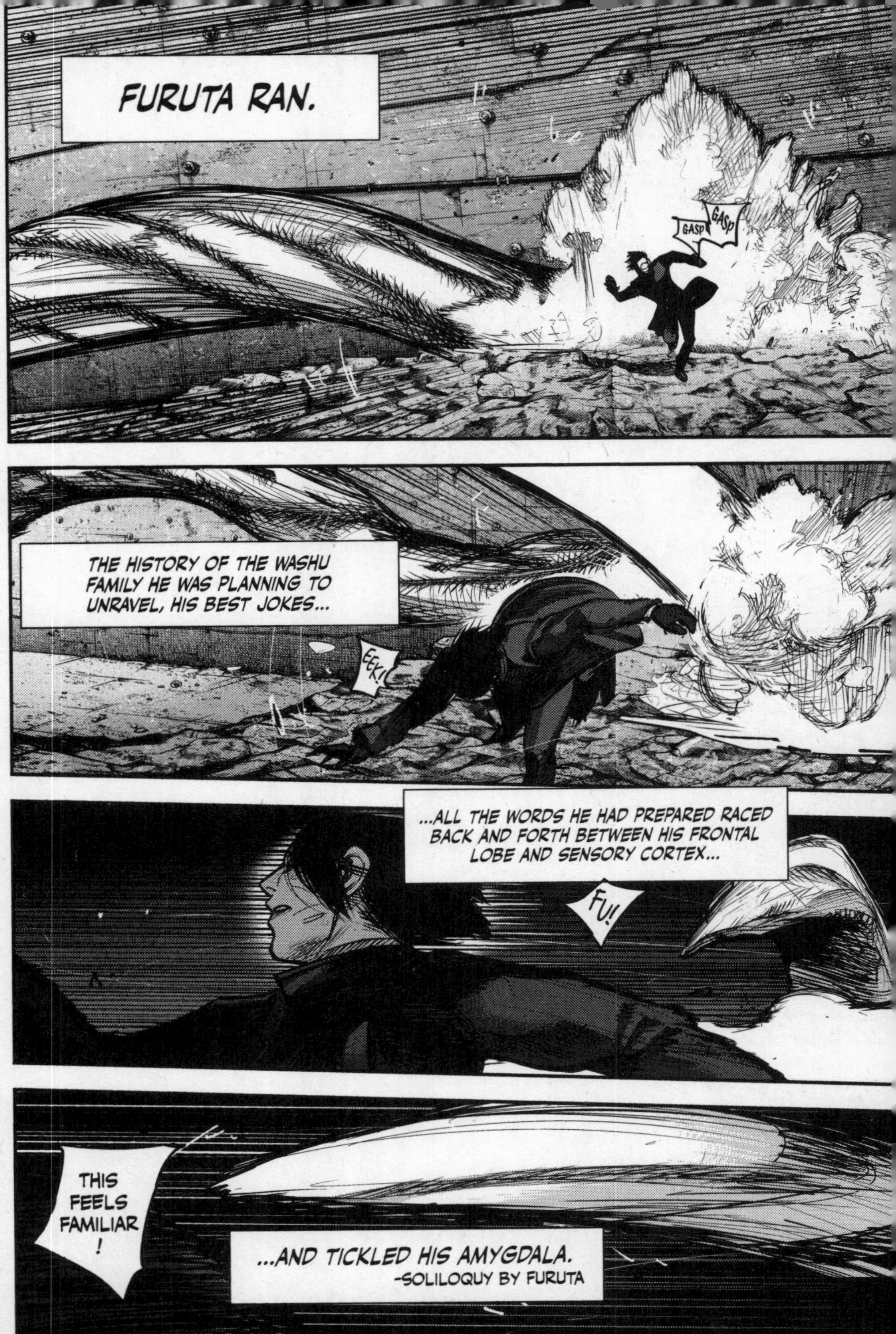
FURUTA RAN.
GASP
GASP
THE HISTORY OF THE WASHU FAMILY HE WAS PLANNING TO UNRAVEL, HIS BEST JOKES...
EEK!
...ALL THE WORDS HE HAD PREPARED RACED BACK AND FORTH BETWEEN HIS FRONTAL LOBE AND SENSORY CORTEX...
FU!
THIS FEELS FAMILIAR!
...AND TICKLED HIS AMYGDALA.
-SOLILOQUY BY FURUTA

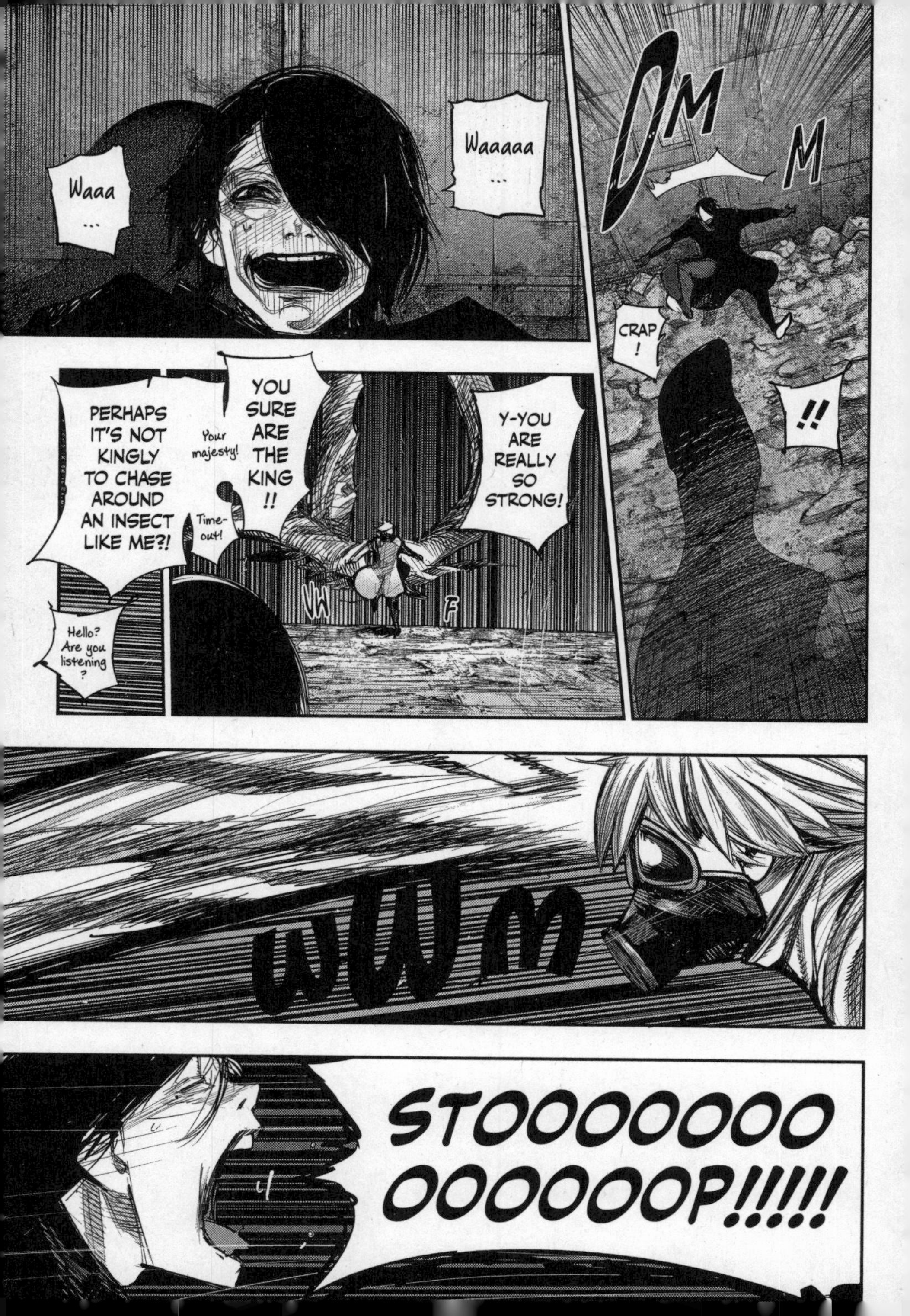
DMM
CRAP!
!!
Waaaaa...
Waaa...
Y-YOU ARE REALLY SO STRONG!
YOU SURE ARE THE KING!!
Your majesty!
PERHAPS IT'S NOT KINGLY TO CHASE AROUND AN INSECT LIKE ME?!
Time-out!
Hello? Are you listening?
WH
F
WWM
STOOOOOOOOOOOOOP!!!!!

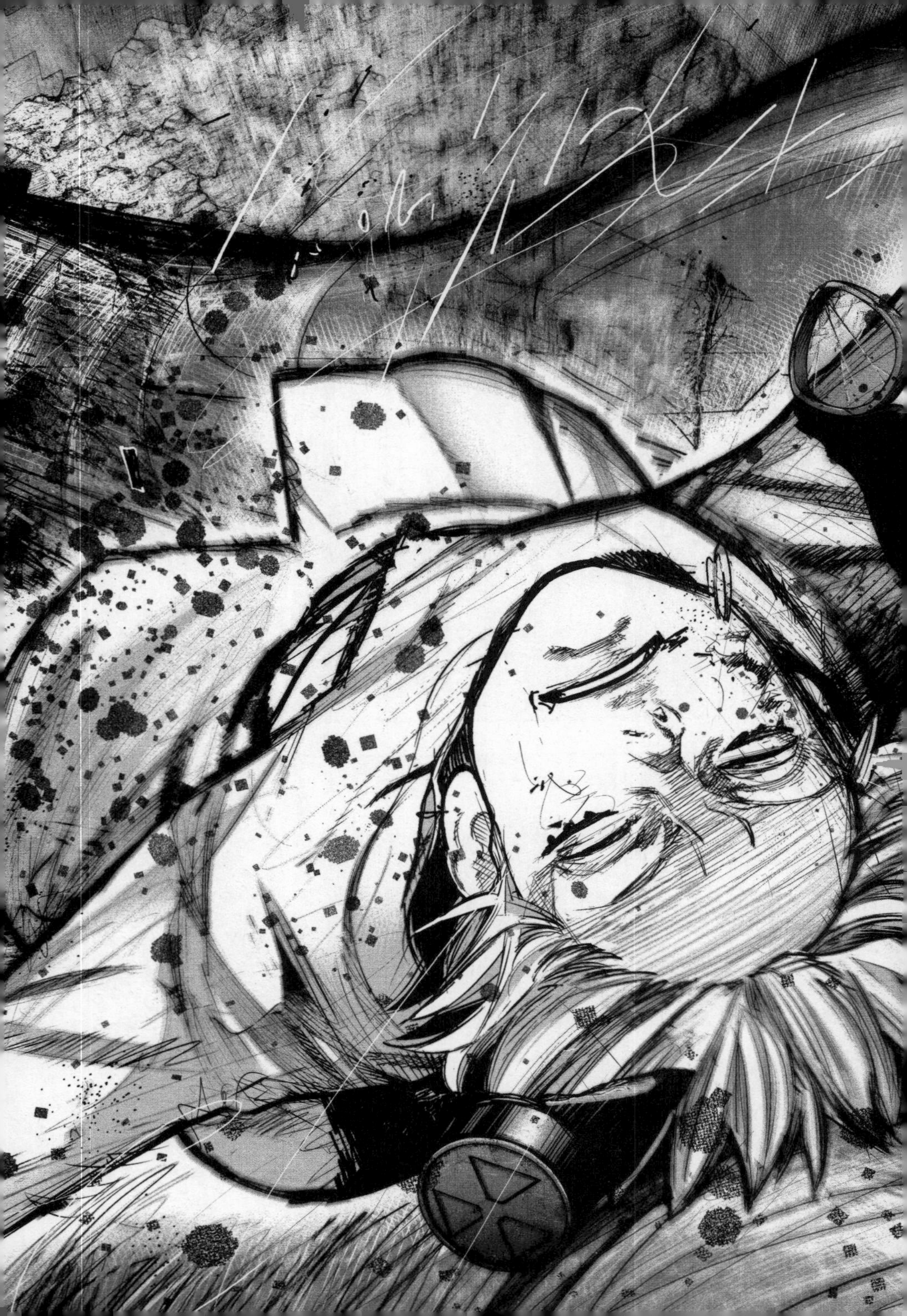

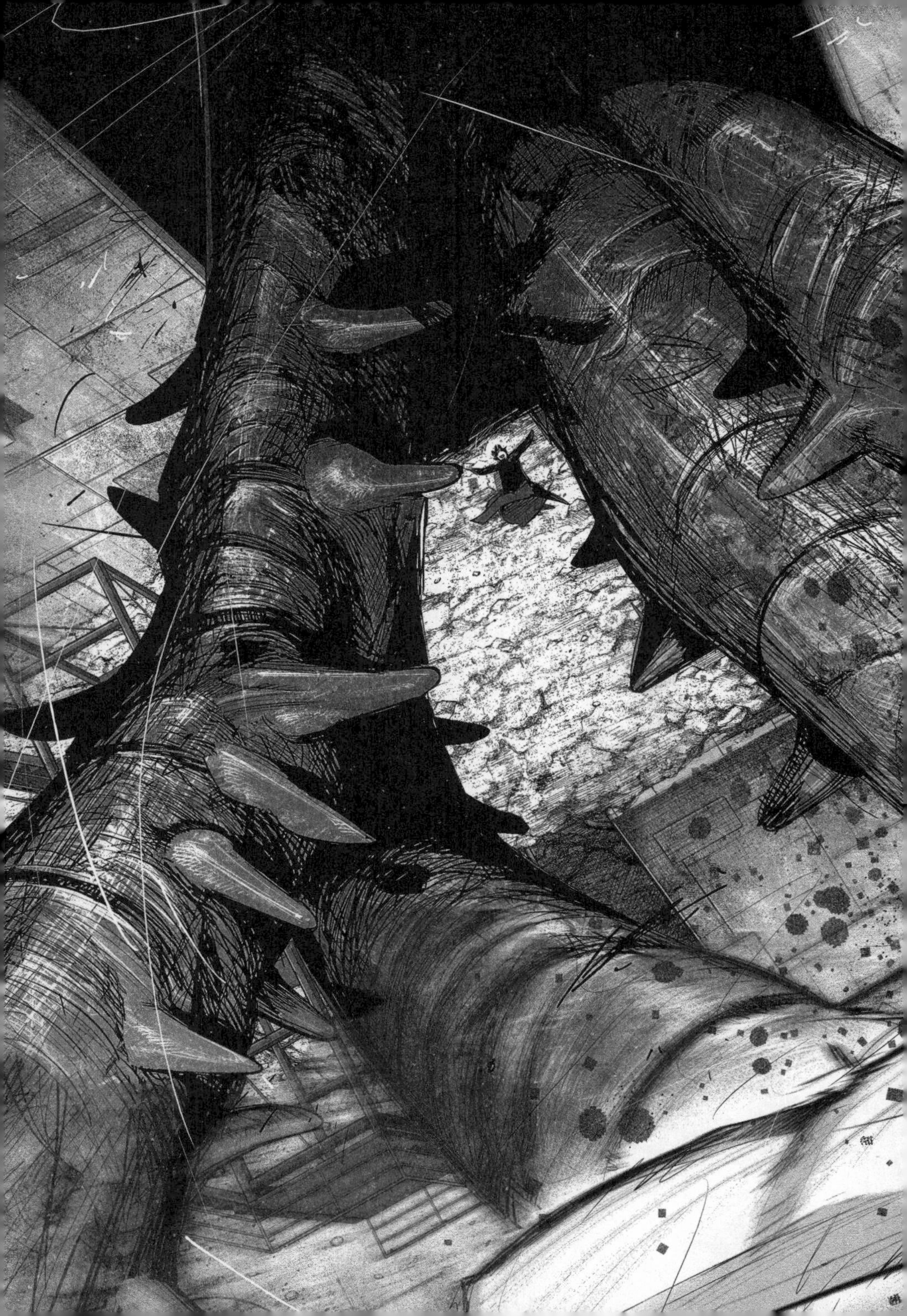

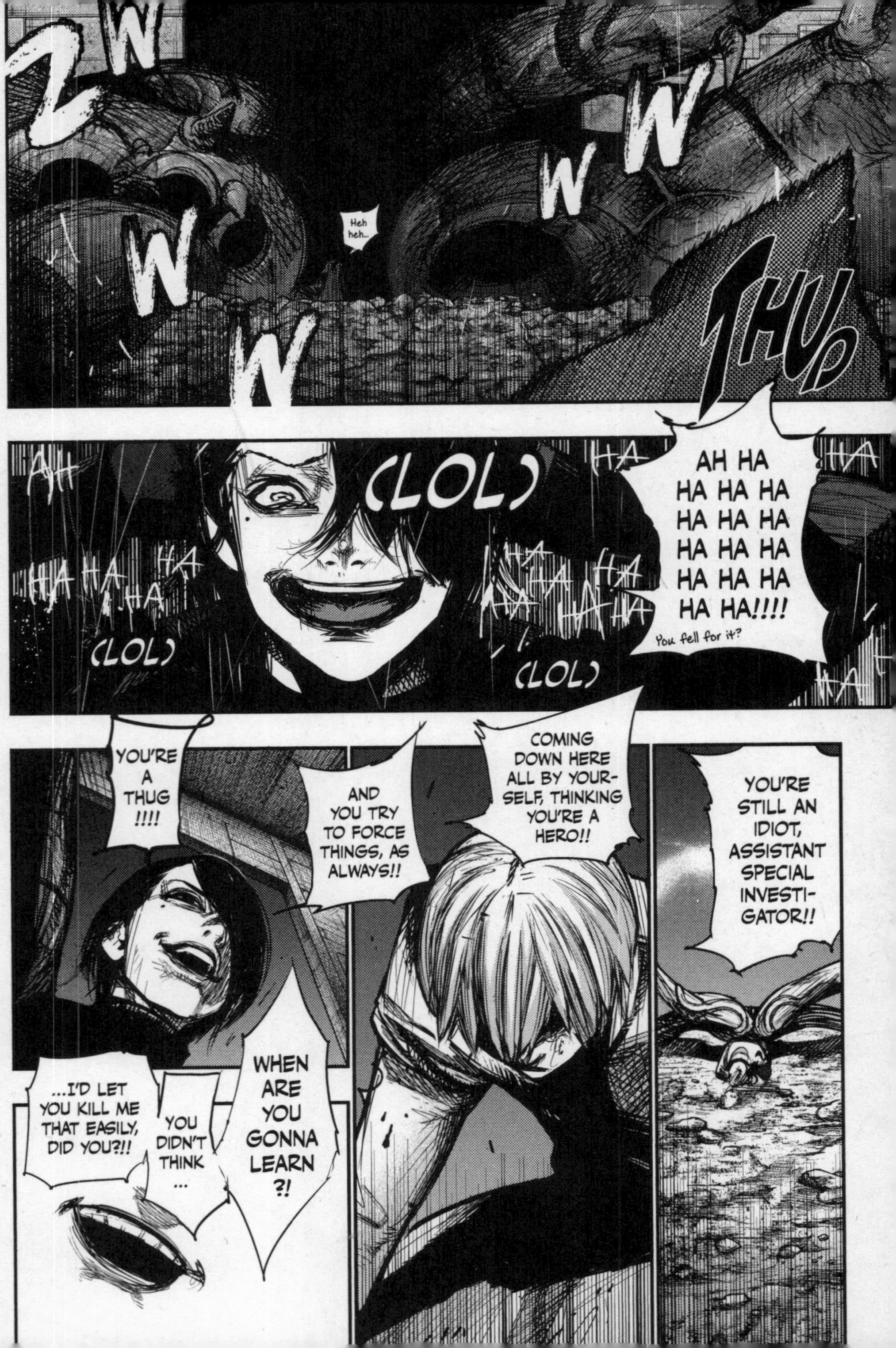
THUD
WWW
Heh heh...
ZWWW
AH HA HA HA HA HA HA HA HA HA HA HA HA HA HA HA HA HA!!!!
You fell for it?
HA
(LOL)
HA HA HA HA HA HA HA
(LOL)
AH
HA HA HA HA
(LOL)
YOU'RE STILL AN IDIOT, ASSISTANT SPECIAL INVESTI-GATOR!!
COMING DOWN HERE ALL BY YOUR-SELF, THINKING YOU'RE A HERO!!
AND YOU TRY TO FORCE THINGS, AS ALWAYS!!
YOU'RE A THUG!!!!
WHEN ARE YOU GONNA LEARN?!
YOU DIDN'T THINK...
...I'D LET YOU KILL ME THAT EASILY, DID YOU?!!

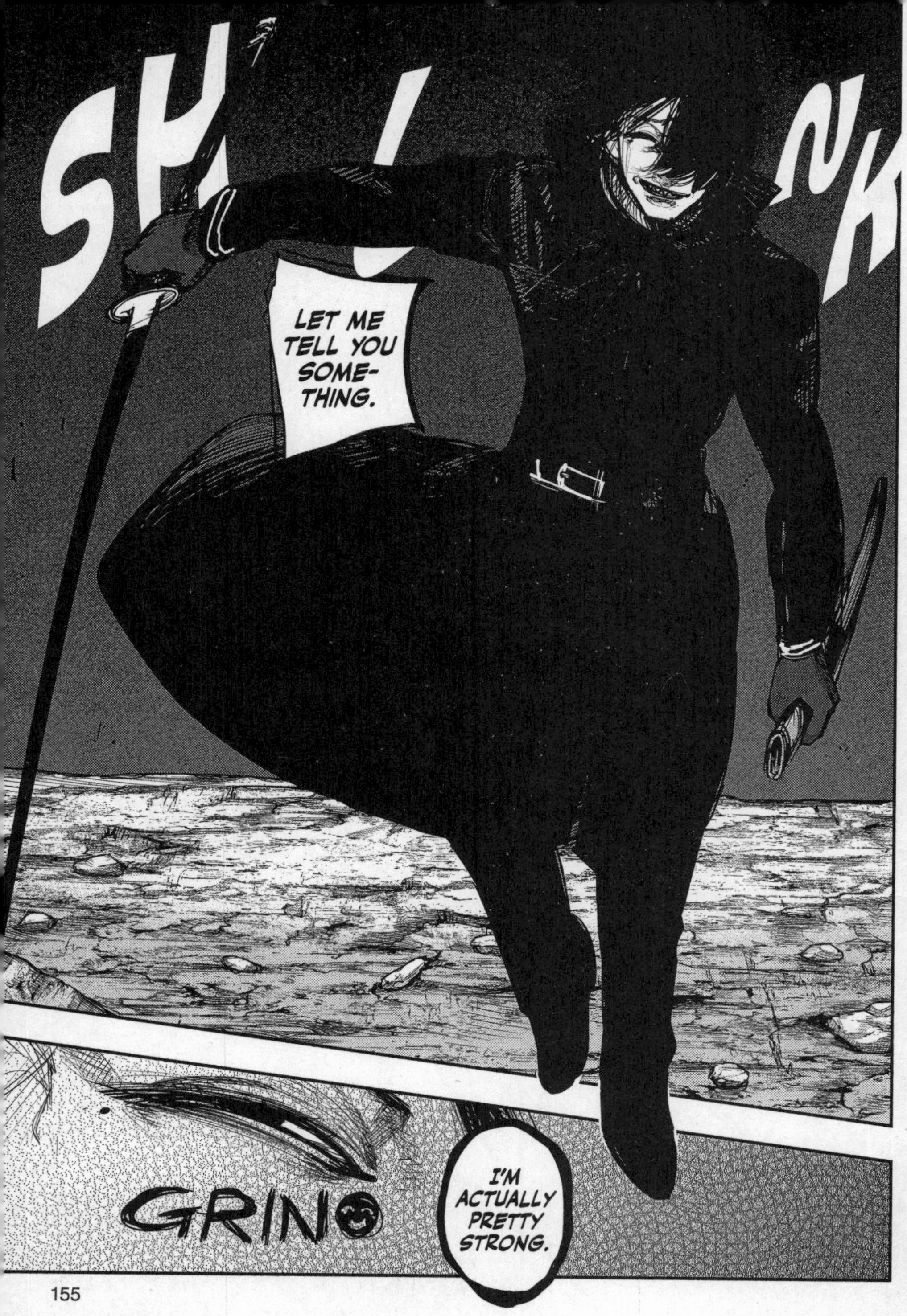
SHINK
LET ME TELL YOU SOME-THING.
I'M ACTUALLY PRETTY STRONG.
GRIN

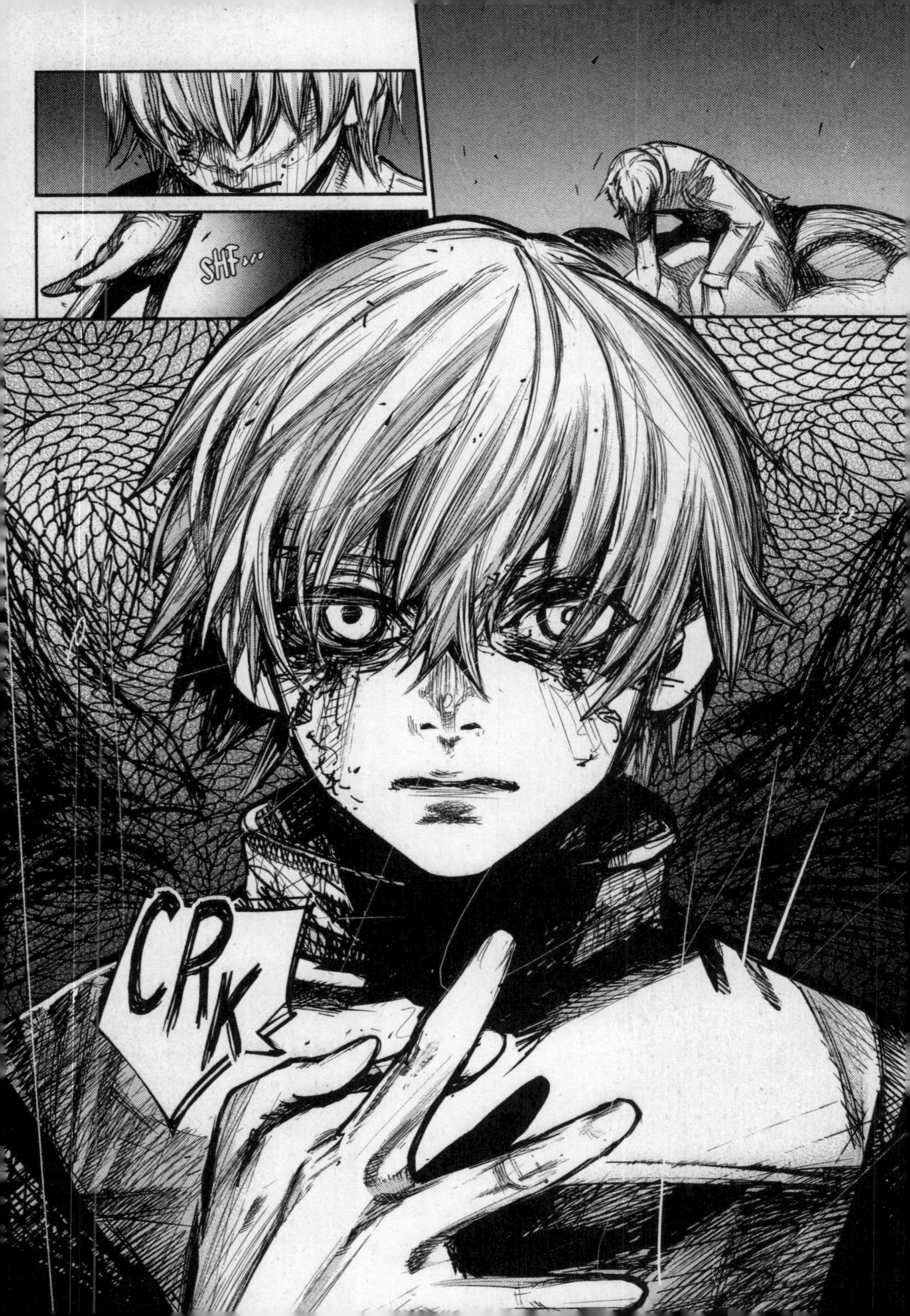
SHF...
CRK

TOKYO GHOUL:re

Sidestep :173

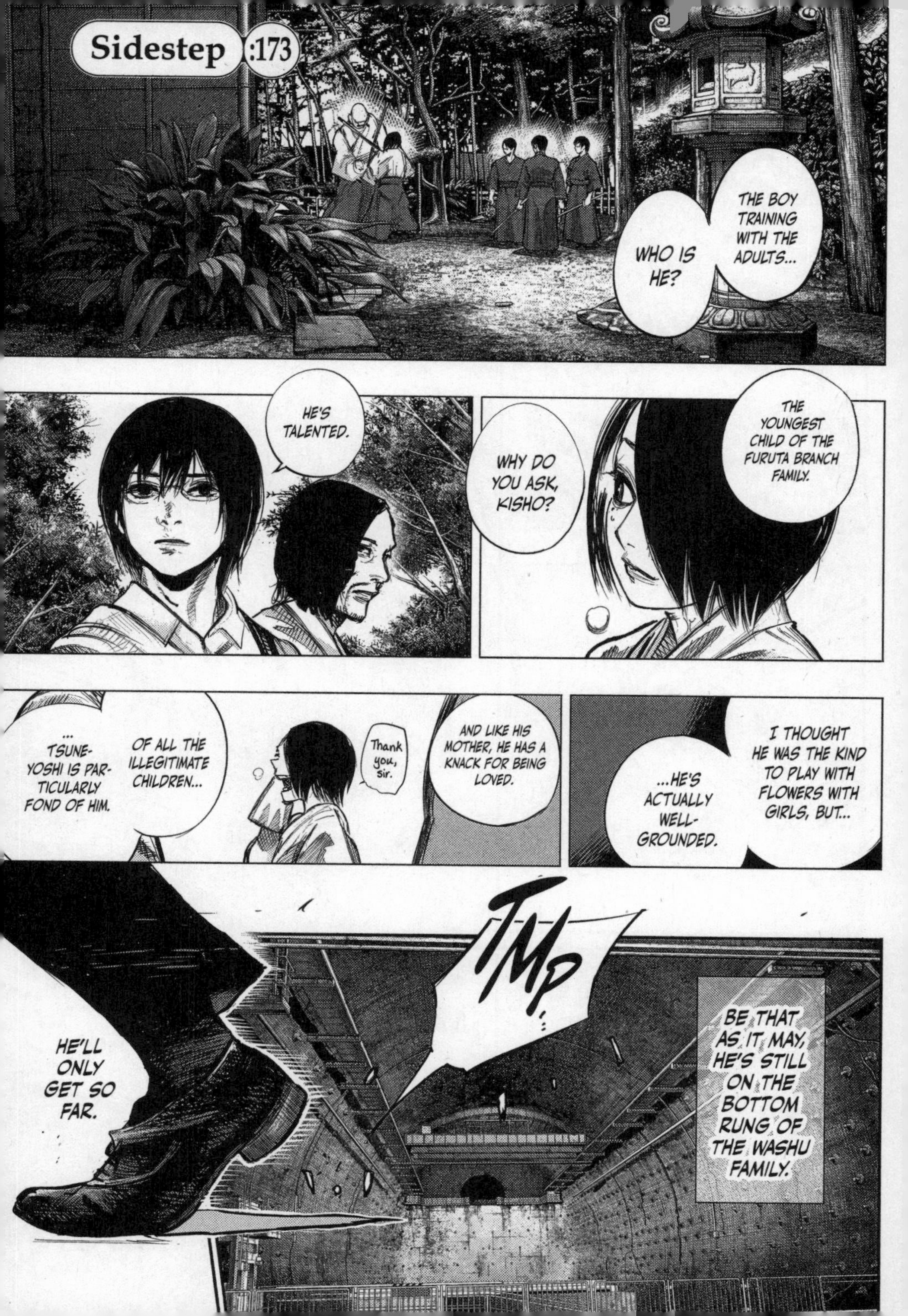
THE BOY TRAINING WITH THE ADULTS...
WHO IS HE?
THE YOUNGEST CHILD OF THE FURUTA BRANCH FAMILY.
WHY DO YOU ASK, KISHO?
HE'S TALENTED.
I THOUGHT HE WAS THE KIND TO PLAY WITH FLOWERS WITH GIRLS, BUT...
...HE'S ACTUALLY WELL-GROUNDED.
AND LIKE HIS MOTHER, HE HAS A KNACK FOR BEING LOVED.
Thank you, sir.
OF ALL THE ILLEGITIMATE CHILDREN...
... TSUNE-YOSHI IS PAR-TICULARLY FOND OF HIM.
BE THAT AS IT MAY, HE'S STILL ON THE BOTTOM RUNG OF THE WASHU FAMILY.
TMP
HE'LL ONLY GET SO FAR.

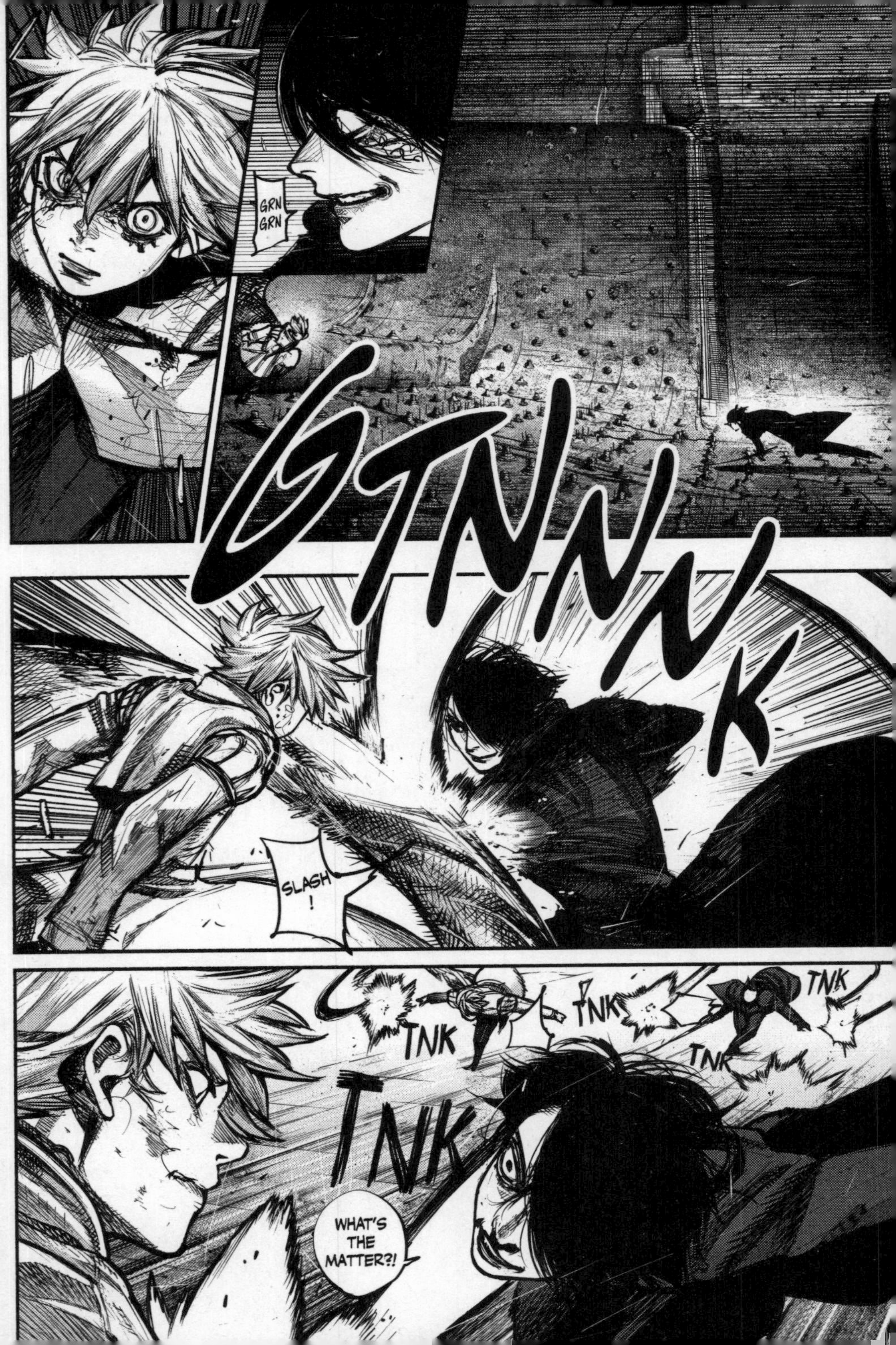
GRN GRN
GTNNNK
SLASH!
TNK
TNK
TNK
TNK
TNK
WHAT'S THE MATTER?!

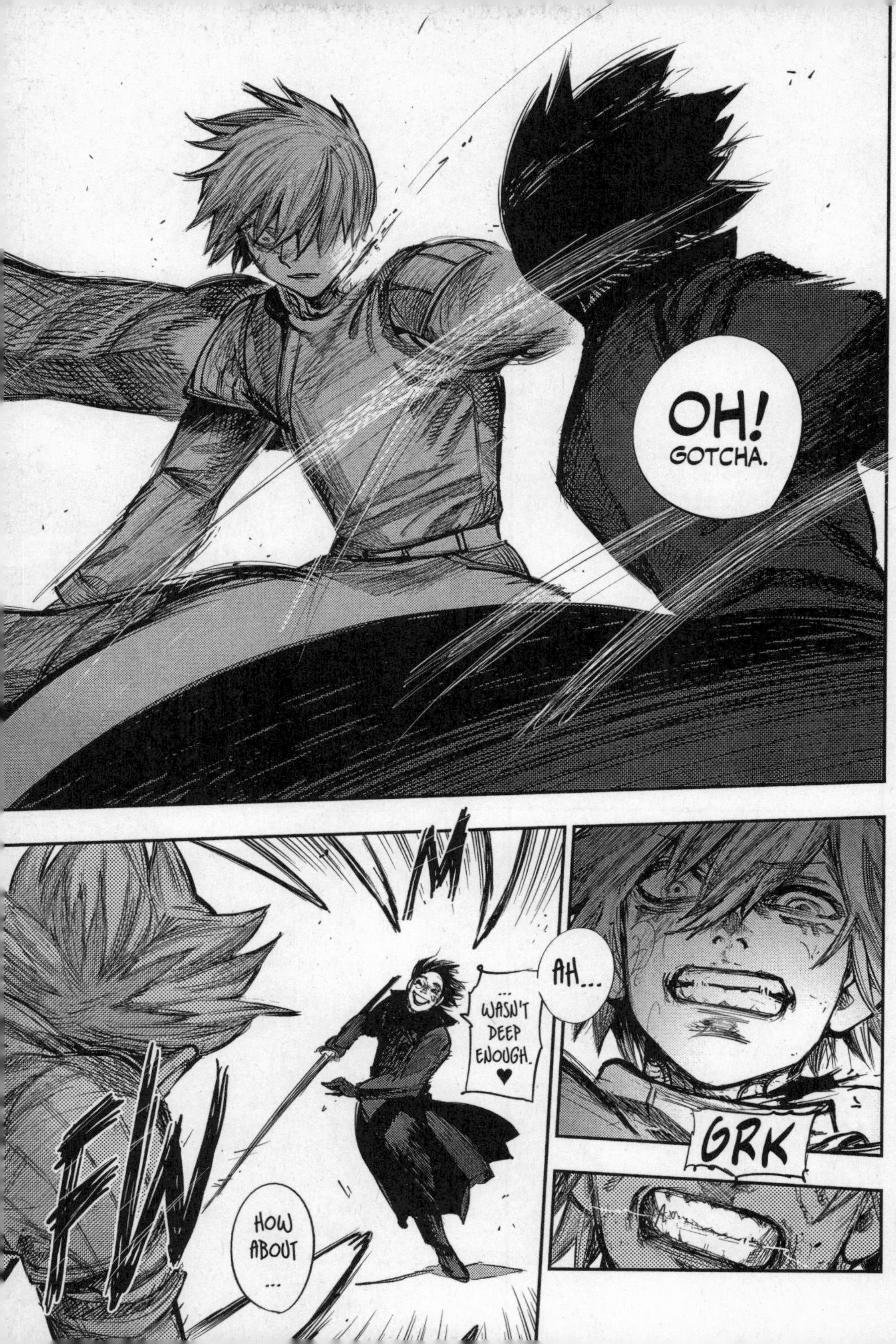
OH! GOTCHA.
AH...
GRK
M
... WASN'T DEEP ENOUGH ♥
HOW ABOUT ...
FW

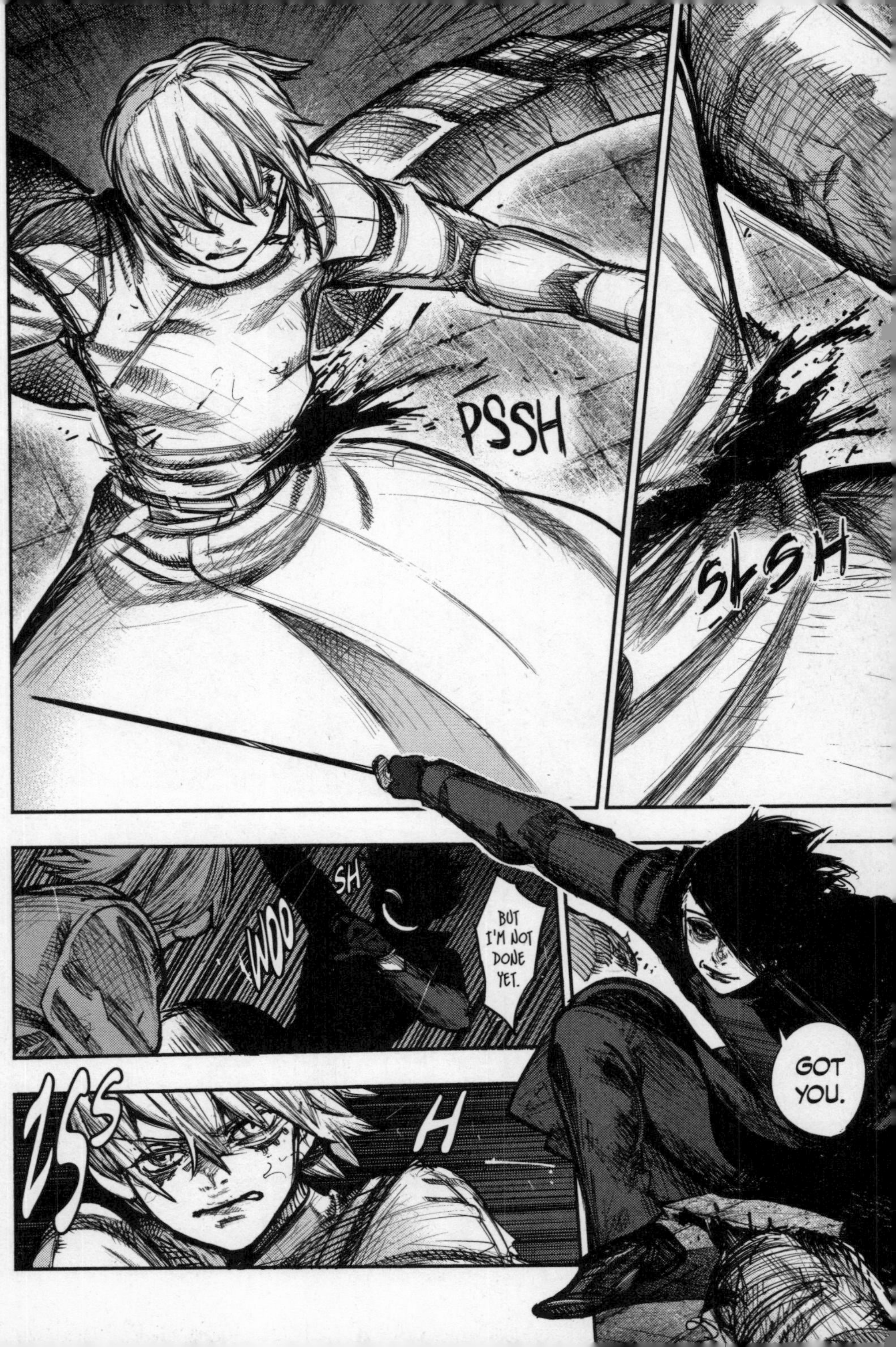
SLSH
PSSH
GOT YOU.
SH
WOO
BUT I'M NOT DONE YET.
ZS
H

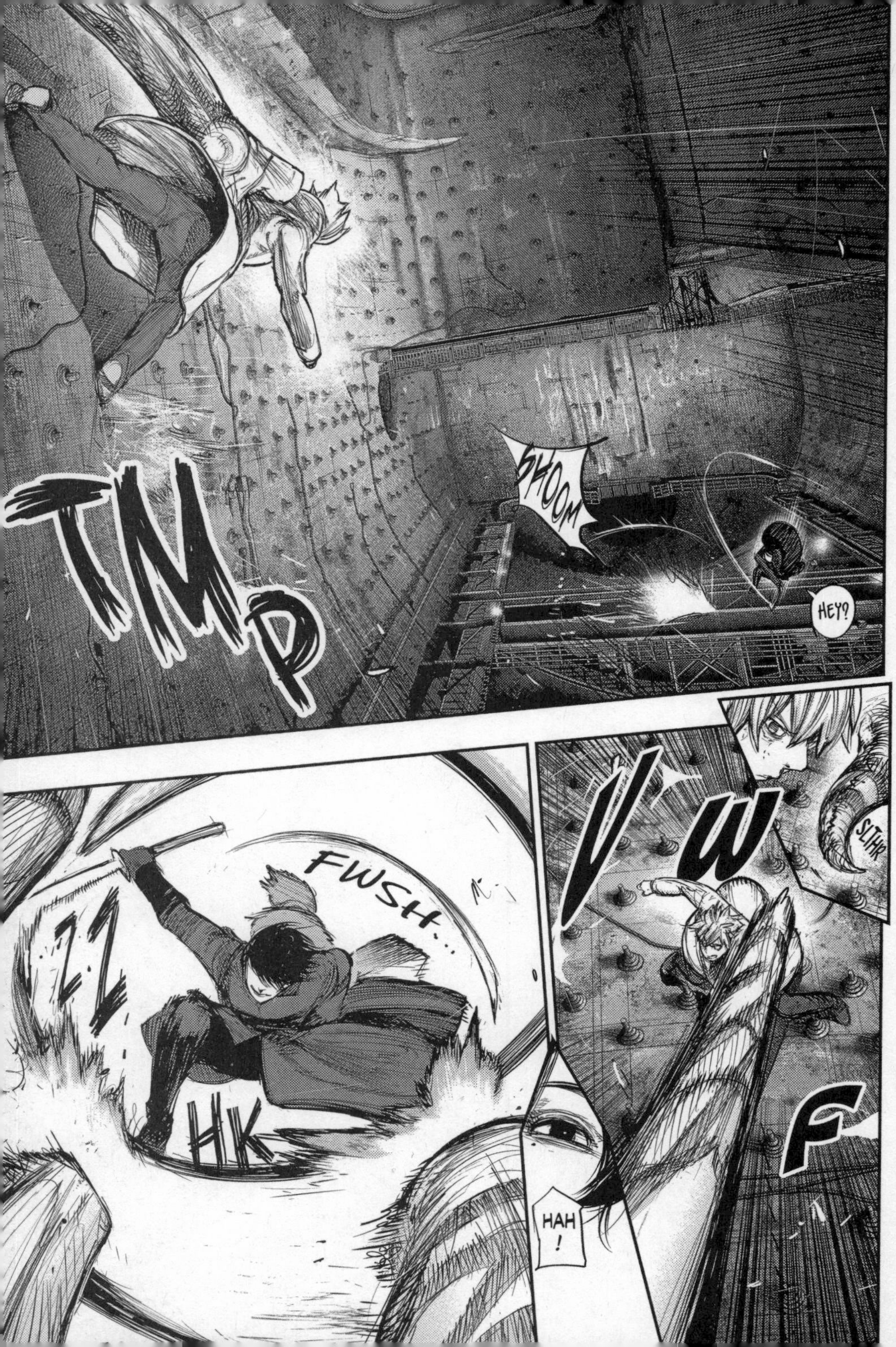
SHOOM
HEY?
TMP
SLTHR
VW
F
HAH!
FWSH...
ZZ
HK

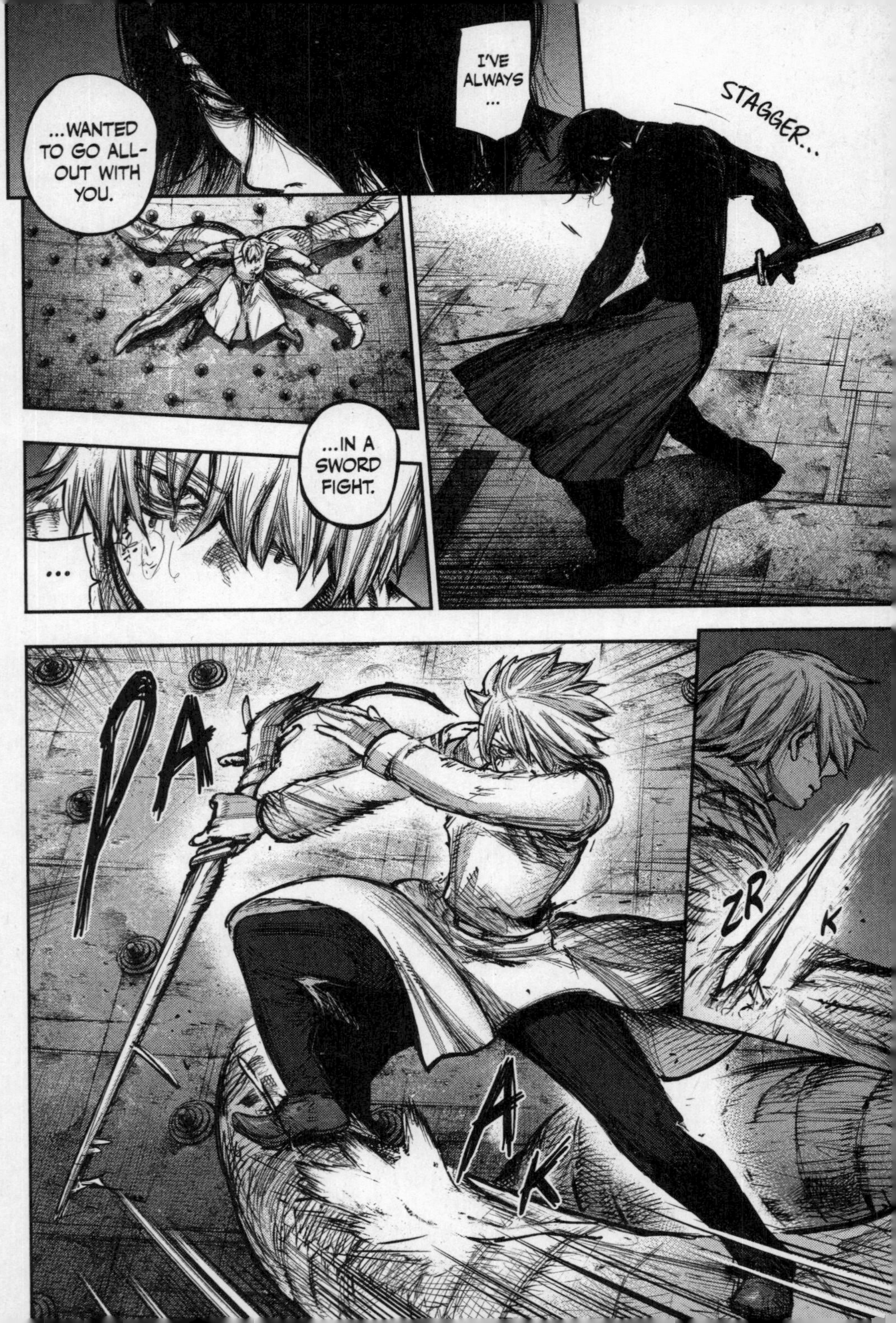
I'VE ALWAYS ...
...WANTED TO GO ALL-OUT WITH YOU.
STAGGER...
...IN A SWORD FIGHT.
...
ZRK
PA
AK

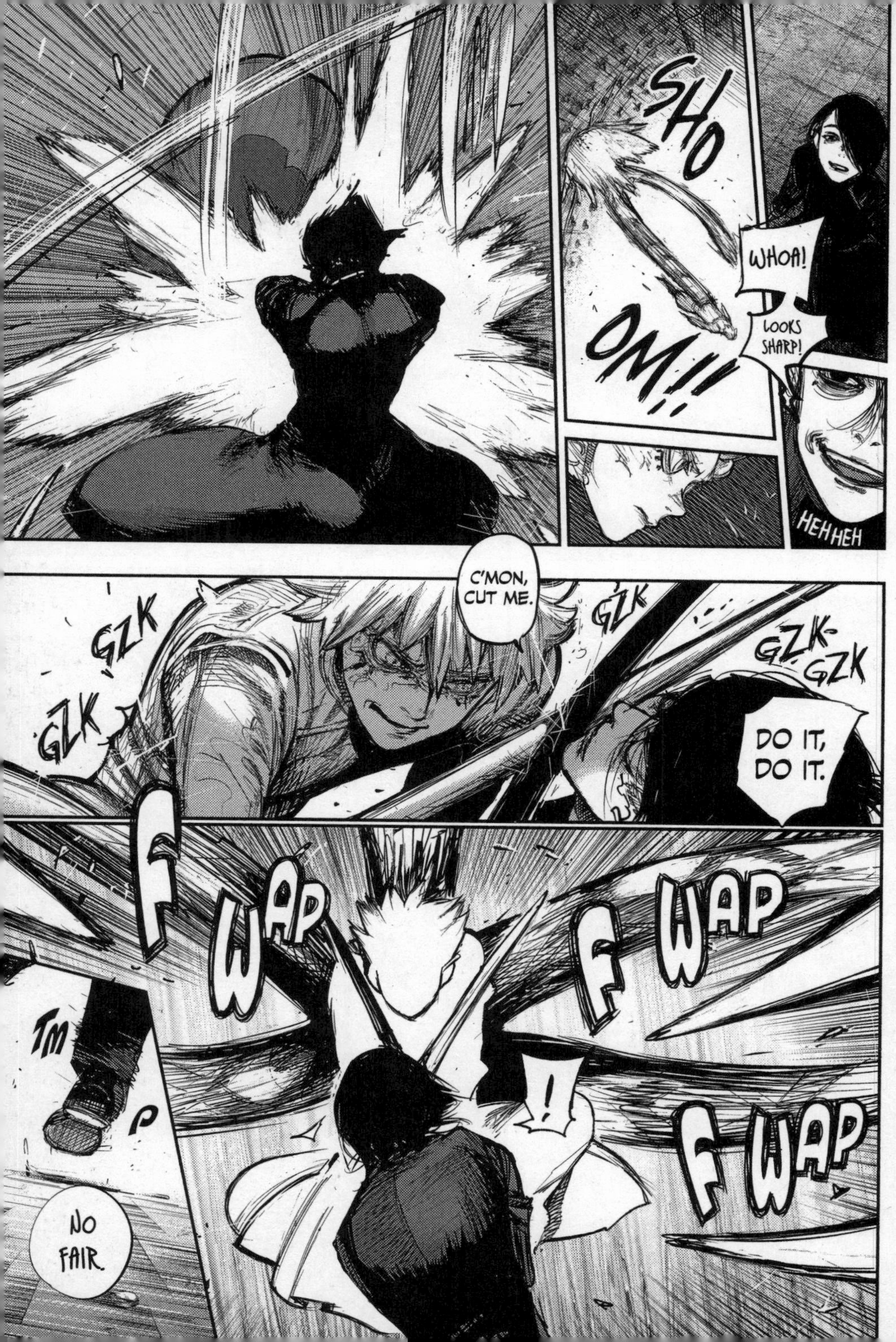
SHOOM!!
WHOA!
LOOKS SHARP!
HEHHEH
C'MON, CUT ME.
GZK
GZK-GZK
DO IT, DO IT.
GZK
GZK
FWAP
FWAP
!
FWAP
TMP
NO FAIR.

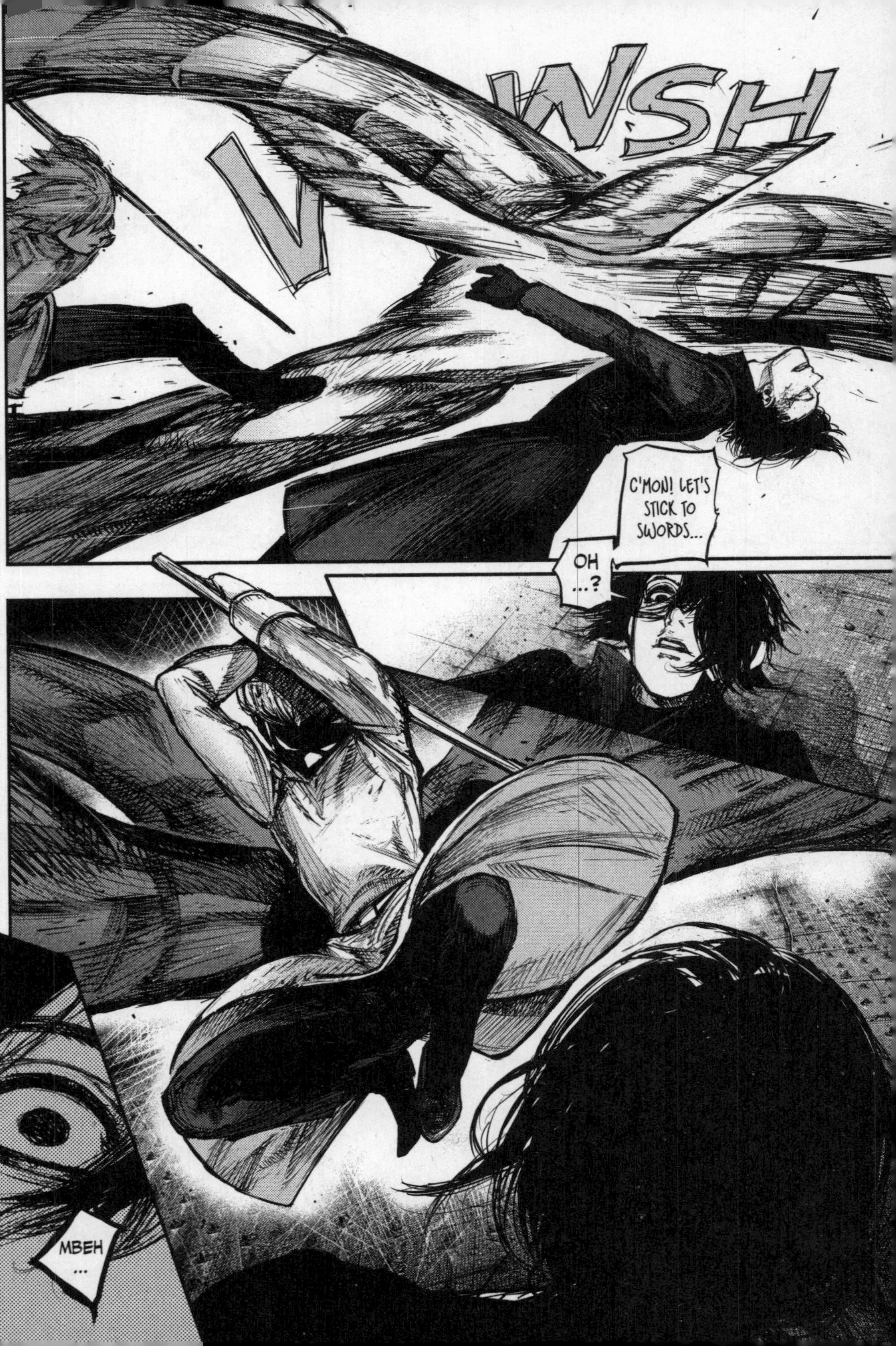
WSH
C'MON! LET'S STICK TO SWORDS...
OH ...?
MBEH ...

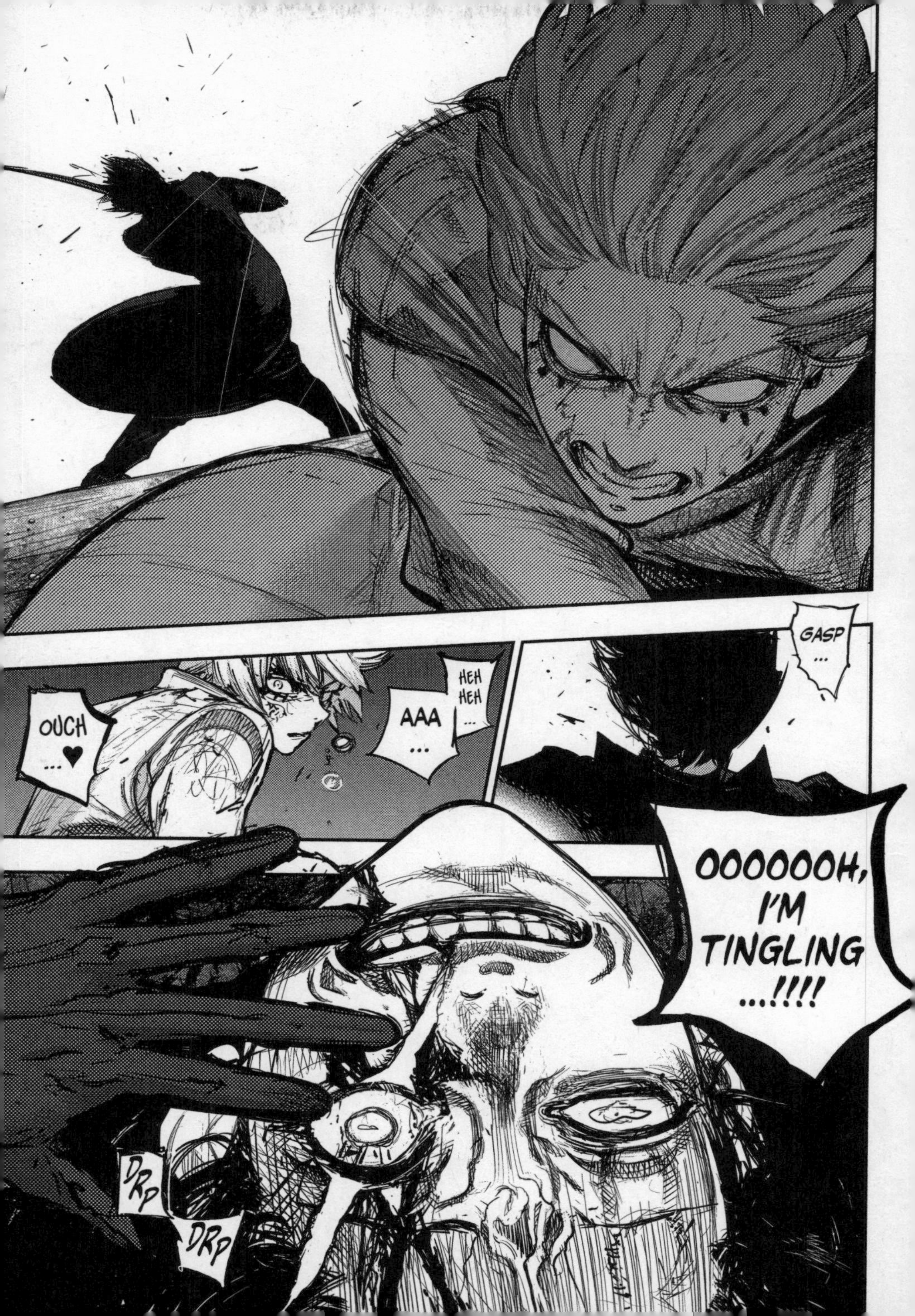
GASP ...
HEH HEH ...
AAA ...
OUCH ...♥
OOOOOOH, I'M TINGLING ...!!!!
DRP
DRP

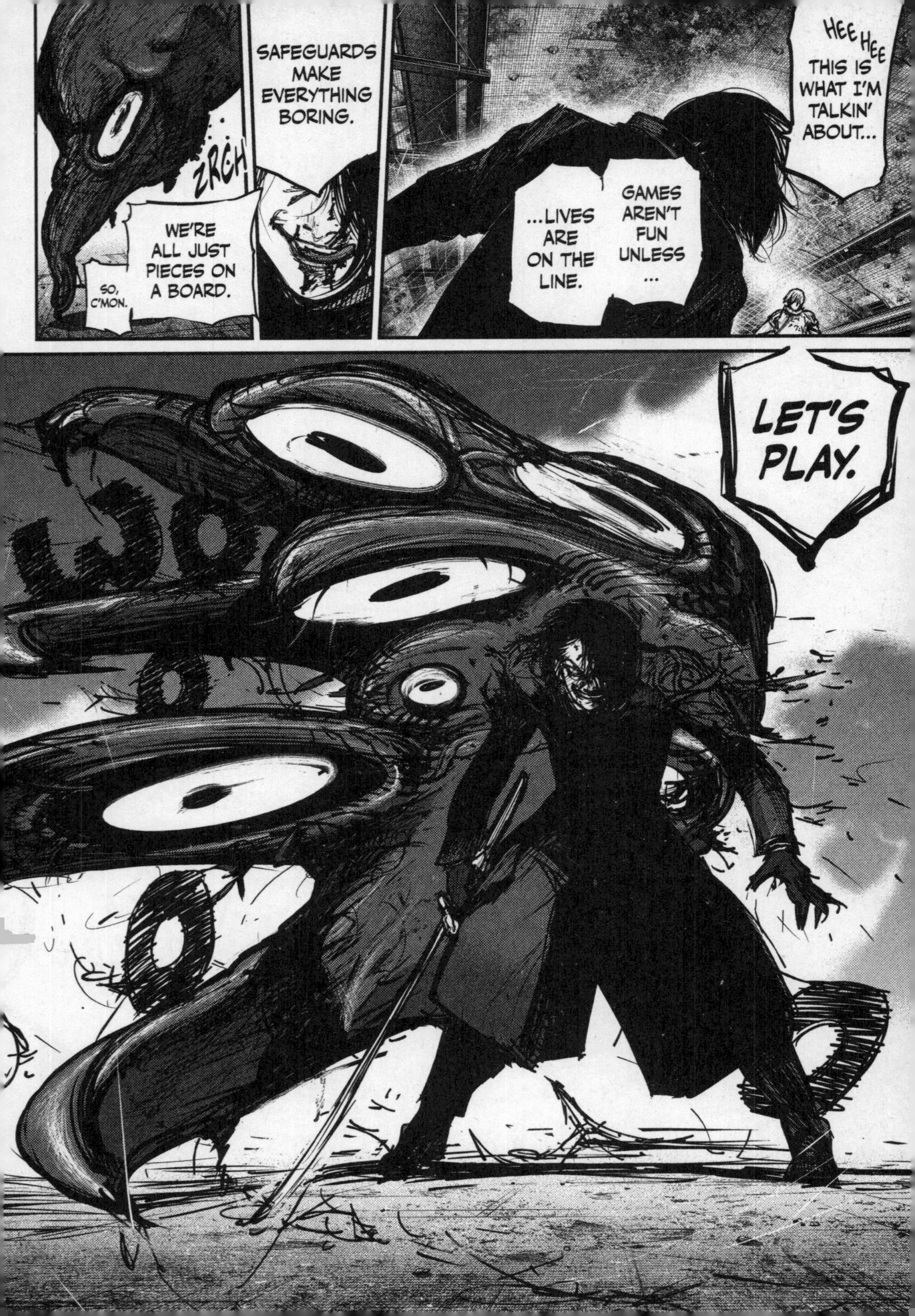
HEE HEE
THIS IS WHAT I'M TALKIN' ABOUT...
GAMES AREN'T FUN UNLESS...
...LIVES ARE ON THE LINE.
SAFEGUARDS MAKE EVERYTHING BORING.
ZRCH
WE'RE ALL JUST PIECES ON A BOARD.
SO, C'MON.
LET'S PLAY.

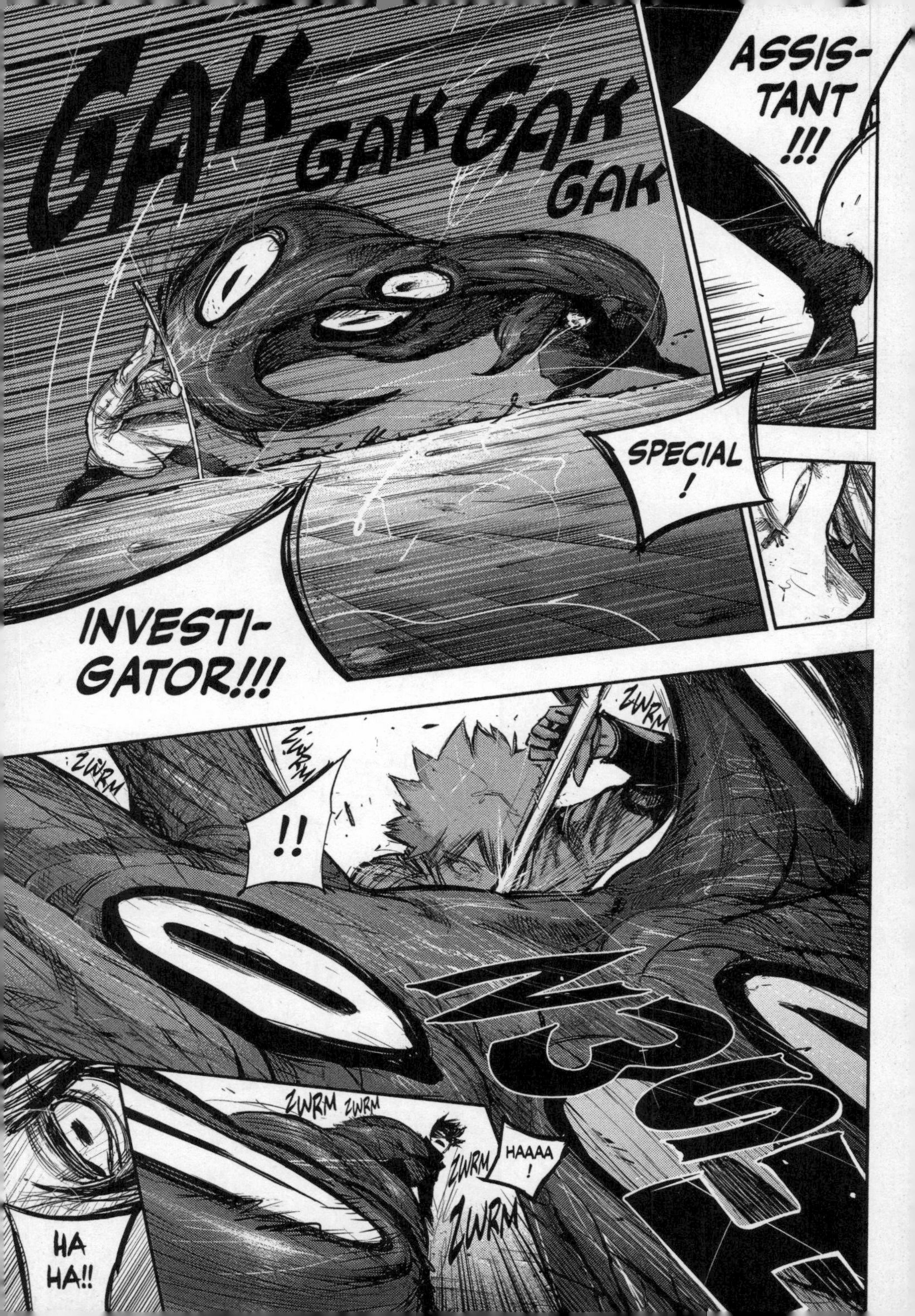
ASSIS-
TANT
!!!
SPECIAL
!
GAK
GAK GAK GAK
GAK
INVESTI-
GATOR!!!
ZWRM
ZWRM
ZWRM
!!
ZWRM ZWRM
HAAAA
!
ZWRM
ZWRM
HA
HA!!

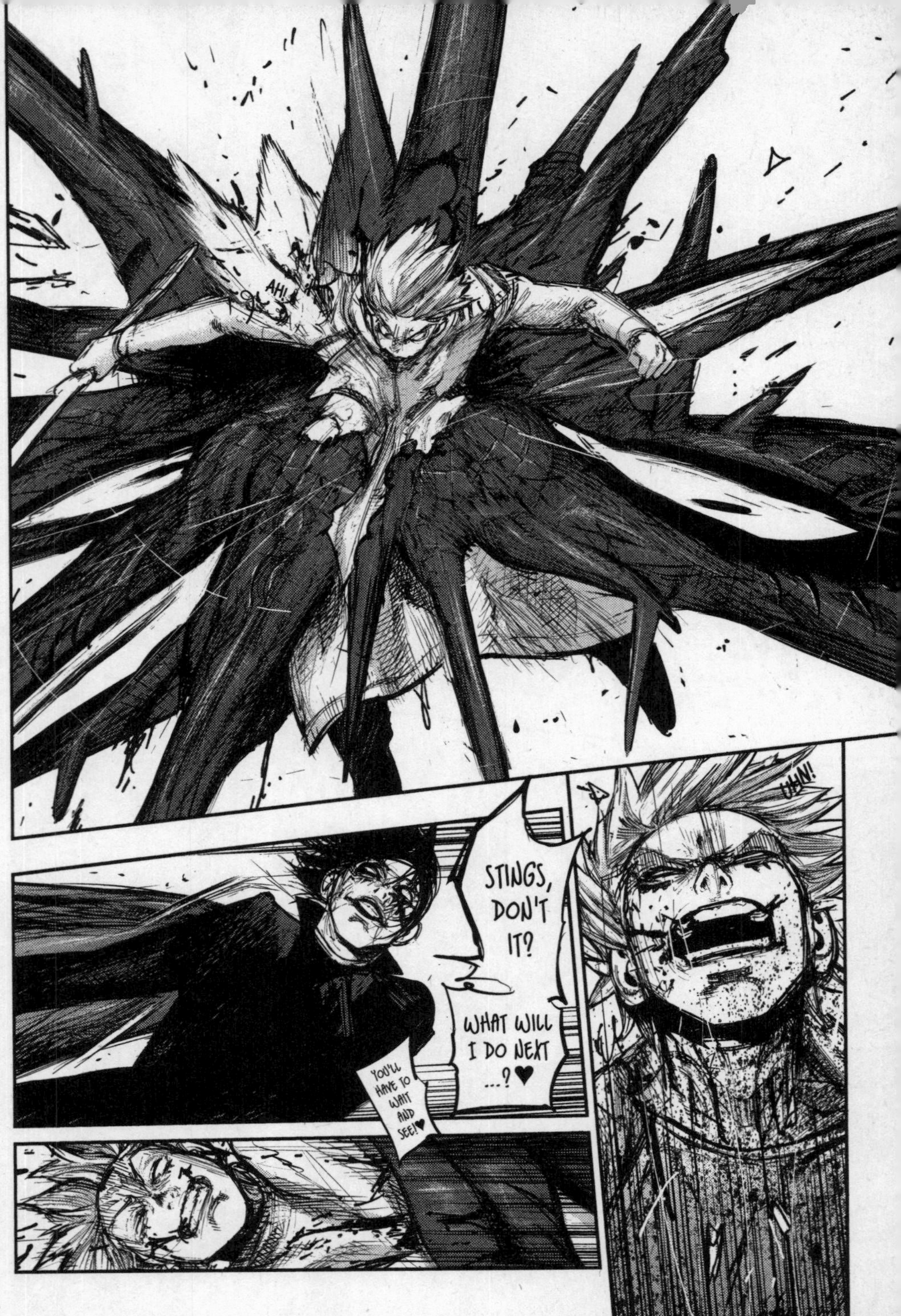
AH!
UHN!
STINGS, DON'T IT?
WHAT WILL I DO NEXT ...?♥
YOU'LL HAVE TO WAIT AND SEE!♥

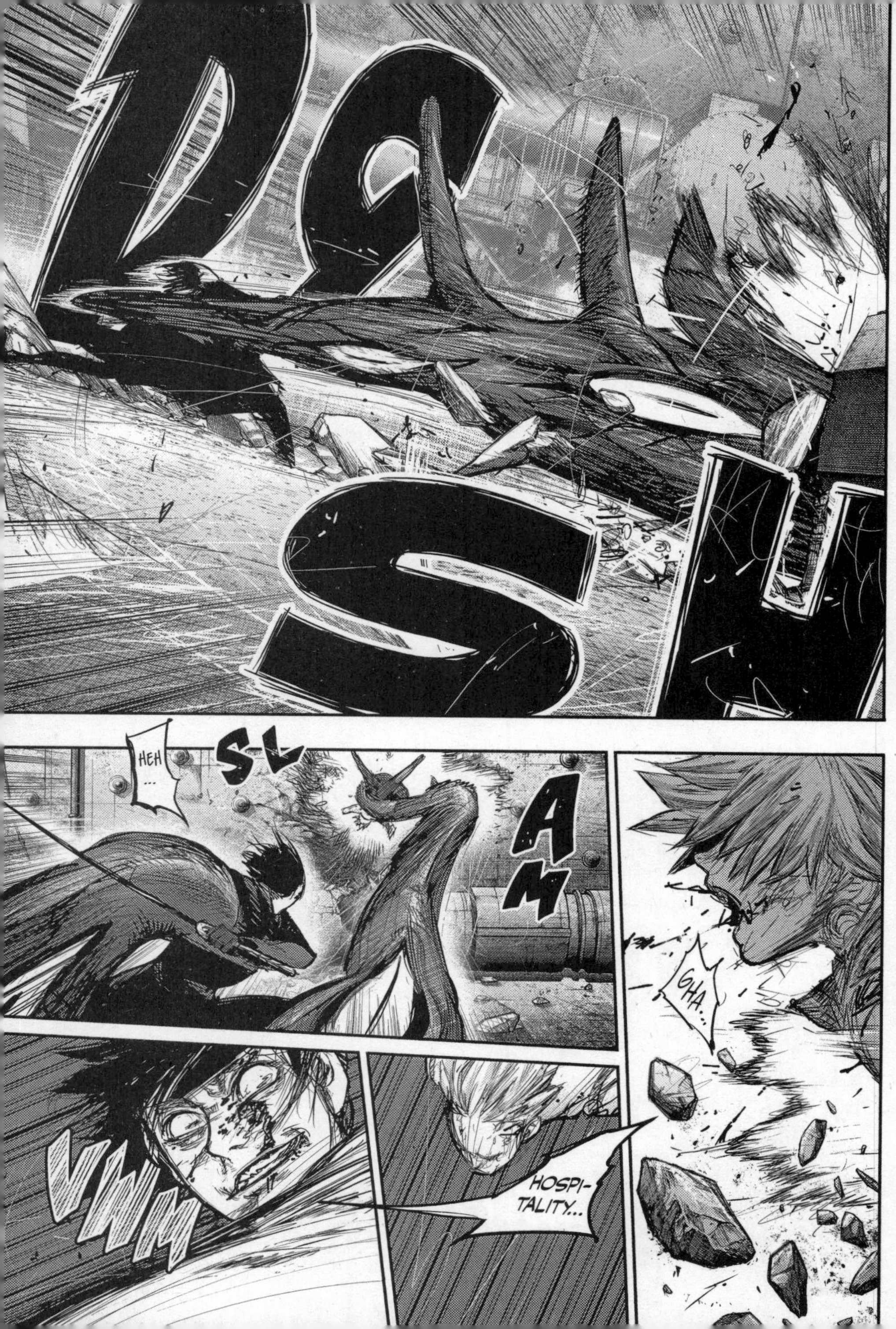
DASH
GHA...
HEH...
SLAM
HOSPI-TALITY...

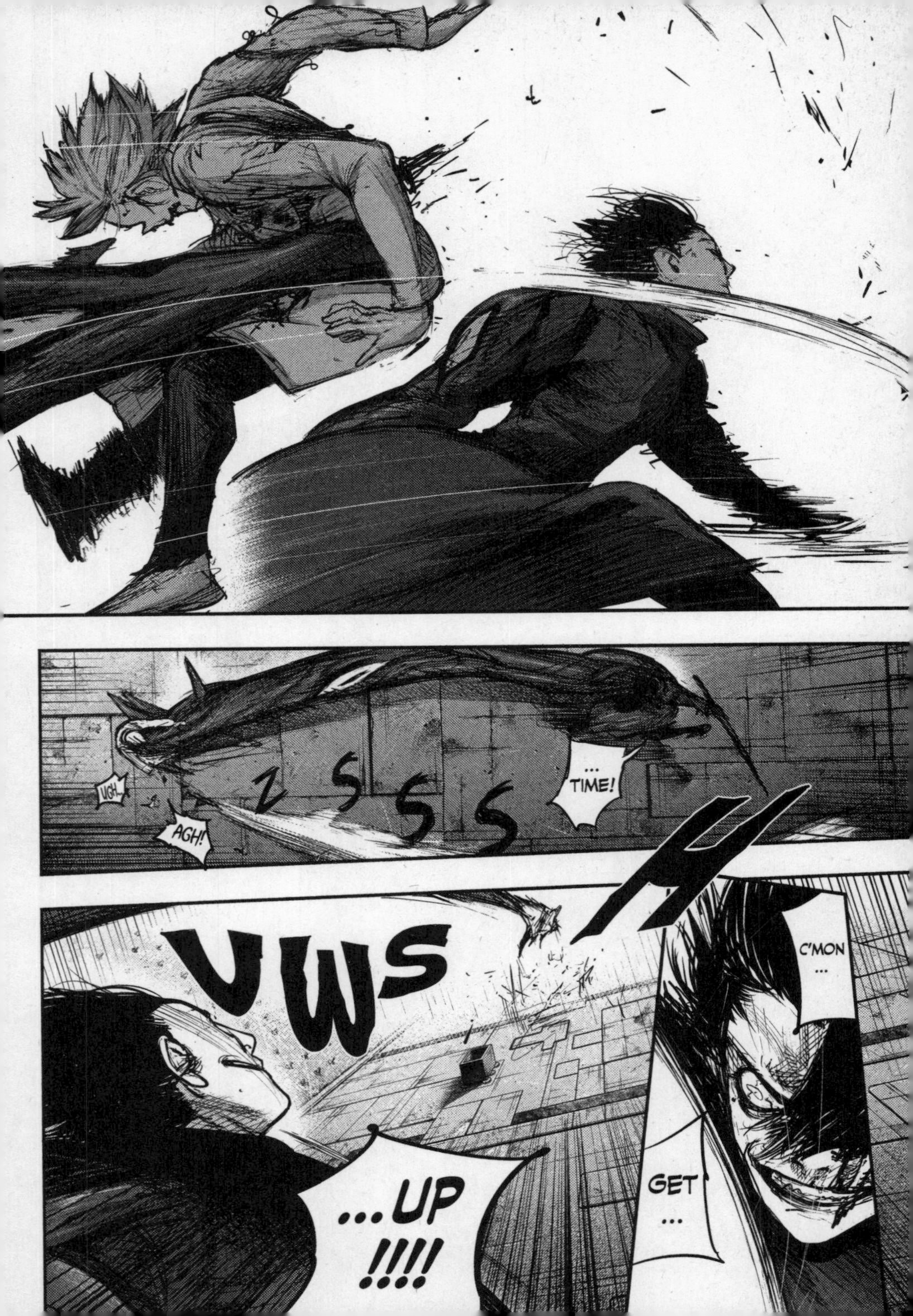
...TIME!
ZSSSS
UGH..
AGH!
C'MON ...
GET ...
VWSH
...UP !!!!

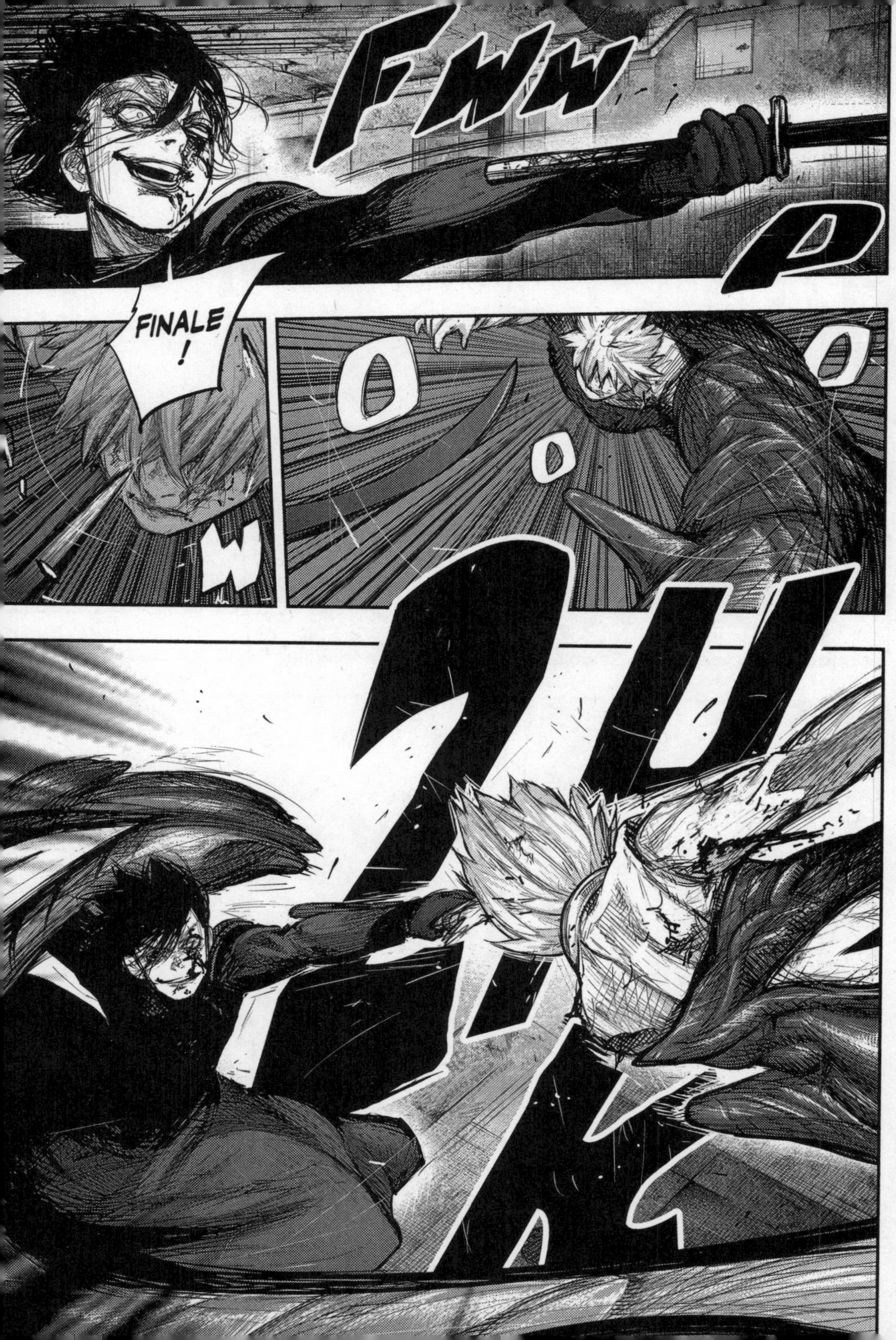
FWW
P
O
O
O
FINALE!
W

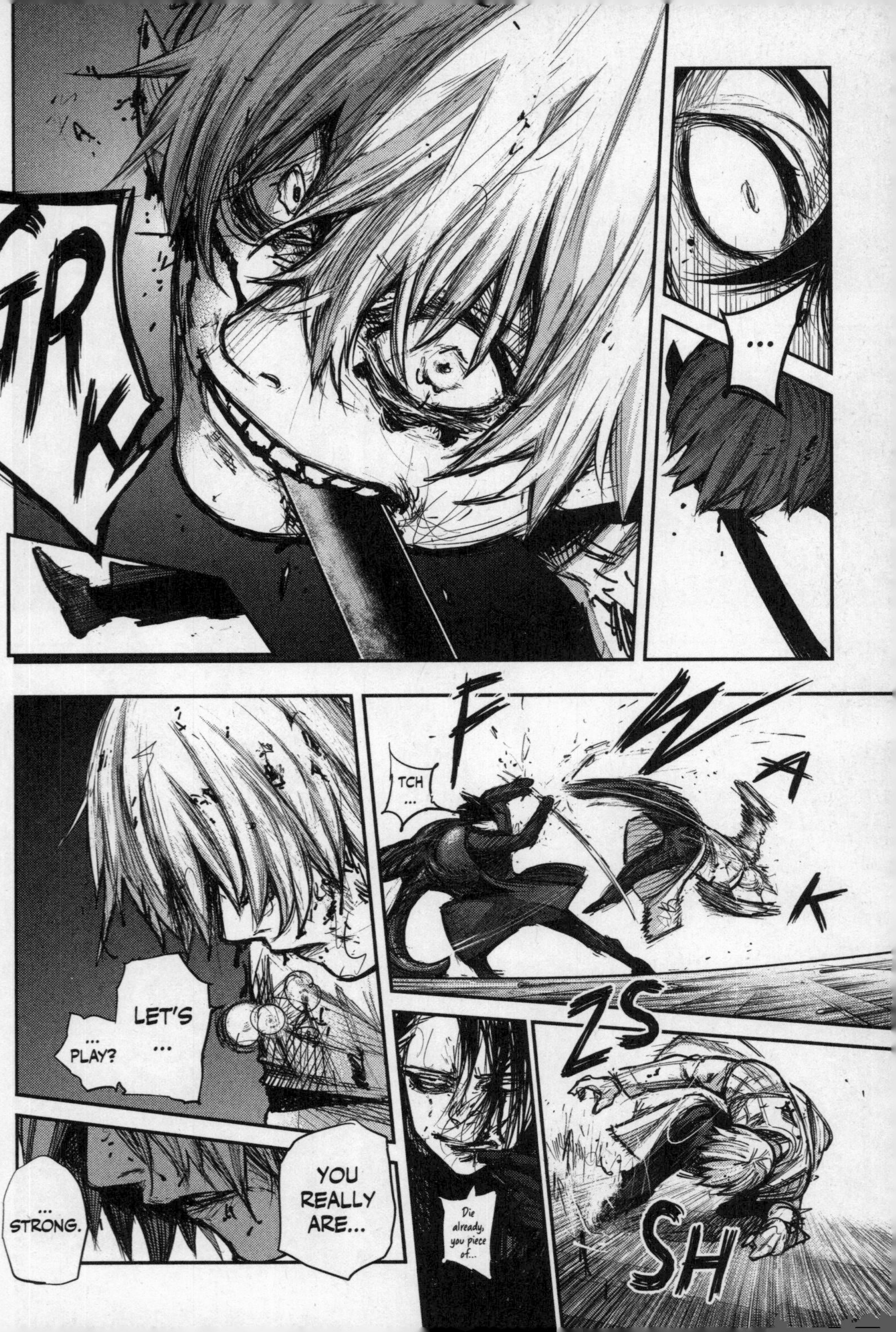
...
GRK
TCH ...
FWAK
ZSSH
Die already, you piece of...
LET'S ...
... PLAY?
YOU REALLY ARE...
... STRONG.

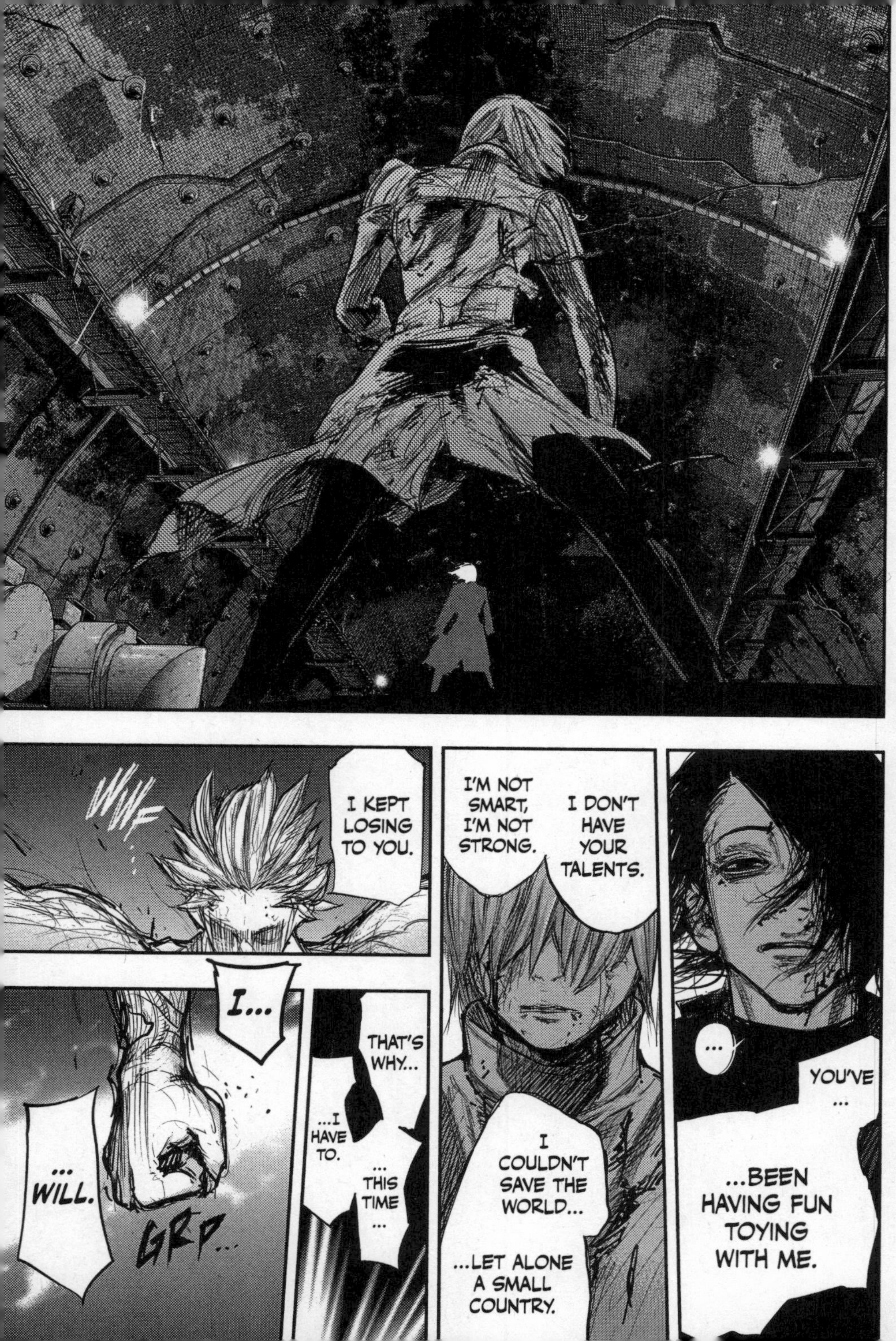
...
YOU'VE ...
...BEEN HAVING FUN TOYING WITH ME.
I'M NOT SMART, I'M NOT STRONG.
I DON'T HAVE YOUR TALENTS.
I COULDN'T SAVE THE WORLD...
...LET ALONE A SMALL COUNTRY.
I KEPT LOSING TO YOU.
WNF
THAT'S WHY...
...I HAVE TO.
... THIS TIME ...
I...
... WILL.
GRP...

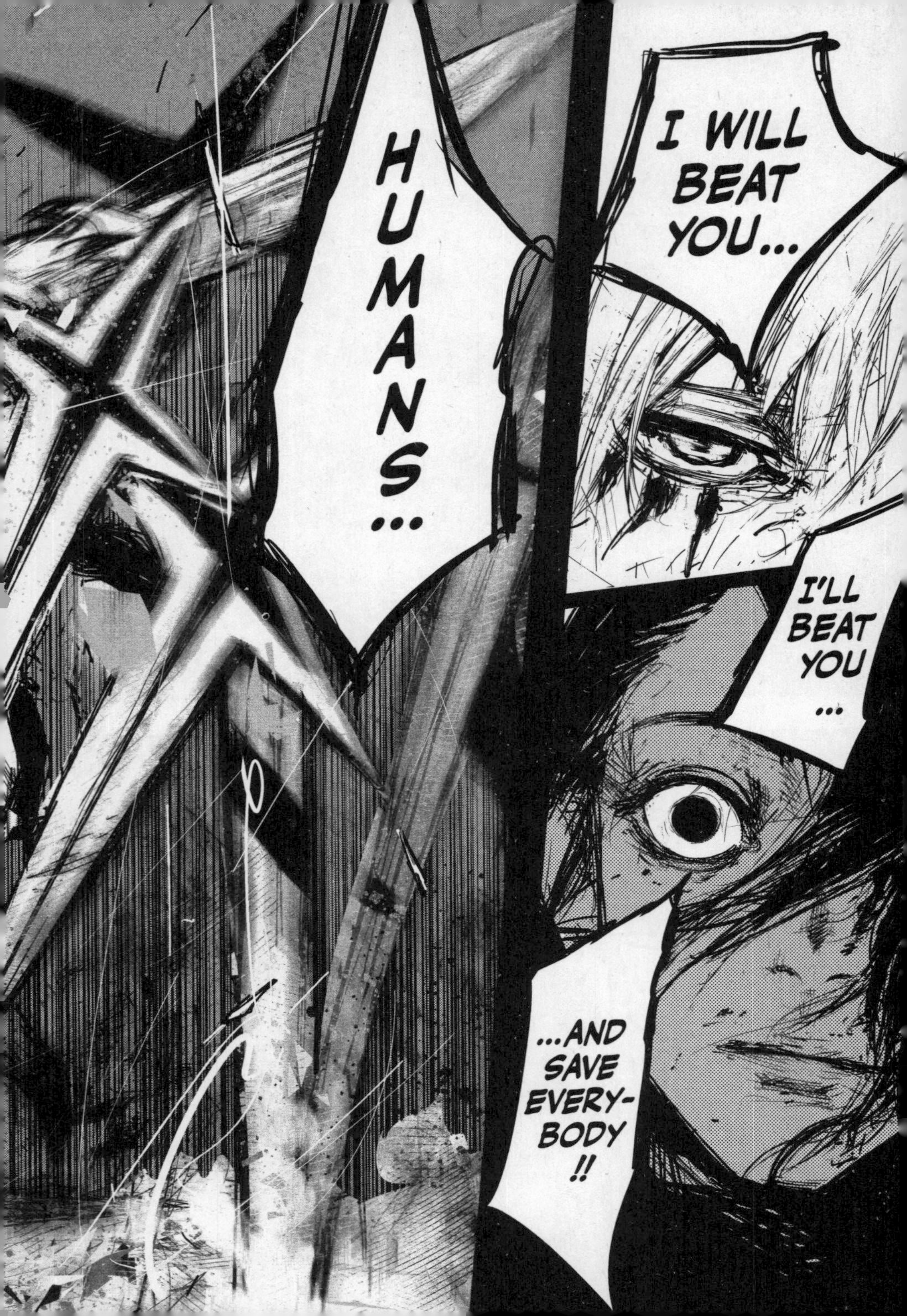
I WILL BEAT YOU...
HUMANS...
I'LL BEAT YOU ...
...AND SAVE EVERY-BODY !!

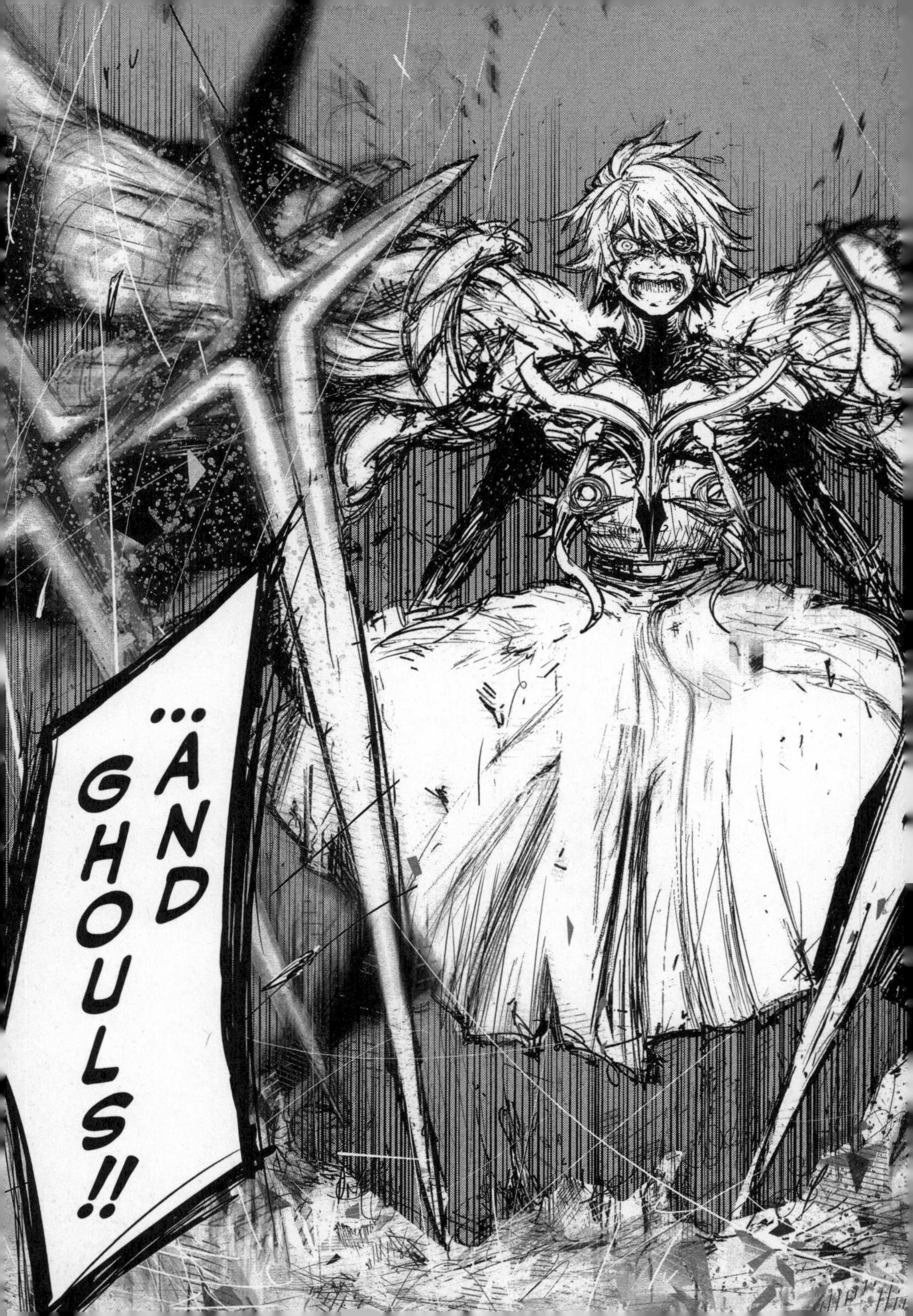
...AND GHOULS!!

TOKYO GHOUL:re

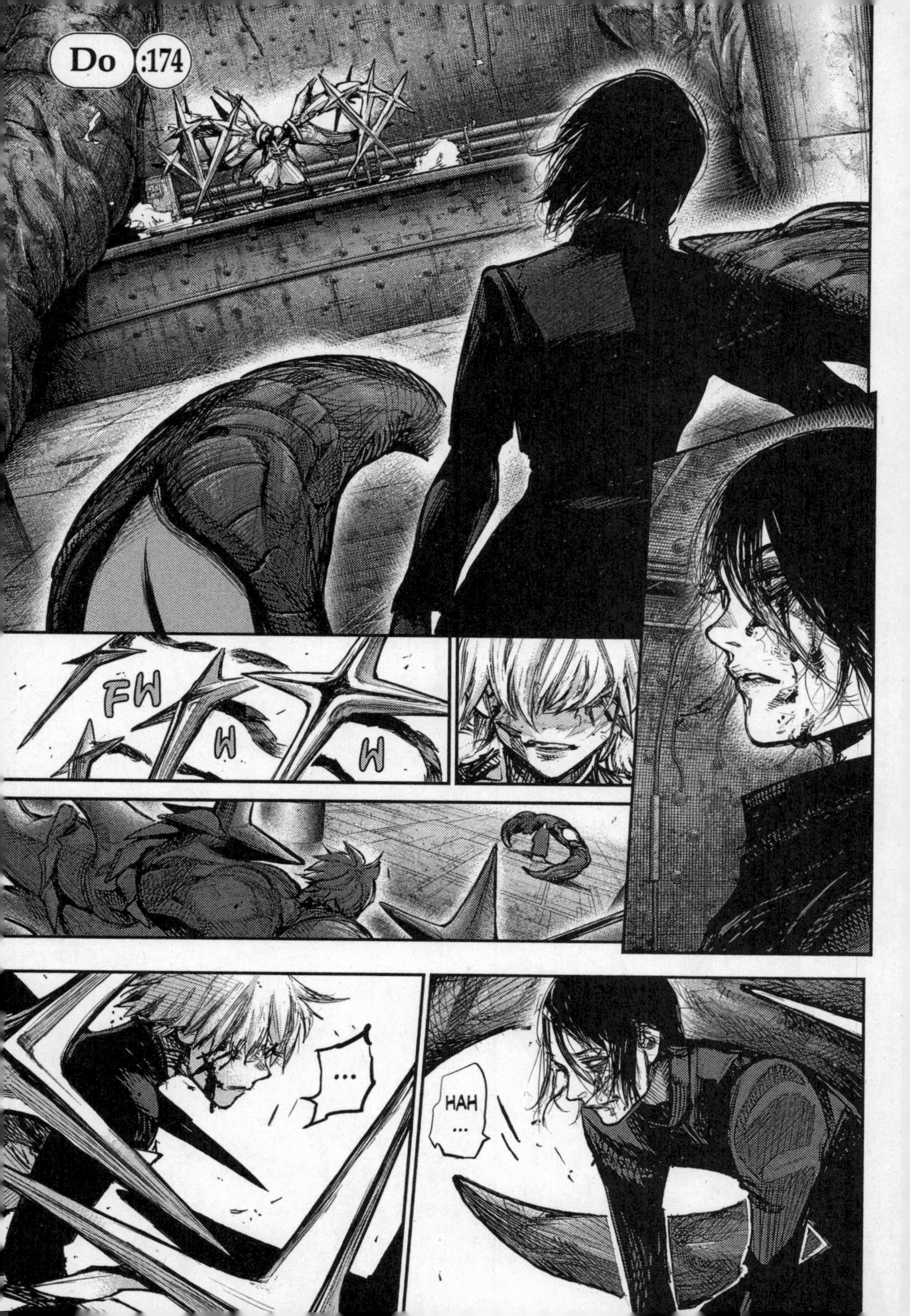
Do :174
FW W W
HAH ...
...

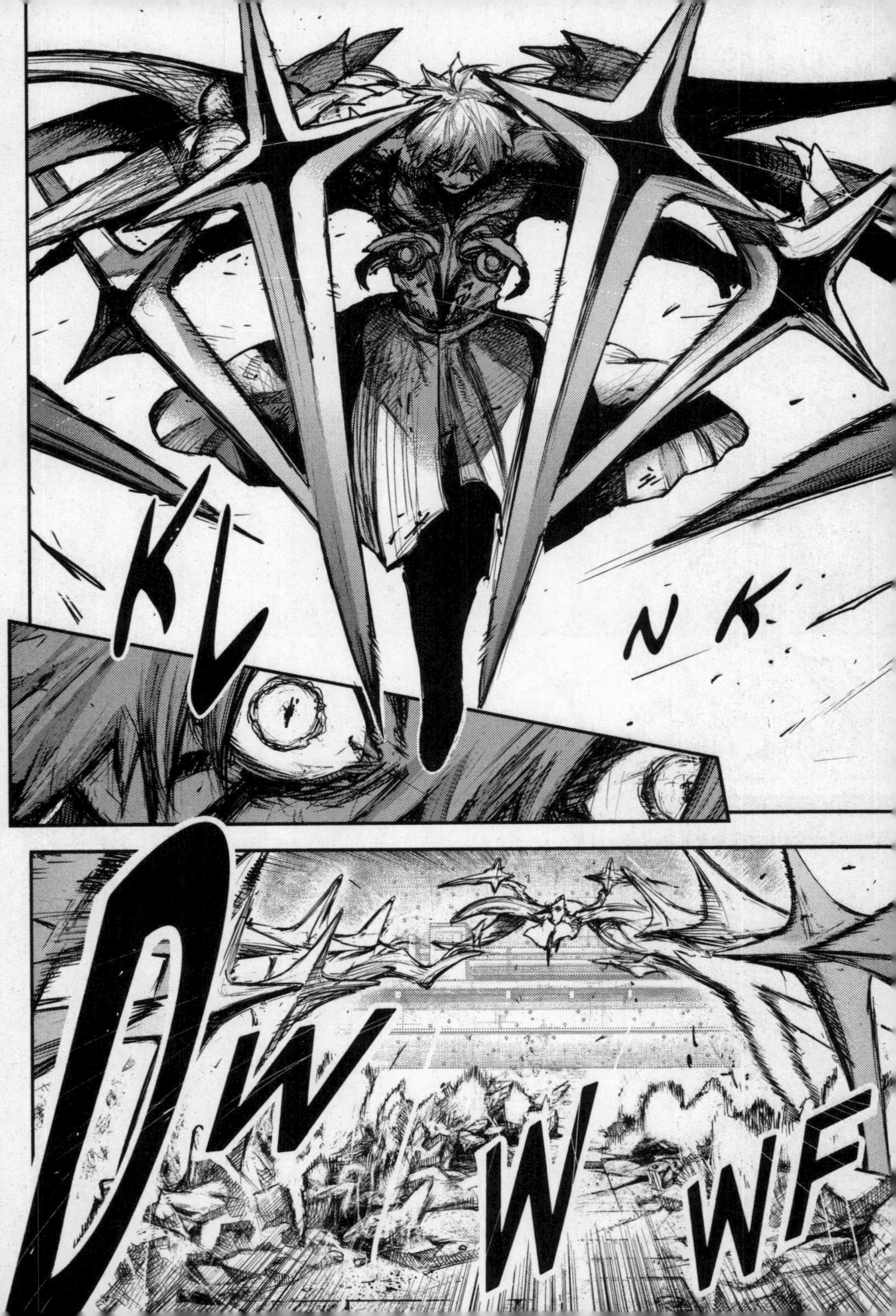
KLNK
DWWWF

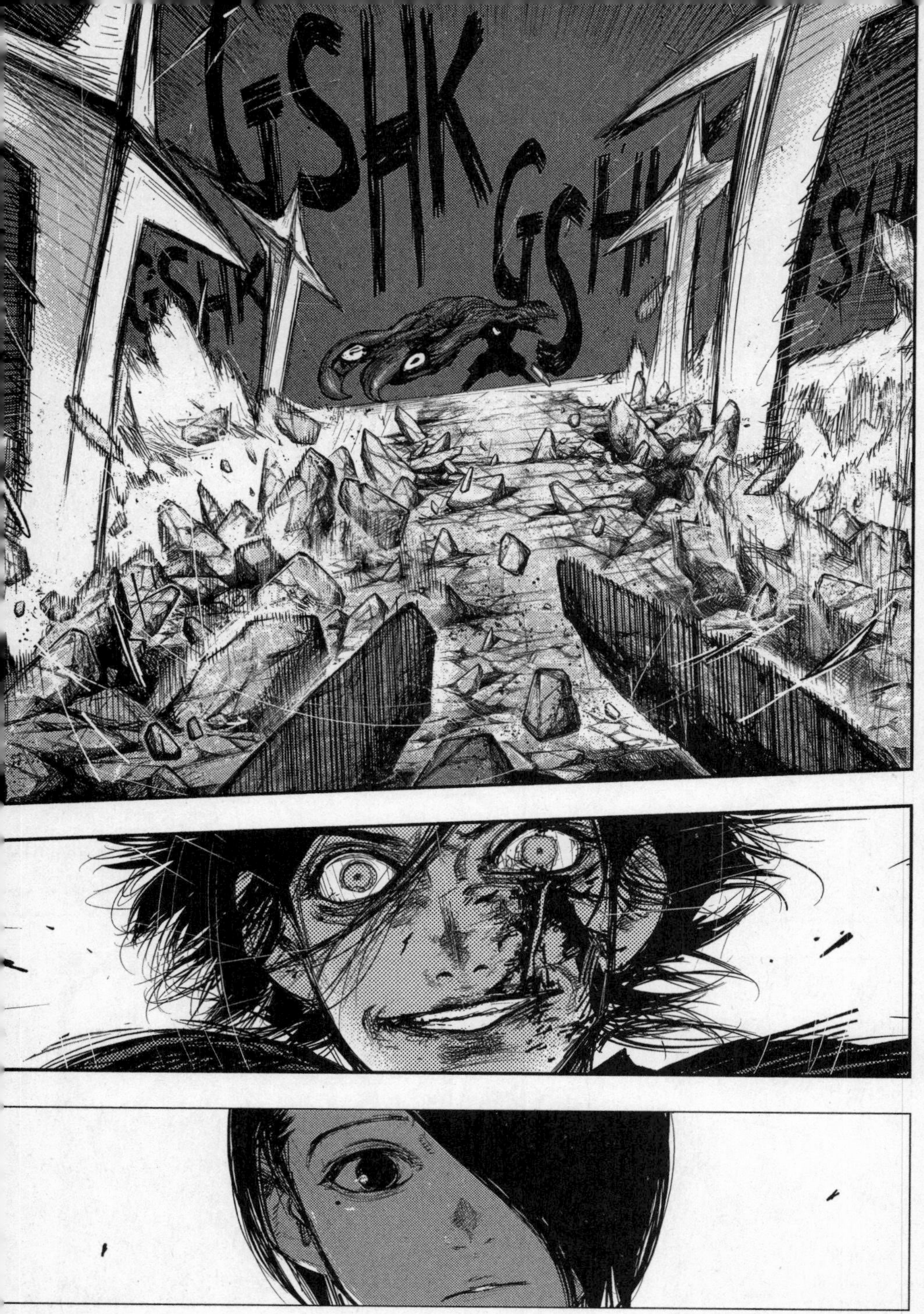
GSHK
GSHK
GSHK

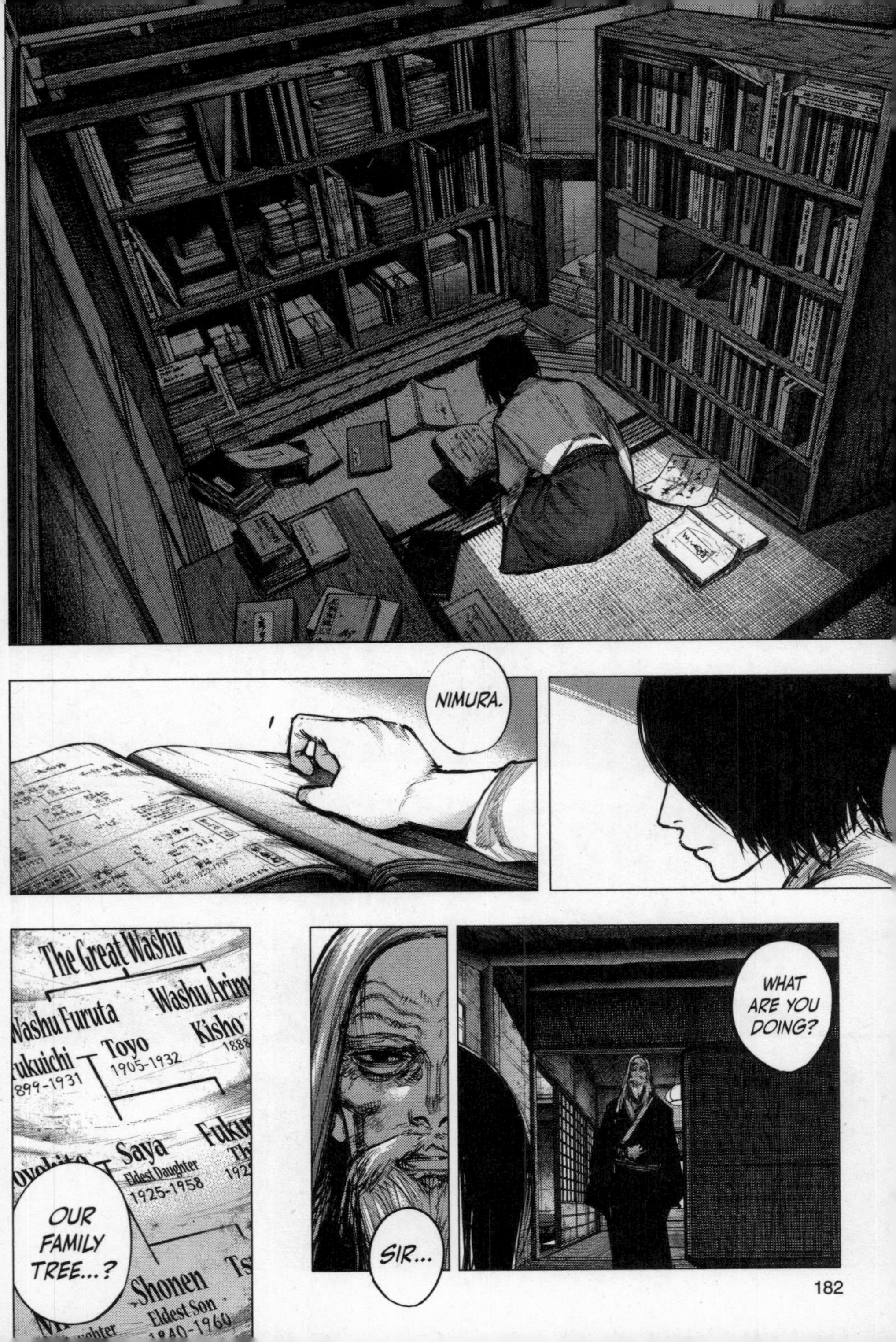
NIMURA.
WHAT ARE YOU DOING?
SIR...
The Great Washu
Washu Furuta
Kisho
Toyo
1905-1932
Saya
Eldest Daughter
1925-1958
Shonen
Eldest Son
OUR FAMILY TREE...?

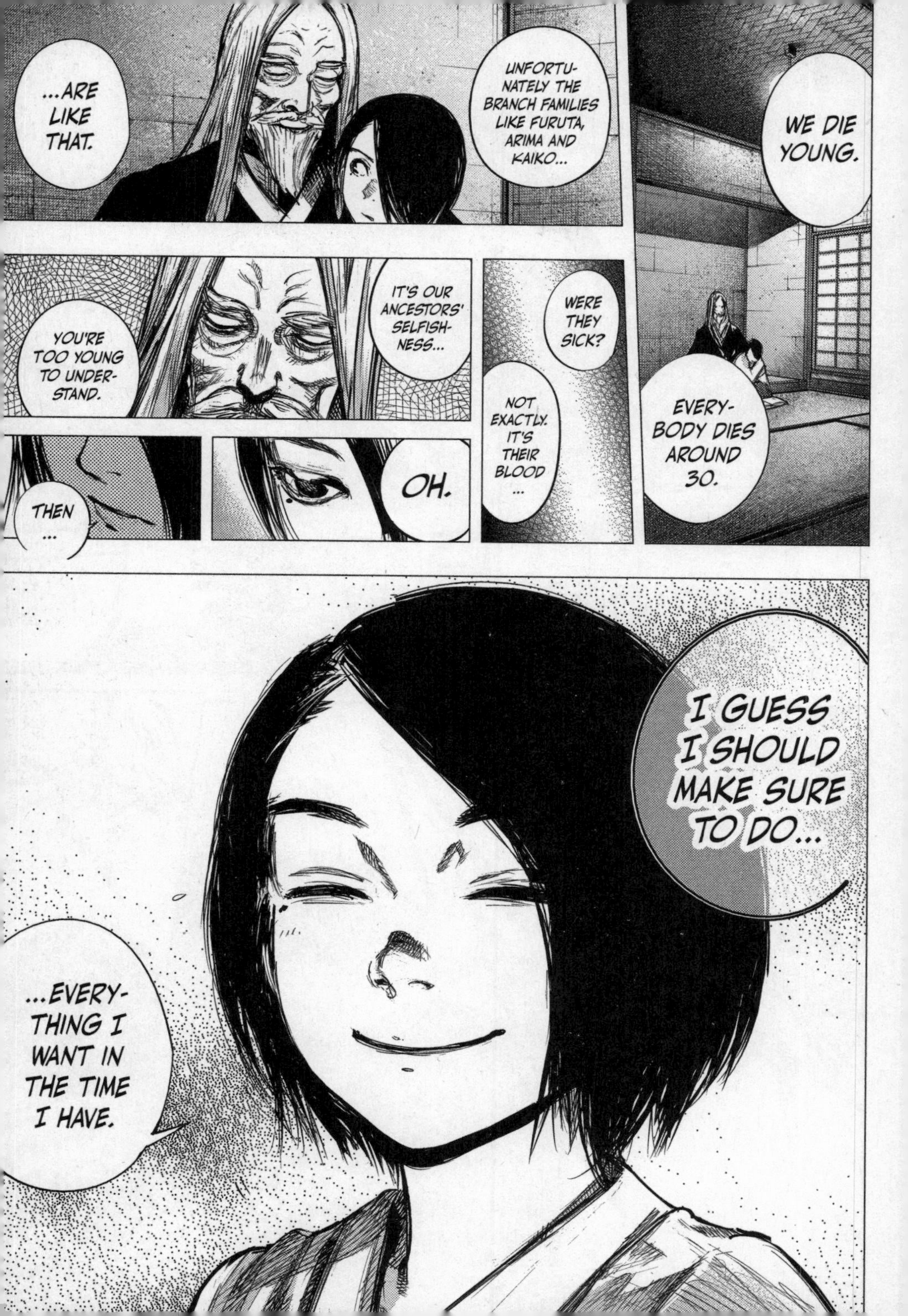
WE DIE YOUNG.
EVERY-BODY DIES AROUND 30.
UNFORTU-NATELY THE BRANCH FAMILIES LIKE FURUTA, ARIMA AND KAIKO...
...ARE LIKE THAT.
WERE THEY SICK?
NOT EXACTLY. IT'S THEIR BLOOD...
IT'S OUR ANCESTORS' SELFISH-NESS...
YOU'RE TOO YOUNG TO UNDER-STAND.
OH.
THEN...
I GUESS I SHOULD MAKE SURE TO DO...
...EVERY-THING I WANT IN THE TIME I HAVE.

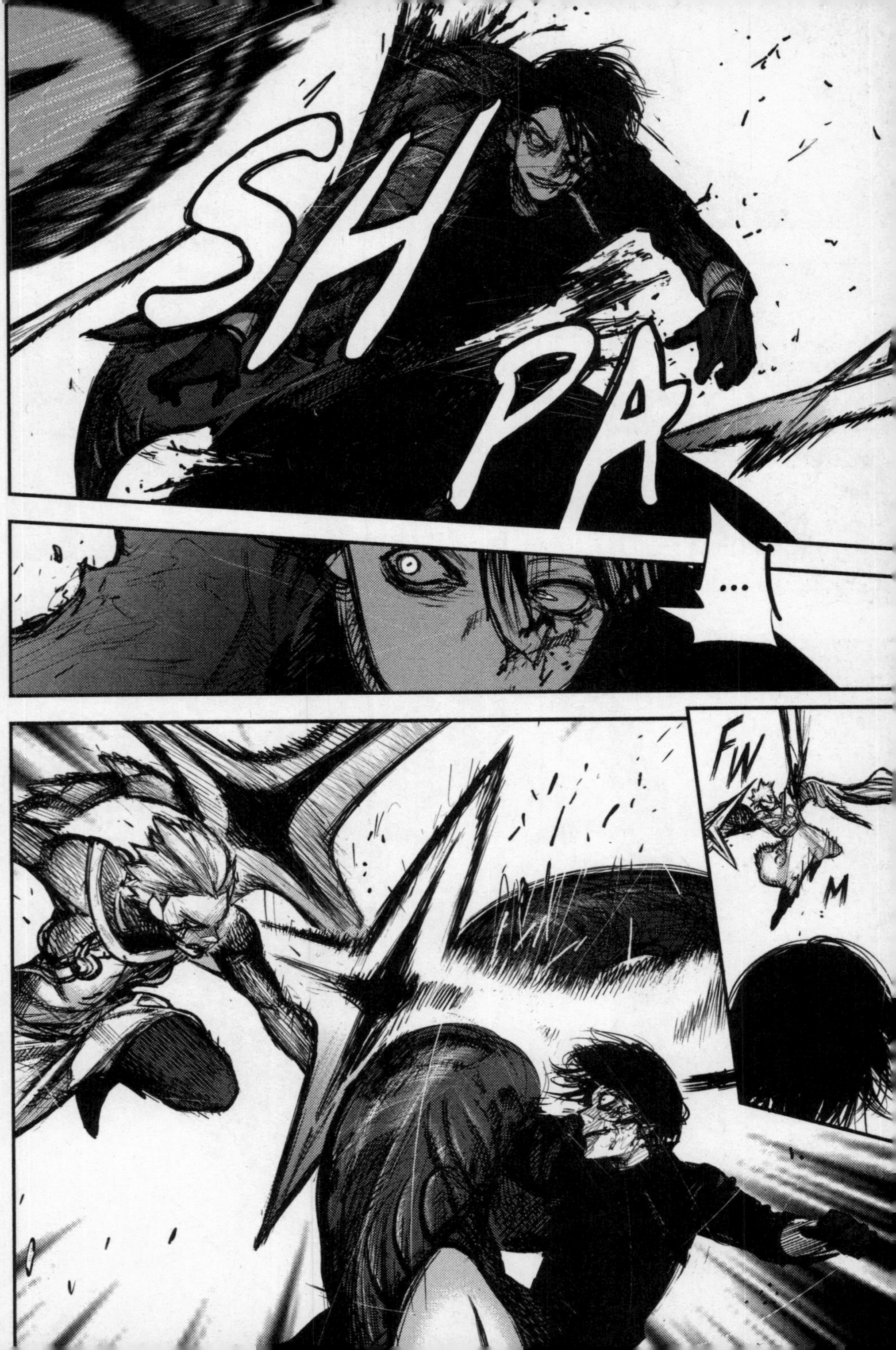
SHPA
...
FWM

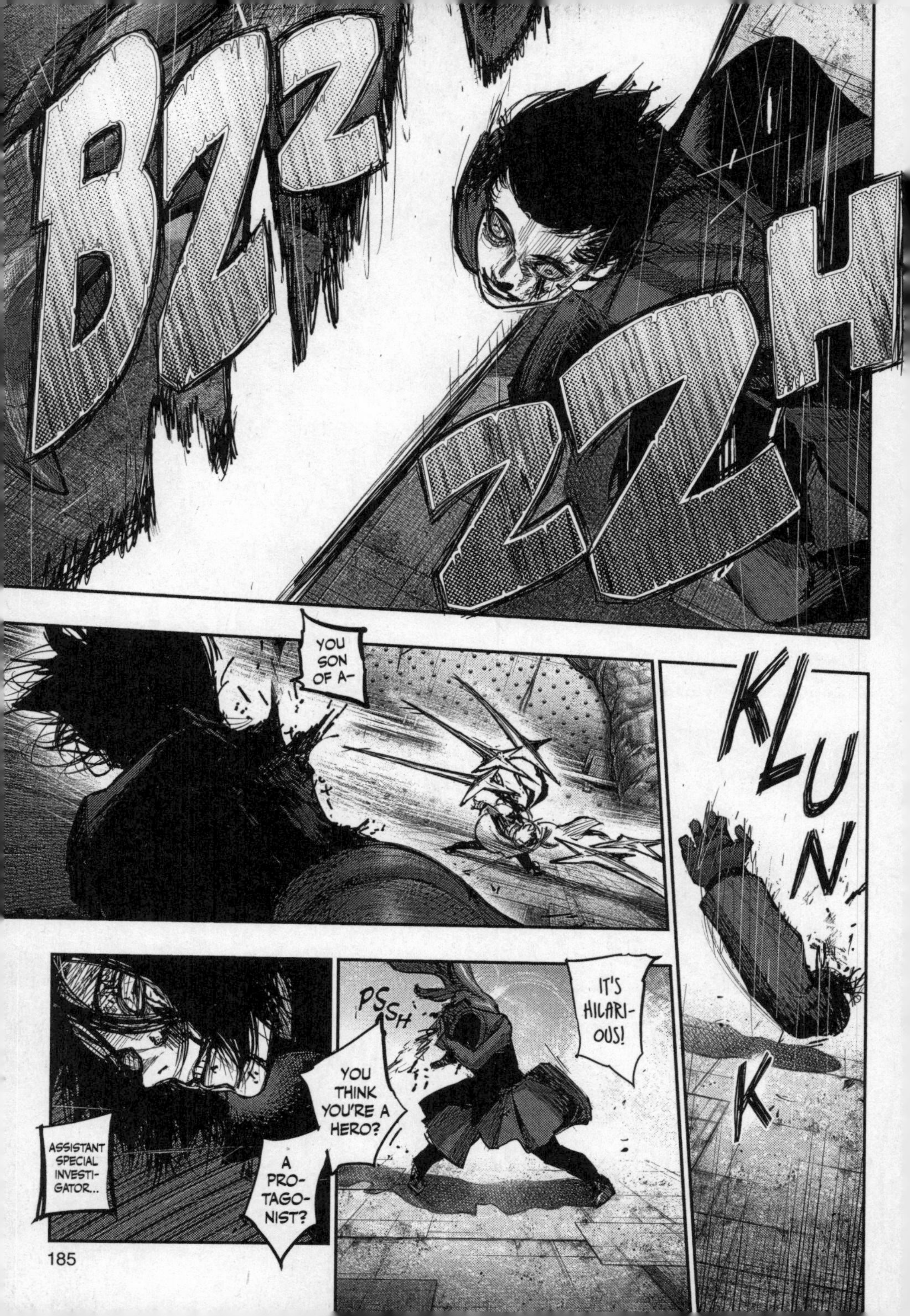
BZZZZH
KLUNK
YOU SON OF A-
IT'S HILARIOUS!
PSSH
YOU THINK YOU'RE A HERO?
A PROTAGONIST?
ASSISTANT SPECIAL INVESTIGATOR...

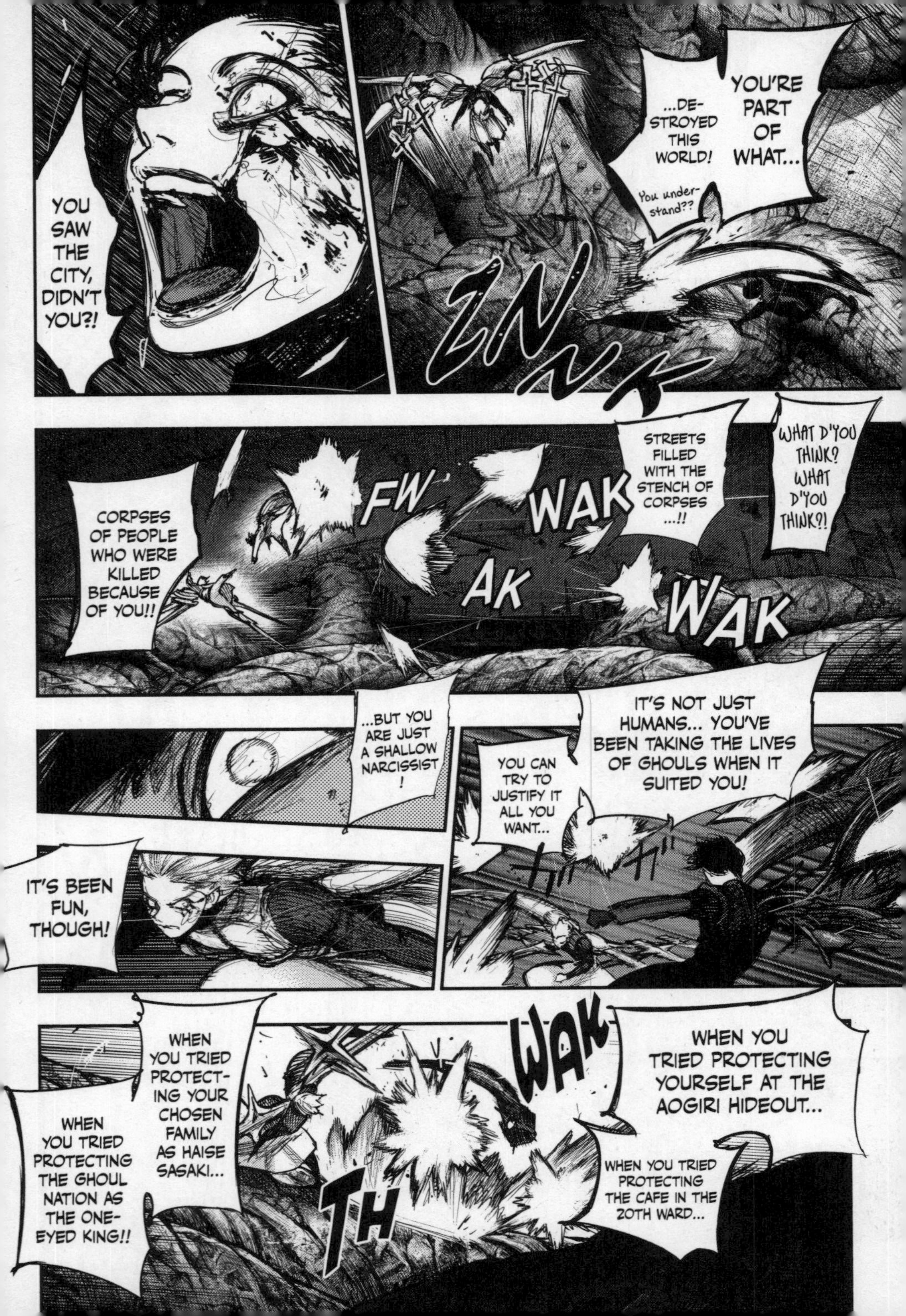
YOU'RE PART OF WHAT...
...DESTROYED THIS WORLD!
You understand??
ZNNK
YOU SAW THE CITY, DIDN'T YOU?!
WHAT D'YOU THINK? WHAT D'YOU THINK?!
STREETS FILLED WITH THE STENCH OF CORPSES ...!!
WAK
FW
WAK
AK
CORPSES OF PEOPLE WHO WERE KILLED BECAUSE OF YOU!!
IT'S NOT JUST HUMANS... YOU'VE BEEN TAKING THE LIVES OF GHOULS WHEN IT SUITED YOU!
YOU CAN TRY TO JUSTIFY IT ALL YOU WANT...
...BUT YOU ARE JUST A SHALLOW NARCISSIST!
IT'S BEEN FUN, THOUGH!
WHEN YOU TRIED PROTECTING YOURSELF AT THE AOGIRI HIDEOUT...
WAK
WHEN YOU TRIED PROTECTING THE CAFE IN THE 20TH WARD...
WHEN YOU TRIED PROTECTING YOUR CHOSEN FAMILY AS HAISE SASAKI...
TH
WHEN YOU TRIED PROTECTING THE GHOUL NATION AS THE ONE-EYED KING!!

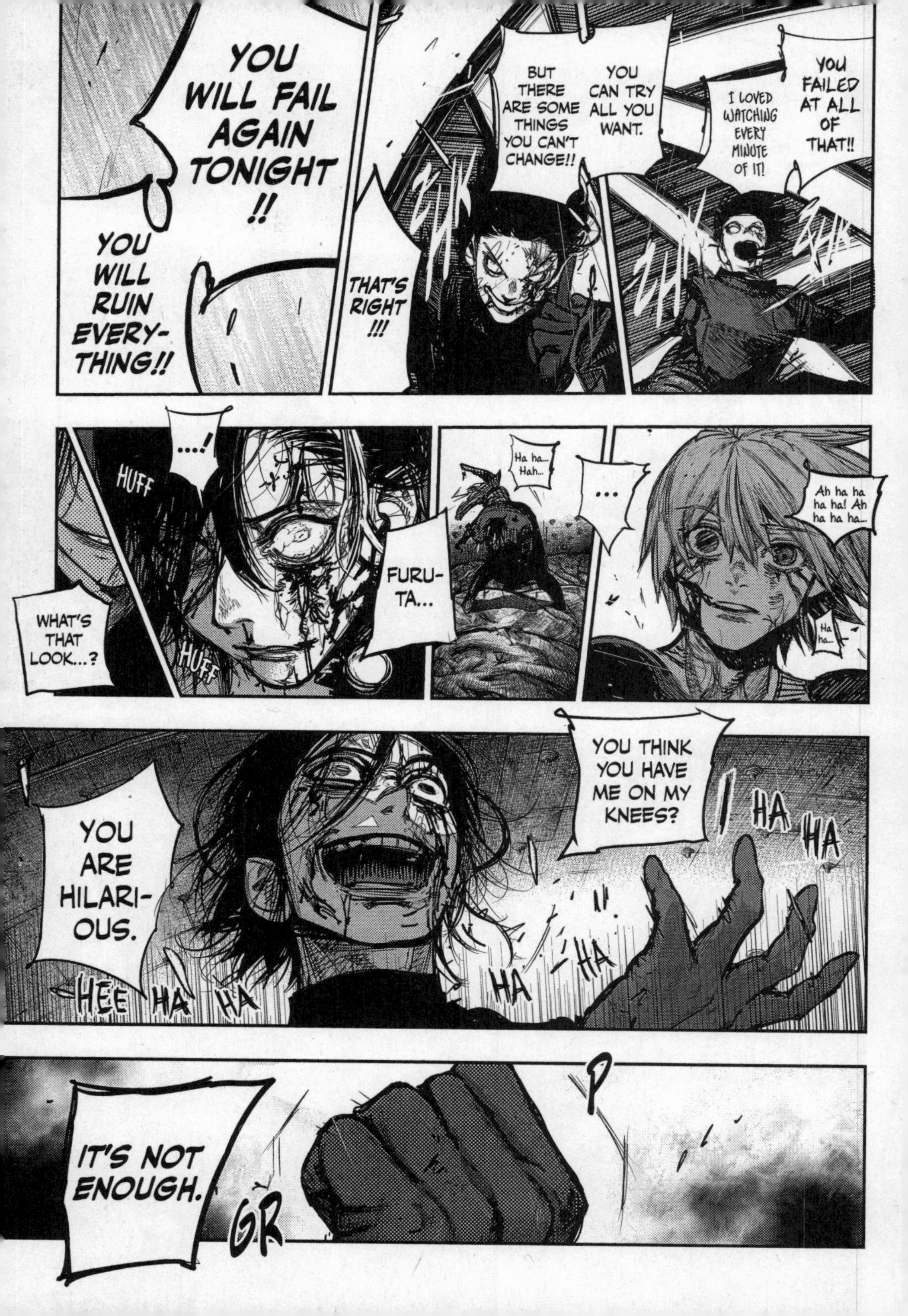
YOU FAILED AT ALL OF THAT!!
I LOVED WATCHING EVERY MINUTE OF IT!
YOU CAN TRY ALL YOU WANT.
BUT THERE ARE SOME THINGS YOU CAN'T CHANGE!!
THAT'S RIGHT!!!
YOU WILL FAIL AGAIN TONIGHT!!
YOU WILL RUIN EVERYTHING!!
Ah ha ha ha ha! Ah ha ha ha...
Ha ha...
...
Ha ha... Hah...
FURU-TA...
...!
HUFF
WHAT'S THAT LOOK...?
HUFF
YOU THINK YOU HAVE ME ON MY KNEES?
HA HA
YOU ARE HILARI-OUS.
HA HA
HEE HA HA
IT'S NOT ENOUGH.
GR

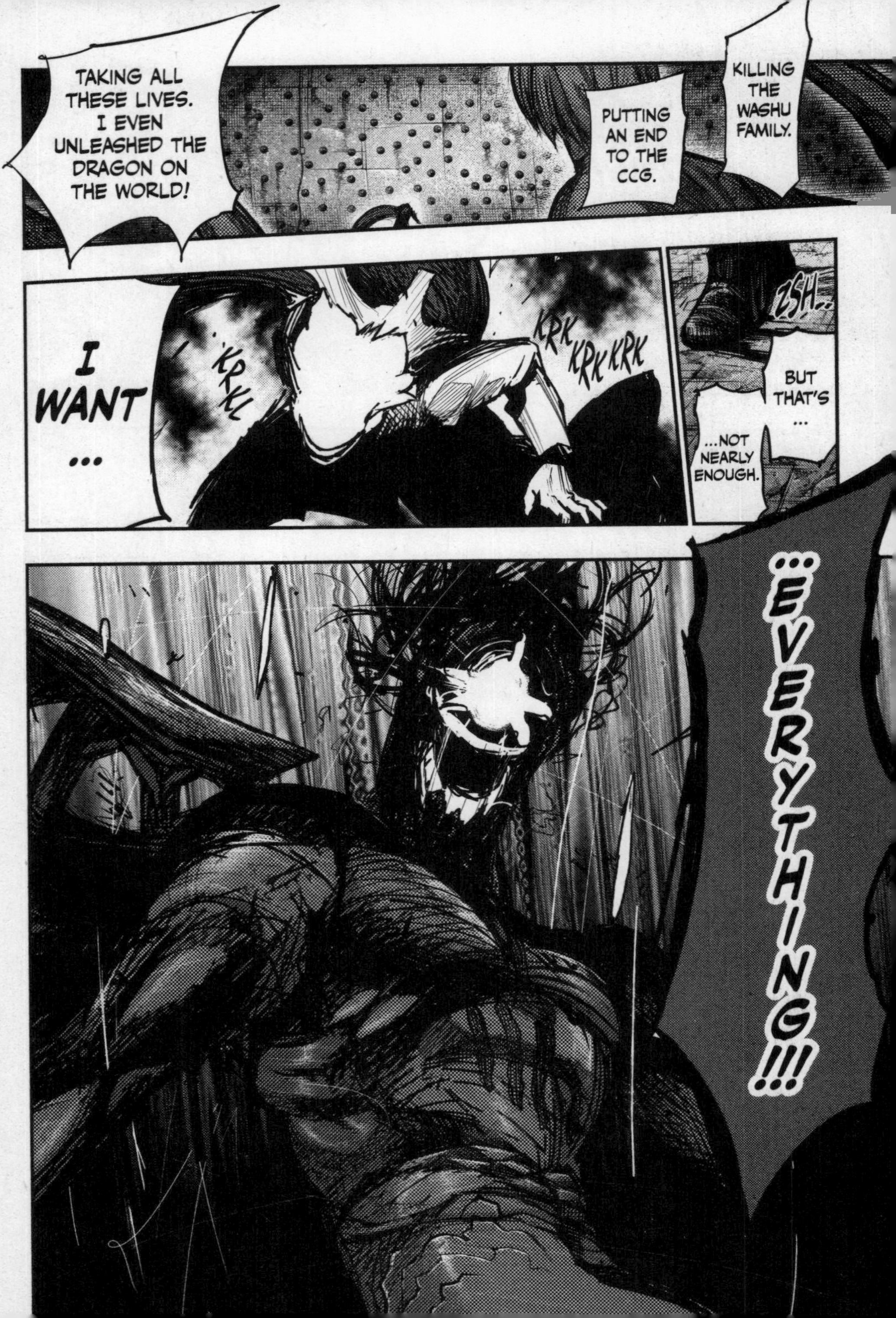
KILLING THE WASHU FAMILY.
PUTTING AN END TO THE CCG.
TAKING ALL THESE LIVES. I EVEN UNLEASHED THE DRAGON ON THE WORLD!
ZSH...
BUT THAT'S...
...NOT NEARLY ENOUGH.
KRK KRK KRK
KRKL
I WANT...
...EVERYTHING!!!

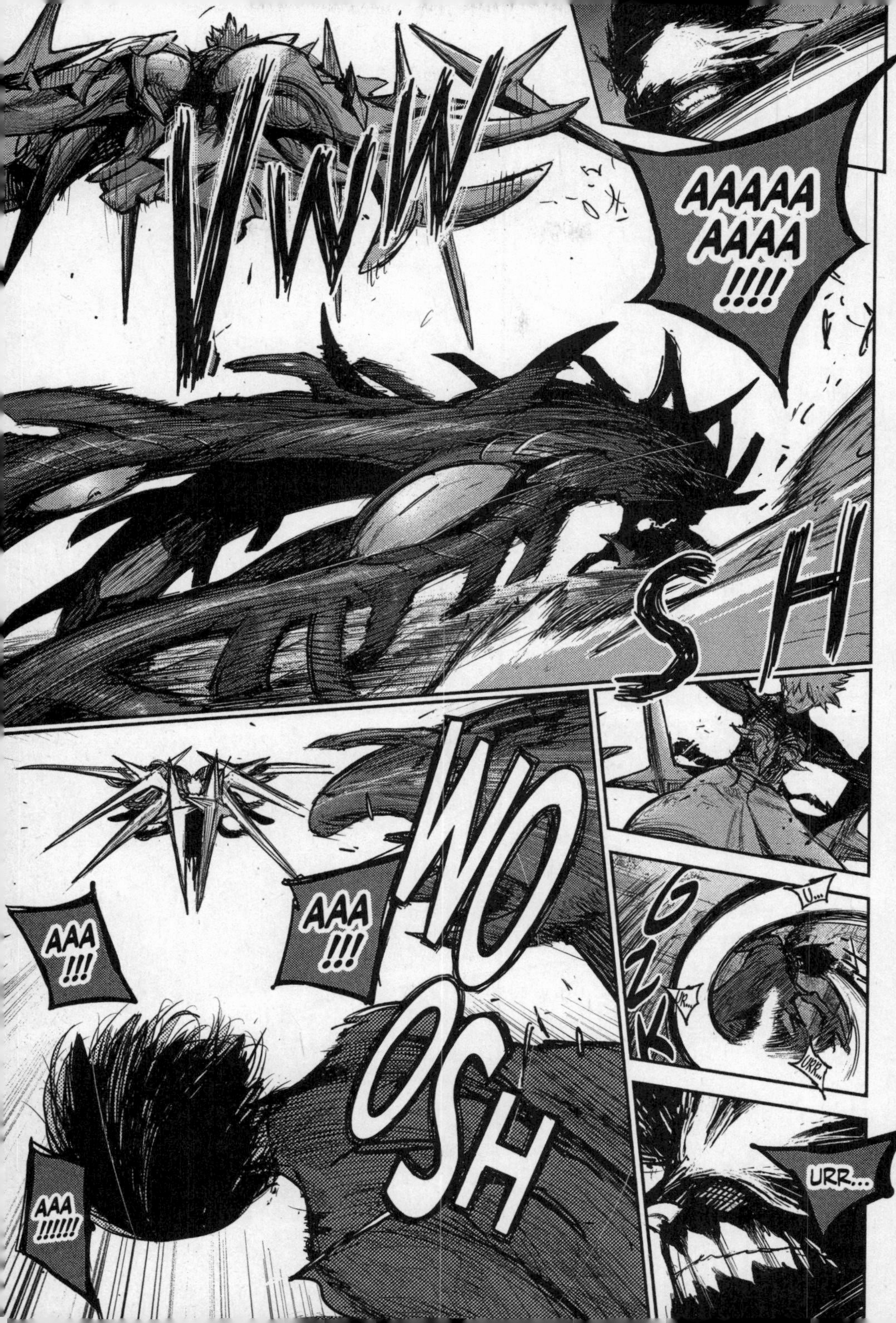
AAAAA AAAA !!!!
VWWW
SH
WOOSH
U...
GZNK
UR...
URR...
URR...
AAA !!!
AAA !!!
AAA !!!!!!

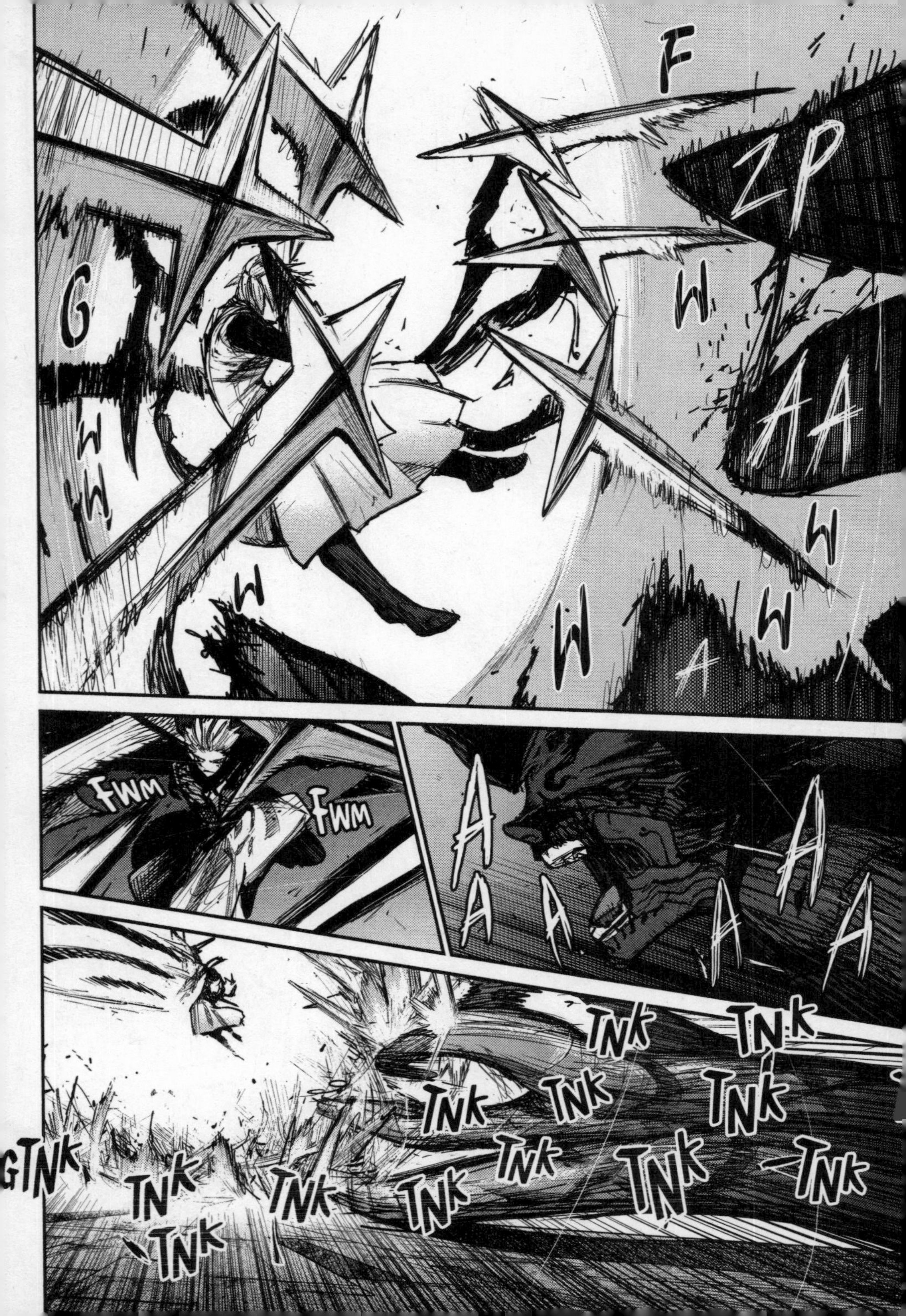

F
ZP
W
AA
W
W
W
A
G
W
W
W
A
A
A
A
A
A
FWM
FWM
TNK
TNK
TNK
TNK
TNK
TNK
TNK
TNK
TNK
TNK
TNK
TNK
GTNK

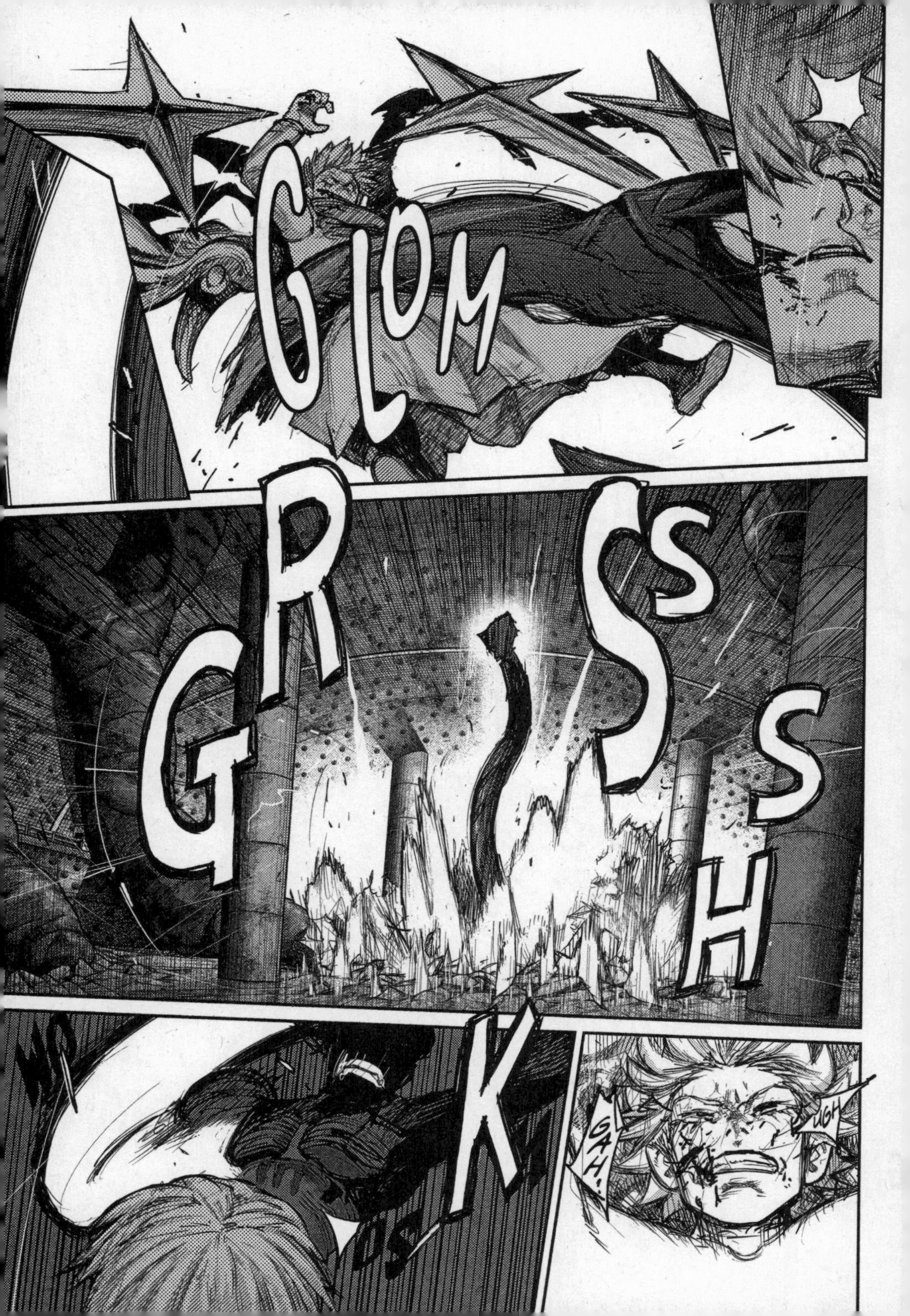
GLOM
GRSSSHK
GAH!
UGH

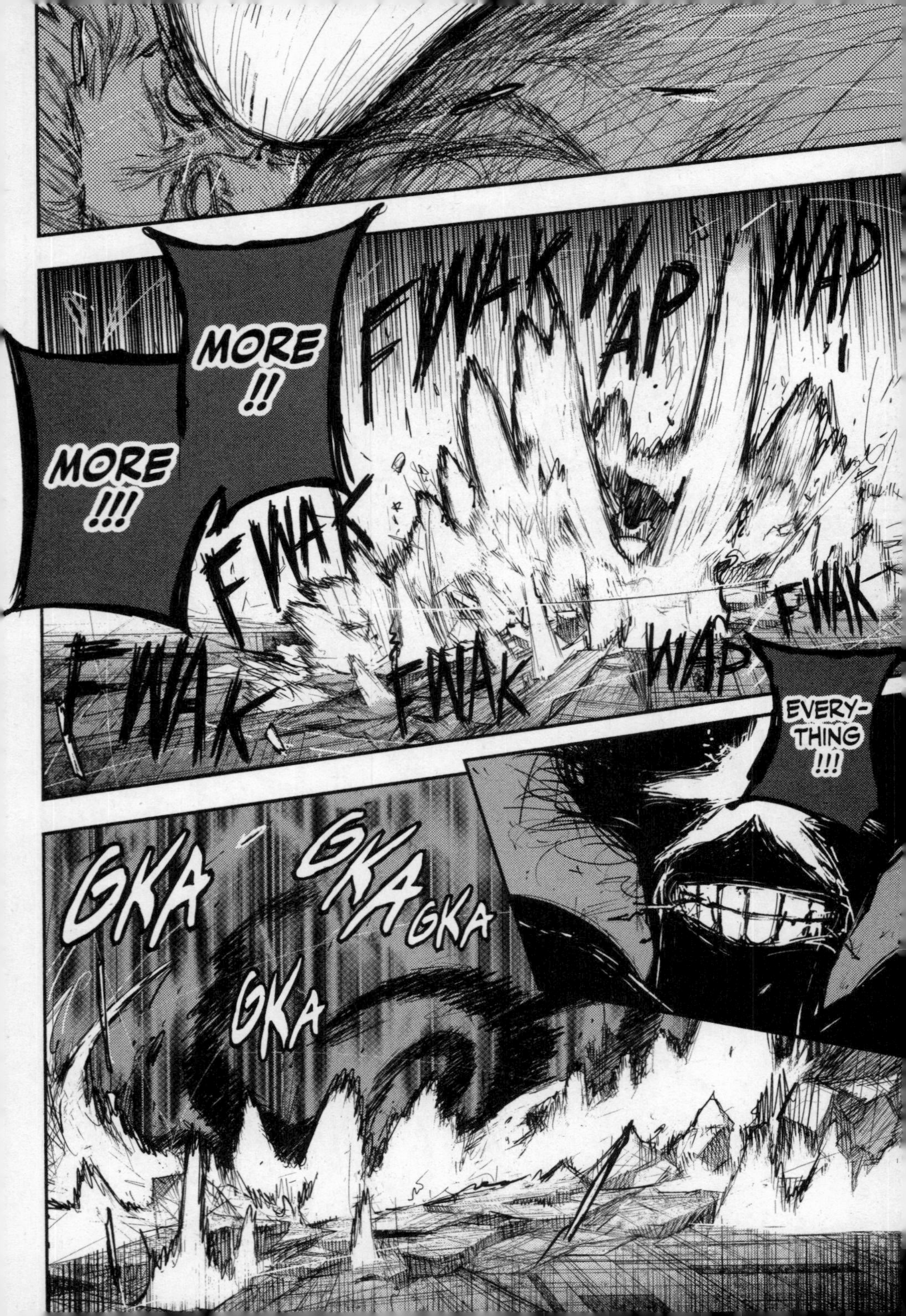
WAP
FWAK WAP
MORE !!
MORE !!!
FWAK
FWAK
WAP
FWAK
FWAK
EVERY-THING !!!
GKA GKA GKA
GKA
GKA

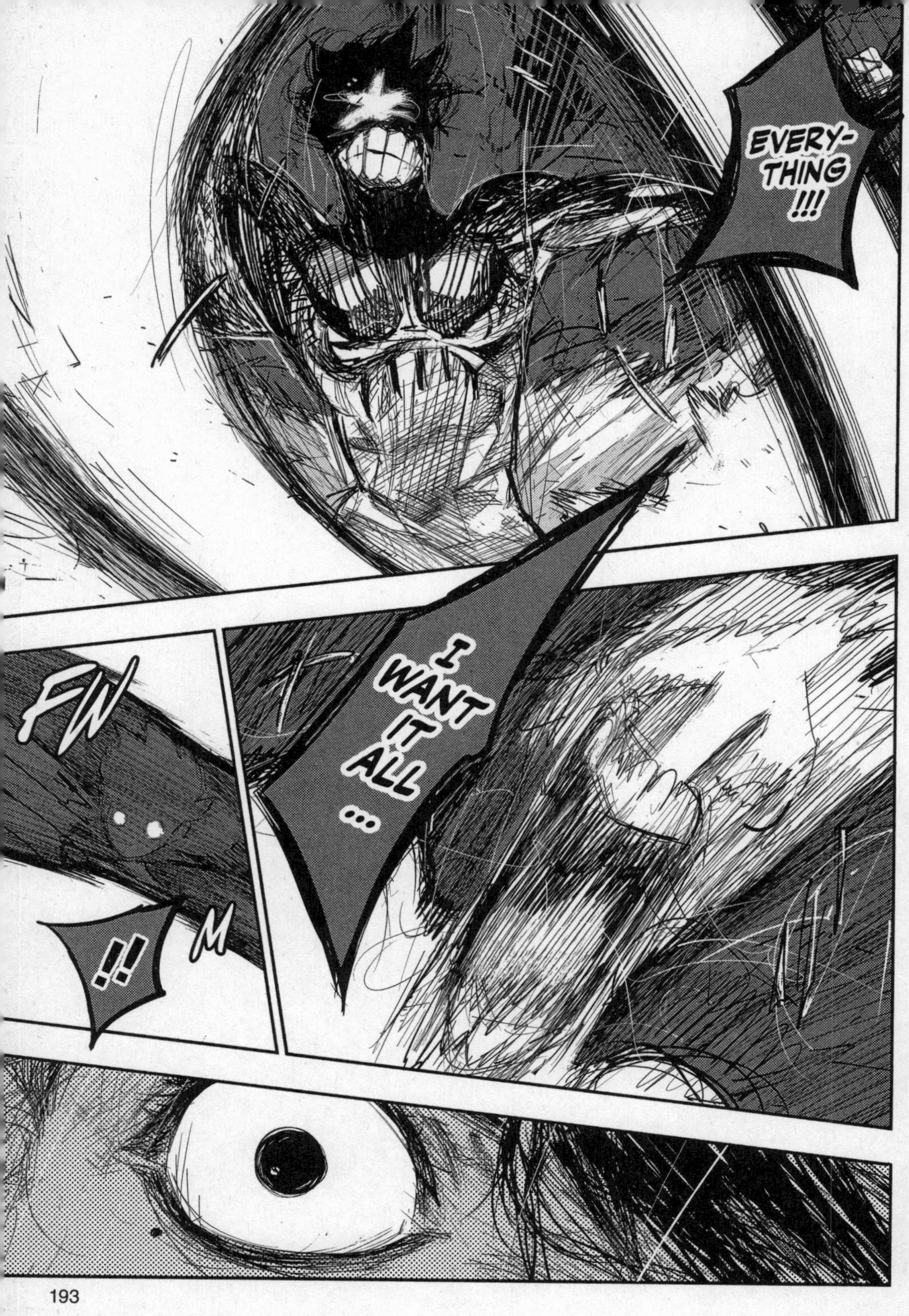
EVERY-THING!!!
I WANT IT ALL...
FWM
!!

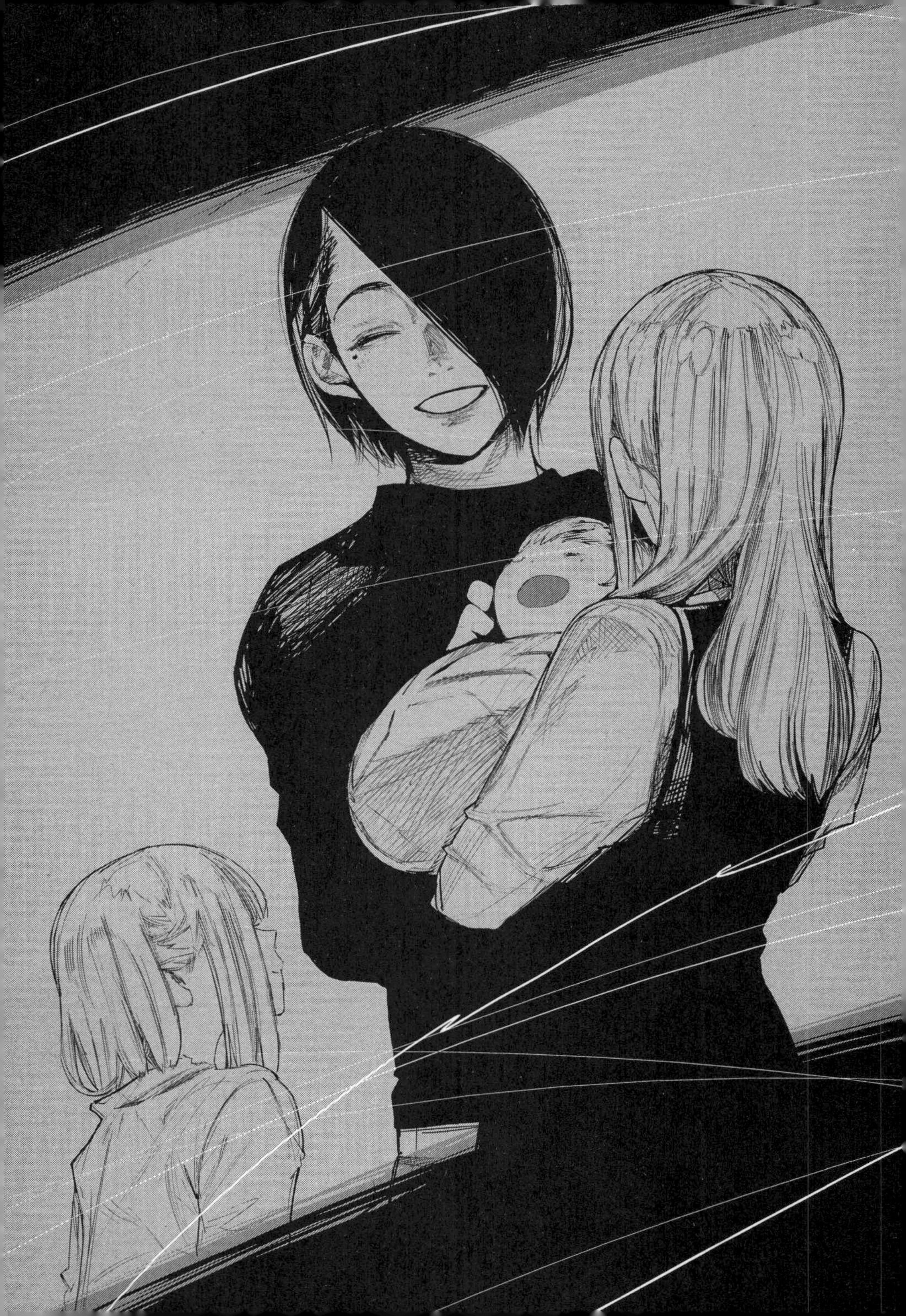

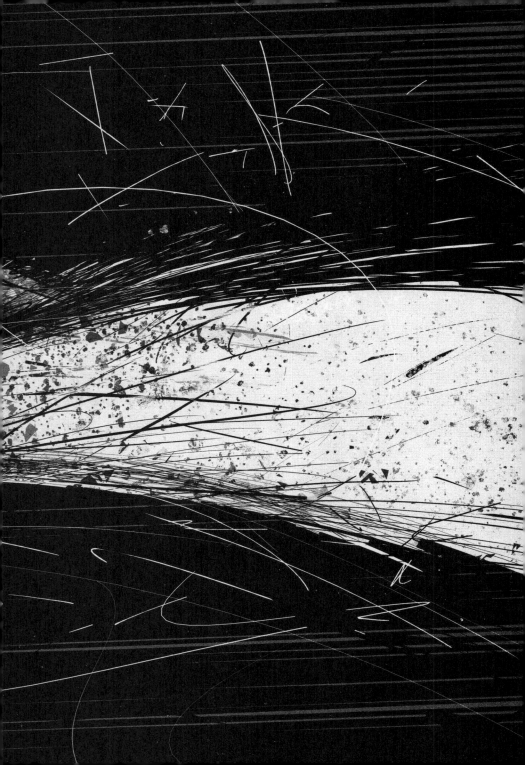

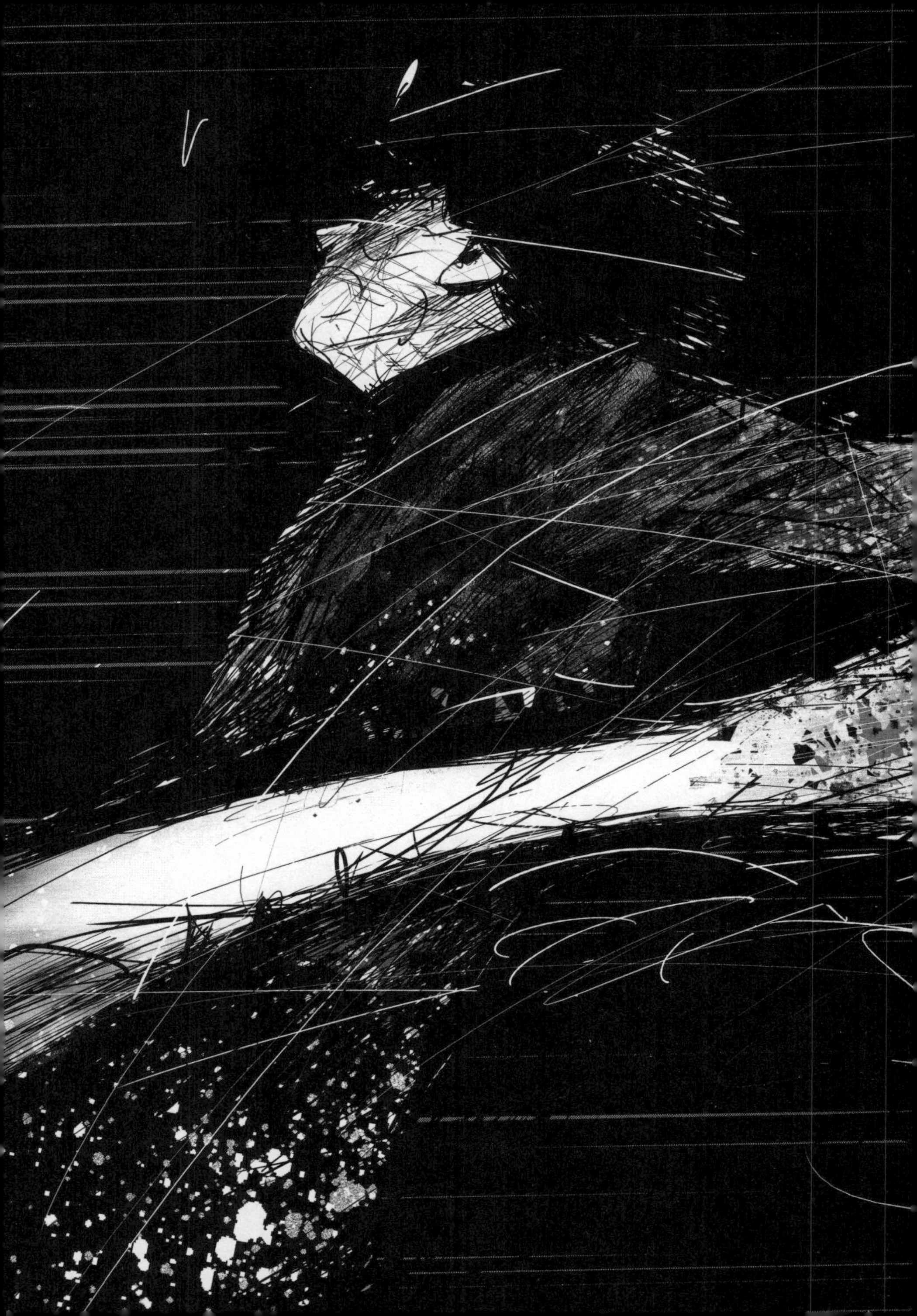

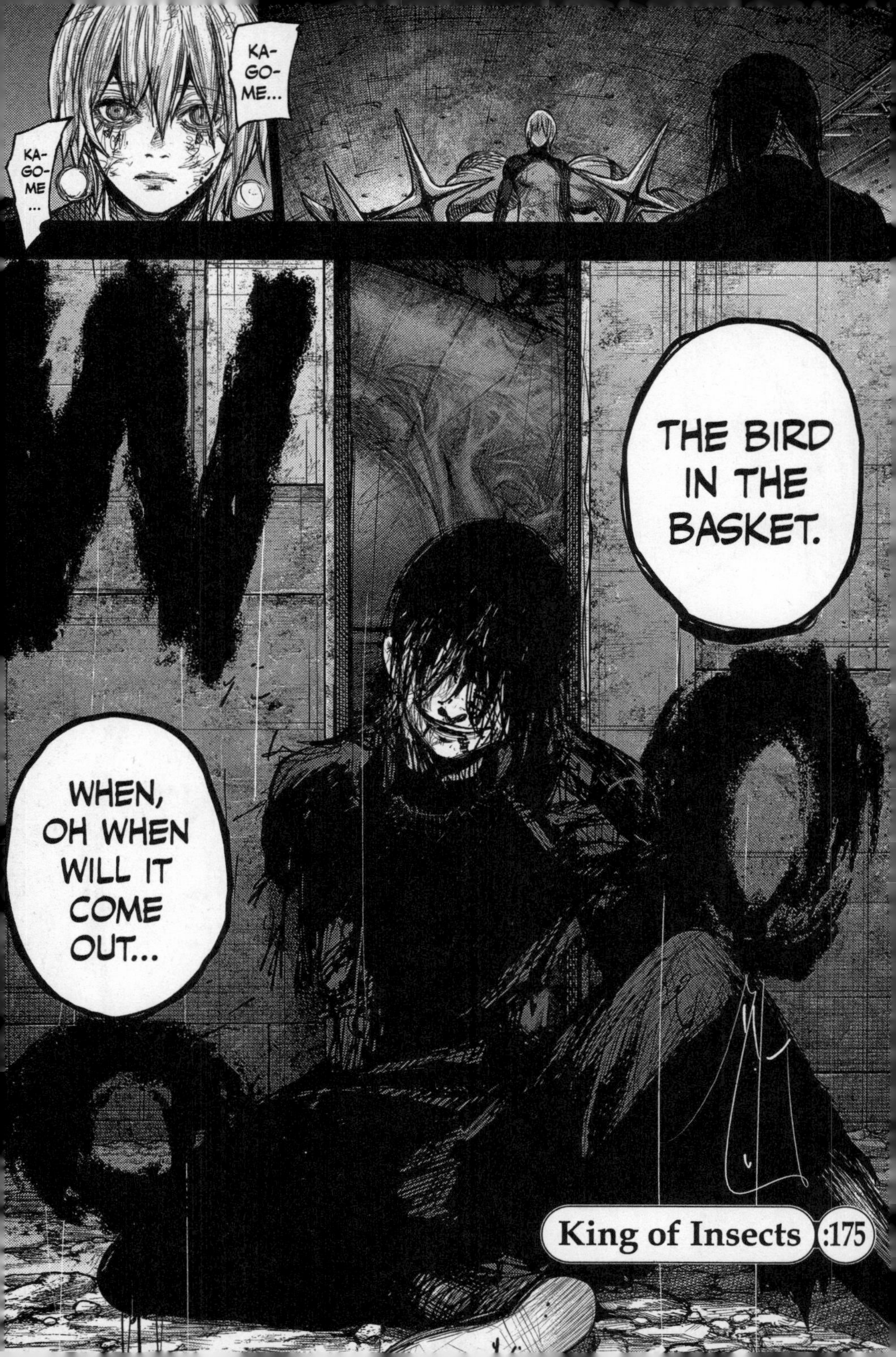
KA-GO-ME...
KA-GO-ME ...
THE BIRD IN THE BASKET.
WHEN, OH WHEN WILL IT COME OUT...

King of Insects :175

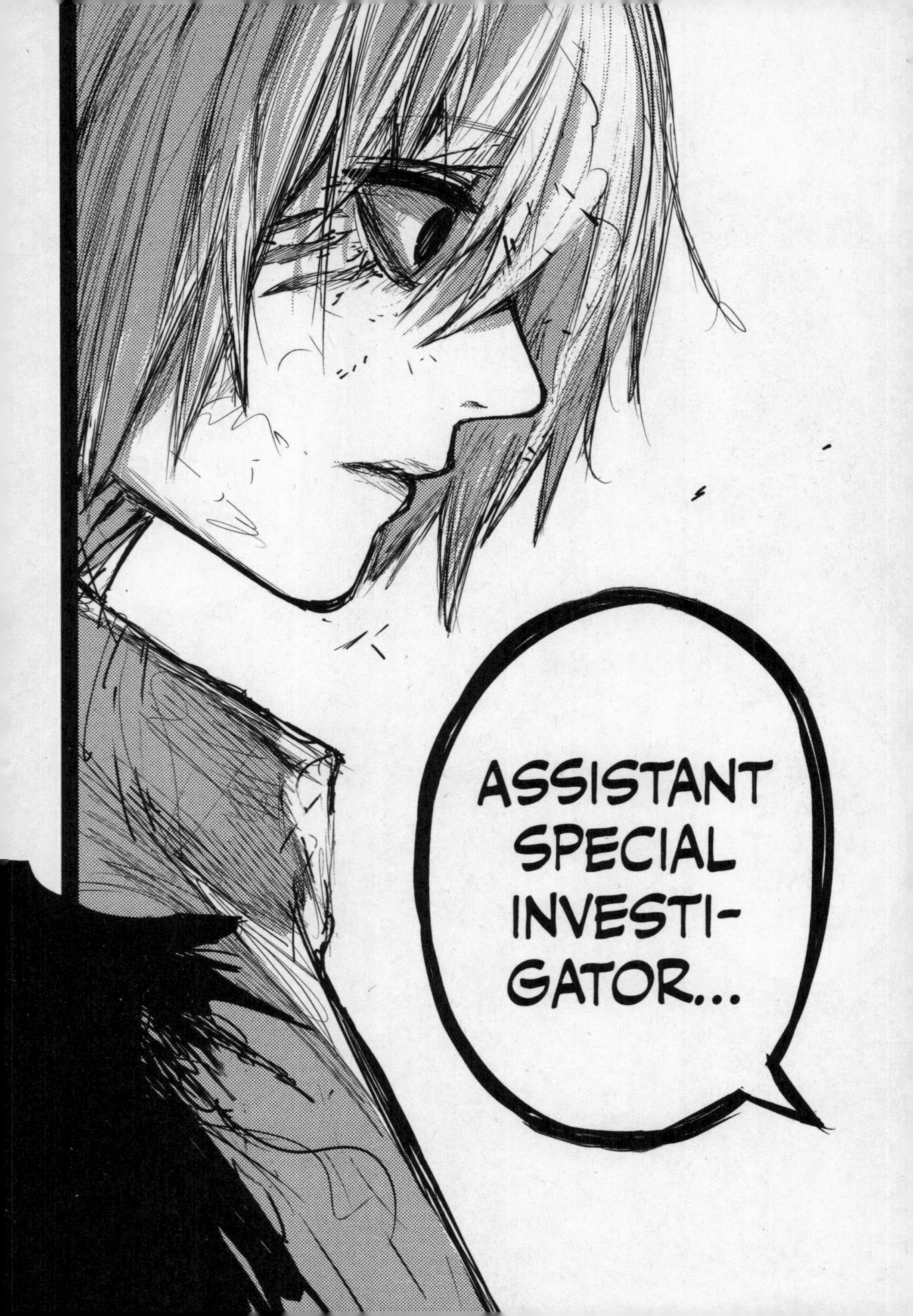
ASSISTANT SPECIAL INVESTI- GATOR...

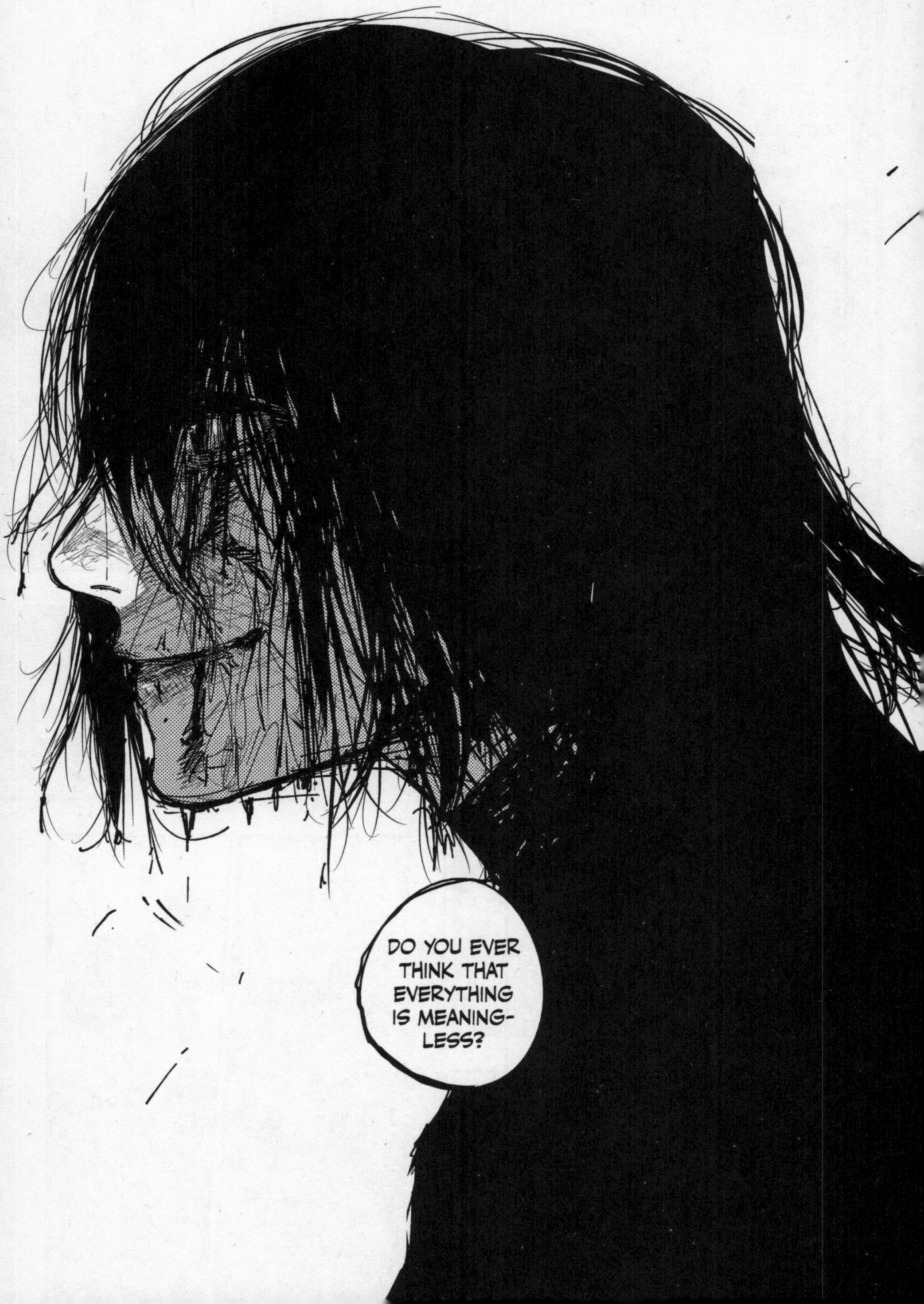
DO YOU EVER THINK THAT EVERYTHING IS MEANING-LESS?

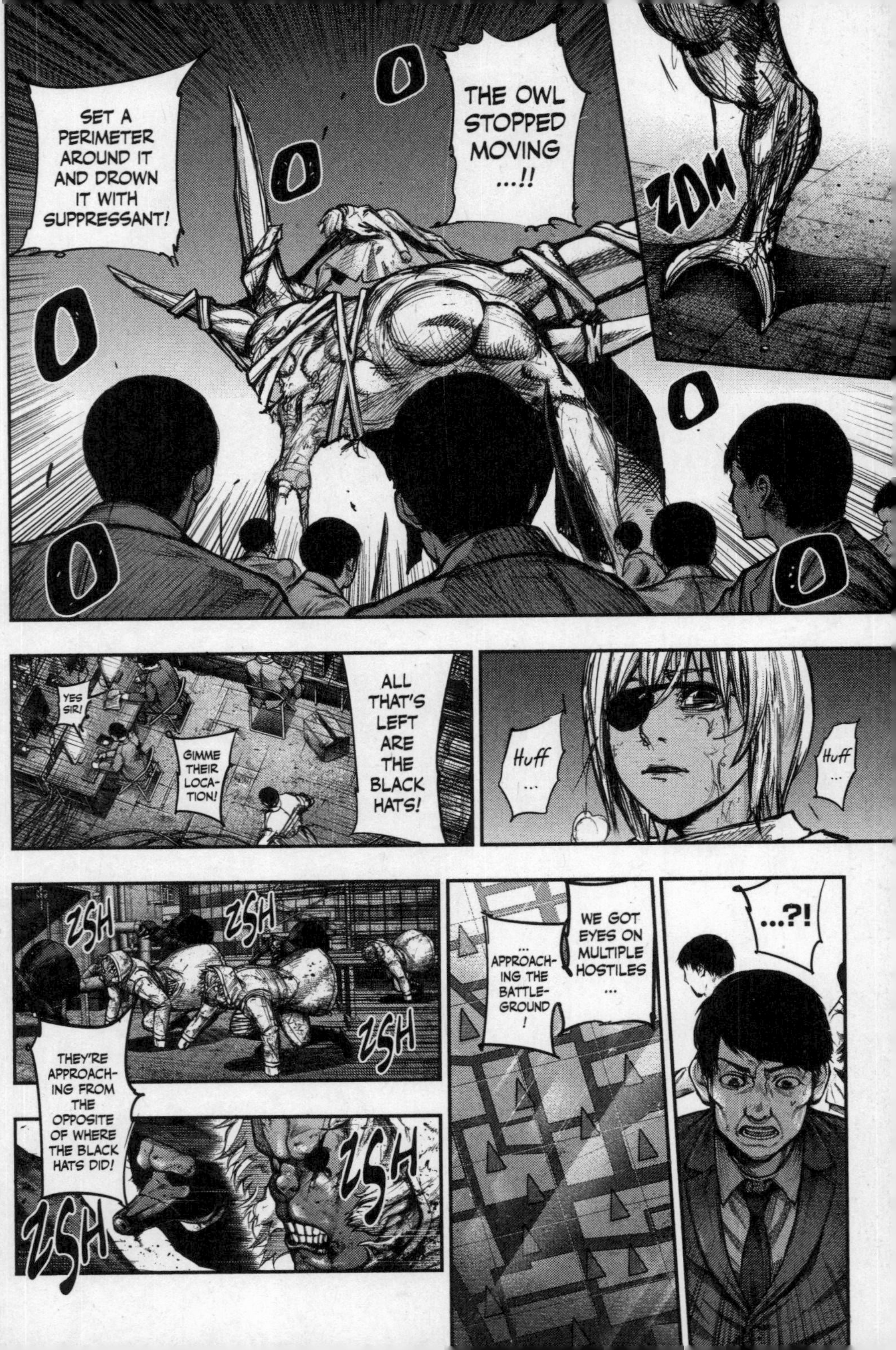
ZDM
THE OWL STOPPED MOVING ...!!
O
O
SET A PERIMETER AROUND IT AND DROWN IT WITH SUPPRESSANT!
O
O
O
O
Huff ...
Huff ...
ALL THAT'S LEFT ARE THE BLACK HATS!
GIMME THEIR LOCATION!
YES SIR!
...?!
WE GOT EYES ON MULTIPLE HOSTILES ...
... APPROACHING THE BATTLE-GROUND !
ZSH
ZSH
ZSH
THEY'RE APPROACHING FROM THE OPPOSITE OF WHERE THE BLACK HATS DID!
ZSH
ZSH

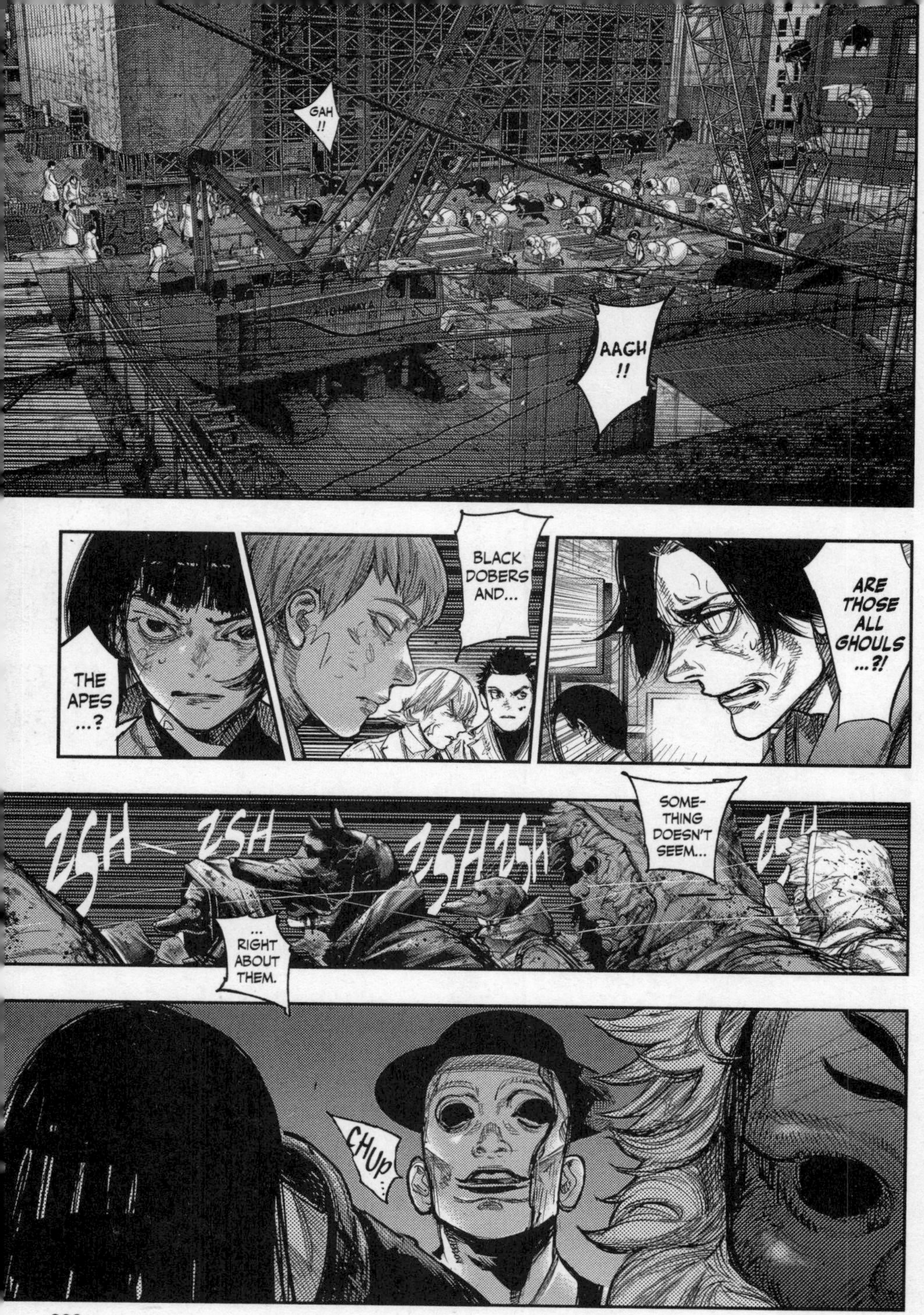
GAH!!
AAGH!!
ARE THOSE ALL GHOULS...?!
BLACK DOBERS AND...
THE APES...?
ZSH
ZSH ZSH
SOMETHING DOESN'T SEEM...
...RIGHT ABOUT THEM.
ZSH
ZSH
CHUP

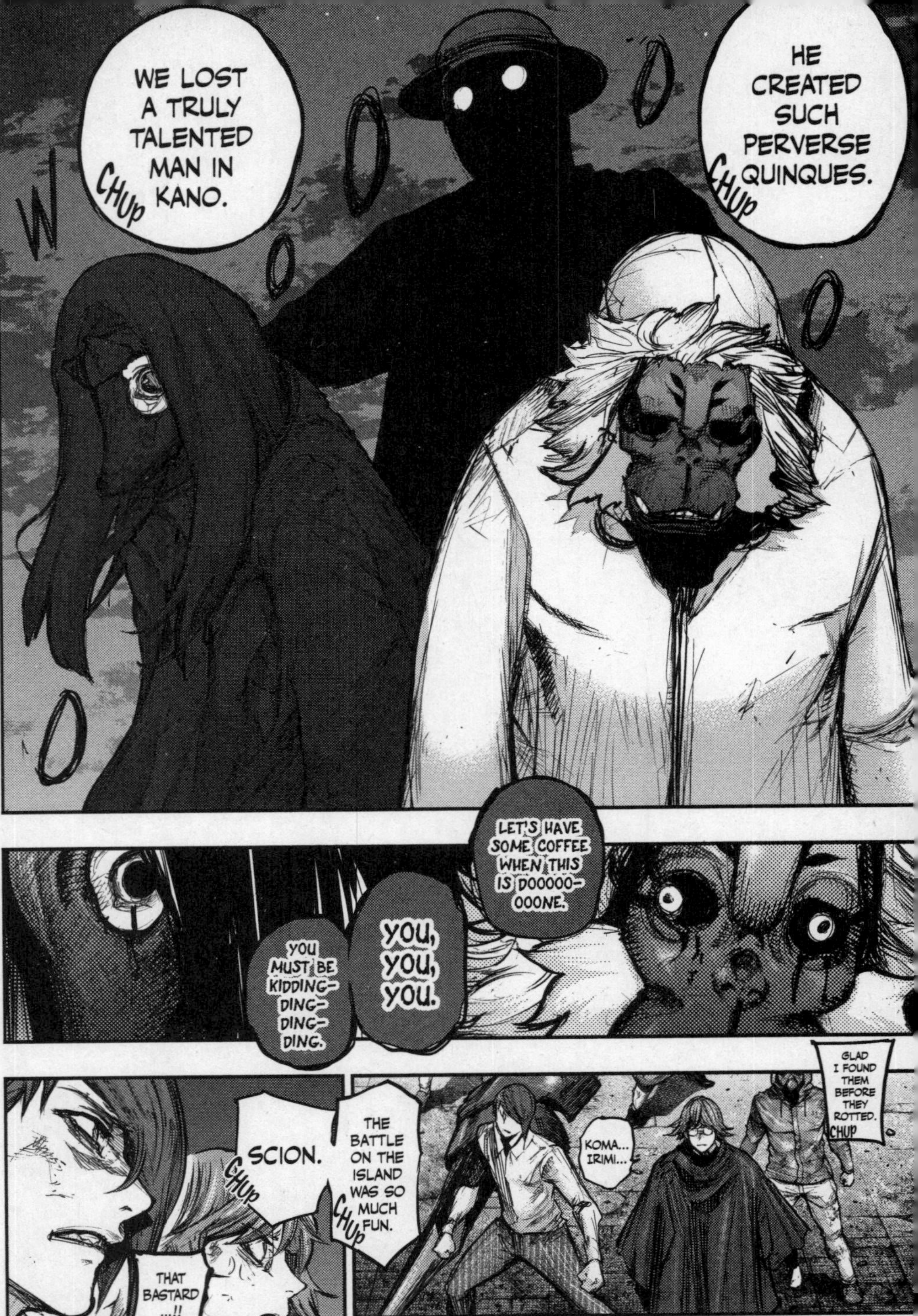
HE CREATED SUCH PERVERSE QUINQUES.
CHUP
WE LOST A TRULY TALENTED MAN IN KANO.
CHUP
W
LET'S HAVE SOME COFFEE WHEN THIS IS DOOOOOO-OOONE.
YOU, YOU, YOU.
YOU MUST BE KIDDING-DING-DING-DING.
GLAD I FOUND THEM BEFORE THEY ROTTED.
CHUP
KOMA... IRIMI...
THE BATTLE ON THE ISLAND WAS SO MUCH FUN.
CHUP
SCION.
CHUP
THAT BASTARD ...!!

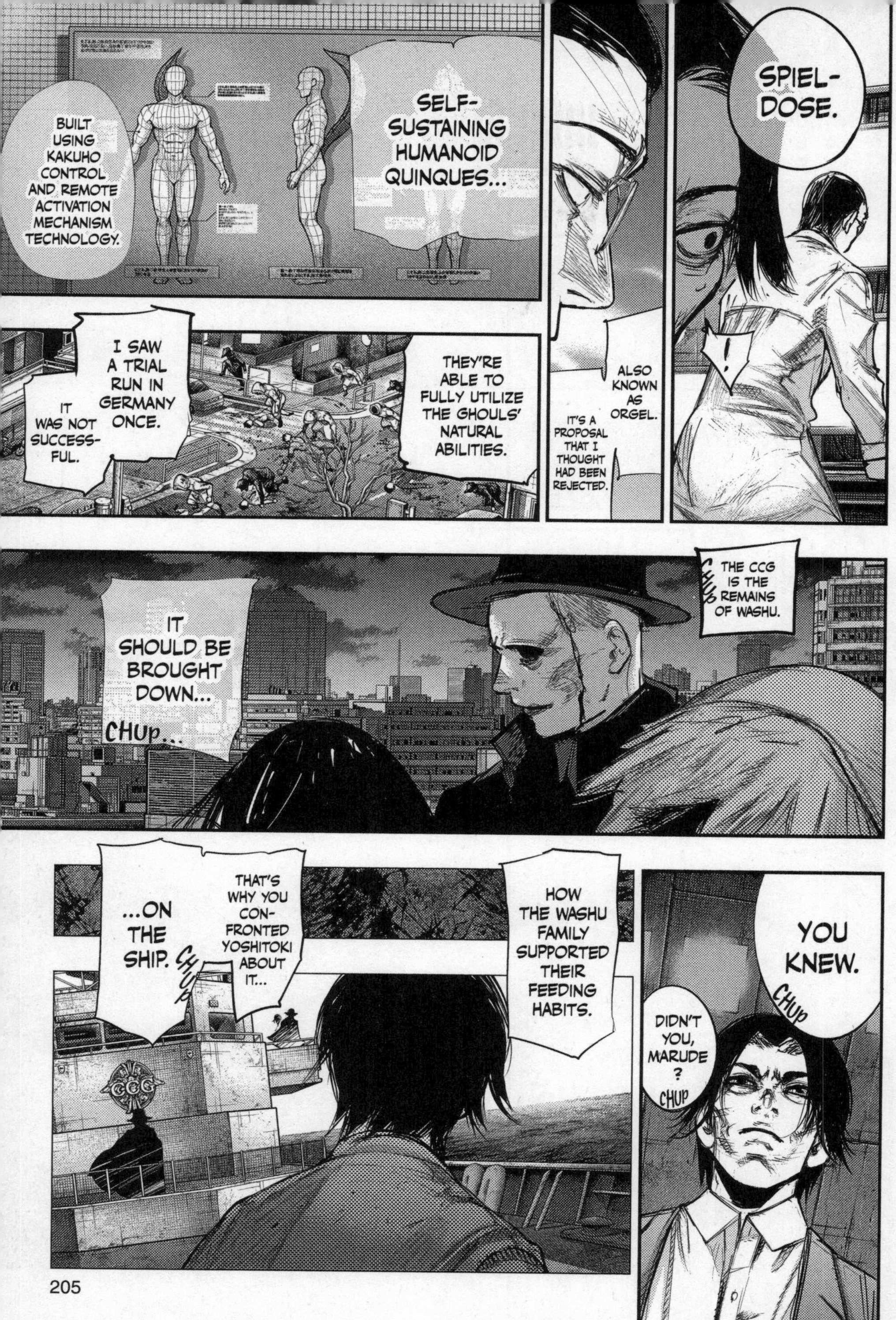
SPIEL-DOSE.
ALSO KNOWN AS ORGEL.
IT'S A PROPOSAL THAT I THOUGHT HAD BEEN REJECTED.
SELF-SUSTAINING HUMANOID QUINQUES...
BUILT USING KAKUHO CONTROL AND REMOTE ACTIVATION MECHANISM TECHNOLOGY.
THEY'RE ABLE TO FULLY UTILIZE THE GHOULS' NATURAL ABILITIES.
I SAW A TRIAL RUN IN GERMANY ONCE.
IT WAS NOT SUCCESS-FUL.
THE CCG IS THE REMAINS OF WASHU.
CHUP
IT SHOULD BE BROUGHT DOWN...
CHUP...
YOU KNEW.
CHUP
DIDN'T YOU, MARUDE?
CHUP
HOW THE WASHU FAMILY SUPPORTED THEIR FEEDING HABITS.
THAT'S WHY YOU CON-FRONTED YOSHITOKI ABOUT IT...
CHUP
...ON THE SHIP.

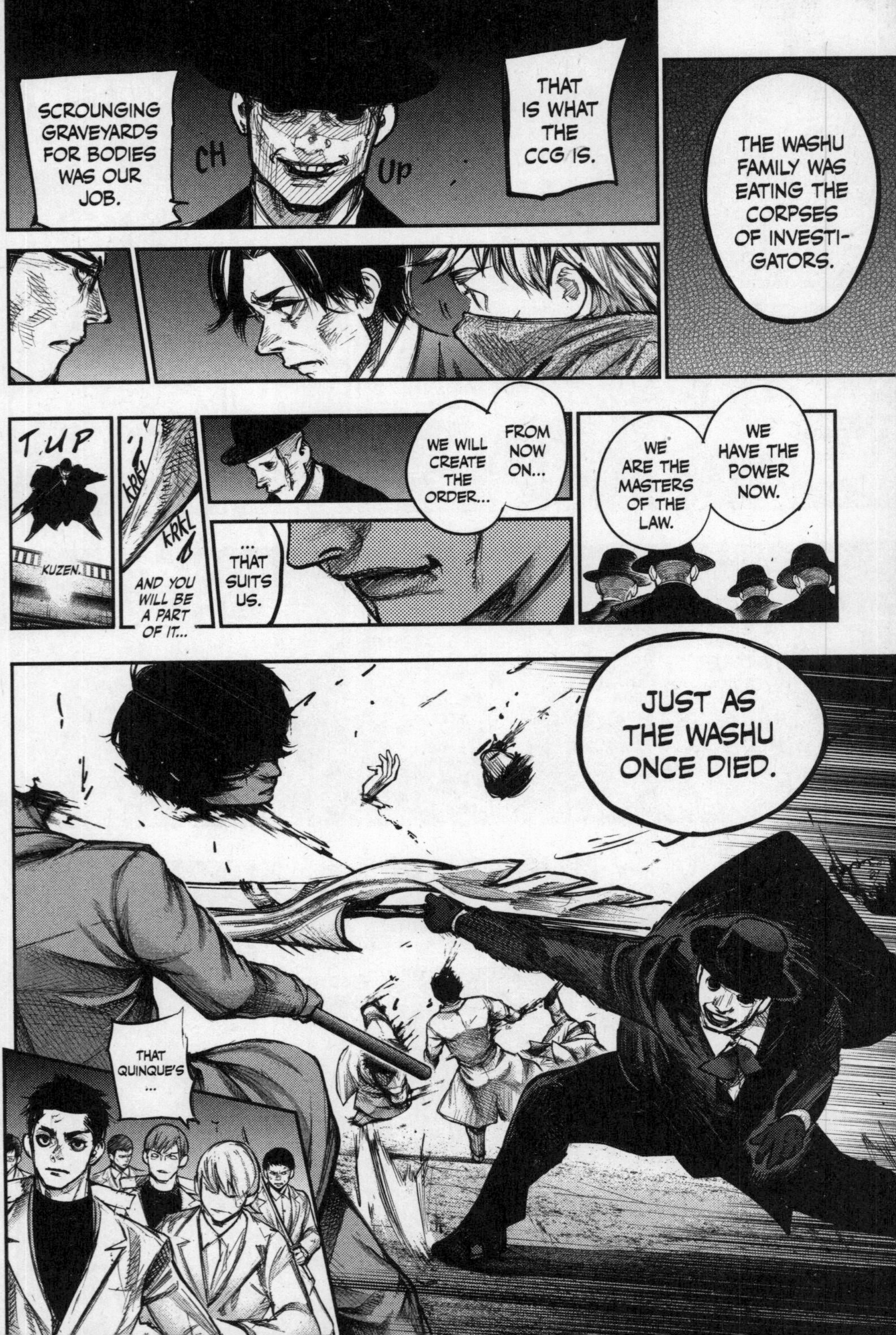
THE WASHU FAMILY WAS EATING THE CORPSES OF INVESTIGATORS.
THAT IS WHAT THE CCG IS.
CH Up
SCROUNGING GRAVEYARDS FOR BODIES WAS OUR JOB.
WE HAVE THE POWER NOW.
WE ARE THE MASTERS OF THE LAW.
FROM NOW ON...
WE WILL CREATE THE ORDER...
... THAT SUITS US.
KRKL
KRKL
AND YOU WILL BE A PART OF IT...
T.UP
KUZEN.
JUST AS THE WASHU ONCE DIED.
THAT QUINQUE'S ...

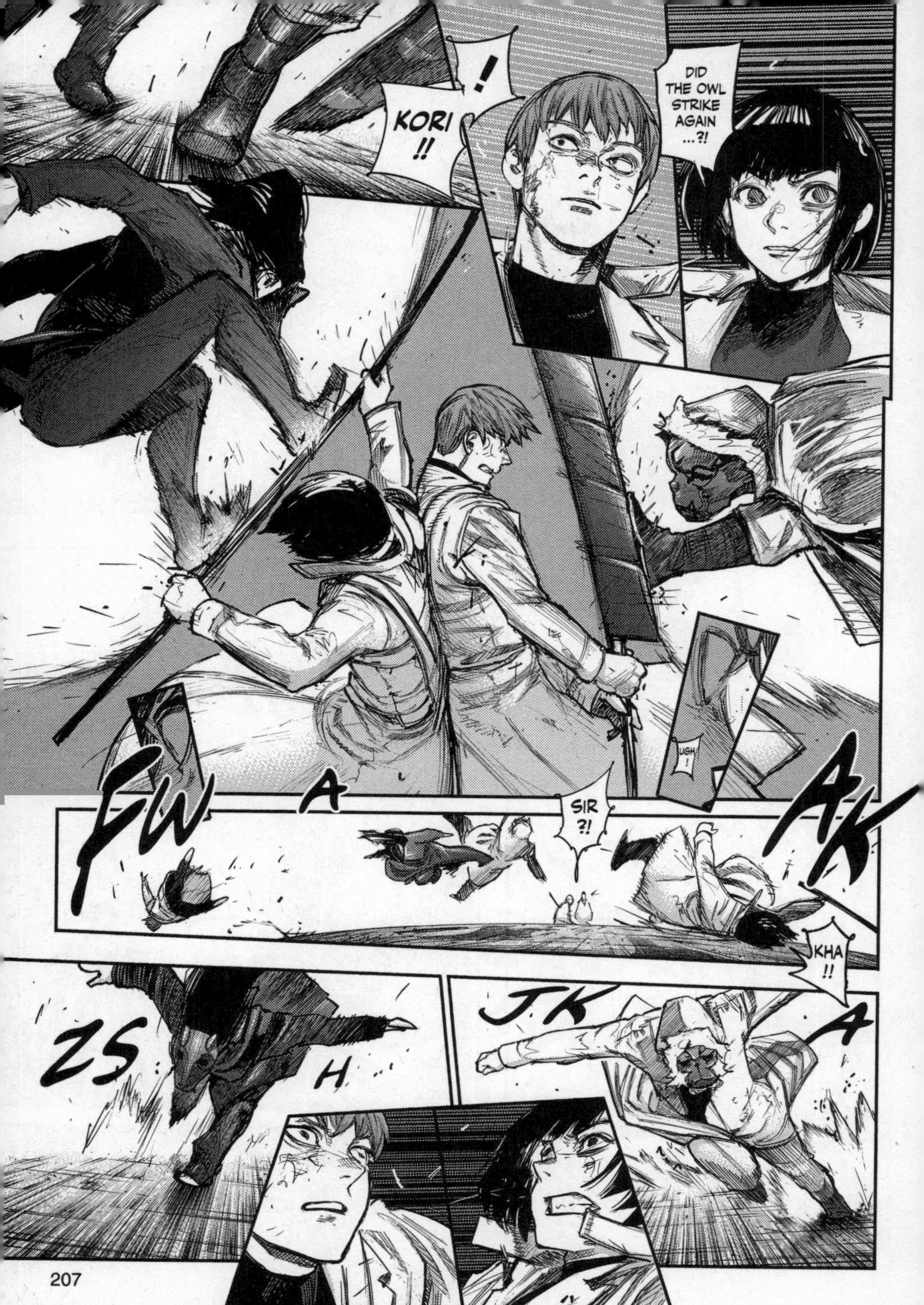
DID THE OWL STRIKE AGAIN ...?!
!
KORI !!
UGH!
FWAAK
SIR ?!
KHA !!
JKA
ZSH

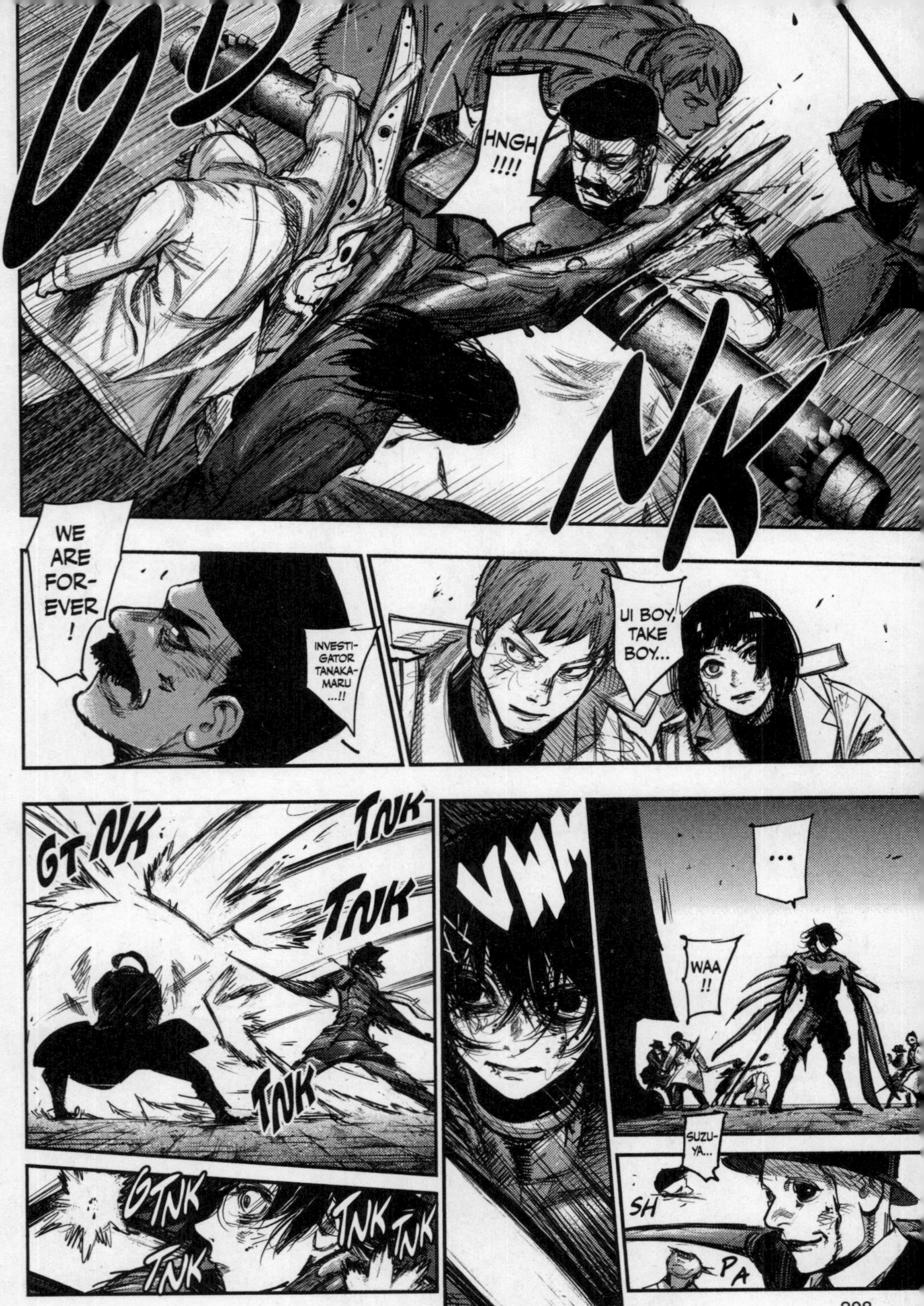
HNGH !!!!
NK
UI BOY, TAKE BOY...
WE ARE FOR-EVER!
INVESTI-GATOR TANAKA-MARU ...!!
...
WAA !!
SUZU-YA...
SH
PA
VWM
GT NK
TNK
TNK
TNK
GTNK
TNK
TNK
TNK
TNK

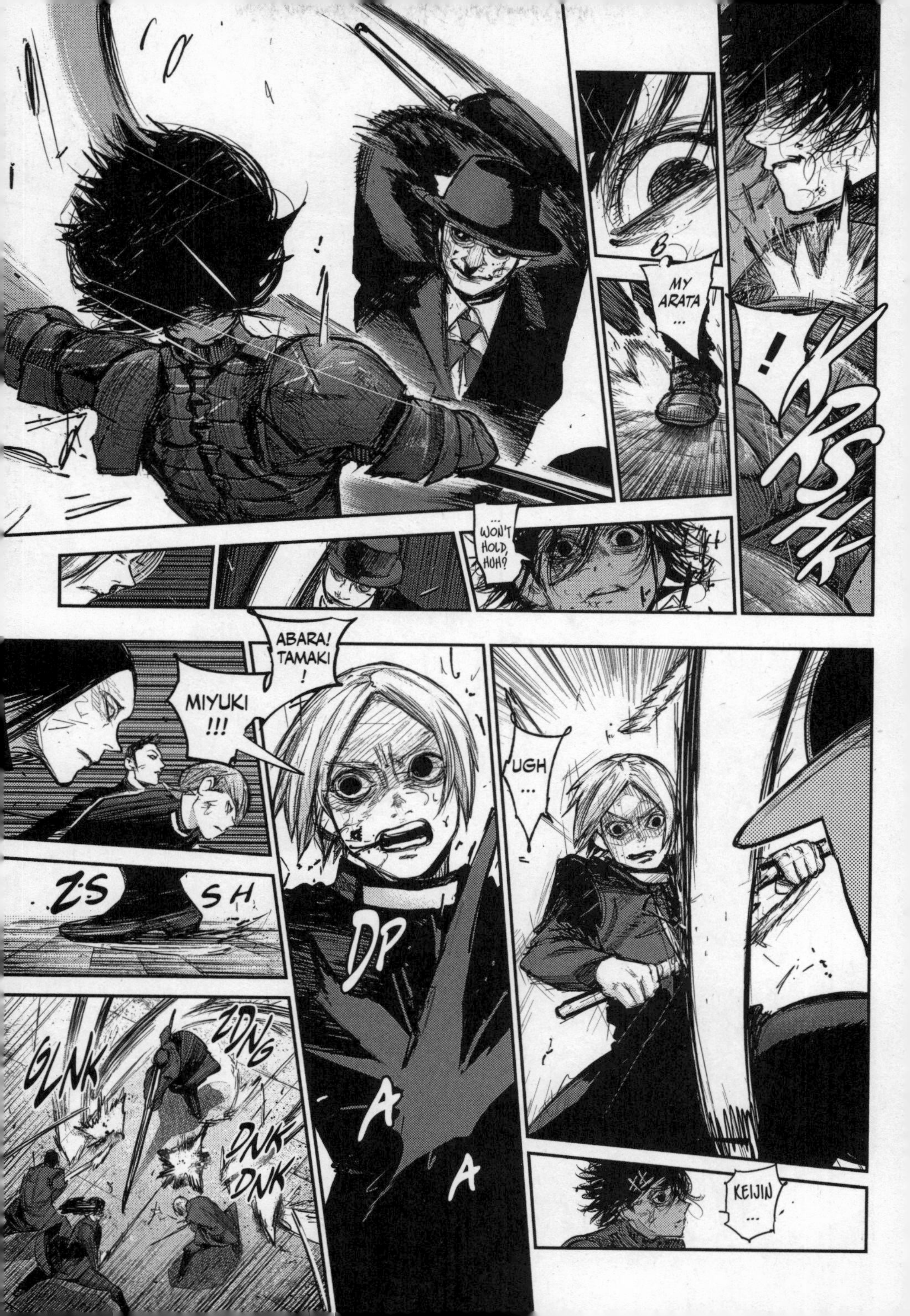
!
KRSHK
MY ARATA ...
... WON'T HOLD, HUH?
UGH ...
KEIJIN ...
ABARA! TAMAKI!
DP
A
A
MIYUKI !!!
Z-S
SH
ZDNG
GLNK
DNK DNK

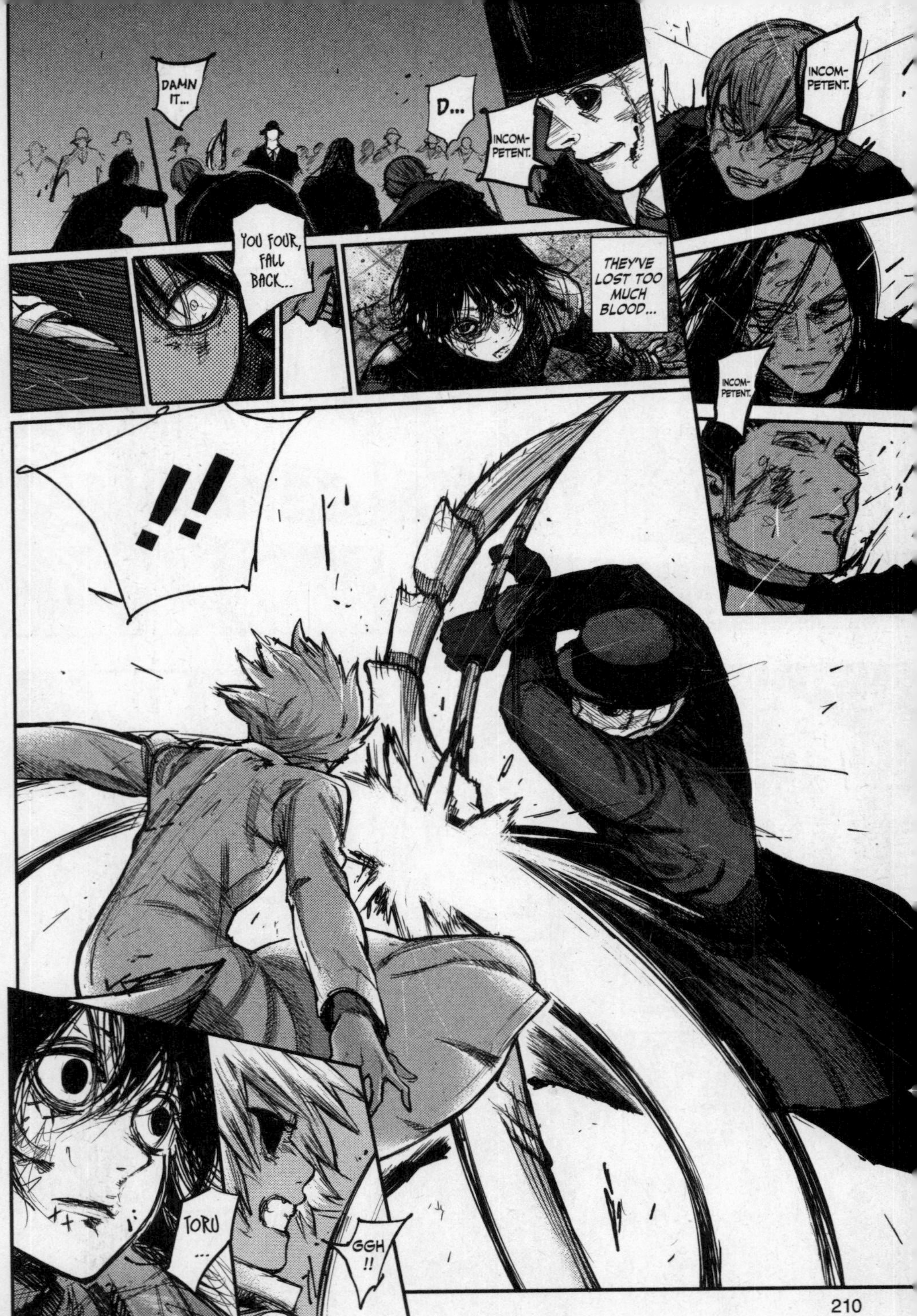
INCOM-
PETENT.
INCOM-
PETENT.
D...
DAMN
IT...
INCOM-
PETENT.
THEY'VE
LOST TOO
MUCH
BLOOD...
YOU FOUR,
FALL
BACK...
!!
GGH
!!
TORU
...

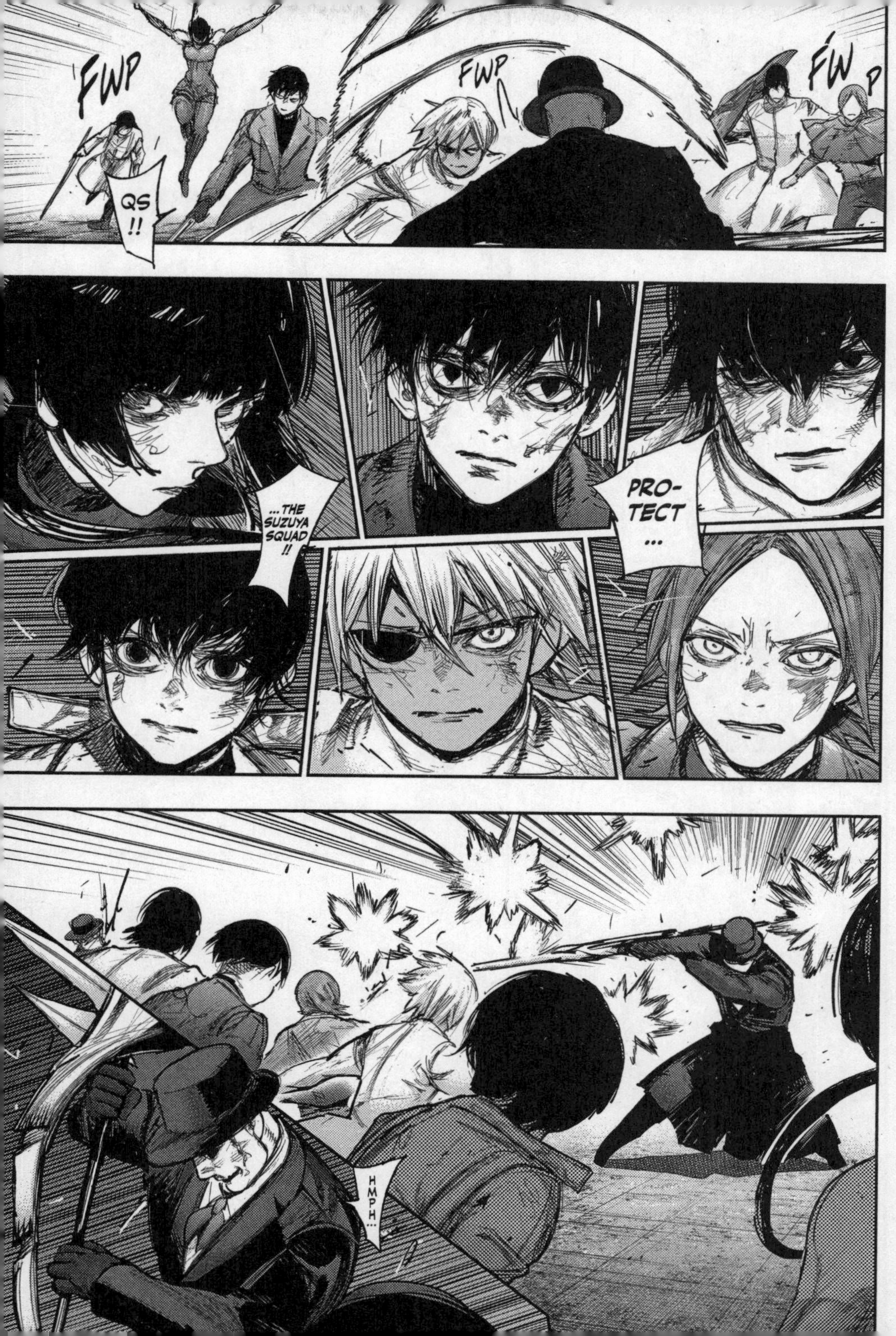
FWP
FWP
FWP
QS !!
PRO-TECT ...
...THE SUZUYA SQUAD !!
HMPH...

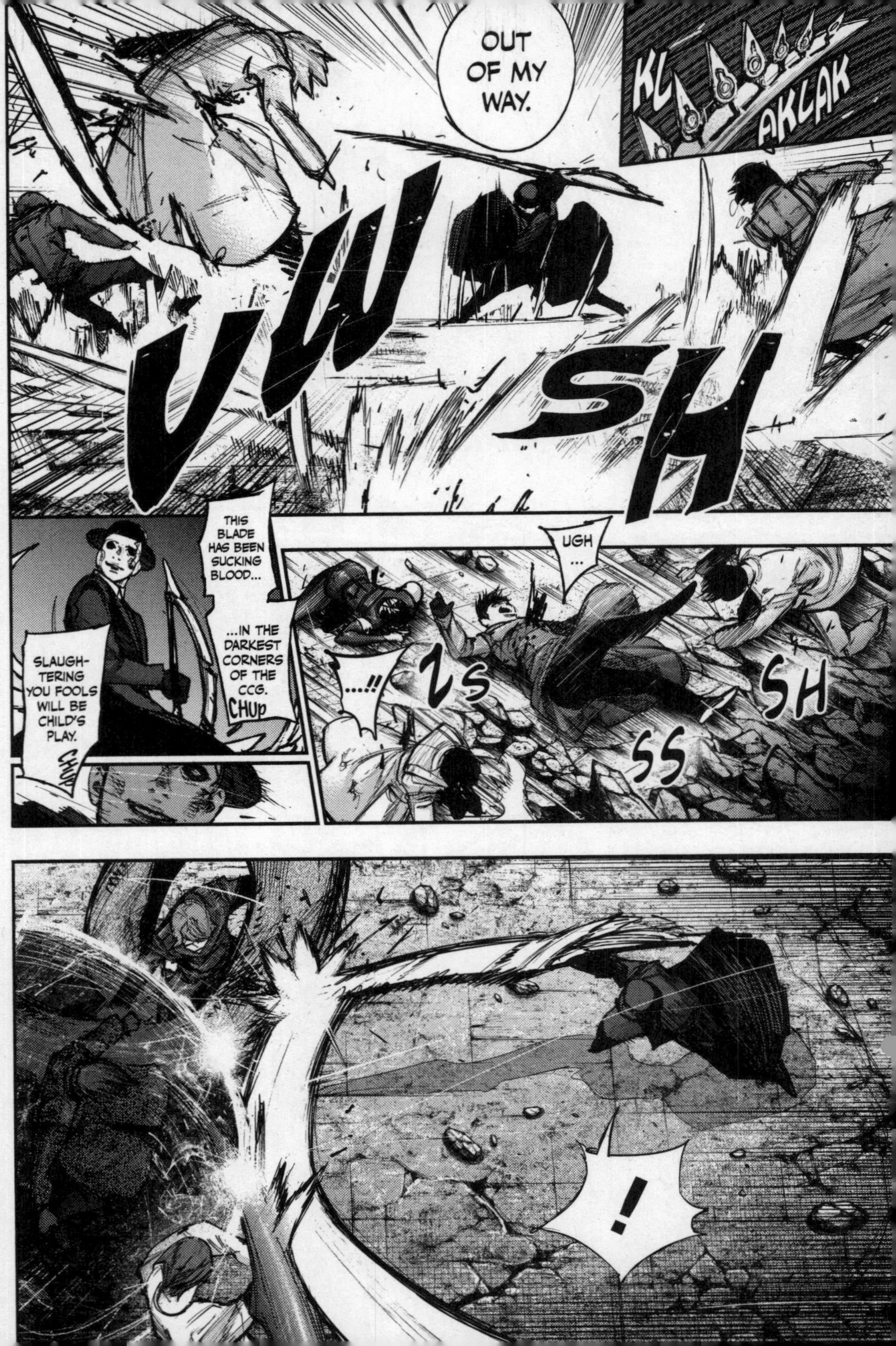
KLAKLAK
OUT OF MY WAY.
VWSH
UGH...
...!!
ZS
SH
SS
THIS BLADE HAS BEEN SUCKING BLOOD...
...IN THE DARKEST CORNERS OF THE CCG.
CHUP
SLAUGHTERING YOU FOOLS WILL BE CHILD'S PLAY.
CHUP
!

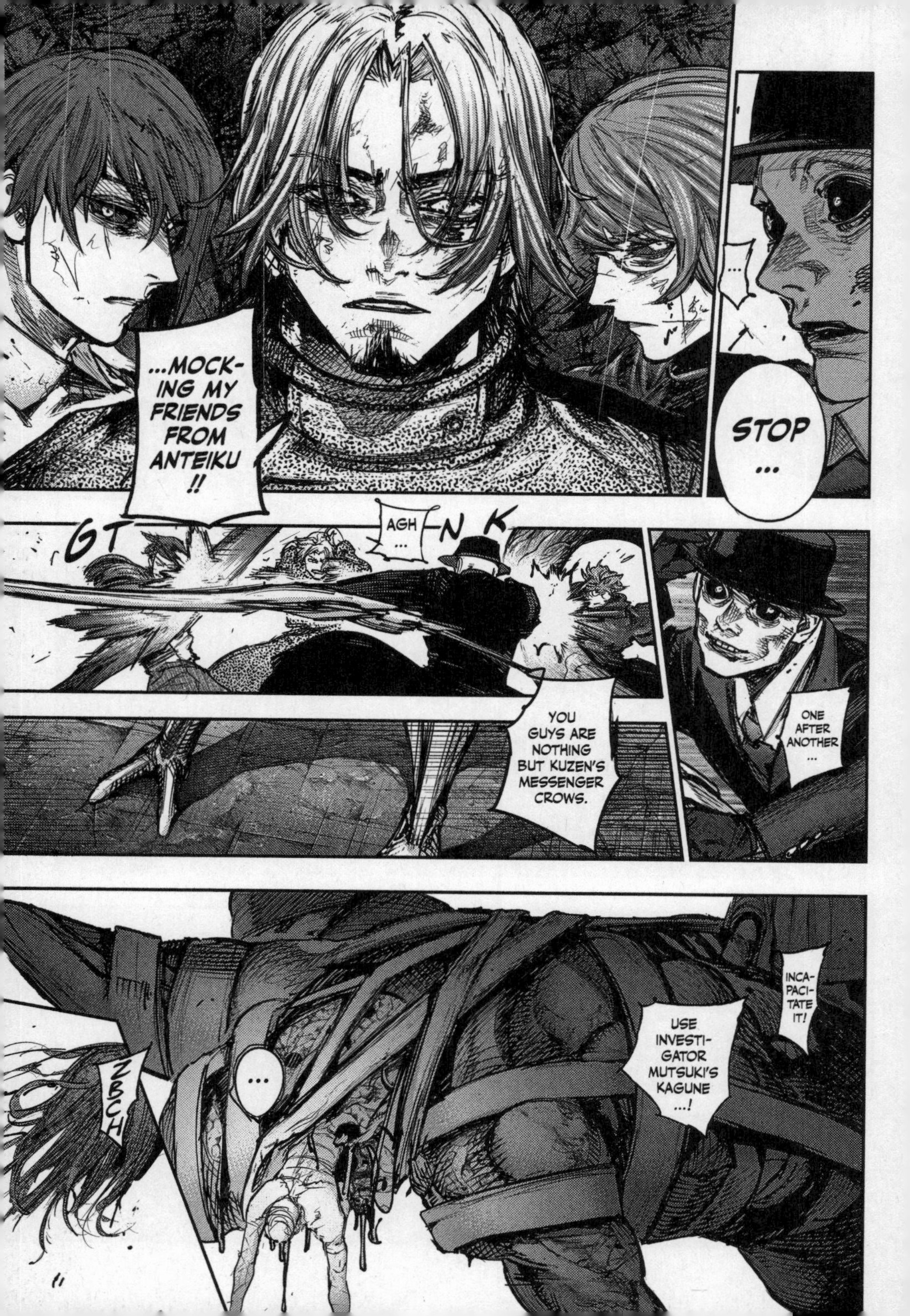
...
STOP ...
...MOCKING MY FRIENDS FROM ANTEIKU !!
ONE AFTER ANOTHER ...
AGH ...
GT
NK
YOU GUYS ARE NOTHING BUT KUZEN'S MESSENGER CROWS.
INCAPACITATE IT!
USE INVESTIGATOR MUTSUKI'S KAGUNE ...!
...
ZBCH

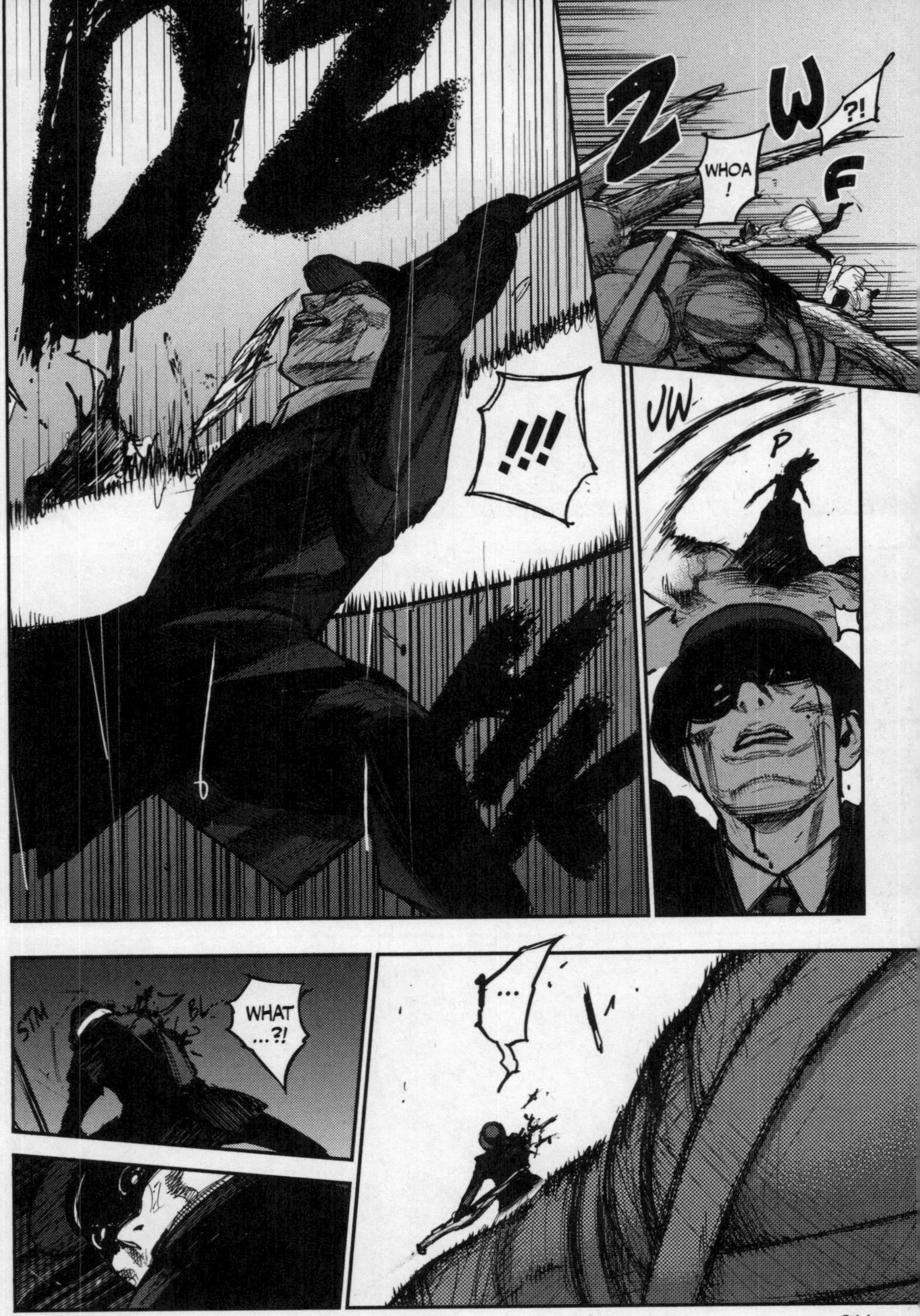
ZWF
?!
WHOA
!
JW
P
DZ
!!!
...
STM
BL
WHAT
...?!

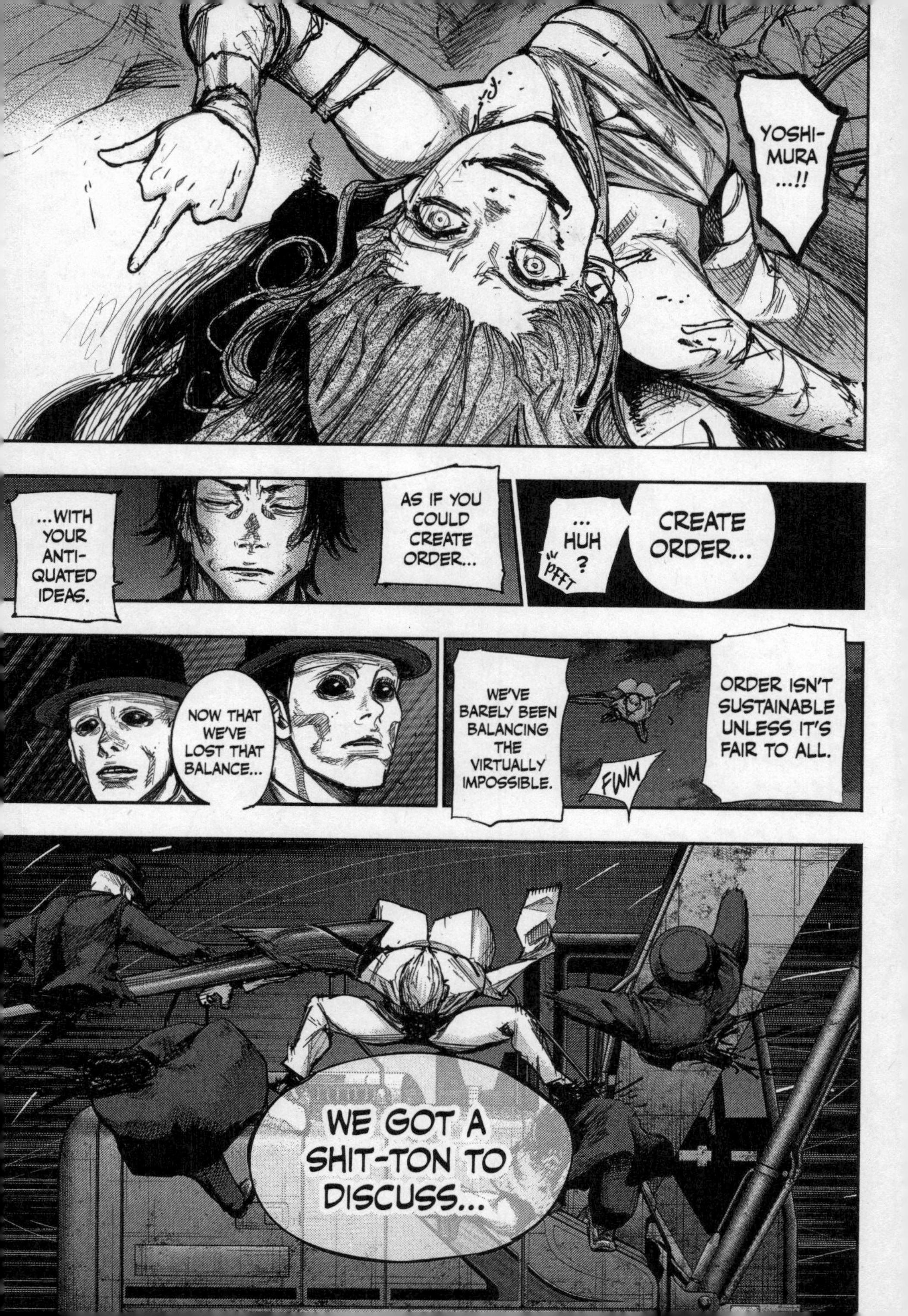
YOSHIMURA ...!!
CREATE ORDER...
... HUH ?
PFFT
AS IF YOU COULD CREATE ORDER...
...WITH YOUR ANTIQUATED IDEAS.
ORDER ISN'T SUSTAINABLE UNLESS IT'S FAIR TO ALL.
FWM
WE'VE BARELY BEEN BALANCING THE VIRTUALLY IMPOSSIBLE.
NOW THAT WE'VE LOST THAT BALANCE...
WE GOT A SHIT-TON TO DISCUSS...

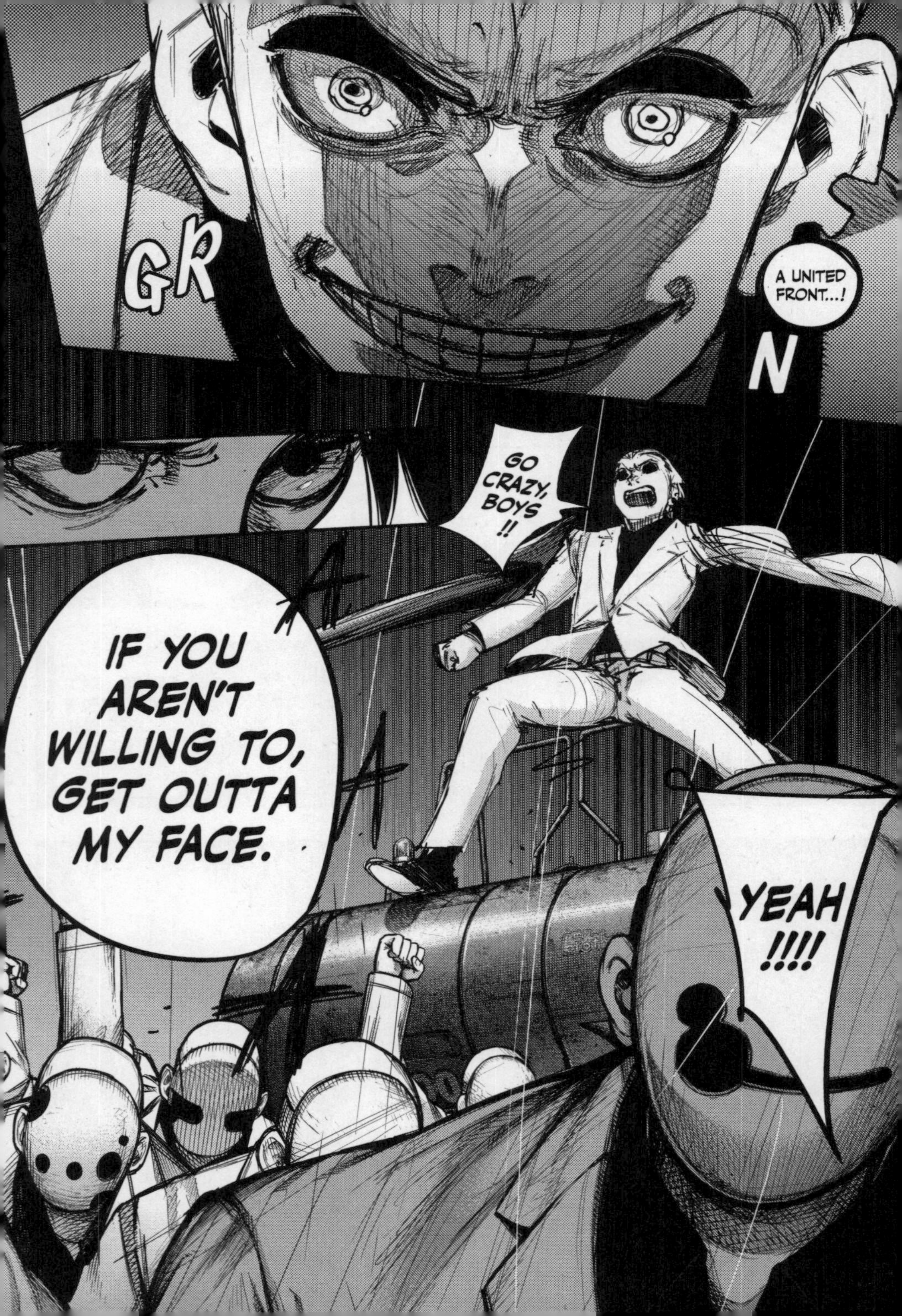
A UNITED FRONT...!
GR
N
GO CRAZY, BOYS!!
IF YOU AREN'T WILLING TO, GET OUTTA MY FACE.
YEAH!!!!

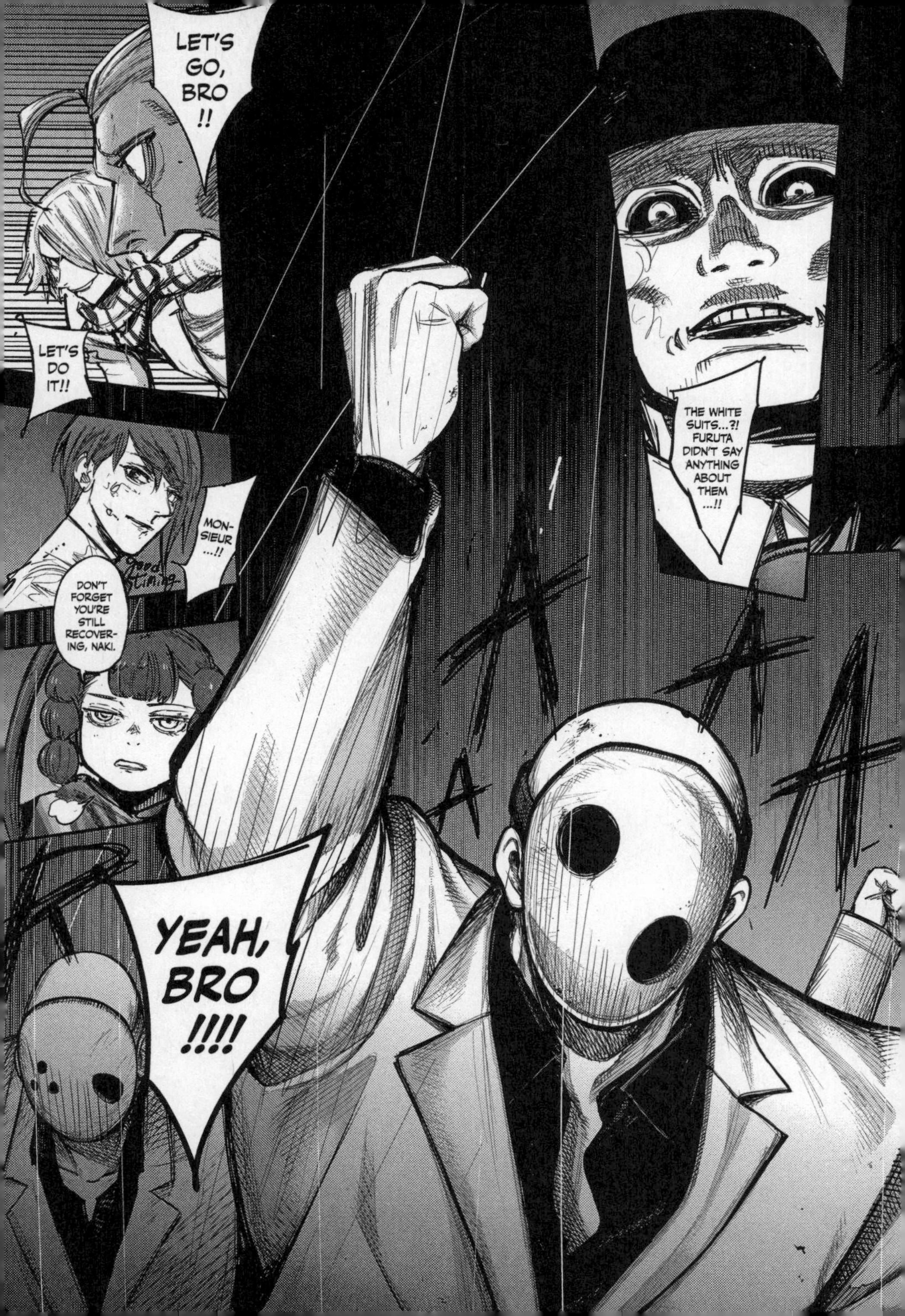
THE WHITE SUITS...?! FURUTA DIDN'T SAY ANYTHING ABOUT THEM ...!!
LET'S GO, BRO !!
LET'S DO IT!!
MON-SIEUR ...!!
DON'T FORGET YOU'RE STILL RECOVER-ING, NAKI.
YEAH, BRO !!!!

TOKYO GHOUL:re

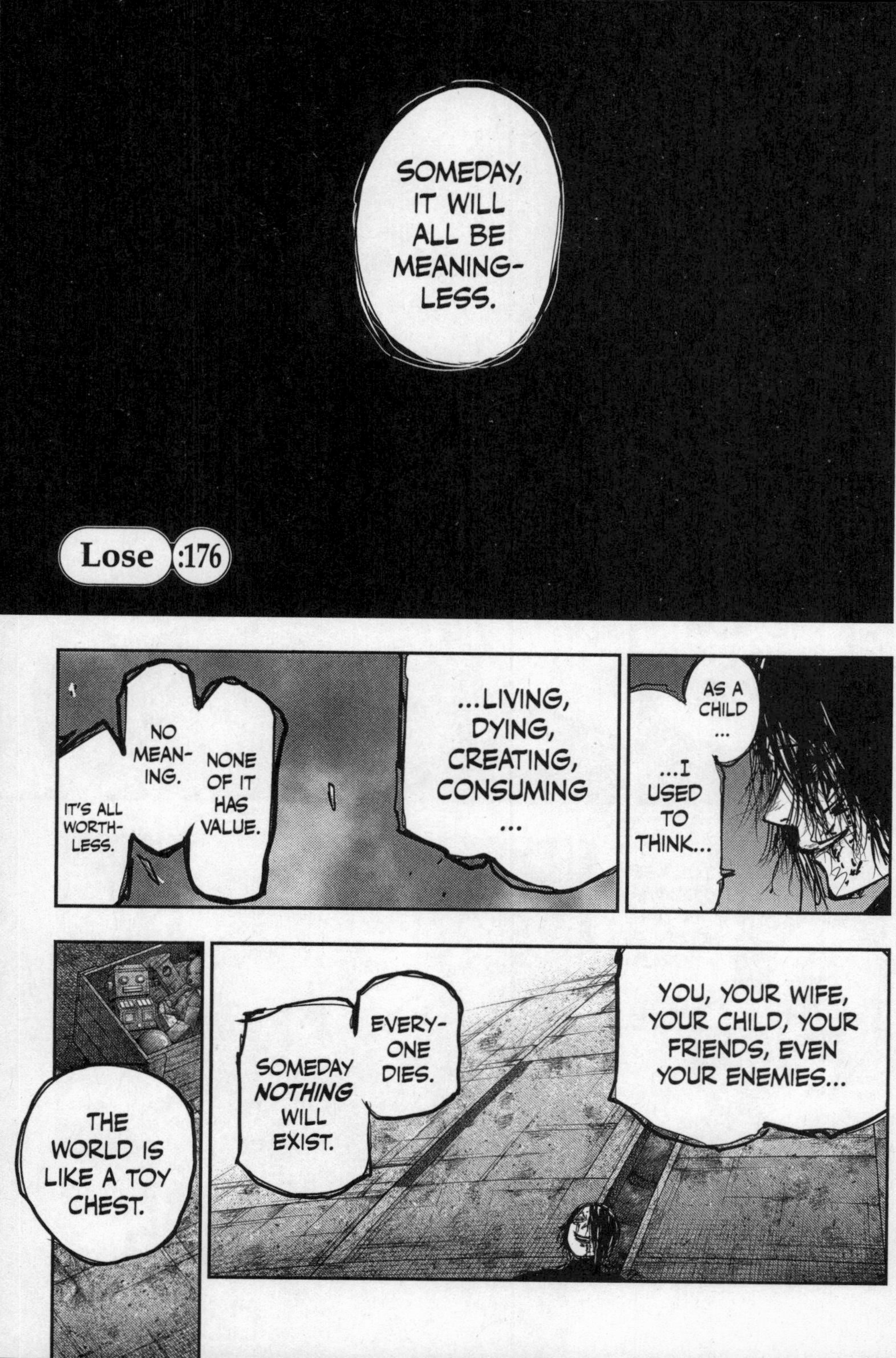
SOMEDAY, IT WILL ALL BE MEANING-LESS.
Lose :176
AS A CHILD...
...I USED TO THINK...
...LIVING, DYING, CREATING, CONSUMING...
NONE OF IT HAS VALUE.
NO MEAN-ING.
IT'S ALL WORTH-LESS.
YOU, YOUR WIFE, YOUR CHILD, YOUR FRIENDS, EVEN YOUR ENEMIES...
EVERY-ONE DIES.
SOMEDAY *NOTHING* WILL EXIST.
THE WORLD IS LIKE A TOY CHEST.

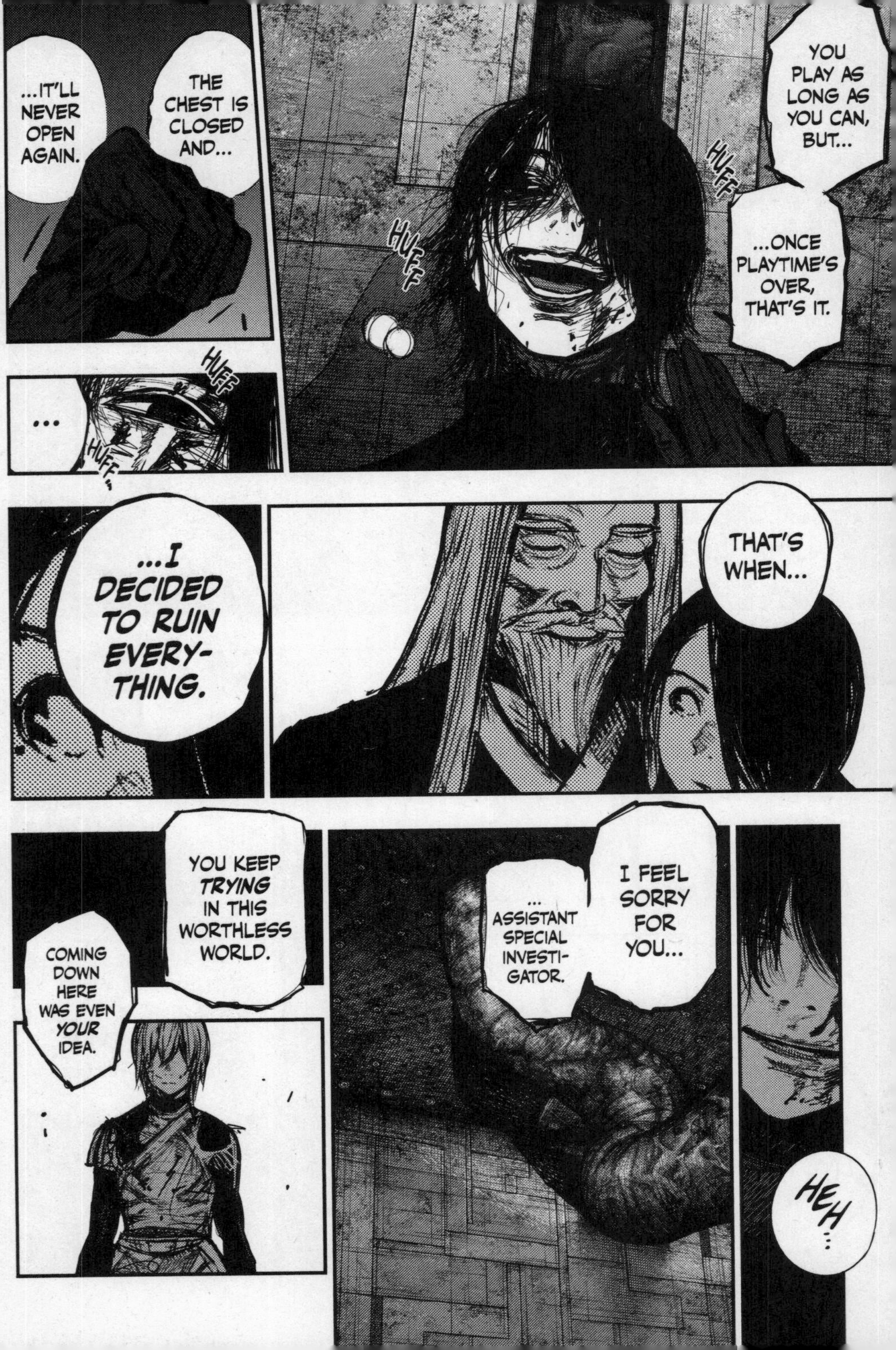
YOU PLAY AS LONG AS YOU CAN, BUT...
HUFF
HUFF
...ONCE PLAYTIME'S OVER, THAT'S IT.
THE CHEST IS CLOSED AND...
...IT'LL NEVER OPEN AGAIN.
HUFF
HUFF
...
THAT'S WHEN...
...I DECIDED TO RUIN EVERYTHING.
HEH...
I FEEL SORRY FOR YOU...
...ASSISTANT SPECIAL INVESTIGATOR.
YOU KEEP TRYING IN THIS WORTHLESS WORLD.
COMING DOWN HERE WAS EVEN YOUR IDEA.

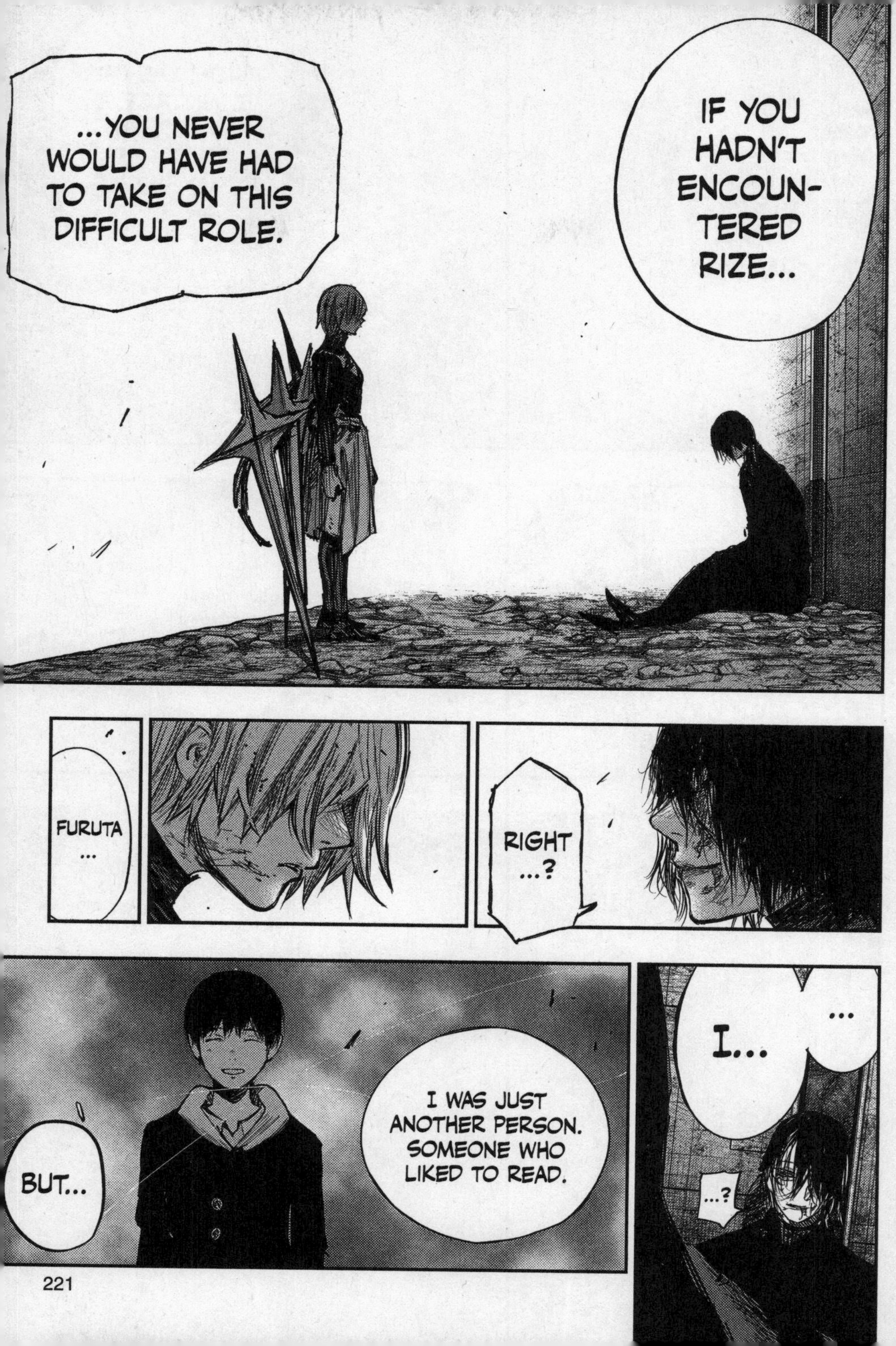
IF YOU HADN'T ENCOUNTERED RIZE...
...YOU NEVER WOULD HAVE HAD TO TAKE ON THIS DIFFICULT ROLE.
RIGHT ...?
FURUTA ...
...
I...
...?
I WAS JUST ANOTHER PERSON. SOMEONE WHO LIKED TO READ.
BUT...

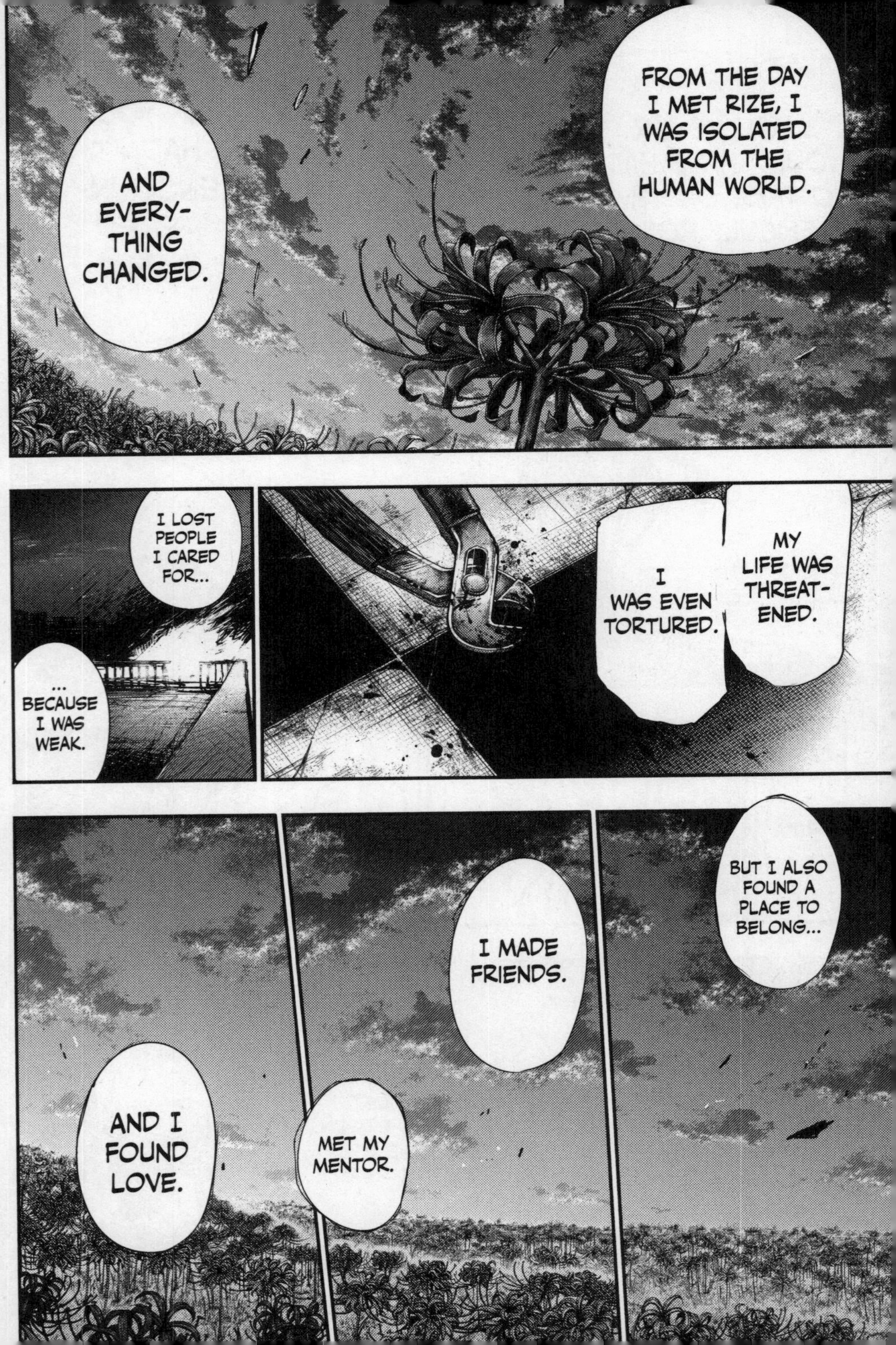
FROM THE DAY I MET RIZE, I WAS ISOLATED FROM THE HUMAN WORLD.
AND EVERY-THING CHANGED.
MY LIFE WAS THREAT-ENED.
I WAS EVEN TORTURED.
I LOST PEOPLE I CARED FOR...
...BECAUSE I WAS WEAK.
BUT I ALSO FOUND A PLACE TO BELONG...
I MADE FRIENDS.
MET MY MENTOR.
AND I FOUND LOVE.

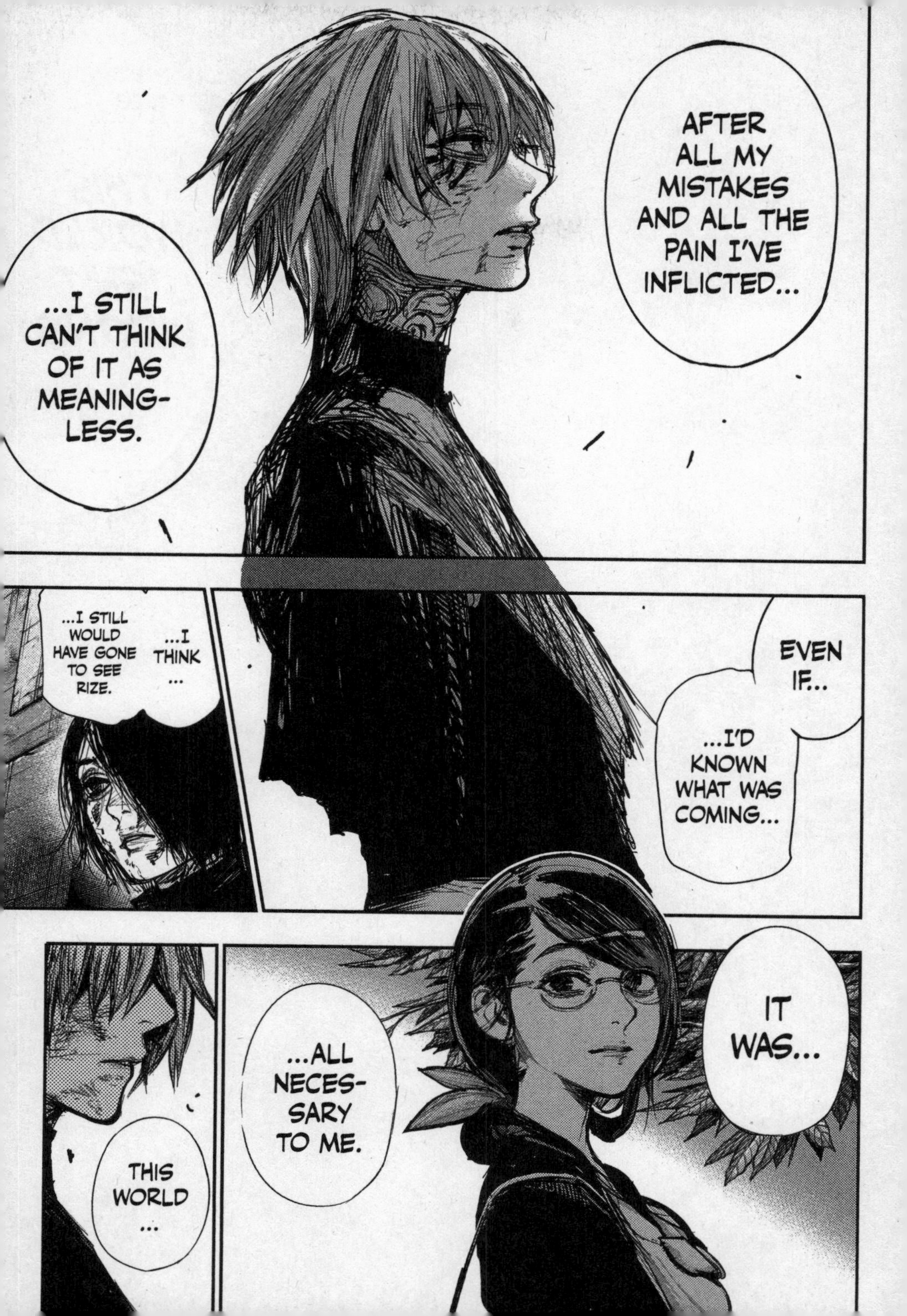
AFTER ALL MY MISTAKES AND ALL THE PAIN I'VE INFLICTED...
...I STILL CAN'T THINK OF IT AS MEANING-LESS.
EVEN IF...
...I'D KNOWN WHAT WAS COMING...
...I THINK ...
...I STILL WOULD HAVE GONE TO SEE RIZE.
IT WAS...
...ALL NECES-SARY TO ME.
THIS WORLD ...

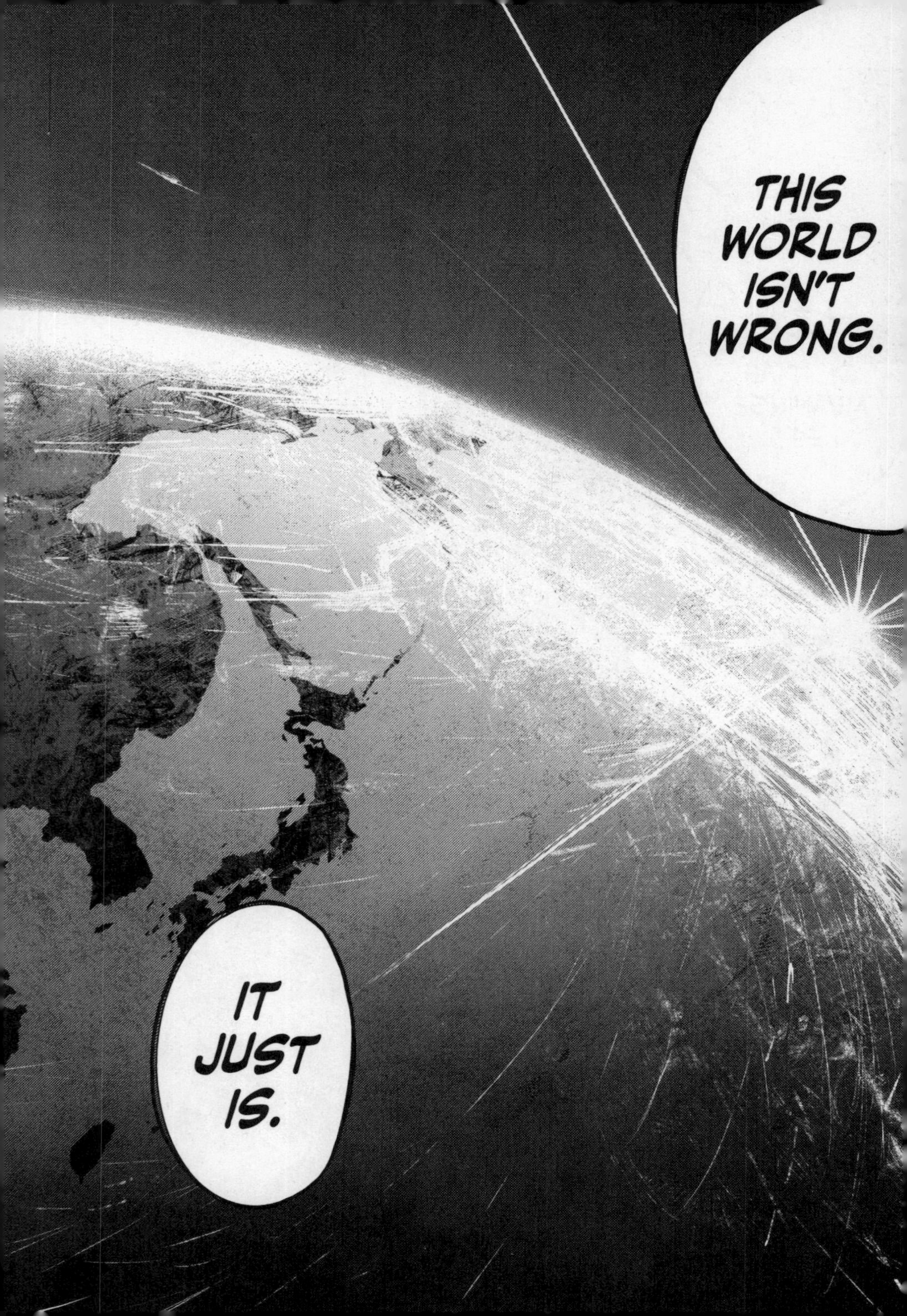
THIS WORLD ISN'T WRONG.
IT JUST IS.

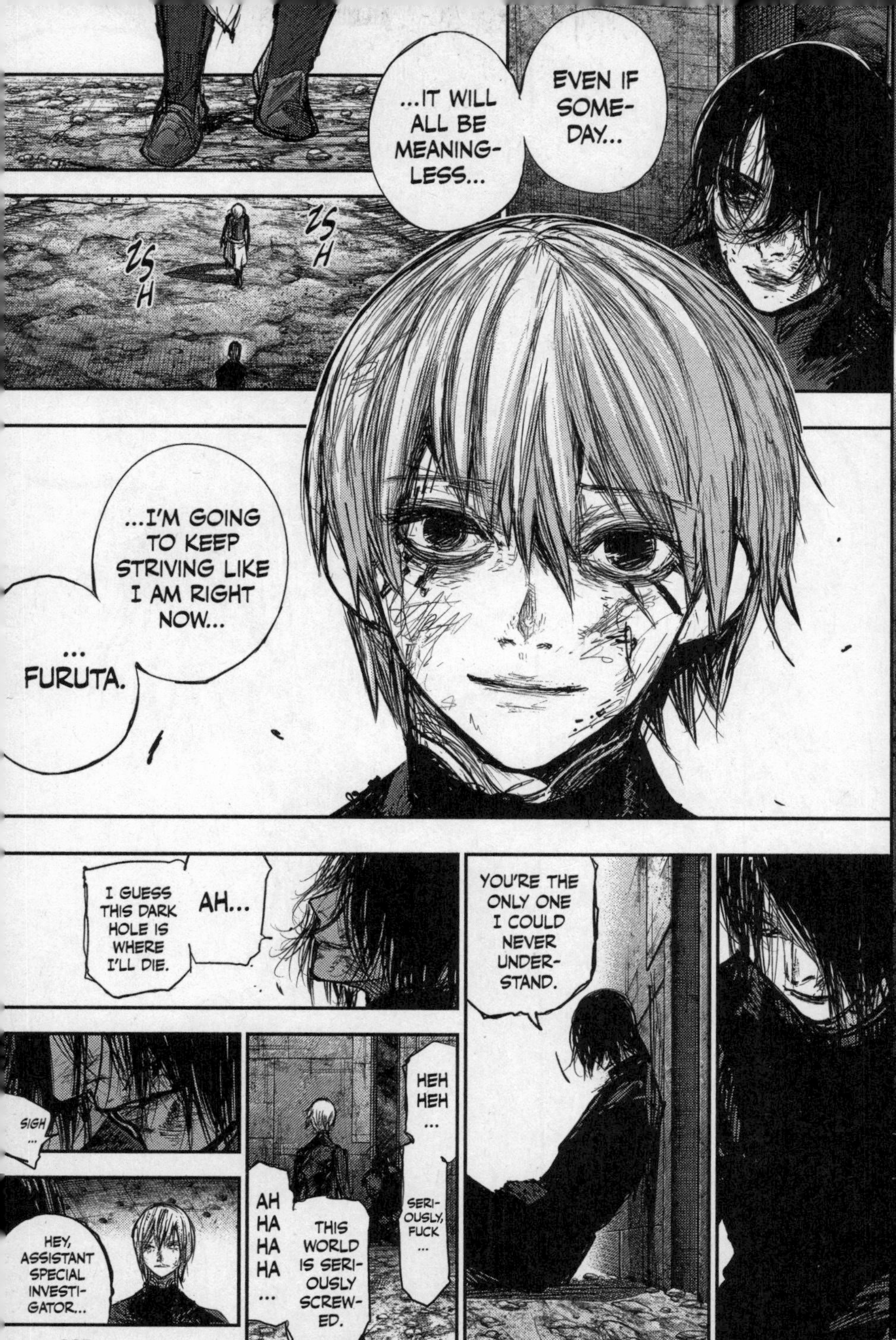
EVEN IF SOMEDAY...
...IT WILL ALL BE MEANINGLESS...
ZSH
ZSH
...I'M GOING TO KEEP STRIVING LIKE I AM RIGHT NOW...
... FURUTA.
YOU'RE THE ONLY ONE I COULD NEVER UNDERSTAND.
AH...
I GUESS THIS DARK HOLE IS WHERE I'LL DIE.
HEH HEH...
SERIOUSLY, FUCK...
THIS WORLD IS SERIOUSLY SCREWED.
AH HA HA HA...
SIGH...
HEY, ASSISTANT SPECIAL INVESTIGATOR...

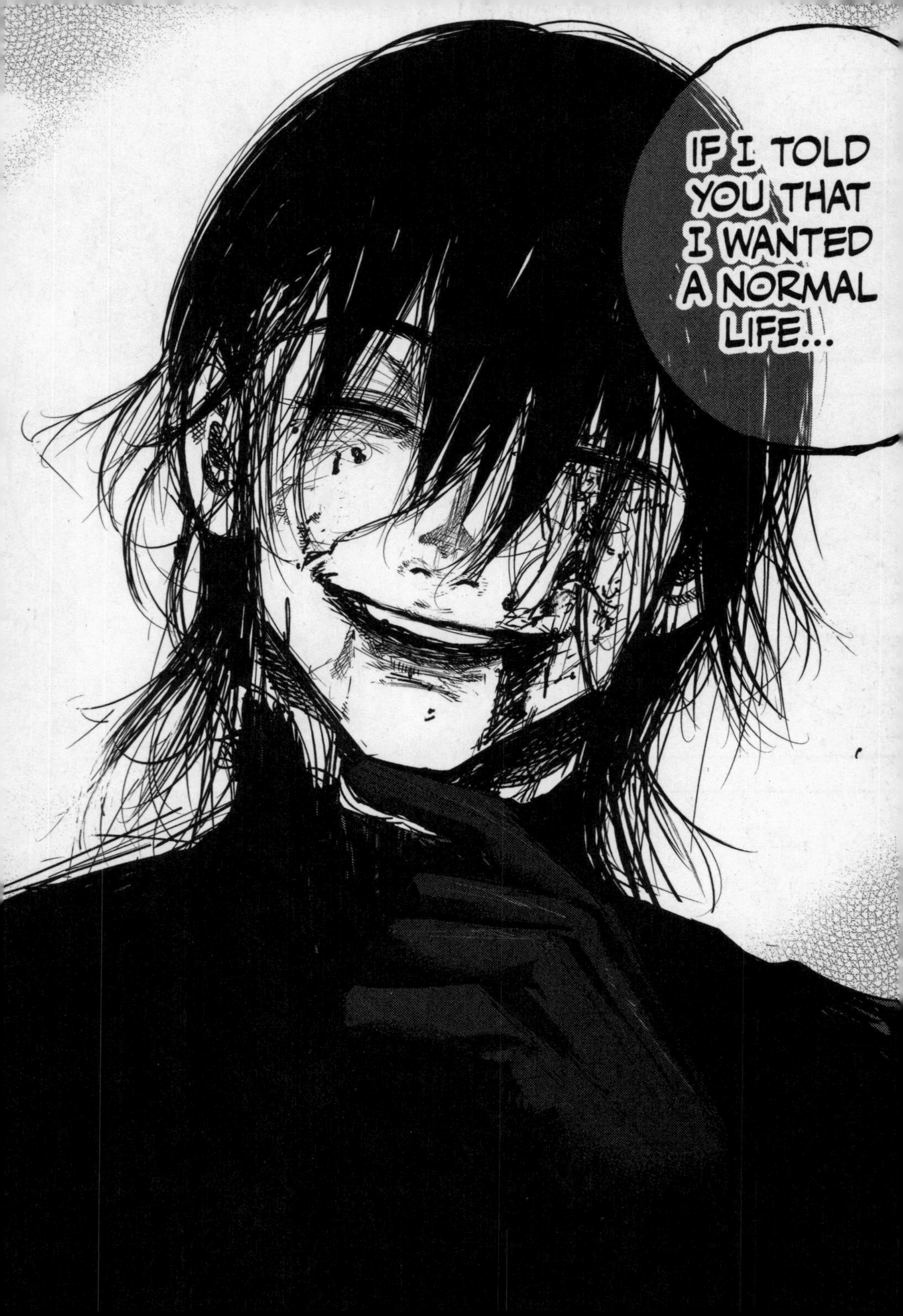
IF I TOLD YOU THAT I WANTED A NORMAL LIFE...

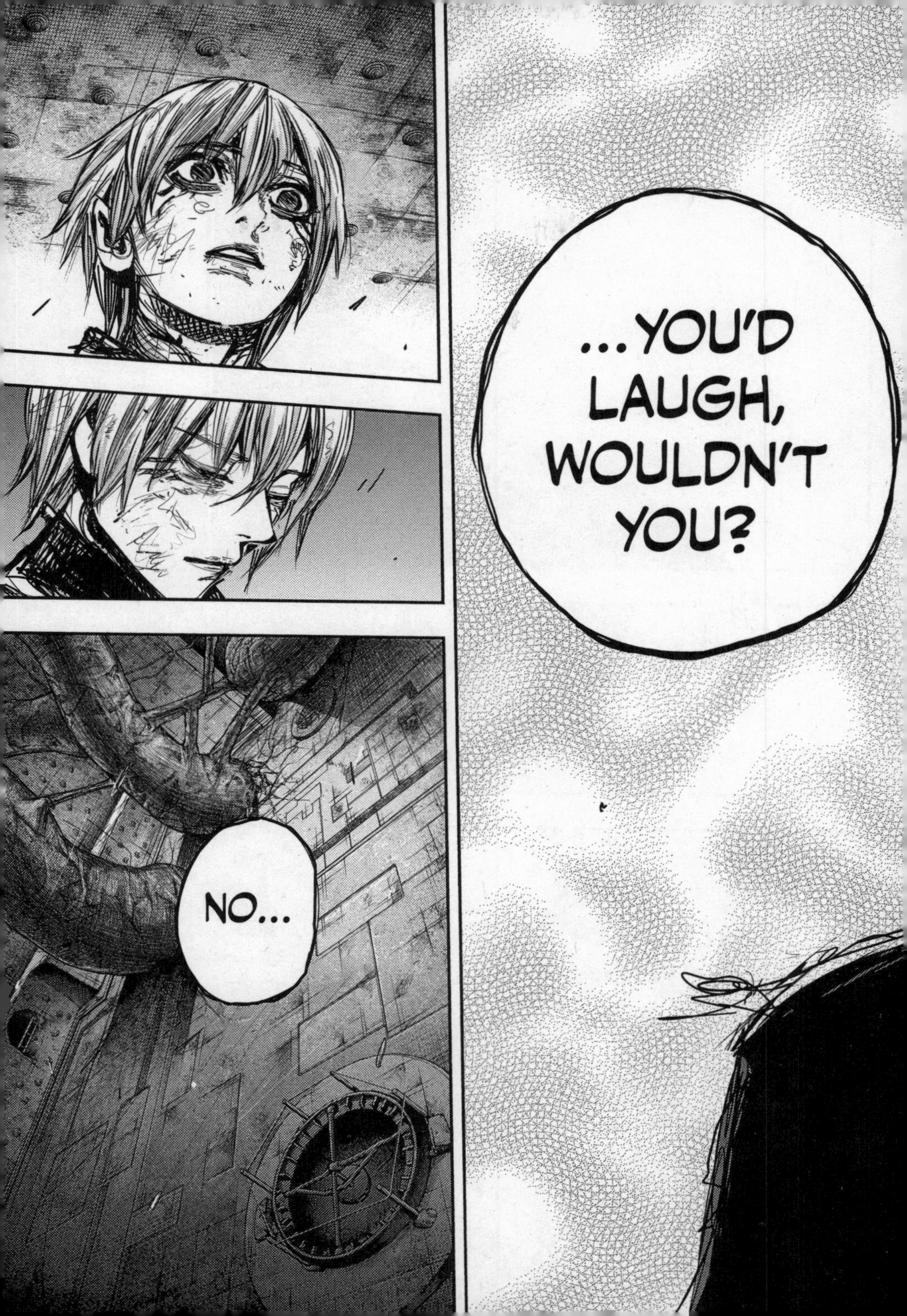
...YOU'D LAUGH, WOULDN'T YOU?
NO...

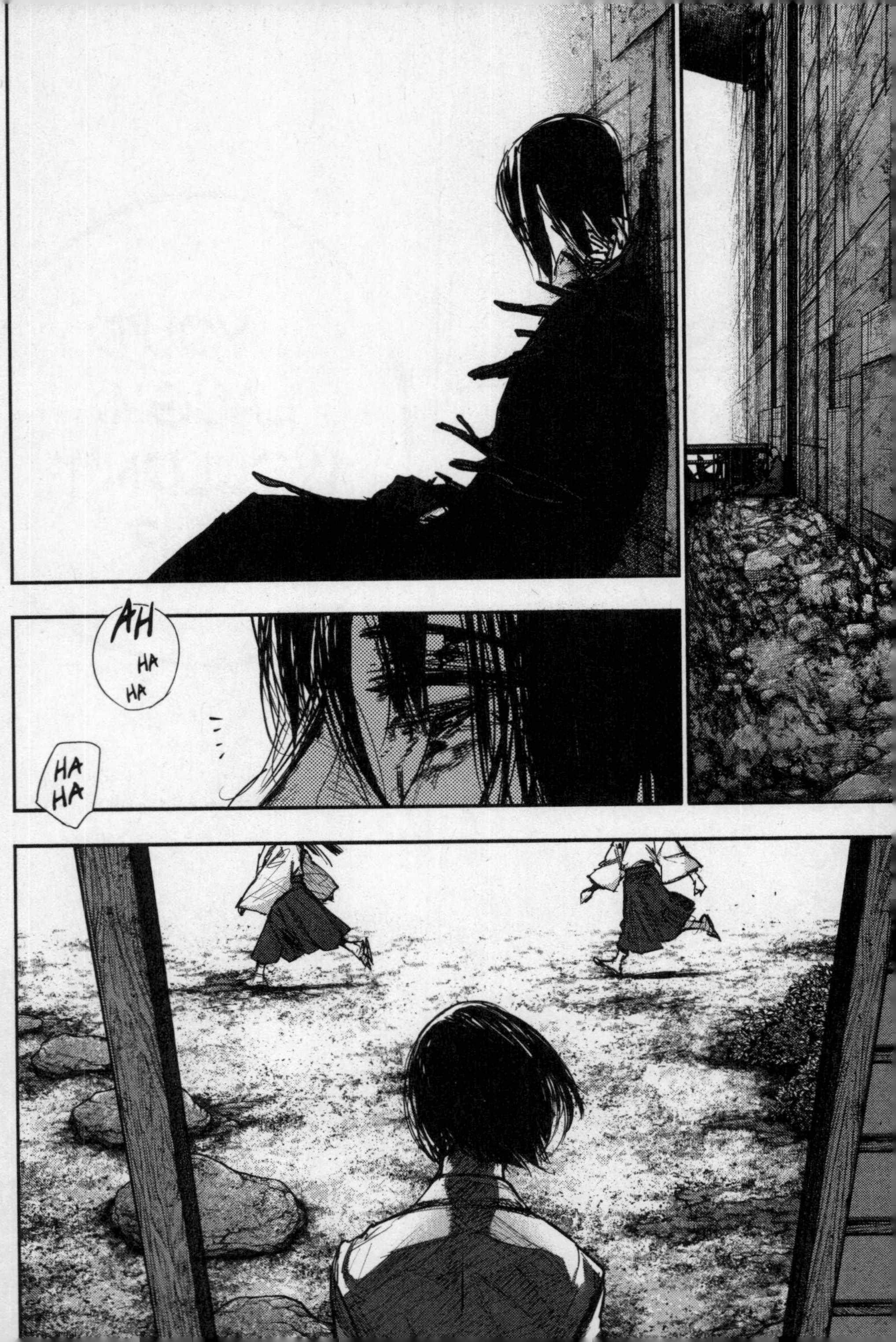
AH HA HA
HA HA

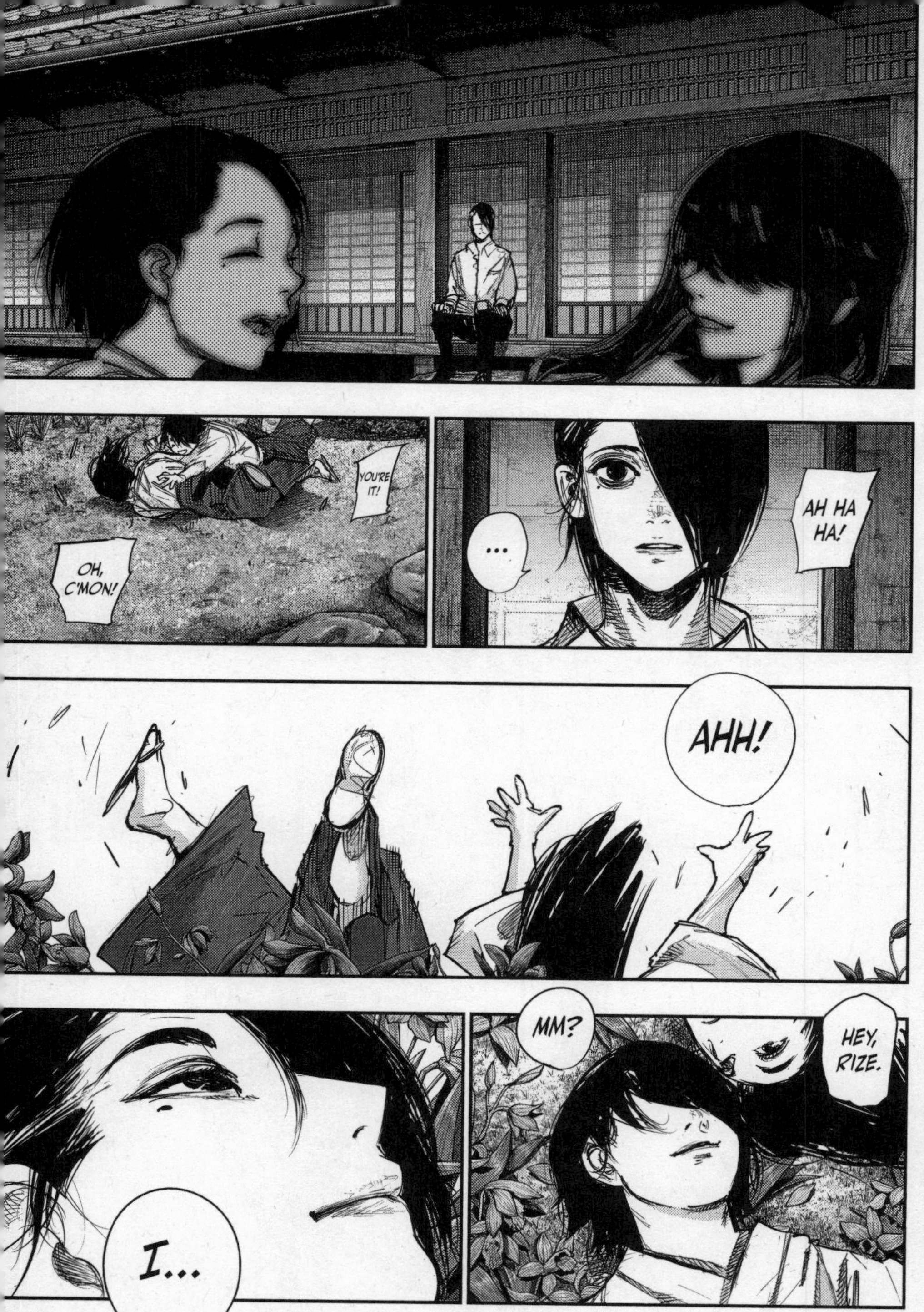
AH HA HA!
...
YOU'RE IT!
OH, C'MON!
AHH!
HEY, RIZE.
MM?
I...

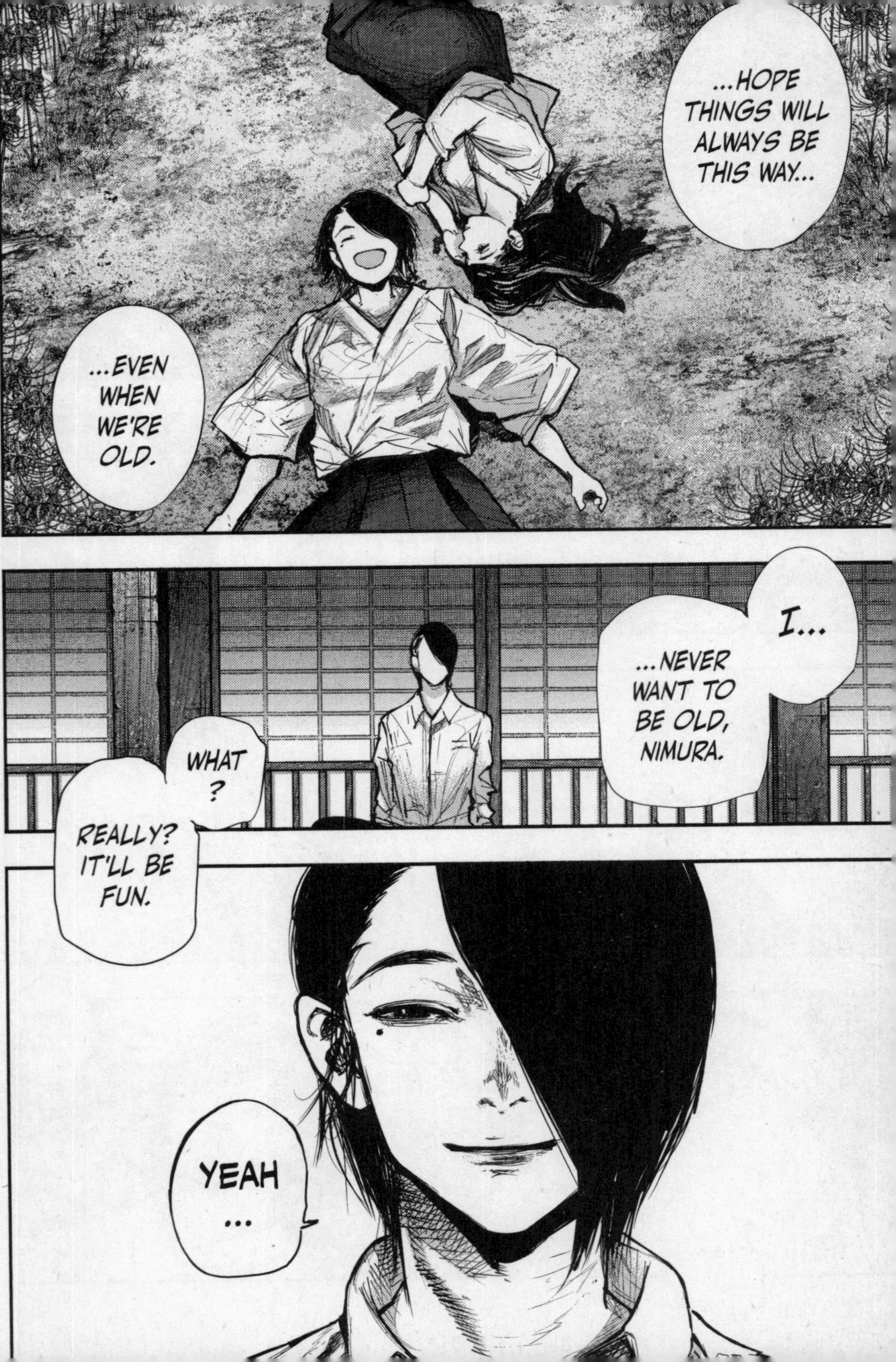
...HOPE THINGS WILL ALWAYS BE THIS WAY...
...EVEN WHEN WE'RE OLD.
I...
...NEVER WANT TO BE OLD, NIMURA.
WHAT?
REALLY? IT'LL BE FUN.
YEAH ...

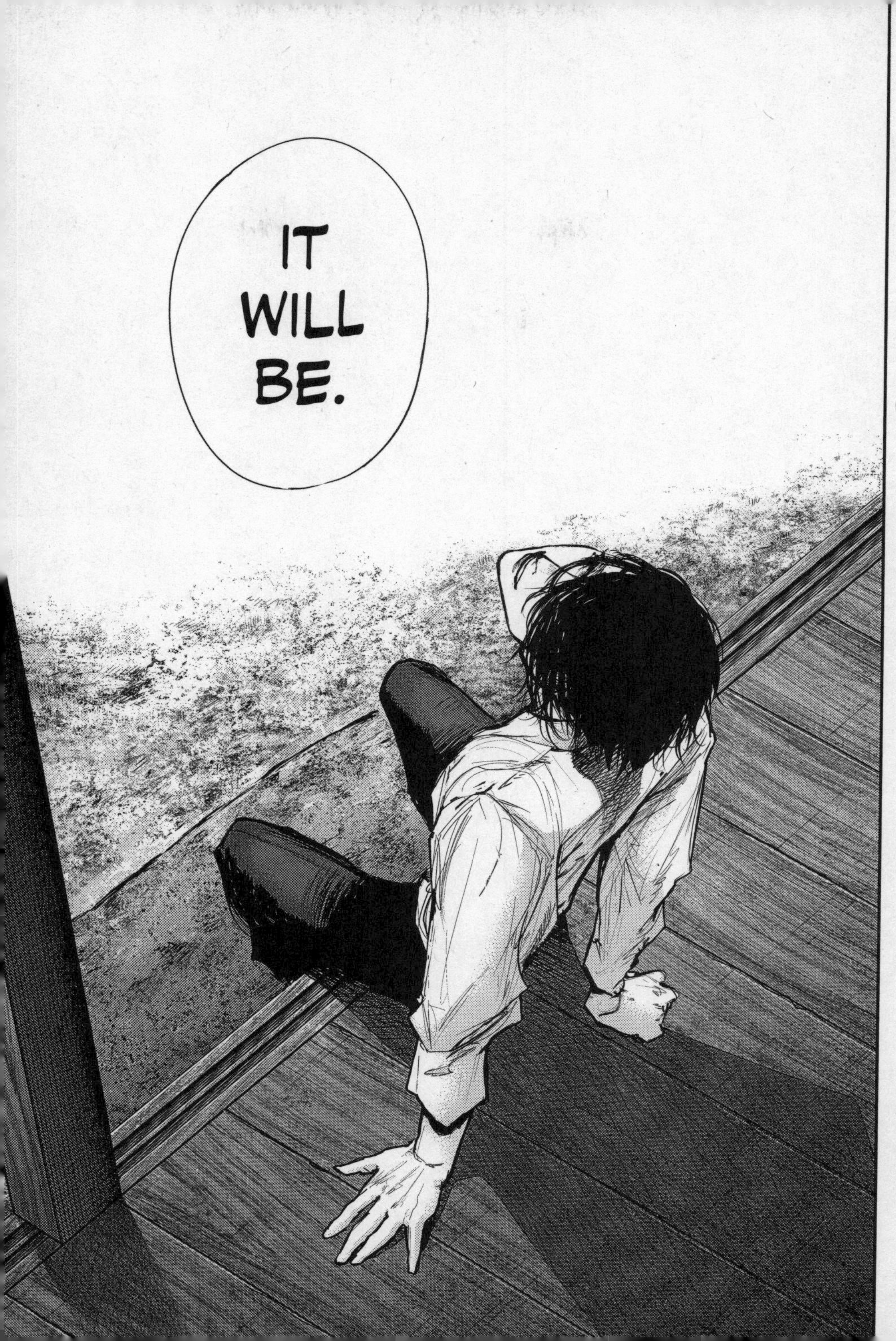
IT WILL BE.

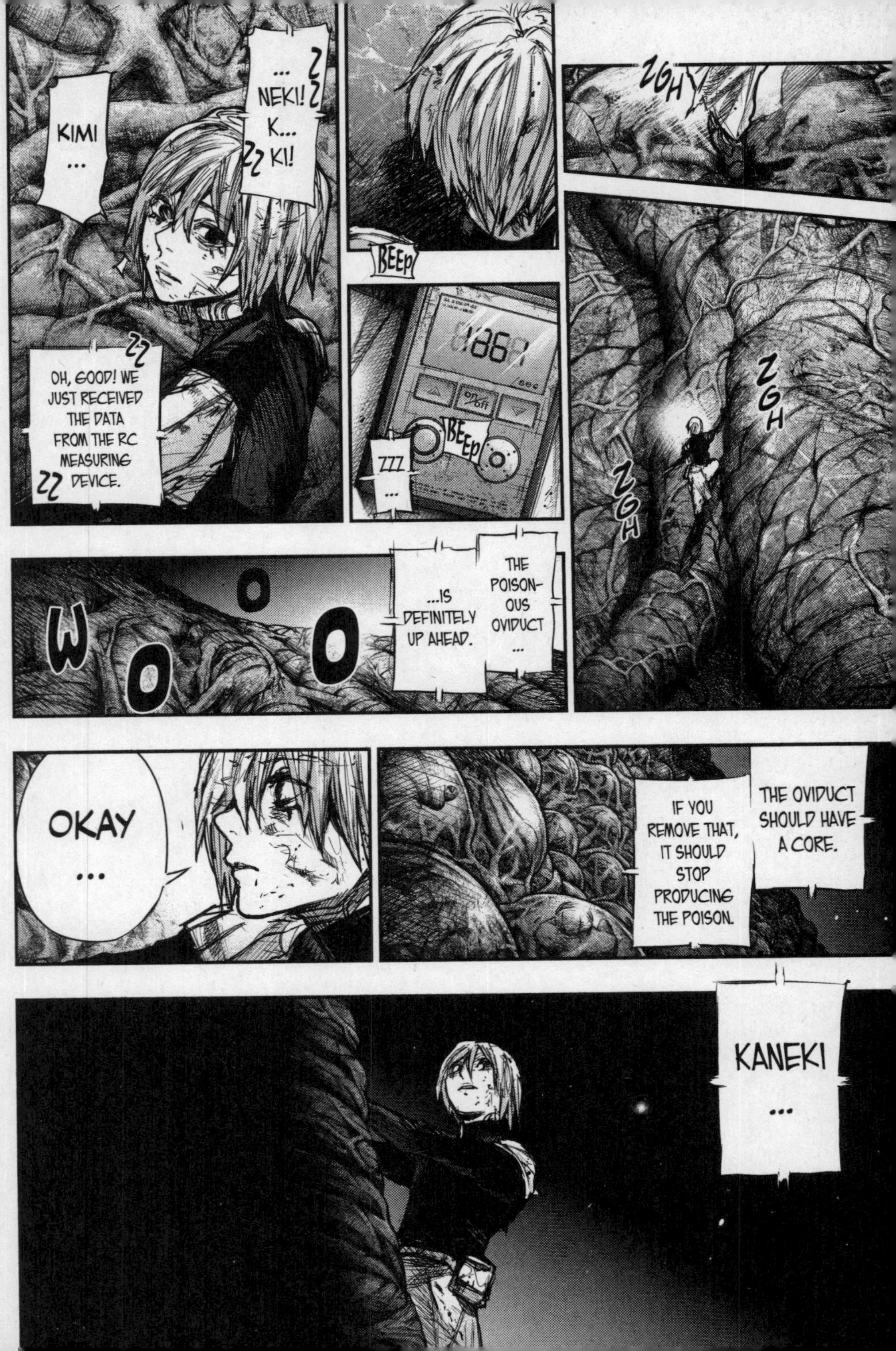
ZGH
BEEP
... NEKI! K... KI!
ZZ
KIMI ...
OH, GOOD! WE JUST RECEIVED THE DATA FROM THE RC MEASURING DEVICE.
BEEP
ZZZ ...
ZGH
ZGH
THE POISON-OUS OVIDUCT ...
...IS DEFINITELY UP AHEAD.
WOOO
THE OVIDUCT SHOULD HAVE A CORE.
IF YOU REMOVE THAT, IT SHOULD STOP PRODUCING THE POISON.
OKAY ...
KANEKI ...

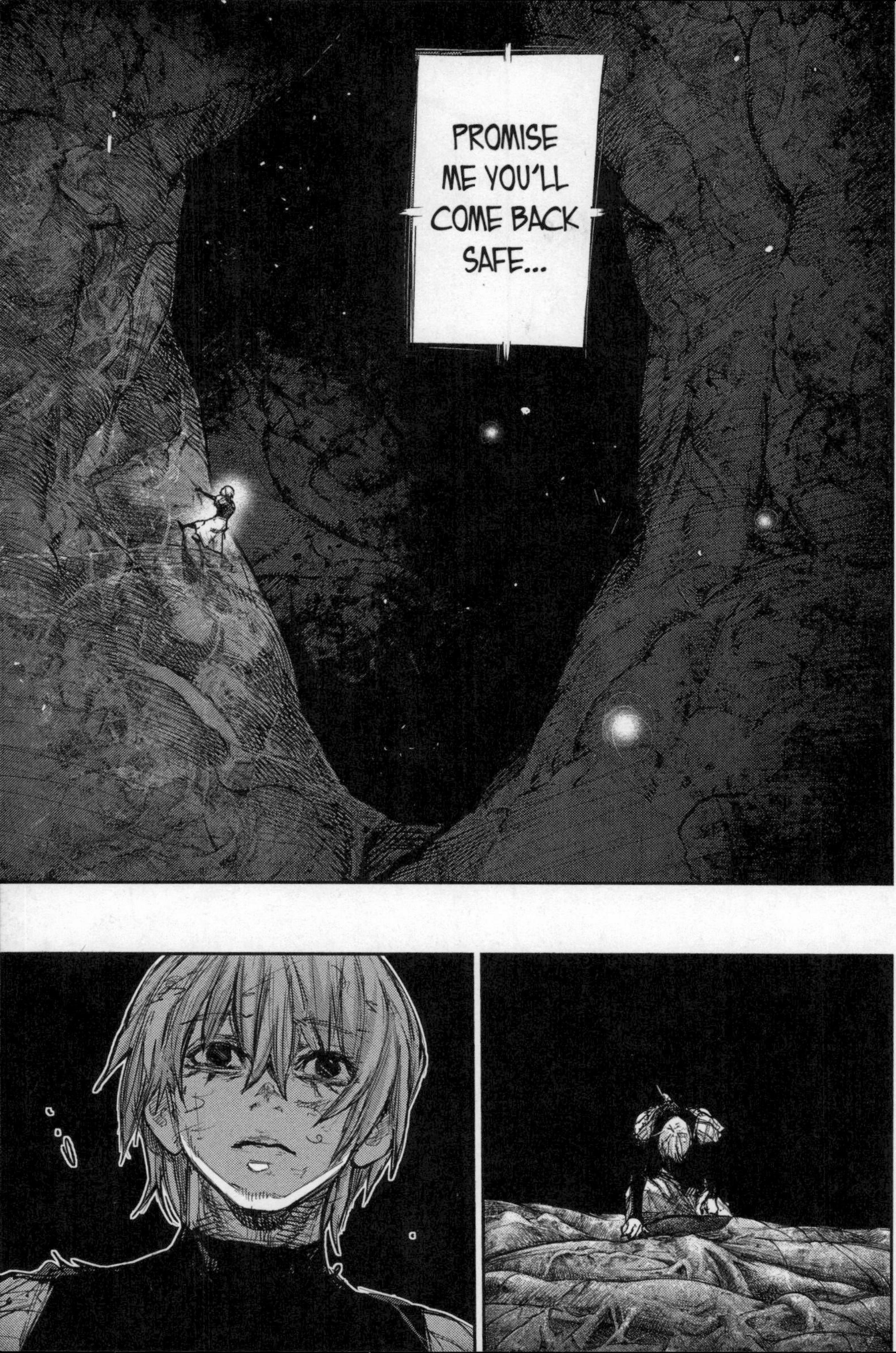
PROMISE ME YOU'LL COME BACK SAFE...

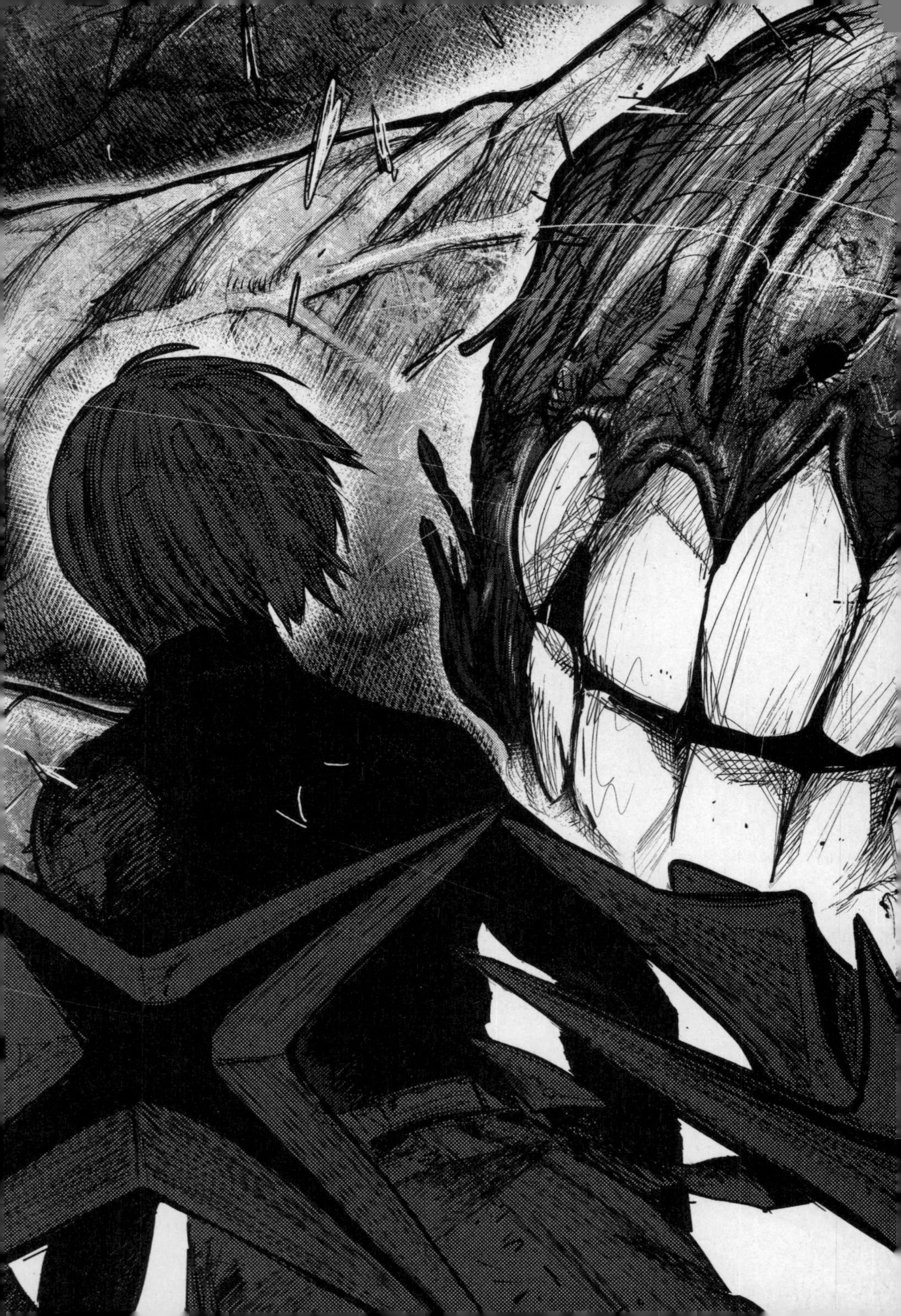

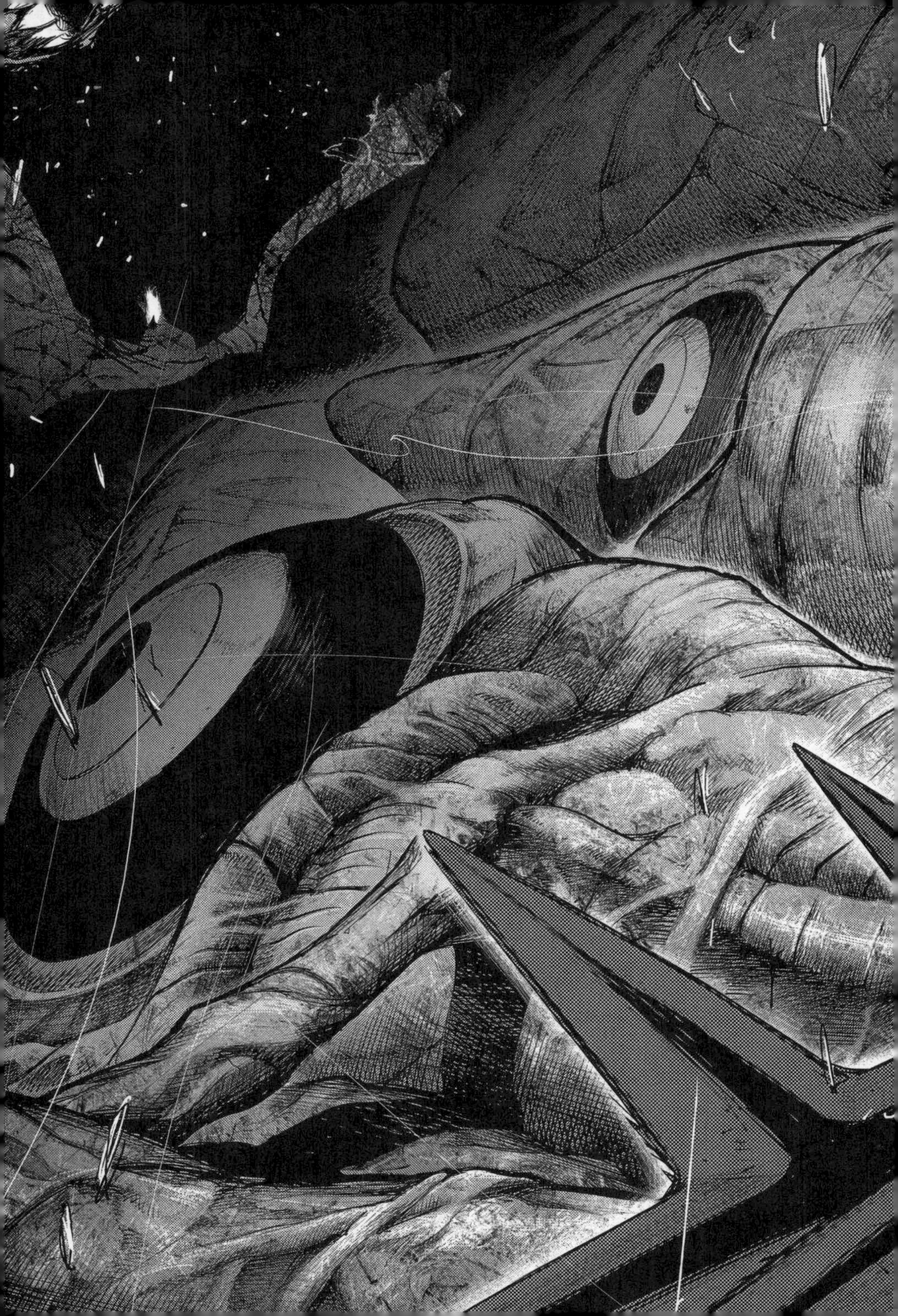

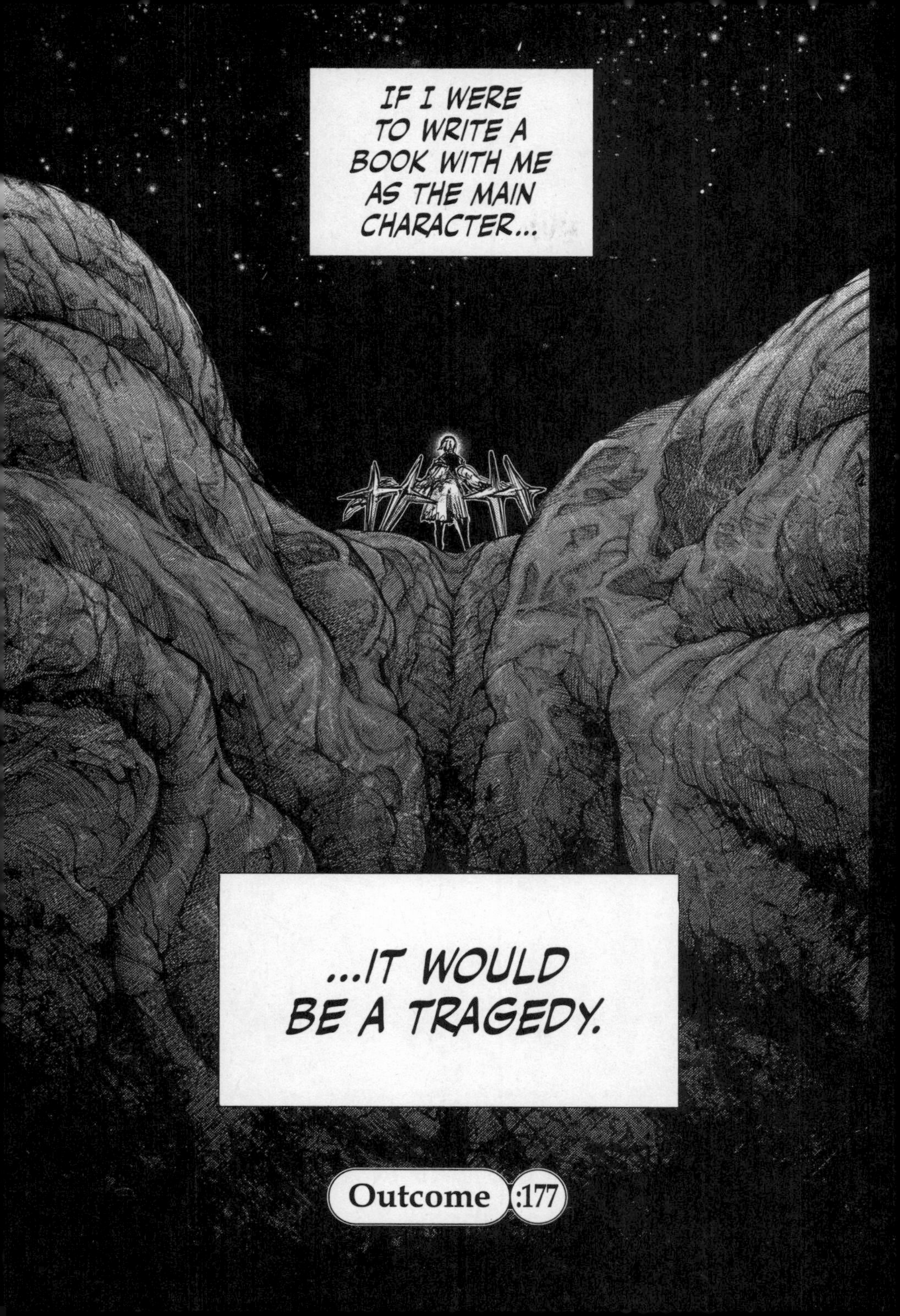
IF I WERE TO WRITE A BOOK WITH ME AS THE MAIN CHARACTER...
...IT WOULD BE A TRAGEDY.
Outcome :177

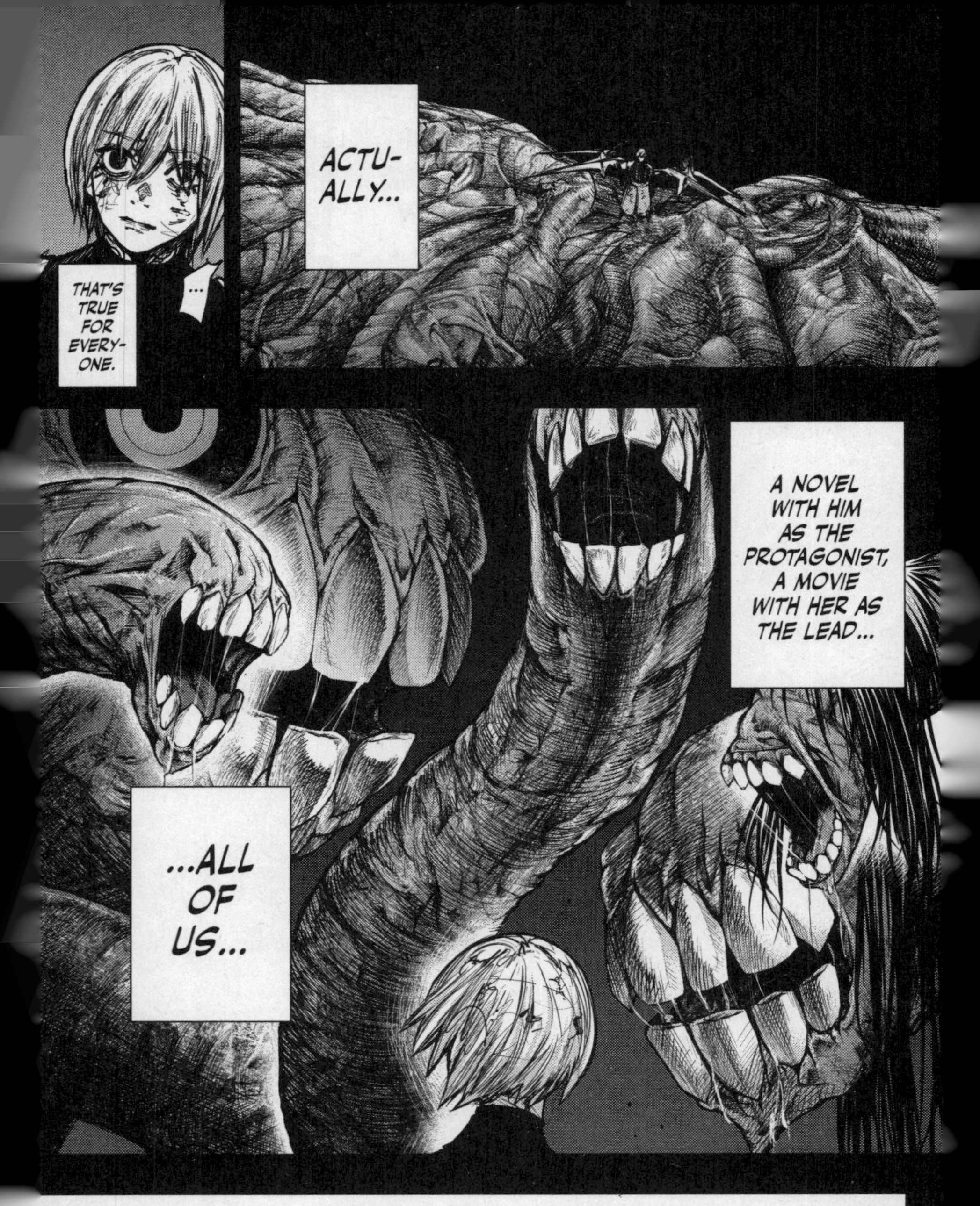
ACTU-ALLY...
...
THAT'S TRUE FOR EVERY-ONE.
A NOVEL WITH HIM AS THE PROTAGONIST, A MOVIE WITH HER AS THE LEAD...
...ALL OF US...
...WE'RE ALL MAIN CHARACTERS IN A TRAGEDY.

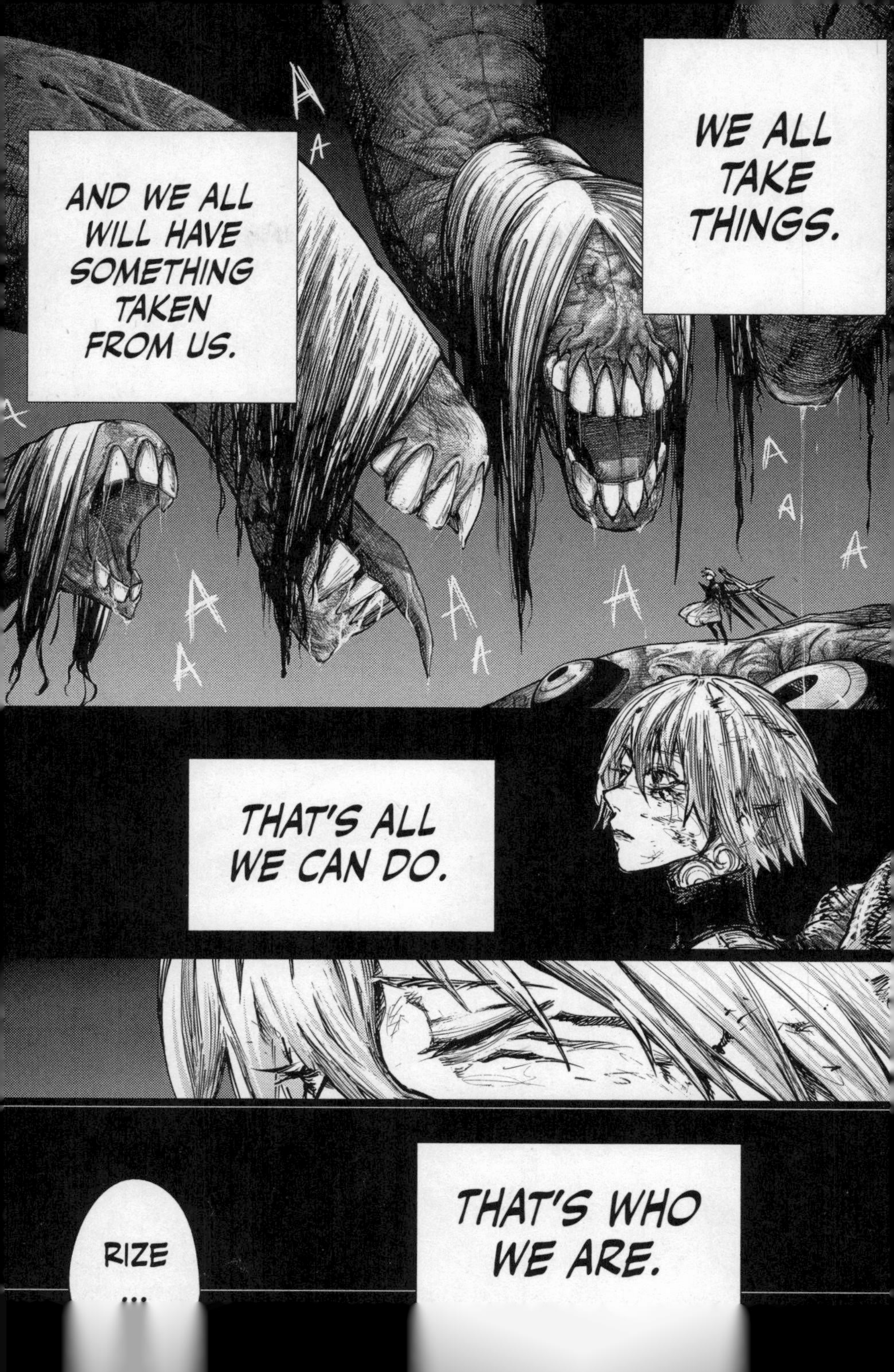
WE ALL TAKE THINGS.
AND WE ALL WILL HAVE SOMETHING TAKEN FROM US.
AAAA
THAT'S ALL WE CAN DO.
THAT'S WHO WE ARE.
RIZE ...

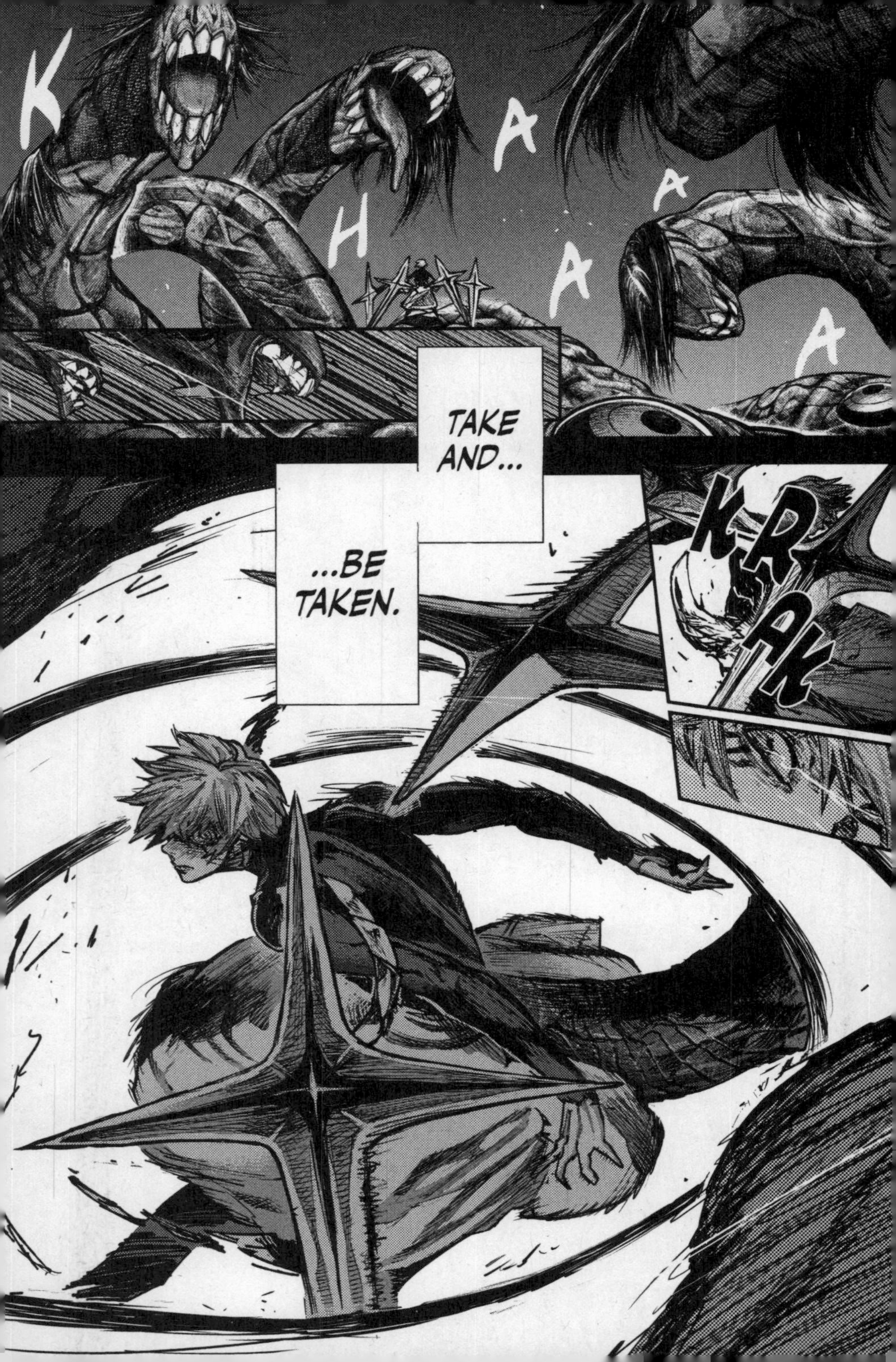
KHAAAA
TAKE AND...
KRAK
...BE TAKEN.

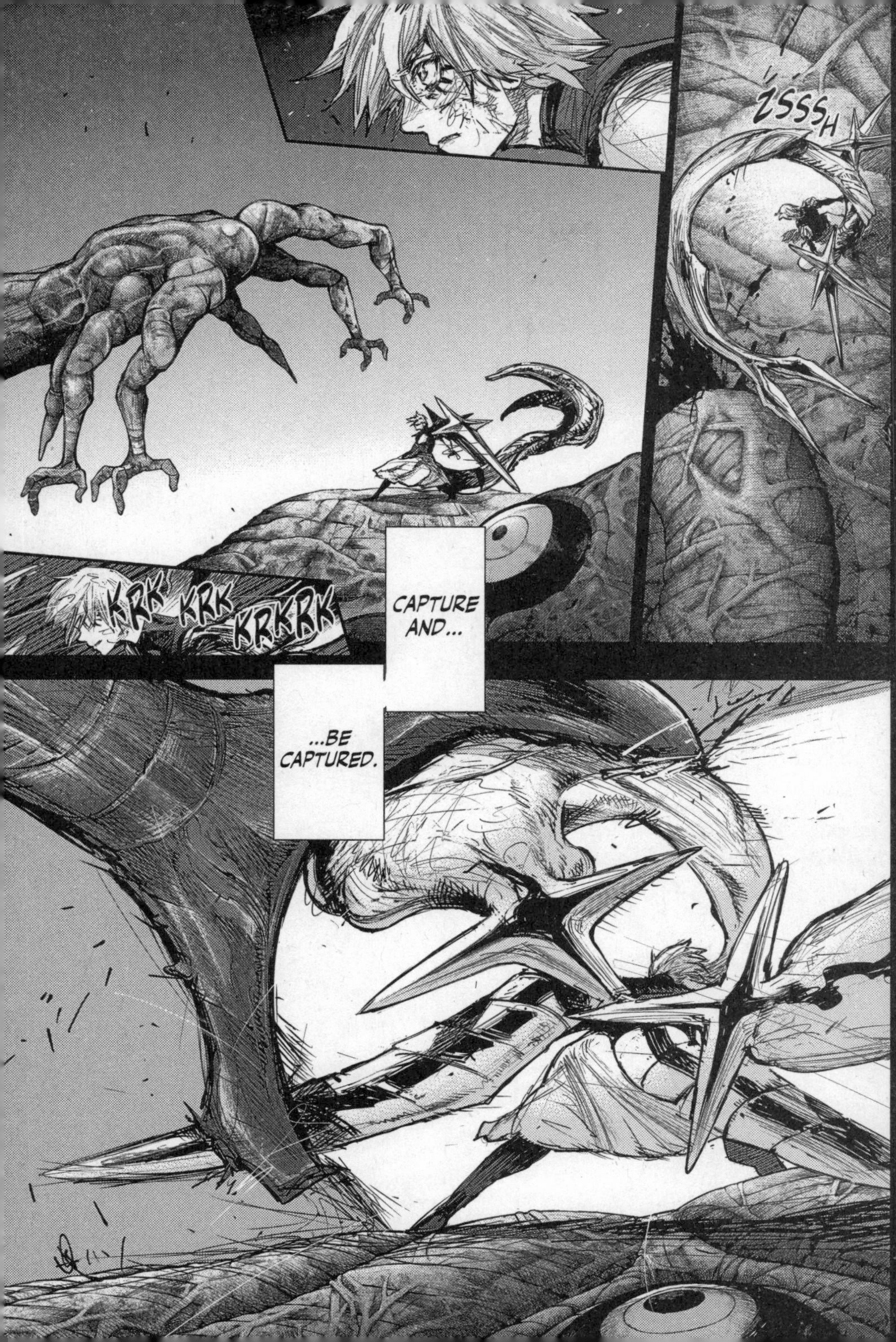
ZSSSH
KRK KRK KRKRK
CAPTURE AND...
...BE CAPTURED.

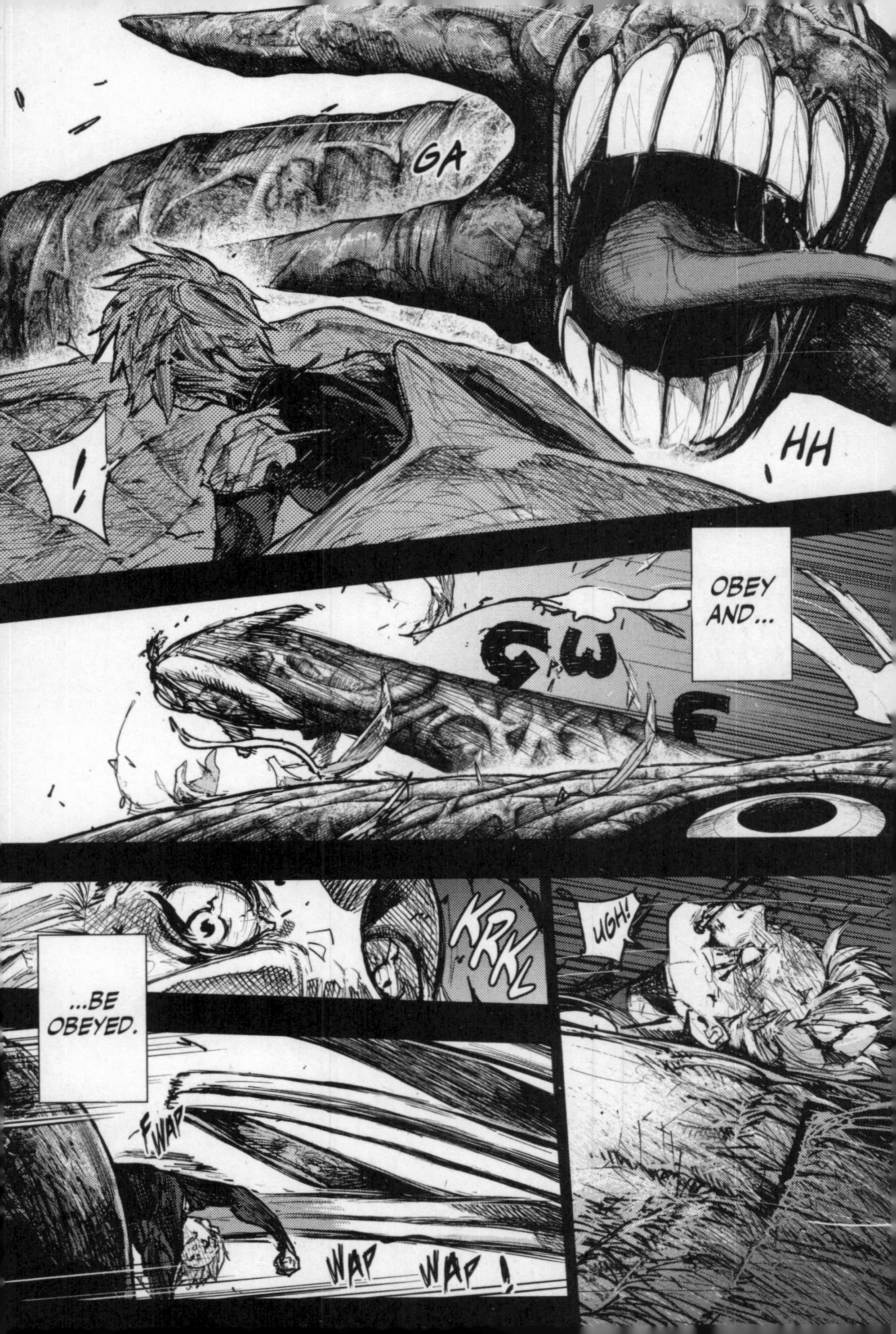
GA
HH
OBEY AND...
CWF
UGH!
KRKL
...BE OBEYED.
FWAP
WAP WAP!

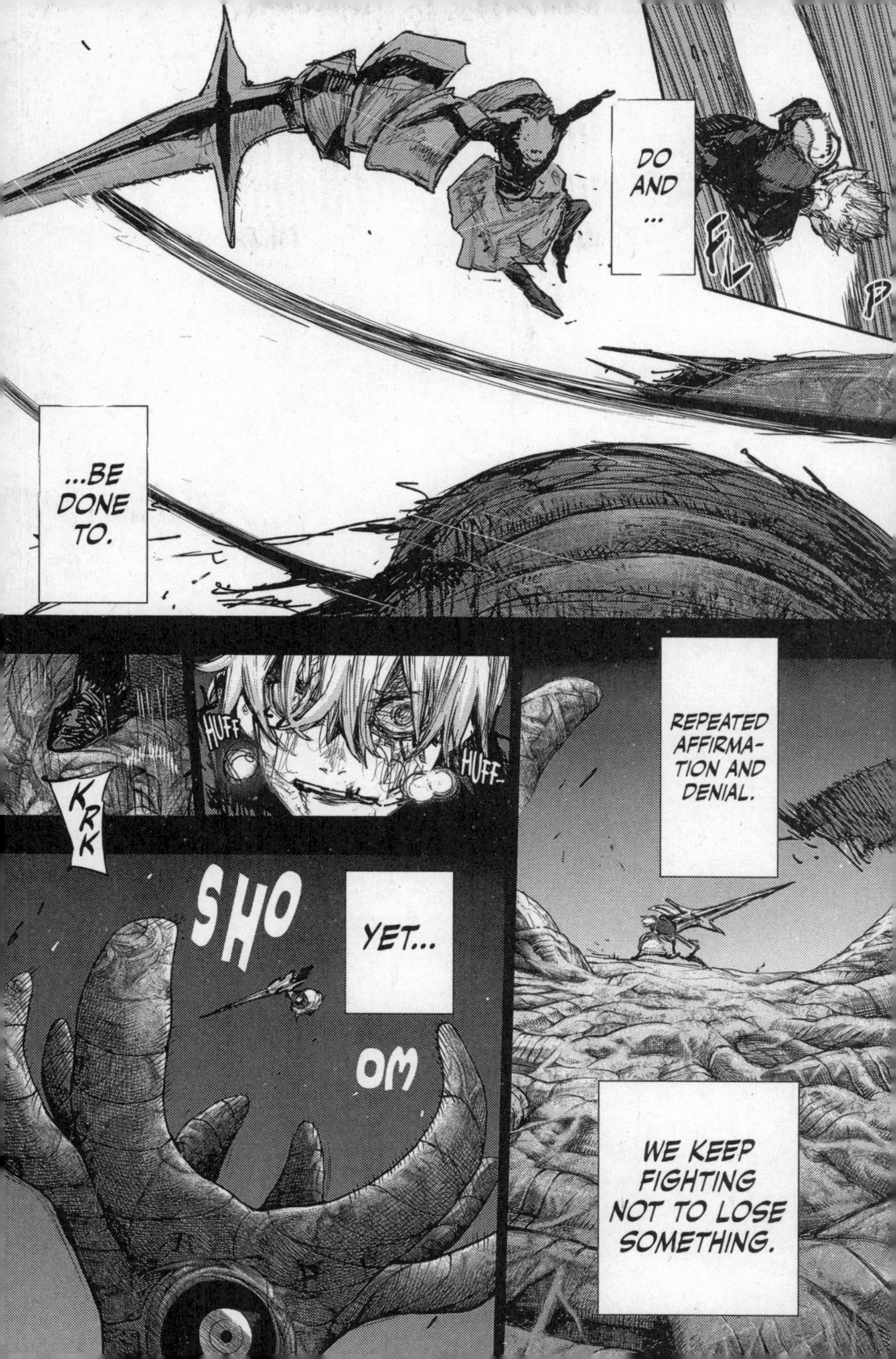
DO AND ...
FL
P
...BE DONE TO.
REPEATED AFFIRMATION AND DENIAL.
WE KEEP FIGHTING NOT TO LOSE SOMETHING.
HUFF
HUFF
KRK
YET...
SHO
OM

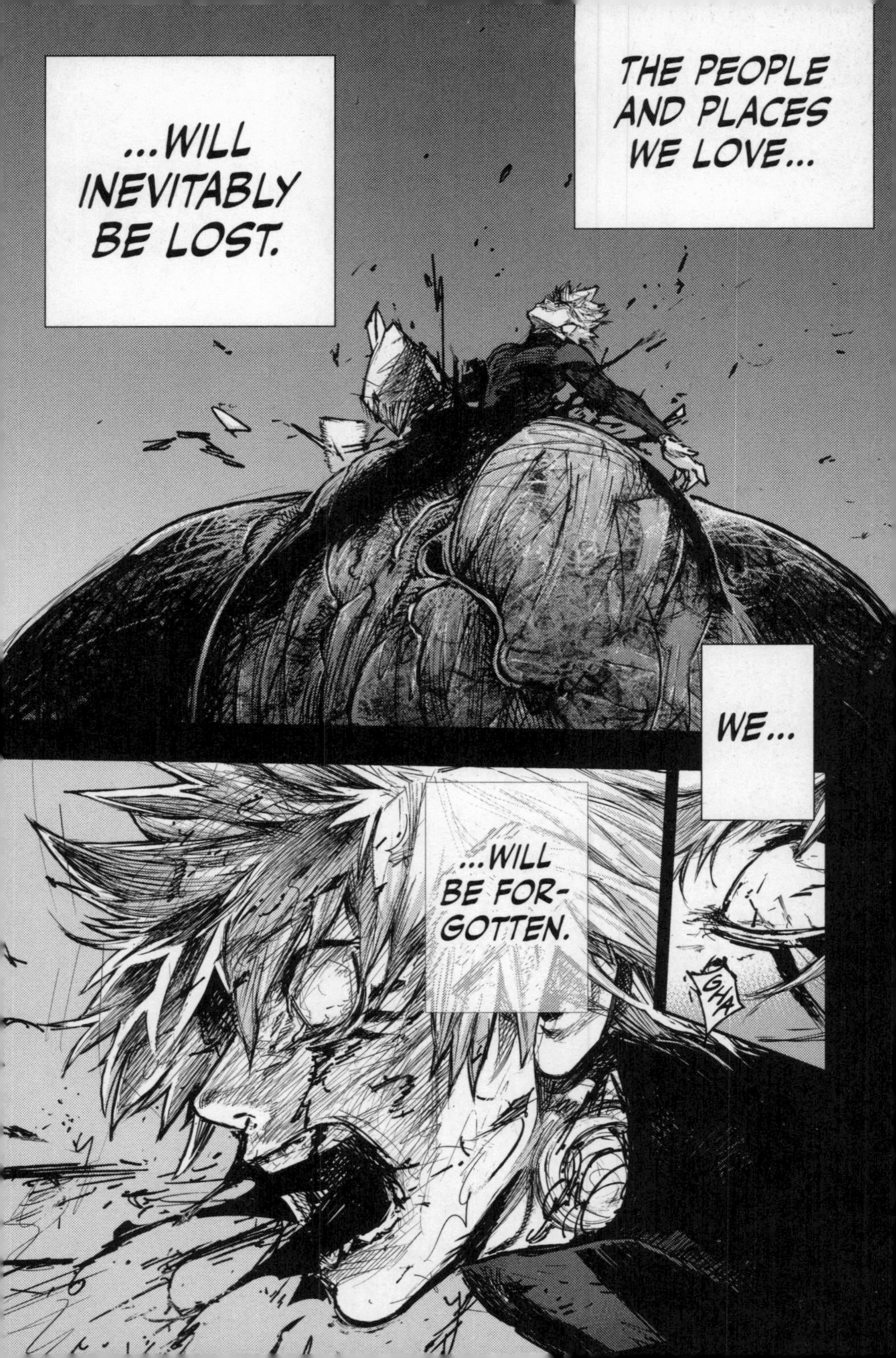
THE PEOPLE AND PLACES WE LOVE...
...WILL INEVITABLY BE LOST.
WE...
GHA
...WILL BE FOR-GOTTEN.

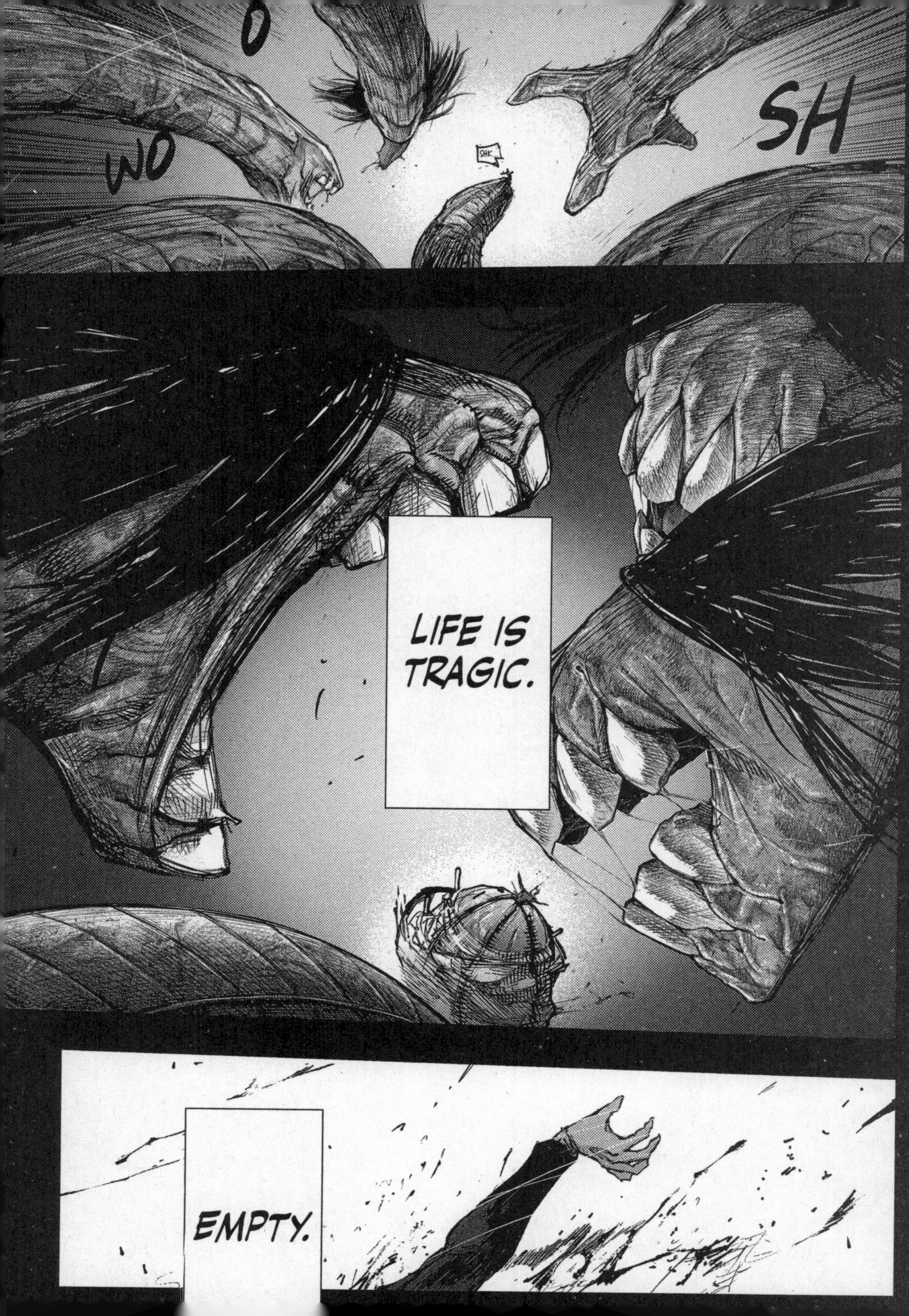
SH
SHK
WO
O
LIFE IS TRAGIC.
EMPTY.

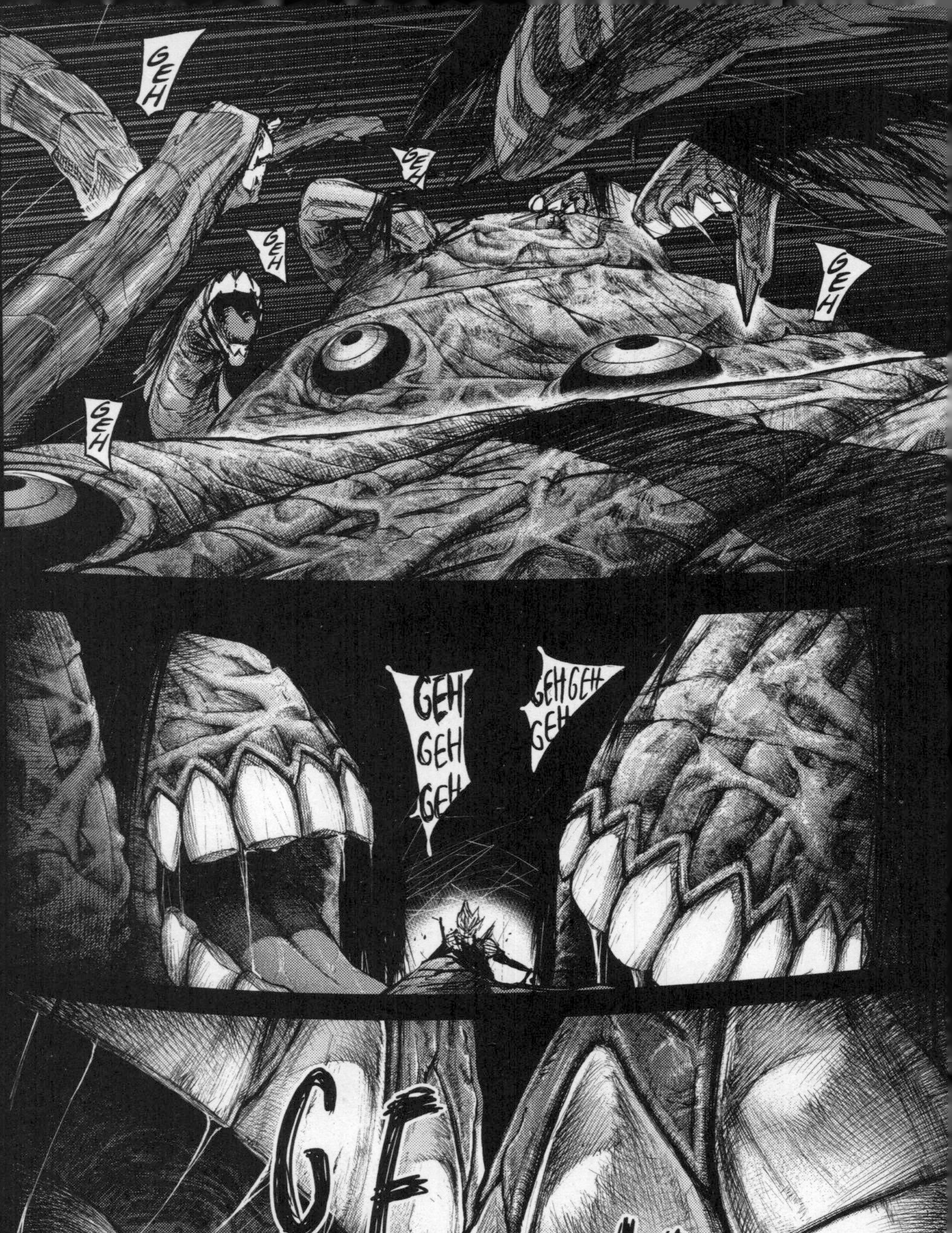
GEH
GEH
GEH
GEH
GEH
GEHGEH GEH
GEH GEH GEH
GEH

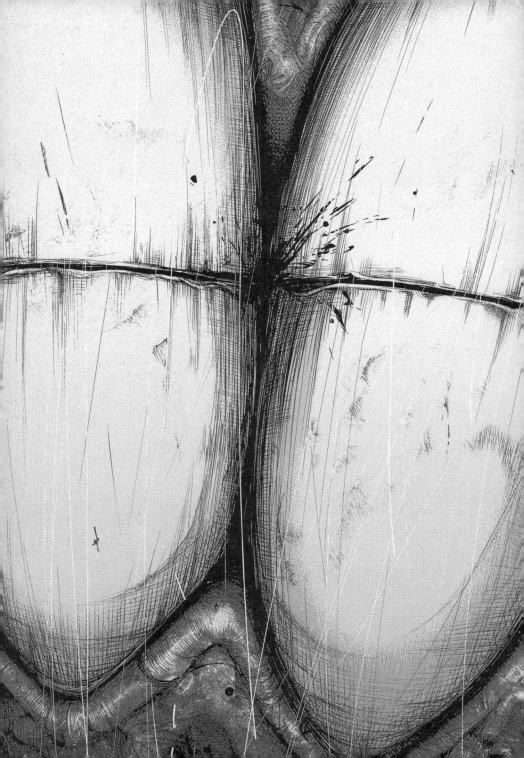

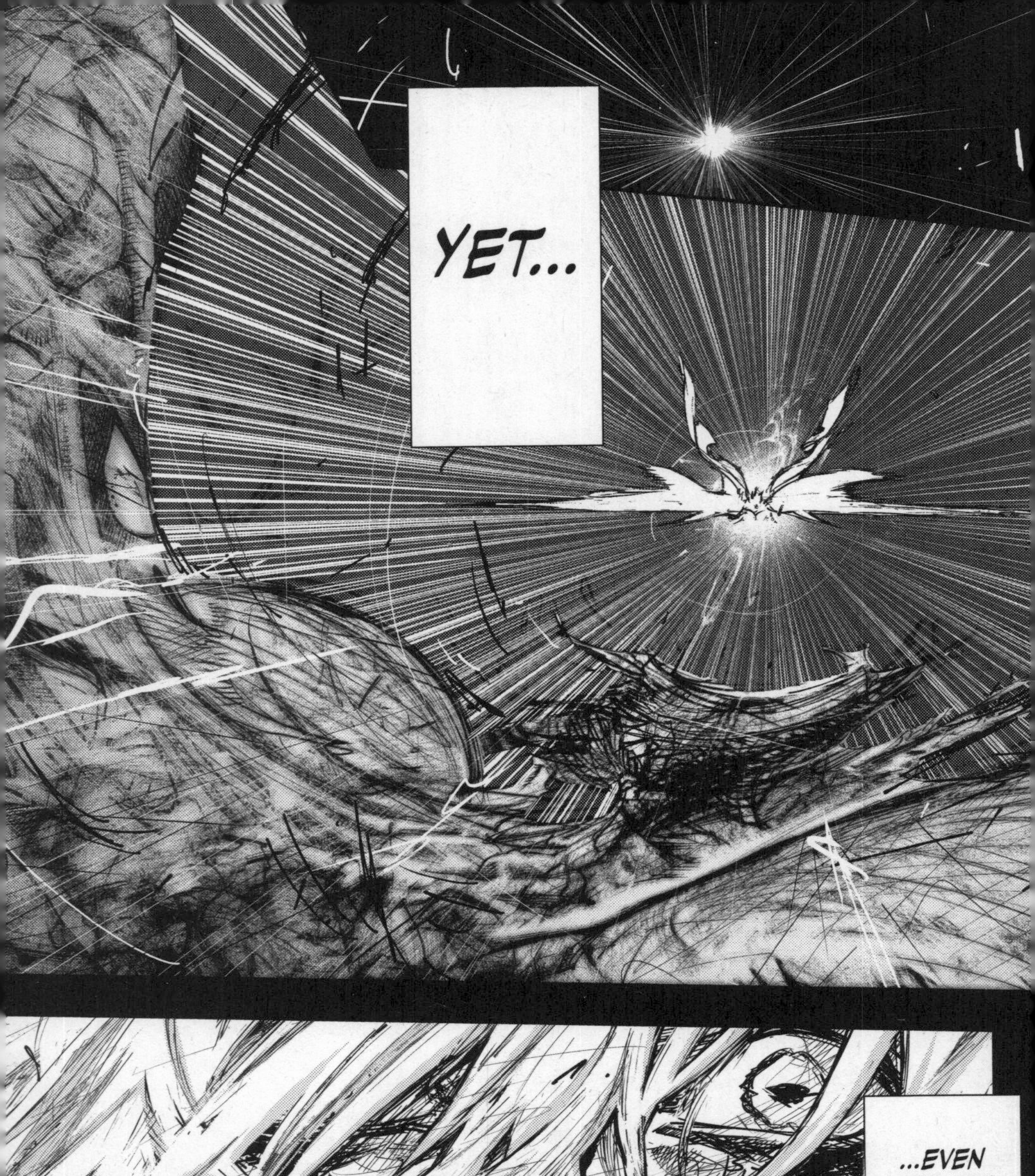
YET...
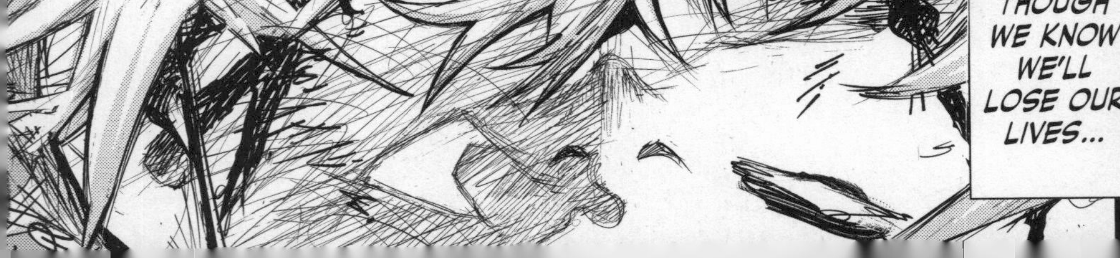
...EVEN THOUGH WE KNOW WE'LL LOSE OUR LIVES...

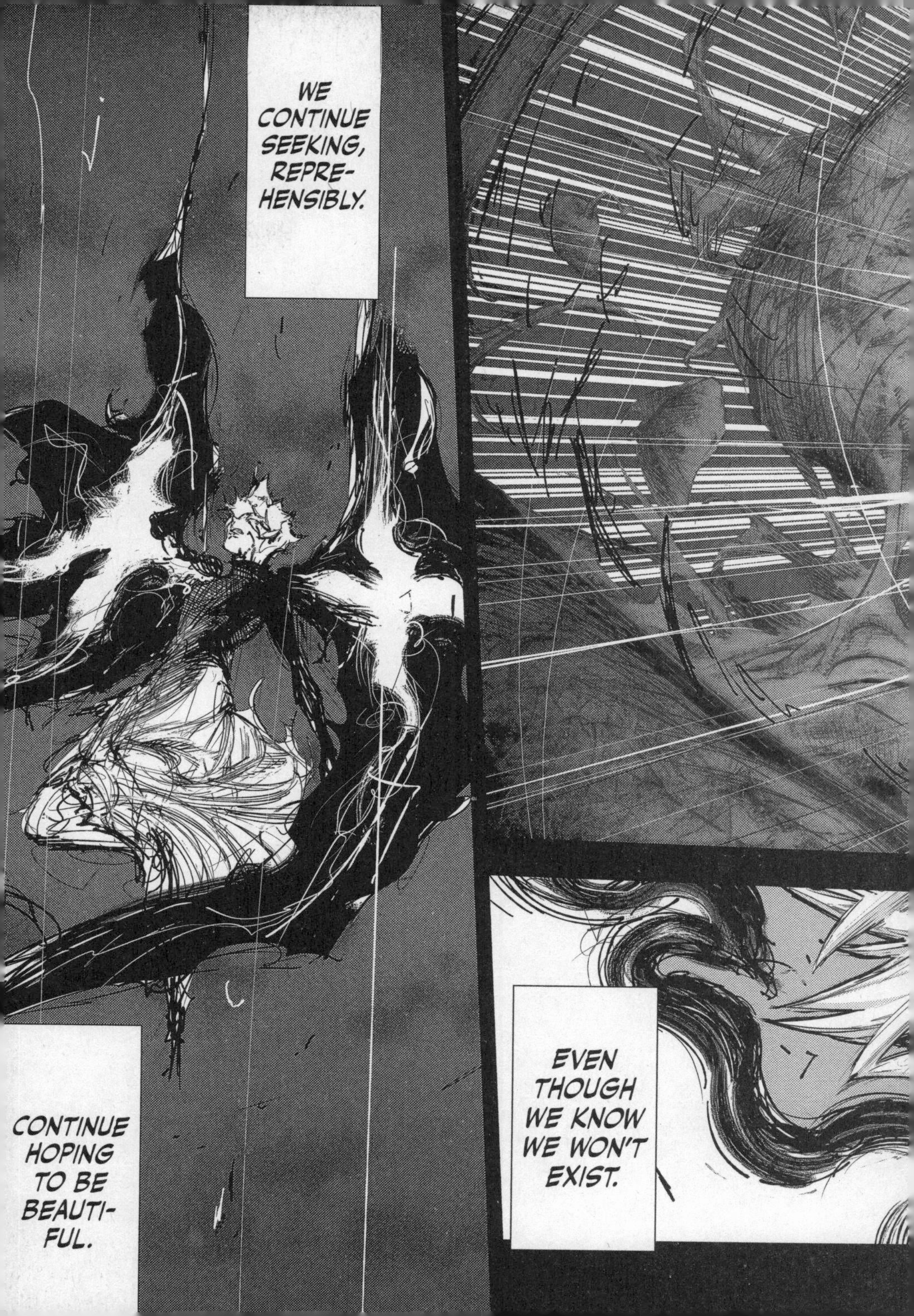
EVEN THOUGH WE KNOW WE WON'T EXIST.
WE CONTINUE SEEKING, REPRE-HENSIBLY.
CONTINUE HOPING TO BE BEAUTI-FUL.

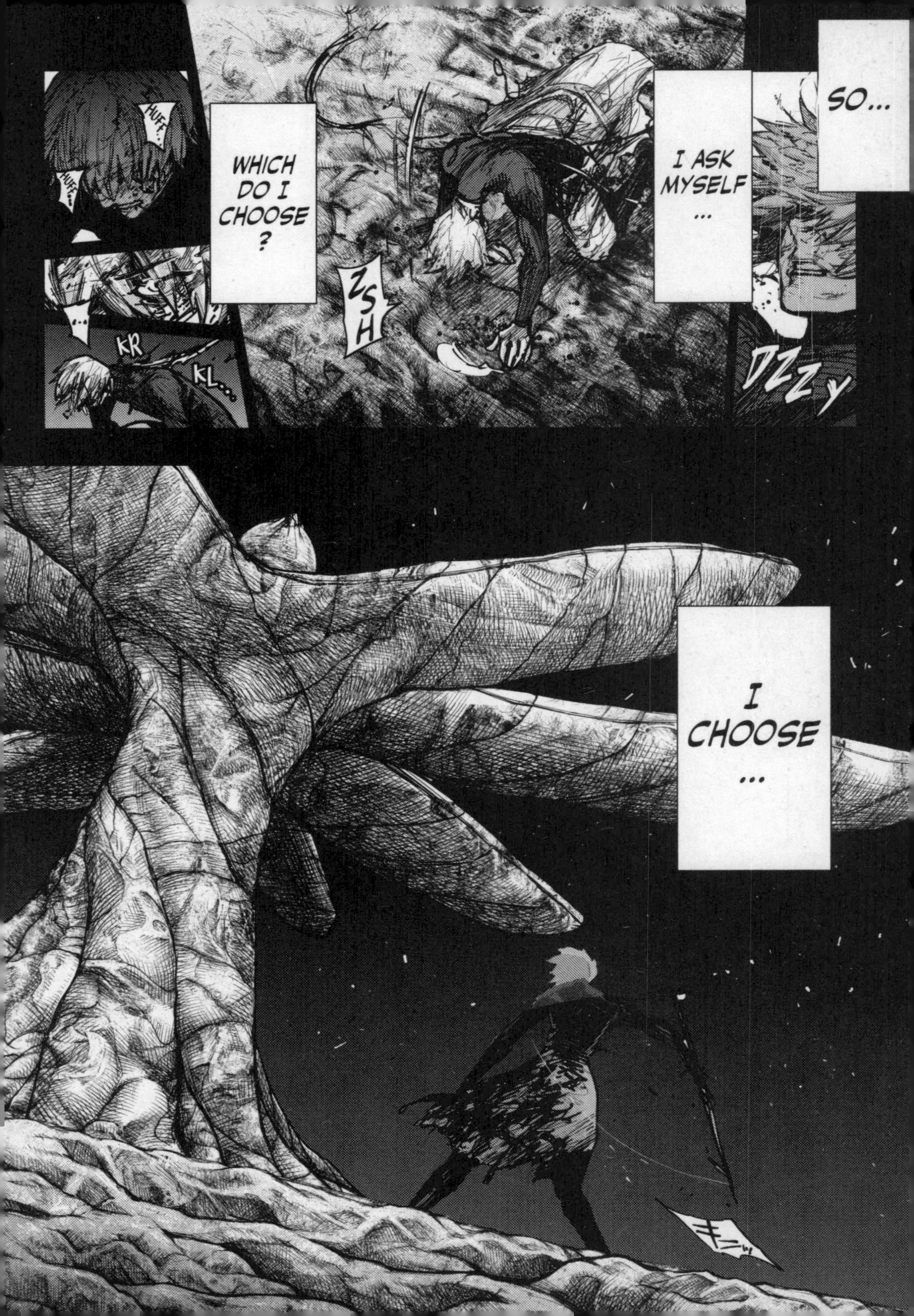
SO...
I ASK MYSELF ...
DZZY
WHICH DO I CHOOSE ?
ZSH
HUFF...
HUFF...
...
KR
KL...
I CHOOSE ...

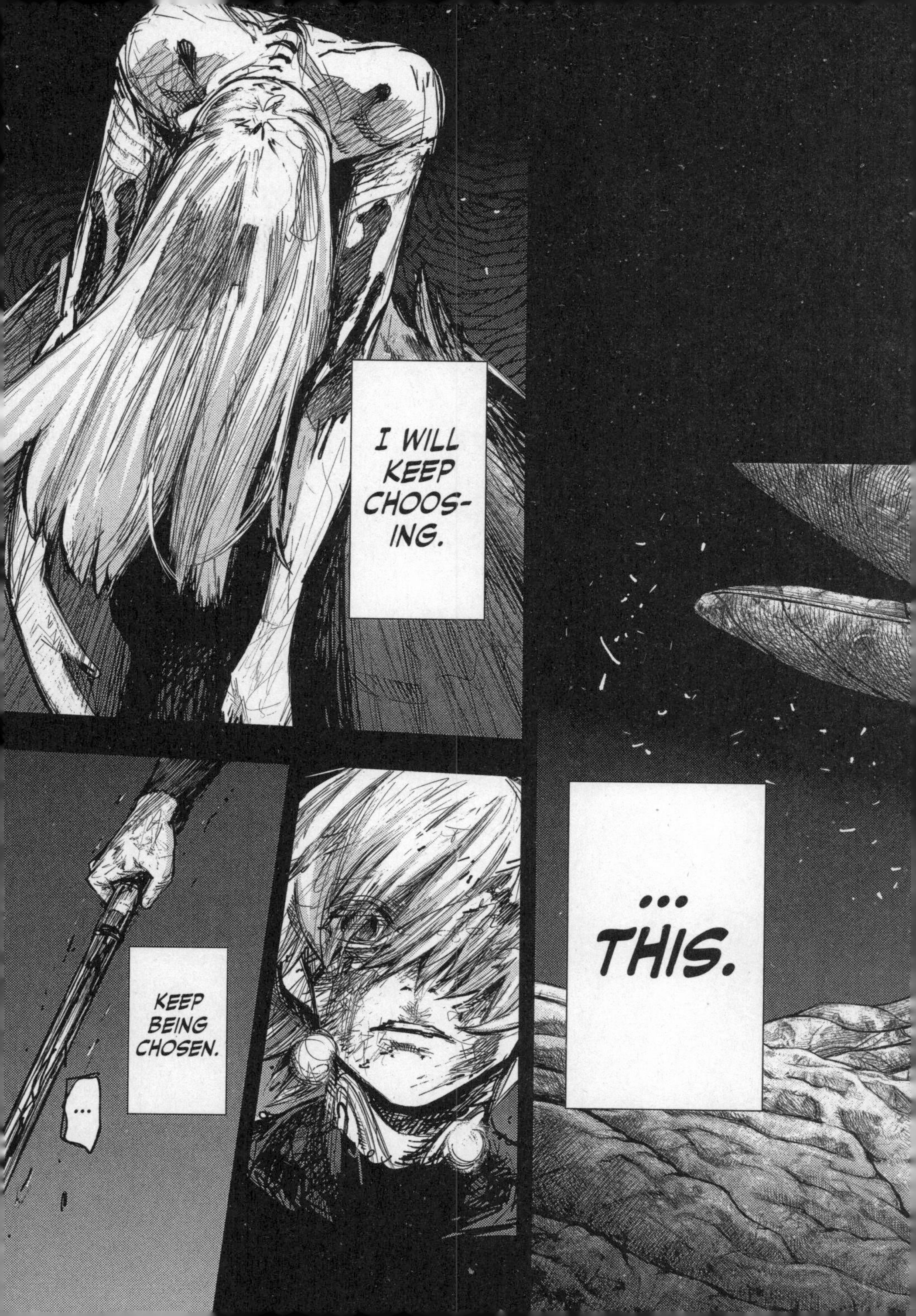
...THIS.
I WILL KEEP CHOOSING.
KEEP BEING CHOSEN.
...

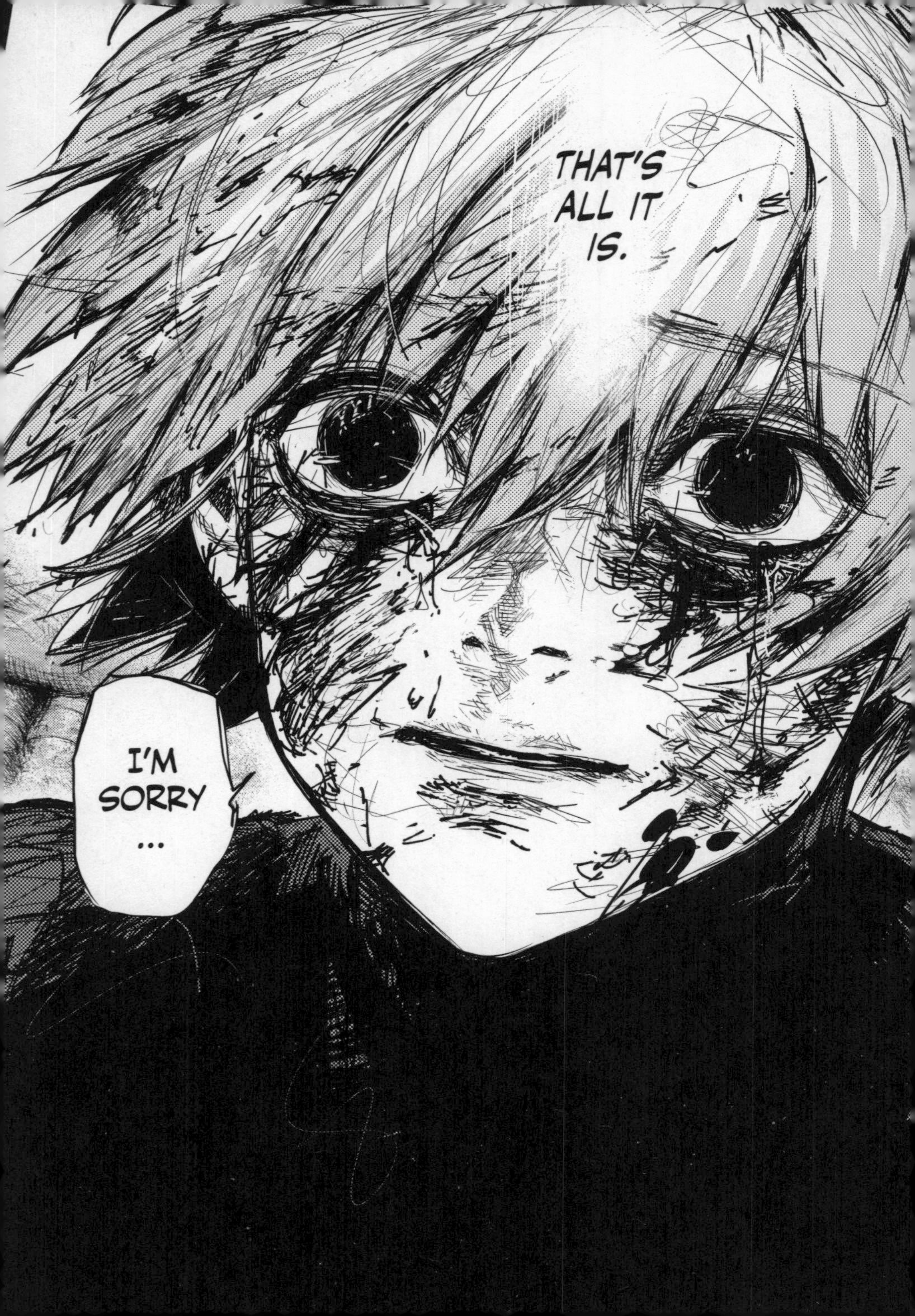
THAT'S ALL IT IS.
I'M SORRY ...

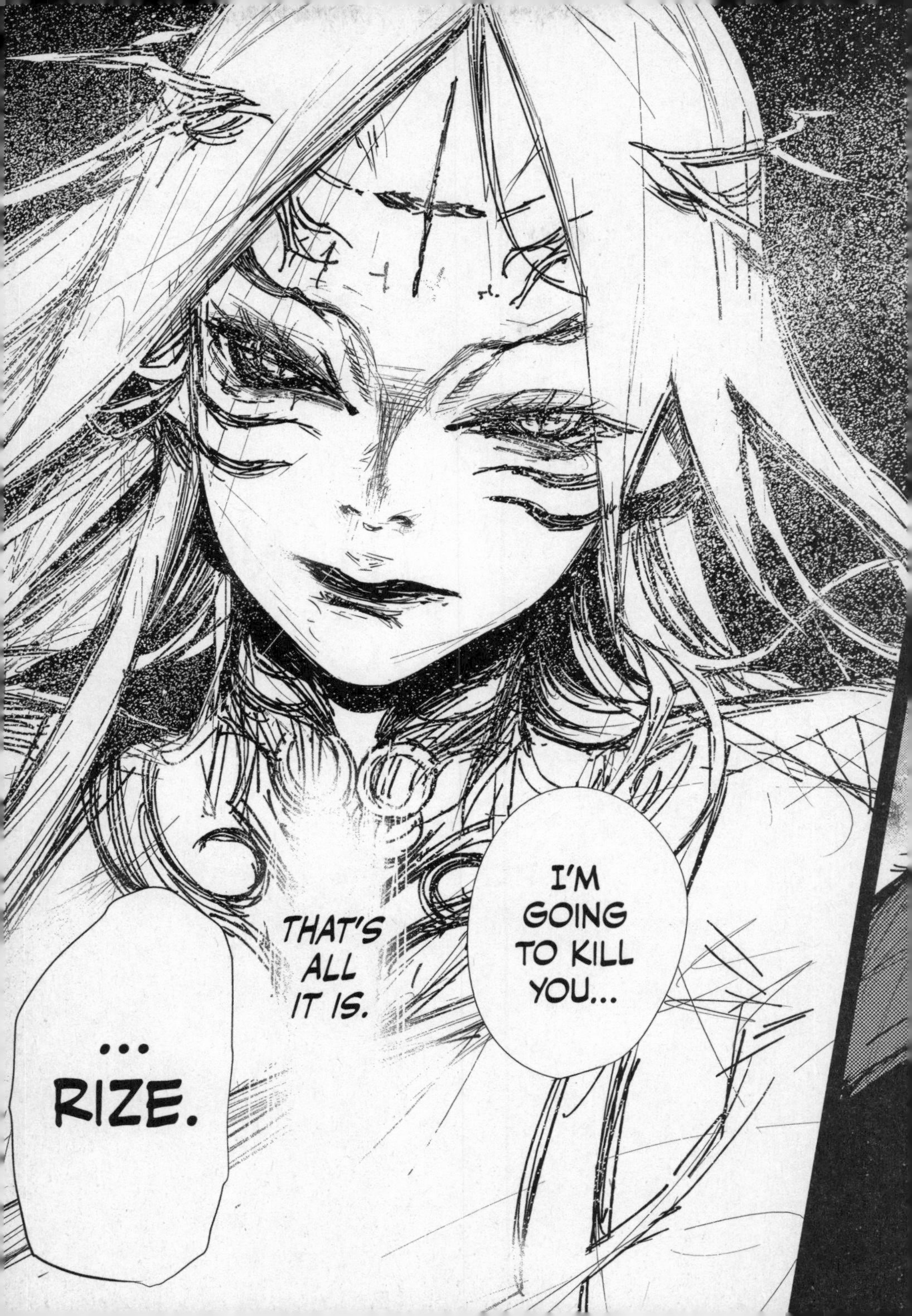
I'M GOING TO KILL YOU...
THAT'S ALL IT IS.
... RIZE.

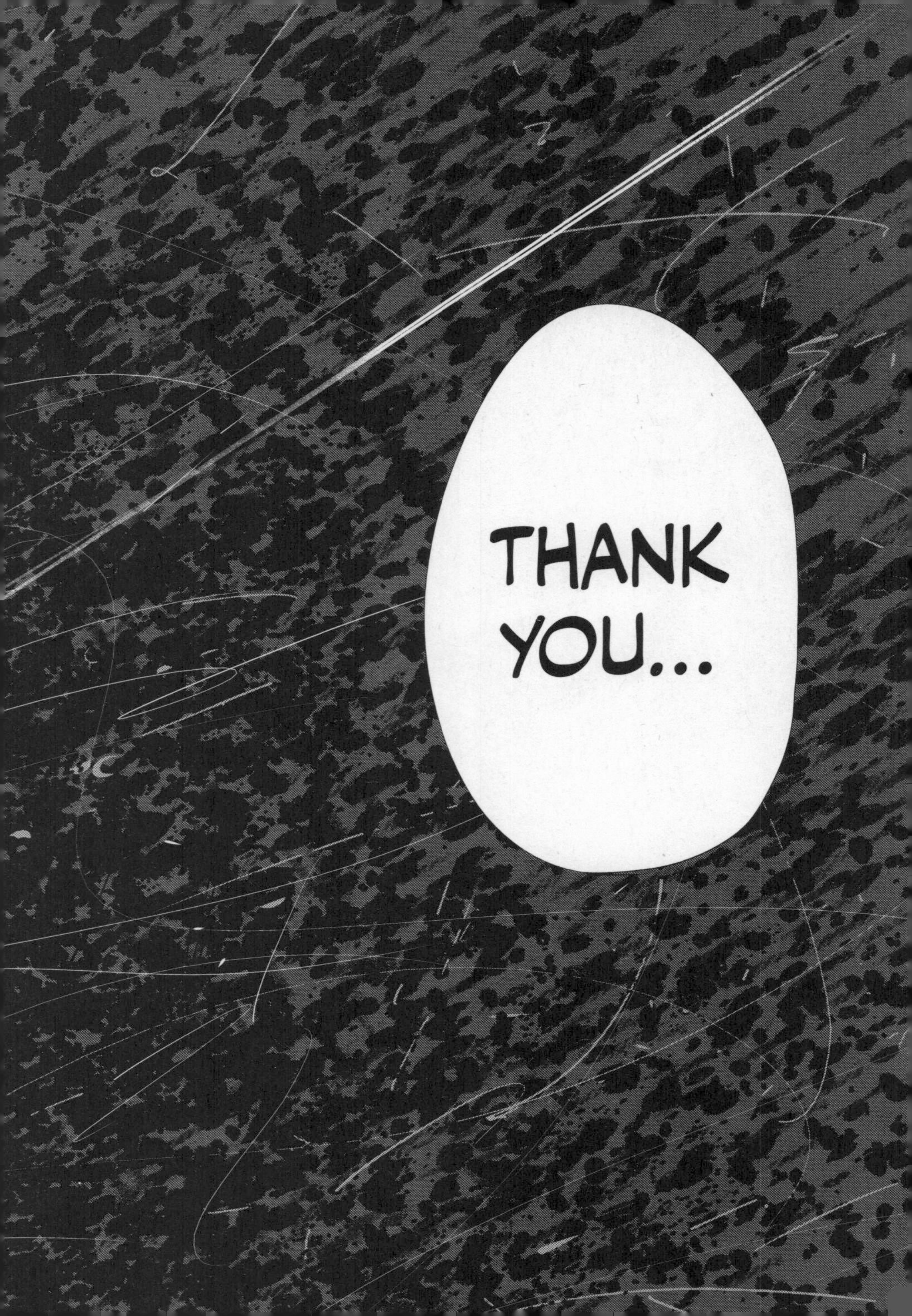
THANK YOU...

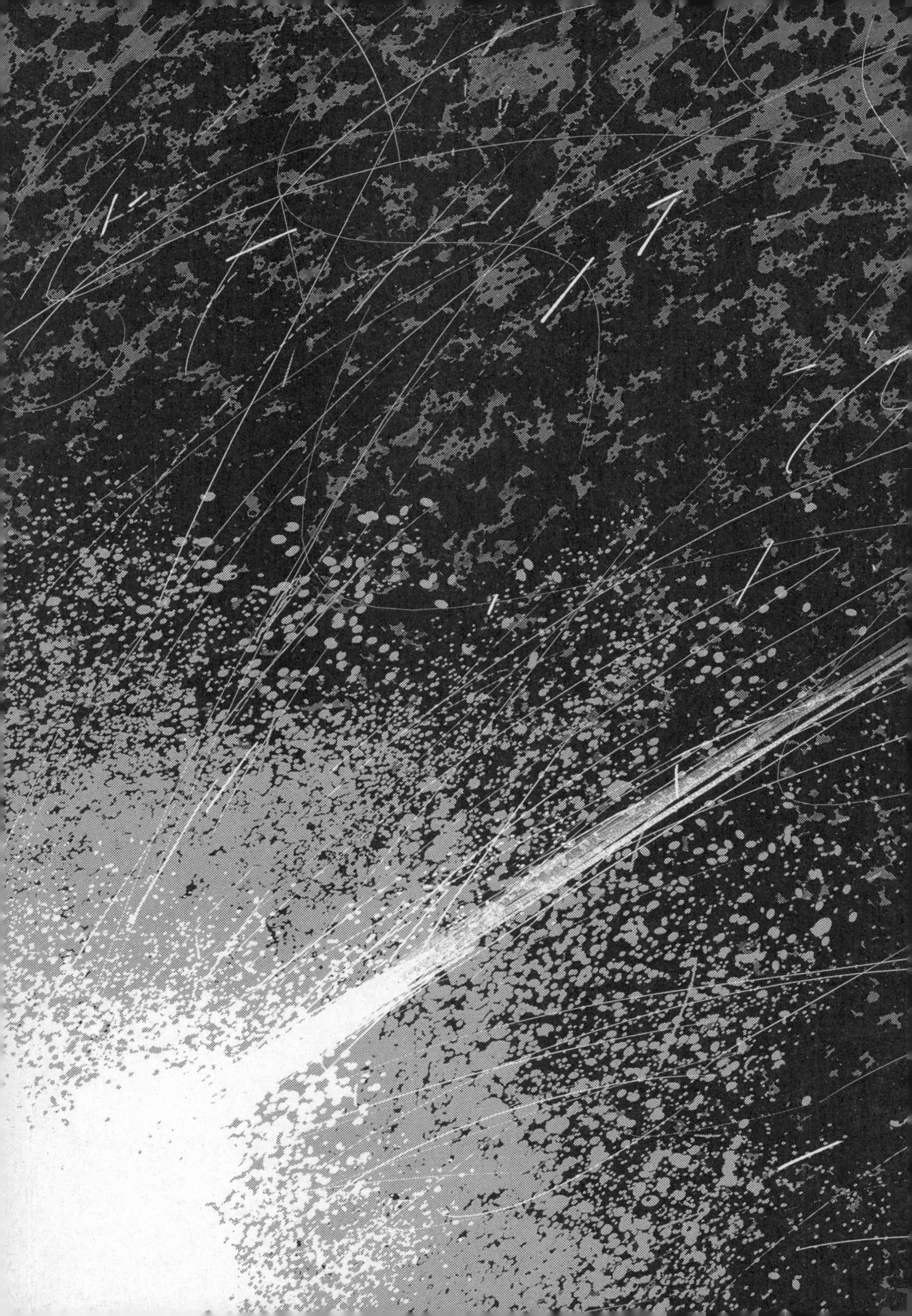

White and Rabbit :178

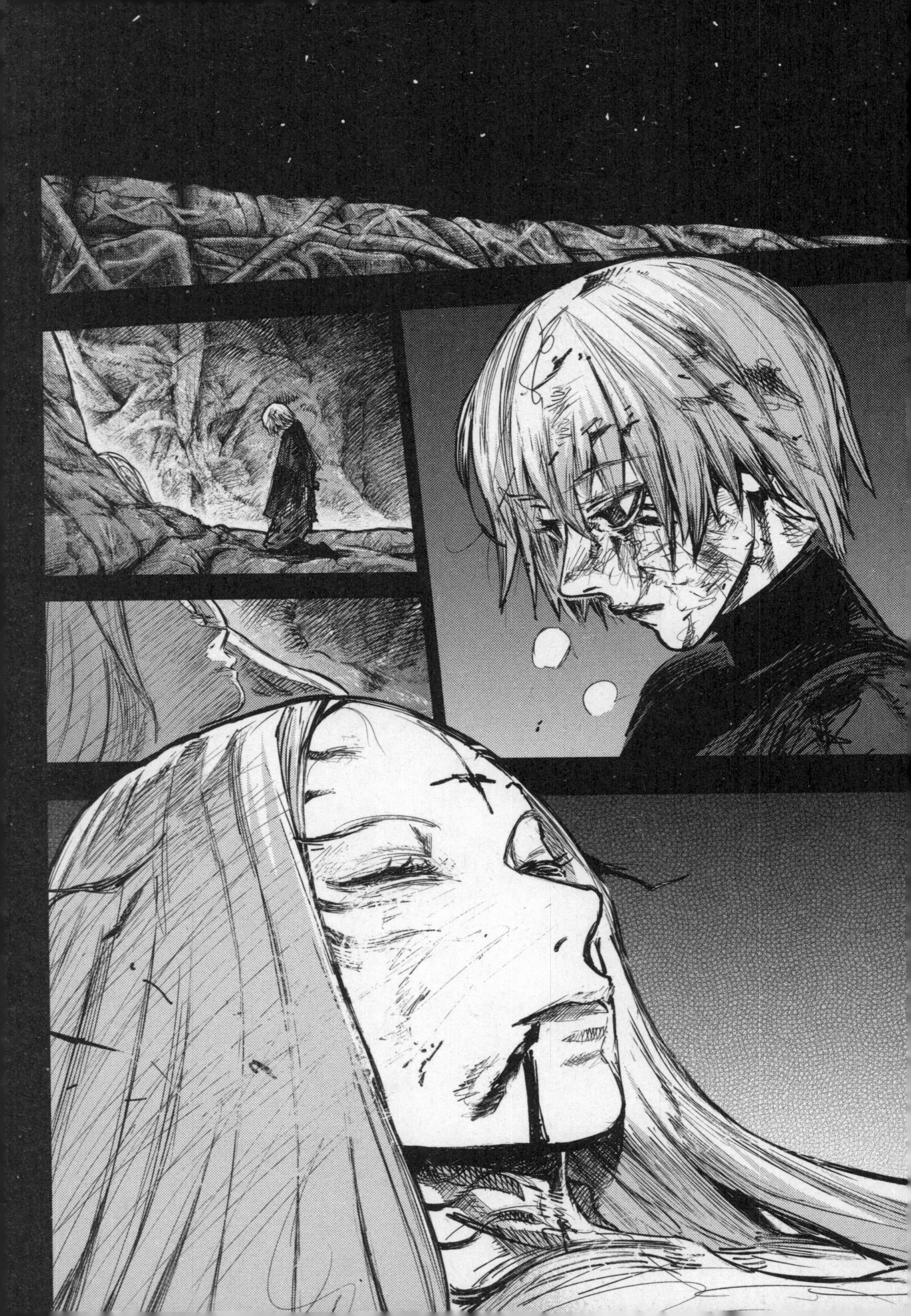

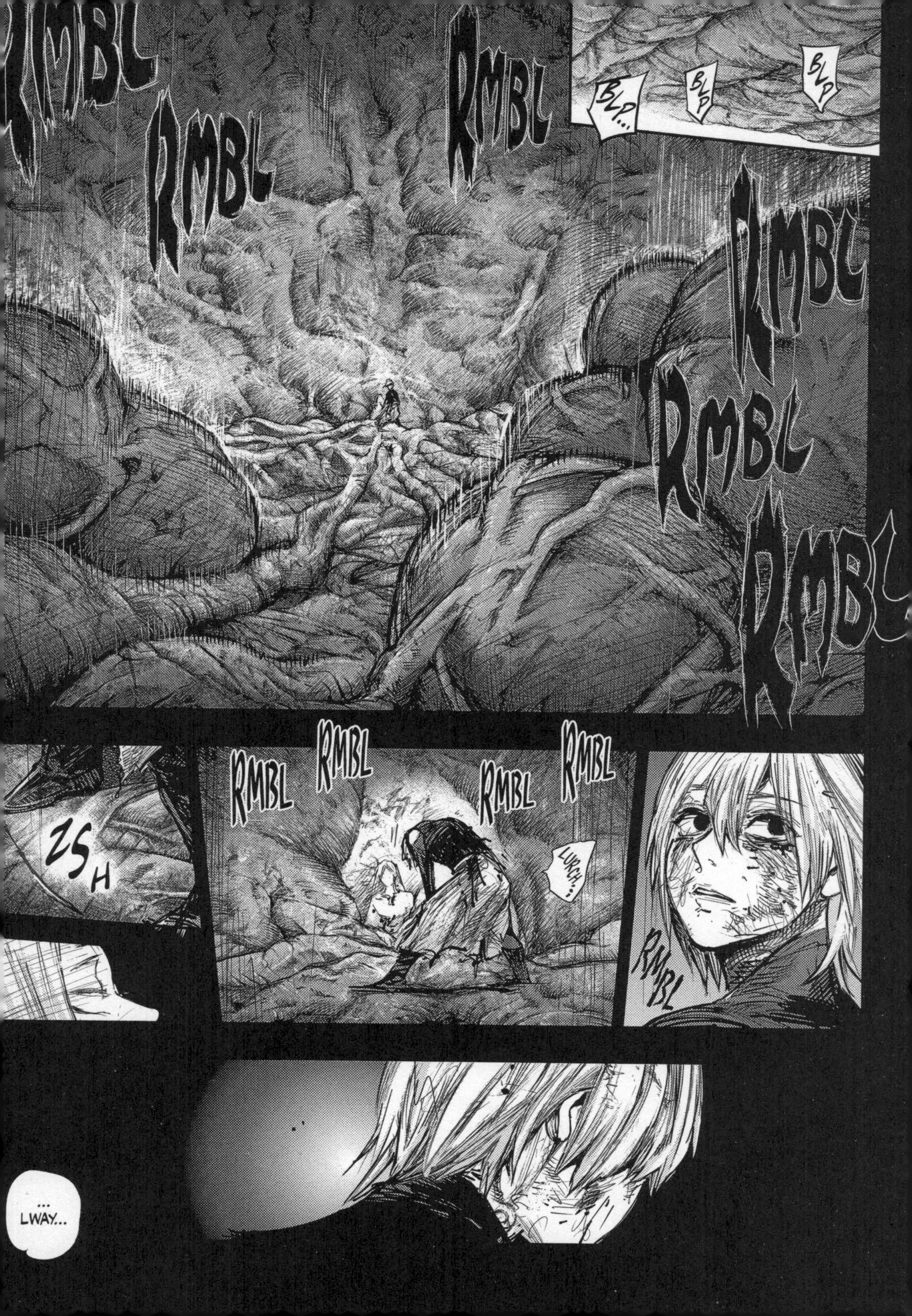
BLP
BLP
BLP...
RMBL
RMBL
RMBL
RMBL
RMBL
RMBL
RMBL
RMBL
RMBL
RMBL
RMBL
LURCH...
ZSH
...LWAY...

RMBL
RMBL
RMBL
RMBL
RMBL
RMBL
RMBL
RMBL
RMBL
DRP
RMBL
DRP
DRP
RMBL
DRP
DRP
DRP
DRP
RMBL
DRP
RMBL

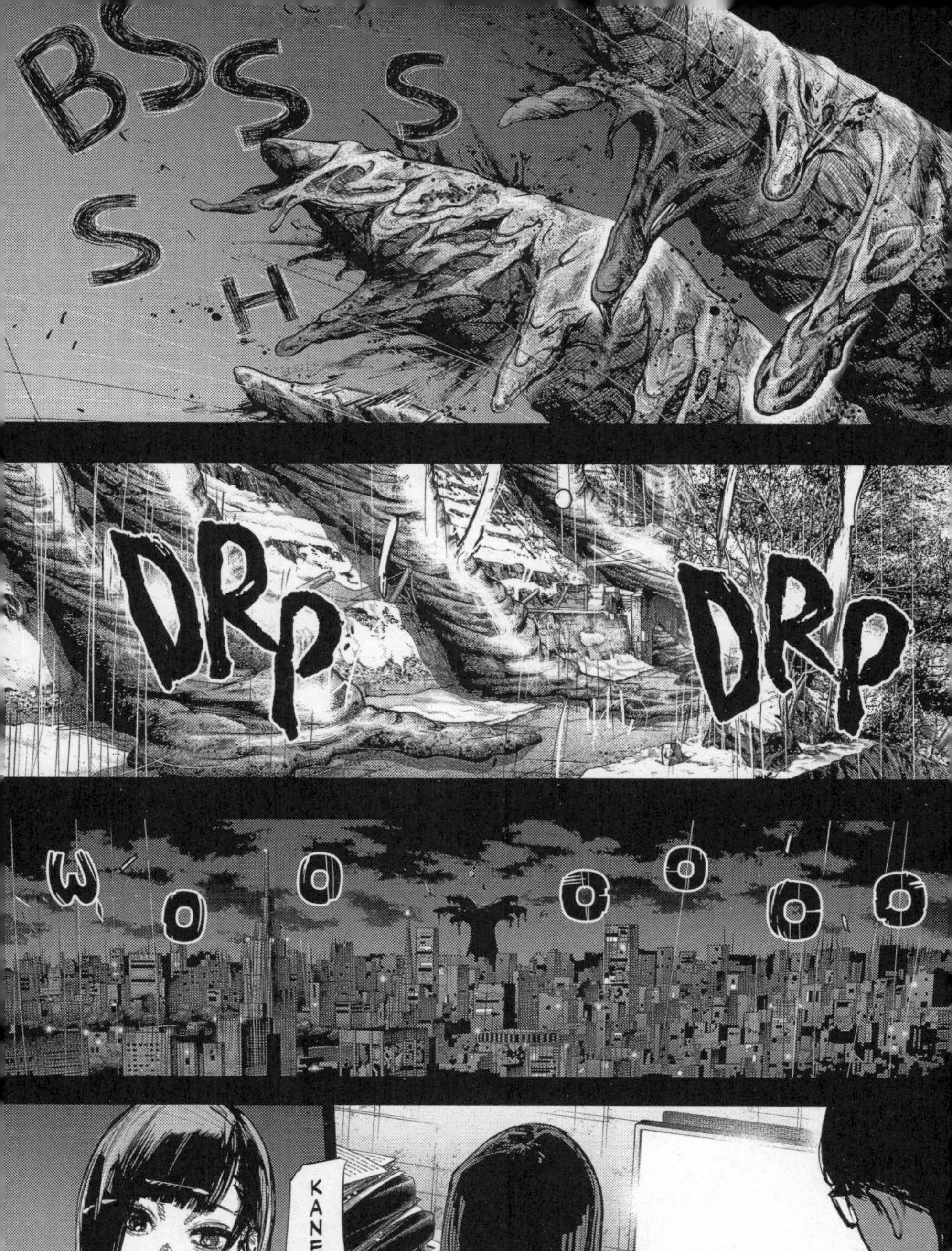
BSSSSH
DRP
DRP
WOOOOOO
KANEKI...

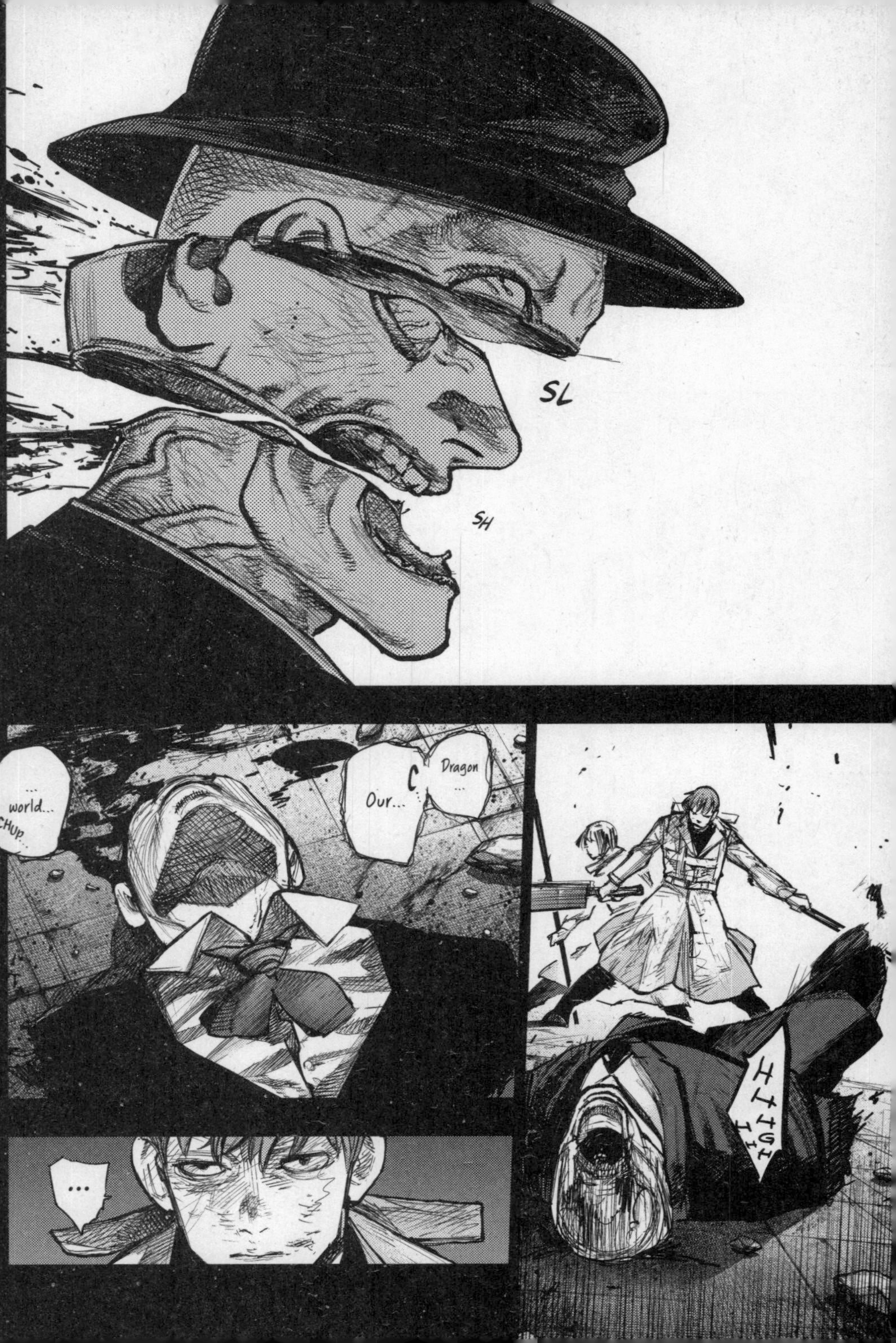
SL
SH
HIIGH
Dragon ...
Our...
... world... CHUp...
...

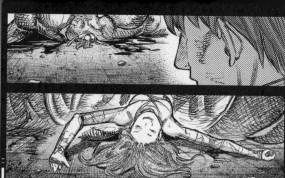

Th-thanks,
Y-Yomo...

Th...

REST,
KOMA.

SOB

SOB

DON'T
MENTION
IT.

TO ALL
PERSON-
NEL...

DAMN
IT...

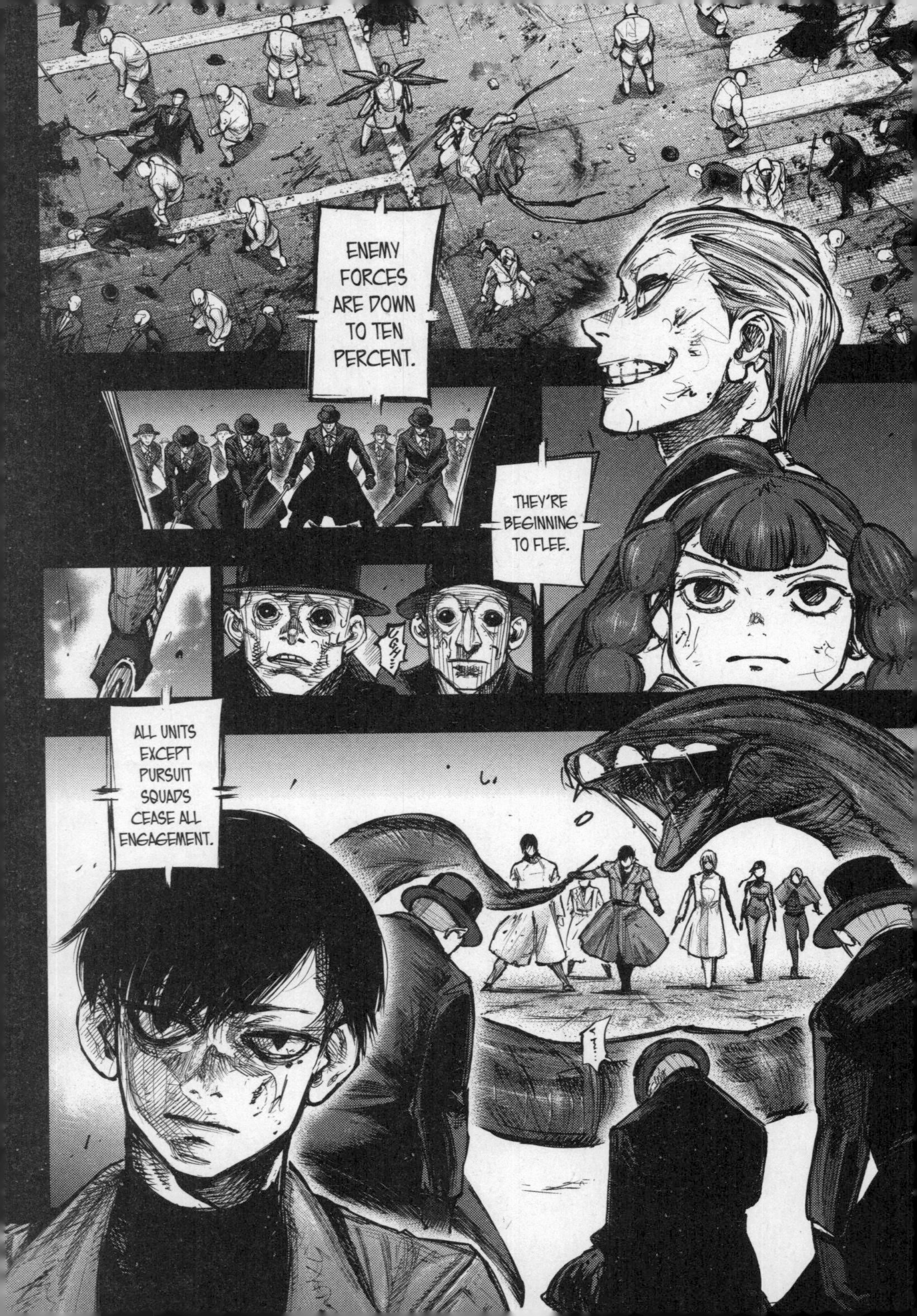
ENEMY FORCES ARE DOWN TO TEN PERCENT.
THEY'RE BEGINNING TO FLEE.
UGH...
ALL UNITS EXCEPT PURSUIT SQUADS CEASE ALL ENGAGEMENT.

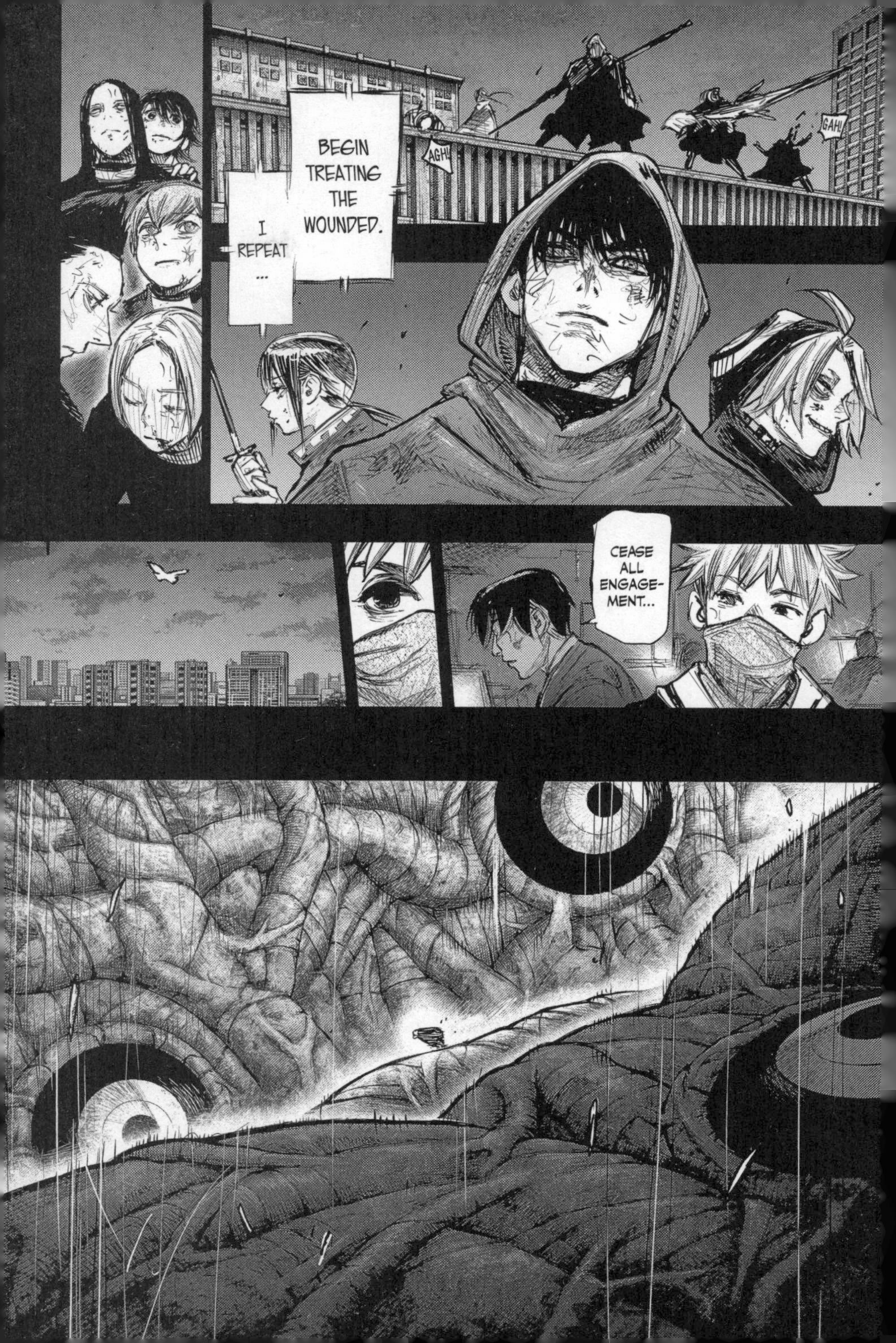
GAH!
BEGIN TREATING THE WOUNDED.
AGH!
I REPEAT ...
CEASE ALL ENGAGE-MENT...

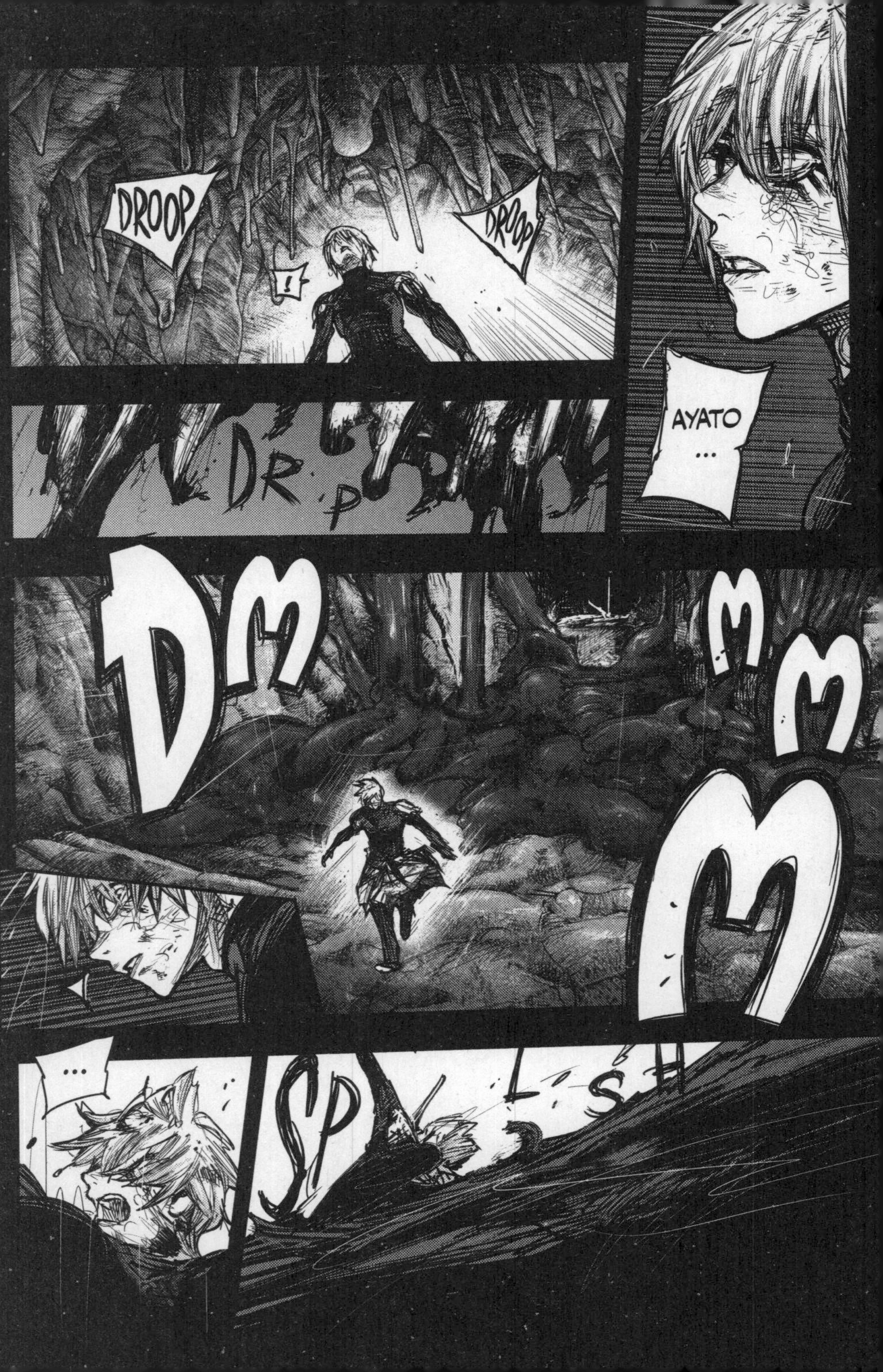

AYATO ...
DROOP
!
DROOP
DRP
DMMMM
SPLSH
...

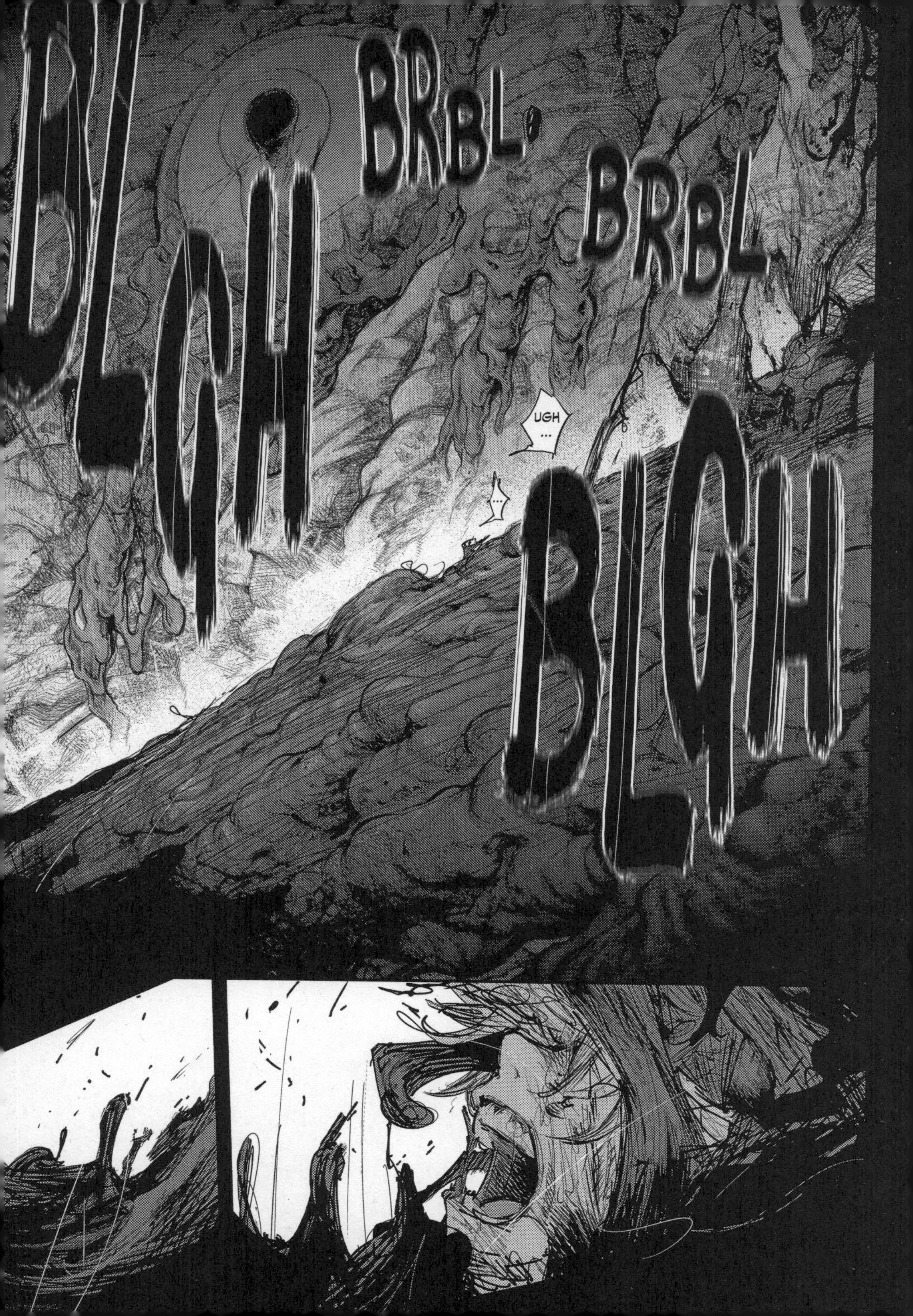
BRBL
BRBL
BLGH
UGH ...
...
BLGH

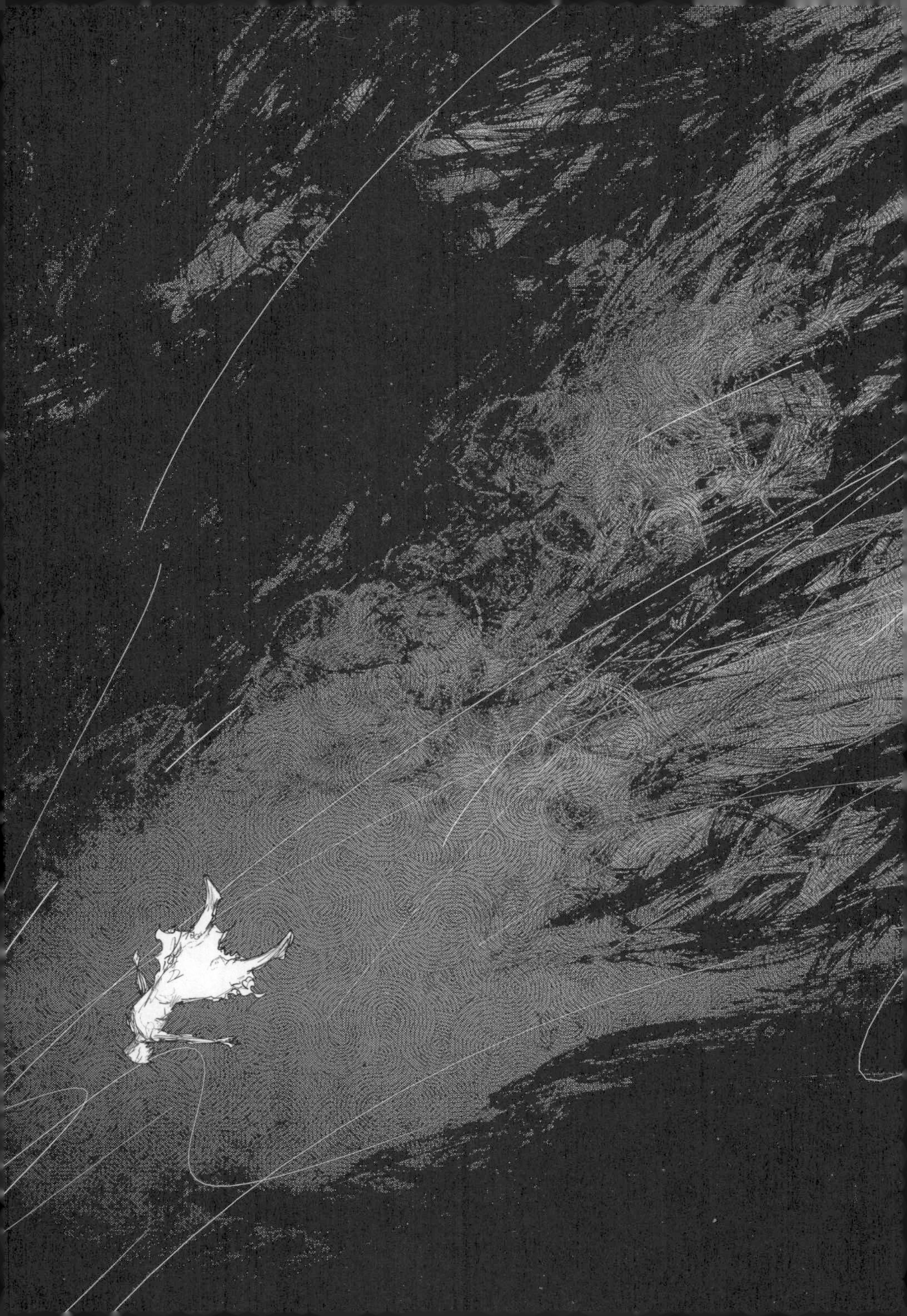

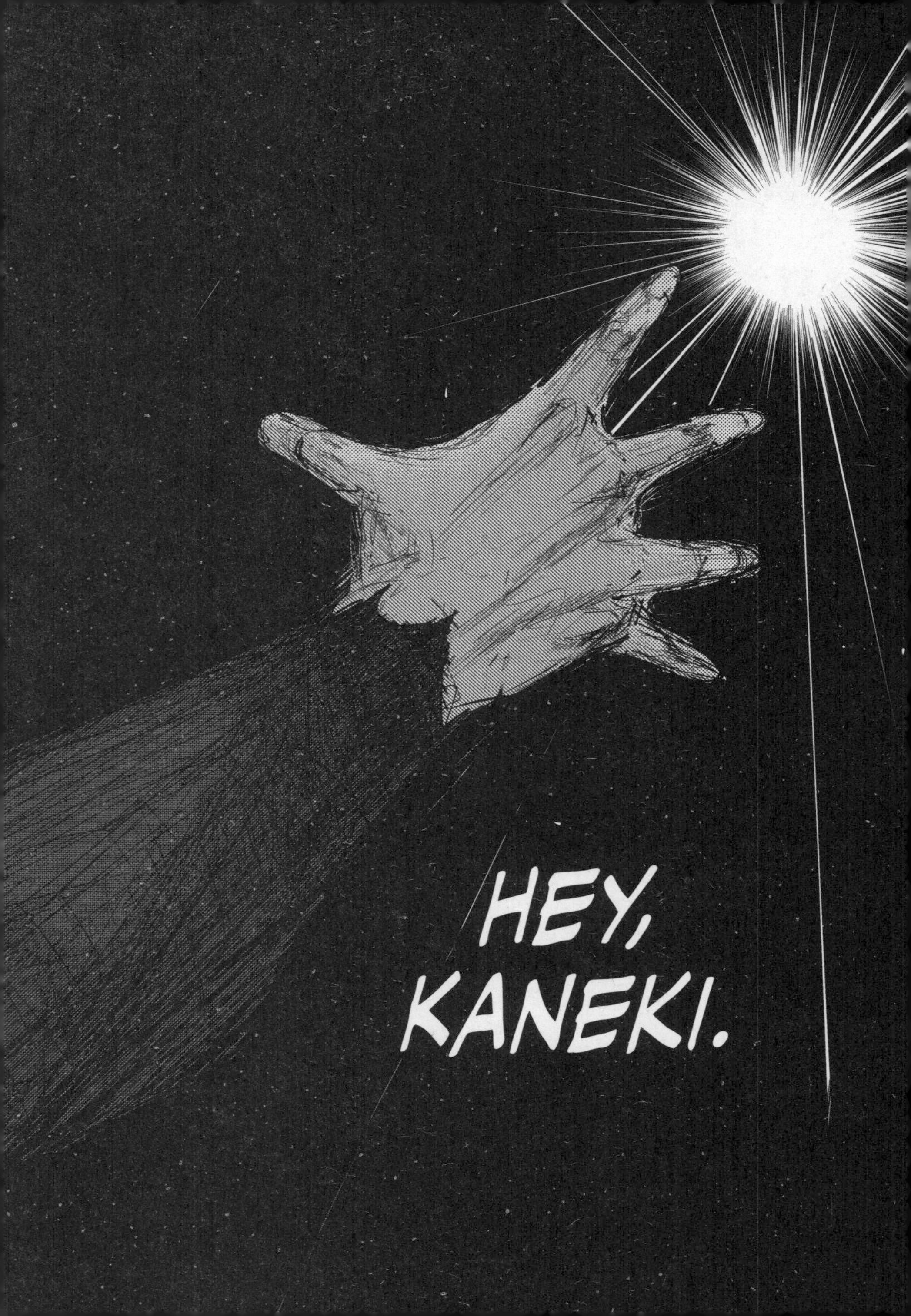
HEY, KANEKI.

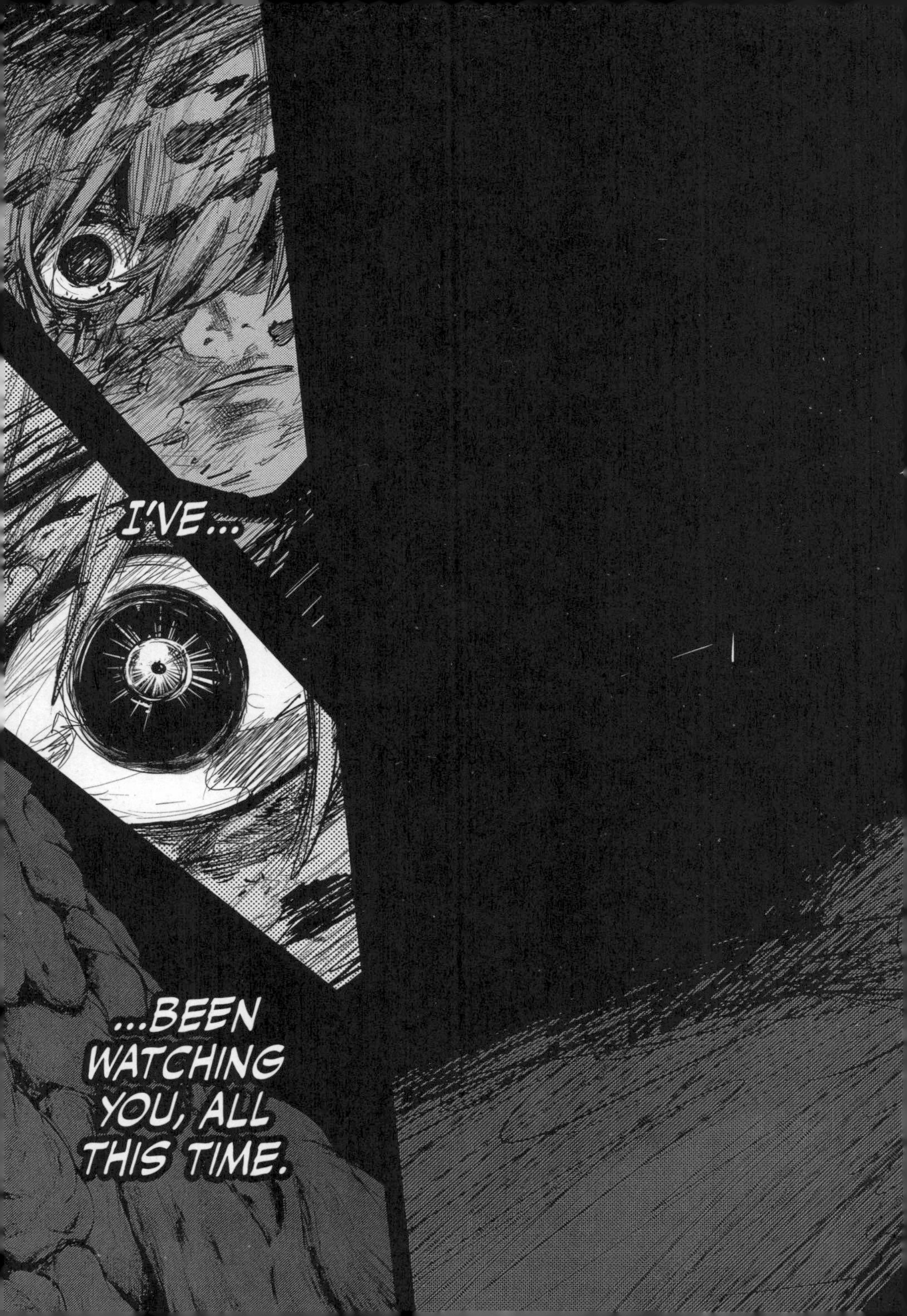
I'VE...
...BEEN WATCHING YOU, ALL THIS TIME.

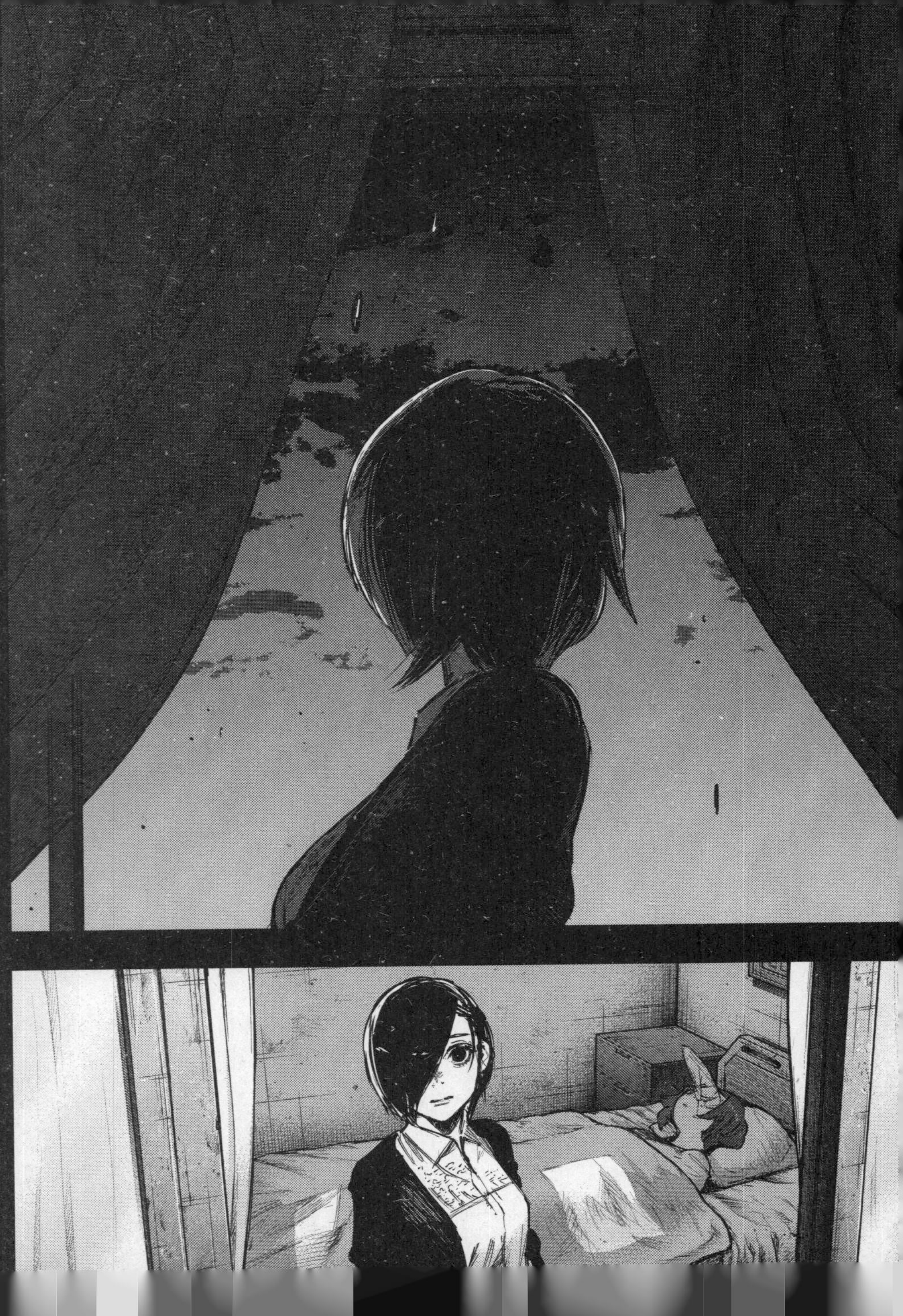

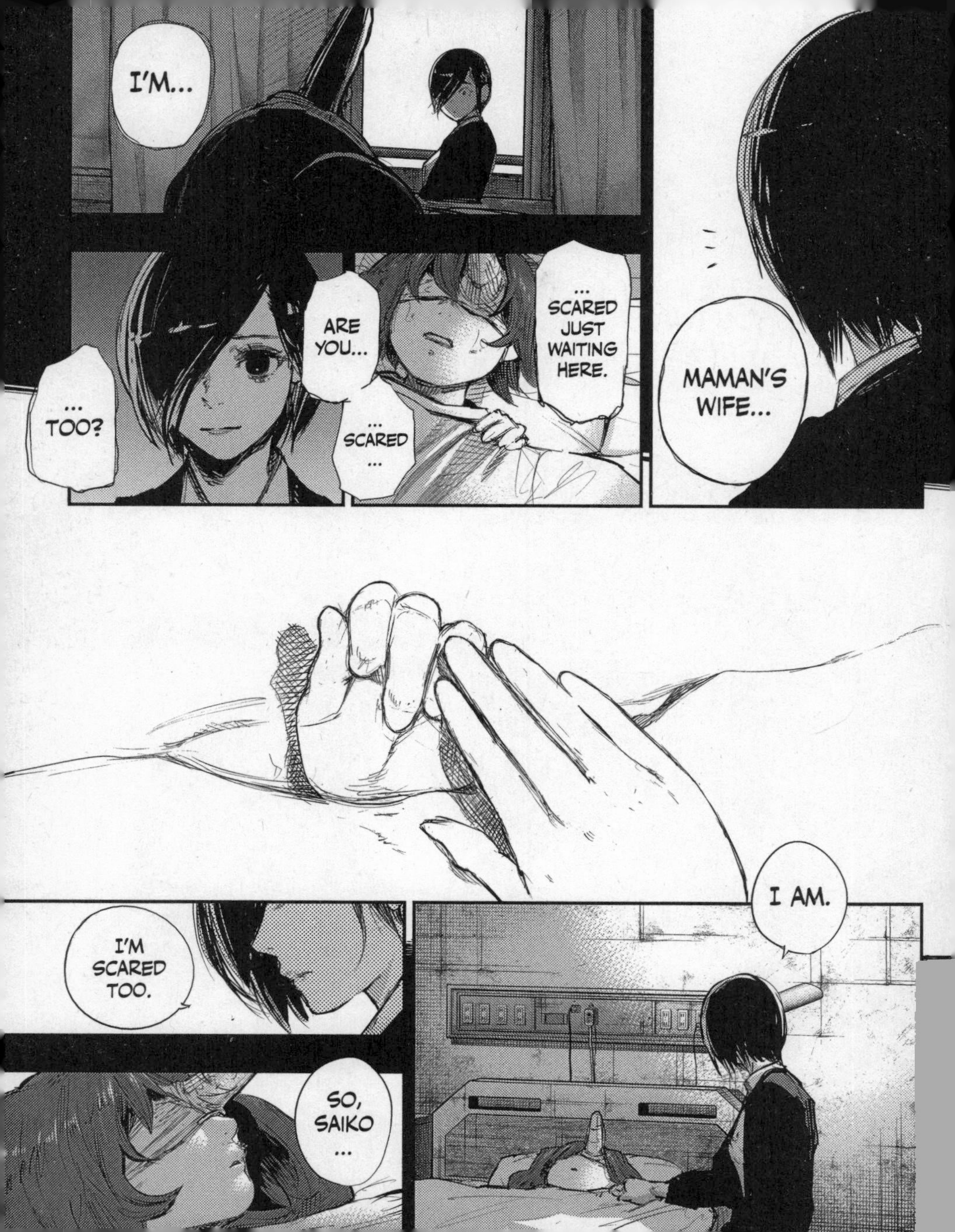
MAMAN'S WIFE...
I'M...
... SCARED JUST WAITING HERE.
ARE YOU...
... SCARED ...
... TOO?
I AM.
I'M SCARED TOO.
SO, SAIKO ...

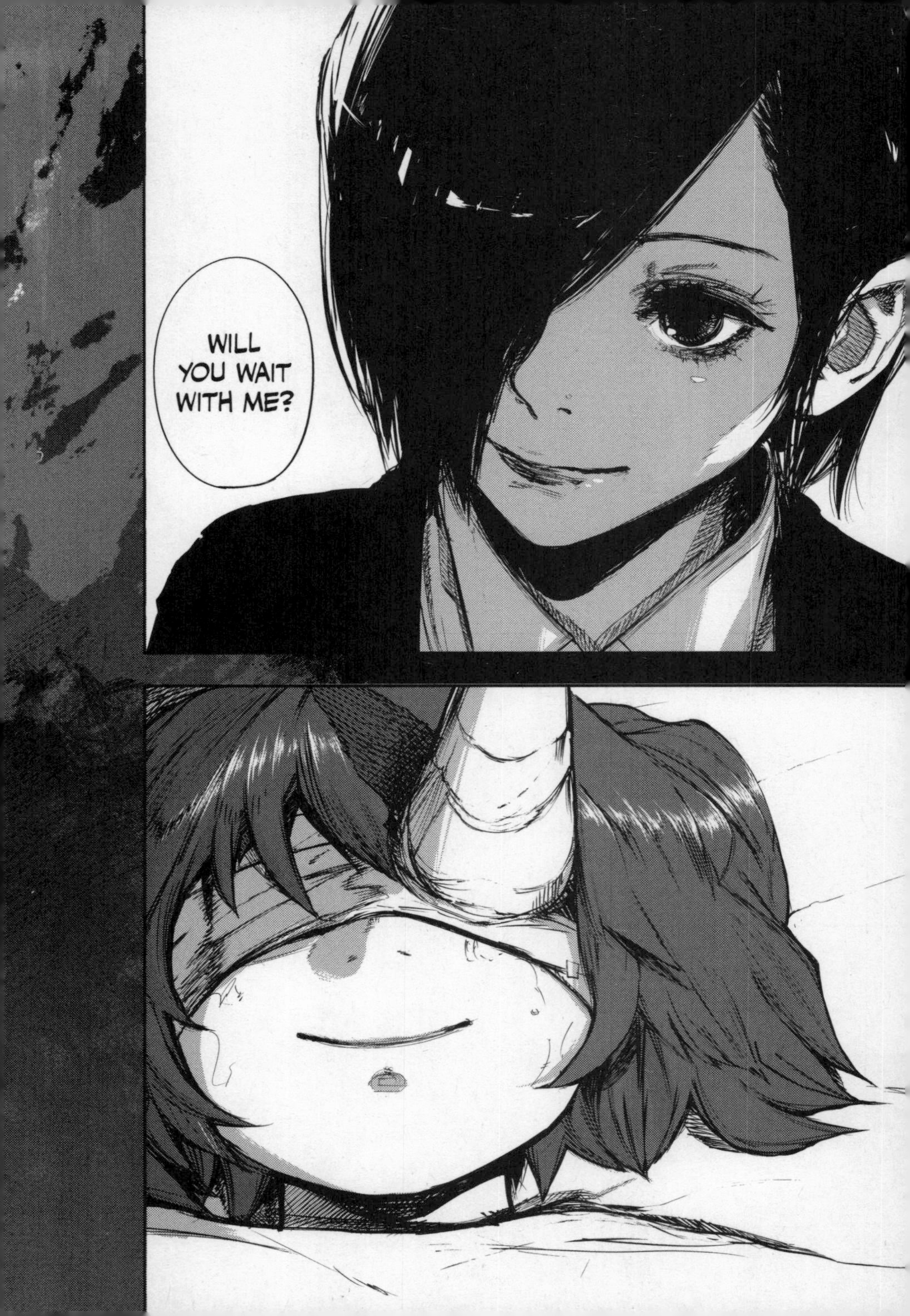
WILL YOU WAIT WITH ME?

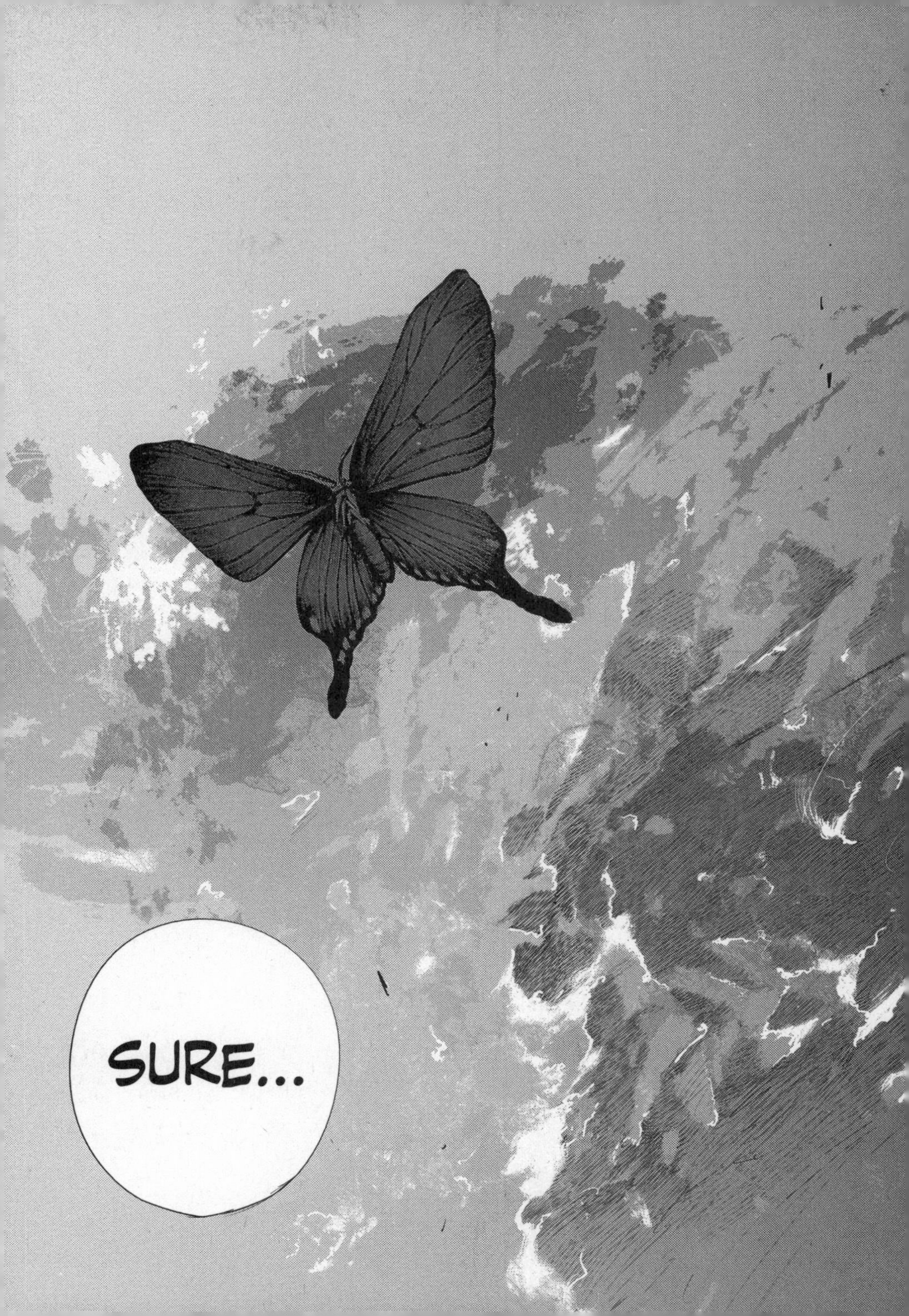
SURE...

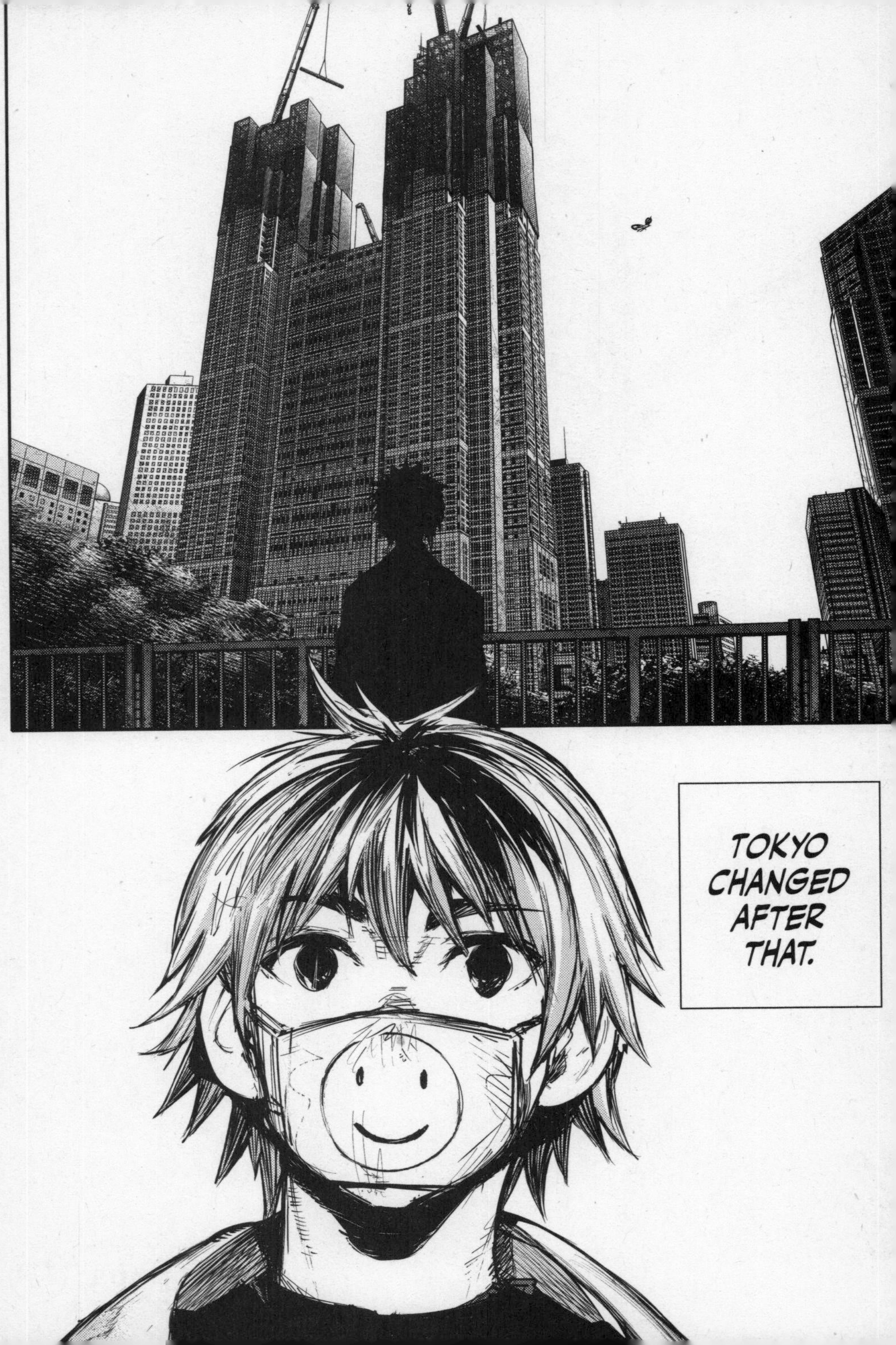
TOKYO CHANGED AFTER THAT.

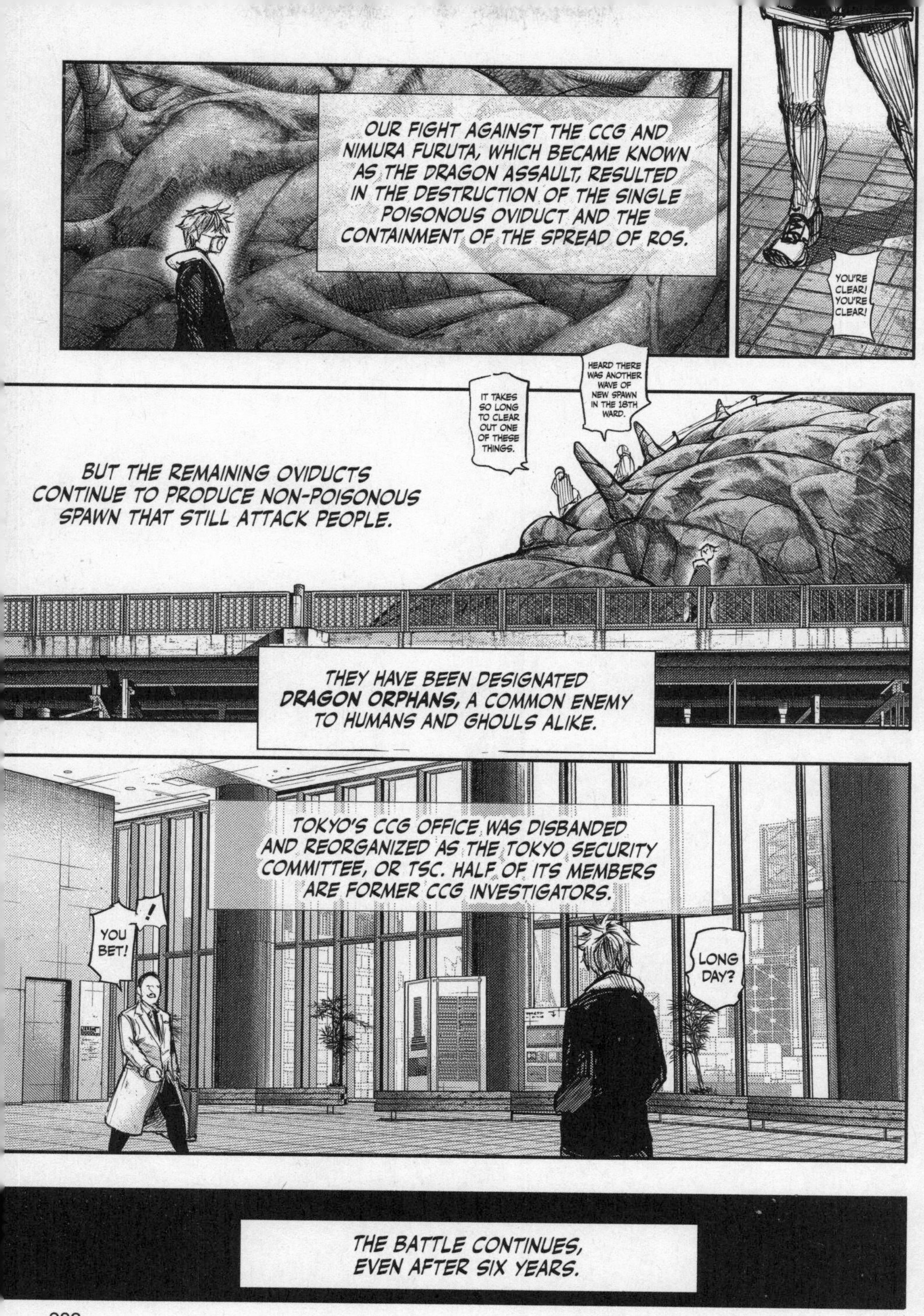
YOU'RE CLEAR! YOU'RE CLEAR!
OUR FIGHT AGAINST THE CCG AND NIMURA FURUTA, WHICH BECAME KNOWN AS THE DRAGON ASSAULT, RESULTED IN THE DESTRUCTION OF THE SINGLE POISONOUS OVIDUCT AND THE CONTAINMENT OF THE SPREAD OF ROS.
HEARD THERE WAS ANOTHER WAVE OF NEW SPAWN IN THE 18TH WARD.
IT TAKES SO LONG TO CLEAR OUT ONE OF THESE THINGS.
BUT THE REMAINING OVIDUCTS CONTINUE TO PRODUCE NON-POISONOUS SPAWN THAT STILL ATTACK PEOPLE.
THEY HAVE BEEN DESIGNATED DRAGON ORPHANS, A COMMON ENEMY TO HUMANS AND GHOULS ALIKE.
TOKYO'S CCG OFFICE WAS DISBANDED AND REORGANIZED AS THE TOKYO SECURITY COMMITTEE, OR TSC. HALF OF ITS MEMBERS ARE FORMER CCG INVESTIGATORS.
LONG DAY?
!
YOU BET!
THE BATTLE CONTINUES, EVEN AFTER SIX YEARS.

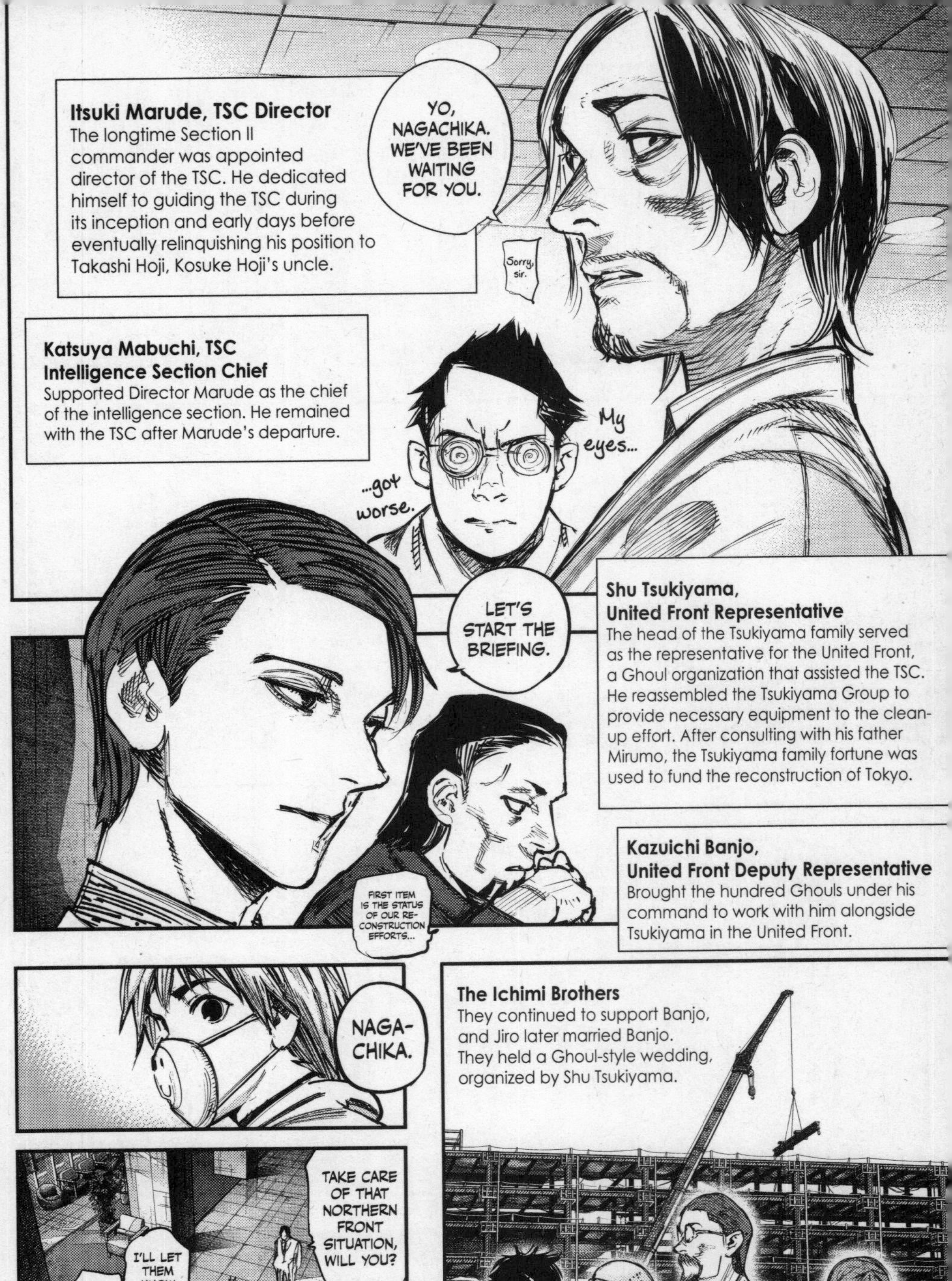
YO, NAGACHIKA. WE'VE BEEN WAITING FOR YOU.
Sorry, sir.
Itsuki Marude, TSC Director
The longtime Section II commander was appointed director of the TSC. He dedicated himself to guiding the TSC during its inception and early days before eventually relinquishing his position to Takashi Hoji, Kosuke Hoji's uncle.
My eyes...
...got worse.
Katsuya Mabuchi, TSC Intelligence Section Chief
Supported Director Marude as the chief of the intelligence section. He remained with the TSC after Marude's departure.
Shu Tsukiyama, United Front Representative
The head of the Tsukiyama family served as the representative for the United Front, a Ghoul organization that assisted the TSC. He reassembled the Tsukiyama Group to provide necessary equipment to the clean-up effort. After consulting with his father Mirumo, the Tsukiyama family fortune was used to fund the reconstruction of Tokyo.
LET'S START THE BRIEFING.
Kazuichi Banjo, United Front Deputy Representative
Brought the hundred Ghouls under his command to work with him alongside Tsukiyama in the United Front.
FIRST ITEM IS THE STATUS OF OUR RE-CONSTRUCTION EFFORTS...
The Ichimi Brothers
They continued to support Banjo, and Jiro later married Banjo. They held a Ghoul-style wedding, organized by Shu Tsukiyama.
NAGA-CHIKA.
TAKE CARE OF THAT NORTHERN FRONT SITUATION, WILL YOU?
I'LL LET THEM KNOW WHEN I GO SEE THEM.
OH ...

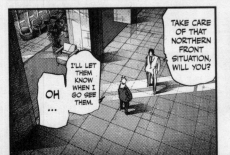

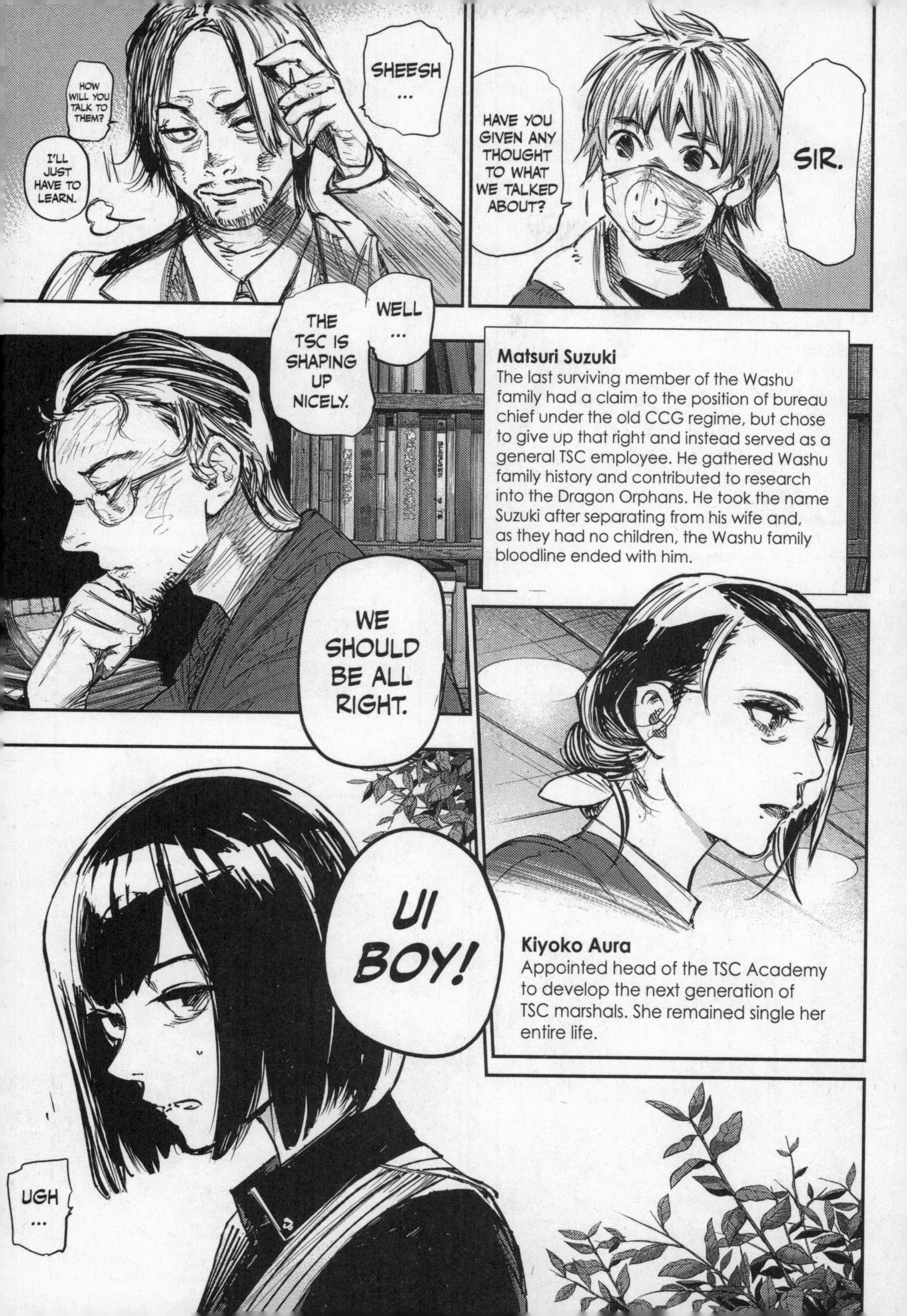
SIR.
HAVE YOU GIVEN ANY THOUGHT TO WHAT WE TALKED ABOUT?
SHEESH ...
HOW WILL YOU TALK TO THEM?
I'LL JUST HAVE TO LEARN.
Matsuri Suzuki
The last surviving member of the Washu family had a claim to the position of bureau chief under the old CCG regime, but chose to give up that right and instead served as a general TSC employee. He gathered Washu family history and contributed to research into the Dragon Orphans. He took the name Suzuki after separating from his wife and, as they had no children, the Washu family bloodline ended with him.
WELL ...
THE TSC IS SHAPING UP NICELY.
WE SHOULD BE ALL RIGHT.
Kiyoko Aura
Appointed head of the TSC Academy to develop the next generation of TSC marshals. She remained single her entire life.
UI BOY!
UGH ...

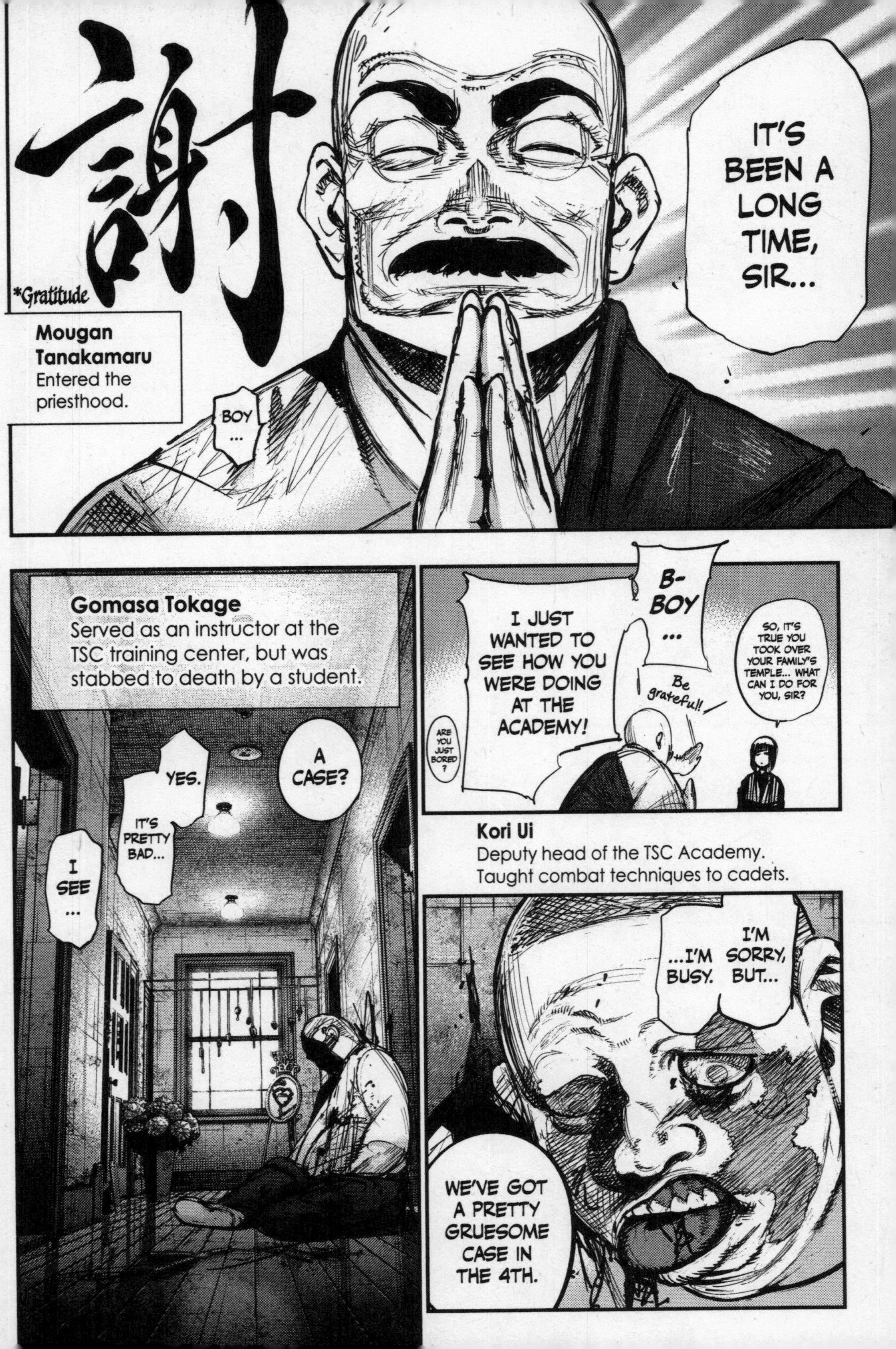
IT'S BEEN A LONG TIME, SIR...
謝
*Gratitude
Mougan Tanakamaru
Entered the priesthood.
BOY ...
SO, IT'S TRUE YOU TOOK OVER YOUR FAMILY'S TEMPLE... WHAT CAN I DO FOR YOU, SIR?
B-BOY ...
Be grateful!!
I JUST WANTED TO SEE HOW YOU WERE DOING AT THE ACADEMY!
ARE YOU JUST BORED?
Kori Ui
Deputy head of the TSC Academy. Taught combat techniques to cadets.
I'M SORRY, BUT...
...I'M BUSY.
WE'VE GOT A PRETTY GRUESOME CASE IN THE 4TH.
Gomasa Tokage
Served as an instructor at the TSC training center, but was stabbed to death by a student.
A CASE?
YES.
IT'S PRETTY BAD...
I SEE ...

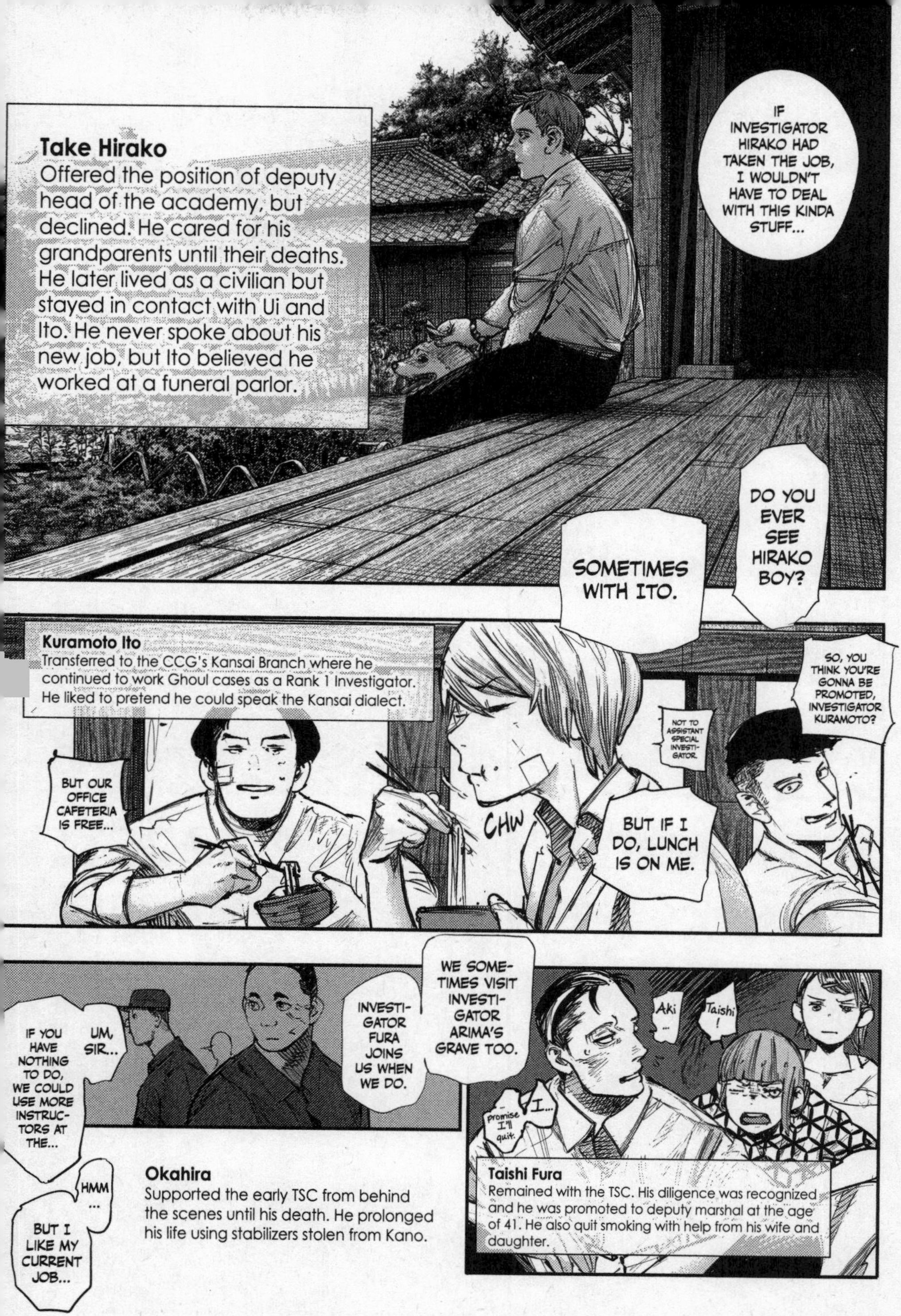
IF INVESTIGATOR HIRAKO HAD TAKEN THE JOB, I WOULDN'T HAVE TO DEAL WITH THIS KINDA STUFF...
Take Hirako
Offered the position of deputy head of the academy, but declined. He cared for his grandparents until their deaths. He later lived as a civilian but stayed in contact with Ui and Ito. He never spoke about his new job, but Ito believed he worked at a funeral parlor.
DO YOU EVER SEE HIRAKO BOY?
SOMETIMES WITH ITO.
SO, YOU THINK YOU'RE GONNA BE PROMOTED, INVESTIGATOR KURAMOTO?
NOT TO ASSISTANT SPECIAL INVESTIGATOR.
BUT IF I DO, LUNCH IS ON ME.
CHW
BUT OUR OFFICE CAFETERIA IS FREE...
Kuramoto Ito
Transferred to the CCG's Kansai Branch where he continued to work Ghoul cases as a Rank 1 Investigator. He liked to pretend he could speak the Kansai dialect.
Taishi!
Aki...
I...
...promise I'll quit.
Taishi Fura
Remained with the TSC. His diligence was recognized and he was promoted to deputy marshal at the age of 41. He also quit smoking with help from his wife and daughter.
WE SOMETIMES VISIT INVESTIGATOR ARIMA'S GRAVE TOO.
INVESTIGATOR FURA JOINS US WHEN WE DO.
UM, SIR...
IF YOU HAVE NOTHING TO DO, WE COULD USE MORE INSTRUCTORS AT THE...
HMM...
BUT I LIKE MY CURRENT JOB...
Okahira
Supported the early TSC from behind the scenes until his death. He prolonged his life using stabilizers stolen from Kano.

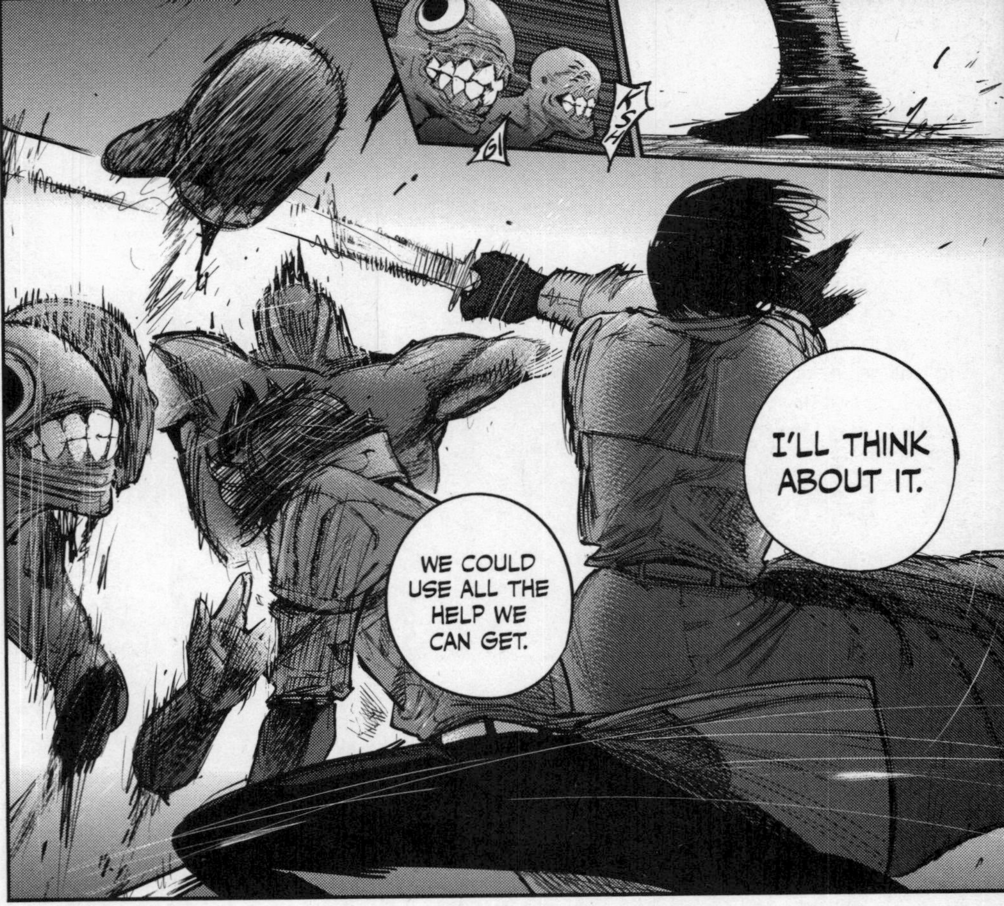
KSH
GI
I'LL THINK ABOUT IT.
WE COULD USE ALL THE HELP WE CAN GET.

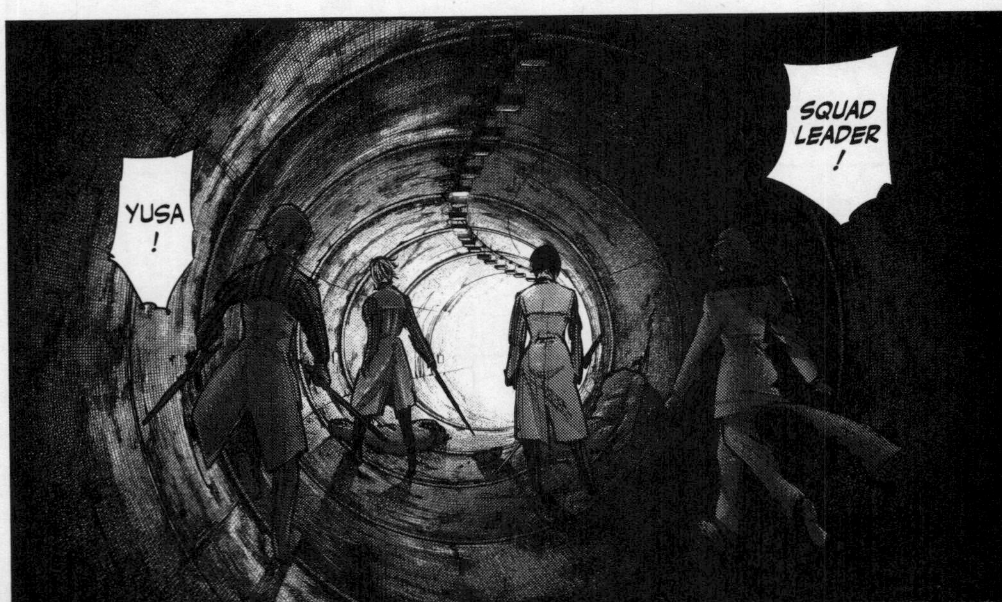
SQUAD LEADER!
YUSA!

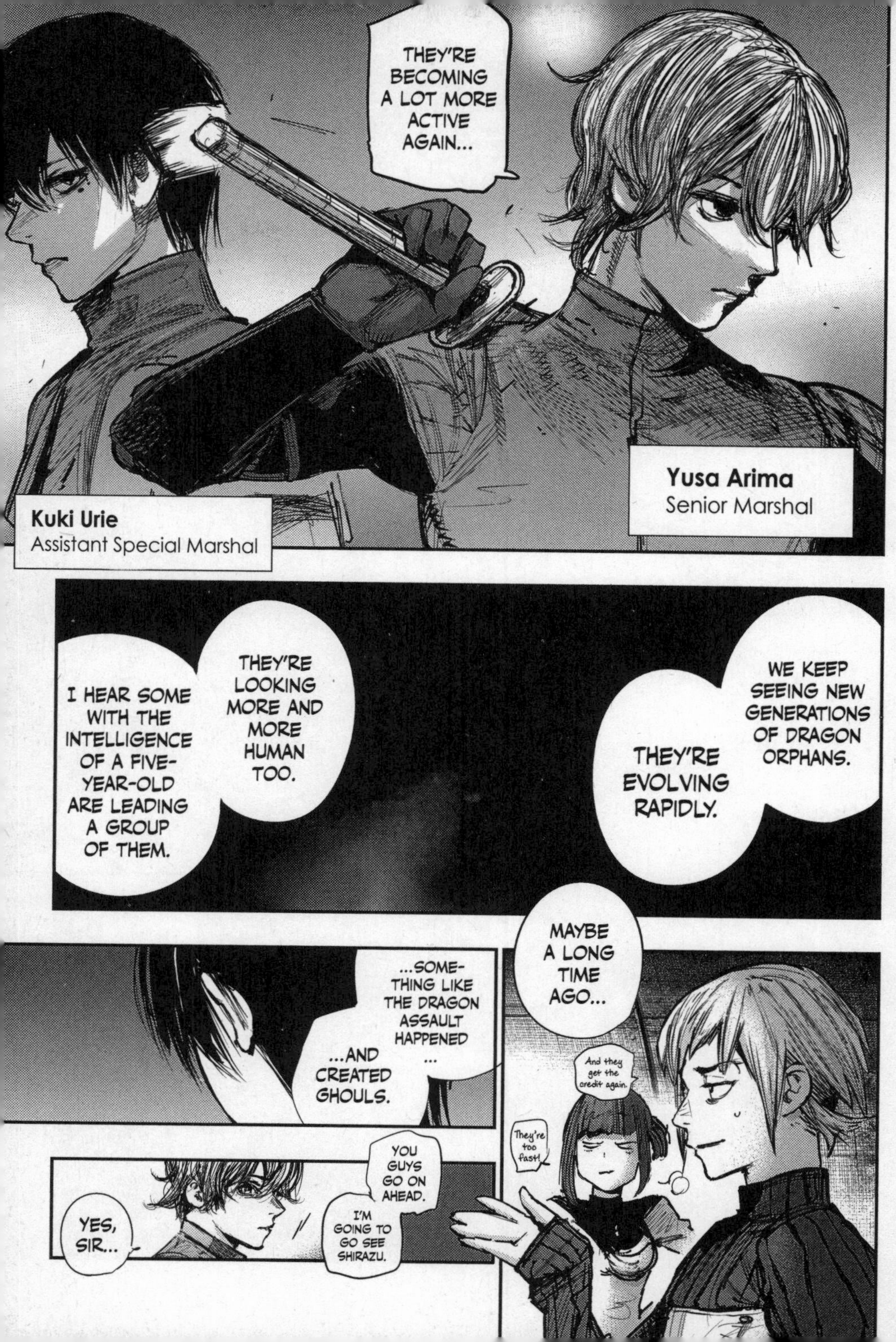
THEY'RE BECOMING A LOT MORE ACTIVE AGAIN...
Yusa Arima
Senior Marshal
Kuki Urie
Assistant Special Marshal
WE KEEP SEEING NEW GENERATIONS OF DRAGON ORPHANS.
THEY'RE EVOLVING RAPIDLY.
THEY'RE LOOKING MORE AND MORE HUMAN TOO.
I HEAR SOME WITH THE INTELLIGENCE OF A FIVE-YEAR-OLD ARE LEADING A GROUP OF THEM.
MAYBE A LONG TIME AGO...
...SOME-THING LIKE THE DRAGON ASSAULT HAPPENED ...
...AND CREATED GHOULS.
And they get the credit again.
They're too fast!
YOU GUYS GO ON AHEAD.
I'M GOING TO GO SEE SHIRAZU.
YES, SIR...

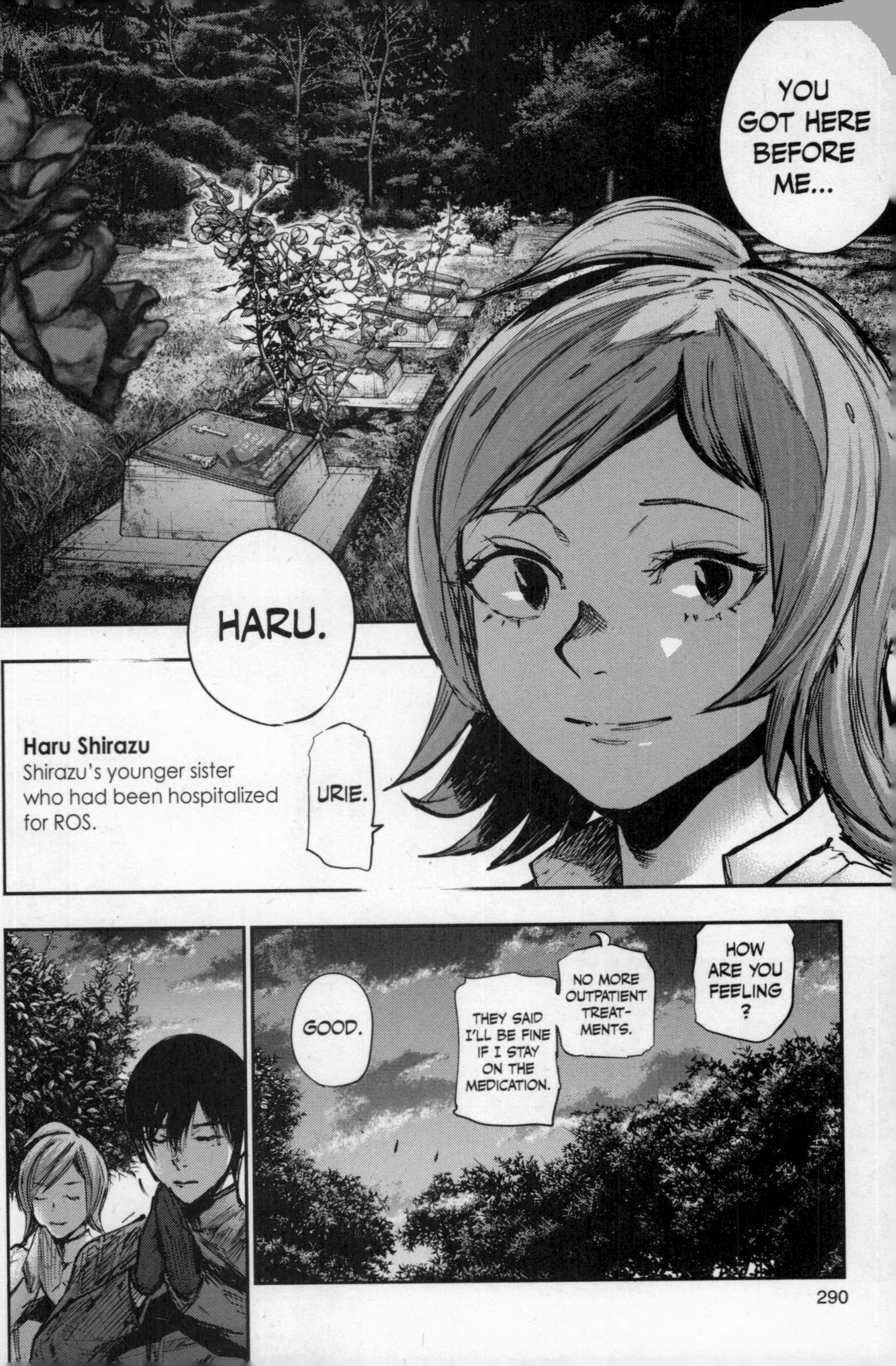
YOU GOT HERE BEFORE ME...
HARU.
URIE.
Haru Shirazu
Shirazu's younger sister who had been hospitalized for ROS.
HOW ARE YOU FEELING?
NO MORE OUTPATIENT TREAT-MENTS.
THEY SAID I'LL BE FINE IF I STAY ON THE MEDICATION.
GOOD.

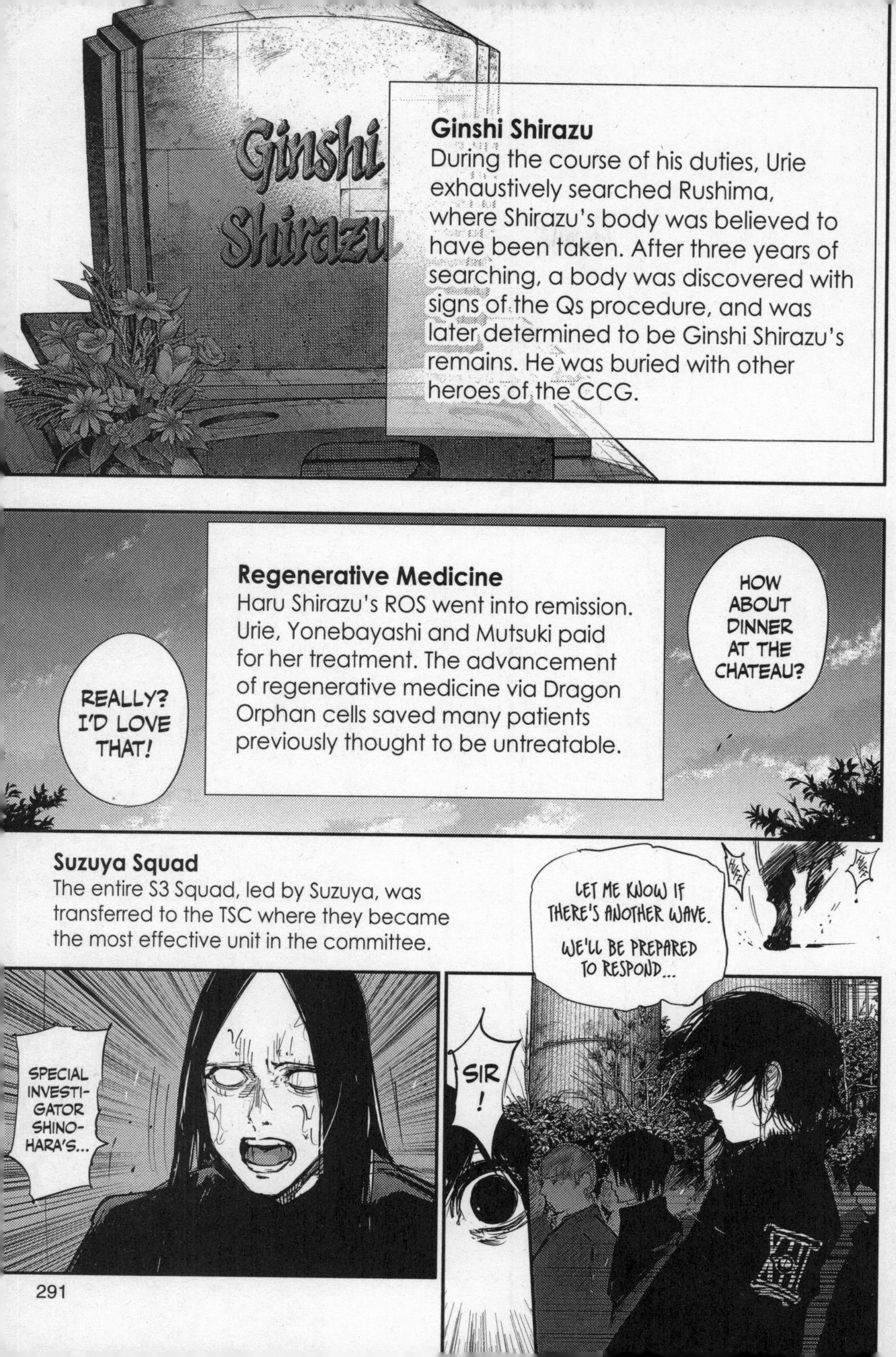
Ginshi Shirazu
Ginshi Shirazu
During the course of his duties, Urie exhaustively searched Rushima, where Shirazu's body was believed to have been taken. After three years of searching, a body was discovered with signs of the Qs procedure, and was later determined to be Ginshi Shirazu's remains. He was buried with other heroes of the CCG.
Regenerative Medicine
Haru Shirazu's ROS went into remission. Urie, Yonebayashi and Mutsuki paid for her treatment. The advancement of regenerative medicine via Dragon Orphan cells saved many patients previously thought to be untreatable.
HOW ABOUT DINNER AT THE CHATEAU?
REALLY? I'D LOVE THAT!
Suzuya Squad
The entire S3 Squad, led by Suzuya, was transferred to the TSC where they became the most effective unit in the committee.
HUFF
HUFF
LET ME KNOW IF THERE'S ANOTHER WAVE.
WE'LL BE PREPARED TO RESPOND...
SIR!
SPECIAL INVESTIGATOR SHINOHARA'S...

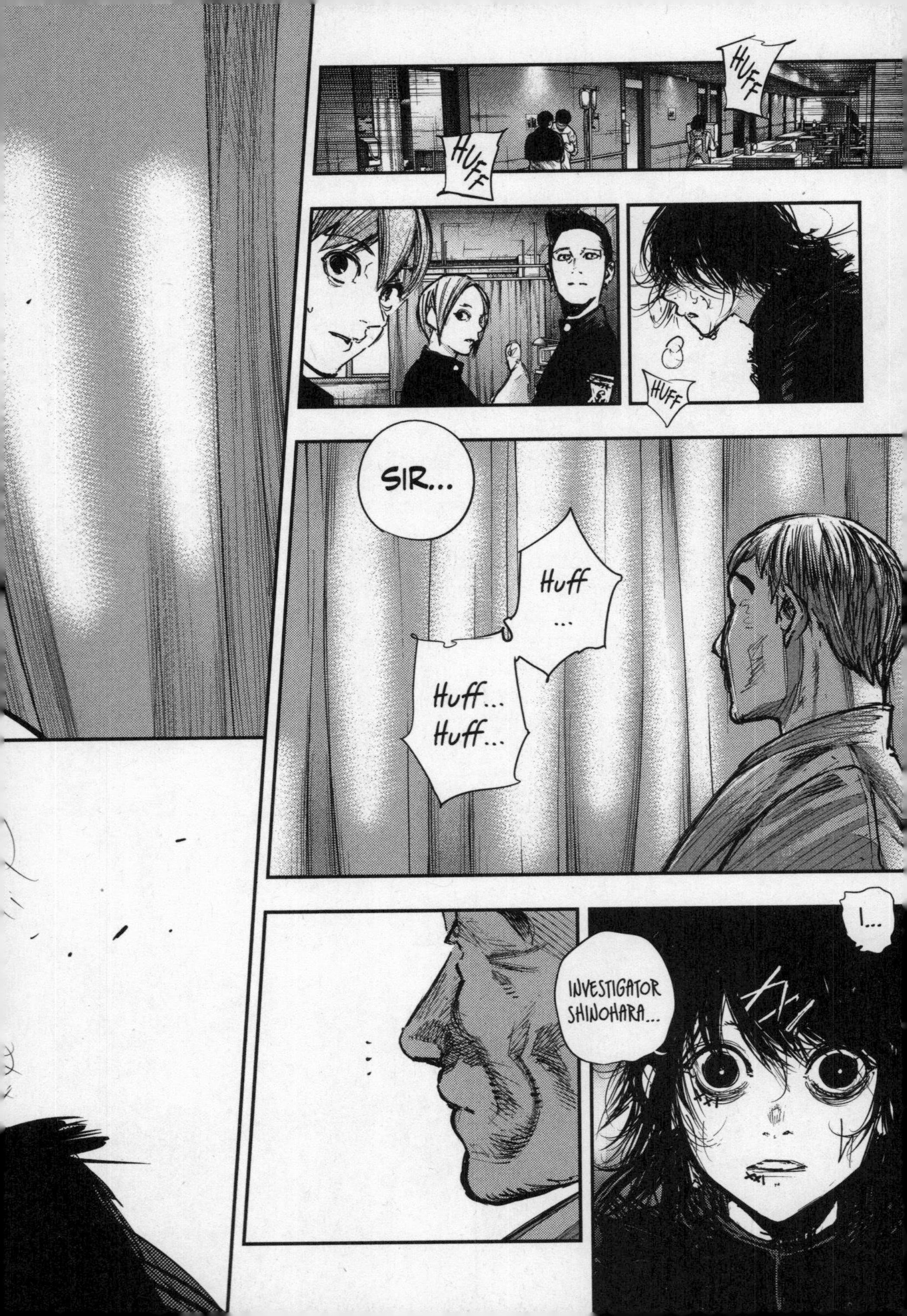
HUFF
HUFF
HUFF
SIR...
Huff...
Huff... Huff...
I...
INVESTIGATOR SHINOHARA...

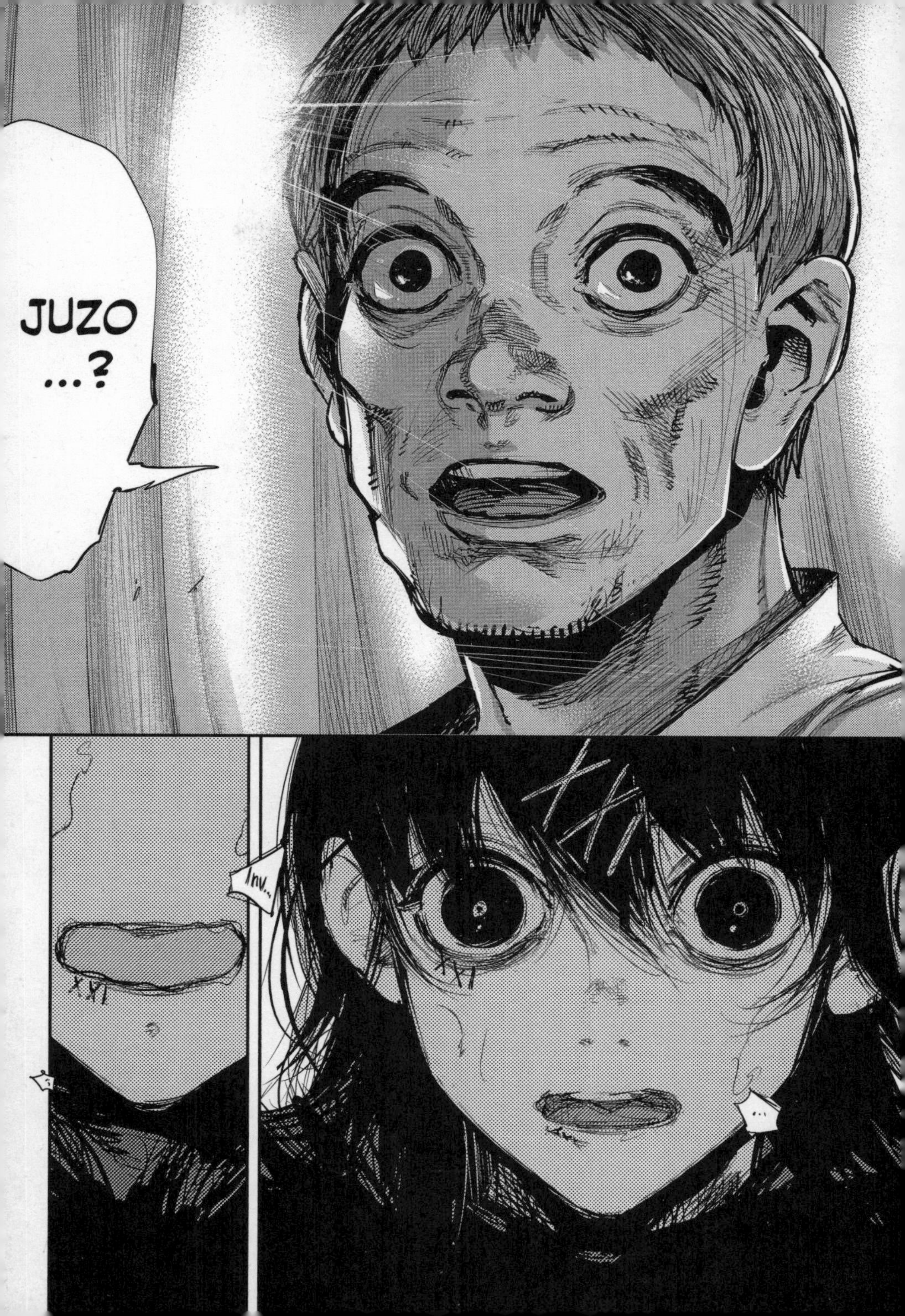
JUZO ...?
Inv...
...
?

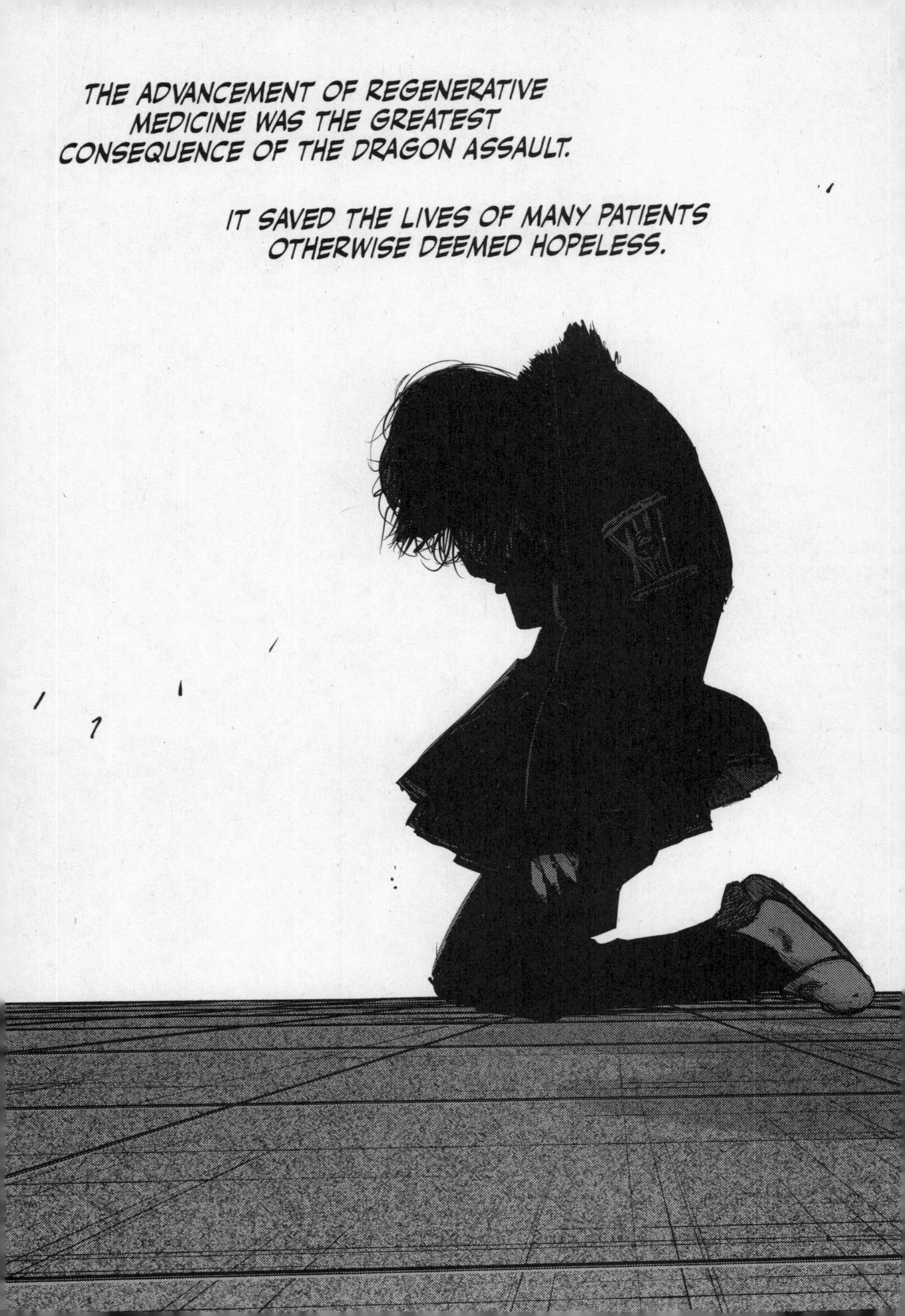
THE ADVANCEMENT OF REGENERATIVE MEDICINE WAS THE GREATEST CONSEQUENCE OF THE DRAGON ASSAULT.
IT SAVED THE LIVES OF MANY PATIENTS OTHERWISE DEEMED HOPELESS.

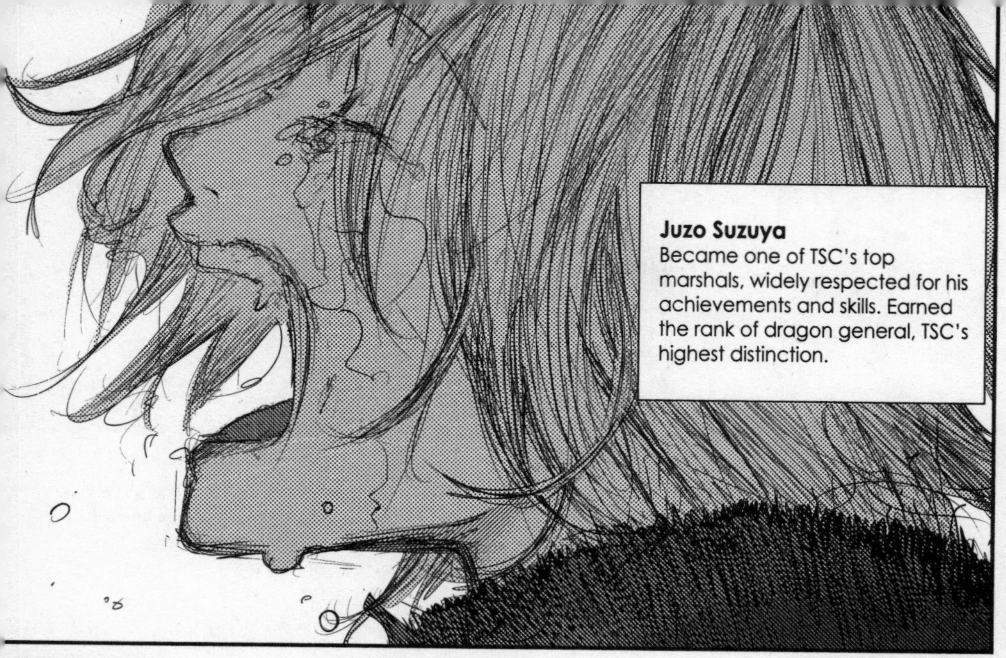

Juzo Suzuya
Became one of TSC's top marshals, widely respected for his achievements and skills. Earned the rank of dragon general, TSC's highest distinction.

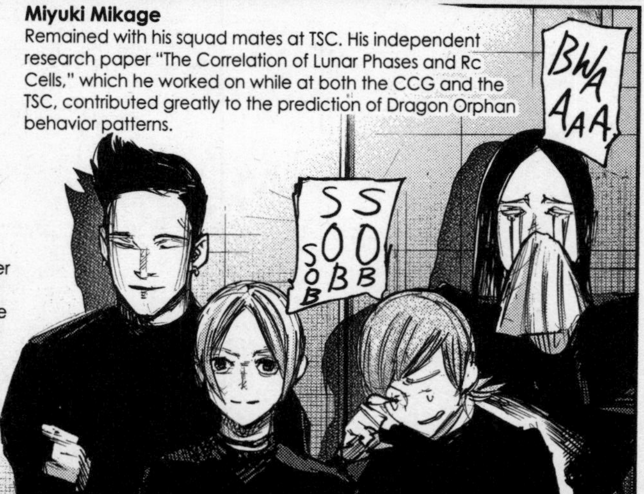
BWAAAA
SOB
SOB
SOB

Miyuki Mikage
Remained with his squad mates at TSC. His independent research paper "The Correlation of Lunar Phases and Rc Cells," which he worked on while at both the CCG and the TSC, contributed greatly to the prediction of Dragon Orphan behavior patterns.

Keijin Nakarai
Worked for the TSC under Juzo as lieutenant dragon general. Withdrew from active field duty after sustaining serious injuries in a battle against Shikorae. Served as an instructor nicknamed "Nakarai the Devil" at the academy under Kiyoko Aura.

Mizuro Tamaki
Worked for the TSC alongside Abara under Suzuya's command. Married a TSC agent from the administrative section. Left active field duty at Abara's suggestion and moved to administrative duties.

Hanbeh Abara
Served throughout his life as Dragon General Suzuya's right-hand man.

Yukinori Shinohara
In a vegetative state for years but made a miraculous recovery thanks to advancements in medicine. He was never involved with the TSC after the dissolution of the CCG. However, he assisted the committee from behind the scenes by keeping in touch with Dragon General Suzuya and Diretor Marude and providing them with advice.

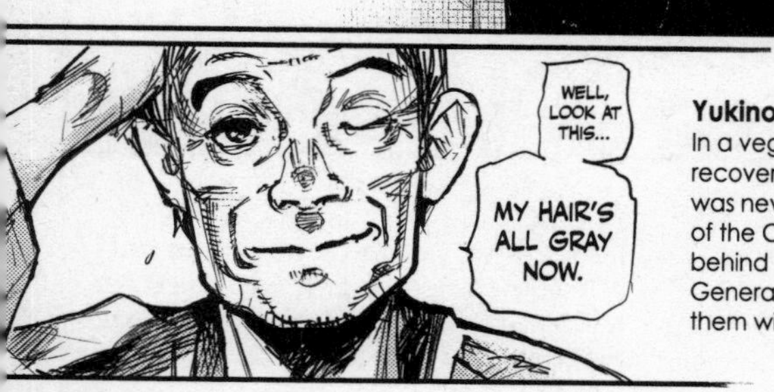
WELL, LOOK AT THIS...
MY HAIR'S ALL GRAY NOW.

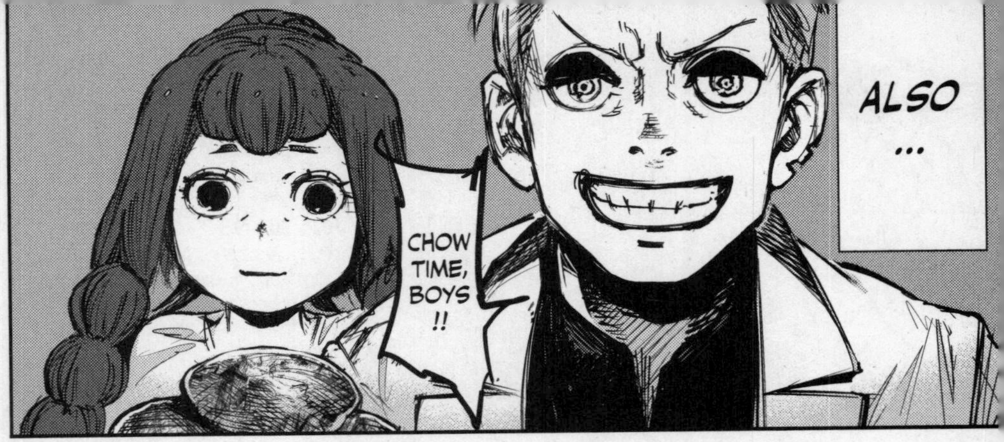
ALSO ...
CHOW TIME, BOYS !!

Miza Kuskarai
Joined the United Front with Naki and the others. She had nine children (six boys, three girls): Shiori (eldest son), Nagi (second son) and Nage (third son) = twins, Mirei (eldest daughter), Marin (second daughter), Zei (fourth son), Sonki (fifth son), Yanagi (sixth son), Warai (third daughter)

Naki Kusakari
Joined the United Front with Tsukiyama and the others. Helped educate Ghoul orphans and trained young Ghoul volunteers who wished to fight on the front lines. Had nine children with Miza.

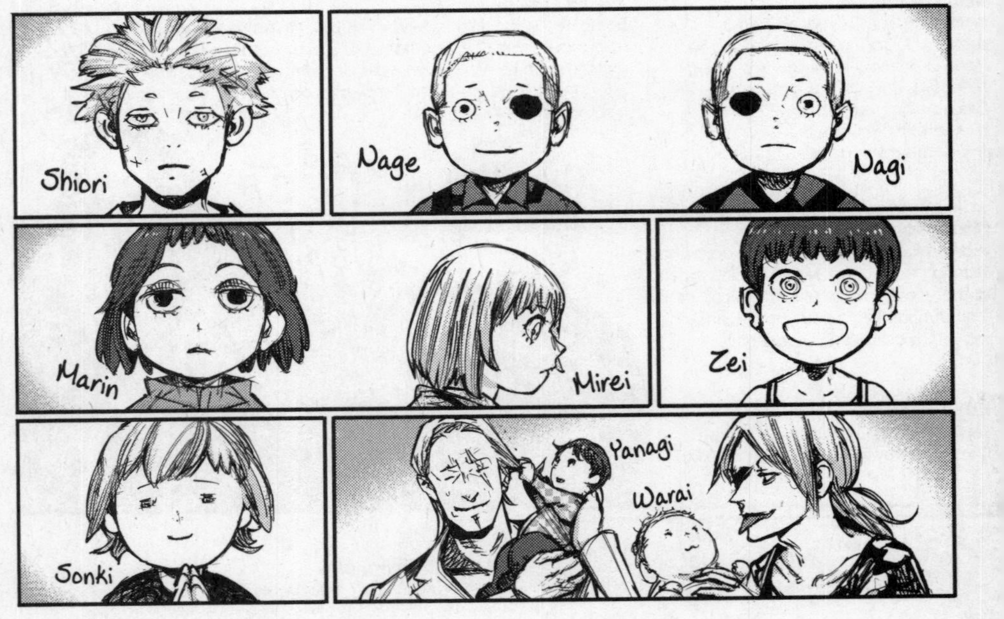
Nagi
Nage
Shiori
Zei
Mirei
Marin
Yanagi
Warai
Sonki

Shosei
Worked with Hoguro in the United Front while taking care of Naki's children. Gained human knowledge and taught it to other Ghouls. Remained loyal to Naki throughout his life.

Hoguro
Fell in love with a human woman he met in the United Front. They were married in a Ghoul-style wedding and lived happily. He remained loyal to Naki throughout his life.

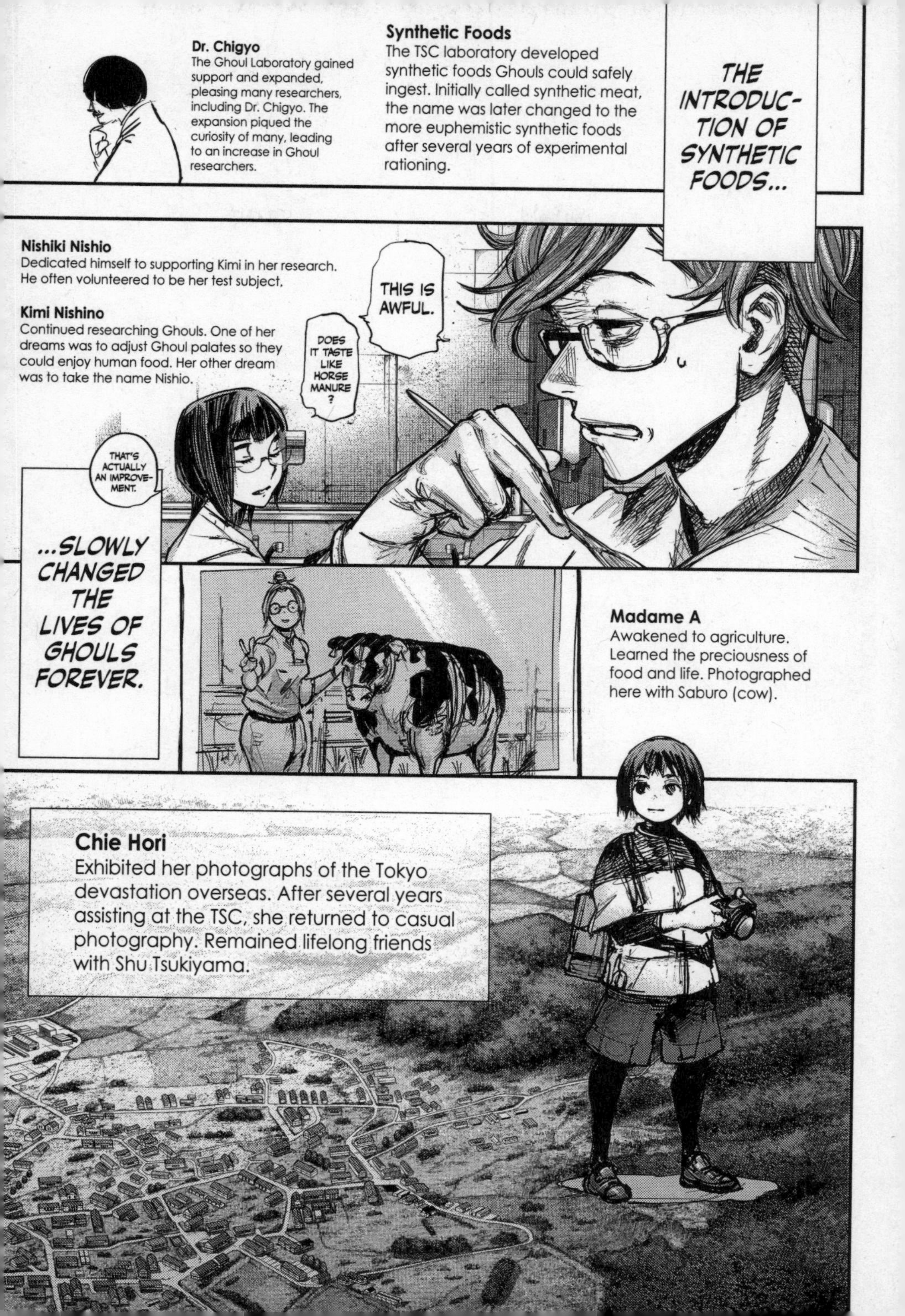
THE INTRODUCTION OF SYNTHETIC FOODS...
Synthetic Foods
The TSC laboratory developed synthetic foods Ghouls could safely ingest. Initially called synthetic meat, the name was later changed to the more euphemistic synthetic foods after several years of experimental rationing.
Dr. Chigyo
The Ghoul Laboratory gained support and expanded, pleasing many researchers, including Dr. Chigyo. The expansion piqued the curiosity of many, leading to an increase in Ghoul researchers.
THIS IS AWFUL.
DOES IT TASTE LIKE HORSE MANURE?
THAT'S ACTUALLY AN IMPROVEMENT.
Nishiki Nishio
Dedicated himself to supporting Kimi in her research. He often volunteered to be her test subject.
Kimi Nishino
Continued researching Ghouls. One of her dreams was to adjust Ghoul palates so they could enjoy human food. Her other dream was to take the name Nishio.
Madame A
Awakened to agriculture. Learned the preciousness of food and life. Photographed here with Saburo (cow).
...SLOWLY CHANGED THE LIVES OF GHOULS FOREVER.
Chie Hori
Exhibited her photographs of the Tokyo devastation overseas. After several years assisting at the TSC, she returned to casual photography. Remained lifelong friends with Shu Tsukiyama.

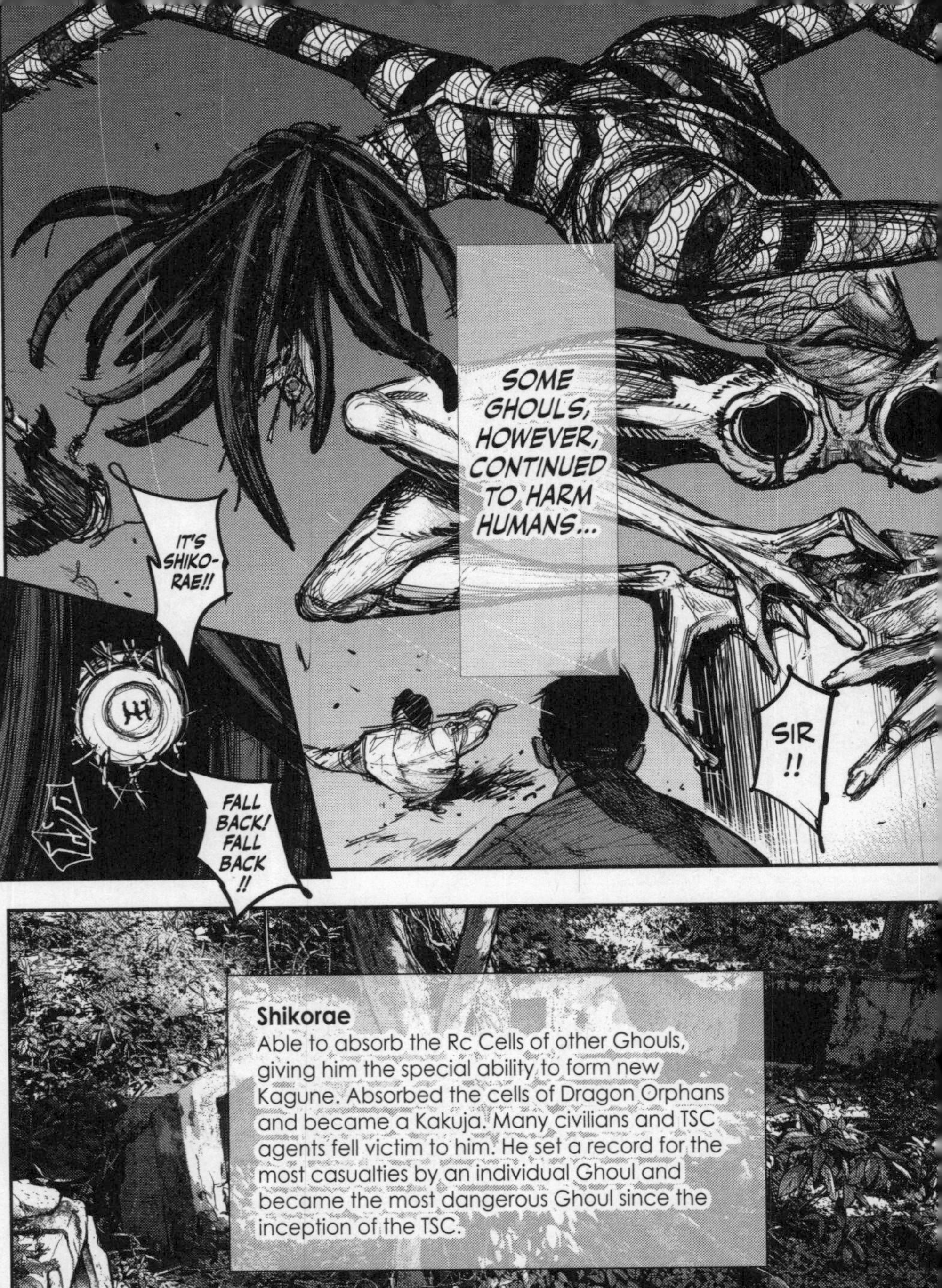
SOME GHOULS, HOWEVER, CONTINUED TO HARM HUMANS...
SIR!!
IT'S SHIKO-RAE!!
FALL BACK! FALL BACK!!
Shikorae
Able to absorb the Rc Cells of other Ghouls, giving him the special ability to form new Kagune. Absorbed the cells of Dragon Orphans and became a Kakuja. Many civilians and TSC agents fell victim to him. He set a record for the most casualties by an individual Ghoul and became the most dangerous Ghoul since the inception of the TSC.

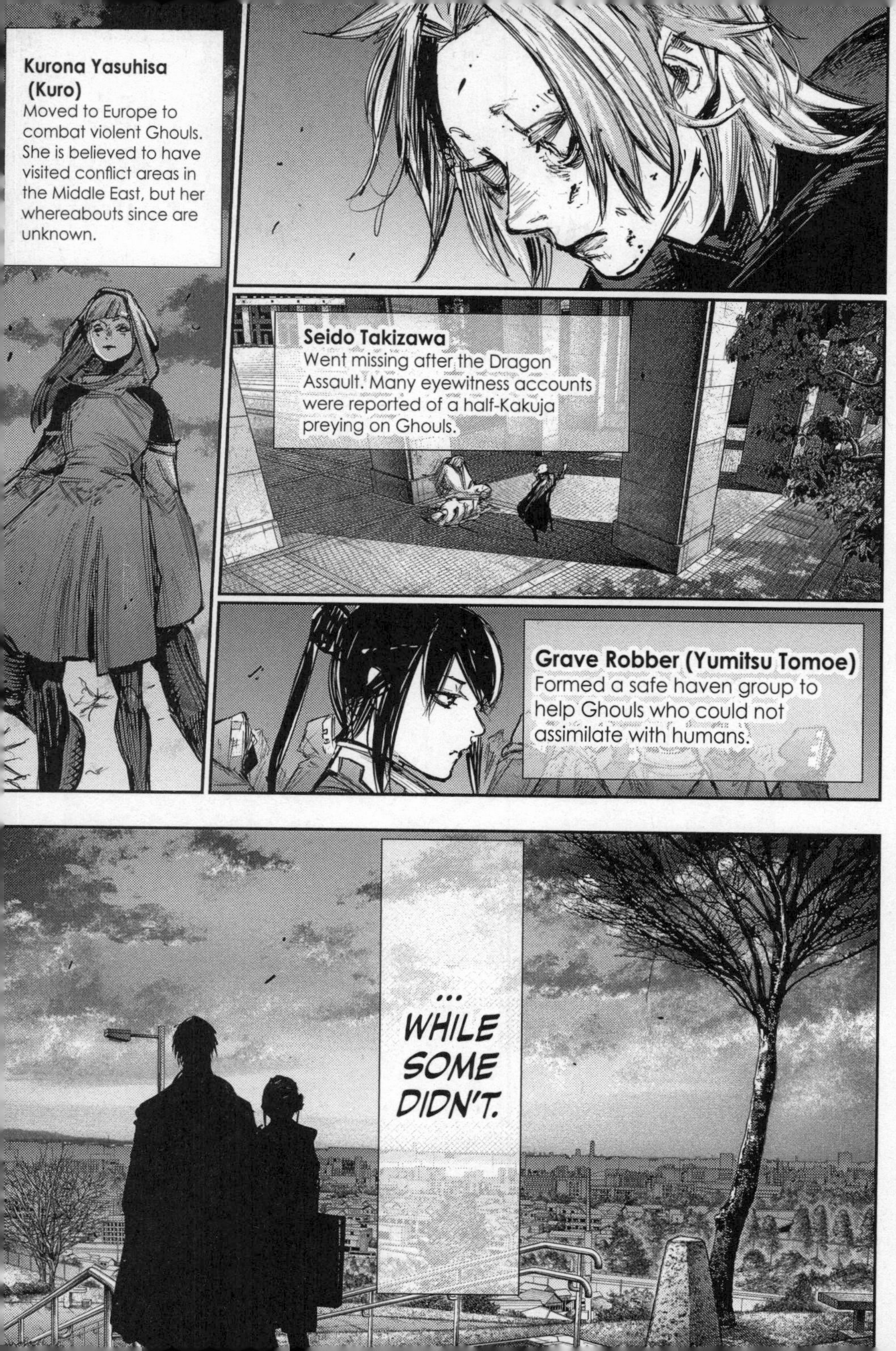
Seido Takizawa
Went missing after the Dragon Assault. Many eyewitness accounts were reported of a half-Kakuja preying on Ghouls.
Grave Robber (Yumitsu Tomoe)
Formed a safe haven group to help Ghouls who could not assimilate with humans.
Kurona Yasuhisa (Kuro)
Moved to Europe to combat violent Ghouls. She is believed to have visited conflict areas in the Middle East, but her whereabouts since are unknown.
... WHILE SOME DIDN'T.

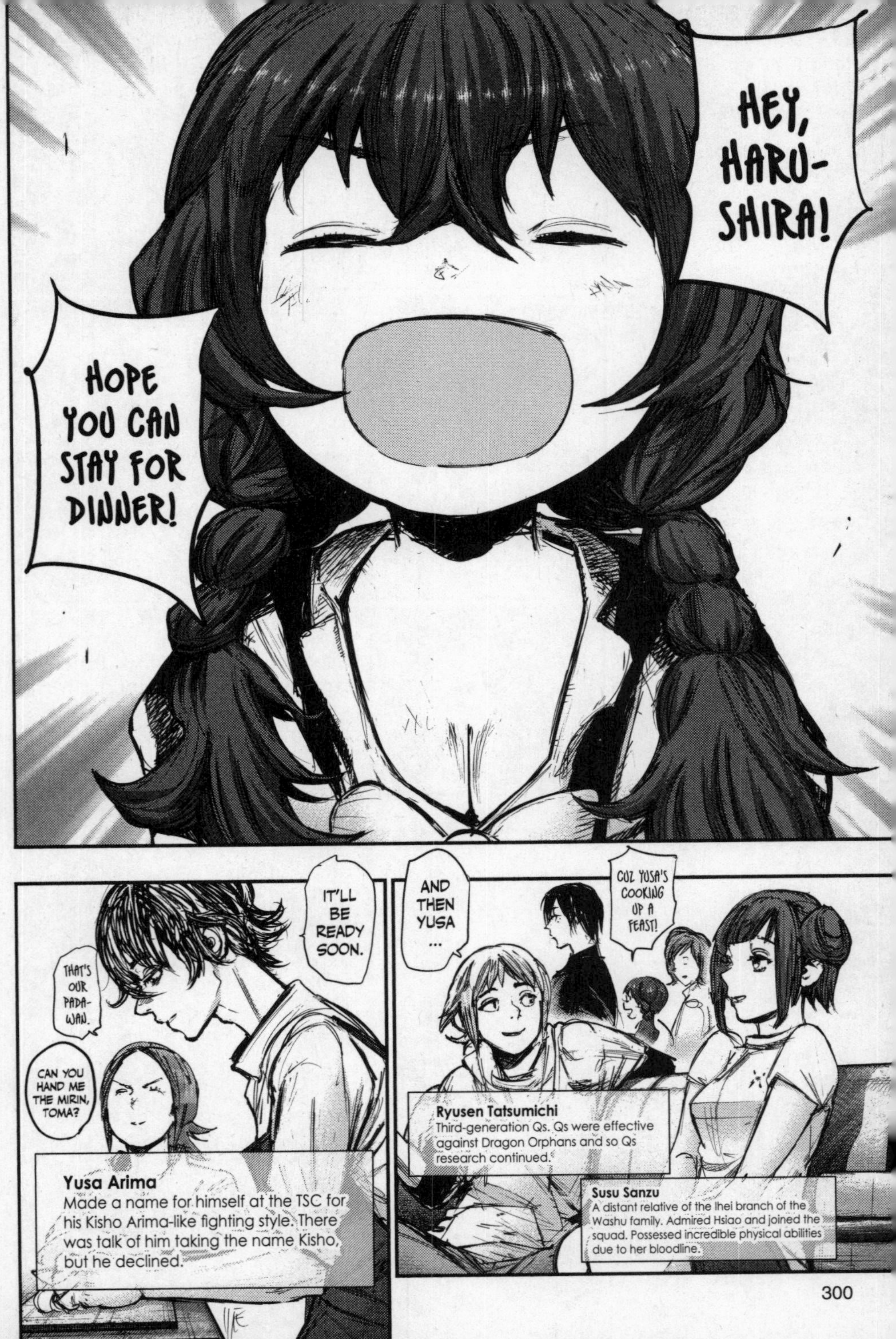
HEY, HARU-SHIRA!
HOPE YOU CAN STAY FOR DINNER!
CUZ YUSA'S COOKING UP A FEAST!
AND THEN YUSA ...
Ryusen Tatsumichi
Third-generation Qs. Qs were effective against Dragon Orphans and so Qs research continued.
Susu Sanzu
A distant relative of the Ihei branch of the Washu family. Admired Hsiao and joined the squad. Possessed incredible physical abilities due to her bloodline.
IT'LL BE READY SOON.
THAT'S OUR PADA-WAN.
CAN YOU HAND ME THE MIRIN, TOMA?
Yusa Arima
Made a name for himself at the TSC for his Kisho Arima-like fighting style. There was talk of him taking the name Kisho, but he declined.

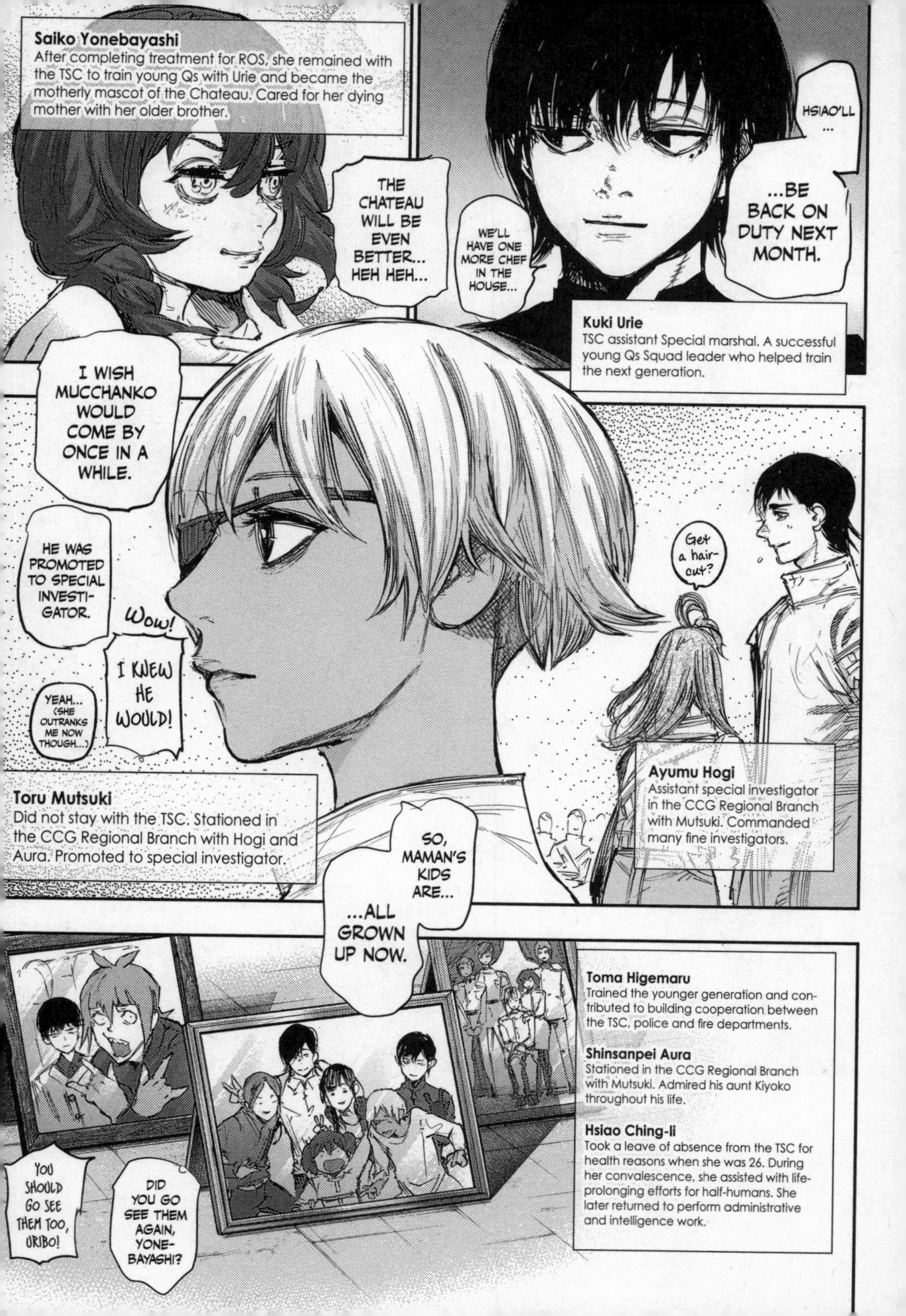
HSIAO'LL ...
...BE BACK ON DUTY NEXT MONTH.
WE'LL HAVE ONE MORE CHEF IN THE HOUSE...
Kuki Urie
TSC assistant Special marshal. A successful young Qs Squad leader who helped train the next generation.
Saiko Yonebayashi
After completing treatment for ROS, she remained with the TSC to train young Qs with Urie and became the motherly mascot of the Chateau. Cared for her dying mother with her older brother.
THE CHATEAU WILL BE EVEN BETTER... HEH HEH...
Get a hair-cut?
Ayumu Hogi
Assistant special investigator in the CCG Regional Branch with Mutsuki. Commanded many fine investigators.
I WISH MUCCHANKO WOULD COME BY ONCE IN A WHILE.
HE WAS PROMOTED TO SPECIAL INVESTI-GATOR.
Wow!
I KNEW HE WOULD!
YEAH... (SHE OUTRANKS ME NOW THOUGH...)
Toru Mutsuki
Did not stay with the TSC. Stationed in the CCG Regional Branch with Hogi and Aura. Promoted to special investigator.
SO, MAMAN'S KIDS ARE...
...ALL GROWN UP NOW.
Toma Higemaru
Trained the younger generation and contributed to building cooperation between the TSC, police and fire departments.
Shinsanpei Aura
Stationed in the CCG Regional Branch with Mutsuki. Admired his aunt Kiyoko throughout his life.
Hsiao Ching-li
Took a leave of absence from the TSC for health reasons when she was 26. During her convalescence, she assisted with life-prolonging efforts for half-humans. She later returned to perform administrative and intelligence work.
DID YOU GO SEE THEM AGAIN, YONE-BAYASHI?
YOU SHOULD GO SEE THEM TOO, URIBO!

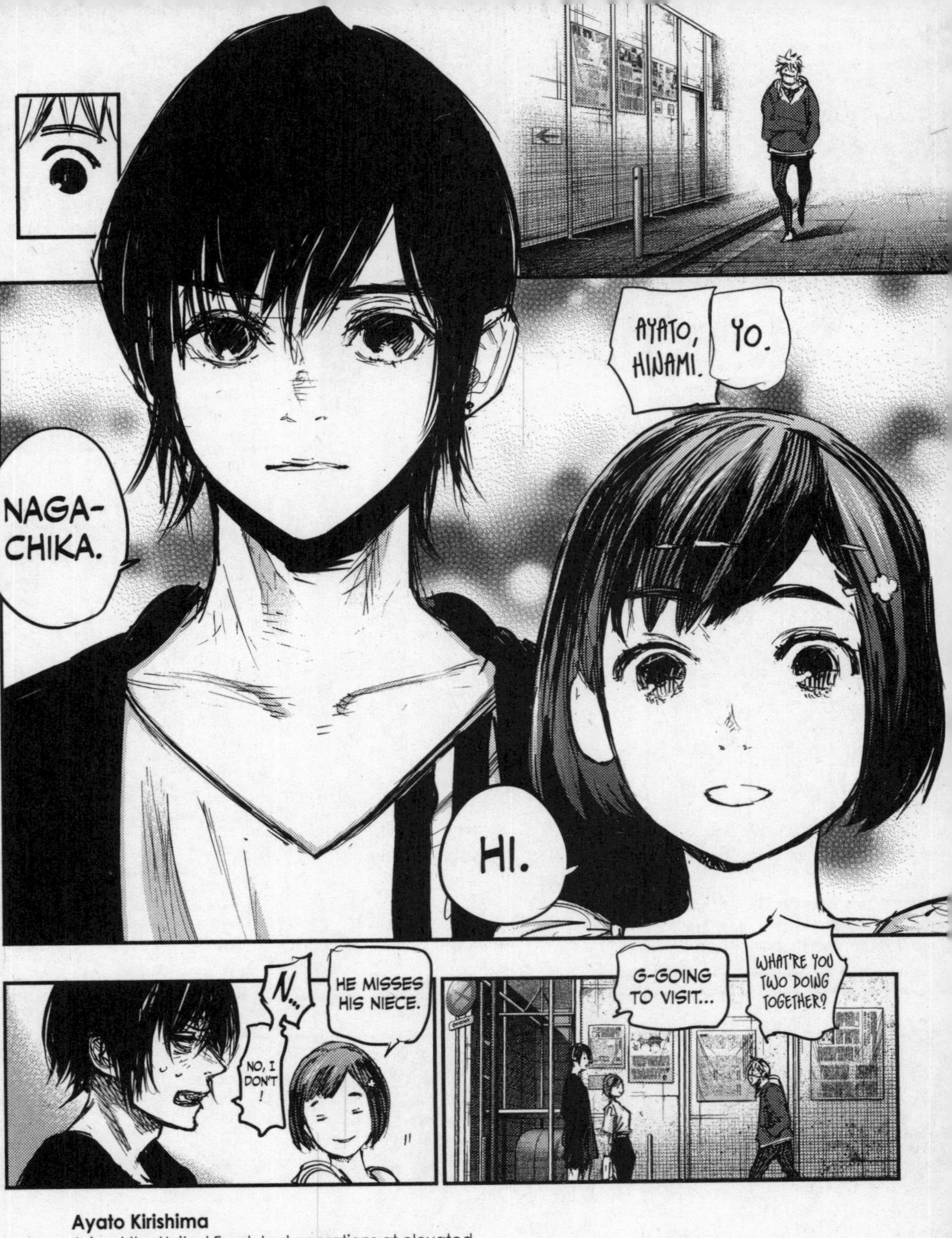
YO.
AYATO, HINAMI.
NAGA-CHIKA.
HI.
WHAT'RE YOU TWO DOING TOGETHER?
G-GOING TO VISIT...
HE MISSES HIS NIECE.
N...
NO, I DON'T!

Ayato Kirishima
Joined the United Front. Led operations at elevated positions that were difficult for marshals to access and eradicated Dragon Orphans with his outstanding leadership.

Hinami Fueguchi
Taught reading and writing at the United Front's orphanage for Ghouls. Accompanied by Ayato when she shopping in rural areas.

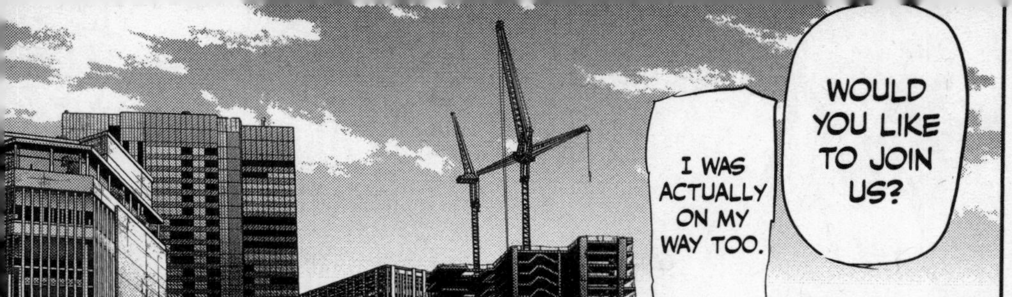
WOULD YOU LIKE TO JOIN US?
I WAS ACTUALLY ON MY WAY TOO.

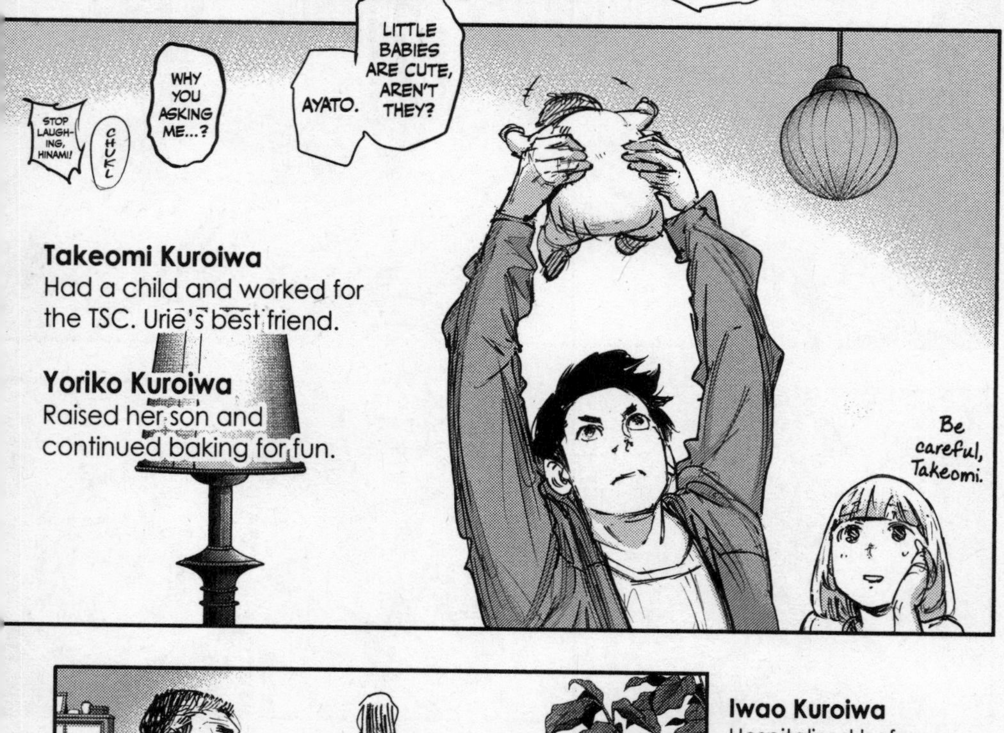
LITTLE BABIES ARE CUTE, AREN'T THEY?
AYATO.
WHY YOU ASKING ME...?
CHUKL
STOP LAUGHING, HINAMI!
Be careful, Takeomi.

Takeomi Kuroiwa
Had a child and worked for the TSC. Urie's best friend.

Yoriko Kuroiwa
Raised her son and continued baking for fun.

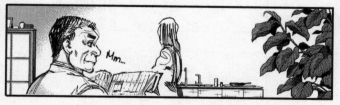

Iwao Kuroiwa
Hospitalized before the Dragon Assault, but served as Marude's aide once his neck healed.

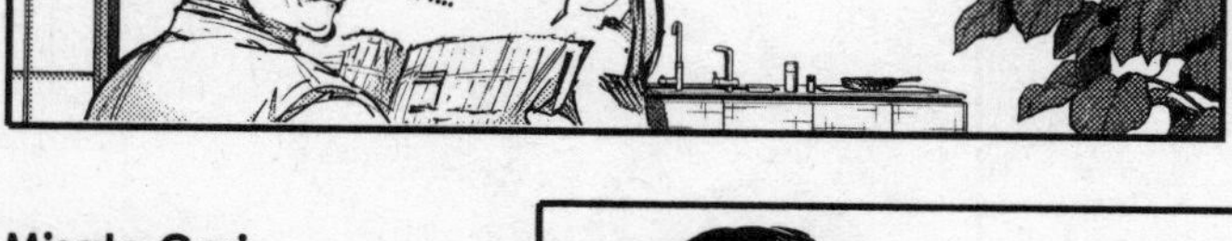
Mm...

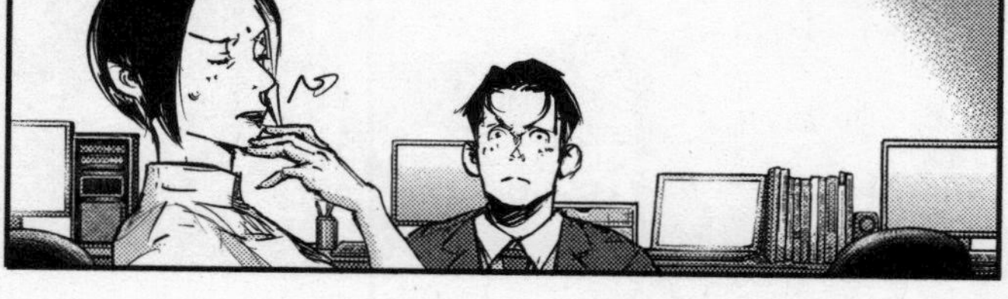

Misato Gori
Worked for the TSC with Iwao Kuroiwa. Wooed by many male marshals for her dedication to work. Has yet to respond to a single marriage proposal.

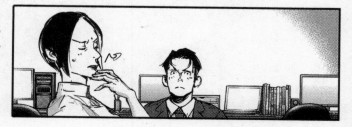

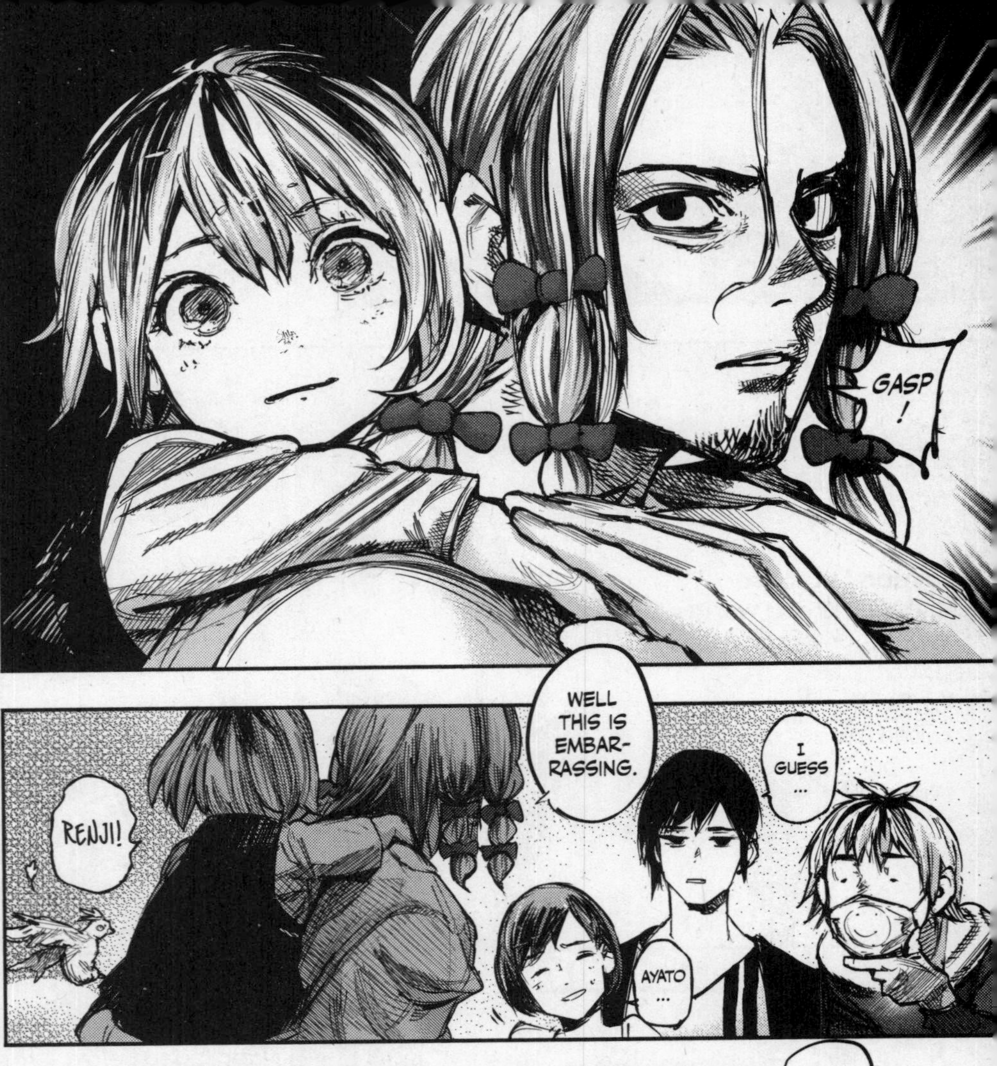
GASP!
WELL THIS IS EMBARRASSING.
I GUESS...
RENJI!
AYATO...

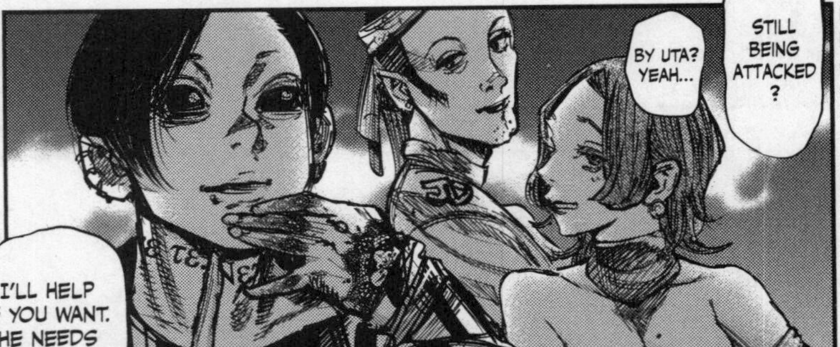
STILL BEING ATTACKED?
BY UTA? YEAH...
I'LL HELP IF YOU WANT. HE NEEDS HIS ASS KICKED.
SURE.

Itori
Enjoyed whatever Uta did. She may have never told him her feelings for him.

Nico
Remained drinking buddies with Itori and Uta. Eventually went south to find love.

Uta
Planned attacks on Yomo, designed masks and silver accessories. Probably lived happily as long as Yomo was alive.

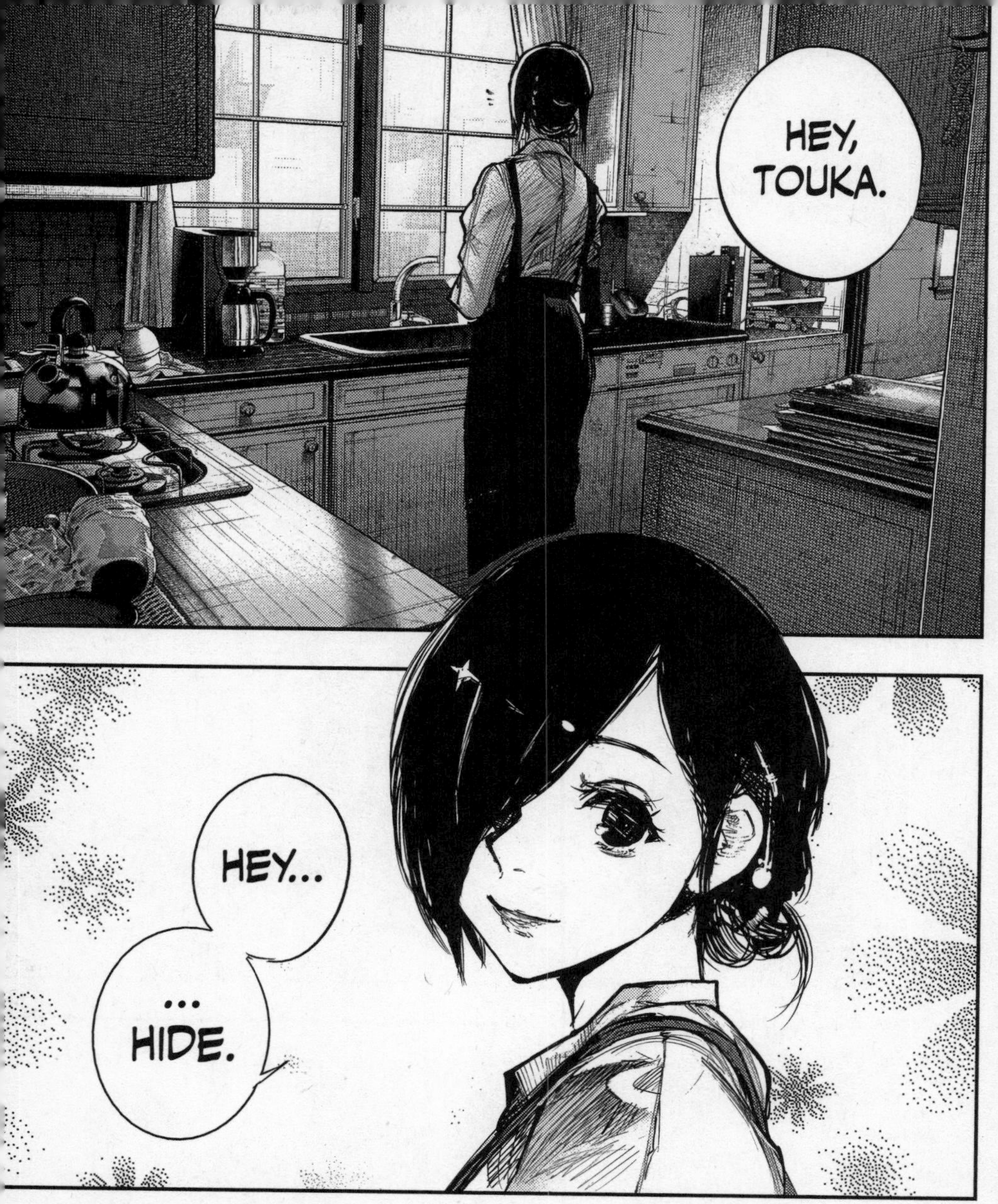
HEY, TOUKA.
HEY...
... HIDE.

Renji Yomo
Often visited Touka and Kaneki between Uta's attacks to see their daughter.

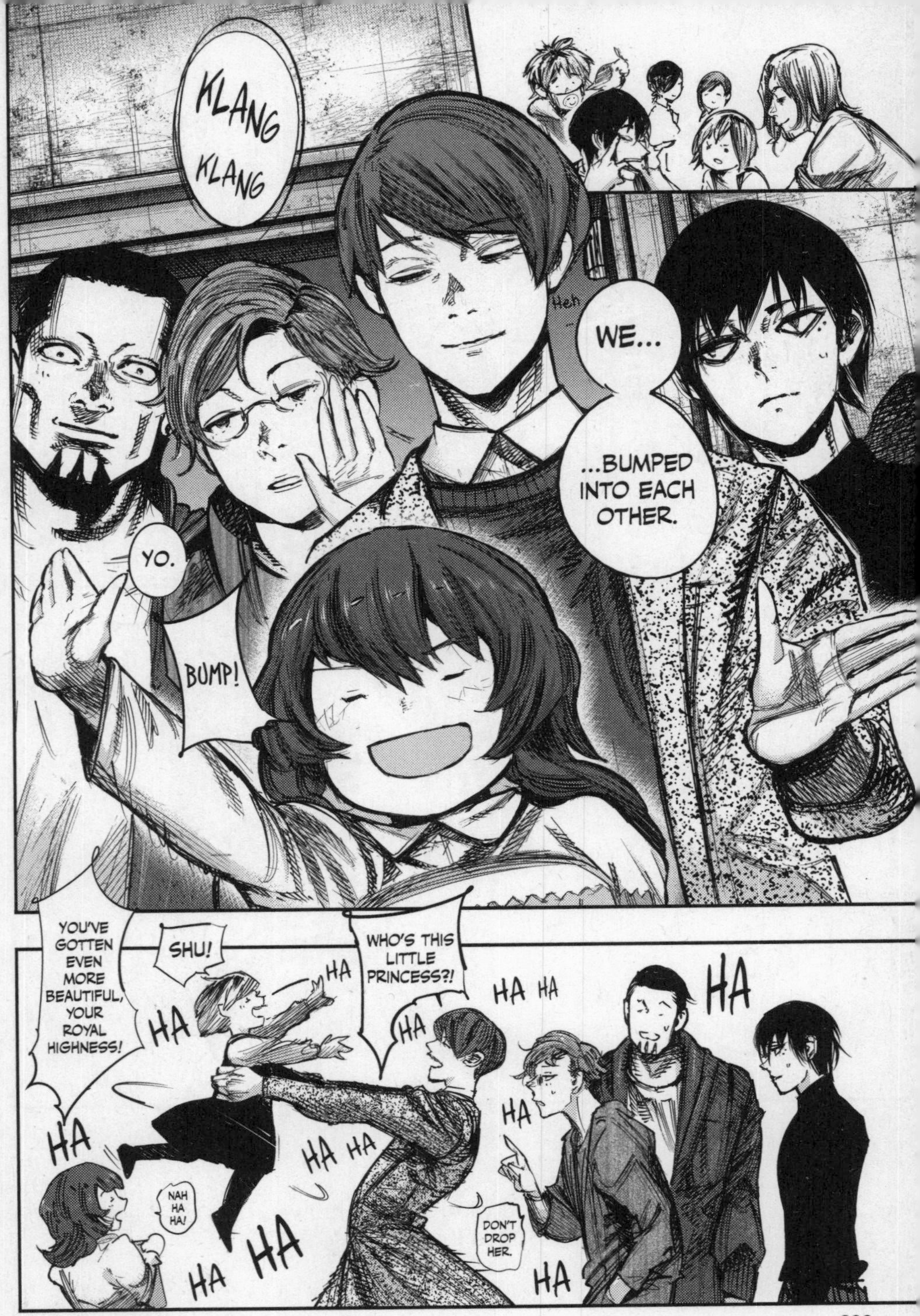
KLANG
KLANG
Heh
WE...
...BUMPED INTO EACH OTHER.
YO.
BUMP!
HA
HA HA
WHO'S THIS LITTLE PRINCESS?!
HA
SHU!
HA
YOU'VE GOTTEN EVEN MORE BEAUTIFUL, YOUR ROYAL HIGHNESS!
HA
HA
HA
DON'T DROP HER.
HA
HA HA
NAH HA HA!
HA
HA
HA

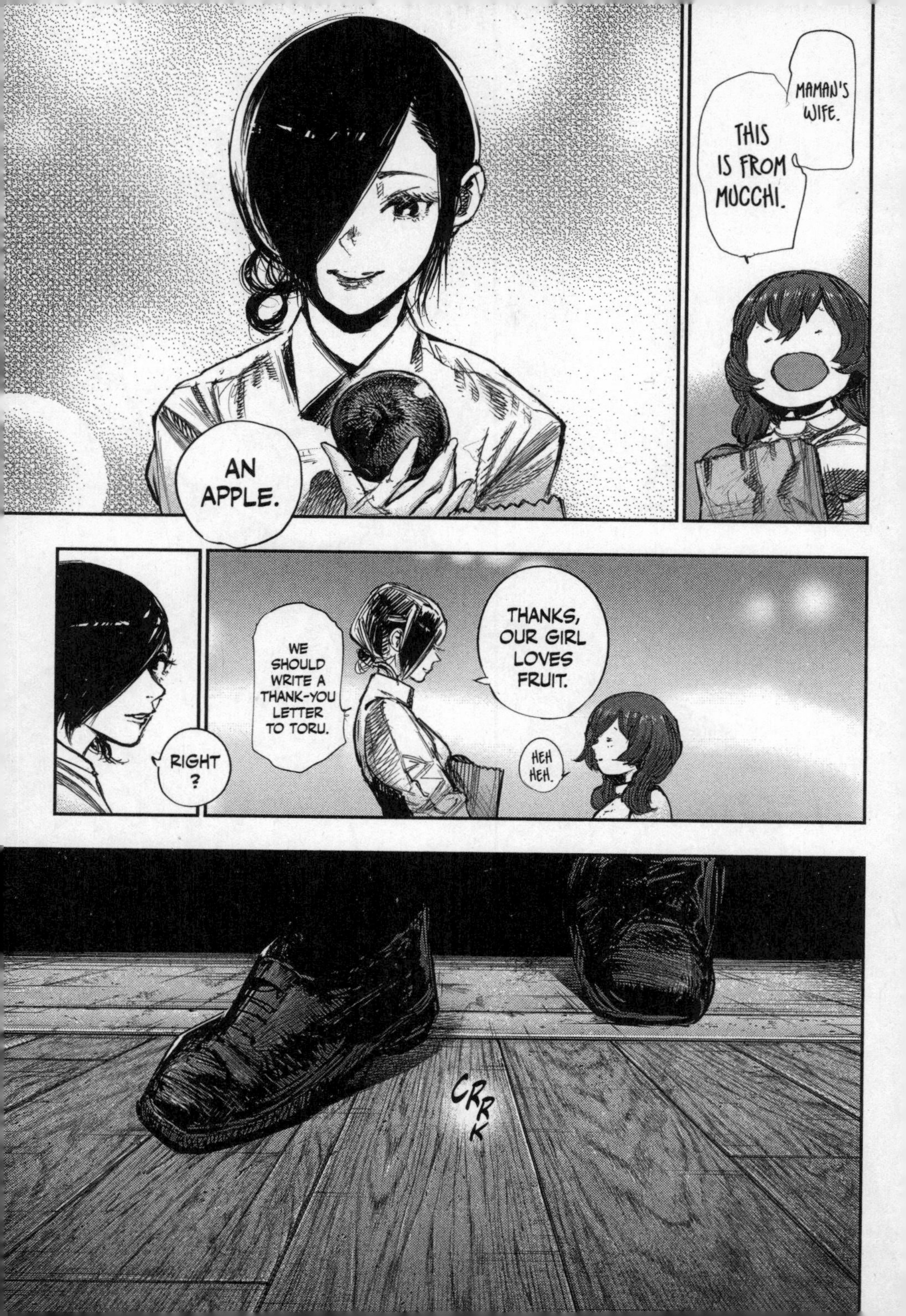
THIS IS FROM MUCCHI.
MAMAN'S WIFE.
AN APPLE.
THANKS, OUR GIRL LOVES FRUIT.
WE SHOULD WRITE A THANK-YOU LETTER TO TORU.
HEH HEH.
RIGHT?
CRRK

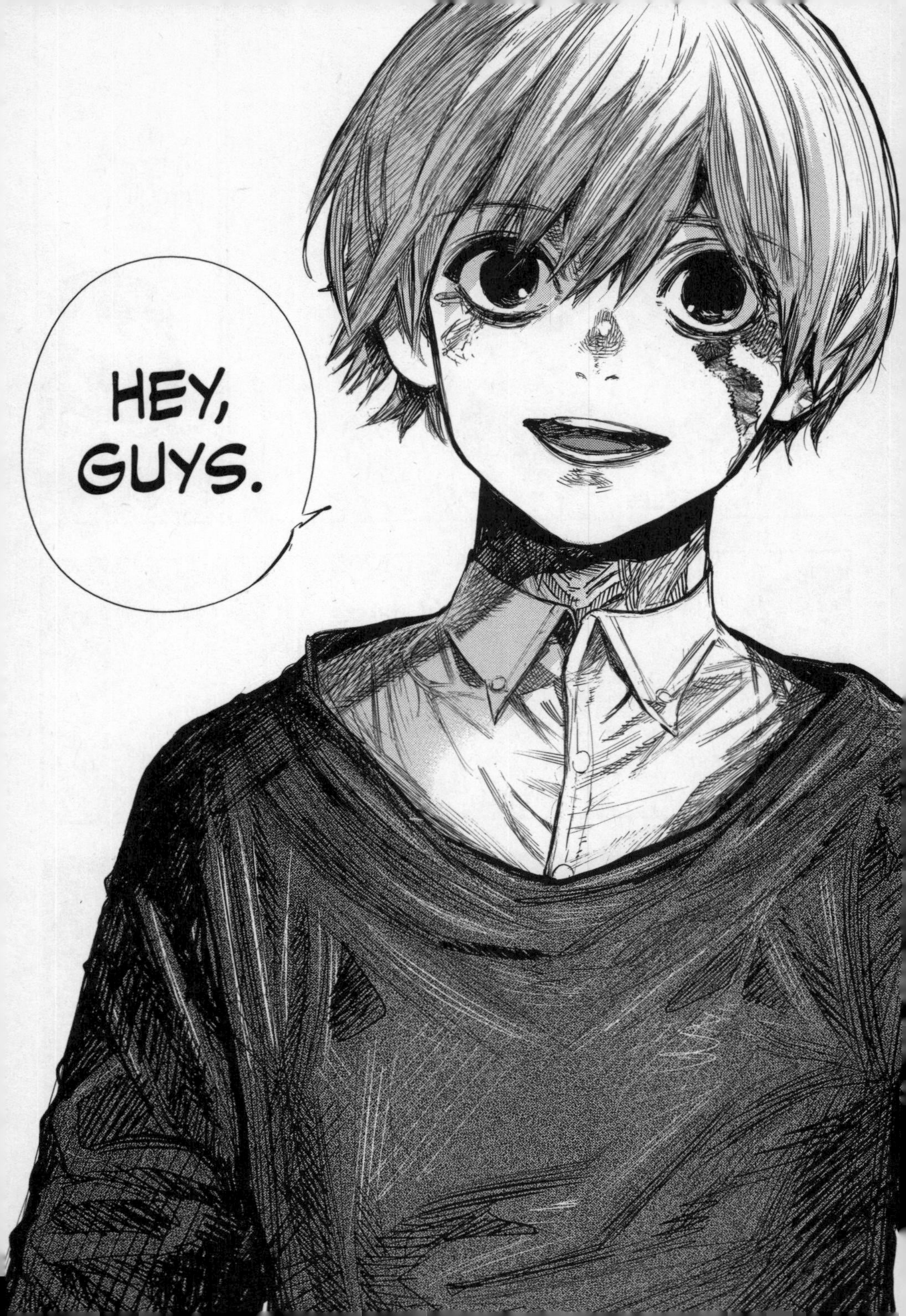
HEY, GUYS.

THE WORLD
KEEPS
CHANGING.

Ken Kaneki

He nearly drowned in the Dragon's fluids after eradicating it, but was rescued by Ayato Kirishima. Returned to the surface in bad shape and slept for two whole weeks. Provided assistance to both the TSC and the United Front.

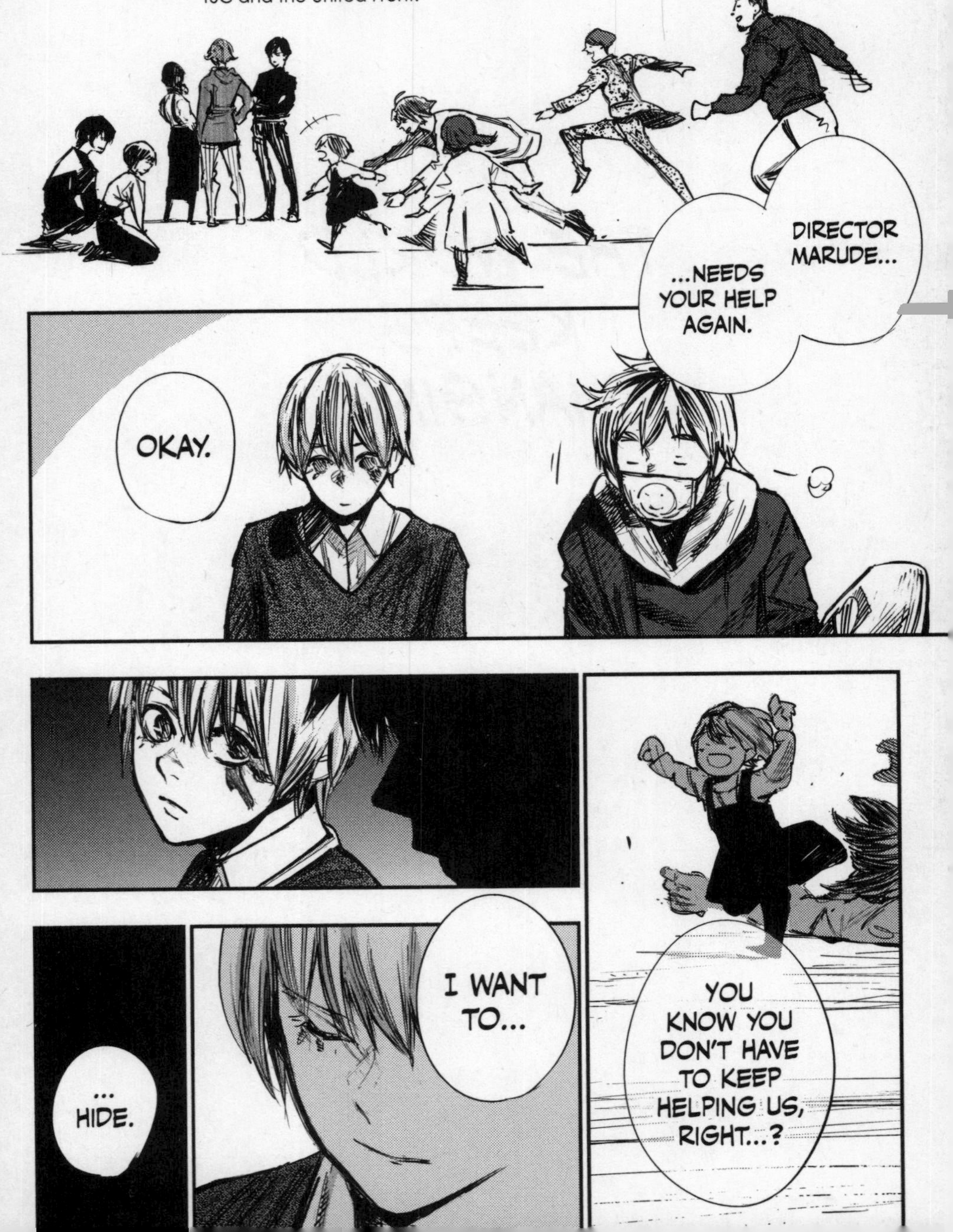
DIRECTOR MARUDE...
...NEEDS YOUR HELP AGAIN.
OKAY.
YOU KNOW YOU DON'T HAVE TO KEEP HELPING US, RIGHT...?
I WANT TO...
...HIDE.

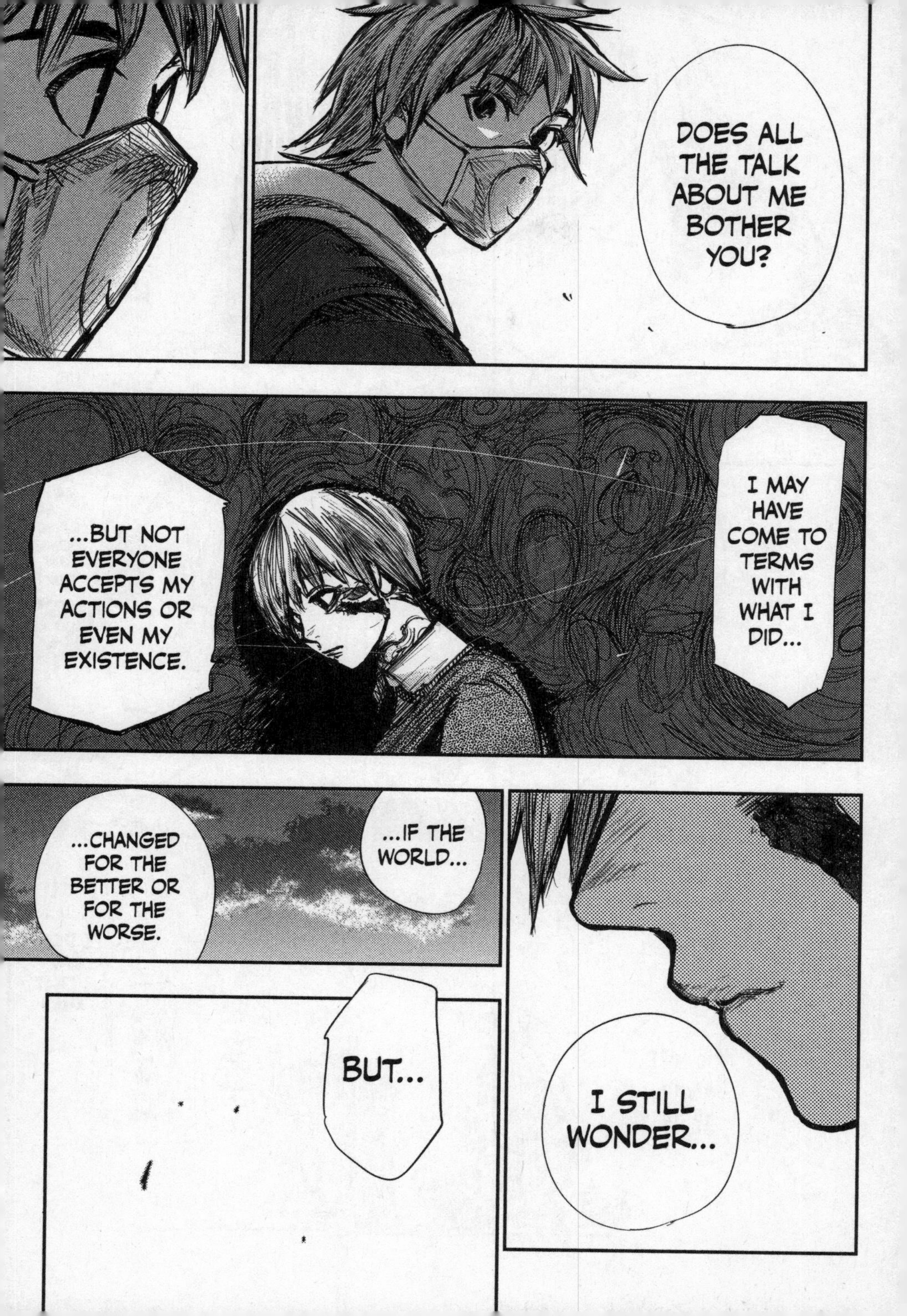
DOES ALL THE TALK ABOUT ME BOTHER YOU?
I MAY HAVE COME TO TERMS WITH WHAT I DID...
...BUT NOT EVERYONE ACCEPTS MY ACTIONS OR EVEN MY EXISTENCE.
I STILL WONDER...
...IF THE WORLD...
...CHANGED FOR THE BETTER OR FOR THE WORSE.
BUT...

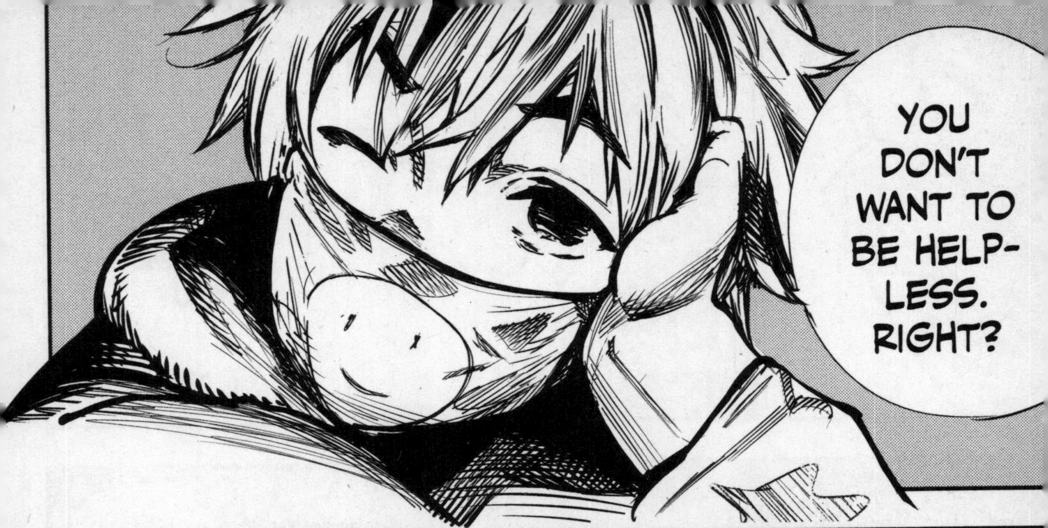
YOU DON'T WANT TO BE HELP-LESS. RIGHT?

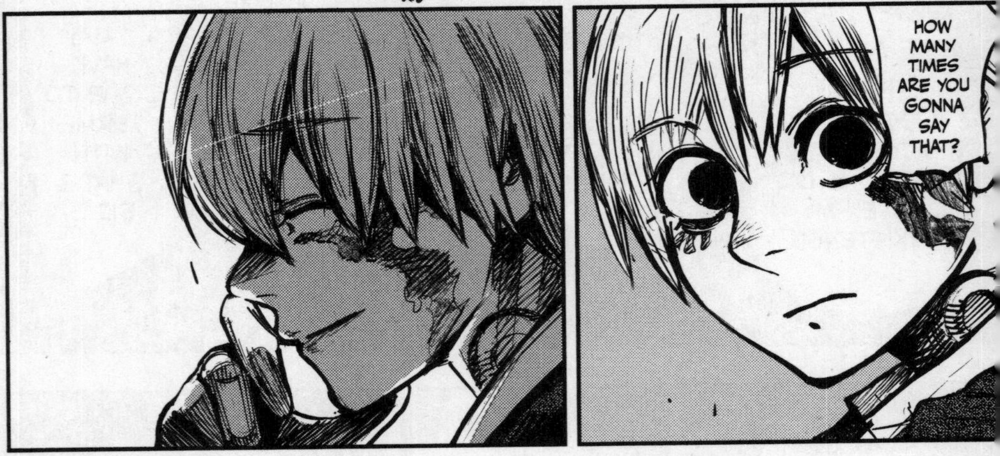
HOW MANY TIMES ARE YOU GONNA SAY THAT?

Hideyoshi Nagachika
Lived in an orphanage after his Ghoul investigator father died when he was in elementary school. Was adopted and later met Ken Kaneki.

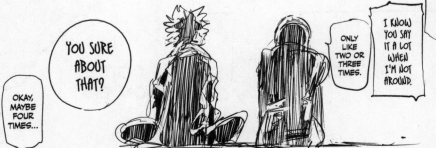

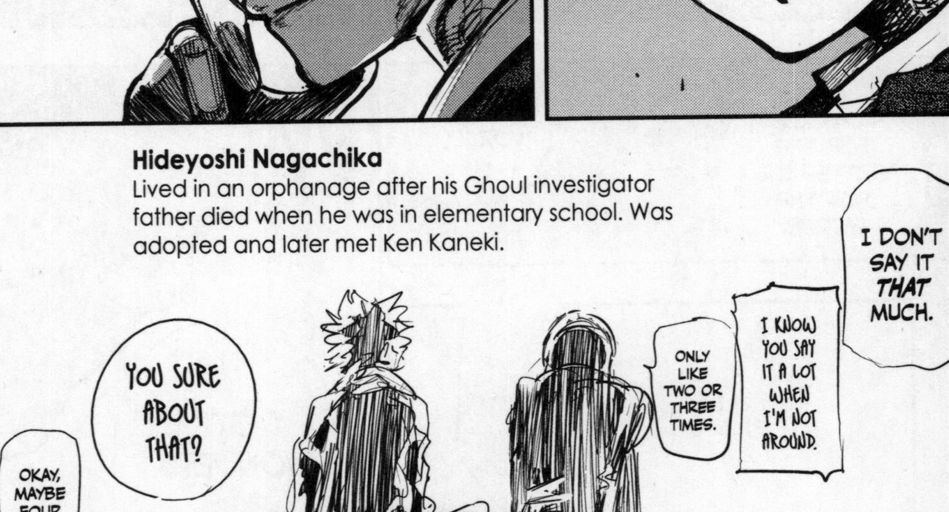
I DON'T SAY IT *THAT* MUCH.
I KNOW YOU SAY IT A LOT WHEN I'M NOT AROUND.
ONLY LIKE TWO OR THREE TIMES.
YOU SURE ABOUT THAT?
OKAY, MAYBE FOUR TIMES...

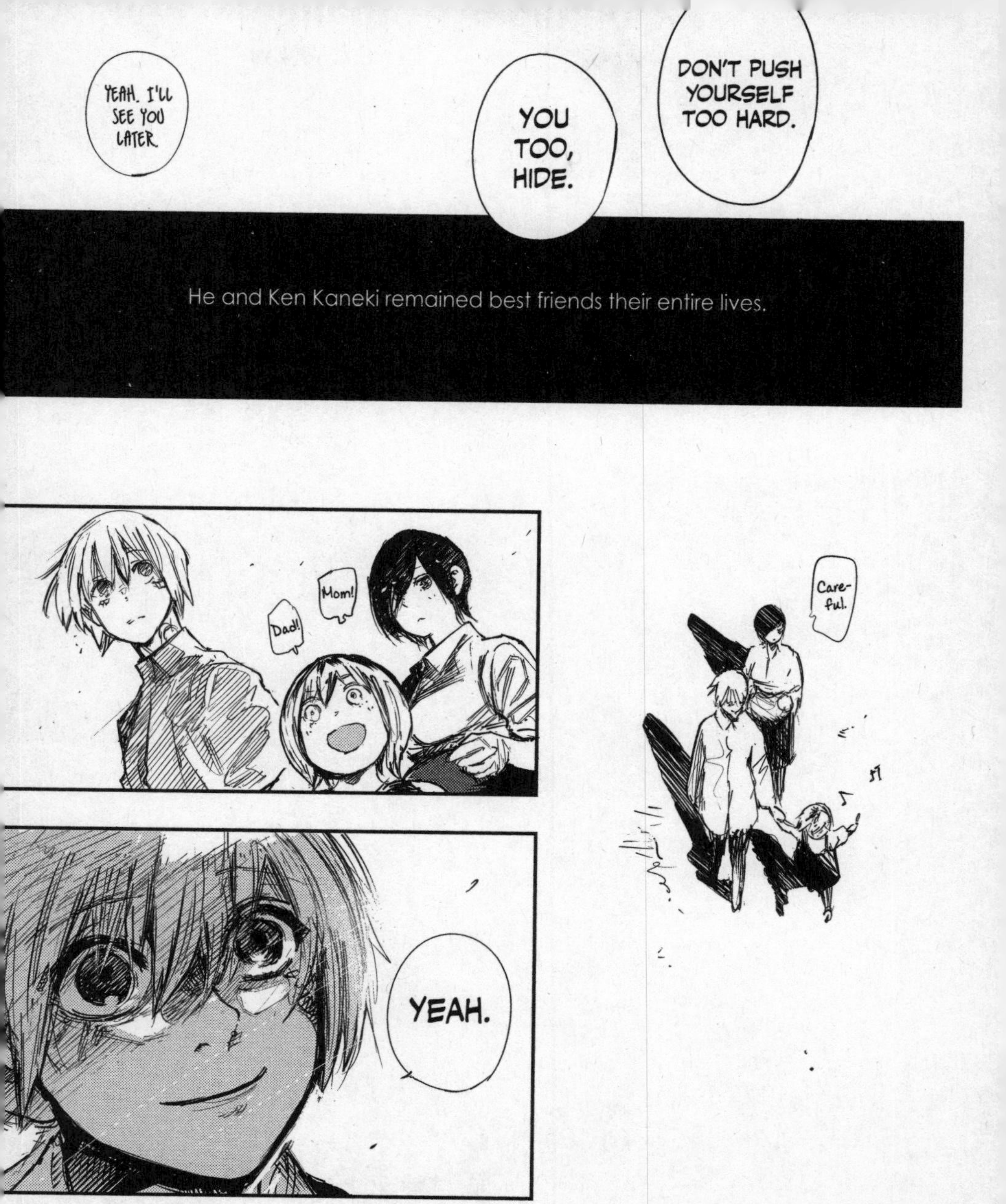
DON'T PUSH YOURSELF TOO HARD.
YOU TOO, HIDE.
YEAH. I'LL SEE YOU LATER.
He and Ken Kaneki remained best friends their entire lives.
Care-ful.
Mom!
Dad!
YEAH.

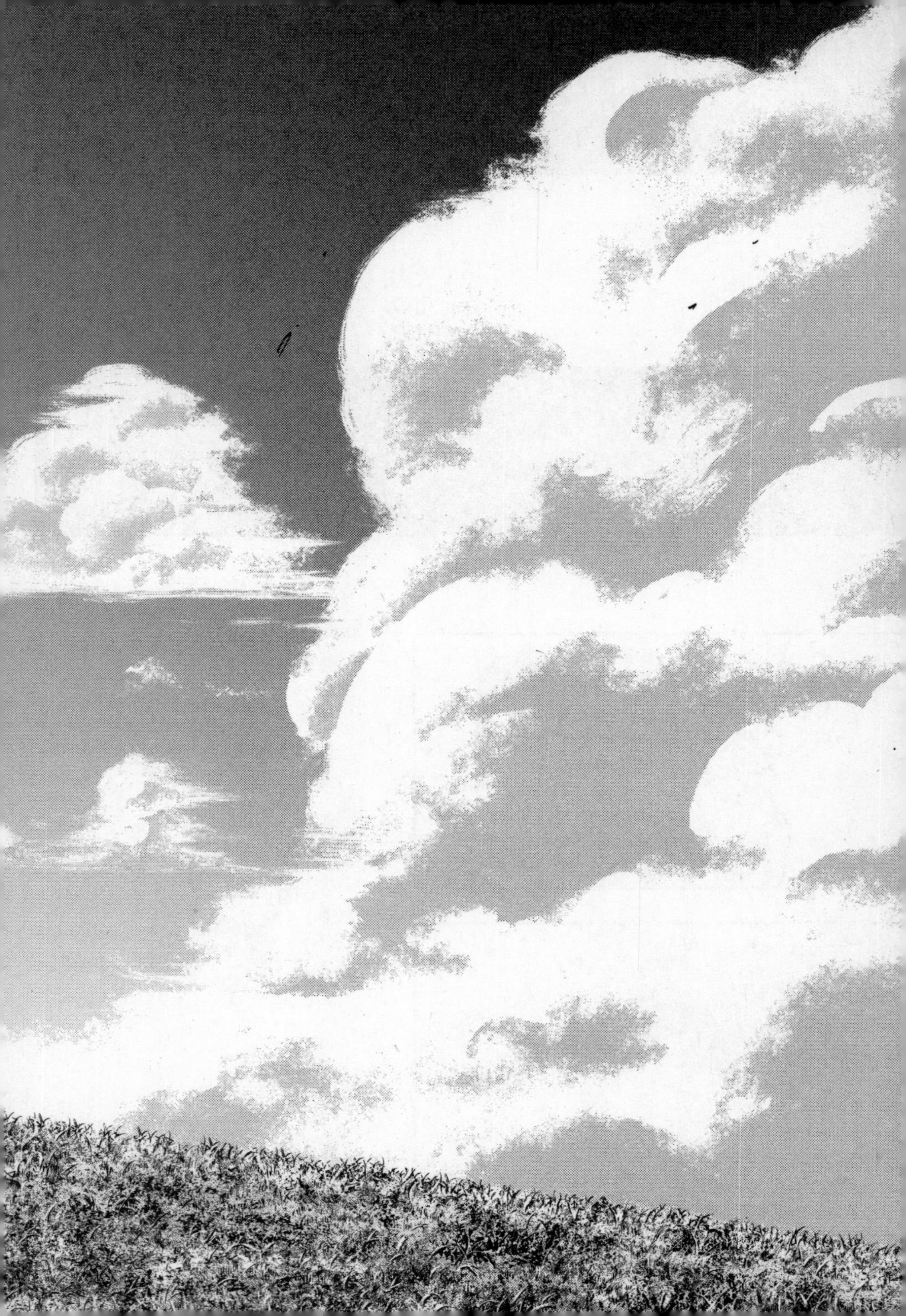

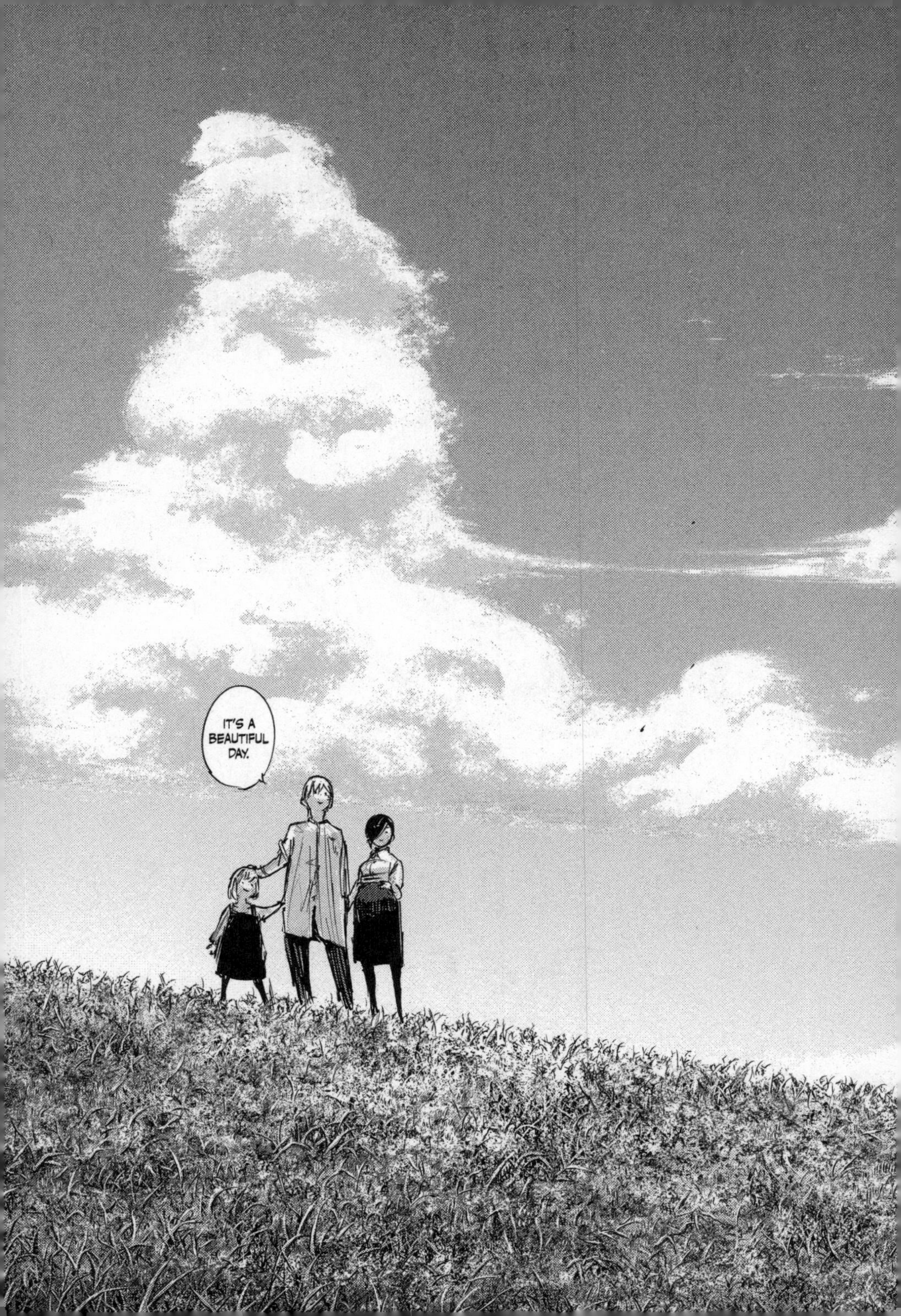
IT'S A BEAUTIFUL DAY.

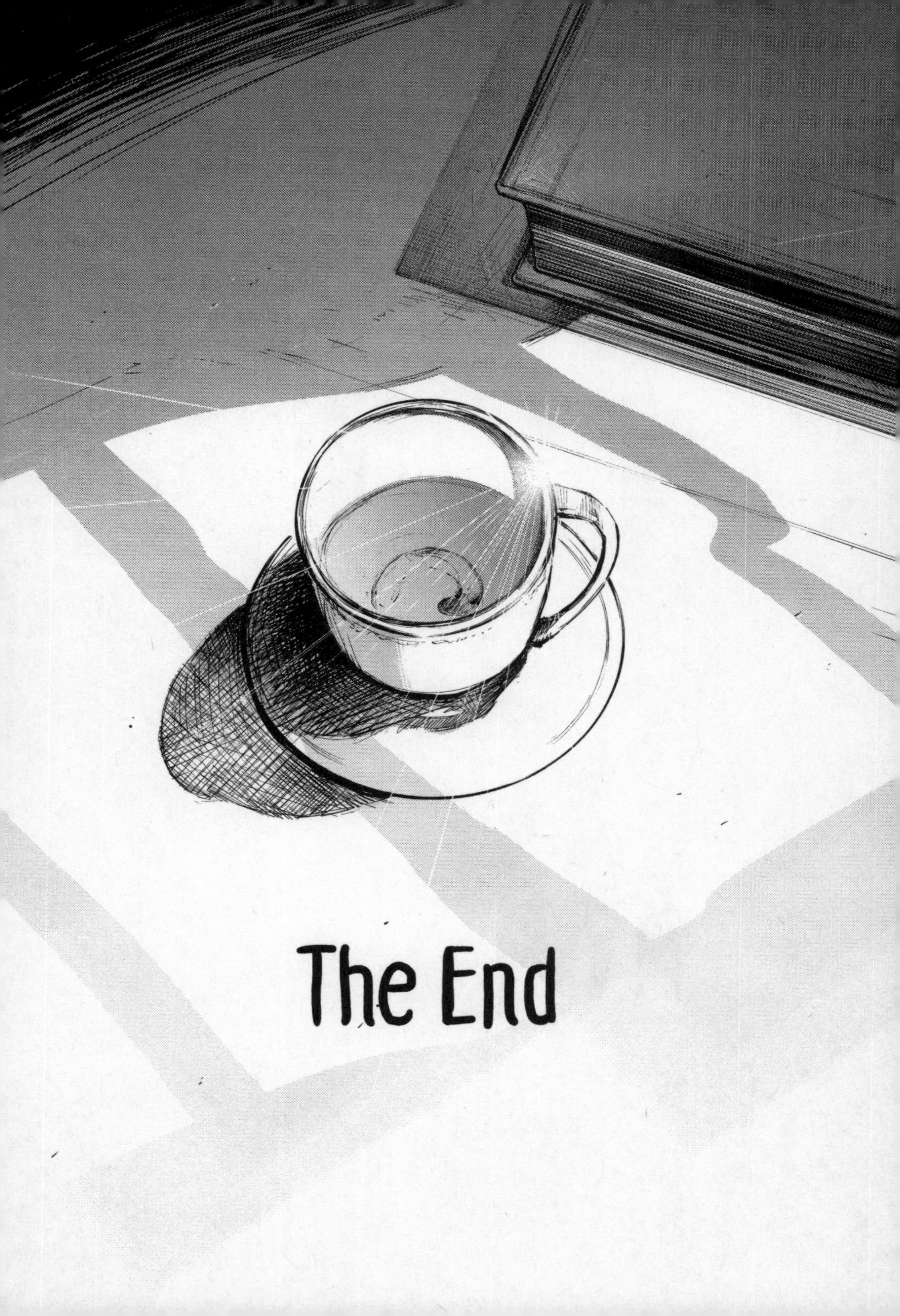
The End

Afterword

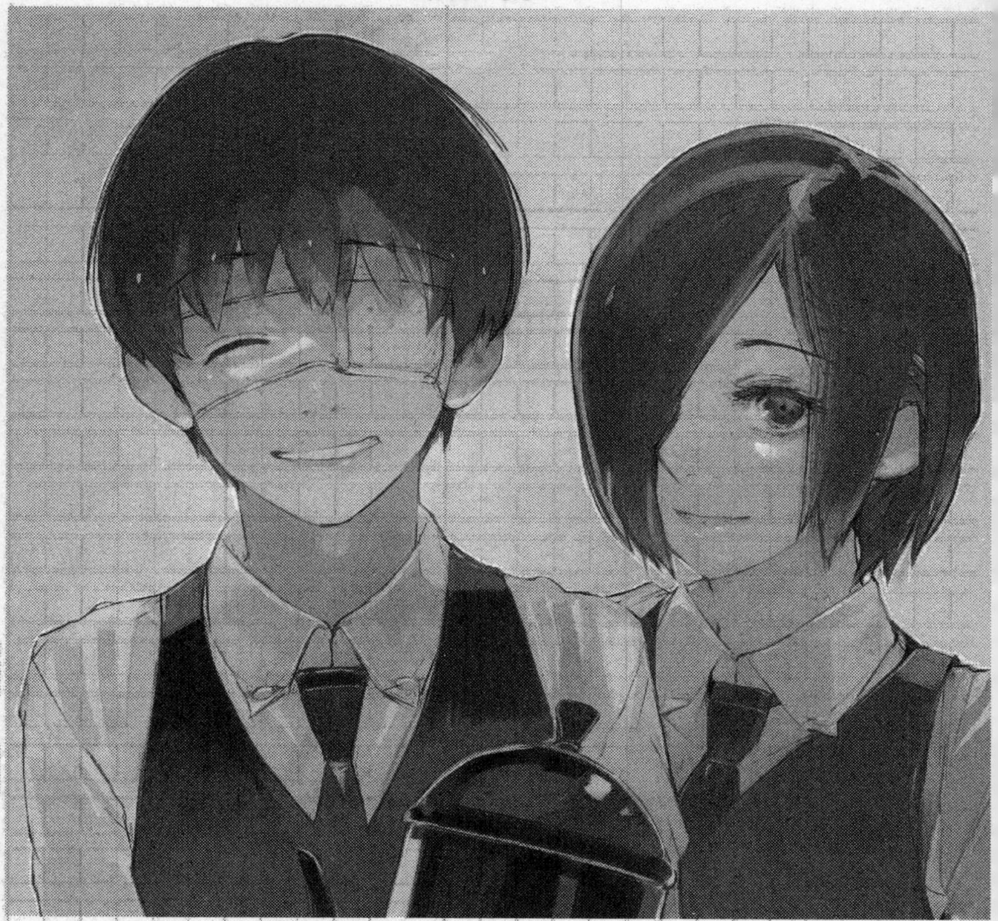

I'm writing this three days after finishing the final chapter.

Normally I include a four-panel comic at the end of every volume, but it didn't feel right to do that for the afterword. So I decided to write it instead.

START ➡

◆ The Beginning

Tokyo Ghoul was first published in September of 2011.

For the seven years since then, I've lived a life of facing one deadline after another. If I took a break, I felt like I'd never be able to write again, so I never asked for hiatus.

Now that the series is done, I can finally live a life free of deadlines!

How did I spend my time before all this started?

If I were to honestly describe what I'm feeling right now, it would be *release*.

That is how closely *Tokyo Ghoul* was tied to my life. It dominated my emotions and time. It even changed my relationships.

There were good times, but a lot bad times as well.

So I finally feel like I've been released from a cage I've been locked in.

"It's just a manga. How bad could it have been?"

You might laugh at me for feeling this way, but manga was a huge obstacle that was always with me. My attitude toward manga changed from around volume 7 of *Tokyo Ghoul*.

I worked in an overly demanding way in order to push myself.

I think I was trying to be like Kaneki while he was being tortured.

I started experiencing health issues.

I was concerned at first, but every few months, I would come down with a variety of symptoms, so eventually I just accepted it.

What I remember most clearly is losing my sense of taste.

Everything tasted the same. The symptoms may be different, but I felt like a Ghoul.

I was shocked to learn how closely the mind is tied to our bodies.

This may disappoint some of my readers, but writing *Tokyo Ghoul* was not a "fun" experience. I hate working!

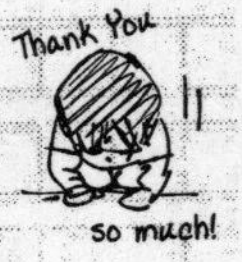

Thank You
so much!

"Why do I write manga?"

I began to question myself.

◆ Childhood

I moved around a lot because of my father's job.

By the time I was in the sixth grade, I had lived in Tokushima, Tokyo, Kanagawa, Saga and Fukuoka. I lived in Taiwan as a kindergartner too.

Making friends then having to leave them was my life. It was hard making close friends.

I naturally became close with my family, but my father was a very strict man, so my home was not a comfortable place.

I liked playing games behind my father's back. I would also draw once in a while.

◆ Drawing

I copied my older sister and started drawing around the first grade.

I would draw fantasy adventure stories with dragons and swords on stacks of paper to make my own manga.

I eventually wanted proper art supplies. Right around that time, a cram school was doing a manga artist set giveaway that you could win by studying and earning points. I studied hard to save up points.

The prize cost a lot of points. I think it took a few months to earn enough points.

I finally had enough points and got the manga artist set. That was the first time I held a G Pen.

When I dipped the nib into ink and drew a line on hard Kent paper, I felt like I opened a forbidden door.

I spent some time pretending to be a manga artist, until one day my hand slipped and I spilled ink all over the tatami mat.

My mother was furious. She, for some strange reason, wiped the ink off the tatami mat with steaming hot rice (high absorption, maybe?). That's me, dejected, watching my mother clean.

I felt so guilty that I permanently sealed up the manga artist set. I wouldn't hold a pen for the next ten years.

If I hadn't spilled the ink, maybe I'd have been a super genius manga artist...

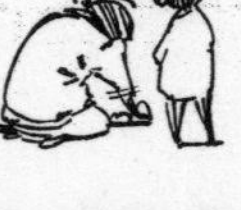

Sui!

CONT'D ➡

◆ My Dream in Elementary School

I remember writing "gymnast" in an essay.

I was an overweight kid until the sixth grade, but I think I was actually pretty athletic.

I was particularly good at floor exercises and horizontal bars. I used to do backflips too.

I never really planned on becoming a gymnast, but I think I felt guilty writing "manga artist" in my essay.

◆ Junior High School

I was a pretty good student. My parents hounded me to study, so I did.

I liked English. I was proud, at the time, that I passed the Grade 2 exam English proficiency test when I was in the seventh grade. (Although I don't understand much English now.)

My parents were upset if I got bad grades. I studied so they wouldn't get on my case.

When I had the best score in school, I told my father about it. He said "keep it up." Looking back now, I think that was his way of praising me, but...

I remember thinking hard work got me nothing.

That's when I couldn't find a purpose in studying anymore.

◆ College ~Moratorium~

I wanted to get away from my parents, so I applied to schools with dorms.

Dorm life was fun. I basically spent all my time playing video games.

My grades were terrible. Dead last in my class. The subjects they taught didn't interest me.

I also started drawing on the internet. I would draw using a mouse at first, then used a pen and tablet. And eventually moved on to drawing color illustrations on a PC.

◆ Job Hunting

While the people around me were job hunting, I did nothing. I couldn't find a job I was interested in.

All the jobs required specialized knowledge learned at school. I wasn't interested in studying so I didn't look for a job.

I felt left behind. Not sure of what I should do.

I fought with my parents a lot.

My father chewed me out so I gave in and finally started looking for a job. My memory of then is a bit hazy, but I supposedly said "I'm dead" to him.

Maybe those words were the last straw. He let me choose another path.

The path that came to mind was "becoming a manga artist."

◆ Moving to Tokyo

I studied manga before moving to Tokyo. My editor Mr. Matsuo got me an assistant's position.

At one point, I had the privilege of working at the studio of Mr. Yasuhisa Hara *(Kingdom)*.

I was a totally useless assistant. I was just an inconvenience to them, but I learned so much.

I remember being awed at seeing a professional artist's work for the first time. It was so powerful, you could almost feel the artist's passion coming off the pages.

Mr. Hara was already a leading artist at the time and continues to be today. I have so much respect for him.

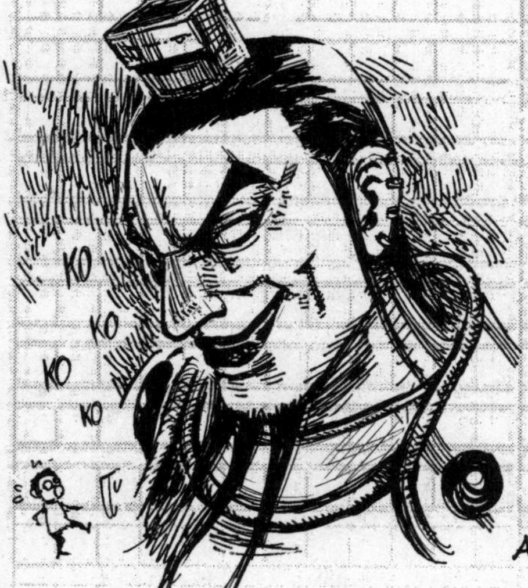
KO
KO
KO
KO

A wall too high...

CONT'D ➡

◆ Happy Moments

I know I've only been bringing up painful memories, but there were a lot of happy moments too.

I got to choose artists I liked to write songs for the anime.

Ling tositesigure
"unravel"

People in The Box
"The Saints"

amazarashi
"Seasons Die One After Another"

Kunimitsu Takahashi
"Incompetence"

For :re

Queen Bee
"HALF"

CöshuNie
"asphyxia"

(They're both still demos, but both songs are really good.)

These songs still bring back memories. I love all of them.

Meeting and talking to Mr. Yoshihiro Togashi of *Hunter x Hunter* through a Hisoka spinoff project is a great memory too.

He was a very charming and cool person.

He sprawled on the floor and showed me how he usually creates his storyboards. I sat on my knees and watched him.

I couldn't tell if it was real or a dream.

He wrote me a letter on the back of a *Hunter X Hunter* storyboard before I met him.

It was for chapter 351 where Hisoka battles Chrollo. It was such a nice gesture. I remember being touched by it.

To this day, I look at it when I need courage. It's a family treasure.

I was simply happy the readers enjoyed my work. Even if it was stressful, knowing people enjoyed it got me through.

That may sound cliché, but it was truly the biggest reward. It basically meant everything.

◆ In Closing

I'm so happy I got to conclude *Tokyo Ghoul*.

Not because I've been freed from it, but because by creating this story, I was able to think about a lot of things, like me, creativity, art and the industry of making "things." I got to meet a lot of great people too.

The last six months of creating *Tokyo Ghoul* was truly a joy. There was so much to discover and appreciate.

"Why am I writing and drawing manga?"

I think it's because that's what I needed. It's a clumsy manga, but I like it.

I have nothing but gratitude for everybody that was involved, the readers, and you for reading this.

Thank you so much.

◆ In Passing

I recently dug up a diary entry I wrote nine years ago.

I want to bring this naive young man to where I am now. I'm putting this out there knowing how embarrassing it is.

Amen to me, nine years ago.

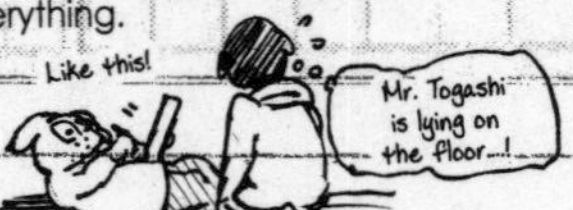
Like this!
Mr. Togashi is lying on the floor...!

7/7/2009

I'm in Tokyo. Living alone.

Looking back at my diary, it becomes so clear how clueless, thoughtless and pathetic I am.

I was such a punk my second year of college (technical college), it makes me laugh. Thinking I grew up a bit since then, I read back some of my recent diary entries... What I wrote isn't much different from back then. I need to grow up...

Why are my diary entries from tech college almost all about my dreams? I really must've been sleeping the whole time...

I'm writing a storyboard I'm taking to Shueisha right now. I'm going at 5:30 p.m. tomorrow... It's a war story. Although I'm not sure I have the skills right now to do a sci-fi story.

I used to wonder what my five years at tech college was for or about things I should've done. I would sometimes feel regret.

But all of that past led to who am I now. My mistakes, struggles, the little bit of success I had, make me who I am.

If I can accept who I am now, that would mean accepting all of my past. All of my failures still live inside me.

If I'm happy now, it's because of who I used to be (and of course) who I am now.

I can't accept everything. But I "kinda" like who I am. That's not so bad, right?

Staff

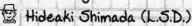

Eda

Ryuji Miyamoto

Mizuki Ide

Matsuzaki

Kazumi Takahata

Nakano

Kota Shugyo

Hashimoto

Haraguchi

Kiyotaka Aihara

Rikako Miura

Nina

Ippo Yaguchi

Akikuni Nakao

Nomaguchi

Abe

Comic Design:

Hideaki Shimada (L.S.D.)

Magazine Design:

Miyuki Takaoka (POCKET)

Akie Demachi (POCKET)

Photography

Wataru Tanaka

Editor

Junpei Matsuo

THANKS

My sister, family

My friends J and

T-hashi

Thank you so much for everything.

07/02/2018

Sui Ishida

● Ichika Kaneki
金木 一花 （カネキ イチカ）

- Almost six ●Blood type: B ●Height/weight: 112cm/18kg
- Favorite food: Apples, Yoriko's bread

Kaneki and Touka's daughter.
Very friendly and energetic.

A natural half-Ghoul. Can eat human food.

SUI ISHIDA is the author of the immensely popular *Tokyo Ghoul* and several *Tokyo Ghoul* one-shots, including one that won second place in the *Weekly Young Jump* 113th Grand Prix award in 2010. *Tokyo Ghoul:re* is the sequel to *Tokyo Ghoul*.

TOKYO GHOUL:re

TOKYO GHOUL:re

VOLUME 16
VIZ SIGNATURE EDITION

Story and art by
SUI ISHIDA

First published in Japan in 2014 by SHUEISHA Inc., Tokyo.
English translation rights arranged by SHUEISHA Inc.

Translation Joe Yamazaki
Touch-Up Art & Lettering Vanessa Satone
Design Shawn Carrico
Editor Pancha Diaz

Printed in the U.S.A.

Published by VIZ Media, LLC
P.O. Box 77010
San Francisco, CA 94107

10 9 8 7 6 5 4 3 2 1
First printing, April 2020

VIZ MEDIA
viz.com

VIZ SIGNATURE
vizsignature.com

ratings.viz.com RATED T+ OLDER TEEN

PARENTAL ADVISORY
TOKYO GHOUL: RE is rated T+ for Older Teen and is recommended for ages 16 and up. This volume contains violence.

Tokyo Ghoul

YOU'VE READ THE MANGA
NOW WATCH THE
LIVE-ACTION MOVIE!

OWN IT NOW ON BLU-RAY, DVD & DIGITAL HD

WITNESS THE ANIME FINALE

STREAM IT. OWN IT.

TOKYO:re
GHOUL:re

FUNIMATION.COM/TOKYOGHOUL
funimation

TOKYO GHOUL
[ILLUSTRATIONS]
z a k k i

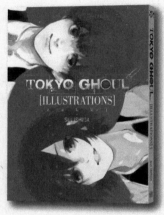

Tokyo Ghoul Illustrations: zakki features artwork and behind-the-scenes notes, commentary and ruminations from *Tokyo Ghoul* creator Sui Ishida. Discover the creative process that brought the hit manga to life, in gloriously ghoulish full color.

TOKYO GHOUL

C O M P L E T E   B O X   S E T   STORY AND ART BY SUI ISHIDA

KEN KANEKI is an ordinary college student until a violent encounter turns him into the first half-human, half-Ghoul hybrid. Trapped between two worlds, he must survive Ghoul turf wars, learn more about Ghoul society and master his new powers.

Box set collects all fourteen volumes of the original *Tokyo Ghoul* series. Includes an exclusive double-sided poster.

COLLECT THE COMPLETE SERIES

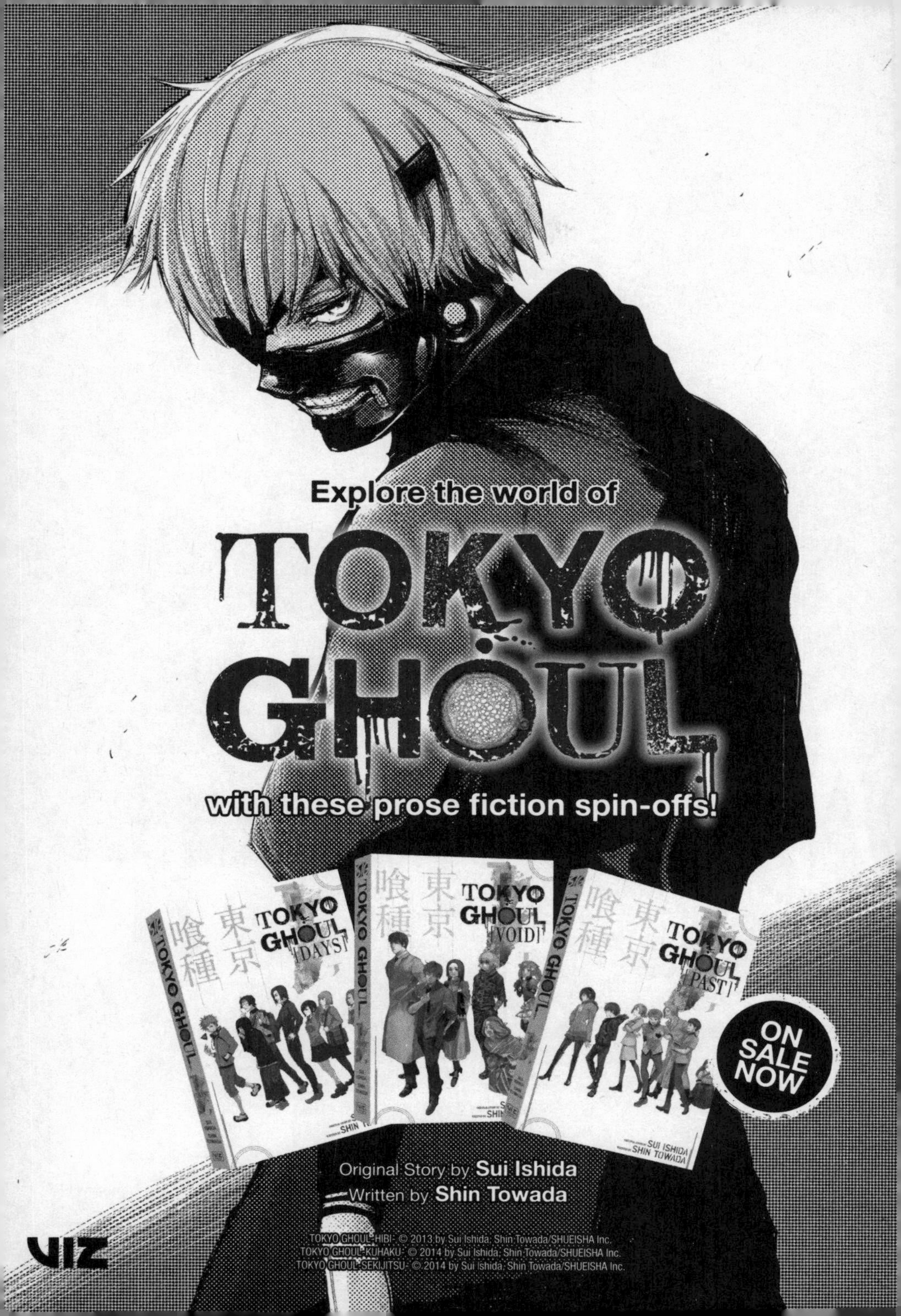

Explore the world of
TOKYO GHOUL
with these prose fiction spin-offs!
東京喰種
TOKYO GHOUL [DAYS]
TOKYO GHOUL [VOID]
TOKYO GHOUL [PAST]
SUI ISHIDA
SHIN TOWADA
ON SALE NOW
Original Story by Sui Ishida
Written by Shin Towada
VIZ
TOKYO GHOUL -HIBI- © 2013 by Sui Ishida, Shin Towada/SHUEISHA Inc.
TOKYO GHOUL -KUHAKU- © 2014 by Sui Ishida, Shin Towada/SHUEISHA Inc.
TOKYO GHOUL -SEKIJITSU- © 2014 by Sui Ishida, Shin Towada/SHUEISHA Inc.

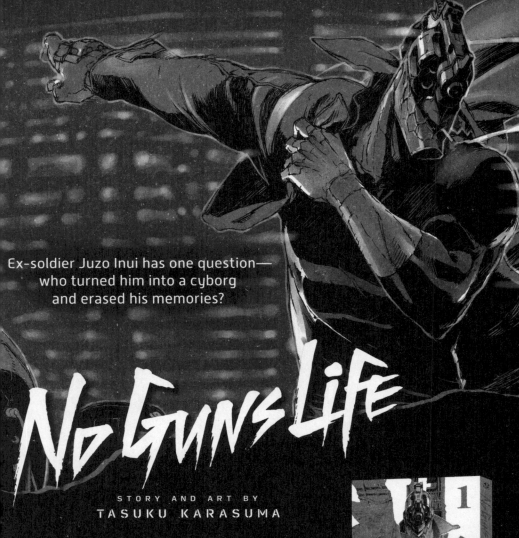

Ex-soldier Juzo Inui has one question—
who turned him into a cyborg
and erased his memories?

No Guns Life

STORY AND ART BY
TASUKU KARASUMA

After the war, cyborg soldiers known as the
Extended were discharged. Juzo Inui is one of
them, a man whose body was transformed, his
head replaced with a giant gun! With no memory
of his previous life—or who replaced his head and
why—Inui now scratches out a living in the dark
streets of the city as a Resolver, taking on cases
involving the Extended.

ABARA
COMPLETE DELUXE EDITION
TSUTOMU NIHEI

A visually stunning work of sci-fi horror from the creator of **BIOMEGA** and **BLAME!**

A vast city lies under the shadow of colossal, ancient tombs, the identity of their builders lost to time. In the streets of the city something is preying on the inhabitants, something that moves faster than the human eye can see and leaves unimaginable horror in its wake.

Tsutomu Nihei's dazzling, harrowing dystopian thriller is presented here in a single-volume hardcover edition featuring full-color pages and foldout illustrations. This volume also includes the early short story "Digimortal."

UZUMAKI

Story and Art by JUNJI ITO

SPIRALS... THIS TOWN IS CONTAMINATED WITH SPIRALS...

Kurouzu-cho, a small fogbound town on the coast of Japan, is cursed. According to Shuichi Saito, the withdrawn boyfriend of teenager Kirie Goshima, their town is haunted not by a person or being but by a pattern: uzumaki, the spiral, the hypnotic secret shape of the world. It manifests itself in everything from seashells and whirlpools in water to the spiral marks on people's bodies, the insane obsessions of Shuichi's father and the voice from the cochlea in our inner ear. As the madness spreads, the inhabitants of Kurouzu-cho are pulled ever deeper into a whirlpool from which there is no return!

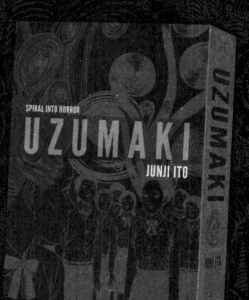

SPIRAL INTO HORROR
UZUMAKI
JUNJI ITO

A masterpiece of horror manga, now available in a
DELUXE HARDCOVER EDITION!

VIZ SIGNATURE

My parents are clueless.

My boyfriend's a mooch.

My boss is a perv.

But who cares? I sure don't.
At least they know who they are.

Being young and dissatisfied
really makes it hard to care
about anything in this world...

solanin

STORY & ART BY INIO ASANO

2009 Eisner Nominee!

AVAILABLE AT YOUR LOCAL BOOKSTORE OR COMIC STORE

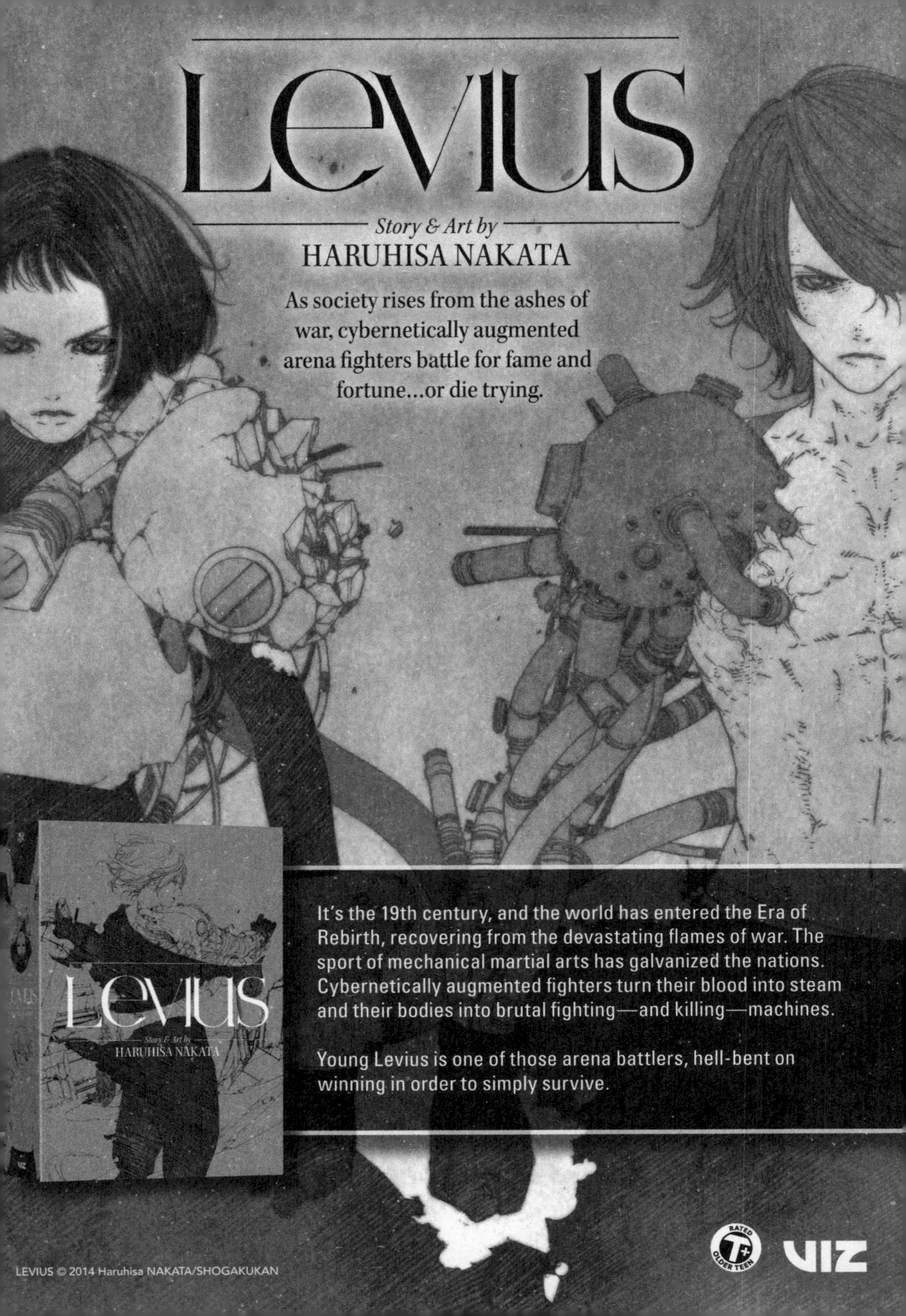
LEVIUS
Story & Art by
HARUHISA NAKATA
As society rises from the ashes of war, cybernetically augmented arena fighters battle for fame and fortune...or die trying.
LEVIUS
Story & Art by
HARUHISA NAKATA
It's the 19th century, and the world has entered the Era of Rebirth, recovering from the devastating flames of war. The sport of mechanical martial arts has galvanized the nations. Cybernetically augmented fighters turn their blood into steam and their bodies into brutal fighting—and killing—machines.
Young Levius is one of those arena battlers, hell-bent on winning in order to simply survive.
RATED T+ OLDER TEEN
VIZ
LEVIUS © 2014 Haruhisa NAKATA/SHOGAKUKAN

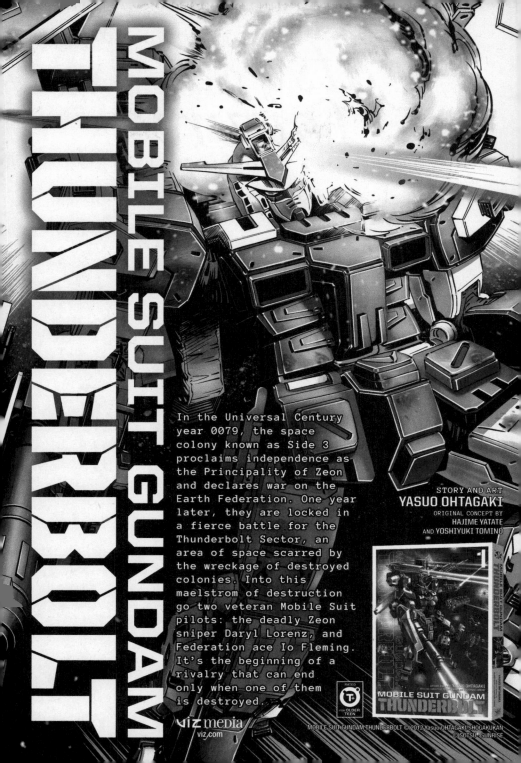

MOBILE SUIT GUNDAM THUNDERBOLT

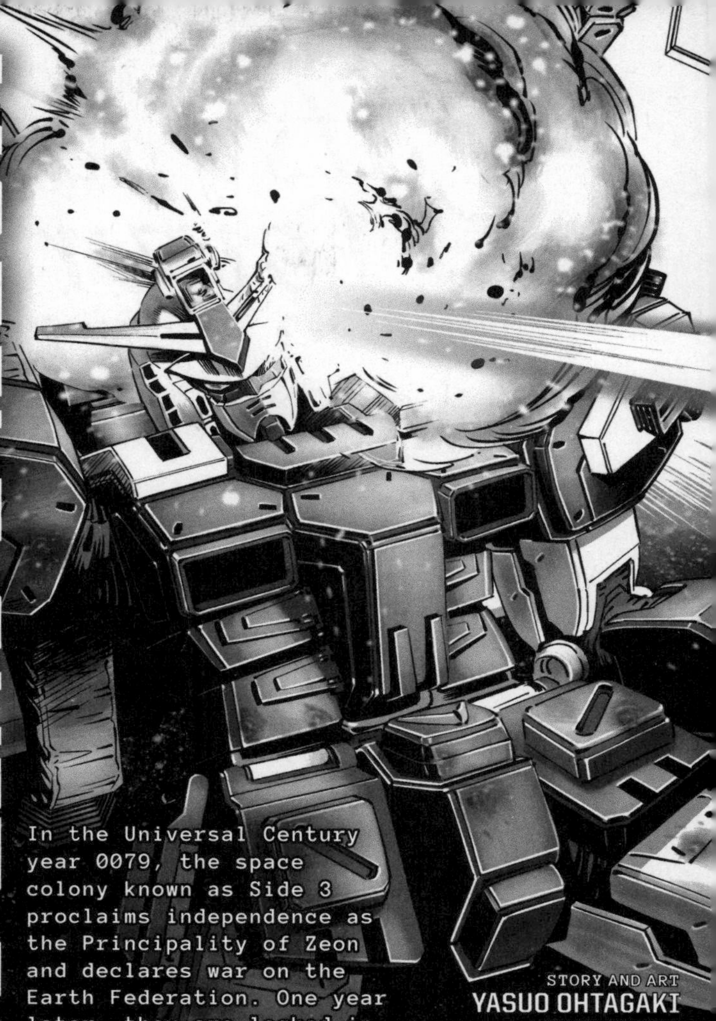

In the Universal Century year 0079, the space colony known as Side 3 proclaims independence as the Principality of Zeon and declares war on the Earth Federation. One year later, they are locked in a fierce battle for the Thunderbolt Sector, an area of space scarred by the wreckage of destroyed colonies. Into this maelstrom of destruction go two veteran Mobile Suit pilots: the deadly Zeon sniper Daryl Lorenz, and Federation ace Io Fleming. It's the beginning of a rivalry that can end only when one of them is destroyed.

STORY AND ART
YASUO OHTAGAKI
ORIGINAL CONCEPT BY
HAJIME YATATE
AND YOSHIYUKI TOMINO

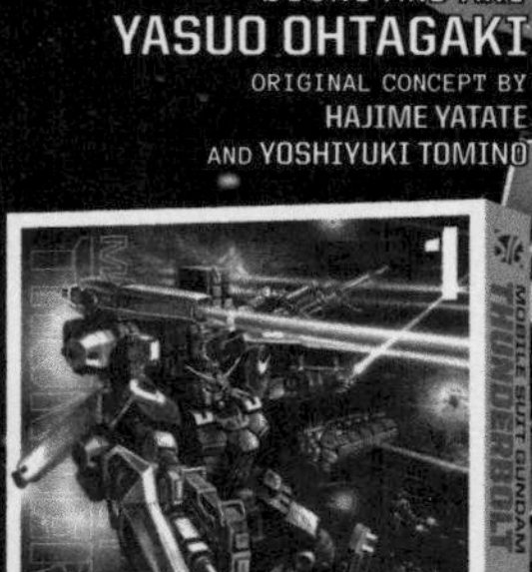
1
MOBILE SUIT GUNDAM
THUNDERBOLT
STORY AND ART BY YASUO OHTAGAKI

RATED T+ FOR OLDER TEEN

viz media
viz.com

Cats of the Louvre
by TAIYO MATSUMOTO

A surreal tale of the secret world of the cats of the Louvre, told by Eisner Award winner Taiyo Matsumoto.

The world-renowned Louvre museum in Paris contains more than just the most famous works of art in history. At night, within its darkened galleries, an unseen and surreal world comes alive— a world witnessed only by the small family of cats that lives in the attic. Until now…

Translated by *Tekkonkinkreet* film director Michael Arias.

TOKYO GHOUL:re

This is the last page.
TOKYO GHOUL:re reads right to left.